Lecture Notes in Computer Science　　14032

The series Lecture Notes in Computer Science (LNCS), including its subseries Lecture Notes in Artificial Intelligence (LNAI) and Lecture Notes in Bioinformatics (LNBI), has established itself as a medium for the publication of new developments in computer science and information technology research, teaching, and education.

LNCS enjoys close cooperation with the computer science R & D community, the series counts many renowned academics among its volume editors and paper authors, and collaborates with prestigious societies. Its mission is to serve this international community by providing an invaluable service, mainly focused on the publication of conference and workshop proceedings and postproceedings. LNCS commenced publication in 1973.

Aaron Marcus · Elizabeth Rosenzweig ·
Marcelo M. Soares
Editors

Design, User Experience, and Usability

12th International Conference, DUXU 2023
Held as Part of the 25th HCI International Conference, HCII 2023
Copenhagen, Denmark, July 23–28, 2023
Proceedings, Part III

 Springer

Editors
Aaron Marcus
Aaron Marcus and Associates
Berkeley, CA, USA

Elizabeth Rosenzweig
World Usability Day and Bubble Mountain
Consulting
Newton Center, MA, USA

Marcelo M. Soares
Southern University of Science
and Technology – SUSTech
Shenzhen, China

ISSN 0302-9743   ISSN 1611-3349 (electronic)
Lecture Notes in Computer Science
ISBN 978-3-031-35701-5   ISBN 978-3-031-35702-2 (eBook)
https://doi.org/10.1007/978-3-031-35702-2

This Springer imprint is published by the registered company Springer Nature Switzerland AG
The registered company address is: Gewerbestrasse 11, 6330 Cham, Switzerland

Foreword

Human-computer interaction (HCI) is acquiring an ever-increasing scientific and industrial importance, as well as having more impact on people's everyday lives, as an ever-growing number of human activities are progressively moving from the physical to the digital world. This process, which has been ongoing for some time now, was further accelerated during the acute period of the COVID-19 pandemic. The HCI International (HCII) conference series, held annually, aims to respond to the compelling need to advance the exchange of knowledge and research and development efforts on the human aspects of design and use of computing systems.

The 25th International Conference on Human-Computer Interaction, HCI International 2023 (HCII 2023), was held in the emerging post-pandemic era as a 'hybrid' event at the AC Bella Sky Hotel and Bella Center, Copenhagen, Denmark, during July 23–28, 2023. It incorporated the 21 thematic areas and affiliated conferences listed below.

A total of 7472 individuals from academia, research institutes, industry, and government agencies from 85 countries submitted contributions, and 1578 papers and 396 posters were included in the volumes of the proceedings that were published just before the start of the conference, these are listed below. The contributions thoroughly cover the entire field of human-computer interaction, addressing major advances in knowledge and effective use of computers in a variety of application areas. These papers provide academics, researchers, engineers, scientists, practitioners and students with state-of-the-art information on the most recent advances in HCI.

The HCI International (HCII) conference also offers the option of presenting 'Late Breaking Work', and this applies both for papers and posters, with corresponding volumes of proceedings that will be published after the conference. Full papers will be included in the 'HCII 2023 - Late Breaking Work - Papers' volumes of the proceedings to be published in the Springer LNCS series, while 'Poster Extended Abstracts' will be included as short research papers in the 'HCII 2023 - Late Breaking Work - Posters' volumes to be published in the Springer CCIS series.

I would like to thank the Program Board Chairs and the members of the Program Boards of all thematic areas and affiliated conferences for their contribution towards the high scientific quality and overall success of the HCI International 2023 conference. Their manifold support in terms of paper reviewing (single-blind review process, with a minimum of two reviews per submission), session organization and their willingness to act as goodwill ambassadors for the conference is most highly appreciated.

This conference would not have been possible without the continuous and unwavering support and advice of Gavriel Salvendy, founder, General Chair Emeritus, and Scientific Advisor. For his outstanding efforts, I would like to express my sincere appreciation to Abbas Moallem, Communications Chair and Editor of HCI International News.

July 2023   Constantine Stephanidis

HCI International 2023 Thematic Areas and Affiliated Conferences

Thematic Areas

- HCI: Human-Computer Interaction
- HIMI: Human Interface and the Management of Information

Affiliated Conferences

- EPCE: 20th International Conference on Engineering Psychology and Cognitive Ergonomics
- AC: 17th International Conference on Augmented Cognition
- UAHCI: 17th International Conference on Universal Access in Human-Computer Interaction
- CCD: 15th International Conference on Cross-Cultural Design
- SCSM: 15th International Conference on Social Computing and Social Media
- VAMR: 15th International Conference on Virtual, Augmented and Mixed Reality
- DHM: 14th International Conference on Digital Human Modeling and Applications in Health, Safety, Ergonomics and Risk Management
- DUXU: 12th International Conference on Design, User Experience and Usability
- C&C: 11th International Conference on Culture and Computing
- DAPI: 11th International Conference on Distributed, Ambient and Pervasive Interactions
- HCIBGO: 10th International Conference on HCI in Business, Government and Organizations
- LCT: 10th International Conference on Learning and Collaboration Technologies
- ITAP: 9th International Conference on Human Aspects of IT for the Aged Population
- AIS: 5th International Conference on Adaptive Instructional Systems
- HCI-CPT: 5th International Conference on HCI for Cybersecurity, Privacy and Trust
- HCI-Games: 5th International Conference on HCI in Games
- MobiTAS: 5th International Conference on HCI in Mobility, Transport and Automotive Systems
- AI-HCI: 4th International Conference on Artificial Intelligence in HCI
- MOBILE: 4th International Conference on Design, Operation and Evaluation of Mobile Communications

List of Conference Proceedings Volumes Appearing Before the Conference

1. LNCS 14011, Human-Computer Interaction: Part I, edited by Masaaki Kurosu and Ayako Hashizume
2. LNCS 14012, Human-Computer Interaction: Part II, edited by Masaaki Kurosu and Ayako Hashizume
3. LNCS 14013, Human-Computer Interaction: Part III, edited by Masaaki Kurosu and Ayako Hashizume
4. LNCS 14014, Human-Computer Interaction: Part IV, edited by Masaaki Kurosu and Ayako Hashizume
5. LNCS 14015, Human Interface and the Management of Information: Part I, edited by Hirohiko Mori and Yumi Asahi
6. LNCS 14016, Human Interface and the Management of Information: Part II, edited by Hirohiko Mori and Yumi Asahi
7. LNAI 14017, Engineering Psychology and Cognitive Ergonomics: Part I, edited by Don Harris and Wen-Chin Li
8. LNAI 14018, Engineering Psychology and Cognitive Ergonomics: Part II, edited by Don Harris and Wen-Chin Li
9. LNAI 14019, Augmented Cognition, edited by Dylan D. Schmorrow and Cali M. Fidopiastis
10. LNCS 14020, Universal Access in Human-Computer Interaction: Part I, edited by Margherita Antona and Constantine Stephanidis
11. LNCS 14021, Universal Access in Human-Computer Interaction: Part II, edited by Margherita Antona and Constantine Stephanidis
12. LNCS 14022, Cross-Cultural Design: Part I, edited by Pei-Luen Patrick Rau
13. LNCS 14023, Cross-Cultural Design: Part II, edited by Pei-Luen Patrick Rau
14. LNCS 14024, Cross-Cultural Design: Part III, edited by Pei-Luen Patrick Rau
15. LNCS 14025, Social Computing and Social Media: Part I, edited by Adela Coman and Simona Vasilache
16. LNCS 14026, Social Computing and Social Media: Part II, edited by Adela Coman and Simona Vasilache
17. LNCS 14027, Virtual, Augmented and Mixed Reality, edited by Jessie Y. C. Chen and Gino Fragomeni
18. LNCS 14028, Digital Human Modeling and Applications in Health, Safety, Ergonomics and Risk Management: Part I, edited by Vincent G. Duffy
19. LNCS 14029, Digital Human Modeling and Applications in Health, Safety, Ergonomics and Risk Management: Part II, edited by Vincent G. Duffy
20. LNCS 14030, Design, User Experience, and Usability: Part I, edited by Aaron Marcus, Elizabeth Rosenzweig and Marcelo Soares
21. LNCS 14031, Design, User Experience, and Usability: Part II, edited by Aaron Marcus, Elizabeth Rosenzweig and Marcelo Soares

47. CCIS 1836, HCI International 2023 Posters - Part V, edited by Constantine Stephanidis, Margherita Antona, Stavroula Ntoa and Gavriel Salvendy

https://2023.hci.international/proceedings

Preface

User experience (UX) refers to a person's thoughts, feelings, and behavior when using interactive systems. UX design becomes fundamentally important for new and emerging mobile, ubiquitous, and omnipresent computer-based contexts. The scope of design, user experience, and usability (DUXU) extends to all aspects of the user's interaction with a product or service, how it is perceived, learned, and used. DUXU also addresses design knowledge, methods, and practices, with a focus on deeply human-centered processes. Usability, usefulness, and appeal are fundamental requirements for effective user-experience design.

The 12th Design, User Experience, and Usability Conference (DUXU 2023), an affiliated conference of the HCI International conference, encouraged papers from professionals, academics, and researchers that report results and cover a broad range of research and development activities on a variety of related topics. Professionals include designers, software engineers, scientists, marketers, business leaders, and practitioners in fields such as AI, architecture, financial and wealth management, game design, graphic design, finance, healthcare, industrial design, mobile, psychology, travel, and vehicles.

This year's submissions covered a wide range of content across the spectrum of design, user-experience, and usability. The latest trends and technologies are represented, as well as contributions from professionals, academics, and researchers across the globe. The breadth of their work is indicated in the following topics covered in the proceedings.

Five volumes of the HCII 2023 proceedings are dedicated to this year's edition of the DUXU Conference:

- Part I addresses topics related to design methods, tools and practices, as well as emotional and persuasive design.
- Part II addresses topics related to design case studies, as well as creativity and design education.
- Part III addresses topics related to evaluation methods and techniques, as well as usability, user experience, and technology acceptance studies.
- Part IV addresses topics related to designing learning experiences, as well as design and user experience of chatbots, conversational agents, and robots.
- Part V addresses topics related to DUXU for cultural heritage, as well as DUXU for health and wellbeing.

The papers in these volumes were included for publication after a minimum of two single–blind reviews from the members of the DUXU Program Board or, in some cases, from Preface members of the Program Boards of other affiliated conferences. We would like to thank all of them for their invaluable contribution, support, and efforts.

July 2023

Aaron Marcus
Elizabeth Rosenzweig
Marcelo M. Soares

12th International Conference on Design, User Experience and Usability (DUXU 2023)

The full list with the Program Board Chairs and the members of the Program Boards of all thematic areas and affiliated conferences of HCII2023 is available online at:

http://www.hci.international/board-members-2023.php

HCI International 2024 Conference

The 26th International Conference on Human-Computer Interaction, HCI International 2024, will be held jointly with the affiliated conferences at the Washington Hilton Hotel, Washington, DC, USA, June 29 – July 4, 2024. It will cover a broad spectrum of themes related to Human-Computer Interaction, including theoretical issues, methods, tools, processes, and case studies in HCI design, as well as novel interaction techniques, interfaces, and applications. The proceedings will be published by Springer. More information will be made available on the conference website: http://2024.hci.international/.

General Chair
Prof. Constantine Stephanidis
University of Crete and ICS-FORTH
Heraklion, Crete, Greece
Email: general_chair@hcii2024.org

https://2024.hci.international/

Contents – Part III

Evaluation Methods and Techniques

Usage and Application of Heatmap Visualizations on Usability User Testing: A Systematic Literature Review

Fabricio Davila$^{(\boxtimes)}$ ⓘ, Freddy Paz ⓘ, and Arturo Moquillaza ⓘ

Pontificia Universidad Católica del Perú, Av. Universitaria, 1801 Lima, Peru
sebastian.davila@pucp.edu.pe, {fpaz,amoquillaza}@pucp.pe

Abstract. Nowadays, high-quality user experience (UX) has become a key competitive factor for product development. User experience methods and techniques investigate how people feel about a system. However, we must take into account that traditional evaluation methods, whether interviews or surveys are based on self-reported data, which are often exposed to social desire. Therefore, by obtaining additional information from the user's interaction with the system being evaluated, besides interviews or surveys, we build a more robust user experience. In this research, we present the outcomes of a Systematic Literature Review (SLR) aimed at uncovering case studies, difficulties, issues, and opportunities related to the use of heatmaps in usability testing. The SLR was carried out using the protocol proposed by Kitchenham and Charters. The research was carried out on August 23, 2022, and a total of 371 articles were retrieved, from which 22 were selected. The results show that a formal process reported in the literature has not been identified that indicates the tasks that an evaluation team should carry out to complement the results of the heatmap application with user tests for a better analysis of usability problems and design errors. On the other hand, it can be seen that the tools necessary to carry out this analysis only obtain information from the user but do not obtain metrics from it or vice versa. According to the results obtained, we can conclude that heatmaps are useful for specialists who perform usability tests with users because the user's interaction with the system to be evaluated can be graphically visualized.

Keywords: Visualization · Heatmap · User Testing · Usability · Literature Review

1 Introduction

Currently, usability is considered one of the most important quality attributes in software development and aims to make the developed product easier to use for its users [1]. Due to the impact of usability on software products, there are various methods to evaluate that they are met within the applications, one of which is usability testing.

Usability testing is a UX research technique, in which a researcher asks a participant to complete certain tasks in a specific interface so that they can observe their behavior and hear their comments [2].

© The Author(s), under exclusive license to Springer Nature Switzerland AG 2023
A. Marcus et al. (Eds.): HCII 2023, LNCS 14032, pp. 3–17, 2023.
https://doi.org/10.1007/978-3-031-35702-2_1

Similarly, today high-quality user experience (UX) has become a key competitive factor in product development. User experience methods and techniques investigate how people feel about a system. However, we must keep in mind that traditional evaluation methods, whether interviews or questionnaires are based on self-reported data, which are often exposed to social desire [3]. Therefore, by obtaining additional information from the user's interaction with the system to be evaluated, besides interviews or questionnaires, we build a more robust user experience.

In this study, we will present the results of a Systematic Literature Review (SLR) to identify the use and application of heatmaps in usability testing. Our main objective is to identify studies that will inform about the implementation of heatmaps in usability testing to understand their advantages, disadvantages, and challenges. To do this, we are following a protocol established by B. Kitchemham and M. Petticrew [4, 5]. With the information obtained, we will be able to identify a series of challenges, applications, and metrics related to the use of heatmaps in usability testing. This will allow us to deepen our understanding of how this technique can be used to evaluate the usability of a software product.

This document is structured as follows. In Sect. 2, we describe the main concepts belonging to the Human-Computer Interaction (HCI) area that was used in this study. In addition, in Sect. 3, we present the conduct of the systematic literature review and, in Sect. 4, we discuss the results of the SLR. Finally, in Sect. 5, we present the conclusions of the research.

2 Background

Next, the main concepts of Human-Computer Interaction (HCI) used in the present research are presented.

2.1 User Experience

According to I. Maslov and S. Nikou [6], user experience is a concept that describes the user's interactions with a product, including perception, learning, and usage. This can be evaluated based on ten facets: legal or ethical, economic, technological, pragmatic, cultural, emotional, social, reciprocal, cognitive, and perceptual. On the other hand, according to ISO 9241–210 [7], user experience refers to the perceptions and responses of a person resulting from the use of a product, system, or service.

2.2 Usability

According to J. Nielsen [2], usability is a quality attribute that represents how user-friendly interfaces are. Usability is defined by five components. The first, the ease of learning component, refers to the fact that the system must be easy to learn. Then, there is the efficiency component, which indicates that once the user has learned to use the system, it must have a high level of productivity. Subsequently, there is the ease of memory component, which refers to the fact that the system must be easy to remember so that if the user stops using it, they do not have to re-learn everything all over again.

Then, there is the error component, which refers to the fact that the system must have a low error rate so that users make the least number of errors and in case they do, they can quickly recover from them. Finally, there is the satisfaction component, which refers to the fact that the system must be pleasant to use so that users are satisfied.

2.3 Usability Test

According to J. Nielsen [2], usability tests are a user experience research methodology. It is the process in which a usability evaluator asks a participant to perform different tasks using one or more specific user interfaces while the usability evaluator observes the behavior of the usability test participant and listens to the feedback from the evaluated interface. The objective varies depending on the study, but they are generally used to identify problems, discover opportunities, or learn about the behavior and preferences of the target user [8].

2.4 Heatmap

Heat maps are an additional tool to usability tests that have been successfully used in the HCI area [3]. They serve to be able to visualize in a friendly way the metrics obtained from the user's interaction with the system. The metrics that are ideal to be shown through a heatmap are the user's clicks, mouse movements, and eye movements of the user participating in the usability test [9].

2.5 Eye Tracking

According to S. Stuart [9], eye tracking is the process of monitoring and measuring the movements and positioning of the eyes during a specific task, without causing any discomfort. The device used for this purpose is commonly referred to as an eye tracker.

2.6 Data Visualization

According to C. Chen, W. Härdle, and A. Unwin [10], data visualization is the representation of data in a graphical form that can be easily understood by readers or viewers. As a result, it is becoming an increasingly important tool in scientific research.

2.7 User Experience Metric

According to Nielsen Group [11], a user experience metric is numerical data that informs usability specialists about some aspect of the user experience of the product being evaluated. These metrics can have high value as they help to improve the quality of designs and identify problems.

3 Systematic Literature Review

The Systematic Literature Review aims to identify the available research related to the phenomenon of interest. Additionally, the methodology proposed by B. Kitchenham and S. Charters [4] has been employed, which consists of the review being carried out in three stages. The first stage, the planning stage of the review, involves defining the needs of the review and developing a proposal for the review for further development. In this stage, the review questions, search strings, and inclusion and exclusion criteria are developed. Then comes the review execution stage, which consists of identifying and selecting the investigations that are related to the final project. Additionally, data extraction is performed for subsequent synthesis in this stage. Finally, the reporting and dissemination stage will facilitate the preparation of the main report generated [4]. For the execution of the process, we use the web tool called Parsifal, using the phases presented above.

3.1 Review Goal

The main goal of this review is to identify studies that report on the implementation of heatmaps in remote usability tests to understand their advantages, disadvantages, and challenges. Additionally, it aims to identify the tools used for creating and generating heatmaps in this context, to find the best way to implement them.

3.2 Review Questions

To achieve the objectives proposed above, the following review questions were formulated.

- **RQ1:** How have heatmaps been used in the application of usability tests?
- **RQ2:** What challenges were addressed by using heatmaps in usability testing? How were they cared for?
- **RQ3:** What are the metrics that have been used when using heatmaps in usability tests?

To review each of the questions, the PICOC criteria were defined, which are included in the B. Kitchenham protocol [4] and were defined by M. Petticrew and H. Roberts [5]. The PICOC criteria are as follows: (1) Population, referring to the object of study, (2) Intervention, related to the aspects that will be studied by the population and how they will be carried out, (3) Comparison, in which the interventions are compared, (4) Outcomes, related to what is wanted or obtained from the systematic review, (5) Context, in which the circumstances under which the studies to be identified were carried out are established. It is important to mention that in this case, the comparison criterion will not be applied because it is not intended to compare the interventions. Table 1 shows the definition of the PICOC criteria.

Table 1. Definition of the general concepts using PICOC

Criterion	Description
Population	Usability testing
Intervention	Heatmap
Comparison	(N.A)
Outcomes	Metrics, impact, advantage, disadvantage, algorithm, tools, challenges
Context	Academic and industrial

3.3 Search Strategy

Search Engines. Four search engines have been considered for the research: SCOPUS, ACM Digital Library, IEEE Digital Library for their relevance in the field of computer engineering, and ALICIA from Concytec as the largest digital collection of scientific and technological production in Peru, where, in addition, the thesis repositories of various Peruvian universities are included.

Search Strings. For the formulation of the chains, it is important to define the keywords obtained from the definition of the PICOC criteria. Subsequently, the search for related words for each concept is carried out. Table 2 shows the grouping of each concept with its related words and the PICOC criterion to which they belong.

Table 2. Keywords and related words

Keyword	Related word	PICOC Criterion
Usability test	UX, user test	Population
Heatmap	Eye track, eyetrack, heatmap	Intervention
Algorithm	Technique	Outcome
Disadvantage	Downside, drawback	Outcome
Metric	Benchmark, criterion, measures	Outcome
Tool	Instrument	Outcome

Then, to build the search chain, the logical operator OR was used for the keywords and synonyms in the same group. On the other hand, the logical operator AND was used to join different groups. It is important to mention that an asterisk was considered at the end of the keywords that present more than one conjunction or a plural form. Next, the search chain is shown as a result of the previously mentioned process.

("heatmap*" **OR** "eye track*" **OR** "eyetrack*" **OR** "heat map*") **AND** ("usability test*" **OR** "UX" **OR** "user test*") **AND** ("algo-rithm*" **OR** "technique*" **OR** "disadvantage" **OR** "downside*" **OR** `"drawback*"` **OR** `"metric*"` **OR** `"benchmark*"` **OR** `"criterion*"` **OR** `"measure*"` **OR** `"tools"` **OR** `"instrument*"`).

For ALICIA, the same string translated into Spanish was used. The search string is shown below.

(`"mapa de calor"` **OR** `"eye track"` **OR** `"seguimiento ocular"`) **AND** (`"pruebas de usabilidad"` **OR** `"UX"`) **AND** (`"algoritmo"` **OR** `"técnica"` **OR** `"desventajas"` **OR** `"métrica"` **OR** `"benchmark"` **OR** `"criterios"` **OR** `"medidas"` **OR** `"herramientas"` **OR** `"instrumentos"`).

Inclusion and Exclusion Criteria. As not all scientific articles can answer the questions posed in the systematic review, Kitchenham establishes the definition of inclusion and exclusion criteria, which help to evaluate which investigations are useful in answering these questions.

For this reason, the study inclusion criteria were:

- IC1: The study describes the different types of heatmaps in usability testing, as well as their challenges.
- IC2: The study reports tools for the implementation of a heatmap module in usability testing.
- IC3: The study describes eye-tracking methods applied to usability testing.

Similarly, the exclusion criteria for discarding investigations are as follows:

- EC1: The study is more than 15 years old.
- EC2: The study is written in a language other than English or Spanish.
- EC3: The study focuses on usability but does not mention heatmap tools.
- EC4: The study focuses on the implementation of heatmaps but not on usability.

3.4 Search Results

After executing the search chain on August 23, 2022, in each of the selected databases, results were obtained, which have been divided into three sections. The first is the total amount of studies found in each of the databases. The second is the number of duplicate studies found in each search engine. Finally, the number of selected studies in each database. The search results by the database are shown in Table 3.

Table 3. Number of extracted, duplicated, and selected studies

Search Engine	# Extracted Studies	# Duplicated Studies	# Selected Studies
Scopus	207	25	11
ACM Digital Library	192	21	8
IEEE Digital Library	20	3	2
ALICIA	2	1	1
Total	**421**	**50**	**22**

Additionally, Table 4 shows the primary studies collected to answer the previously posed research questions.

Table 4. Selected primary studies

ID	Study	Quote	Search Engine
S01	A Scenario-based Analysis of Front-facing Camera Eye Tracker for UX-UI Survey on Mobile Banking App	[12]	IEEE Xplore
S02	A Visualization Tool for Eye Tracking Data Analysis in the Web	[13]	ACM Digital Library
S03	An Evaluation Framework for User Experience Using Eye Tracking, Mouse Tracking, Keyboard Input, and Artificial Intelligence: A Case Study	[14]	Scopus
S04	An eye-tracking study of web search interaction design patterns	[15]	ACM Digital Library
S05	Automated areas of interest analysis for usability studies of tangible screen-based user interfaces using mobile eye tracking	[16]	Scopus
S06	Comparative study of user experience evaluation techniques based on mouse and gaze tracking	[17]	ACM Digital Library
S07	Enhanced representation of web pages for usability analysis with eye tracking	[18]	ACM Digital Library
S08	Exploring Relationships Between Eye Tracking and Traditional Usability Testing Data	[19]	Scopus
S09	Eye Gaze Tracking for Human Computer Interaction	[20]	ACM Digital Library
S10	Eye tracking for screening design parameters in adjective-based design of yacht hull	[21]	Scopus
S11	Eye Tracking: Background, Methods, and Applications	[9]	Scopus
S12	Proceedings of the 20th Congress of the International Ergonomics Association (IEA 2018): Volume V: Human Simulation and Virtual Environments, Work With Computing Systems (WWCS), Process Control (Vol. 822)	[22]	Scopus
S13	Remote Usability Testing Using Eyetracking	[23]	Scopus
S14	Sistema de rastreo ocular para la experiencia del usuario en los contenidos de la página web en la empresa grupo CELLCH	[24]	ALICIA
S15	Social Computing and Social Media: Design, User Experience and Impact: 14th International Conference	[25]	Scopus

(continued)

Table 4. (*continued*)

ID	Study	Quote	Search Engine
S16	U-index: An Eye-Tracking-Tested Checklist on Webpage Aesthetics for University Web Spaces in Russia and the USA	[26]	ACM Digital Library
S17	Usability and eye tracking: Analysis of the home pages of international universities: Do they clearly show the objectives of the institution?	[27]	IEEE Xplore
S18	Usability and UX of Learning Management Systems: An Eye- Tracking Approach	[6]	Scopus
S19	UX Heatmaps: Mapping User Experience on Visual Interfaces	[3]	ACM Digital Library
S20	UXmood—A Tool to Investigate the User Experience (UX) Based on Multimodal Sentiment Analysis and Information Visualization	[28]	Scopus
S21	Web Usability Testing With Concurrent fNIRS and Eye Tracking	[29]	Scopus
S22	WebGazer: Scalable Webcam Eye Tracking Using User Interactions	[30]	ACM Digital Library

3.5 Data Extraction

Once the selection of articles according to the inclusion and exclusion criteria was completed, a data extraction form was developed which allowed to organize of the most relevant information from each article to answer the previously raised research questions. Table 5 shows the data extraction form, which includes the field name, description, and the question related to which it will provide an answer with its filling.

Table 5. Data extraction form

Field	Description	Answers the RQ
ID	Assigned code to each research. Will start with the letter 'S' followed by a number	All RQs
Title	Study title	All RQs
Publication year	Year of publication of the research	All RQs
Authors	Authors who have participated in the research	All RQs
Language	Language in which the research was developed	All RQs

(*continued*)

Table 5. (*continued*)

Field	Description	Answers the RQ
Country	Country of origin of the research	All RQs
Search Engine	Search engine where the location was found	All RQs
Link	Link to the research	All RQs
Procedures and activities	Description of the procedures and activities to be carried out upon implementation	RQ1
Artifact	Description and list of artifacts used in heatmap tests for usability	RQ1
Algorithm	Algorithms used in the implementation of heatmaps in usability tests	RQ1
Challenges	Description of the challenges in implementing heatmaps in usability tests	RQ2
Advantages and disadvantage	Description of the advantages and disadvantages in implementing heatmaps in usability tests	RQ2
Problem solved	Description of the problems solved by implementing heatmaps in usability tests	RQ2
Metrics	Description of the metrics used when using heatmaps in usability tests	RQ3

4 Data, Analysis, and Results

After reviewing the 22 primary studies, it was observed that the majority come from Europe. This evidences that in Europe, heatmap research is considered an additional resource for usability tests. On the other hand, it is important to mention that the number of investigations is increasing, as evidenced in the year 2019. Finally, the relevant information from each study was compiled in the extraction form, and with this, the questions posed for the systematic review were answered.

4.1 Answer to Review Question RQ1

The answer to the question posed for the systematic review of "How have heatmaps been used in the application of usability tests?" is addressed by grouping twenty investigations, from which, taking into account the particular stages of each investigation, four stages were identified which are shown in Table 6.

Table 6. Stages for the generation of heatmaps in the application of usability tests.

Number	Step	Studies that report the challenge	Number of studies
1	Model training to be used for data acquisition	S01, S13, S20	3
2	Selection of the user sample and the system to be evaluated	S01, S02, S03, S04, S06, S07, S08, S10, S12, S13, S14, S15, S16, S17, S18, S19, S20, S21, S22	19
3	Execution of the usability test	S01, S02, S03, S04, S06, S07, S08, S10, S12, S13, S14, S15, S16, S17, S18, S19, S20, S21, S22	19
4	Display of the information generated by the interaction between the user and the system through a heatmap	S02, S03, S04, S06, S08, S09, S10, S11, S13, S15, S16, S19	12

The following is a description of each stage in obtaining heatmaps.

1. Training of the model to be used in data acquisition: To obtain data on the interaction between the user and the system, it is important to train the developed software using a data model [E01, E10 & E12] to obtain more precise and specific results according to the scenario to be applied. This training can be performed using data sets, such as the Face Expression Recognition Plus [E20].
2. Selection of User and System Sample for Evaluation: To perform a usability test, obtain the expected results, and finally visualize them through a heatmap, it is important to select an appropriate sample of users for each scenario [S01, S02, S03, S04, S06, S07, E08, E10, E12, S13, S14, S15, S16, S17, S18, S19, S20, S21 & S22]. One factor to consider is the age of the evaluated users [E18 & E20] because they have to be within the target audience of the system's users.
3. Usability Test Execution: To obtain the metrics that provide more information about the interaction between the users and the system, different methods have been used to provide both quantitative and qualitative results [S03, S13 & S15]. Among the main methods, the use of surveys to determine the user's opinion about the system under evaluation is used. On the other hand, as qualitative methods, there is eye-tracking [S10 & S16], which determines which area of interest the users have by the time they fixate on it. On the other hand, it is possible to analyze the user's emotions through audio or facial gestures [S08 & S19]. The data collected from each evaluation serves for a more effective analysis of the usability problems or design errors that may present the system's graphical interfaces [S01, S02, S03, S04, S06, S07, S08, S10, S12, S13, S14, S15, S16, S17, S18, S19, S20, S21, and S22].
4. Display of Information Generated by User and System Interaction through Heat Map: Finally, after generating the data to be evaluated, it is displayed through useful graphs

for the evaluators. One of the existing graphs is the heatmap [S02, S03, S04, S06, S08, S09, S10, S11, S13, S15, S16 & S19], which shows the number of user fixations [S02, S08, S09, S11, S16 & S18] on sectors of the screen through different shades of color. The colors used are yellow, blue, and red, with yellow being the least intense shade and red being the most intense shade. On the other hand, the fixations shown can be divided by quantity and time [S15, S19 & S20], providing new possibilities for analysis.

4.2   Answer to Review Question RQ2

The answer to the question posed for the systematic review of "What challenges were addressed when using heatmaps in usability tests and how were they addressed?" is addressed by a group of twelve studies, which are synthesized into three main challenges (Table 7).

Table 7. Challenges addressed when using heatmaps in usability testing.

Number	Step	Studies that report the challenge	Number of studies
1	Ineffective visualization of the data collection of the user's interaction with the system's stimulus	S02, S03, S04, S06, S08, S09, S11, S16, S19	9
2	Search for new criteria other than efficiency and accuracy in usability tests	S02, S08, S09, S10, S15, S19	6
3	Display of the information generated by the interaction between the user and the system through a heatmap	S06, S08, S13	3

A description of each of the challenges shown along with the solutions proposed in the literature is presented below.

1. Ineffective Visualization of User-Stimulus Interaction Data Collection: After obtaining the data from the result of the user's interaction with the system, it is important to visualize these for the researchers [S02]. Therefore, one of the proposed alternatives is heatmaps [S02, S03, S04, S06, S08, S09, S11, S16 & S19], which help in better evaluating the user experience as the information resulting from the user's interaction with the system [S03] can be easily visualized through colors in various screen areas [S04] depending on the frequency with which the sector is interacted with.
2. Searching for New Criteria Different from Effectiveness and Accuracy in Usability Tests: Usability tests often only evaluate the effectiveness and accuracy of systems. However, due to the high competitiveness of the market, it is not enough to analyze these indicators as users will remain unsatisfied [S02, S08 & S15]. Therefore, to

obtain new evaluation criteria that allow for a better analysis of the user experience and software quality, the use of data-gathering methods that show the user's interaction with the system is proposed, such as eye tracking [S09, S10 & S19], so that new criteria can be obtained that help researchers build a user-friendly and satisfying system.

3. High Cost of Specialized Tools for Information Gathering and Data Generation to Complement Test Results: Obtaining additional information that complements the data obtained from the user's interaction with the system presents high-cost alternatives. Firstly, in the case of using additional equipment besides the software, a laboratory must be present or, otherwise, many replicas of the equipment, which generates high costs [S08 & S13]. On the other hand, there are also paid alternatives for generating heatmaps, in which only paying enables analysis options and does not allow access to the source code. Among them, we have HotJar or MouseFlow [E06]. As an alternative, there are Open-Source tools, such as WebGazer.js or SearchGazer.js [E06], which allow obtaining information from the user's interaction with the system at no cost and with the possibility of obtaining the source code.

4.3 Answer to Review Question RQ3

The answer to the question posed for the systematic review of "What metrics have been used when using heatmaps in usability tests?" is addressed by the grouping of nineteen studies, which are synthesized into three main metrics which are visualized in Table 8.

Table 8. Metrics used when using heatmaps in usability tests

Number	Step	Studies that report the challenge	Number of studies
1	Number of user fixations on screen sectors	S02, S03, S04, S05, S06, S07, S08, S09, S10, S11, S12, S13, S14, S16, S17, S18, S21, S22	19
2	User fixation time on screen sectors	S02, S15, S16	3
3	Position of the clicks made by users on screen sectors	S03, S06	2

Below is the description of each of the displayed metrics.

1. Number of user fixations on-screen sectors: One of the main metrics for generating heatmaps is the number of user fixations on-screen sectors [S02, S03, S04, S06, S07, S08, S10, S12, S13, S14, S15, S16, S17, S18, S19, S20, S21 & S22]. This capture is performed using eye tracking, which determines the areas in which users have observed most frequently.
2. User fixation time on screen sectors: Like the number of screen fixations, the user's fixation time in the various screen areas [S02, S15 & S16] is available. This metric is obtained by capturing eye movement so that the screen areas with which the user interacts the most can be identified.

3. Position of the clicks made by users on-screen sectors: This metric shows us which sectors of the screen have the highest number of clicks by the user [S03 & S06]. This shows us which are the screen areas with which the user interacts the most. With this, said metric is shown on the heatmap according to the number of clicks in each zone with the colors yellow, blue, and red, with yellow being the least intense and red being the most intense.

5 Conclusion

As a result of the systematic review carried out using the B. Kitchenham protocol, it was determined that a formal process has not been identified in the literature that indicates the tasks that an evaluation team should perform to complement the results of heatmap application with user testing for better analysis of usability problems and design errors.

Additionally, while some tools reported in the literature were identified, these are not easily available to the academic or industrial community because they do not provide the ability to obtain the metrics necessary for generating heatmaps or only provide information on the user's interaction with the system but do not provide the ability to perform an analysis effectively and efficiently.

Finally, it was identified that heatmaps are useful for specialists who carry out usability testing with users because it is possible to visually display the user's interaction with the system being evaluated, such as the areas of gaze fixation on the screen.

Acknowledgment. We express our gratitude to the "HCI, Design, User Experience, Accessibility & Innovation Technologies (HCI DUXAIT)" research group from Pontificia Universidad Católica del Perú (PUCP) for their support throughout the entire research process.

References

1. Paz, F.: Método para la evaluación de usabilidad de sitios web transaccionales basado en el proceso de inspección heurística. 275 (2017)
2. Nielsen, J.: Usability engineering. Academic Press, Boston (1993)
3. Georges, V., Courtemanche, F., Senecal, S., Baccino, T., Fredette, M., Leger, P.-M.: UX Heatmaps: Mapping User Experience on Visual Interfaces. In: Proceedings of the 2016 CHI Conference on Human Factors in Computing Systems, pp. 4850–4860. ACM, San Jose California USA (2016). https://doi.org/10.1145/2858036.2858271
4. Kitchenham, B., Charters, S.: Guidelines for performing Systematic Literature Reviews in Software Engineering (2007)
5. Petticrew, M., Roberts, H.: Systematic Reviews in the Social Sciences. 354 (2006)
6. Maslov, I., Nikou, S.: Usability and UX of learning management systems: an eye- tracking approach. In: 2020 IEEE International Conference on Engineering, Technology and Innovation (ICE/ITMC). pp. 1–9. IEEE, Cardiff, United Kingdom (2020). https://doi.org/10.1109/ICE/ITMC49519.2020.9198333
7. International Organization for Standardization: ISO 9241–210: Ergonomics of human-system interaction – Part 210: Human-Centred Design for Interactive Systems, Geneva (2010)
8. Rubin, J., Chisnell, D.: Handbook of usability testing: how to plan, design, and conduct effective tests. Wiley Pub, Indianapolis, IN (2008)

9. Stuart, S. (ed.): Eye Tracking: Background, Methods, and Applications. Springer US, New York, NY (2022). https://doi.org/10.1007/978-1-0716-2391-6

10. Chen, C., Härdle, W., Unwin, A.: Handbook of Data Visualization. Springer Berlin Heidelberg, Berlin, Heidelberg (2008). https://doi.org/10.1007/978-3-540-33037-0

11. Nielsen Norman Group: UX Metrics and ROI. Nielsen Norman Group (2016)

12. Sunhem, W., Pasupa, K.: A scenario-based analysis of front-facing camera eye tracker for UX-UI survey on mobile banking app. In: 2020 12th International Conference on Knowledge and Smart Technology (KST), Pattaya, Chonburi, Thailand, pp. 80–85. IEEE (2020). https://doi.org/10.1109/KST48564.2020.9059376

13. Menges, R., Kramer, S., Hill, S., Nisslmueller, M., Kumar, C., Staab, S.: A visualization tool for eye tracking data analysis in the web. In: ACM Symposium on Eye Tracking Research and Applications, Stuttgart Germany, pp. 1–5. ACM (2020). https://doi.org/10.1145/3379156.3391831

14. Souza, K.E.S. de, et al.: An evaluation framework for user experience using eye tracking, mouse tracking, keyboard input, and artificial intelligence: a case study. Int. J. Hum.–Comput. Interact. **38**, 646–660 (2022). https://doi.org/10.1080/10447318.2021.1960092

15. Dimitrakopoulou, D., Faliagka, E., Rigou, M.: An eye-tracking study of web search interaction design patterns. In: Proceedings of the 20th Pan-Hellenic Conference on Informatics, Patras Greece, pp. 1–6. ACM (2016). https://doi.org/10.1145/3003733.3003795

16. Batliner, M., Hess, S., Ehrlich-Adám, C., Lohmeyer, Q., Meboldt, M.: Automated areas of interest analysis for usability studies of tangible screen-based user interfaces using mobile eye tracking. AIEDAM **34**, 505–514 (2020). https://doi.org/10.1017/S0890060420000372

17. Aviz, I.L., Souza, K.E., Ribeiro, E., de Mello Junior, H., Seruffo, M.C. da R.: Comparative study of user experience evaluation techniques based on mouse and gaze tracking. In: Proceedings of the 25th Brazillian Symposium on Multimedia and the Web, pp. 53–56. ACM, Rio de Janeiro Brazil (2019). https://doi.org/10.1145/3323503.3360623

18. Menges, R., Tamimi, H., Kumar, C., Walber, T., Schaefer, C., Staab, S.: Enhanced representation of web pages for usability analysis with eye tracking. In: Proceedings of the 2018 ACM Symposium on Eye Tracking Research & Applications, pp. 1–9. ACM, Warsaw Poland (2018). https://doi.org/10.1145/3204493.3214308

19. Wang, J., Antonenko, P., Celepkolu, M., Jimenez, Y., Fieldman, E., Fieldman, A.: Exploring relationships between eye tracking and traditional usability testing data. Int. J. Hum.-Comput. Interact. **35**, 483–494 (2019). https://doi.org/10.1080/10447318.2018.1464776

20. Drewes, H.: Eye Gaze Tracking for Human Computer Interaction. 167 (2010)

21. Dogan, K.M., Suzuki, H., Gunpinar, E.: Eye tracking for screening design parameters in adjective-based design of yacht hull. Ocean Eng. **166**, 262–277 (2018). https://doi.org/10.1016/j.oceaneng.2018.08.026

22. Bagnara, S., Tartaglia, R., Albolino, S., Alexander, T., Fujita, Y. (eds.): IEA 2018. AISC, vol. 822. Springer, Cham (2019). https://doi.org/10.1007/978-3-319-96077-7

23. Chynał, P., Szymański, J.M.: Remote usability testing using eyetracking. In: Campos, P., Graham, N., Jorge, J., Nunes, N., Palanque, P., Winckler, M. (eds.) INTERACT 2011. LNCS, vol. 6946, pp. 356–361. Springer, Heidelberg (2011). https://doi.org/10.1007/978-3-642-23774-4_29

24. Suxe Ramírez, M.A.: Sistema de rastreo ocular para la experiencia del usuario en los contenidos de la página web en la empresa grupo CELLCH – Huaraz; 2017 (2019. https://hdl.handle.net/20.500.13032/11961)

25. Meiselwitz, G. (ed.): Social Computing and Social Media: Design, User Experience and Impact, HCII 2022. Springer, Cham (2022). https://doi.org/10.1007/978-3-031-05061-9

26. Bodrunova, S.S., Yakunin, A.V.: U-index: an eye-tracking-tested checklist on webpage aesthetics for university web spaces in Russia and the USA. In: Marcus, A., Wang, W. (eds.) DUXU 2017. LNCS, vol. 10288, pp. 219–233. Springer, Cham (2017). https://doi.org/10.1007/978-3-319-58634-2_17

27. Lago, B.L., Pereira, V.C., Cardoso, J.M.: Usability and eye tracking: Analysis of the home pages of international universities: Do they clearly show the objetives of the institution? In: 2018 13th Iberian Conference on Information Systems and Technologies (CISTI), Caceres, pp. 1–5. IEEE (2018). https://doi.org/10.23919/CISTI.2018.8399462

28. Da Silva Franco, R.Y., et al.: UXmood - a tool to investigate the user experience (UX) based on multimodal sentiment analysis and information visualization (InfoVis). In: 2019 23rd International Conference Information Visualisation (IV), Paris, France, pp. 175–180. IEEE (2019). https://doi.org/10.1109/IV.2019.00038

29. Bhatt, S., Agrali, A., McCarthy, K., Suri, R., Ayaz, H.: Web usability testing with concurrent fNIRS and eye tracking. In: Neuroergonomics, pp. 181–186. Elsevier (2019). https://doi.org/10.1016/B978-0-12-811926-6.00030-0

30. Papoutsaki, A., Sangkloy, P., Laskey, J., Daskalova, N., Huang, J., Hays, J.: WebGazer: Scalable Webcam Eye Tracking Using User Interactions 7 (2016)

A Comparison Between Performing a Heuristic Evaluation Based on a Formal Process Using a System and the Traditional Way: A Case Study

Adrián Lecaros(✉) ⓘ, Arturo Moquillaza ⓘ, Fiorella Falconi ⓘ, Joel Aguirre ⓘ, Alejandro Tapia ⓘ, and Freddy Paz ⓘ

Pontificia Universidad Católica del Perú, Av. Universitaria 1801, San Miguel, Lima 32, Lima, Peru
{adrian.lecaros,ffalconit,aguirre.joel}@pucp.edu.pe,
{amoquillaza,a.tapiat,fpaz}@pucp.pe

Abstract. The heuristic evaluation belongs to the usability inspection methods and is considered one of the most popular methods since it allows the discovery of over 75% of the total usability problems involving only 3 to 5 usability experts. However, certain problems and challenges have been identified during their execution. One of the identified problems is the lack of validation scenarios that demonstrate the contributions and benefits of incorporating systems that provide support for heuristic evaluation. Although there are case studies that could support the problems described above, the literature has shown that these are quite scarce and, for the most part, are software products that are used as support tools for certain elements to be evaluated, such as, for example, visual clarity of the system, page links validations and readability. For this reason, since there are no validation scenarios that demonstrate the contributions and benefits of the automation of heuristic evaluations through software products, the result is that there is a low level of confidence in usability evaluators to use a system that supports the heuristic evaluation process, for so the inspection continues to be carried out manually. As a part of previous research, a software product was implemented to support the five steps (planning, training, evaluation, discussion, and report) of a previously selected formal process to perform heuristic evaluations. To test the previously developed software product, a case study that demonstrates the contributions and benefits of incorporating the web application developed as a support tool for heuristic evaluation was proposed, and it has been of the utmost importance since it has allowed performing a comparative analysis between the evaluation when is performed by using the selected formal process through a template contained in an MS Excel format document, and by using the web application developed as a result of the aforementioned previous research. The results demonstrated that a higher average result was obtained, for the team that used the implemented system, in all the established criteria. The interpretation of the results can be summarized with the fact that the system obtained a better perception by the team who used it than the results obtained by the team that used the evaluation template.

Keywords: Human-computer Interaction · Usability · Heuristic Evaluation · Process · BPMN

A. Marcus et al. (Eds.): HCII 2023, LNCS 14032, pp. 18–29, 2023.
https://doi.org/10.1007/978-3-031-35702-2_2

1 Introduction

Nowadays, usability is a very important aspect of the User Experience in the context of interaction between users and software products since it establishes a fundamental role in users' use, acceptance, and interaction with those software products [1]. Moreover, the heuristic evaluation belongs to the usability inspection methods [2] and is considered one of the most popular methods since it allows the discovery of over 75% of the total usability problems involving only 3 to 5 usability experts [3]. However, specific problems and challenges were identified during their execution.

One identified problem is the need for validation scenarios that demonstrate the contributions and benefits of incorporating systems that support heuristic evaluation. Although there are case studies that could support the problems described above, the literature has shown that these are quite scarce and, for the most part, are software products that are used as support tools for certain elements to be evaluated, such as, for example, visual clarity of the system [4], page links validations and readability [5].

For this reason, since there are no validation scenarios that demonstrate the contributions and benefits of the automation of heuristic evaluations through software products, the result is that there is a low level of confidence in usability evaluators to use a system that supports the heuristic evaluation process, for so the inspection continues to be carried out manually.

As a part of previous research, a software product was implemented to support the five steps (planning, training, evaluation, discussion, and report) of a previously selected formal process to perform heuristic evaluations [6] through the construction of 3 modules: (1) heuristic selection, (2) evaluation execution, and (3) results and reports modules. Those modules were implemented through a defined architecture, a low-level prototype design, and the construction of the system through the AUP methodology, in which each completed module meant an increment for the software as a minimum viable product.

To test the previously developed software product, a case study that demonstrates the contributions and benefits of incorporating the web application developed as a support tool for heuristic evaluation was proposed, and it has been of the utmost importance since it has allowed performing a comparative analysis between the evaluation when is performed by using the selected formal process through a template contained in an MS Excel format document, and by using the web application developed as a result of the aforementioned previous research.

To be able to perform it, a comparative case study and validation instruments were first designed, where the composition of the teams, the scenarios to be compared, and the scope of the study were defined, where one of those scenarios considers the execution of the process, by a first team of 3 evaluators (2 engineers and 1 master), as is currently being carried out (manually), and the other, considers the execution of the process using the web application by a second team of 3 evaluators with the same level of expertise as the first one.

The software product to perform the evaluation was an e-commerce website. The selected heuristics were focused on transactional websites to find more problems related to that scope. The first team found 22 usability problems, and the second one found 21, and to measure the perception of both groups, TAM criteria were defined by proposing questions that needed to be answered on a scale of 1 to 5, where 1 represented a highly negative perception, and 5 represented a highly positive perception, that allowed to quantify the results obtained by the answers of the proposed questions of each criterion: (1) ease of use, (2) perceived usefulness and (3) intention to use (2).

After that, the case study was carried out, where the results obtained by both scenarios were compiled, and the perception of the evaluators who performed heuristic evaluation by using the MS Excel template and the proposed system were compared through a T-Student test (since the samples belonged to a normal population) to check if the populations were statistically significant and to confirm if, indeed, better indicators have been obtained by the team that used the developed web application.

The obtained results demonstrated that a higher average result was obtained for the team that used the implemented system in all the established criteria, and two of these were statistically significant after the numerical experimentation (ease and intention of use). The interpretation of the results can be summarized with the fact that the proposed heuristic evaluation support system obtained a better perception by the evaluators who used it in comparison with the perception results obtained by the team that used the evaluation template. Although 2 of the 3 criteria were statistically significant, the usefulness perception criterion could also reach this condition if the number of evaluators is increased.

This paper is structured as follows: In Sect. 2, we describe the main concepts belonging to the Human-Computer Interaction area used in the study. In Sect. 3, we present the results of previous research where a selected formal process to perform heuristic evaluations was selected as the basis of an automated software product that supports that process. In Sect. 4, we present the elaboration of the case study that allowed to compare the execution of the selected formal process by using a system and the traditional way. In Sect. 5, we present the execution and results of the case study. Finally, in Sect. 6, we present the conclusions of the research, and the future works to be done.

2 Background

In this section, we present the main concepts related to this work.

2.1 Usability

Usability, according to ISO 9241–210-2019 [7], is the "extend to which a system, product or service can be used by specified users to achieve specified goals with effectiveness, efficiency, and satisfaction in a specified context of use".

Additionally, Jacob Nielsen [8] defines it as the evaluation of five attributes the user interface of a system must have, which are the following:

- Learnability: The system should be easy to learn so that the user can perform some tasks with the system as quickly as possible.
- Efficiency: The system should be efficient during its use to provide the highest level of productivity possible.
- Memorability: The system should be easy to remember so that the casual user can use it again after a period of leaving it without the need to relearn how it works.

- Errors: The system should provide a low error rate so that users make as few errors as possible and can quickly recover from them. Errors considered catastrophic must not occur.
- Satisfaction: The system should be pleasant to use so that users are subjectively satisfied while using it.

2.2 Heuristic Evaluation

According to Andreas Holzinger [2], Heuristic Evaluation (HE) belongs to usability inspection methods and is the most common informal method. For its execution, it requires usability experts who can identify if the dialogue elements or other interactive software elements follow the established principles of usability.

According to Jacob Nielsen [8], the heuristic evaluation allows the inspection of what is good and bad in the interface of a system, which could be done through one's own opinion or, ideally, using well-defined guidelines. The author also maintains that the main goal of the evaluation is to find usability problems in the design of an interface that is carried out through a group of evaluators who will inspect and judge it through usability principles called heuristics. Additionally, a single evaluator can find only 35% of the usability problems in an interface; however, each evaluator usually encounters different types of problems; for this reason, he recommends the participation of 3 to 5 evaluators to obtain the best cost-benefit ratio. These evaluations are performed singularly, and then, upon completion, the results are compared for overall usability analysis.

2.3 Heuristic Evaluation Formal Process

According to Freddy Paz [9], it consists of a framework that has a base in the analysis of case studies that will provide a structured way to execute the heuristic evaluation to reduce the different interpretations that arise now of its use. An example of the formal process is the one defined by the author, who establishes five phases for its execution: (1) planning, (2) training, (3) evaluation, (4) discussion, and (5) report.

3 Selecting a Heuristic Evaluation Formal Process and Developing a Software Product that Used It as the Basis

As part of a previous investigation [6], a comparative analysis of the formal processes or protocols found in a systematic review of the literature was carried out, where the formal process, with duly defined steps of Paz [9], turned out to be the one that obtained the best results. For this reason, the modeling of the process was carried out through the BPMN notation to ensure that the evaluators who use it can interpret it in only one way. The general process diagram is divided into five steps: (1) planning, (2) training, (3) evaluation, (4) discussion, and (5) reporting. Figure 1 shows the elaborated BPMN diagram.

Then, using this formal process as a basis, the construction of a system was carried out that allowed the automation of the heuristic evaluation process through the development of 3 modules that allowed the previously described steps to be covered: (1) selection of heuristics, (2) execution of the evaluation and (3) results and reports.

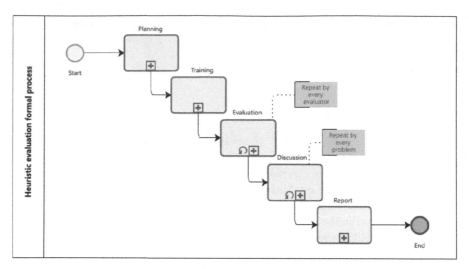

Fig. 1. General process flow diagram

Those modules were implemented through a defined architecture, a low-level prototype design, and the construction of the system through the AUP methodology [10], in which each completed module meant an increment for the software as a minimum viable product.

The software product was validated at each stage by a software engineering expert who gave improvement recommendations for each module that were applied to obtain an optimally built software product. In addition, when the construction of the last module was finished, a heuristic evaluation was carried out with usability experts, which allowed us to find certain usability problems that were solved to obtain a final version of the system.

After having completed the development of the system, it was necessary to verify if its use contributed to a better perception in comparison to the previously used MS Excel template, for which a case study was designed that allowed to carry out the analysis that will be explained in the next section.

4 Elaboration of the Case Study

The approach of a case study that demonstrates the contributions and benefits of incorporating the web application developed as a support tool for heuristic evaluation has been of the utmost importance since it has allowed a comparative analysis to be carried out between how the traditional execution of the selected formal process was, through a template contained in an MS Excel format document, and between the developed web application.

For this reason, the comparative case study and validation instruments were first designed, where the composition of the teams, the scenarios to be compared, and the scope were defined, where one of these considers the execution of the process as is currently being carried out, and the other, the execution of the process using the developed web application.

Then, the case study was carried out where the results obtained by both scenarios were compiled, and the perception of the evaluators of the execution of the evaluation using the template in MS Excel format and the proposed system to confirm if, indeed, better indicators have been obtained using the developed web application.

For the design of the comparative case study, there were two scenarios: (1) a group that performs the heuristic evaluation using the selected formal process using a template in Excel format, and (2) another group that performs the evaluation using the developed web application. The evaluators that made up the teams are usability experts, since they already have considerable experience performing heuristic usability evaluations of software products.

The evaluated website was Linio Perú, which is an online store that distributes products of various categories, such as cell phones, consoles, home products, and sports, among others, and is characterized for being one of the largest and most popular online shopping portals in the country.

The flow of the case study consisted of evaluating both scenarios with the respective support tool to carry out the heuristic evaluation, where each team must be trained first on how to apply the formal process and then execute the evaluation to finally fill out a questionnaire that allows knowing the perception about the tool for each team member. Figure 2 shows the flow in detail.

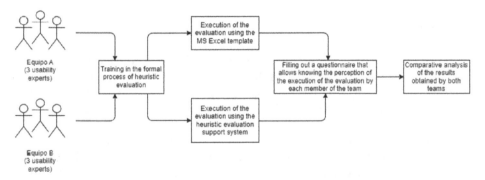

Fig. 2. Case study execution flow

Likewise, to make the comparison between the perception of the execution of the evaluation, TAM criteria were used, validated by Davis [11], and were adapted for the present case study where the following were selected: (1) perception of ease of use, (2) perceived usefulness and (3) intent of use. Figure 3 shows the relationship between the criteria.

Each criterion is measured based on a scale from 1 to 5, where the lowest corresponds to a highly negative perception and the highest to a highly positive perception. It is worth mentioning that each criterion consists of questions that were rated with said scale by the evaluators to then obtain the final average for each criterion.

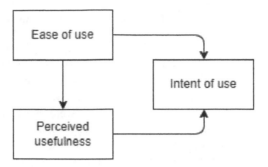

Fig. 3. Relationship between TAM criteria

Finally, to compare the results obtained by each evaluator, a Shapiro-Wilk test is performed to determine if the samples belong to a normal population whose hypotheses are as follows:

- H_0: The evaluated data belong to a normal population.
- H_1: The data evaluated does not belong to a normal population.

Depending on the results for each criterion, at a significance level of 0.05, the T-Student or Mann-Whitney U test needs to be used to determine which of the two tools is the best.

5   Execution and Results of the Case Study

For the execution of the case study presented, six usability experts were contacted who participated in a heuristic evaluation of the Linio Perú website, following the selected formal process and using Paz's heuristics for transactional websites [12]. After managing to contact the experts, they were divided into two teams according to their titles, so an engineer and two bachelors participated in each team.

The execution of the case study by Team A consisted of the use of a template contained in an MS Excel file, which is the one currently used to carry out the heuristic evaluations following the formal process and was adapted for the present case study. On the other hand, Team B used the developed heuristic evaluation support system, which is the proposal presented to carry out heuristic inspections, as a better alternative to the evaluation template.

Once all the evaluators completed the individual evaluation in the submitted template, they were sent an invitation to participate virtually in a group meeting per team to discuss, rate, and offer possible solutions to the problems. In total, the Team A and Team B evaluators found 22 and 21 usability problems, respectively, which were supported by screenshots of the inspected interfaces.

Likewise, on the day of the group meeting, the evaluators reviewed each of the problems found by their team, where each evaluator provided more details about their individual problems, according to what was reported in the evaluation template or in the system. to decide if they were considered in the final list of problems. After completing the review, a final list of 20 usability problems was obtained for both Team A, and Team B. Figure 4 shows the number of problems that were identified by Team B for each transactional website heuristic.

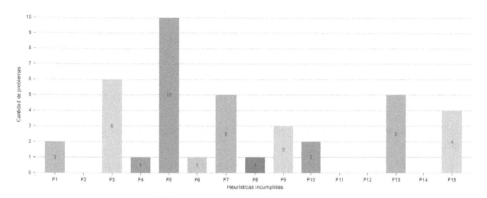

Fig. 4. Relationship between TAM criteria – Team B

Additionally, each evaluator rated the final list of problems according to their severity and frequency, where a scale of 0 to 4 was used, where 0 means that they do not agree that it is a usability problem or that the frequency is less than 1%, while 4 means that the problem is catastrophic or that the frequency is greater than 90% respectively. Figure 5 shows the criticality, which is the severity and frequency summed up, of each problem of the final list by every member of Team B.

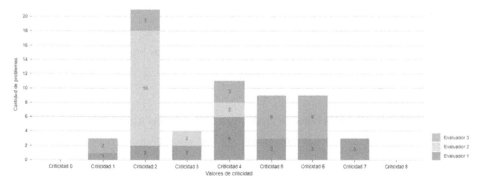

Fig. 5. Criticality by evaluator v.s. number of problems – Team B

Finally, the evaluators proposed possible solutions for each of the problems on the final list, where they placed suggestions on how to improve the design of the interfaces and functionalities.

Once the evaluation was completed by both teams, each evaluator was asked to complete a survey that would allow the evaluation of the TAM criteria (ease of use, perceived usefulness, and intent of use) through the proposed questions for the case study and a couple of open questions that sought to find out what they thought about the time and effort spent on the evaluation. Table 1 shows the questionnaire.

Table 1. TAM criteria questionnaire

Ease of use
Using the formal evaluation process support tool in my heuristic inspections would allow me to complete the evaluations more quickly
Using the formal evaluation process support tool would improve my performance in heuristic inspections
Using the formal evaluation process support tool in my heuristic inspections would increase my productivity
Using the formal evaluation process support tool would improve the effectiveness of my heuristic inspections
I would find the formal evaluation process support tool useful in my heuristic inspections
Perceived usefulness
Learning to use the tool to support the formal evaluation process would be easy for me
I would find it easy to make the formal evaluation process support tool do what I want it to do
My interaction with the formal process support tool could be clear and understandable
I would consider that the support tool for the formal evaluation process is flexible to interact with
It would be easy for me to become an expert in using the formal evaluation process support tool
I would consider the formal evaluation process support tool to be easy to use
Intent of use
I would intend to use the formal evaluation process support tool in my heuristic inspections
I would promote the use of the tool to support the formal evaluation process to perform heuristic inspections
Using the tool to support the formal evaluation process would increase interest in performing heuristic inspections
I would love to use the formal evaluation process support tool in my heuristic inspections
I would use the formal evaluation process support tool for as an alternative to perform heuristic inspections
Open questions
Has the use of the tool allowed the evaluation to be carried out more quickly? Detail your answer
Has the use of the tool reduced the effort expended in generating the final reports? Detail your answer

Then, to compare the results obtained by the evaluators, the Shapiro-Wilk test was performed to determine if the samples belonged to a normal population whose hypotheses were as follows:

- H_0: The evaluated data belong to a normal population.
- H_1: The data evaluated does not belong to a normal population.

The results of the said test are shown in Table 2, where the mean, standard deviation, significance level, and p-value of each team are presented.

Table 2. Shapiro-Wilk test for TAM criteria

Team	Criterion	Mean	Standard deviation	Significance level	p-value
Team A	Ease of use	3.27	0.46	0.05	**0.13**
	Perceived usefulness	3.39	0.42	0.05	**1.00**
	Intent of use	3.00	0.87	0.05	**0.38**
Team B	Ease of use	**4.47**	0.31	0.05	**0.99**
	Perceived usefulness	**4.28**	0.63	0.05	**0.44**
	Intent of use	**4.53**	0.12	0.05	**0.13**

As each criterion of both teams has a p-value greater than the significance level (0.05), that meant that each of the samples belonged to a normal distribution, so the T-Student test was used to make the comparison to check if the populations were statistically significant. Table 3 shows the result of said test.

Table 3. T-Student test results

Criterion	Team	Mean	Standard deviation	Significance level	p-value
Ease of use	Team A	3.27	0.46	0.05	**0.02**
	Team B	**4.47**	0.31	0.05	**0.02**
Perceived usefulness	Team A	3.39	0.42	0.05	0.11
	Team B	**4.28**	0.63	0.05	0.11
Intent of use	Team A	3.00	0.87	0.05	**0.04**
	Team B	**4.53**	0.12	0.05	**0.04**

After performing the T-Student test, it is verified that the populations of the ease and the intent of use are statistically significant (p-value less than the level of significance), so it is concluded that Team B obtained a better perception (average) than Team A in these criteria, which means that the system has been better perceived than the template in Excel. Although there is also greater perceived usefulness for Team B compared to Team A, it cannot be concluded that this result is statistically significant since the p-value was higher than the significance level; however, this last point could be improved if the number of evaluators participating in the case study is increased.

6 Conclusions and Future Works

The results achieved for the validation of the software product that supports Paz's heuristic evaluation formal process in a scenario that demonstrates the contributions and benefits of incorporating the web application developed as a support tool for heuristic evaluation have been the following:

- A comparative case study was designed to carry out a heuristic evaluation of Linio Perú through two scenarios: an evaluation team that uses the evaluation template and another that performs the evaluation using the developed system obtained in previous research. Then, the validation instruments were defined, which consisted of perception surveys using TAM criteria, whose results would be validated through numerical experimentation to verify which of the two scenarios obtained a better perception by the evaluators.
- The case study proposed in the previous point was carried out, where the two evaluation teams were made up of three evaluators (an engineer and two bachelors) who carried out the evaluation using the evaluation support tool, respectively. Then, a perception survey was applied to them with the TAM criteria questionnaire, where a higher average result was obtained, for the team that used the implemented system, in all the established criteria, and two of these were statistically significant after the numerical experimentation (ease and intention of use).

The interpretation of the results can be summarized with the fact that the proposed heuristic evaluation support system obtained a better perception by the evaluators who used it in comparison with the perception results obtained by the team that used the evaluation template. Although 2 of the 3 criteria were statistically significant, the usefulness perception criterion could also reach this condition if the number of evaluators is increased.

In addition, since the means of both teams for the perceived usefulness criterion are high, it could be concluded that the selected process was considered useful by usability evaluators.

The results are consistent with previous research since the use of a tool that contributes in a certain way to the execution of a heuristic evaluation allows the evaluation process to be significantly streamlined and facilitated.

Additionally, the results obtained can be generalized by carrying out the proposed case study with more groups of evaluators to obtain a greater number of perception results about the use of the template in comparison with the use of the proposed system.

For future works, the possibility of executing the same case study is proposed but with different groups of evaluators who have master or doctoral degrees to obtain additional validation from professionals with vast professional experience in the HCI area.

In addition, it has been proposed to carry out case studies in software products other than transactional websites, with the use of other groups of heuristics according to the case presented, to evaluate that the use of the heuristic evaluation support system can be extended effectively to other software domains and that its perception will be as satisfactory as in the original case study.

Acknowledgments. This work is part of the research project "Virtualización del proceso de evaluación de experiencia de usuario de productos de software para escenarios de no presencialidad" (virtualization of the user experience evaluation process of software products for non-presential scenarios), developed by HCI-DUXAIT research group. HCI-DUXAIT is a research group that belongs to the PUCP (Pontificia Universidad Católica del Perú).

This work was funded by the Dirección de Fomento a la Investigación at the PUCP through grant 2021-C-0023.

References

1. Huang, Z.: Usability of tourism websites: a case study of heuristic evaluation. New Rev. Hypermedia Multimed. **26**, 55–91 (2020). https://doi.org/10.1080/13614568.2020.1771436
2. Holzinger, A.: Usability engineering methods for software developers. Commun. ACM. **48**, 71–74 (2005). https://doi.org/10.1145/1039539.1039541
3. Paz Espinoza, F.A.: Método para la evaluación de usabilidad de sitios web transaccionales basado en el proceso de inspección heurística. Pontif. Univ. Católica del Perú. 275 (2018). file:///C:/Users/UTM-BIBLIOTECA/Downloads/PAZ_FREDDY_USABILIDAD_SITIOS_WEB_%20INSPECCI%C3%93N_HEUR%C3%8DSTICA.pdf
4. Ghazali, M., Sivaji, A., Abdollah, N., Khean, C.N.: Visual Clarity Checker (VC2) to support heuristic evaluation: to what extent does VC2 help evaluators? Proc. - 2016 4th Int. Conf. User Sci. Eng. i-USEr 2016. 182–187 (2017). https://doi.org/10.1109/IUSER.2016.7857957
5. Ahmad, W.F.W., Sarlan, A., Ezekiel, A., Juanis, L.: Automated Heuristic Evaluator. J. Informatics Math. Sci. **8**, 301–306 (2016)
6. Lecaros, A., Moquillaza, A., Falconi, F., Aguirre, J., Tapia, A., Paz, F.: Selection and modeling of a formal heuristic evaluation process through comparative analysis. In: Soares, M.M., Rosenzweig, E., and Marcus, A. (eds.) Design, User Experience, and Usability: UX Research, Design, and Assessment, pp. 28–46. Springer, Cham (2022). https://doi.org/10.1007/978-3-031-05897-4_3
7. International Organization for Standardization: ISO 9241-210-2019. (2019)
8. Nielsen, J.: Usability Engineering. Morgan Kaufmann Publishers Inc., San Francisco, CA, USA (1993)
9. Paz, F., Paz, F.A., Pow-Sang, J.A., Collazos, C.: A formal protocol to conduct usability heuristic evaluations in the context of the software development process. Int. J. Eng. Technol. **7**, 10–19 (2018). https://doi.org/10.14419/ijet.v7i2.28.12874
10. Edeki, C.: Agile Unified Process. Int. J. Comput. Sci. Mob. Appl. IJCSMA. **1**, 13–17 (2013)
11. Davis, F.D.: Perceived usefulness, perceived ease of use, and user acceptance of information technology. MIS Q. Manag. Inf. Syst. **13**, 319–339 (1989). https://doi.org/10.2307/249008
12. Paz, F.: Heurísticas de usabilidad para sitios web transaccionales. Pontif. Univ, Católica del Perú (2013)

A Review of Usability Guidelines for E-Commerce Website Design

Martin Maguire[✉]

School of Design and Creative Arts, Loughborough University, Leicestershire LE11 3TU, UK
m.c.maguire@lboro.ac.uk

Abstract. E-commerce websites often fail in their primary objective of making purchasing easy for customers. This paper reviews recommendations for making a website more usable and improving its conversion rate. General issues that are important to users are to create a home page with clear calls to action, support the navigation process, create an effective page layout and writing style, optimise the checkout process, design for responsiveness or mobile use, make the website accessible, demonstrate credibility and promote user trust, minimise page load times and manage customer reviews and feedback. The broader issue of considering the whole user experience is discussed and the need for designers to strike a balance between usability and business goals.

Keywords: E-commerce · Usability · User experience · Web-design · User-interface design guidelines

1 Introduction

This paper reviews usability issues of website design for e-commerce (electronic commerce). Unless a website meets the needs of the intended users it will not meet the needs of the organisation providing it and fewer products and services will be purchased. Web site development should be user-centred, evaluating the evolving design against user requirements. The first step is to define the business objectives, the intended context of use and key scenarios of use. This helps prioritise design and provides a focus for evaluation. Effective usability helps the user by making tasks easy and intuitive, minimising steps and roadblocks, supporting what users do (tasks) and how they do it, and providing satisfaction in completing a task. This in turn leads to higher revenues, loyal customers, and an increased brand value [1]. Since a good conversion rate for e-commerce is around 2.5 to 3%, there is always the opportunity to improve it. This paper presents key guidelines for improving e-commerce website usability.

2 Homepage or Landing Page

The homepage creates the first impression on the minds of visitors – at least for those who have commenced browsing the site by going through the front door. It is imperative that site visitor can find exactly what they are looking for when they arrive. e-Commerce websites need to display numerous product offerings rather than just displaying one or two products on the homepage. By displaying very few products on the homepage, this narrows down customer's choice from the start [2].

Customers generally look for special offers, discounts, or best deals so it is reasonable to provide the best offers at the home page. It is most likely that customers will review special offers so it should strike a chord on the first attempt. The goal of e-Commerce website is not just better user experience, but also to increase sales and improve bottom-line results [2].

2.1 Establish Brand Identity

That immediate visual identification is vital - if any website has a disconnect between its appearance and its content, customers will likely be put off. If an e-commerce an site doesn't quite match up to what the company claims, visitors are less likely to trust it, and therefore less likely to make a purchase [3].

The visual identity of a website needs to match the expectations of the customers. If the website sells toys, then it probably needs to have a colourful and cheerful design. If it sells high-end or expensive products, then it needs to look elegant with high quality images of the products. If the company is selling medical services or products, it should look clean and have a re-assuring calm quality, while if it is sells sporting goods, it probably needs a dynamic and sporty appearance. Establishing a clear brand identity and sticking to it is the best strategy since easily recognisable brands have much better exposure and brand awareness [3].

2.2 Minimize Content

Regardless of the ease and speed at which visitors can accomplish their goals from the landing page, it will be diminished by crowding the page and doing so with information that does not help to convert customers. A mass of text will be off-putting to users if for example it was a website for painting or photography classes [4]. While adverts are also often important for a website, the user experience will be reduced if they compete to strongly with the website content or create too much clutter.

2.3 Organise Content

Information that is not grouped together and identified is difficult to absorb for the users. Grouping the related information together with a headline that identifies it will improve usability. Key elements that should be included and stand out are:

- Headline – to confirm that the visitor is in the right place.
- Image – to reinforce what the page is about and quickly highlight the product qualities.
- Price – Every shopper wants to know the bottom line.
- Availability – Shoppers will want to know if the product is in stock, in the size or style they want.
- Additional Information – In case it is needed to help the shopper make the decision to purchase e.g., shipping and returns.

- Calls to action (CTA) – Every landing page must ask its visitors to take the action that the page is designed to encourage. The page should have a single or at least a main conversion goal, towards which the call-to-action leads, and the main CTA must be clearly visible [4]. (See section: 'Navigation' for further details.)

3 Navigation

3.1 Make Navigating Easy

One of the core elements in driving conversions is user-friendly navigation. It must be easy for visitors to find what they are looking for. The availability of a sitewide search function can speed up the process.

Nothing confuses customers more than trying to find where to click next. If it's not clear how they move onto the next stage in their purchase, they won't waste time, they'll just leave and find one that makes their life easier. So, if the customer is visiting with a particular product in mind, it should require minimal effort to find what they are looking for, so providing simple navigation tools is very important [5]. Simple navigation resources (tabs, drop-down menus, etc.) instead of multiple sidebars and navigation widgets makes finding the correct option much simpler for the user.

As emphasised by [6], user-friendly navigation is a core element in driving conversions and fundamentally, the site should make it as easy as possible for a visitor to find what they are looking for. It has been said that a complex navigation maze, requiring a complex series of clicks is the biggest problem for users [2]. The designer needs to give tactical thought to the navigation structure of the website to ensure that customers can locate information, compare products, and make payment with a minimum of clicks [2].

The availability of a site-wide search function can speed up the process. Alternatively, navigation tools should be both easy to find and functional. Links to the next or previous product pages can help users browse the site efficiently and navigation bars should promote the most critical pages [6].

The search bar, CTAs, and checkout button should also be prominent features on the pages. Wherever a user finds themselves on the website, the cart and checkout should only be a click away. CTAs give visitors a hint as to what to do next. It could be an 'add to cart' button, a link to their cart/basket, a button to click to continue shopping, and so on. They should be easy to see and follow a sensible path through to purchase. Don't make people think - let them complete their transaction without any fuss. If this not made easy, sales will be lost, especially from impulse shoppers.

If the company wants to upsell customers, CTAs can allow the company to do that. If the website is selling a battery-operated toy, a button that shows up offering to add batteries to the basket is a quick and simple opportunity to increase the value of that sale. CTAs should be helpful and relevant - something that makes sense in the context of the purchase they're making - that way the website will look helpful rather than looking like the aim is to get as much money from the customer as possible [3].

3.2 Primary Navigation

It is equally important to have an intuitive and engaging primary navigation so that users can find information they are looking for quickly with minimal clicks. Initially, users will tend to look at the main content area to see if there is anything of interest and may navigate from there. They might be interested in the gallery or search tool to find items e.g. holidays that meet their criteria. Next, users will explore the primary navigation controls present in a sidebar to the left, right, or top of a page on inner pages. These controls allow users to surf effortlessly on the website [2]. If these categories don't help, they will then tend to look at the footer of the page. The design of the website home page should focus on these aspects in this order [7]. The easier and more interesting the website is for the audience, the more likely they are to stay on the site, buy the product they are looking for, and return in future. Mundane or unintuitive primary navigation will have the opposite effect [2].

3.3 Breadcrumb Line or Progress Bar

A breadcrumb is text-based navigation that shows the user their current location in the site hierarchy. A similar feature is a progress bar that shows how far the user has got to through a process such as completing an online survey to specify details for a quote. If the existing e-commerce site does not have breadcrumbs, it may result in customer discomfort if unable to find their exact location in site. Highly time-effective, breadcrumbs help in reducing site abandonment and prevent the consumer from going off track while placing an order.

For example: Home > > Women > > Clothing > > Jackets.

Not only do breadcrumb lines give the user their location within the site, but it also provides shortcuts within the site hierarchy. This is a standard navigational element in e-commerce websites that users look for and rely on [2].

4 Search Engine Effectiveness

Site search usability can be a useful tool to promote both the internal and external search functionality and product findability. Online shoppers tend to expect a site search box in the top right-hand corner (or top centre) of an ecommerce store and up to 43% of visitors to retail sites go directly to the internal search function. Optimized search functionality can lead to increased site usage and should drive those visitors with purchase intent directly to the product they are looking for. One way to increase usability is to provide a drop-down of popular searches (based on the first few characters typed) which users can select as a short cut. Keeping the last search within the bar after a search has been performed is another technique that may be of value depending on the context of use. This allows users to easily amend their query if it hasn't brought up the products they were looking for [6].

Search engine optimization (SEO) can be another asset for improving site usability, driving consumers to the website based on their searches. To increase conversion rates once consumers are onsite, it is first essential to generate online traffic to the website [6].

5 Responsive Design

Statistics show that mobile traffic has surpassed desktop traffic and Google now focuses on mobile responsiveness as a key ranking factor. However, reports have shown that only a small proportion of people, 12%, find shopping on mobile to be convenient. So, fixing the design and making it easier and more convenient for visitors to browse easily can help a company match the competition [6]. Hence businesses need to make sure that their websites are mobile friendly. Mobile transactions are expected to account for 44.2% of retail eCommerce sales ($728 billion) in the USA in 2025 [8]. To maintain usability, ecommerce platforms must ensure that their mobile sites are compatible and up to date with the latest technologies. For example, incorporating device features like fingerprint scanning or digital wallets makes for a more comfortable mobile shopping experience [6].

For better mobile optimisation, the size of key buttons, reducing the amount of text on product pages, and simplifying the site navigation should be considered. The mobile checkout should also offer options such as credit card scanning to save customers time manually entering these details. It is also crucial that the mobile site exists on the same domain as the desktop store. Having multiple domains can confuse potential customers and affect the conversion rate [1].

Regarding payment methods such as Apple Pay, Android Pay and PayPal, providing these as options can make a big difference to mobile e-commerce conversion rates, especially for impulse purchases. If a customer simply needs to use a fingerprint rather than type out all of their details on a tiny keyboard, it's much easier for them to convert a prospective product and buy it although care should be taken that they don't purchase a product by mistake [3].

Mobile devices have enabled consumers to multitask while they're on the go. According to Statista, mobile devices account for the majority of all web pages. Many sites are now indexed with Google's mobile-first indexing. The crawling, indexing, and ranking systems of Google make it possible for a website to rank better on mobile-initiated searches.

Mobile users don't navigate a website the way desktop users do. Usually, they want to look for something particular and they want to find it fast. That's why it is necessary to shorten the mobile user journey. This can be done by using:

- Click-to-call buttons
- Click-to-scroll buttons
- Pinch-and-zoom for product photos
- Sticky navigation bars
- Pop-ups designed for mobile [1].

6 Make the Website Accessible

Websites that fail to consider accessibility in the design of their online stores are not providing a shopping experience with maximum usability. Businesses seeking to improve traffic and visitor retention must provide an ecommerce UX that caters to all its users, including those who are disabled, have sight or hearing impairments. Providing an inclusive ecommerce experience and improving the site accessibility should be a top priority since universal design is usable for anyone, regardless of ability [6].

Upgrades to the website accessibility are simple to implement and contribute to the overall user experience. Features like search by voice, keyboard navigation, and alt-tag descriptions will improve the site flow and customer engagement. Accessibility considerations are often inexpensive to implement and provide significant value to the consumers. All they require for execution is a bit of thoughtfulness and know-how. The more customers that can make a purchase on the website, the greater total conversions, and revenue [6].

6.1 Follow WCAG Standards

Web content accessibility guidelines, also known as WCAG, are created so that websites can meet the needs of people with disabilities. These are updated regularly so it is necessary to check them regularly to see the latest updates. WCAG's guidelines aim to address the most common barriers that prevent people from using various digital platforms. The policies cover a variety of success criteria for creating an excellent digital experience and ensuring that it complies with the regulations. The guidelines help to avoid discriminating against any site visitors since everyone is entitled to have a good site experience. Following WCAG is also an effective way to create good usability and improve user experience in general [9].

7   Page Layout

A customer's pathway to the products should be clear, straightforward, and effortless. At the same time, information should be differentiated between the homepage and product or category pages.

To facilitate sales, users should understand which products and services are available to them and best suited for their needs. It is necessary to choose a landing page that displays all the options available to customers and promotes the content in the most eye-catching way possible. With each new product page, new information should be presented in an uncluttered and well-organized manner. Listings should be done in a concise way that clearly identifies the availability of other options. For example, in size, style, or colour.

A high contrast colour scheme can make the store more readable for all users, as can offering text alternatives to images. If the website integrates video, captions for sound effects, and subtitles will help to clarify the message. The inclusion of customer ratings and reviews can also be a helpful tool to integrate into the various pages. The more informed a consumer is, the more likely they are to see a product through to checkout [1].

7.1 Font Visibility

Selecting the right typography and deciding on what font type, font size, and font colour to use is an aspect that should be considered. A company may spend a lot of money on a cutting-edge e-commerce platform to achieve robust performance, but the site will not work well if this very basic and crucial aspect of website designing is neglected. Choosing the right colour combination, font size, and font colour ensures that visitors do not have any problem viewing product details and that they find relevant information they are looking for in the shortest possible time. So, every element should be designed to achieve this goal [2].

7.2   Creating a Visual Hierarchy

On average, it takes 2.6 s for a person to create a first impression of a website once they land on the page. It's something that happens involuntarily, meaning the page has to be optimised for the users. Therefore, it is necessary that pages are simple for users to understand what they're looking at. If the website is overwhelming and draws attention to many different elements, the user won't know what to focus on, which doesn't translate to a good user experience. Thus, it is necessary to create a visual hierarchy that will guide visitors to the most critical elements of the site. It might mean placing essential elements in natural focus on the pages, such as images or CTAs. By providing a visual hierarchy for website users, they can find the products and pages that are important to them, and at the same time, usability will improve [1].

The following are aspects to remember when designing a visual hierarchy for site usability:

Alignment: Visitors usually read from top to bottom and left to right in an F pattern.

Colour: Vibrant hues appeal better to the visitor's eye.

Contrast: Different colours either emphasize or de-emphasize page elements.

White or Negative Space: Sufficient white space is important to help make a web page uncluttered and to give it a clear structure. Generally, the more space is provided, the more comfortable it is for the user to view.

Size: A suitable text size has an impact on how understandable a page is, making it easier to read while not being distracting [1].

7.3   Readability

Readability refers to the ability of website visitors to comprehend and digest the content of the site. If the website has issues with readability, there's a high chance it will frustrate users, and they end up leaving so potential customers will be lost. Therefore, the designer needs to take steps to ensure that the website is easy to understand, the intent is clear, and organization of content is effective. Having adequate white space, proper paragraph formatting, and creating bullet point lists will make the site content more readable. Placement of design elements should also be considered, such as banners, videos, images, sidebars, and text boxes on the site so that they won't distract users when navigating.

7.4 Website Patterns

A web design pattern, also known as a user interface design pattern, is a set of guidelines for designing a user interface aspect or component. Web design patterns are developed for specific user experience challenges and can be adopted and implemented by any website.

8 Checkout Process

According to Invesp's infographic "Shopping Cart Abandonment Rate Statistics" [10], 11% of surveyed shoppers abandoned their carts because the checkout process was too long or complex. A user may be asked for the same information twice, or redundant information e.g., the state where they live as well as their zip code, making the process less efficient and less usable [6].

8.1 Simplify the Checkout Process

An effective checkout process that makes purchasing quick and simple will lead to more conversions and reduce cart abandonment. Ideally, checkout should be a two to three step process that includes adding to cart, payment information, and shipping or contact information. The amount of information that the site needs to collect from customers should also be trimmed down. For instance, a checkbox may be provided to autofill shipping information when it matches the billing address.

Similarly, the site should also provide an option to check out as a guest. A guest checkout option allows people to see something and buy it without having to become a member. As the website will need to get their billing and shipping details, name, and email address in order to fulfil the order, one approach is to allow a guest checkout but add a tick box at the end of the process to create an account. Instead of stopping the visitor's flow from seeing the product to buying it, this lets them complete that process before they decide if they want to sign up, making it a smoother process [3].

For existing customers, the option to save credit card information allows for a more seamless transaction the next time they visit the e-commerce store [6].

Very often, the 'Add to Cart' action button in an e-Commerce website is either not well designed or not strategically placed to grab prospective buyer's attention. It should therefore be obvious, bright, and prominent in comparison to other features on product page such as wish-lists, view product, email to friend, or check out buttons. Less important functions can be lighter coloured buttons or simple text links. Confirmation that an order was successful after payment is also necessary and reassuring for the customer.

8.2 Have a Save Cart Function

A mistake often made in e-commerce has been to make the online experience as similar to street-level retail as possible. If a user visits a store in their local shopping centre, they would not expect to be able to fill a shopping cart, leave it in the store thoroughfare to go elsewhere, and expect to find it untouched it when they returned. But that is what many ecommerce shoppers expect as part of the nature of online shopping. Going from one site to another takes seconds. Very often, with different discounts, promotions and shipping charges, the only way to compare the price of a basket of goods is to add the products to the ecommerce cart and get a total price, then go to the next site and do the same. Usability suffers when the shopper returns to the site from which they want to buy a product, and are required to refill their cart [4].

8.3 Communicate Good Security

It is best to let customers know that their credit card information is secure. For instance, a paragraph can be placed on the top part of the 'Place Order' page which will make the checkout security more visible on the website. (See also the section: 'Security and accepted payment methods'.)

9 Trust and Credibility

E-commerce websites run on the fundamental principle of trust. In order to win customer's trust it is very important to take into account customer psychology. Lack of secure site (https) or lack of a certification by an Internet trust organization can prevent customers from buying from the store. Online businesses must provide security against misuse of confidential information and clearly display privacy policies. Providing guarantees as well as client testimonials of actual clients will help in improving credibility of the site. It is equally important to provide details for contacting the organization such as physical address, email address and phone number [2].

10 Reviews and Feedback

Reviews are one of the ways that online shoppers help decide between different products or different providers and to reassure themselves that the product or service on offer is legitimate and does what it claims to do? E-commerce websites should therefore include reviews and feedback sections, displaying customers' opinions about the product. Reviews and feedback are important because they function as part of the brand's credibility. They also encourage the company to build a good and honest relationship with customers and not just hide bad reviews [3].

All businesses are likely to get a bad review at some point but it should be used as an opportunity to resolve the issue by replying appropriately and offering assistance. The more reviews the company gets, means there are people buying the company's products or services which means that they are seen as legitimate. In addition to the website's own review section, links can also be provided to external review sites like TrustPilot or Google. These sources provide more credibility, since the businesses have no control over which reviews are posted - so visitors know that whatever the star rating is, that is an accurate reflection [3].

11   Building a Positive Experience

Building an eCommerce website is a situation where providing an outstanding user experience is of major importance. E-commerce websites have a specific target: to get sales. The website's success is not just measured by the number of visitors coming to the website but also the conversion rate and revenue. Ultimately, as the company is dictating the customers' journey; it is necessary to imagine being the customer and review the flow critically [11]. For example, is it easy to find the information the customer needs? Does the site appear trustworthy? Is it easy to look around? Is the checkout process simple and secure?

Comparison testing is a practical way to identify issues with the usability of an ecommerce site. Conducting randomized experiments based on two prototypes for comparison, or one prototype and a competitor, is a simple way to trial individual elements of the ecommerce site (e.g., a new menu system or page layout) and the whole experience. Tests are a cost-effective way to develop the store in alignment with consumer demands. They predict how users will react to changes and can therefore help to foresee any issues. Testing is this way provides an opportunity to identify consumer needs and better address them [6].

One of the key mistakes in eCommerce websites is overwhelming customers with too much information. Good UI and UX design should guide customers to their goal without overloading them with information. The information available should also be relevant to the page they're on and the needs they have before moving to the next page. What information might someone want before they decide to add that product to their basket? It is important not overwhelm users with irrelevant information, but just to provide what is necessary. For example, don't hide shipping costs - Shopify reported that 56% of online shoppers abandoned their baskets due to unexpected costs at the checkout stage [4].

Despite their importance of good usability and user experience (UX), they are often confused for one another and one or both may not be achieved. The International Organization for Standardization (ISO) defines the two as follows:

- Usability: the effectiveness, efficiency and satisfaction with which specified users achieve specified goals in particular environments.
- User Experience: a person's perceptions and responses that result from the use or anticipated use of a product, system or service.

The following simple example shows the difference between usability and user experience on an e-commerce site:

A customer arrives on the landing page for a product they want to buy. They add the product to their shopping cart quickly and easily, and checkout with minimal effort. The page would score high on a usability scale.

But the shopper was hoping to get a better sense of the product by looking at images taken from different angles and reading customer reviews. They were also not sure if the retailer was reputable. Without the images, reviews and credibility assurances, the customer was left uncertain whether they were wise to buy from this site. This page would score low on a user experience scale.

This illustrates the fact that it is possible to have good usability without good UX [4].

12   Security and Accepted Payment Methods

This is one of the essential attributes that differentiates eCommerce websites to any other website. eCommerce websites must build more trust with customers if they are to feel comfortable and confident with it. Especially as eCommerce websites are the top targets of cyberattacks.

All eCommerce websites should have an SSL certificate, without question. SSL encrypts and secures information and makes sensitive details like passwords and card details unreadable to protect against theft. In addition, security is required to meet PCI compliance for any business that accepts credit card payments.

Using alternative checkout and payment methods, like PayPal or Amazon checkouts, is another way to increase the likelihood of a visitor completing a purchase. If someone can use a system they already know and trust, they will be more confident in making that purchase - especially if they know they can get their money back should they never receive their items. Having that extra layer of backup can make a wavering visitor into an actual customer [3].

13   Consistency with Existing Designs

Some designers want to try to be more creative when designing a website or to try something new. While creativity is valuable for the brand image, it can work better for elements such as marketing than it does for the website's overall functionality and design. In trying to shake things up or reinvent the wheel, this might not translate to a good user experience for the site visitors who are used to traditional site designs. The following are some of the standard elements that people expect when visiting a website, according to a study:

- A logo at the top of the screen.
- Contact information or buttons on the top right of the screen.
- Primary horizontal menu navigation in the header on the top of each page.
- A search bar in the header.
- Social media icons in the footer [1].

14   Minimise Page Load Times

Website visitors may leave a webpage when it doesn't load within a few seconds. A slow loading site impacts the UX because people are annoyed whenever a web page takes more than three seconds to load, creating a poor user experience. That's why it is necessary to optimise site speed [1].

Reducing load time should be a priority for ecommerce platforms that seek to remain competitive and can benefit the search engine rankings, as some web search platforms now consider speed in their indexing. One of the easiest ways to increase the speed of page loading is to ensure all the images are an appropriate size, typically 640 x 640 or 800 x 800 pixels for e-commerce images to provide visual appeal while remaining efficient. Another way to improve page speed is to reduce the number of redirects on the website (points where an existing URL has to be converted) telling visitors and Google Search that a page has a new location. Every redirect contributes to the HTTP request and response process. Business continuity software can help survey the website for any redirects that are not needed or have been accidentally duplicated [6].

It is of course preferable to provide feedback on the process taking place so that if page load and responses times do increase, the user is at least informed that something is happening and that it is worth waiting.

15   Marketing and Analytics

Marketing and analytics tools can help understand user behaviour and boost user traffic When designing and building the site, including an analytics function such as Google Tag Manager, can give a deeper insight into what people do while they're looking around, and where they might drop out of the process. Including the appropriate cookies and pixels, will allow setting up of targeted remarketing campaigns that highlight products directly to the people who have already shown an interest in them.

SEO is one of the main ways to grow website traffic since it is necessary to be visible online. It is necessary to think carefully about how the e-commerce site is going to be structured. As well as providing an intuitive structure for users, avoiding duplicate content is important, and a sensible architecture will help search engines crawl the site.

Another useful strategy is to include a blog since this provides opportunities to rank for relevant keywords and provide useful information to potential customers. A site with a well-maintained, insightful blog will have more credibility than one without [3]. Creating high-quality blog content that is helpful and relevant to the target audience helps in product buying decisions. Providing links to them from specific product page(s) helps users to find them [7].

16   Usability Goals v Business Goals

Although it is important to create e-commerce websites that are easy to use, the company selling the products or services also have the goals that they wish to maximize. For example, adverts may appear within the page where the user is interested which they may find distracting. The following table provides examples of website design where usability goals have to be reconciled with business goals (Table 1):

Table 1. Comparison of usability and business goals for a video streaming service

Aim: Make the shopping process easy	Aim: Maximize number of users or subscribers
Present only the chosen product when being view	Show accessories that the user might also buy
Provide guest checkout without needing to set up an account	Encourage account creation to provide offers and track future usage
Present clean image without additional clutter	Present large image of partner company to encourage further exploration
Provide delivery time and cost options	Make the fastest delivery the default option to encourage users to select it

While design for business goals are accepted in the e-commerce world, the design should not be misleading so as to compromise or negatively affect what the user wants to achieve.

17 Conclusion

This paper has reviewed key usability guidelines for e-commerce website design drawing from a number of sources. Success of e-Commerce websites lies in improving user experience, keeping it simple, and winning client's trust. This will not only result in converting potential clicks into final transaction payment, but also strongly influence the customer to revisit the website in future. It is important however to consider the whole user experience which includes receiving items, possibly returning them and visiting the physical shop. As purchasing behaviors evolve, shopping is now a more social experience and one where customers are influenced by recommendations based on knowledge of their tastes and preferences. These processes need to be made transparent so that users understand how they work and have trust in them.

References

1. Anderson, J.: 8 Best practices to improve the usability of your ecommerce website, Poll the People, 28 July 2022. https://pollthepeople.app/website-usability/. Accessed 8 Mar 2023
2. Mc. Grath, E.: Top 9 E-commerce usability guidelines. https://www.usabilitygeek.com/top-9-e-commerce-usability-guidelines/. Accessed 8 Mar 2023
3. SpiderGroup: 8 key points in building an eCommerce website, September 2019. https://www.spidergroup.com/blog/8-key-points-in-building-an-ecommerce-website. Accessed 8 Mar 2023
4. Da Cambra, S.: 7 guidelines for ecommerce usability, Invesp. https://www.invespcro.com/blog/7-guidelines-for-ecommerce-usability/. Accessed 8 Mar 2023
5. Krug, S.: Don't make me think revisited: a common-sense approach to web and mobile usability, New Riders, Third Edition (2014)

6. Cooper, M.: How to optimize your shop based on usability, Big Commerce. https://www.big commerce.co.uk/blog/ecommerce-usability/. Accessed 8 Mar 2023
7. Arriloa, B.: How to improve your website navigation: 7 essential best practices. Search Eng. J. https://www.searchenginejournal.com/technical-seo/website-navigation/. Accessed 8 Mar 2023
8. Merchant Savvy: Global mobile ecommerce statistics, Trends and Forecasts (2022). https://www.merchantsavvy.co.uk/mobile-ecommerce-statistics. Accessed 8 Mar 2023
9. World Wide Web Consortium, Web Accessibility Initiative: WCAG 2 Overview. https://www.w3.org/WAI/standards-guidelines/wcag/. Accessed 8 Mar 2023
10. Invesp: Shopping Cart Abandonment Rate Statistics. https://www.invespcro.com/blog/shopping-cart-abandonment-rate-statistics-infographic/. Accessed 8 Mar 2023
11. Gibbons, S.: Journey mapping 101, Nielsen Norman Group, December 2018. https://www.nngroup.com/articles/journey-mapping-101/. Accessed 8 Mar 2023

User Generated Inverted Item Evaluation (UGIIE)

Denys J. C. Matthies[1]([✉]), Jagankumar Kothandan[2], Wenhan Sun[1,3], and Anke Dittmar[2]

[1] Technical University of Applied Sciences Lübeck, Lübeck, Germany
denys.matthies@th-luebeck.de
[2] University of Rostock, Rostock, Germany
[3] East China University of Science and Technology, Shanghai, China

Abstract. Measuring short-term User Experience (UX) of interactive systems is often assessed by standardized questionnaire-based methods. As standardized methods are broadly applicable, they deploy a great variety of questions. Depending on the target system, certain questions may appear irrelevant and annoying, while others may even bias the participant. This paper proposes an alternative UX evaluation method, the User Generated Inverted Item Evaluation (UGIIE). It utilizes a think-aloud technique to elicit only relevant items for a system-tailored questionnaire and employs an item inversion to increase critical reflection. Utilizing four user studies, UGIIE is benchmarked through a comparative study with two common UX methods, meCUE and UEQ. We found UGIIE to decrease users' frustration when filling out the questionnaire. UGIIE also indicates to provide a higher consistency in feedback when comparing the participants' quantitative rating and qualitative comments. UGIIE's drawback is the rather time-consuming preparation. Our study results suggest a preparation with a minimum of five participants to discover at least 80% of all relevant items for a UGIIE questionnaire. However, when testing much larger numbers of participants, UGIIE can be executed without the presence of an experimenter and thus becomes increasingly efficient.

Keywords: User Experience (UX) · Evaluation Method/Technique

1 Introduction

Research and development in the User Experience (UX) field is constantly growing, receiving high interest from industries and academia. UX is generally described as a result of an interaction between the user, the system and the context [1]. According to the ISO 9241-210, UX is defined as a person's *"perceptions and responses that result from the use or anticipated use of a product, system or service"* [2]. This formal definition is supplemented by other interpretations where the user experience *"also explores how a person feels about using a product, i.e., the experiential, meaningful and valuable aspects of the product use"* [3].

A. Marcus et al. (Eds.): HCII 2023, LNCS 14032, pp. 44–68, 2023.
https://doi.org/10.1007/978-3-031-35702-2_4

These definitions therefore indicate that measuring a realistic UX impression may be challenging. This is because the person's *feelings* and *perceptions* are highly subjective, manifold, individual, and thus ambiguous. Consequently, researchers and practitioners have developed a vast collection of standardized evaluation methods. To an extent, these methods measure a person's perception of the system before, during, and after the interaction. These UX evaluation methods are mostly questionnaire-based and aim to be broadly applicable. However, based on practitioners experiences, the results can occasionally be ambiguous and inaccurate. Other issues also arise where UX questionnaires are perceived as being inappropriate, as a number of questions fail to apply to the current tested system.

This paper proposes a new evaluation method, the *User Generated Inverted Item Evaluation (UGIIE)*. This method focuses on measuring short term UX by targeting a single behavioral episode having a defined beginning and end. The quality of the proposed method has been benchmarked by a comparative evaluation approach, in which the participants completed four diverse tasks. Each task involved an interactive product (1. flying a drone, 2. handling an unknown smartphone application, 3. setting up a mobile projector, and 4. using Instagram on a smartphone). The participant's UX was measured by: *User Experience Questionnaire (UEQ)*, *Modular Evaluation of Key Components of UX (meCUE)*, and *User Generated Inverted Item Evaluation (UGIIE)*.

Although UGIIE is also a questionnaire-based evaluation method, its core idea differentiates it from existing methods. UGIIE is based on the concept of *Reverse Brainstorming* [4], which is a creative technique that attempts to locate constructive ideas and solutions by simply inverting the goal. This deception releases the human brain from thought processes reliant on old structures, enabling the participant to reflect on the topic or system from a different angle. This allows a more creative problem-solving [5] and explains why UGIIE tends to achieve a slightly more critical reflection, resulting in greater consistency in the feedback of the actual UX during the study and final quantitative rating. Based on our results, it is suggested to run UGIIE with at least five participants individually to extract the required parameters for the inverted item questionnaire (*see* Fig. 10). UGIIE seems to only apply relevant items, which also decreases the users' frustration when filling out the questionnaire. Considering we utilized a combination of qualitative and quantitative analysis, results are still extracted in a reasonably short amount of time.

2   Background

2.1   Understanding User Experience

The design of products and services increasingly focuses on user enjoyment, while simultaneously supporting fundamental human needs and values [6, 7]. Meanwhile, User Experience (UX) exists as a core aspect of product development [8]. UX is generally understood as inherently dynamic, given the ever-changing internal and emotional state of a person and difference in the circumstances during and after an interaction with a product [9,10]. While it is relevant to evaluate short-term experience [11], investigating the temporal change of UX [10, 12] is also essential. When referring to the long-term use of interactive systems, products, and services, Kujala et al. [13] state the importance of the following UX attributes: attractiveness of the system, ease of use, utility, and degree of usage.

In HCI, understanding UX is regarded as an important issue. Several techniques, such as interviews, observations, surveys, story-telling, and diaries among others [14] have been explored. Numerous peripheral factors, such as peer groups, used products, and the environment substantially influence the UX that the interaction evokes [15]. The following aspects directly influence the experience evoking directly from user-product interaction: individual values, emotions, expectations, and prior experiences among similar products [16,17]. The "best-practise" to measure such attitudinal data is to conduct it either on a small scale, such as in the lab, or on a large scale by using surveys [18,19]. Within this century, the HCI field has substituted usability concerns with the UX. A methodological shift from a quantitative to a qualitative approach occurred, as noted by Bargas et al. [20].

2.2   Relationship of User Experience and Usability

User Experience (UX) and usability are fundamental for a successful product and service delivery. According to the ISO 9241-11, usability is defined as *"the extent to which a product can be used by specified users to achieve specified goals with effectiveness, efficiency and satisfaction in a specified context of use"* [21]. Long time the term UX remained vague and was widely used as a synonym for other terms [22]. This changed when the concept of usability was defined by ergonomics research in the early 1980's. The concept of usability, however, has gradually evolved into a definition that captures the quality of use [23]. Hertzum [24] describes six different perspectives on usability: universal usability, situational usability, perceived usability, hedonic usability, organizational usability, and cultural usability.

In contrast, UX focuses on the individual experience, rather than effectively and efficiently achieving a goal within the context of product use [9,20,23]. Hassenzahl [25] and Bevan et al. [23], however, point out that usability and UX are both underpinned by an element of satisfaction. Therefore, this clarification can be added to the ISO 9241-11. Nevertheless, differences exist between UX and usability. UX focuses on lived experiences [26], whereas usability focuses on evaluating task performance. Also, UX is highly subjective [10]. Usability, however, is objectively measurable using typical measures, such as the task completion time, number of clicks, error rate, etc. Another way to measure usability is considering the user's *"satisfaction"*, which is also a core aspect of UX evaluations. As the UX addresses a range of other subjective qualities, usability may also be a subset of the UX [22].

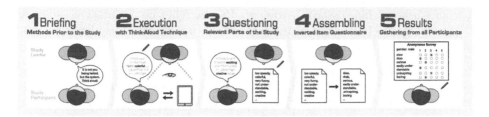

Fig. 1. The UGIIE technique features five phases. In a short (1) Briefing the participant is explained important considerations, such as to think aloud. At the (2) Execution phase of the study, the user is interacting with the target system. A (3) Questioning post study helps to elicit additional attributes describing the subject's experience. (4) Assembling the inverted item questionnaire is a crucial step. Once the questionnaire is compiled, the (5) Results are gathered from all participants.

3   User Generated Inverted Item Evaluation (UGIIE)

This method is based on initial qualitative user feedback [27], which is then transformed into quantitative measurable results. Using clear user instructions and classic methods, this technique has potential to overcome common drawbacks of standardized quantitative methods. It particularly circumvents the problem of user's failing to independently undertake a critical reflection by assessing a semi-negative questionnaire that is compiled from the user's gathered feedback. This methodology appropriates the idea of a creativity technique, the *"Brainstorm Paradox/Reverse Brainstorming"* [4], which attempts to discover constructive ideas and solutions through goal inversion. The human brain is released from relying on old structures, enabling the participant to view the topic from a different perspective. This has been discovered and utilized for creative problem solving as early as 1974 [5]. To perform a successful evaluation, a study leader and a suggested minimum of five participants are required. This minimum enables the finding of at least ~80% of all relevant items (*see* Fig. 10). However, we suggest a number of eight participants. In fact, the sample size between eight and twelve will also yield a larger finding of the majority of all usability problems [28,29]. To improve post-processing and subsequent analysis, it is suggested to include audio and video recordings, while having an additional observer taking notes. Once the questionnaire is compiled, UGIIE can be executed without the presence of the experimenter (Fig. 1).

3.1   Classification

From the later introduced criteria *(see section: Related Work)* based on Vermeeren's taxonomy [3], UGIIE could be classified as follows:

Origin: Similar to most UX assessment methods, the UGIIE framework was developed in a scholarly context.

Type of Gathered Information: Although UGIIE relies on qualitative feedback [27], it transforms it into quantitative feedback, which can be analyzed by statistical means.

Type of Applications/Designs: UGIIE is applicable to a large variety of applications, such as testable multimedia information systems (e.g., smartphone interfaces, games, interactive installations etc.). While other application fields (e.g., on-site with users) may be possible, they have yet to be tested.

Data Sources: The proposed evaluation method is based on the *"think aloud method"* [30] and can be performed individually or in groups. A specific user group is not necessary. However, an *"expert"* would need to extract the attributes and compile the questionnaire.

Location: Any location, such as a lab environment or the field is possible that allows the study leader to track the user's experiences using the *"think aloud method"* [30]. Remote-environments, namely when the participant is at a different location and using a web-based service, may create complications, but is not impossible using a technical workaround.

Period of Experience: UGIIE operates most effectively at a single behavioural episode with a defined beginning and end (e.g., task or period in which the user explores some specific feature). It also works for a typical test session (e.g., one hour of performing a task).

Development Phases: The proposed method is sufficient for interactive products, such as fully functional products and functional prototypes.

Technical Requirements: UGIIE does not require any specialized equipment. However, it requires a *"trained UX examiner"*, to extract the items and to prepare the questionnaire. Conducting it remotely requires technical applications.

The method itself consists of five phases; briefing, execution, questioning, assembling the attribute list, and gathering results. The work-flow is explained in the subsequent sections.

3.2   I. Briefing

Prior to executing the user study, a short briefing phase is required. There are few important factors to consider:

- The briefing phase should be kept as short as possible
- Providing the user with suggestions on potential interaction methods with the system should be avoided. Where techniques, such as paper prototyping [31] or an obvious *"Wizard of OZ"* [32] are used, providing a short explanation to avoid confusion is recommended.
- Important: It is imperative to inform the user that there are no incorrect interaction methods. User interaction is not being tested, but the system in which they are interacting with. Any occurring problems thus stem from flaws in the system design, not from their lack of proficiency.

– *"Think aloud"* [30]: The participants should be sensitized to articulate every single thought aloud during their interaction. This allows easy tracing of their thought processes over the interaction sequences.

3.3   II. Execution

Exploration. Providing a short exploration phase prior to evaluating the actual task is recommended. This phase should remain short and provide the user with an opportunity to adjust with confronting a new system, as they would in a real scenario.

Testing. While there are different ways to test multimedia information systems, a user test need not be purposeful to achieve prescribed goals. It can also be performed in an exploratory way by the user without a specific aim. Nevertheless, in scientific literature, an effective and gap-less user test is based on different use cases [33] and scenarios. These scenarios have to be created initially, which the study participant subsequently experiences. The user will be requested to follow certain tasks, and or, achieve objectives. The user will also be requested to use the *"think aloud method"*, where the study leader will record the attributes mentioned based on the user's current experience.

3.4   III. Questioning

Free Talk/Reflection. Once the participant has completed all the required tasks, encouraging the user to discuss their overall experience is highly recommended instead of starting the questioning immediately. It is important to give the user an opportunity to discuss their mindset, before questions steer the user in a specific direction.

Questions. Some users may have failed to take initiative in offering their insights. It may be relevant to elicit attributes by questioning the user about particular moments in which joy and discomfort was experienced. This aspect is crucial to facilitate discussion about their experience, namely their perceptions and feelings. Furthermore, questions about specific user decisions should be asked to prevent confusion. Where necessary, a small set of questions concerning which features require feedback, can be prepared beforehand.

3.5   IV. Assembling Item List

Collecting Attributes. During the questioning process, the participants will have used different attributes to describe their experiences. For example: "too speedy, colorful, very funny, not understandable, creative, exciting...". These attributes should be listed. Moreover, the participants can be asked to describe their experience of the evaluated system in a post-questioning process. These adjectives would also need to be added to the item list.

Inverting Attribute List. Following the interviews with all the study participants, the attribute list should be fairly substantial by now. It is worth mentioning that we experienced the attributes list to be shorter when performing group interviews. New, creating an inverted item list by using the opposites of all attributes (e.g. "too speedy→ slow, colourful→drab, very funny→serious, not understandable→easy to understand, creative→uninspired, exciting→boring"), is the next and most crucial step.

3.6 V. Results Gathering

Anonymous Rating. The next stage requires the users to rate the inverted item list. It is important to communicate that the performed rating will be treated anonymously. (Requesting the user's gender, age, and other relevant data is still acceptable and should be done.) For the rating, a 7-point Likert scale [34] appears suitable, but other scales may fit also [35]. The study participants are now prepared to rate the system on attributes, which are actually the opposite of their own valuation. This may foster an increased critical reflection, since the attributes are contrary to their opinion (and mostly negative when they had a positive experience). This method provides the participants with an opportunity to reflect on a level with greater profundity.

Note: The process of compiling the inverted item list is time consuming, since it can only be completed after gathering attributes from several participants. If the participant is no longer physically present, the questionnaire can still be sent via a small online survey to the participant. However, long temporal gaps between completing the study and filling out the questionnaire should be avoided.

Analysis. After all the results are collected, the overall average of each opposite attribute can be analyzed or converted into the original attribute. For example, the majority may have rated the attribute *"boring"* with a 3, The item be inverted into the original attribute, *"exciting"*, which would result in a rating of 5 (based on a 7-point Likert scale). The gathered data can now be analyzed by statistical means. Although ratings on a Likert scale is strictly spoken non-parametric data [36], a 7-point scale to account for parametric data is also suitable. Literature proposes that both are feasible [37], as the drawn conclusions may not necessarily differ [38].

4 Evaluating UGIIE

Based on past experiences, we found that study participants tended to feel increasingly annoyed when required to answer a large number of unsuitable questions from standardized methods. Literature has also shown goal inversion [4] to enable a more creative and impartial judgement and problem solving [5]. Therefore, UGIIE will potentially provide a more critical impression of the user experience and decrease user frustration during the post-questioning process (*see Hypotheses*). To evidence this, the UGIIE will be benchmarked against established UX methods (*see Methodology*). Three experiments were designed, in which the UX of different products were measured. Finally, the results are presented and more general conclusions will be drawn (*see Results*).

4.1 Hypotheses

Hypothesis 1: UGIIE will yield a greater critical and consistent evaluation compared to other UX methods.

Hypothesis 2: UGIIE will apply a more relevant criteria for evaluation than standard UX questionnaire.

Hypothesis 3: UGIIE will be rated as less annoying compared to other standard questionnaires.

4.2 Methodology

To evidence the hypotheses, a comparative approach is used, in which different evaluation techniques are evaluated. Two established methods were used to compare their performances against the newly developed UGIIE method.

1. *User Experience Questionnaire (UEQ)*
2. *Modular Evaluation of Key Components of User Experience Questionnaire (meCUE)*
3. *User Generated Inverted Item Evaluation (UGIIE)*

4.3 Procedure

At the beginning of each experimental study, the participants were briefly introduced to the product. After completing the task, each user was asked to fill out a questionnaire in which they had to provide demographic data and rate the system with the help of a questionnaire. A drone, an unknown smartphone app, a projector, and the Instagram smartphone app were deliberately chosen from a broad range of interactive products. Four unique situations were examined and assessed: a group of users with no involvement in utilizing the product (drone), a group of users with great involvement in utilizing the product (unknown smartphone app), a group of users with a blend of limited understanding in utilizing the product (projector), and a group of users using a familiar smartphone app (Instagram). Experiment 4 was conducted remotely via a video-communication tool. At the end of each experiment, the users were requested to fill the survey questionnaires to measure the user experience of using the device. The users were also requested to mark the questions in the questionnaires which they found inappropriate. All four experiments were audio-taped with the participant's consent (Figs. 2 and 3).

Fig. 2. Study participant getting familiar with the drone using the manual (A) and eventually performing the given tasks (B).

4.4 Task 1: Drone

The participants were seated at a table, while having a drone and wireless controller laid in front of them. The study leader sat next to them and read the tasks aloud, which were recorded down on a sheet of paper. A secretary accompanied the study leader and noted the protocol of the user's mentioned attributes. Subsequently, the users were requested to envision themselves as a drone pilot and test the drone by performing a series of tasks. Users can read the user manual at the beginning of the experiment or between the experimental tasks. The first task is to raise the drone roughly at the user's eye level and land it instantly on the marked position. The second task requires lifting the drone roughly to

Fig. 3. Study participants performing the task on the smartphone (C) and filling out a questionnaire after the experiment (D)

the user's knee level and move the drone to hit the target (empty water bottle). The user will then land the drone immediately next to the target. The final task requires the user to fly the drone from one marked position to another.

4.5   Task 2: Unknown Smartphone App

The participants were seated at a table, while having a smartphone (model: iPhone 5) laid in front of them. The study leader sat next to them and read the tasks aloud, which were recorded on a sheet of paper. Beside the study leader, a secretary was taking protocol of the user's mentioned attributes. The users are then requested to envision themselves in a scenario where they need to create a sale advertisement to sell an old wristwatch using a specific mobile app they were not familiar with. Several sub-tasks, such as taking a photo of watch, were included (Fig. 4).

4.6   Task 3: Projector

The participants were seated at a table, while having a mini projector (UNIC UC 46+) laid in front of them. The study leader sat next to them and read the tasks aloud, which were recorded on a sheet of paper. Beside a study leader, a secretary was taking protocol of the user's mentioned attributes. The users are requested to envision a scenario in which, during their thesis defence, the projector in the conference room experienced some issues. Subsequently, they were provided with a small portable projector to complete the thesis presentation. Users can read the user manual at the beginning of the experiment or between the experimental task. The first task is to connect the mini projector to the power supply and modify the setting to get a clear image output. The second task is to connect the laptop with the mini projector to project the thesis presentation slides onto the

 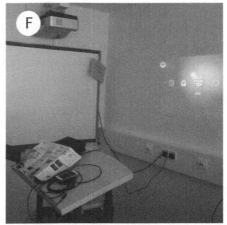

Fig. 4. Study participant performing the think-aloud technique during the experiment (E) and setting up the projector (F).

screen. The third task is to connect the projector to the smartphone by remotely using WiFi (Fig. 5).

4.7   Task 4: Familiar Smartphone App

Fig. 5. Experimenter observing the study participant interacting with their smartphone during experiment 4.

Since this experiment was carried out during the COVID-19 pandemic, the study participant was located in a remote location from the experimenter. A pre-condition for this study was that participants were an Instagram user. The participant used their own Android smartphone for the study. For the first task, the user was required to set up the camera from a side-angle to allow the experimenter to gain a greater impression of the participant's performance. The experimenter guided the user through several use cases, which included: taking photos and uploading them; taking short videos and uploading them; searching the experimenters Instagram account and adding him as a friend; interacting with the experimenter via Instagram's chat, like, and comment feature. Finally, the experimenter asked the participant to customize their account, such as filling in an account description.

4.8   Participants

To perform the comparative evaluation of the three UX assessment techniques, 21 participants were invited to take part in the first three experiments. One participant was excluded afterwards. All participants were university students. The majority of the participants were male (85%) and the remaining were female (15%). The age of the participants ranged between 20yrs to 47yrs ($M = 25.7$yrs).

The fourth study also featured 20 participants aged between 20yrs to 47yrs ($M = 24.55$yrs). Since we were interested in comparing UX techniques and not the products itself, we neglected an age and gender balancing.

4.9 Data Gathering

As the UGIIE questionnaire needs to be generated during the experiment, we asked the first 10 participants to fill out the UEQ and meCUE questionnaires in alternating order. We decided not to ask participants to fill out more than two questionnaires to prevent unnecessary annoyance, as this could negatively bias the provided data from a third questionnaire.

To ensure comparability of all three questionnaires (UEQ, meCUE, and UGIIE), the rating scale was transformed to a common scale. All participants were asked to rate each attribute for all UX questionnaires using a 7-point Likert scale [34]. The following rating was applied: Strongly Disagree (1) to Strongly Agree (7). With each question, the participant could indicate whether the question was inappropriate and inapplicable. Although when the question was marked as such, the participant was still required to answer it regardless.

One participant that performed experiment 1–3 was declared an outlier since he provided unrealistic and incomplete answers. After removing this single dataset, we accumulated 30 valid questionnaires for each experiment, x10 meCUE, x10 UEQ, and x10 UGIIE, resulting in 120 filled questionnaires in total.

To gather the items for the UGIIE method, the mentioned attributes were extracted from the audio tapes. Noting these attributes during the experiment would be less time consuming. The analysis of the audio tapes resulted in the identification of 17 items for experiment 1 *(see* Table 1 and 2*)*, 14 item for experiment 2, 15 attributes for experiment 3, and 15 attributes for experiment 4.

4.10 Results

Addressing Hypothesis 1. Following the hypothesis, the rating of a system using a standardized posteriori questionnaire, may not be sufficiently critical or very reflective of the actual user experience. To investigate this, the ratings of common attributes, which were used for all three UX methods, were compared *(Common items – see* Table 1 and 2*)*.

Experiment 1 - Drone, six common attributes were identified: Easy, Understandable, Annoying, Attractive, Clear, Exciting.

Experiment 2 - Smartphone (unfamiliar App), four common attributes were identified: Easy, Attractive, Clear, Good.

Experiment 3 - Projector, four common attributes were identified: Understandable, Easy, Good, and Attractive.

Experiment 4 - Projector (Instagram), four common attributes were identified: Attractive, Friendly, Easy, and Practical.

Data Analysis: Although statistical significance is lacking among most single attributes *(see* Fig. 6), a *one-way ANOVA for independent samples* could evidence a statistical significance for a couple of attributes.

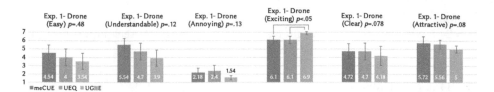

Fig. 6. Displaying all common attributes among the three questionnaires (UEQ, meCUE, UGIIE). UGIIE demonstrated to be somewhat closer to the baseline: the drone was rated to be very exciting.

In experiment 1, every participant found it very "exciting" flying the drone, which UGIIE ($M = 6.9$; $SD = .31$) emphasized significantly stronger ($F_{2,27} = 3.92$; $p < .05$) than meQUE ($M = 6.1$; $SD = .87$) and UEQ ($M = 6.1$; $SD = .87$), as confirmed by a Tukey HSD post-hoc analysis. For the other common attributes, it could be said that UGIIE emphasizes the user experience slightly stronger than other questionnaires. When there was a positive trend, UGIIE showed more positive results. When there is a negative trend, UGIIE showed a slightly more negative trend. However, these observations at all other attributes are not backed with a statistical difference ($p > .05$).

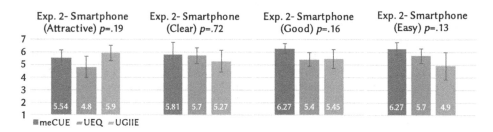

Fig. 7. Displaying all common attributes among the three questionnaires (UEQ, meCUE, UGIIE). UGIIE did not show a significant different rating with the first smartphone experiment.

In experiment 2, all common attributes showed consistency across all three questionnaires ($p > .05$), see Fig. 7.

In experiment 3, the user had to setup a poorly designed low-budget WiFi projector. None of the participants were satisfied, as they stated during the experiment that the product had a bad output, was poor quality, and operated insufficiently. The participants were hardly able to accomplish the given task. Taking this as a baseline, the scores of the meQUE ($M = 4.6$; $SD = 1.78$) and UEQ ($M = 4.9$; $SD = 1.45$) do not reflect these "bad" experiences. Those tests score a neutral to positive tendency. In contrast, UGIIE ($M = 2.5$; $SD = 1.71$) shows a significantly more critical rating, which is confirmed by a one-way ANOVA for independent samples $F_{2,27} = 6.26$; $p < .05$, as well as a post-hoc

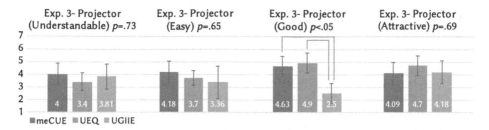

Fig. 8. Displaying all common attributes among the three questionnaires (UEQ, meCUE, UGIIE). UGIIE demonstrated to be somewhat closer to the baseline: the projector was perceived to be very bad).

analysis by a Tukey HSD. For other attributes UGIIE coincides with the other methods, although it is striking that UGIIE yields either similar ratings or more critical ratings closer to the qualitative statements. Considering the qualitative feedback during the studies as a ground truth baseline, the rating of all common attributes for both meQUE ($M = .61$; $SD = .65$) and UEQ ($M = .68$; $SD = .58$), deviated higher than the rating of UGIIE ($M = .28$; $SD = .43$). A statistical difference using a one-way ANOVA for independent samples $F_{2,39} = 2.02$; $p = .14$ could not be indicated from this rather low sample size (Fig. 8).

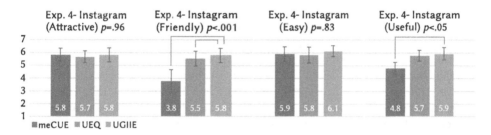

Fig. 9. Displaying all common attributes among the three questionnaires (UEQ, meCUE, UGIIE). UGIIE demonstrated to be somewhat closer to the baseline: the Instragram Smartphone app was perceived significantly different to meCUE results).

In experiment 4, we evaluated a sophisticated smartphone app (Instagram) optimized for great user experience. Every participant was positive about the app, as it was a requirement that participants were frequent users. For the attribute "friendly", meQUE ($M = 3.8$; $SD = 1.8$) provided a significant understatement compared to UEQ ($M = 5.5$; $SD = .1.18$) and UGIIE ($M = 5.8$; $SD = 1.14$), following a one-way ANOVA ($F_{2,27} = 5.85$; $p < .001$) and a Tukey HSD post-hoc analysis (*see Figure* 9). Another difference was found in the item "useful". MeQUE ($M = 4.8$; $SD = .92$) again under-performed while UGIIE ($M = 5.9$; $SD = .99$) showed a significantly better and more realisitc result, as it coincided with results gathered from the UEQ ($M = 5.7$; $SD = .82$). A one-way

ANOVA ($F_{2,27} = 4.1$; $p = .023$) made the discovery, while a Tukey HSD test confirmed the result. Other common attributes, such as "attractive" and "easy" did not significantly differ ($p > .05$) and seemed constant across all three tests.

Considering qualitative as ground truth, (1) UGIIE was indicated to be slightly more critical at some attributes and even significantly different to four attributes, which also coincides with the user statements and, (2) the tendency of UGIIE to deviate less from the baseline compared to meCUE and UEQ, allows the conclusion that hypothesis 1 is acceptable.

Addressing Hypothesis 2. A simultaneous advantage and disadvantage of commonly applied UX methods, is the variety of the questions asked. These UX methods are advantageous as they can assess a variety of different systems. However, this also requires answering a large amount inappropriate questions, which may be perceived as bothersome and time consuming. In fact, the meCUE Questionnaire incorporates 33 questions, in which 22 were found to be inappropriate across all experiments. Therefore, only $M = 33.33\%$ ($SD = 8.9$) of all attributes were considered appropriate. The UEQ Questionnaire includes 26 attributes, where approximately 20 were considered unsuitable across all experiments. Thus, only $M = 24.35\%$ ($SD = 4.79\%$) of all attributes were suitable. In contrast, the UGIIE accumulated, on average, 15 different attributes across all experiments. Less than two items were considered inappropriate across all participants. Therefore, $M = 88.41\%$ ($SD = 8.83\%$) of all attributes were perceived as appropriate.

A one-way ANOVA for independent samples ($F_{3,6} = 42.5$; $p < .001$) suggests a strong significance comparing all UX questionnaires. A Tukey HSD Test confirms that the UGIIE yields significantly more appropriate attributes compared to the meCUE ($p < .01$) and the UEQ ($p < .01$). In terms of appropriate attributes, there are no significant differences between the meCUE and the UEQ. Therefore, this data confirms hypothesis 2 in that UGIIE applies more relevant attributes than classical UX methods, which is due to the sheer nature of how a UGIIE questionnaire is developed.

Addressing Hypothesis 3. The participants were requested to think aloud during the experiment, as well as during the time when filling out the questionnaire. Commenting on the participant's reaction was avoided to prevent imbuing any biases. It was striking that most participants stated that several items in the standard questionnaires were unrelated. Comments from the participants are as follows:

P12: *"It [–the attribute to be rated–]] is not specific."* P10: *"[Several attributes were] out of Scope"* P2: *"It is too open, the questionnaire."* P17: *"I am unable to answer the questions, it does not reflect my real experience"* P21: *"It [–the question–] is too unspecific."* P1: *"It's difficult to answer the question which is not applicable."* P4: *"It is not related."* P14: *"[This question is] exaggerated."*

Another feedback from the questionnaire was the apparent excess of similar items. The majority of participants stated that they were irritated by the high similarity in questions, having felt they had addressed a similar question prior. Once the participants took part in more than one experiment and used the UGIIE, the majority concluded that UGIIE was quick to fill out and did not include irrelevant questions. Based on the many qualitative feedback, hypothesis 3 can thus be confirmed, as the UGIIE method creates less annoyance compared to other standard questionnaires (UEQ and meCUE) that often show unsuitable questions and questions of high redundancy.

5 Discussion

The proposed UX method: User Generated Inverted Item Evaluation (UGIIE) features certain advantages in contrast to standardized UX questionnaires. Still, drawbacks and challenges are an inevitable aspect of its development.

5.1 Advantages

Critical Reflection and Consistent Feedback. Due to the poor usability of some products we tested, it was evident that the participants experienced difficulties. Their negative experiences were also confirmed by the attributes they used to describe their situation at that particular moment. However, these experiences were reflected differently with a standardized questionnaire. UGIIE's inverted item questionnaire, which is contrary to their own valuation, potentially enabled a more critical reflection. The results appeared more consistent, as they greater coincided with the users' actual qualitative feedback spoken aloud during the experiment. This finding is also somewhat underpinned by our subjective observation that most participants were slightly surprised when asked to fill in UGIIE. Participants also seemed more cautious when rating the items on UGIIE.

Appropriate Attributes. Due to the nature of UGIIE, it includes more appropriate questions than standardized questionnaires. From the ascertained outcome, only 24.35% of these attributes in UEQ method were rated as appropriate, 33.3% of all attributes were considered proper in meCUE questionnaire, and 88.4% of all attributes were considered appropriate in UGIIE. Although standard questionnaires may not require a preparation time, the costs of creating UGIIE questionnaires are still relatively low when compiling it based on a small number of users, such as five. The benefits indicated from the results, namely more appropriate questions, reveal that UGIIE is a worthwhile investment.

Subjectively Less Annoying Questions. In comparison to commonly used questionnaires, which usually deploy up to 33 items that may be partly redundant, UGIIE is significantly more compact. In over four experiments, we extracted 15 relevant items on average. The participant's qualitative discussion statements concerning the rated attributes of the questionnaires reveal that the UGIIE method was experienced as less annoying and less frustrating compared to the standard UX methods.

Broad Applicability. The nature of UGIIE does not require it to be bound to a specific domain - *see Experiment 1–4*. It is applicable in a variety of scenarios, which do not necessarily need to be within interactive products. However, one still needs to rigorously experiment and prove its usefulness for a variety of other products and systems.

5.2 Further Insights

Extracting a Reasonable Number of Attributes. Extracting items is an essential step for the UGIIE technique. It was identified that after five times running the experiment, at least 80% of the total attributes were discovered (based on our investigations with 10 runs). This suggests that very few participants sufficiently develop a reasonable and precise conclusion of the outcome.

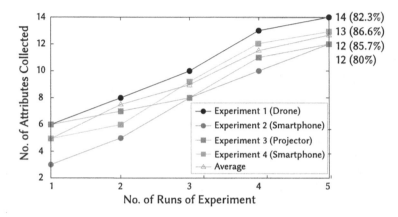

Fig. 10. Five runs seem to be sufficient in to extract a reasonable number of attributes. In our experiments, we could find at least 80% of the total attributes found after 10 runs.

Reasonable Time Consumption. Compiling the tailored inverted questionnaire requires the experimenter to expend extra time. For instance, in our last experiment, we took around 2 h to develop the questionnaire by fast-forwarding through the audio recordings of 10 users, although the actual use case test only lasted around 15 min per user. However, once compiled, the presence of the experimenter is no longer necessary. Also, the time participants require to fill the questionnaire is shorter compared to standardized questionnaires. This is advantageous when testing a greater number of users.

UEQ Comparison. On the one hand, the User Experience Questionnaire (UEQ) provides a comprehensive impression of UX, ranging from classical usability aspects to user experience aspects. However, the six scale with the 26 items constrains the UX measurement to certain limited items. On the other hand, UEQ does not require significant reading efforts from the participants and can be completed within five minutes. Another advantage is that UEQ is of no cost.

meCUE Comparison. MeCUE is based on statements and considers the affection of product use. With the meCUE questionnaire, the authors express that it has the advantage of assessing major UX components in a comprehensive manner. However, the questions are often redundant and lengthy, creating annoyances with the survey method. Nevertheless, meCUE may be relevant to researchers, as it is applicable to any User Experience surveys in a variety of interactive systems.

5.3 Challenges

Preparation Time Required. The UGIIE method features a custom questionnaire, which requires preparation in advance. This creates a delay between the actual execution of the study and administering the posterori evaluation. To counter this, items from other users who are testing the system were collected first. The generated inverted questionnaire was then deployed straightaway with other users, once they completed using the system. Alternatively, the UGIEE questionnaire could be sent to the users some days after testing the system. Recapturing their UX with a time-distance, may enable a greater critical and consistent reflection. However, this also yields drawbacks, as the users may have forgotten their actual experience of the system during the execution. If just testing a single-digit number of users, UEQ and meCUE have a time-cost advantage.

Item Extraction Can Cause Complications. In some exceptional cases, problems may arise, namely when the system is tested with a passive user who is reserved in character. Although previously prompted to use the think-aloud technique, such a user may still fail to use their initiative to discuss their thought processes aloud. This creates difficulties in capturing the user's actual experience. Continuing to prompt the user to discuss their experience, may create user dissatisfaction and imbue a sense of bias. In this case, the chances of failing to capture a realistic UX may increase. Only a greater sample size of users can mitigate this issue.

5.4 Methodological Limitations

Evaluating Evaluation Tools. The optimum method to evaluate an evaluation tool remains contentious. While a comparative approach may be superior, it also has limitations. An issue which arises is that each method uses their own rating scale. Moreover, a comparison is not necessarily fair, as different UX methods are tailored to specific domains. To ensure the best comparison possible, two similar UX questionnaires were selected for interactive systems. The same rating scale, a 7-point Likert scale, was applied.

Participants. In reality, there is no ideal user. Instead, the individual factor is very well pronounced, which underpins much of UX research. Therefore, a high number of participants and trials are suggested to counterbalance the individual factor, and thus enable generalized and valid conclusions. As each experiment (including: preparation, execution, filling the questionnaire) lasted around an hour, roughly around three hours per participant (~80 h total study time), a reasonable cut-off point was necessary. This point was defined when a minimum of 10 questionnaires were completed for each method. Running statistical means with an increased number of participants, may have contributed to more significant results and possibly fully proving the first hypothesis.

Ground Truth UX. As there is no physiological technology to measure the actual UX, we considered qualitative feedback expressed during the study as the ground truth UX, which we compared with the quantitative ratings.

6   Related Work

6.1   Overview of UX Evaluation Methods

There are various User Experience evaluation methods within the market. A few common ones are: AttrakDiff, Experience Sampling Method (ESM), Game experience questionnaire (GEQ), User Experience Questionnaire (UEQ), TRUE Tracking Realtime User Experience, Modular Evaluation of Key Components of UX (meCUE) questionnaire, Attrak-Work questionnaire etc. Several overviews of UX assessment techniques have been conducted [39]. For instance, Isomursu et al. [40] particularly highlights those surveying transient feelings. [41] lists a collection of more extensive methods for designing pleasurable products. Vermeeren et al. arranges UX evaluation strategies into three gatherings, namely by the type of measures the method focuses on: Sensory characteristics, Articulation or Meaning and Emotional response [3]. The AAAC [42] gathered and developed design and assessment techniques for effective interactive systems. Furthermore, Isomursu [43] arranged alternative UX assessment techniques that focus on understanding user emotions.

However, the broadest collection includes 96 UX assessment techniques [44]. Based on the current individual UX evaluation strategies [3], inferences can be drawn as to which techniques are rare or successful, and what their qualities and shortcomings are. This overview is briefly summarized [3] by using eight criteria, based on their value in interest:

Origin: It is striking that 70% of all strategies root in the scholar community. Still, it is plausible that a large number of UX assessment strategies, categorized by industry, remain undiscovered.

Type of Gathered Information: Around 33% of the strategies were accounted for giving quantitative information, 33% qualitative information and 33% both.

Type of Applications/Designs: 73% of the strategies are moderately application-autonomous. However, most UX techniques aim to evaluate: web services, mobile software, PC software, and hardware designs.

Data Sources: The majority (80%) can be utilized with single users. 17% use a user groups, as a conceivable source of data (e.g., AttrakWork questionnaire, outdoor play observation scheme, Living Lab, product personality assignment).

Location: Lab, field, or on the web? About half of all strategies are only applicable at a single location: in the lab (67%), in the field (52%), or on the web (40%). All other UX evaluation strategies can be applied in multiple contexts and locations.

Period of Experience: 63% of all strategies can be utilized for considering UX of single behavioural episodes and 59% are suggetsed to be applied in a single test session. 36% of all techniques can manage long-term use.

Development Phases: 39% of all methods are to be used to assess the system's UX in an early development stage. However, the vast majority of all strategies (~80%) can be utilized as a part for later as well as early development stages.

Technical Requirements: Most techniques (67%) are accounted for not requiring any unique equipment or programming. Remote utilization, such as by means of a website is conceivable in about half of all cases (e.g., multiple sorting methods, ServUX, audio narrative, activity experience sampling, SUMI, etc.).

From the above UX evaluation framework, User Experience Questionnaire (UEQ) and a Modular Evaluation of Key Components of UX (meCUE Questionnaire) provide exceptional advantages, as similarities exist with our proposed method. UEQ and meCUE both provide a complete UX impression, ranging from classic usability aspects to user experience aspects. Moreover, it introduces an analytic apparatus to precisely translate the outcome effectively. UEQ and meCUE are also highly accessible, being of no cost [45]. Therefore, comparing UGIIE with these established UX questionnaires may produce interesting results.

6.2   Quantitative UX Evaluation Methods for Single Episodes

Quantitative evaluations represents the user's subjective feelings towards the item they utilize in a measurable way enabling a comparison. Estimating a valid impression on UX the user encounters with a design or service generally requires gathering input from a large user group. The most efficient way is using an online survey [45]. Common UX techniques are mostly questionnaire-based, which provide a quantitative analysis. As previously stated, the User Experience Questionnaire (UEQ), and a Modular Evaluation of Key Components of UX (meCUE), were selected based on their advantages and high similarities to our proposed method.

User Experience Questionnaire (UEQ). The principal objective of the UEQ is to enable a prompt estimation of the user experience of interactive products [46]. The user experience questionnaire contains six scales with 26 items in total (Attractiveness, Efficiency, Perspicuity, Dependability, Stimulation, Novelty) [45]. UEQ features a bi-polar item scale, which can be rated on seven steps. For example, one item would be annoying <> enjoyable. This rating scale has been benchmarked [47] with data sets containing information from a 163 item assessment. These assessed items secured an extensive variety of applications, such as: complex business applications (98), advancement tools (4), web shops or services (37), social networks (3), versatile applications (13), and a few other products(8). UEQ has also been applied in research context and counts to a common technique to measure UX [48].

meCUE - A Modular Evaluation of Key Components of UX. The meCUE questionnaire [49] is described by its creators as *"a freely accessible, experimentally established questionnaire, which centers around the particular securing of user focused audits and their experience of interactive technical product'* [50]. It is a particular UX evaluation scale adapted from the Thüring and Mahlke's CUE- model [51] and composed of 33 items partitioned into 4 dimensions: instrumental and non-instrumental product perception, emotions, consequence and overall judgment. Inside each sub-scale, respondents are requested to evaluate their agreement level with proclamations on a 7-point Likert scale [34] from 1 "strongly disagree" to 7 "strongly agree". All questions are positively worded and required, as expressed in the instructions. As indicated by its' authors, the main advantage of meCUE when contrasted with existing questionnaire is to survey the significant segments of UX in a comprehensive manner. The psychometric properties of the questionnaire have been evaluated through a few investigations [49]. Furthermore, *"meCUE can be applied in UX reviews on a wide range of interactive systems"* [50]. The meCUE questionnaire has recorded logical properties, particularly taking into account the evaluation of both hedonic and pragmatic perspectives and is depicted as reasonable for all specific circumstances. Using a more *"common-sensual"* decision from a pragmatic-only scale is not ideal for the present purpose [50].

7 Conclusion

This paper presented an alternative UX evaluation technique, the User Generated Inverted Item Evaluation (UGIIE). The core idea is adapted from reverse brainstorming, in which the user's mind is freed from thought processes bound by limiting grids of goal inversion. Based on the think-aloud technique and a post-questioning method, only the relevant attributes that describe the system were evaluated and later inverted, before being subject to participant ratings. By comparing UGIIE against two common UX questionnaires (UEQ and meCUE), we discovered that in some circumstances, UGIIE was rated as being significantly more basic for a few traits. This coincides with the subjective user explanation and the general factual contrast of UGIIE compared to a baseline average calculated from the UEQ and meCUE. Moreover, a UGIIE questionnaire incorporates more relevant questions and is thus considered to be less annoying for the participant to complete. Incidentally, this positively impacts the UX of the evaluation process itself. Although standard questionnaires may not require preparation time, applying UGIIE becomes increasingly advantageous when testing greater number of users. However, aiming to gather quick insights on UX with just a single digit number of users, standard questionnaires or qualitative questioning seem to provide the most time-efficient solution.

Appendix

Table 1. Displaying the collected attributes and the corresponding inverted items for the first two experiments.

No.	User Generated	Inverted Item	No.	User Generated	Inverted Item
1	very sensitive	→ insensitive	1	too small	→ big
2	lightweight	→ heavy	2	good appearance	→ bad
3	not understandable	→ understandable	3	little bit slow	→ fast
4	unclear	→ clear	4	no direct feedback	→ direct feedback
5	hard to accomplish	→ easy to accomplish	5	dislike	→ like
6	uncontrollable	→ controllable	6	unclear	→ clear
7	problematic	→ straightforward	7	not responsive	→ responsive
8	very cheap	→ expensive	8	attractive	→ unattractive
9	attractive	→ unattractive	9	easy to find	→ difficult to find
10	confusing	→ simple	10	easy to use	→ difficult to use
11	complicated	→ uncomplicated	11	high quality	→ inferior
12	responsive	→ unresponsive	12	user friendly	→ not user friendly
13	colourful	→ colourless	13	understandable	→ not understandable
14	fun	→ boring	14	confusing	→ simple
15	enjoyable	→ annoying			
16	not easy	→ easy			
17	hard to learn	→ easy to learn			
1	**Drone**		**2**	**Smartphone**	**(unfamiliar App)**

Table 2. Displaying the collected attributes and the corresponding inverted items for the last two experiments.

No.	User Generated	Inverted Item	No.	User Generated	Inverted Item
1	noisy	→ quiet	1	attractive	→ unattractive
2	unclear (UI)	→ understandable	2	clear	→ unclear
3	not interesting	→ interesting	3	featured	→ featureless
4	confusing	→ clear	4	aesthetic	→ unsightly
5	bad output	→ good output	5	intuitive	→ abstract
6	fast	→ slow	6	intelligent	→ non-intelligent
7	insufficient	→ sufficient	7	fast	→ slow
8	difficult	→ easy	8	relaxing	→ stressful
9	poor quality	→ good quality	9	pleasant	→ unpleasant
10	small and portable	→ big and unhandy	10	interesting	→ dull
11	attractive	→ unattractive	11	friendly	→ unfriendly
12	useful	→ not useful	12	customized	→ non-modifiable
13	difficult to navigate	→ easy to navigate	13	easy to use	→ difficult to use
14	frustrating	→ pleasuring	14	useful	→ useless
15	challenging	→ not demanding	15	convenient	→ inconvenient
3	**Projector**		**4**	**Smartphone**	**(Instagram)**

References

1. Lallemand, C., Gronier, G., Koenig, V.: User experience: a concept without consensus? exploring practitioners' perspectives through an international survey. Comput. Hum. Behav. **43**, 35–48 (2015)
2. FDIs, I.: 9241-210: 2009. ergonomics of human system interaction-part 210: Human-centered design for interactive systems (formerly known as 13407). International Organization for Standardization (ISO). Switzerland (2009)
3. Vermeeren, A.P., Law, E.L.-C., Roto, V., Obrist, M., Hoonhout, J., Väänänen-Vainio-Mattila, K.: User experience evaluation methods: current state and development needs. In: Proceedings of the 6th Nordic Conference on Human-Computer Interaction: Extending Boundaries, pp. 521–530. ACM (2010)
4. Wilson, C.: Brainstorming and beyond: a user-centered design method. Newnes (2013)
5. Rickards, T.: Problem-Solving Through Creative Analysis. Wiley (1974)
6. N. Corporation: Inspired human technology (2005)
7. Seidel, M., Loch, C.H., Chahil, S.: Quo vadis, automotive industry? a vision of possible industry transformations. Eur. Manag. J. **23**(4), 439–449 (2005)
8. Väänänen-Vainio-Mattila, K., Roto, V., Hassenzahl, M.: Towards practical user experience evaluation methods. Meaningful measures: valid useful user experience measurement (VUUM), pp. 19–22 (2008)
9. Hassenzahl, M.: User experience (ux): towards an experiential perspective on product quality. In: Proceedings of the 20th Conference on l'Interaction Homme-Machine, pp. 11–15. ACM (2008)
10. Law, E.L.-C., Roto, V., Hassenzahl, M., Vermeeren, A.P., Kort, J.: Understanding, scoping and defining user experience: a survey approach. In: Proceedings of the SIGCHI Conference on Human Factors in Computing Systems, pp. 719–728. ACM (2009)
11. Kujala, S., Väänänen-Vainio-Mattila, K.: Value of information systems and products: understanding the users' perspective and values. J. Inf. Technol. Theory Appl. (JITTA) **9**(4), 4 (2009)
12. Karapanos, E., Zimmerman, J.F., Forlizzi, J., Martens, J.: user experience over time: an initial framework. In: Proceedings of the 27th International Conference on Human Factors in Computing Systems, pp. 729–738 (2009)
13. Kujala, S., Roto, V., Väänänen-Vainio-Mattila, K., Karapanos, E., Sinnelä, A.: Ux curve: a method for evaluating long-term user experience. Interact. Comput. **23**(5), 473–483 (2011)
14. Johanson, B., Fox, A., Winograd, T.: The interactive workspaces project: experiences with ubiquitous computing rooms. IEEE Pervasive Comput. **1**(2), 67–74 (2002)
15. Arhippainen, L., Tähti, M.: Empirical evaluation of user experience in two adaptive mobile application prototypes. In: MUM 2003. Proceedings of the 2nd International Conference on Mobile and Ubiquitous Multimedia, no. 011, pp. 27–34, Linköping University Electronic Press (2003)
16. Dewey, J.: Art as experience: New york: Gp putnam's sons (1980)
17. Forlizzi, J., Ford, S.: The building blocks of experience: an early framework for interaction designers. In: Proceedings of the 3rd Conference on Designing Interactive Systems: Processes, Practices, Methods, and Techniques, pp. 419–423. ACM (2000)

18. W. Albert and T. Tullis, Measuring the user experience: collecting, analyzing, and presenting usability metrics. Newnes, 2013
19. Law, E.L.-C.: The measurability and predictability of user experience. In: Proceedings of the 3rd ACM SIGCHI Symposium on Engineering Interactive Computing Systems, pp. 1–10. ACM (2011)
20. Bargas-Avila, J.A., Hornbæk, K.: Old wine in new bottles or novel challenges: a critical analysis of empirical studies of user experience. In: Proceedings of the SIGCHI Conference on Human Factors in Computing Systems, pp. 2689–2698. ACM (2011)
21. W. ISO, 9241-11. ergonomic requirements for office work with visual display terminals (vdts). Int. Organ. Standard. **45**, 9 (1998)
22. Roto, V.E.: User experience white paper (2011). http://www.allaboutux.org/uxwhitepaper
23. Bevan, N., Carter, J., Harker, S.: ISO 9241-11 revised: what have we learnt about usability since 1998? In: Kurosu, M. (ed.) HCI 2015. LNCS, vol. 9169, pp. 143–151. Springer, Cham (2015). https://doi.org/10.1007/978-3-319-20901-2_13
24. Hertzum, M.: Images of usability. Int. J. Hum.-Comput. Interact **26**(6), 567–600 (2010)
25. Hassenzahl, M.: The effect of perceived hedonic quality on product appealingness. Int. J. Hum.-Comput. Interact. **13**(4), 481–499 (2001)
26. Kaye, J.: Evaluating experience-focused HCI. In: CHI 2007 Extended Abstracts on Human Factors in Computing Systems, pp. 1661–1664. ACM (2007)
27. Patton, M.Q.: How to use qualitative methods in evaluation. No. 4, Sage (1987)
28. Nielsen, J., Landauer, T.K.: A mathematical model of the finding of usability problems. In: Proceedings of the INTERACT 1993 and CHI 1993 Conference on Human Factors in Computing Systems, pp. 206–213. ACM (1993)
29. Schmettow, M.: Sample size in usability studies. Commun. ACM **55**(4), 64–70 (2012)
30. Van Someren, M., Barnard, Y., Sandberg, J.: The think aloud method: a practical approach to modelling cognitive (1994)
31. Snyder, C.: Paper prototyping: the fast and easy way to design and refine user interfaces. Morgan Kaufmann (2003)
32. Dahlbäck, N., Jönsson, A., Ahrenberg, L.: Wizard of OZ studies-why and how. Knowl.-Based Syst. **6**(4), 258–266 (1993)
33. Cockburn, A.: Writing effective use cases, the crystal collection for software professionals. Addison-Wesley Professional Reading (2000)
34. Likert, R.: A technique for the measurement of attitudes. Arch. Psychol. (1932)
35. Maurer, T.J., Pierce, H.R.: A comparison of likert scale and traditional measures of self-efficacy. J. Appl. Psychol. **83**(2), 324 (1998)
36. Norman, G.: Likert scales, levels of measurement and the "laws" of statistics. Adv. Health Sci. Educ. **15**(5), 625–632 (2010)
37. Sullivan, G.M., Artino, A.R., Jr.: Analyzing and interpreting data from likert-type scales. J. Grad. Med. Educ. **5**(4), 541–542 (2013)
38. Murray, J.: Likert data: what to use, parametric or non-parametric? Int. J. Bus. Soc. Sci. **4**(11) (2013)
39. ENGAGE: Report on the evaluation of generative tools and methods for 'emotional design, Deliverable D15.3 EU project Engage 520998 (2006)
40. Isomursu, M.: User experience evaluation with experimental pilots. Proc. UXEM (2008). www.cs.tut.fi/ihte/CHI08_workshop/papers.shtml
41. Jordan, P.: Designing pleasurable products. An introduction to the new human (2000)

42. H. D9j. Final report on wp9 (2008)
43. Isomursu, M., Tähti, M., Väinämö, S., Kuutti, K.: Experimental evaluation of five methods for collecting emotions in field settings with mobile applications. Int. J. Hum. Comput. Stud. **65**(4), 404–418 (2007)
44. Roto, V., et al.: All about ux - information for user experience professionals (2010)
45. Santoso, H.B., Schrepp, M., Isal, R., Utomo, A.Y., Priyogi, B.: Measuring user experience of the student-centered e-learning environment. J. Educ. Online **13**(1), 58–79 (2016)
46. Laugwitz, B., Held, T., Schrepp, M.: Construction and evaluation of a user experience questionnaire. In: Holzinger, A. (ed.) USAB 2008. LNCS, vol. 5298, pp. 63–76. Springer, Heidelberg (2008). https://doi.org/10.1007/978-3-540-89350-9_6
47. Schrepp, M., Olschner, S., Schubert, U.: User experience questionnaire (ueq) benchmark. praxiserfahrungen zur auswertung und anwendung von ueq-erhebungen im business-umfeld," Tagungsband UP13 (2013)
48. Hartmann, J.: User experience monitoring: Über die notwendigkeit geschäftskritische online-prozesse permanent zu überwachen. i-com Zeitschrift für interaktive und kooperative Medien **10**(3), 59–62 (2011)
49. Minge, M., Riedel, L.: mecue-ein modularer fragebogen zur erfassung des nutzungserlebens. Mensch Comput. 89–98 (2013)
50. Lallemand, C., Koenig, V.: How could an intranet be like a friend to me?: why standardized UX scales don't always fit. In: Proceedings of the European Conference on Cognitive Ergonomics 2017, pp. 9–16. ACM (2017)
51. Thüring, M., Mahlke, S.: Usability, aesthetics and emotions in human-technology interaction. Int. J. Psychol. **42**(4), 253–264 (2007)

Comparing Two Sets of Usability Heuristics in a User Experience Evaluation: A Case Study in an E-Commerce Mobile Application

Freddy Paz[1]([✉]) [iD], Allisson Huaracha[2] [iD], Freddy-Asrael Paz-Sifuentes[3] [iD],
Arturo Moquillaza[1] [iD], Adrián Lecaros[1] [iD], Fiorella Falconi[1] [iD], Joel Aguirre[1] [iD],
and Alejandro Tapia[1] [iD]

[1] Pontificia Universidad Católica del Perú, San Miguel 15088, Perú
{fpaz,amoquillaza,atapiat}@pucp.pe, {adrian.lecaros,ffalconit,
aguirre.joel}@pucp.edu.pe
[2] Universidad Peruana de Ciencias Aplicadas, San Isidro 15076, Perú
u201823932@upc.edu.pe
[3] Universidad Nacional Pedro Ruiz Gallo, Lambayeque, Perú
fpaz@unprg.edu.pe

Abstract. Nowadays, user experience (UX) is relevant in constructing software products since companies intend to offer their customers the best possible interaction experience. Given the current competition on the market and the several websites available, guaranteeing customer satisfaction could mean choosing one company over another. For this reason, user experience is studied through evaluation methods to determine how satisfying the interaction experience is. One of the most used methods is the heuristic evaluation which involves a group of experts verifying whether the design proposal complies with a set of principles called "heuristics". Usually, the most preferred principles by practitioners are the ten heuristics proposed by Jakob Nielsen. However, these principles fail to cover some critical characteristics that must be analyzed in software products of specific categories. This situation has generated the proposal of new sets of heuristics focused on elements not considered by the traditional approach. A representative case is Inostroza's heuristics to assess mobile applications. However, their effectiveness has not been validated in other domains. The purpose of this research is to explore whether the new set of heuristics (SMASH) is appropriate and accurate for the evaluation of e-commerce applications that are at the same time mobile-based. Through a comparative study, it has been possible to identify small details that need to be covered.

Keywords: Human-Computer Interaction · Heuristic evaluation · Mobile apps · User-centered design · Interface design · Comparative study

1 Introduction

The user experience (UX) is a quality attribute that has arisen from the usability concept, and nowadays, it is relevant to attend UX to guarantee the end user's satisfaction [1]. In software products, this concept is considered by development teams who aim to develop an attractive and interactive systems that are friendly to use and allows the achievement of the user's objectives [2]. In this scenario, multiple methods have been developed, all with well-defined procedures and specific tasks to identify design issues and opportunities for improvement of the interaction interfaces [3].

Heuristic evaluation (HE) is one of the most recognized and used methods by the scientific community and specialists for evaluating not only the user experience (UX) but also the usability of interactive systems and digital services [4]. The method consists of identifying if the design of the interaction interfaces meets a set of guidelines called "heuristics" [5]. Usually, the ten usability heuristics proposed by Jakob Nielsen are used in most of the cases; however, researchers have proven these guidelines are imprecise when they are used to analyze software products of specific categories [6]. Aspects and characteristics only present in certain applications have led scholars to develop new instruments that can be used in a heuristic evaluation process [7]. Mobile applications are a clear example that the interaction must be inspected differently than traditional websites. During UX tests, observers concentrate on the ergonomics and the user's physical interactions with the application, which are features not covered by conventional proposals [8]. Likewise, the system's performance and its effectiveness are attributes that determine whether the application is perceived positively. Given the several features that must be examined in mobile apps, Inostroza et al. [9] elaborated a new proposal to perform an extensive evaluation of usability and user experience in this domain. Even though studies and evidence show the results are favorable, there is uncertainty about its accuracy for e-commerce applications.

Software products framed into the e-commerce category as well present particular features similar to mobile applications [10]. The research question addressed by this study is whether the heuristics proposed by Inostroza for mobile applications, are also applicable to those apps that, in addition to being constructed for mobile devices, are used for e-commerce. According to Granollers [11], some aspects must be considered to ensure a satisfactory user experience (UX) when assessing applications focused on the purchase and sale of products/services. In this domain, there are factors related to purchasing decision-making, financial transaction, sensitive data security, information search, and post-sales services, that affect the user experience (UX) during the entire purchase process and, therefore, must be analyzed. In this sense, although Inostroza's proposal is effective for inspecting mobile apps, academics have not still proven if it is appropriate for transactional e-commerce mobile applications.

E-commerce applications have become an essential tool and a relevant means by which companies offer their products and services. The appearance of COVID-19 has increased the use and importance of this technology [12]. Online sales increased due to non-mobilization policies in most countries worldwide, which caused companies to be concerned about the quality of their applications. Under this scenario, usability and user experience (UX) have become two relevant attributes because they can determine the preference of one application over another. In the current competitive market with several options available on the Internet, people will buy from a company that offers an application whose interface is visually attractive and whose interaction is friendly and guides users to achieve their objectives [13]. However, most of these e-commerce applications have been designed and are accessible through mobile devices. Because of the relevance of these types of software products, it is necessary to have a tool that allows evaluating the quality to guarantee a proper level of usability and a satisfactory interaction experience.

In this study, Inostroza's heuristics (SMASH) are tested in the e-commerce domain. In this way, it is possible to verify if the new proposal is suitable for applications that are both, e-commerce, and touchscreen software applications for mobile devices. This study is not only to improve SMASH but is also intended to be used as a guide for future evaluations whose purpose is to improve the quality of software products.

2 Related Works

User experience is a term currently widely used by designers and developers, not only immersed in the software development process but also within the areas of Communications and Marketing of a company [14]. This concept is related to the people's perceptions and responses that result from the use or anticipated use of a product, system, or service [15]. If this definition is explored in the Software Engineering domain, then user experience (UX) can represent the satisfaction degree and impressions generated by a certain software product before, during, and after the interaction of the users with it. This study is focused on e-commerce mobile applications that, besides fitting into the category of software products, present interaction interfaces with specific features [8]. In addition, it is important to highlight that the usability, as well as the functionality provided by the application, plays an important role in the users' perception of the software product. If the software product has the capability to be easy to use, understandable, and easy to learn, then it generates a positive feeling in the people who use it [16]. A positive impact on the end users' perception will generate not only that they use the application again, but also that they recommend it to other possible customers.

Usability is not the only factor that must be studied when inspecting the user experience. The application's functionality is in the same way relevant and can impact the opinions and perceptions of end users [17]. According to the software quality guidelines established by the International Organization for Standardization, the application must allow the achievement of the user's goals [18]. Considering this recommendation for the area of electronic commerce, it is possible to determine that the software product should provide mechanisms in a way in which users can make a purchase satisfactorily [19]. Some elements are required to ensure a friendly shopping experience. The application must provide complete and well-organized information about the products and services offered. Likewise, the application must provide a section of reviews and comments from previous customers of the products, and in this sense, allow users to make a conscientious purchase decision. Another important aspect of e-commerce is guaranteeing a safe environment at the time of purchase. The application must allow a secure and reliable mechanism for the financial transaction. Similarly, the company is obliged to ensure that sensitive data such as personal information or credit cards are not usurped, published, or accessible by third parties.

The user experience is a broad concept that addresses even other factors further the usability of the graphical user interfaces (GUI). A positive experience must be offered not only during the purchase but also after this process, and because of this, the application must provide possibilities for post-sale attention. Given the high competitiveness currently present on the Internet that can be visible across the several available e-commerce mobile applications, factors such as the assurance of the usability and user experience through the entire purchase process can represent the key to success in the market. Because of this scenario, specialists have worked on developing new instruments that contemplate a complete evaluation of these attributes in specific domains.

In a previous work [20], through a systematic literature review, it was possible to determine that heuristic evaluation is one of the most relevant methods for academics and industry professionals. The reasons by which this method is selected is because it is low cost and does not require complex procedures. According to studies conducted by Nielsen [21], only three to five specialists are required to identify 75% of usability problems presented in the graphical interfaces of a software product. In addition, the procedure to be followed is not highly costly in resources. The process consists in that the Human-Computer Interaction specialists must comprehensively review each of the graphical interfaces that are the goal of the inspection. During this review, professionals must identify non-compliance with a set of guidelines called "heuristics" [5]. Each of the non-compliances will subsequently be classified as a usability problem. Later, the usability problems are consolidated and classified according to their severity level.

The most challenging phase of the heuristic evaluation method is finding the availability of usability and user experience experts. Although the assessment process does not require many resources, it can be complicated to find specialists who have enough expertise to identify, based on their experience, the design problems that interfaces of the application present. Although the formal literature establishes that specialists must be from the HCI area, there is a discussion among different authors about the type of professionals that should participate in a heuristic inspection process [22]. However, this method turns out to be appropriate for teams with little budget and time available that want to ensure the quality of the software product they are developing. Even if it may be challenging to come up with specialists, a lot of knowledge is not required to correctly interpret the heuristics and verify whether the design proposal complies with the established good practices.

The most reported, well-known, and used heuristics are the ten principles proposed by Nielsen [23]. This proposal has demonstrated effectiveness and can be used with confidence to obtain valuable results on the condition that the application is a website. Nevertheless, some categories of software products present special interaction characteristics such as mobile applications [8]. Ergonomics factors and touch-screen features must be considered for a comprehensive inspection in which specific (domain-related) usability issues are also addressed. Given this scenario and the need for a more accurate instrument, Inostroza et al. [9] developed SMASH, a set of smartphone's usability heuristics. In this new proposal, in addition to covering the usability elements considered by Nielsen's approach, other characteristics are addressed. The most representative elements in this new proposal are the physical interaction, the ergonomics factors, the customization, the efficiency of use, and the performance.

The Inostroza's proposal was elaborated with basis on the Nielsen's heuristics, and for this reason, many of the usability aspects that were considered in the original proposal are also contemplated in the new approach. Table 1 illustrates the new elements that have been incorporated for a better evaluation of mobile applications. Likewise, it is possible to observe the elements that have remained from the previous proposal.

Table 1. Set of heuristics proposed by Inostroza et al. [9] for evaluating mobile applications.

ID	Heuristic	New category?
TMD1	Visibility of system status	NO
TMD2	Match between system and the real world	NO
TMD3	User control and freedom	NO
TMD4	Consistency and standards	NO
TMD5	Error prevention	NO
TMD6	Minimize the user's memory load	NO
TMD7	Customization and shortcuts	YES
TMD8	Efficiency of use and performance	YES
TMD9	Esthetic and minimalist design	NO
TMD10	Help users recognize, diagnose, and recover from errors	NO
TMD11	Help and documentation	NO
TMD12	Physical interaction and ergonomics	YES

Inostroza's study shows that favorable results are obtained with the new proposed heuristics when used to evaluate mobile applications. However, the motivation of this research is to determine if this new set is also valid for assessing e-commerce mobile applications. This uncertainty arises because e-commerce applications that are as well transactional, present additional features that should be inspected [10, 17]. In addition, these applications must have appropriate functionality that helps users to make a purchase decisively and without obstacles. Moreover, since the user experience involves not only the perceptions generated during the interaction but also before and after, it is important to provide options in the e-commerce application for pre-sale and post-sale services. Many of these features were identified in a previous research conducted by Granollers [11] and cataloged as relevant and required to be considered in a heuristic evaluation. However, these elements are not part of Inostroza's proposal, which leads scholars to formulate the following research question: are the new heuristics proposed by Inostroza an appropriate instrument to evaluate mobile e-commerce applications?

In this study, a comparative analysis is presented in which the results of using traditional heuristics are compared against the new Inostroza's approach, in the context of evaluating a mobile application for e-commerce in Peru. The purpose of this study, besides validating the new assessment instrument, is to find opportunities to improve the tool. Through this experiment, it has been possible to identify aspects that should also be considered by the new heuristics. This research also hopes to serve as a guide for academics and professionals who perform heuristic evaluations in this domain.

3   A Comparative Case Study

In this research, the results of the Nielsen's principles and the Inostroza's heuristics are contrasted. The intention was to determine whether the innovative proposal developed by Inostroza covers most of the issues identified by the conventional tool. Likewise, a relevant aspect of this study was to corroborate if the new heuristics are suitable and valid for e-commerce mobile applications.

The experimental case study consisted of a user experience assessment through the heuristic evaluation method of the mobile application of a popular retail store in Peru. To execute the inspection process, the formal approach proposed by Paz et al. [22] for conducting heuristic inspections of software products was used. In this approach, five well-defined phases for the conduction are established: (1) Planning, (2) Training, (3) Evaluation, (4) Discussion, and (5) Reporting.

Initially, the evaluation manager must define the purpose of the evaluation, the sections of the application that must be inspected, identify the participants, and select the most appropriate heuristics. For this study, the support of six professionals in the area of Software Engineering was requested. Since the purpose was to compare the results obtained by the two groups of heuristics (Nielsen and Inostroza) and also to avoid any bias, two teams of three people each were formed (Team A and Team B). Likewise, to maintain the balance in both groups, an attempt was made to group the participants in a way in which they all had the same degree of expertise. Table 2 details the profile of the participants and the team to which they belonged during the case study. It is important to mention that all the specialists who participated in this study voluntarily and kindly agreed to be part of this evaluation. There was no monetary compensation for their work and contribution to this research. Before starting their participation, all this information was communicated, and an informed consent document was signed, which specified the academic nature of this research and the promise of anonymity and free disposition to conclude their participation at any time.

Table 2. Profile of the participants and assigned team.

ID	Profile of the participant	Assigned Team
P01	Student of the Doctoral Program in Engineering	Team A
P02	Master's degree in Software Engineering	Team A
P03	Informatics Engineer	Team A
P04	Student of the Doctoral Program in Engineering	Team B
P05	Master's degree in Computer Science	Team B
P06	Informatics Engineer	Team B

Both teams (Team A and Team B) followed the entire process with all its phases to execute the heuristic evaluation. However, each team used a different set of heuristics. Team A used the traditional proposal of Jakob Nielsen, while team B used the novel proposal developed by Rodolfo Inostroza. Figure 1 describes the assigned distribution of the assessment tools for each team in the experimental case study.

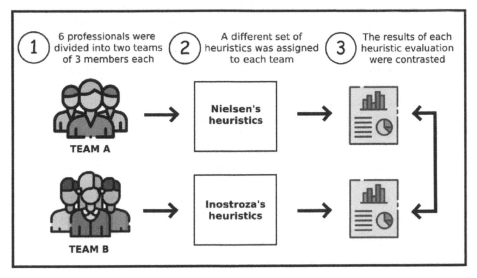

Fig. 1. Assignment of usability heuristics for each of the teams.

The evaluation methodology defines a training phase in those scenarios where the specialists do not know much about the inspection process or the selected heuristics. However, in this study, all the participants had extensive knowledge of the procedure, since all of them had previously conducted a heuristic evaluation and also, belong to a research group in Human-Computer Interaction. Likewise, the sets of heuristics were of previous knowledge because at the time of contacting the specialists, they had been provided with the instruments, and they had been given a considerable period of time for using the heuristics with dominance during the evaluation. In this sense, a training phase was not necessary to conduct the experimental case study.

The heuristic evaluation was executed in synchronous and asynchronous activities. First, the scope was defined. The objective was to examine the user experience (UX) and usability degree of the mobile application of one of the most relevant e-commerce companies in Peru. The scope consisted of all the graphical user interfaces involved in the purchasing process. Subsequently, an Excel template was elaborated for the usage of the evaluators. This digital document was used to report the identified design issues individually. The specialists were grouped, maintaining homogeneous teams, and they were given a week to complete the evaluation independently using the assigned set of heuristics (Table 2 and Fig. 1).

Once the evaluators finished with the individual inspection, the teams were brought together in two separate Zoom rooms to continue with the discussion phase. Zoom is currently one of the most established videoconference tools in the market for academic purposes [24] because, in addition to allowing a meeting, it allows breakout rooms, screen sharing, and a digital whiteboard for interactive notes between users. The purpose of this synchronous activity was to consolidate the diverse results (templates that describe the identified usability problems) into a single consolidated list per team. The discussion took approximately about one hour of work.

When each of the teams finished consolidating the list of identified problems, they proceeded with another individual asynchronous activity which consisted of establishing the severity of each problem. To establish the severity, the ranking proposed by Nielsen was used [25], which goes from 0 to 4, where 0 means that it is not a usability problem and 4 represents that it is a catastrophic usability problem that is imperative to fix. For the specialists to complete this task, they were given a total of three days.

When all the scores were collected, the members of each team got together to start the reporting phase. Teams calculate averages of the individual scores and prepare the final report. This document details not only the interface problems but also the positive aspects and recommendations to correct the identified issues.

In the final phase of the experiment, once the teams had the two reports completed, we proceeded with the comparative analysis. In this analysis, the number of problems and the aspects identified by each team were compared to validate and corroborate the most effective proposal of heuristics in this domain. In this way, it was also possible to identify if the heuristic sets cover all the elements that are relevant in e-commerce mobile applications.

4 Analysis of the Results

The heuristic evaluation of the mobile e-commerce application was carried out during the first week of January 2023. Specialist used their own mobile device to inspect the graphical user interfaces. Some participants had previous experience using the mobile application; however, two of them had to install the application for the first time. The cell phone models that were used in this experimental case study were: Apple iPhone X, Apple iPhone 13, Xiaomi 12 Lite, Samsung Galaxy S20 FE, Samsung Galaxy S22, and Samsung Galaxy A12.

The scope of the evaluation involved the main purchase process, and in some cases some specialists purchased some products to experience the entire flow of interaction. During the inspection, specialists were requested to review all the elements that facilitate the purchase. According to the comments offered by the participants, some even simulated positioning themselves in the user's situation and under certain scenarios to identify compliance with the heuristics. Figure 2 illustrates some of the interfaces that were examined during the heuristic evaluation.

The results of the assessment demonstrate that more critical issues can be identified when Inostroza's proposal is employed. Team A identified a total of twenty-five (25) design problems, while Team B identified thirty-one (31) issues. Nevertheless, fifteen (15) of the total problems identified by both teams are similar. From this fact it can be concluded that ten (10) problems can be identified only when the Nielsen's proposal is used and eighteen and (16) problems can only be determined with the support of the Inostroza's approach. However, these results could be explained because of the level of expertise of the participants instead of the instruments used. This conclusion is due to some of the problems that have been identified as usability problems, they were not classified as non-compliance with any of the heuristics. Despite this, specialists established that they were indeed usability problems.

Fig. 2. Graphical user interfaces of the e-commerce mobile application that was evaluated.

There are times when specialists, instead of reviewing interfaces in search of non-fulfillment with heuristics, identify problems without their support. These scenarios occur when the specialists are highly experienced in the software domain being tested, and due to their expertise, they identify problems without considering the heuristics. It is because of these situations that scholars can determine if the heuristics are largely covering the evaluation of all aspects that are relevant in a software application of this category. Since this situation took place in this experimental case study, it is possible to evidence problems that address aspects that are not related to any of the established heuristics. Tables 3 and 4 detail the most critical problems identified by teams A and B, respectively, in the interface design of the software product. Likewise, it is possible to visualize the unfulfilled heuristic. In certain cases, it was noticed that despite being a usability and user experience (UX) issue, there was no heuristic related.

Table 3. Most critical problems identified by Team A

N°	Description of the Problem	Heuristics Related
P01	The application does not provide in some cases detailed information on products and services	No heuristic related
P02	The application provides error messages with technical expressions that are not understandable to the user	N2, N9
P03	The same product or service is offered multiple times by the company without clearly highlighting the difference	N4, N8
P04	There are occasions where the application does not indicate to the user that it is processing information through icons	N1
P05	The application forces the users to log in several times for no apparent reason	No heuristic related

Table 4. Most critical problems identified by Team B

N°	Description of the Problem	Heuristic Related
P01	The application allows users to choose products and services that do not have stock availability. This situation is shared at the time of indicating the delivery address	No heuristic related
P02	Unable to sign in with Facebook even though the option is available. The action leads to an error state	No heuristic related
P03	The application allows you to make a purchase that can be rejected after a few minutes by email	No heuristic related
P04	Although there is a progress bar on the current status of the order, it always appears as "purchase received" and does not change even if the product is delivered	No heuristic related
P05	There are no clearly defined customization options and shortcuts for frequent customers	TMD7

5 Conclusions and Future Works

Usability and user experience (UX) are very relevant factors nowadays for the success of software products. An understandable interaction interface and a satisfactory user experience can make a difference in a highly competitive market with several options available. For this reason, specialists and professionals have developed evaluation methods that make it possible to determine through well-defined steps whether the applications meet the minimum requirements. One of these methods is the heuristic evaluation which is widely reported in the literature.

Usually, the most recognized set of heuristics to evaluate software products are the ten principles proposed by Nielsen. However, some findings have evidence that these guidelines do not provide appropriate results when used to evaluate applications with specific features. This is the scenario of applications designed for mobile devices that present characteristics related to touchscreen interactions, ergonomics, customization, physical interactions, performance, and efficiency. Due to this, Inostroza et al. worked on a new proposal of heuristics to evaluate mobile applications. However, considering that some mobile applications are also e-commerce products, and there are additional considerations that must be covered, is Inostroza's proposal still a proper tool to assess the user experience of this specific category of software product? In this research, the authors validate through an experimental case study whether the Inostroza's approach is applicable to evaluate e-commerce mobile applications.

The case study consisted of a heuristic evaluation of the mobile application of one of the best-known retail companies in Peru, focused on electronic commerce. For this, the authors requested the support of six professionals from the HCI area, who voluntarily agreed to participate and were divided into two homogeneous teams. Each team was assigned a different set of heuristics. While team A used the principles proposed by Nielsen, Team B used the heuristics proposed by Inostroza et al. Later, the results were compared with the purpose of identifying the precision degree of each proposal.

The results demonstrate that it is possible to identify more usability problems when Inostroza's proposal is employed in a heuristic evaluation to assess the usability and user experience in e-commerce mobile applications. However, it was also possible to determine that Inostroza's heuristics do not cover all aspects that must be addressed in an evaluation of e-commerce mobile applications. Aspects related to decision-making, financial transaction, sensitive data security, information search, post-sales services also affect the user experience (UX) and are not covered by the proposals used in this experimental case study. In this sense, as future work, the Inostroza proposal could be improved to obtain a tool that is more effective in addressing all the elements that are important in this type of applications. Likewise, more case studies can be conducted under other contexts to generalize and complement the obtained results.

Acknowledgments. The authors thank all the professionals involved in the case study who have made possible the development of this study. This research is highly supported by the *HCI, Design, User Experience, Accessibility, and Innovation Technology Research Group* (HCI-DUXAIT). HCI-DUXAIT is a research group of Pontificia Universidad Católica del Perú (PUCP) – Perú.

References

1. Jantan, R., Kamaruddin, N., Abidin, S.Z., Said, T.S., Ramli, H.: Value in exchange: the importance of user interaction as the center of user experiences. Int. J. Innov. Creat. Change **11**(10), 75–83 (2020)
2. Farooqui, T., Rana, T., Jafari, F.: Impact of Human-Centered Design Process (HCDP) on software development process. In: Proceedings of the 2nd International Conference on Communication, Computing and Digital systems (C-CODE 2019), pp. 110–114. Institute of Electrical and Electronics Engineers (2019). https://doi.org/10.1109/C-CODE.2019.8680978
3. Fernandez, A., Insfran, E., Abrahão, S.: Usability evaluation methods for the web: A systematic mapping study. Inf. Softw. Technol. **53**(8), 789–817 (2011). https://doi.org/10.1016/j.infsof.2011.02.007

4. Lecaros, A., Paz, F., Moquillaza, A.: Challenges and opportunities on the application of heuristic evaluations: a systematic literature review. In: Soares, M.M., Rosenzweig, E., Marcus, A. (eds.) HCII 2021. LNCS, vol. 12779, pp. 242–261. Springer, Cham (2021). https://doi.org/10.1007/978-3-030-78221-4_17

5. Nielsen, J., Molich, R.: Heuristic evaluation of user interfaces. In: Proceedings of the SIGCHI Conference on Human Factors in Computing Systems (CHI 1990), pp. 249–256. Association for Computing Machinery (1990). https://doi.org/10.1145/97243.97281

6. Díaz, J., Rusu, C., Collazos, C.A.: Experimental validation of a set of cultural-oriented usability heuristics: e-Commerce websites evaluation. Comput. Stand. Interfaces 50, 160–178 (2017). https://doi.org/10.1016/j.csi.2016.09.013

7. Quiñones, D., Rusu, C.: Applying a methodology to develop user eXperience heuristics. Comput. Stand. Interfaces 66, 103345 (2019). https://doi.org/10.1016/j.csi.2019.04.004

8. Inostroza, R., Rusu, C., Roncagliolo, S., Jimenez, C., Rusu, V.: Usability heuristics for touchscreen-based mobile devices. In: Proceedings of the Ninth International Conference on Information Technology – New Generations (ITNG 2012), pp. 662–667. Institute of Electrical and Electronics Engineers (2012). https://doi.org/10.1109/ITNG.2012.134

9. Inostroza, R., Rusu, C., Roncagliolo, S., Rusu, V., Collazos, C.A.: Developing SMASH: a set of SMArtphone's uSability heuristics. Comput. Stand. Interfaces 43, 40–52 (2016). https://doi.org/10.1016/j.csi.2015.08.007

10. Paz, F.: Applying a new questionnaire to evaluate the usability of Peruvian e-government websites. In: Soares, M.M., Rosenzweig, E., Marcus, A. (eds) HCII 2022. LNCS, vol 13321, pp. 460–472. Springer, Cham (2022). https://doi.org/10.1007/978-3-031-05897-4_32

11. Granollers, T.: Validación experimental de un conjunto heurístico para evaluaciones de UX de sitios web de comercio-e. In: Proceedings of the 11th Colombian Computing Conference (CCC 2016), pp. 1–8. Institute of Electrical and Electronics Engineers (2016). https://doi.org/10.1109/ColumbianCC.2016.7750783

12. Galhotra, B., Dewan, A.: Impact of COVID-19 on digital platforms and change in E-commerce shopping trends. In: Proceedings of the Fourth International Conference on IoT in Social, Mobile, Analytics and Cloud (I-SMAC 2020), pp. 861–866, Institute of Electrical and Electronics Engineers (2020). https://doi.org/10.1109/I-SMAC49090.2020.9243379

13. Paz, F., et al.: Validation of a questionnaire to evaluate the usability in the Peruvian context. In: Soares, M.M., Rosenzweig, E., Marcus, A. (eds.) HCII 2021. LNCS, vol. 12779, pp. 327–336. Springer, Cham (2021). https://doi.org/10.1007/978-3-030-78221-4_22

14. Liu, C., Pan, Z., Zhang, C., Miao, W.: Nonheritage creative product design and development and marketing strategies for computer vision and user experience. Secur. Commun. Networks 2022, 9685280 (2022). https://doi.org/10.1155/2022/9685280

15. International Organization for Standardization: ISO/IEC 9241-210:2019, Ergonomics of human-system interaction – Part 210: Human-centred design for interactive systems. Geneva, Switzerland (2019)

16. Nielsen, J.: Usability 101: Introduction to Usability (2012). https://www.nngroup.com/articles/usability-101-introduction-to-usability/ Accessed 01 Feb 2023

17. Bonastre, L., Granollers, T.: A set of heuristics for user experience evaluation in e-commerce websites. In: Proceedings of the Seventh International Conference on Advances in Computer-Human Interactions (ACHI 2014), pp. 27–34, International Academy, Research and Industry Association (2014)

18. International Organization for Standardization: ISO/IEC 25010:2011, Systems and software engineering – Systems and software Quality Requirements and Evaluation (SQuaRE) – System and software quality models. Geneva, Switzerland (2011)

19. Paz, F., Paz, F.A., Pow-Sang, J.A.: Experimental case study of new usability heuristics. In: Marcus, A. (ed.) DUXU 2015. LNCS, vol. 9186, pp. 212–223. Springer, Cham (2015). https://doi.org/10.1007/978-3-319-20886-2_21

20. Paz, F., Pow-Sang, J.A.: A systematic mapping review of usability evaluation methods for software development process. Int. J. Software Eng. Appl. **10**(1), 165–178 (2016)
21. Nielsen, J.: How to Conduct a Heuristic Evaluation (1994). https://www.nngroup.com/art icles/how-to-conduct-a-heuristic-evaluation/ Accessed 01 Feb 2023
22. Paz, F., Paz, F.A., Pow-Sang, J.A., Collazos, C.: A formal protocol to conduct usability heuristic evaluations in the context of the software development process. Int. J. Eng. Technol. **7**(2.28), 10–19 (2018)
23. Nielsen, J.: 10 Usability Heuristics for User Interface Design (2020). https://www.nngroup. com/articles/ten-usability-heuristics/ Accessed 01 Feb 2023
24. Stefanile, A.: The transition from classroom to zoom and how it has changed education. J. Soc. Sci. Res. **16**(1), 33–40 (2020). https://doi.org/10.24297/jssr.v16i.8789
25. Nielsen, J.: Severity Ratings for Usability Problems (1994). https://www.nngroup.com/art icles/how-to-rate-the-severity-of-usability-problems/. Accessed 01 Feb 2023

Detect and Interpret: Towards Operationalization of Automated User Experience Evaluation

Angeline Sin Mei Tsui[1]([envelope]) [iD] and Anastasia Kuzminykh[2] [iD]

[1] Huawei Technologies Canada Inc., Markham, Canada
angelines.tsui@huawei.com
[2] Faculty of Information, University of Toronto, Toronto, Canada
anastasia.kuzminykh@utoronto.ca

Abstract. The evaluation of user experience (UX) with software products is widely recognized as a critical aspect of supporting a product lifecycle. However, existing UX evaluation methods tend to require high levels of human involvement in data collection and analysis. This makes the ongoing UX monitoring particularly challenging, especially given the increasing number of products, growing user base and associated data. Thus, there is a strong demand in developing UX evaluation systems that are able to automatically track UX and provide insights on required design improvements. The few existing frameworks for such automated systems can help identify user-centric metrics for UX evaluation, but mostly focus on providing recommendations on best practices of determining metrics and tend to reflect only parts of the UX. Moreover, these frameworks predominantly rely on high-level UX concepts, but do not necessarily allow measurements to reveal the underlying causes of UX challenges. In this paper, we demonstrate how the above-mentioned challenges can be addressed through a combination of data gathering and analysis paths employed by the traditional UX evaluation methods. Our paper contributes to the field by providing a review of existing automated UX evaluation approaches and common UX evaluation data collection methods, and offering a two-tier measurement approach for developing automated UX evaluation system, which augments the reflective power of traditional UX evaluation methods.

Keywords: Evaluation Methods and Techniques · UX · User Experience · Automatic UX Evaluation

1 Introduction

Evaluating user experience (UX) for software products is considered as an essential element in the success of the product lifecycle. The goals of the UX evaluation can be broadly summarized into two aspects: (i) to evaluate whether the product meets users' needs; (ii) to provide product teams and designers with insights on how, why and what aspects of the design can be improved. The evaluation of UX includes (but not limited to) evaluating users' perception, thoughts, preferences, feelings and behaviors in their

A. Marcus et al. (Eds.): HCII 2023, LNCS 14032, pp. 82–100, 2023.
https://doi.org/10.1007/978-3-031-35702-2_6

interactions with the products/systems/services [1]. Thus, the nature of UX necessarily involves subjective aspects that are dependent on the specific context and also not directly observable, which significantly complicates the generalization of UX evaluation.

Over the past decades, researchers have explored and developed a great variety of methods to assess whether users have positive UX when and/or after interacting with a product. These methods range from subjectively asking users to report their experiences (e.g., via questionnaire) to objectively inferring UX through users' behaviors, allowing researchers to identify which method(s) should be employed in different contexts and how to best evaluate UX from different types of users' data. However, with the diversity of methods and their context-dependences, this research requires high involvement of human specialists, particularly in terms of high levels of human involvement in data collection and analysis [2, 3].

The strong reliance of the research process on human expert work further complicates the growing need for constantly monitoring UX over time across large numbers of products. In the technology industry, it is particularly important to evaluate UX regularly and ensure users have positive UX with the products in order to keep companies competitive in the fast paced and constantly expanding market. Thus, with a rapid-growing number of technology products and its associated users' base, many companies have been actively exploring the possibility of employing automated UX evaluation systems to track UX regularly and frequently. However, most of the existing automated UX evaluation methods tend to provide a static status of whether UX is positive or negative, lacking insights that guide product teams in identifying areas of improving product design for better UX.

In this paper, we introduce an approach for addressing the above-mentioned UX evaluation challenges through a combination of data gathering and analysis paths employed by the existing UX evaluation methods. In particular, the contributions of this paper include a review of existing automated UX evaluation approaches, review of widely used UX evaluation methods structured according to the different types of data they provide, and, finally, a two-tier measurement approach for developing automated UX evaluation system.

The rest of the paper is organized as follows. We first provide an overview of the existing approaches to automated UX evaluation and discuss the associated challenges. We then present a review of common traditional IX evaluation methods, structured around different types of data collection, alongside with a discussion of the strength and limitations for each type of data. Finally, we propose a two-tier measurement approach to developing automated systems for UX evaluation and discuss how it can address the needs in the UX field.

2   Approaches to Automated UX Evaluation

Past research has suggested several frameworks for automating the process of UX evaluation. These frameworks tend to provide instruction on how to define metrics for measuring users' usage and action when users interact with the products/services.

One of the early examples include the AARRR framework, introduced by McClure [4] for tracking product performance. The elements in the AARRR framework represent

5 sequential stages of customer lifecycle in a company, which are Acquisition (getting new customers), Activation (tracking existing customers' activity), Retention (retaining existing customers), Revenue (maximizing income from customers) and Refer (motivating existing customers to refer new customers to the company). Using the AARRR frameworks, researchers can define metrics to measure users' experience based on different stage of the customer lifecycle. For instance, if the product team focuses on recruiting new customers, they can track the number of users visiting the product's site and how many of users convert to new customers via registration. Or if the product team focuses on retaining existing customers, they can track the number of repeated users (e.g., users logging into/using the product more than once per week). These metrics directly measure consumers' conversion rate in terms of stages in a typical customers' lifecycle and their usage of the product, thus serving a proxy of UX in the product.

Interestingly, the earlier frameworks are strongly influenced by marketing and product sales funnel strategies, which limits their applicability for measuring users' experience. Rodden, Hutchinson and Fu [5] were among the first researchers to point out that marketing framework (e.g., AARRR) mainly evaluates the business or technical performance of a product. Metrics included in these frameworks primarily use PULSE metrics (i.e., page views, uptime, latency, several-day active users and earnings) that are related to the state of UX, such as low uptime means the product has a lot of outage and will likely lead to poorer UX. However, the authors suggested that these metrics cannot directly measure UX and sometimes these metrics could have ambiguous interpretation in the direction of the UX state. For example, an increase in page view could either mean that the page is popular or users are confused with the interface and they need to revisit the same page repeatedly to understand how to complete a task. In response, the authors have suggested the HEART metric framework to develop user-centric metrics for evaluating users' happiness, engagement, adoption, retention and task success. For example, the authors proposed metrics that measure users' satisfaction score via survey as measurement of happiness and metrics that measure users' number of visits on the product's console as measurement of engagement. By developing metrics that assess users' attitude and behaviors in the products, product teams can evaluate UX on a large scale and make data-driven decision on the UX state of the products.

Work in the domain of product data science also leveraged massive users' data to build in-house online controlled experimentation platforms to assess the influences of new features, designs or changes of software product and services [6–8]. Online controlled experiments, also called as A/B tests, involve randomly assigning users to different variants (e.g., different versions of websites that include different features of the product). Often, in a typical A/B test scenario, we have two different variants: the control variant where users are assigned to the current system that has no changes in design; the treatment variant where users are assigned to the system that incorporates the new design. Researchers measure whether there is any statistically significant difference in users' behaviors (i.e., a proxy of user experience) between the control and treatment variants to evaluate the impact of the new design. Many leading software companies, including Microsoft, Amazon and Google, have relied on online controlled experiments to decide on the new design/changes in their products, the research on online controlled experiments has grown substantially in the past decade [9].

Given the importance of measuring users' behavior to reflect UX of the new design/changes in software products, a number of works have focused on providing guidelines of how to define correct metrics [10–12]. Researchers at Microsoft have defined four different types of metrics to evaluate the new design effect (i.e., treatment effect) on the product: (i) Data quality metrics are used to evaluate whether the results of the experiment is reliable and can be trusted, such as the ratio of samples between the control and treatment groups; (ii) Overall evaluation criteria metrics, also known as the North Star or goal metrics, are used to evaluate whether the new design/changes of the products are successful in driving better business value and users' satisfaction, thus reflecting an improvement in UX. This type of metrics defines the success of the new design/changes of the products and has been a key focus on the research in the online controlled experiments literature [10, 12]; (iii) Guardrail metrics are used to reflect whether the new design/changes of the products are leading to a better UX, but they cannot directly reflect the success of the new design/changes. In other words, this type of metrics supplement the overall evaluation criteria metrics and they guard against situations where the overall evaluation criteria metrics may give us wrong direction of UX changes; (iv) Local feature and diagnostic metrics, also known as debugging metrics, are used to identify reasons of the movements of overall evaluation criteria metrics and guide the product teams to interpret why the new design leads to changes in UX.

To summarize, research on automated UX frameworks have moved from predominant focus on measuring company's marketing and business outcomes to measuring more direct and user-centered UX outcomes. With the advancement of technology, many companies can track large amount of users' log data, allowing companies to collect UX metrics that describe users' behaviors when users interact with the product in recent automated UX frameworks (e.g., [5]). However, all these automated frameworks have primarily focused on measuring users' behavioral log data. As UX is multi-dimensional and can be better revealed from different type of users' data, we need to explore how to collect various kinds of users' data to measure UX in a more holistic way. In addition, ample research has been conducted on defining UX metrics in the context of online controlled experiments, however, not all companies can conduct online controlled experiments on a regular basis.

Given the importance of tracking UX continuously, there is a particular interest in developing approaches to an automated UX evaluation system, which can provide researchers with a comprehensive guidelines of measuring UX with a wide range of various UX methods in a non-experimental context.

3 Traditional UX Evaluation: Types of Users' Data Collected in UX Evaluation

In this section, we review traditional UX evaluation methods and related literature, structured according to four types of users' data: self-reported data, behavioral, physiological data, and expert evaluation. For each type of data collection, we review its specifics of reflecting user experience, discussing the strength and limitations of each type of data collection.

3.1 Users' Self-reported Data

Measuring UX by collecting users' self-reported data is one of most common approaches in UX evaluation [2, 13]. Traditionally, most researchers evaluate UX qualitatively, such as user interviews and think aloud procedure that asks participants express what they think (think aloud) as they are performing task when interacting with the product [14, 15]. While qualitative UX evaluation methods provide researchers with detailed information about UX, these methods tend to collect data from a small set of users and are limited in generalizability to broader user groups. To collect users' self-reported data on a larger scale, researchers have utilized other approaches and the more common approaches are the use of questionnaire and users' online reviews.

Questionnaire is a widely used method for UX evaluation. Typically, a UX questionnaire involves Likert scale [16] where there are one to multiple items asking users to rate whether they agree with a statement (e.g., whether you are satisfied with the product) on a scale from small number that represents strongly disagreement to large number that represents strongly agreement. There is a variety of questionnaires that measure different aspects of UX in the field. For example, some questionnaires are more focused on one to several core UX aspects, such as usability [17, 18], how the aesthetics of a website supports positive UX [19, 20] and the degree of perceived mental efforts users needed for completing their task with the product [21, 22]. In contrast, other questionnaires aim to measure UX more holistically, which include (but not limited to) users' perceptions and feelings (e.g., hedonic aspect that generally describes users' overall perception and enjoyment) and how the product supports users' task completion (e.g., ergonomic aspect that generally describes effectiveness and efficiency). Examples of these questionnaires include AttrakDiff [23] and the user experience questionnaire [24]. Apart from designing different questionnaires that measure various aspects of UX, extensive research have been devoted in standardizing questionnaires as researchers need to ensure the questionnaires are good in psychometric quality, namely whether the questionnaires are valid (i.e., measuring what they are supposed to measure, which is UX) and reliable (i.e., consistently producing the same results when applying the same questionnaire in the same setup across raters or within raters or over-time) [25, 26].

Another commonly used approach in UX evaluation is to collect and analyze data from users' feedback in online review. Nowadays, users often leave product reviews on internet platforms, social media and users' community sites. These users' online reviews contain user-generated content that provides the product/service providers with enriched text reflecting how users think and feel (thus their UX) after using the product/service and with design insights on which aspect(s) of the product/service need improvements [27, 28]. To leverage the large amount of user-generated text data and draw UX insights, researchers often use sentiment analysis [29] to identify whether the users' reviews are positive, negative or neutral. For example, in the tourism industry, users often share their reviews publicly on internet platforms, such as sharing their opinion about the hotel stay on a Facebook group, twitter or google review. These reviews, along with the users' rating, can influence other users' purchasing decision, thus it is necessary to analyze and keep track of the users' emotions (whether they are generally positive or negative) towards the hotel and Airbnb accommodations via sentiment analysis [30, 31]. In addition, researchers made use of different types of text mining and machine learning methods (e.g., NLP, neural network, latent direchlet allocation) to extract information that can indicate which aspects of the product/service support UX and how these aspects contribute to positive UX in different degrees [32, 33]. For instance, Xu and colleagues [34] extracted features of hotel services from the reviews and later conducted regression-based model to investigate how different factors (e.g., travel purpose, hotel star levels) contribute to positive UX. More recently, researchers also developed conceptual models that provide detailed steps of how to combine sentiment analysis and machine learning methods when identifying relationship between the extracted text information with different UX aspects (e.g., [35, 36]). To summarize, the massive text data from users' online reviews provide researchers a way to extract information that evaluates the existing product/service and informs design of the product/service supporting positive UX.

Advantages and Limitations. While questionnaires aim to reflect users' feeling and experience in using the product, users may not truly report their real UX [36, 37]. Furthermore, the response rate of questionnaires tends to be low and likely to vary across different types of participants [38]. Together, users' difficulties in reporting real UX via questionnaire and low response rate can lead to issues with validity and sample representations of the user group [39, 40]. In comparison to questionnaire, online users' review data is proposed to be better in revealing different groups of users experience the product and also reflect different groups of users [35]. However, the information about UX is merely dependent on the details of the online reviews from users. If the users do not provide the information of why their UX is poor in a clear and/or detailed way, there would be difficult for researchers to extract meaningful information from users' online review [36].

3.2 Users' Behavioral Data

Analytical users log-based trackers, such as Google Analytics [41] and Hotjar [42], provide researchers with tools that automatically collect users' log web activity though users' interaction with the product websites, such as users' session duration, average number of pages viewed per session and bounce rate. These analytical trackers can collect user behavioral metrics described in the second section reviewing the "Approaches to Automated UX Evaluation" and thus can help infer whether users have a positive or negative UX when interacting with the products.

An extensive studied area in users' behaviors examines how users' mouse/cursor movement reflects the state of the UX when users interact with the website or platform. In the context of measuring UX on a website, analytical tools such as Hotjar [42] can generate heat maps and click maps that describe how users navigate the website and whether users click on the designed features. In addition, these tools can also track the depth that users scroll down the website (i.e., scroll map), indicating where users stop interacting with or reading the information on the website. These users' mouse/cursor movement maps provide important information for product teams and designers to understand whether users navigate or click on elements of the product website in an expected way, thus helping the product team and designers to find out where on the website need improvements for better UX.

In addition to offering insights on where the website or product page designs, users' mouse/cursor movements are considered as a measure of users' attention, cognitive processes and personality traits [43, 44]. Past studies have identified several mouse/cursor patterns in the website contexts that can reveal users' usability and UX when interacting with the product (see [43] for a review). Lee and Chen [45] had identified three types of mouse movements: straight pattern, fixed pattern and guide pattern. Users illustrating straight pattern often had short pauses on the screen at the beginning and later directly move their cursors towards the target element (e.g., a link) on the website without the need of further navigation. Therefore, straight pattern indicates that users know what they are looking for and can decide on what action needed to complete their task, which may suggest the task is relatively easy. Fixed pattern is found when users fixate their cursors to some fixed regions on the screen (e.g., right-side of the website) when processing information on the screen. After the users processed the information well, it is often followed by a straight pattern. A fixed pattern (followed by a straight pattern) often indicates how the information on the screen supports users' searching for relevant information/complete a task. Guide pattern refers to continuous users' cursor movements on the screen rather than the interrupted movements such as straight and fixed patterns. This pattern occurs when users are searching around as some kind of guide in exploring information on the website (e.g., hovering the menu of the website while scrolling down), thus reflecting how users pay attention on the website and whether users' navigation pattern matches with the product design or not. Mueller and Lockerd [46] identified the hesitation pattern in which users' cursor hover over some elements on the screen without taking any actions (e.g., hovering over the clink instead of clicking on it). This pattern often suggests challenges that users might experience with a task, which complicates their decision-making process. Together, prior studies have identified mouse movement patterns that allow researchers to infer whether the website design matches with users' expectation and can provide positive UX to users. However, these studies mainly use qualitative analysis with small sample sizes to identify the above-mentioned movement patterns, limiting the generalizability and reliability of these findings to larger data sets and different settings. To overcome such limitation, recent studies with larger sample sizes have utilized machine learning algorithms to extract mouse features (e.g., trajectory, mouse coordinates, path distance and time measures) examine how these features relate to users' engagement [47], emotion [48] and preferences [49].

Advantages and Limitations. Users' behavioral data collection is often considered as an automatic way of examining UX because it can be scalable to different products and also the data are massive. However, users' behaviors may not always reflect exactly what they feel and experience when interacting with products as the correlation between attitudinal data and behaviors is often moderate in magnitude at best [50, 51] and non-linear [52]. Sometimes, as suggested in previous studies [5], users' behavioral data can be ambiguous in interpretation, thus requiring researchers to carefully interpret the changes and magnitude of users' behavioral metrics when evaluating UX [14, 53].

3.3   Users' Physiological Data

There is an increasing trend in measuring users' physiological responses in evaluating UX. Common physiological responses include eye movements [54], facial expressions (e.g., facial EMG) [55], heart rates [56], electrical activity of the brain via electroencephalography (EEG) [57] and skin conductance via electrodermal activity (EDA) or skin conductance responses (SCR) [58]. Physiological response measurements are regarded as more sensitive reflections of users' affective and cognitive processing states, such as users' arousal, stress, emotions, attention and mental workloads [59]. These sensitive tools provide researchers with useful approximations for assessing UX of products that are strongly related to real-time users' affective and arousal states, such as video games [60] or virtual reality (VR) systems.

In the gaming industry, evaluating users' emotions, arousal and cognitive loads can inform designers on the game features that need improvements for smooth and fun game UX during different design stages (e.g., prototype stage) [61]. For example, eye-tracking data from users can better inform researchers what users paid attention to the interface and also users' emotional state when compared to merely measuring UX from users' self-report [62]. Similarly, researchers have utilized EEG to evaluate game players' pleasure and excitement under different multi-player games. Some researchers examined how users' EEG signals vary in a cooperative game environment as compared to a competitive game environment, providing insights to designers about incorporating social interaction elements in the game [63, 64]. As one type of physiological measurement is likely to be limited in revealing the full real-time UX during video game playing, researchers also have developed frameworks to integrate and analyze different physiological measurements, including EEG, EDA, facial EMG, eyetracking data, to offer a comprehensive evaluation UX for video games [65].

The use of physiological measurements is also commonly employed for the UX evaluation of virtual reality (VR) systems [66]. VR provides users with a simulated environment with scenes, people and objects that appear to be realistic, such that users have an experience and a feeling that they are immersed in the simulated environment. As VR strongly relies on users' perception, researchers also employ physical and physiological measures to evaluate real-time user experience about how users perceive and process information in the virtual world. Due to its cross-modal nature, VR and its applications have specific user experience that is inherent to the technology itself. One of the major UX aspect of interest in VR system is the sense of presence. Presence refers to the VR experience when users feel being existed or being immersed into the virtual world. While earlier studies measured VR users' presence through post-experience questionnaire (e.g., [67]), more researchers have utilized different physiological methods, such as heart rates, EEG and EDA, as additional measures of users' UX presence in real time and identify factors that contributing positive VR presence experience. The findings of the correlations between physiological responses and users' presence reported from questionnaire is mixed. Some studies have found that users' presence questionnaire scores (i.e., stronger feeling of presence) are positively correlated with heart rate and skin conductance [68, 69] whereas others reported weak correlations between these measurements [70, 71]. On the other hand, studies measuring neural responses demonstrated slightly more consistent findings as multiple studies have shown that EEG signals (e.g., gramma bands) are correlated to positive presence experience [71, 72]. Taken together, with a surge of the use of physiological methods in measuring VR UX, our understanding of VR UX and how to use different types of methods to evaluate VR UX is still evolving.

Advantages and Limitations. Users' physiological data collection can provide researchers with a sensitive tool to evaluate users' real time cognitive and affective states. It is nevertheless very costly, in terms of testing and time of data collection, as it often requires testing users in laboratory settings (e.g., EEG). In addition, it requires skilled researchers to analyze physiological data, making the cost of collecting each user's data higher. Because of the cost of data collection, studies using physiological measurement often are small in sample size, limiting the generalization of the data to a boarder UX evaluation setting. Although more recent studies have examined how to collect physiological data from users in a non-laboratory setting (e.g., wearable devices, [73]) or methods that can reduce costs of running experiments with users (e.g., [74]), sample size is still small and cannot be extended to large-scale data collection.

3.4 Expert Evaluation

Expert evaluation methods, also known as usability inspection methods[1] or usability engineering, are designed to help researchers evaluate usability of software systems and/or user interfaces (UI). Typically, usability inspection methods involve one or several evaluators, such as designers and product managers, to evaluate user interaction and identify usability problems through the lens of how users interact with the software systems/UI. As usability inspection methods do not involve real users and can be used at early design development stages (e.g. "prototype" stage), these methods can reduce the cost of identifying usability problems of software/UI [75].

There are a number of usability inspection methods in the Human-Computer Interaction field (see [76] for a review). Examples of usability inspection methods include Heuristic evaluation [77], cognitive walkthrough [78], pluralistic usability walkthrough [79], complexity analysis [80]. Among all usability inspection methods in the literature, heuristic evaluation and cognitive walkthrough are two most popular methods.

Heuristic evaluation guides evaluators to identify usability problems of a system/UI using 10 usability principles that were identified by Nielsen and his colleague [77]. Each evaluator is informed about a typical usage scenario and then asked to identify as many

---

[1] According to ISO 9241-210:2010, 2.13 [1], usability is the "extent to which a system, product or service can be used by specified users to achieve specified goals with effectiveness, efficiency and satisfaction in a specified context of use". In other words, usability refers to how the product/system/UI can help users to complete specific goals in an easy and satisfactory way. In this paper, we would not provide an overview of the differentiation between usability and UX as this is not our primary content and research interest. Instead, we take the perspective of other researchers (e.g., ISO 9241-210:2010, 2.15 [1], [92]) that usability is a part of UX and also a measure of UX because UX additionally includes (but not limited to) users' perceptions and feelings when users interact with the products or systems. Thus, we review usability inspection methods as a way to collect experts' data as a proxy of users' data that measures and evaluates UX.

usability problems of the system/UI as they can using the 10 usability principles individually. Once all evaluators completed their evaluations, an observer would aggregate all the identified usability problems in a list. The observer would present the list of the usability problem to each evaluator and ask each evaluator to rate the severity of the usability problems. When rating the severity of the problems, evaluators can judge the problem in terms of its frequency, whether the problem is easy to solve and whether the problem persistently bothering the user. The aggregated severity rating of the usability problems can provide the designers with insights on which design aspects of the system/UI should be improved first. In contrast, experts using cognitive walkthrough evaluate a system/UI by taking the perspective of how users complete their tasks.

Cognitive walkthrough method is based on Lewis & Polson's model of learning by exploration that describes the cognitive processes of how a typical user explores and learns how to successfully perform a task via a software/UI [78, 81]. Before evaluation, researchers first need to identify the user group and background (including users' knowledge) and the representative tasks with a list of actions that are required to complete the tasks with the system/UI. For the evaluation of the system/UI, evaluators walk through four steps of typical human-computer interaction: (i) users set a goal that needs to be completed with the system/UI; (ii) users find ways of accomplishing the goal with the system/UI; (iii) users select the action that will best support them to accomplish the goal; (iv) users take the selected action and evaluate whether the system/UI help them accomplish the goal based on the system/UI's feedback [78, 82]. In short, by considering users' knowledge and how users take different steps and actions to achieve their goals, cognitive walkthrough can evaluate whether there is a match between users' mental model and the system design.

More recently, researchers have suggested usability inspection methods that can quantify usability of the system/UI as a whole. For example, Sobiesiak and Keefe [80] have developed a list of criteria and metrics that guide experts to evaluate the complexity of each step that a user needs to go through to complete a task. The evaluation can produce a score for each task and can be compared across different versions of the system/UI to identify which version is the best in terms of usability. Similarly, Rohrer and colleagues [83] also have proposed the Practical Usability Rating by Experiment (PURE) system that helps researchers to develop a scorecard system that evaluates the ease of use for each step of a user's task. This approach also generates a score for the whole task that indicates the usability of the system, thus providing another way to quantify usability when comparing different versions of the system design and also tracking the usability of the same system over time. On the other hand, as the existing usability inspection methods were mainly developed in early 1990s, some researchers extended or developed new sets of heuristics/guidelines to evaluate usability in features/products in other domains, such as smartphone/mobile applications (e.g., [84]). This also led to studies that aimed to provide researchers with methods and instructions for developing new usability heuristic sets [85, 86].

Advantages and Limitations. Expert evaluation methods (also known as usability inspection methods) are widely used in the HCI field as a cost-effective way in evaluating UX. Yet, there are several limitations of this method in UX evaluation. First, evaluators are assumed to be able to evaluate the system/UI from the users' perspective. Evaluators' ability to evaluate the system/UI from users' angles are highly related to the accuracy of the hypothetical users' task scenario or users' route to complete their goals [76]. Thus, the UX or product team needs to conduct sufficient research to identify the most accurate typical scenario that their target users would undergo, but the identification of the typical scenario can be difficult for products that are very new or innovative to the market.

Furthermore, the quality of evaluation also depends on the expertise of the evaluators. It was suggested that novice evaluators often identified less usability problems and found it difficult to evaluate system/UI without the knowledge in the field of Human Factors and/or Human-Computer Interaction [77, 87, 88]. While this limitation can be partially solved by providing novice evaluators more guidelines and grouping evaluators together for a collaborative evaluation [89–91], but the problem remains unsolved completely because novice evaluators can still have difficulties in understanding expected users' mental model and lack the necessary HCI knowledge.

4   A Two-Tier Framework for Automated UX Evaluation

Given a rapid growth of the number of technology products, their expanding user bases as well as the resulting surging interest in approaches to developing automated UX evaluation systems, it becomes particularly important to understand how these automated solutions can leverage the advantages of traditional UX evaluation methods and overcome the current focus on static status of UX. Specifically, while there is a pressing need for monitoring UX scoring, it is equally important to associate the identified issues with diagnostic information, which would provide designers with insights on how specific aspects of UX should be improved. Correspondingly, in this section, we propose a two-tier framework for automating the process of UX evaluation and discuss how it allows lower human involvement in both data collection and diagnostic analysis by combining different types of users' data, commonly collected through traditional UX evaluation methods.

The proposed framework distinguishes two types of measurements: UX signals and UX diagnostics. UX signals measurements aim to reflect the state of different aspects of UX (higher-tiered measurements), while the associated UX diagnostics measurements point to the potential causes of UX challenges (lower-tiered measurements). This two-tier measurement approach allows researchers to design an automated system such that it associates UX scoring indicating measurements with the data that provides product teams insights on the required UX improvements.

4.1   First-Tier Measurements: UX Signals

We view the first-tier measurements – UX signals – as metrics that are defined based on whether they can simply reflect the UX status of a feature/product at that particular stage of the corresponding UX journey. For example, metrics that evaluate whether a feature/product supports users to have positive UX when users first start interacting with the feature/product. These metrics are intended to provide monitoring of the UX status of the product, i.e., to signal the product/design team if something is potentially wrong with a given aspect of the product's UX. We suggest that UX signals might include the following types of metrics.

1. User *behavioral log metrics* that reflect the general interaction patterns between the users and the product. For example, the average time that users interact with the product can indicate whether users spent a reasonable time on completing a task. If the time is much longer than the product team's expected time of completing a task, this may indicate poor efficiency and negative UX. Similarly, high bounce rate of a documentation page that aims to provide users instructions of how to use the product (i.e., rate that users left the page without interacting with any components on the page) may indicate poor UX as users may find the information on the page not useful and thus leave the page without interacting with it. Other examples may include dwell time (i.e., amount of time users takes analyzing website before clicking to the search results), average click through rate of a feature of the product (i.e., number of clicks per user on a feature), number of page view per user and number of sessions per user. All these examples can reveal a general picture of users' engagement and/or interaction with a website/web platform of the product, thus signaling whether the UX is positive or negative. Consistent with Deng & Shi [10], we suggest using rate metrics as UX signals because it has bounded values from 0 to 1 and is less skewed that allows better comparison of UX scores and reflections of UX status over time.

2. *Questionnaire* metrics that measure overall users' satisfaction and/or experience of the product. For example, a low average rating of a question asking users how satisfied they are when interacting with the product on a scale signals poor UX with the product. Or a low average rating of a question asking users the ease of learning how to use the product indicates the product has low learnability and suggests poor UX.

3. Sentiment analysis of *online review*, categorizing users' opinion into three types: positive, neutral or negative, can signify whether the product as a whole have a positive UX or negative UX.

4. *Business* or *marketing* metrics that primarily measure the performance of the product can indicate whether UX is positive or not. For example, a high retention rate, a measure of the percentage of users who continue to use the product over a given period of time, can be an indicator of positive UX as users value your product and choose to continue using the product. However, these metrics tend to reflect the long-term effects of whether feature/product support positive UX, rather than reflecting the short-term effects of whether feature/product support positive UX.

5. A score of *expert evaluation*, a quantified score that represents usability of the product, can also reveal whether the product can have a positive UX or not.

The above-mentioned example metrics are considered as UX signals as they can indicate whether UX of a feature/product is positive or negative. It is important to note that these metrics cannot indicate the potential causes of poor UX status. For example, a low click through rate of a feature on the product website – a behavioral metric – can imply users are not engaged with the feature, thus possibly reflect poor UX. However, the rate cannot reveal a potential underlying cause of why users do not find the features useful in their interaction with the product. As UX signal metrics mainly signify if the UX is positive or negative, they may reflect multiple UX challenges. For example, when the average rating of the overall users' satisfaction of the product is low, it can be caused by multiple factors including inefficient interaction with the product and/or ineffectiveness in which the users frequently fail to complete their task. Correspondingly, we further introduce the second-tier measurements that are collected to helps diagnose the potential underlying causes of the UX status.

4.2 Second-Tier Measurements: UX Diagnostics

While UX signals metrics simply indicate an existence of a potential UX issue, second-tier measurements – UX diagnostics – are the metrics intended to help product teams understand the potential underlying causes of these issues, including why the UX status is low and/or understand the UX signal metric's dynamics. In other words, UX diagnostics metrics, associated with specific UX signals, provide insights to what may lead to the low UX status that indicated by the UX signals metrics. Examples of UX diagnostics include:

1. Users' *behavioral* or *log* metrics, describing the potential flows of how users interact with the product and/or complete a task with the product, are UX diagnostic that can reveal why users fail in completing task and/or why the task is not efficient in support positive UX. For example, a high average error rate and a high average rate of repeating the same command on the task may suggest that users encounter an unexpectedly high number of errors when completing their task, thus providing a potential explanation of why the UX signal metric, such as a low average task completion rate and long users' average time of interacting with the product are observed. Other examples like the number of repeated visits to FAQ/documentation page can potentially imply the instruction is unclear, thus suggesting the materials has low learnability that supports users to complete their task when using the product.
2. Text information from users' *online reviews* and/or users' *issue tickets* can provide insights on what the users' problems are and which features/areas of the product that users found unhelpful in supporting their UX. In our experience, using NLP method to extract text information for identifying frequent UX problems from users' issue tickets can be a very useful way in unraveling core problems in the product. For example, the ticket analysis indicated that users consistently failed to solve a problem alone while there is a solution provided on the FAQ page, it may be because that the solution on the FAQ page is not easy for users to comprehend and/or users did not find the solution on the page, thus suggesting the product team to further investigate why the FAQ page cannot support users for a positive UX.
3. *Technical* metrics that reflect the operating performance of the product/system is another type of UX diagnostic metrics. Examples of these technical metrics included page loading time (i.e., average time that users need to wait until the information of the page is fully displayed on the users' screen) and frequency of 404 error reports. All these metrics can direct the product team to potential problems of the system/technical area of the product that fail to support users for positive UX.
4. The usability problems identified in *expert evaluation* can directly point the product team to the areas of improvement of the product. For example, while both heuristic evaluation and cognitive walkthrough provide experts instructions on evaluating the ease and usability of the product, these methods also instruct the expert evaluators

to elaborate the usability problems that they have identified and explain why this is a problem to the users. Thus, this information can directly provide insights to the product team of what they need to improve in their product design for better UX.

Although some traditional UX evaluation methods collect physiological data to evaluate users' response, we do not consider physiological response in either UX signals or UX diagnostics metrics. Our rationale is that collection and analysis of users' physiological data require high involvements of human experts. Additionally, physiological response data are challenging to track automatically and typically are not collected by companies across the user base and/or over time.

5 Conclusion

Evaluating user experience in an automatic system is becoming an urging need to help companies keep track of their product performance and stay competitive on the market. However, most of the current automated UX evaluation systems and traditional UX methods often require high involvements in human experts to collect and analyses data. Most of the existing frameworks for automatic UX evaluation often provide a snapshot of the state of UX, but lack the data to develop insights into the potential underlying causes of UX problems. In this paper, we synthesized traditional UX evaluation methods based on the type of data and proposed a two-tier metrics approach to develop automated UX evaluation systems that can both evaluate the UX status and identify potential underlying causes of UX challenges.

Acknowledgment. We would like to thank Dr. Hrag Pailian for his comments and discussion at the earlier stages of the development of the two-tier UX measurement approach.

References

1. ISO 9241-11:2018(en), Ergonomics of human-system interaction — Part 11: Usability: Definitions and concepts. https://www.iso.org/obp/ui/#iso:std:iso:9241:-11:ed-2:v1:en
2. Inan Nur, A., Santoso, H. B., Hadi Putra, P.O.: The method and metric of user experience evaluation: a systematic literature review. In: 2021 10th International Conference on Software and Computer Applications, Kuala Lumpur Malaysia, pp. 307–317. ACM (2021)
3. Hussain, J., et al.: A multimodal deep log-based user experience (UX) PLATFORM for UX evaluation. Sensors **18**, 1622 (2018). https://doi.org/10.3390/s18051622
4. McClure, D.: Startup Metrics for Pirates (13:03:16 UTC)
5. Rodden, K., Hutchinson, H., Fu, X.: Measuring the user experience on a large scale: user-centered metrics for web applications. In: Proceedings of the SIGCHI Conference on Human Factors in Computing Systems, Atlanta, Georgia, USA, pp. 2395–2398. ACM (2010)
6. Kohavi, R., Deng, A., Frasca, B., Walker, T., Xu, Y., Pohlmann, N.: Online controlled experiments at large scale. In: Proceedings of the 19th ACM SIGKDD International Conference on Knowledge Discovery and Data Mining, Chicago, Illinois, USA, pp. 1168–1176. ACM (2013)
7. Fabijan, A., Dmitriev, P., Olsson, H.H., Bosch, J.: The benefits of controlled experimentation at scale. In: 2017 43rd Euromicro Conference on Software Engineering and Advanced Applications (SEAA), Vienna, Austria, pp. 18–26. IEEE (2017)

8. Gupta, S., Ulanova, L., Bhardwaj, S., Dmitriev, P., Raff, P., Fabijan, A.: The anatomy of a large-scale experimentation platform. In: 2018 IEEE International Conference on Software Architecture (ICSA), Seattle, WA, pp. 1–109. IEEE (2018)
9. Gupta, S., et al.: Top challenges from the first practical online controlled experiments summit. SIGKDD Explor. Newsl. **21**, 20–35 (2019). https://doi.org/10.1145/3331651.3331655
10. Deng, A., Shi, X.: Data-driven metric development for online controlled experiments: seven lessons learned. In: Proceedings of the 22nd ACM SIGKDD International Conference on Knowledge Discovery and Data Mining, San Francisco, California, USA, pp. 77–86. ACM (2016)
11. Dmitriev, P., Wu, X.: Measuring metrics. In: Proceedings of the 25th ACM International on Conference on Information and Knowledge Management, Indianapolis, Indiana, USA, pp. 429–437. ACM (2016)
12. Dmitriev, P., Gupta, S., Kim, D.W., Vaz, G.: A dirty dozen: twelve common metric interpretation pitfalls in online controlled experiments. In: Proceedings of the 23rd ACM SIGKDD International Conference on Knowledge Discovery and Data Mining, Halifax, NS, Canada, pp. 1427–1436. ACM (2017)
13. Robinson, J., Lanius, C., Weber, R.: The past, present, and future of UX empirical research. Commun. Des. Q. Rev. **5**, 10–23 (2018). https://doi.org/10.1145/3188173.3188175
14. Shyr, C., Kushniruk, A., Wasserman, W.W.: Usability study of clinical exome analysis software: top lessons learned and recommendations. J. Biomed. Inform. **51**, 129–136 (2014). https://doi.org/10.1016/j.jbi.2014.05.004
15. Joachim, V., Spieth, P., Heidenreich, S.: Active innovation resistance: an empirical study on functional and psychological barriers to innovation adoption in different contexts. Ind. Mark. Manag. **71**, 95–107 (2018). https://doi.org/10.1016/j.indmarman.2017.12.011
16. Likert, R.: A technique for measurement of attitudes. Arch. Psychol. **140**, 5–55 (1932)
17. Brooke, J.: SUS: a retrospective. J. Usability Stud. **8**, 29–40 (2013)
18. Lewis, J.R.: Critical review of "the usability metric for user experience." Interact. Comput. **25**, 320–324 (2013). https://doi.org/10.1093/iwc/iwt013
19. Moshagen, M., Thielsch, M.T.: Facets of visual aesthetics. Int. J. Hum. Comput. Stud. **68**, 689–709 (2010). https://doi.org/10.1016/j.ijhcs.2010.05.006
20. Lavie, T., Tractinsky, N.: Assessing dimensions of perceived visual aesthetics of web sites. Int. J. Hum. Comput. Stud. **60**, 269–298 (2004). https://doi.org/10.1016/j.ijhcs.2003.09.002
21. Sauro, J., Dumas, J.S.: Comparison of three one-question, post-task usability questionnaires. In: Proceedings of the SIGCHI Conference on Human Factors in Computing Systems, Boston, MA, USA, pp. 1599–1608. ACM (2009)
22. Paas, F.G.W.C., Van Merriënboer, J.J.G.: The efficiency of instructional conditions: an approach to combine mental effort and performance measures. Hum. Factors **35**, 737–743 (1993). https://doi.org/10.1177/001872089303500412
23. Hassenzahl, M., Platz, A., Burmester, M., Lehner, K.: Hedonic and ergonomic quality aspects determine a software's appeal. In: Proceedings of the SIGCHI Conference on Human Factors in Computing Systems, The Hague, The Netherlands, pp. 201–208. ACM (2000)
24. Laugwitz, B., Held, T., Schrepp, M.: Construction and evaluation of a user experience questionnaire. In: Holzinger, A. (ed.) USAB 2008. LNCS, vol. 5298, pp. 63–76. Springer, Heidelberg (2008). https://doi.org/10.1007/978-3-540-89350-9_6
25. Sauro, J., Lewis, J.R.: Quantifying the User Experience: Practical Statistics for User Research. Elsevier, Morgan Kaufmann, Amsterdam (2016)
26. Schankin, A., Budde, M., Riedel, T., Beigl, M.: Psychometric properties of the user experience questionnaire (UEQ). In: CHI Conference on Human Factors in Computing Systems, New Orleans, LA, USA, pp. 1–11. ACM (2022)

27. Abrahams, A.S., Fan, W., Wang, G.A., Zhang, Z.J., Jiao, J.: An integrated text analytic framework for product defect discovery. Prod. Oper. Manag. **24**, 975–990 (2015). https://doi.org/10.1111/poms.12303
28. Qi, J., Zhang, Z., Jeon, S., Zhou, Y.: Mining customer requirements from online reviews: a product improvement perspective. Inf. Manag. **53**, 951–963 (2016). https://doi.org/10.1016/j.im.2016.06.002
29. Ding, X., Liu, B., Zhang, L.: Entity discovery and assignment for opinion mining applications. In: Proceedings of the 15th ACM SIGKDD International Conference on Knowledge Discovery and Data Mining, Paris, France, pp. 1125–1134. ACM (2009)
30. Park, E., Kang, J., Choi, D., Han, J.: Understanding customers' hotel revisiting behaviour: a sentiment analysis of online feedback reviews. Curr. Issue Tour. **23**, 605–611 (2020). https://doi.org/10.1080/13683500.2018.1549025
31. Cheng, M., Jin, X.: What do Airbnb users care about? An analysis of online review comments. Int. J. Hosp. Manag. **76**, 58–70 (2019). https://doi.org/10.1016/j.ijhm.2018.04.004
32. Guo, Y., Barnes, S.J., Jia, Q.: Mining meaning from online ratings and reviews: tourist satisfaction analysis using latent Dirichlet allocation. Tour. Manag. **59**, 467–483 (2017). https://doi.org/10.1016/j.tourman.2016.09.009
33. Vu, H.Q., Li, G., Law, R., Zhang, Y.: Exploring tourist dining preferences based on restaurant reviews. J. Travel Res. **58**, 149–167 (2019). https://doi.org/10.1177/0047287517744672
34. Xu, X., Wang, X., Li, Y., Haghighi, M.: Business intelligence in online customer textual reviews: understanding consumer perceptions and influential factors. Int. J. Inf. Manag. **37**, 673–683 (2017). https://doi.org/10.1016/j.ijinfomgt.2017.06.004
35. Yang, B., Liu, Y., Liang, Y., Tang, M.: Exploiting user experience from online customer reviews for product design. Int. J. Inf. Manag. **46**, 173–186 (2019). https://doi.org/10.1016/j.ijinfomgt.2018.12.006
36. Hussain, J., Azhar, Z., Ahmad, H.F., Afzal, M., Raza, M., Lee, S.: User experience quantification model from online user reviews. Appl. Sci. **12**, 6700 (2022). https://doi.org/10.3390/app12136700
37. Podsakoff, P.M., MacKenzie, S.B., Lee, J.-Y., Podsakoff, N.P.: Common method biases in behavioral research: a critical review of the literature and recommended remedies. J. Appl. Psychol. **88**, 879–903 (2003). https://doi.org/10.1037/0021-9010.88.5.879
38. Holtom, B., Baruch, Y., Aguinis, H., A Ballinger, G.: Survey response rates: trends and a validity assessment framework. Hum. Relat. **75**, 1560–1584 (2022). https://doi.org/10.1177/00187267211070769
39. Sivo, S., Saunders, C., Chang, Q., Jiang, J.: How low should you go? Low response rates and the validity of inference in IS questionnaire research. JAIS **7**, 351–414 (2006). https://doi.org/10.17705/1jais.00093
40. Singh, A.S., Masuku, M.B.: Sampling techniques and determination of sample size in applied statistics research: an overview. Int. J. Econ. Commer. Manag. **2**, 1–22 (2014)
41. Analytics Tools & Solutions for Your Business - Google Analytics. https://marketingplatform.google.com/about/analytics/
42. Hotjar: Website Heatmaps & Behavior Analytics Tools. https://www.hotjar.com/
43. Katerina, T., Nicolaos, P.: Mouse behavioral patterns and keystroke dynamics in end-user development: what can they tell us about users' behavioral attributes? Comput. Hum. Behav. **83**, 288–305 (2018). https://doi.org/10.1016/j.chb.2018.02.012
44. Meidenbauer, K.L., Niu, T., Choe, K.W., Stier, A.J., Berman, M.G.: Mouse movements reflect personality traits and task attentiveness in online experiments. J. Personal. (2022). https://doi.org/10.1111/jopy.12736
45. Griffiths, L., Chen, Z.: Investigating the differences in web browsing behaviour of chinese and european users using mouse tracking. In: Aykin, N. (ed.) UI-HCII 2007. LNCS, vol. 4559, pp. 502–512. Springer, Heidelberg (2007). https://doi.org/10.1007/978-3-540-73287-7_59

46. Mueller, F., Lockerd, A.: Cheese: tracking mouse movement activity on websites, a tool for user modeling. In: CHI 2001 Extended Abstracts on Human Factors in Computing Systems, Seattle Washington, pp. 279–280. ACM (2001)
47. Arapakis, I., Leiva, L.A.: Predicting user engagement with direct displays using mouse cursor information. In: Proceedings of the 39th International ACM SIGIR Conference on Research and Development in Information Retrieval, Pisa, Italy, pp. 599–608. ACM (2016)
48. Yamauchi, T., Xiao, K.: Reading emotion from mouse cursor motions: affective computing approach. Cognit. Sci. **42**, 771–819 (2018). https://doi.org/10.1111/cogs.12557
49. SadighZadeh, S., Kaedi, M.: Modeling user preferences in online stores based on user mouse behavior on page elements. JSIT. **24**, 112–130 (2022). https://doi.org/10.1108/JSIT-12-2019-0264
50. Smith, J.R., Terry, D.J., Manstead, A.S.R., Louis, W.R., Kotterman, D., Wolfs, J.: The attitude-behavior relationship in consumer conduct: the role of norms, past behavior, and self-identity. J. Soc. Psychol. **148**, 311–334 (2008). https://doi.org/10.3200/SOCP.148.3.311-334
51. Sauro, J.: Linking UX Attitudes to Future Website Purchases – MeasuringU. https://measuringu.com/ux-purchases/
52. Bechler, C.J., Tormala, Z.L., Rucker, D.D.: The attitude-behavior relationship revisited. Psychol. Sci. **32**, 1285–1297 (2021). https://doi.org/10.1177/0956797621995206
53. Kohavi, R., Deng, A., Longbotham, R., Xu, Y.: Seven rules of thumb for web site experimenters. In: Proceedings of the 20th ACM SIGKDD International Conference on Knowledge Discovery and Data Mining, New York, USA, pp. 1857–1866. ACM (2014)
54. Fu, B., Noy, N.F., Storey, M.-A.: Eye tracking the user experience – an evaluation of ontology visualization techniques. SW **8**, 23–41 (2016). https://doi.org/10.3233/SW-140163
55. Zaman, B., Shrimpton-Smith, T.: The FaceReader: measuring instant fun of use. In: Proceedings of the 4th Nordic Conference on Human-Computer Interaction: Changing Roles, Oslo, Norway, pp. 457–460. ACM (2006)
56. Lane, R., Mcrae, K., Reiman, E., Chen, K., Ahern, G., Thayer, J.: Neural correlates of heart rate variability during emotion. Neuroimage **44**, 213–222 (2009). https://doi.org/10.1016/j.neuroimage.2008.07.056
57. Zheng, W.-L., Zhu, J.-Y., Lu, B.-L.: Identifying stable patterns over time for emotion recognition from EEG. IEEE Trans. Affect. Comput. **10**, 417–429 (2019). https://doi.org/10.1109/TAFFC.2017.2712143
58. Dawson, M.E., Schell, A.M., Filion, D.L., Berntson, G.G.: The electrodermal system. In: Cacioppo, J.T., Tassinary, L.G., Berntson, G. (eds.) Handbook of Psychophysiology, pp. 157–181. Cambridge University Press, Cambridge (2007)
59. Calvo, R.A., D'Mello, S.: Affect detection: an interdisciplinary review of models, methods, and their applications. IEEE Trans. Affect. Comput. **1**, 18–37 (2010). https://doi.org/10.1109/T-AFFC.2010.1
60. Nacke, L.E.: Games user research and physiological game evaluation. In: Bernhaupt, R. (ed.) Game User Experience Evaluation. HIS, pp. 63–86. Springer, Cham (2015). https://doi.org/10.1007/978-3-319-15985-0_4
61. Bernhaupt, R.: User experience evaluation methods in the games development life cycle. In: Bernhaupt, R. (ed.) Game User Experience Evaluation. HIS, pp. 1–8. Springer, Cham (2015). https://doi.org/10.1007/978-3-319-15985-0_1
62. Courtemanche, F., Léger, P.-M., Dufresne, A., Fredette, M., Labonté-LeMoyne, É., Sénécal, S.: Physiological heatmaps: a tool for visualizing users' emotional reactions. Multimedia Tools Appl. **77**(9), 11547–11574 (2017). https://doi.org/10.1007/s11042-017-5091-1
63. Wehbe, R.R., Kappen, D.L., Rojas, D., Klauser, M., Kapralos, B., Nacke, L.E.: EEG-based assessment of video and in-game learning. In: CHI 2013 Extended Abstracts on Human Factors in Computing Systems, Paris, France, pp. 667–672. ACM (2013)

64. Wehbe, R.R., Nacke, L.E.: Towards understanding the importance of co-located gameplay. In: Proceedings of the 2015 Annual Symposium on Computer-Human Interaction in Play, London, United Kingdom, pp. 733–738. ACM (2015)

65. Nacke, L.E., Stellmach, S., Sasse, D., Niesenhaus, J., Dachselt, R.: LAIF: a logging and interaction framework for gaze-based interfaces in virtual entertainment environments. Entertain. Comput. **2**, 265–273 (2011). https://doi.org/10.1016/j.entcom.2010.09.004

66. Halbig, A., Latoschik, M.E.: A systematic review of physiological measurements, factors, methods, and applications in virtual reality. Front. Virtual Real. **2**, 694567 (2021). https://doi.org/10.3389/frvir.2021.694567

67. Witmer, B.G., Singer, M.J.: Measuring presence in virtual environments: a presence questionnaire. Presence **7**, 225–240 (1998). https://doi.org/10.1162/105474698565686

68. Deniaud, C., Honnet, V., Jeanne, B., Mestre, D.: The concept of "presence" as a measure of ecological validity in driving simulators. J. Interact. Sci. **3**(1), 1–13 (2015). https://doi.org/10.1186/s40166-015-0005-z

69. Lemmens, J.S., Simon, M., Sumter, S.R.: Fear and loathing in VR: the emotional and physiological effects of immersive games. Virtual Real. **26**, 223–234 (2021). https://doi.org/10.1007/s10055-021-00555-w

70. Dey, A., Phoon, J., Saha, S., Dobbins, C., Billinghurst, M.: A neurophysiological approach for measuring presence in immersive virtual environments. In: 2020 IEEE International Symposium on Mixed and Augmented Reality (ISMAR), Porto de Galinhas, Brazil, pp. 474–485. IEEE (2020)

71. Athif, M., et al.: Using biosignals for objective measurement of presence in virtual reality environments. In: 2020 42nd Annual International Conference of the IEEE Engineering in Medicine & Biology Society (EMBC), Montreal, QC, Canada, pp. 3035–3039. IEEE (2020)

72. Arake, M., et al.: Measuring task-related brain activity with event-related potentials in dynamic task scenario with immersive virtual reality environment. Front. Behav. Neurosci. **16**, 779926 (2022). https://doi.org/10.3389/fnbeh.2022.779926

73. Michaelis, J.R., et al.: Describing the user experience of wearable fitness technology through online product reviews. Proc. Hum. Factors Ergon. Soc. Annu. Meet. **60**, 1073–1077 (2016). https://doi.org/10.1177/1541931213601248

74. Cano, S., Araujo, N., Guzman, C., Rusu, C., Albiol-Perez, S.: Low-cost assessment of user experience through EEG signals. IEEE Access **8**, 158475–158487 (2020). https://doi.org/10.1109/ACCESS.2020.3017685

75. Nielson, J.: Usability inspection methods. Presented at the Conference Companion on Human Factors in Computing Systems, April 1994

76. Hollingsed, T., Novick, D.G.: Usability inspection methods after 15 years of research and practice. In: Proceedings of the 25th Annual ACM International Conference on Design of Communication, El Paso, Texas, USA, pp. 249–255. ACM (2007)

77. Nielsen, J., Molich, R.: Heuristic evaluation of user interfaces. In: Proceedings of the SIGCHI Conference on Human Factors in Computing Systems Empowering People - CHI 1990, Seattle, Washington, United States, pp. 249–256. ACM Press (1990)

78. Lewis, C., Polson, P.G., Wharton, C., Rieman, J.: Testing a walkthrough methodology for theory-based design of walk-up-and-use interfaces. In: Proceedings of the SIGCHI Conference on Human Factors in Computing Systems Empowering People - CHI 1990, Seattle, Washington, United States, pp. 235–242. ACM Press (1990)

79. Bias, R.: The pluralistic usability walkthrough: coordinated empathies. In: Nielsen, J., Mack, R.L. (eds.) Usability Inspection Methods, pp. 63–76. Wiley, New York (1994)

80. Sobiesiak, R., O'Keefe, Ti.: Complexity analysis: a quantitative approach to usability engineering. In: CASCON 2011: Proceedings of the 2011 Conference of the Center for Advanced Studies on Collaborative Research, pp. 242–256 (2011)

81. Polson, P.G., Lewis, C., Rieman, J., Wharton, C.: Cognitive walkthroughs: a method for theory-based evaluation of user interfaces. Int. J. Man Mach. Stud. **36**, 741–773 (1992). https://doi.org/10.1016/0020-7373(92)90039-N
82. Lewis, C., Wharton, C.: Cognitive walkthroughs. In: Handbook of Human-Computer Interaction, pp. 717–732. Elsevier (1997)
83. Rohrer, C.P., Wendt, J., Sauro, J., Boyle, F., Cole, S.: Practical usability rating by experts (PURE): a pragmatic approach for scoring product usability. In: Proceedings of the 2016 CHI Conference Extended Abstracts on Human Factors in Computing Systems, San Jose, California, USA, pp. 786–795. ACM (2016)
84. Joyce, G., Lilley, M.: Towards the development of usability heuristics for native smartphone mobile applications. In: Marcus, A. (ed.) DUXU 2014. LNCS, vol. 8517, pp. 465–474. Springer, Cham (2014). https://doi.org/10.1007/978-3-319-07668-3_45
85. Quiñones, D., Rusu, C., Rusu, V.: A methodology to develop usability/user experience heuristics. Comput. Stand. Interfaces **59**, 109–129 (2018). https://doi.org/10.1016/j.csi.2018.03.002
86. Hermawati, S., Lawson, G.: Establishing usability heuristics for heuristics evaluation in a specific domain: is there a consensus? Appl. Ergon. **56**, 34–51 (2016). https://doi.org/10.1016/j.apergo.2015.11.016
87. Nielsen, J.: Finding usability problems through heuristic evaluation. In: Proceedings of the SIGCHI Conference on Human Factors in Computing Systems - CHI 1992, Monterey, California, United States, pp. 373–380. ACM Press (1992)
88. de Lima Salgado, A., de Mattos Fortes, R.P.: Heuristic evaluation for novice evaluators. In: Marcus, A. (ed.) DUXU 2016. LNCS, vol. 9746, pp. 387–398. Springer, Cham (2016). https://doi.org/10.1007/978-3-319-40409-7_37
89. Botella, F., Alarcon, E., Peñalver, A.: How to classify to experts in usability evaluation. In: Proceedings of the XV International Conference on Human Computer Interaction - Interacción 2014, Puerto de la Cruz, Tenerife, Spain, pp. 1–4. ACM Press (2014)
90. Solano, A., Collazos, C.A., Rusu, C., Fardoun, H.M.: Combinations of methods for collaborative evaluation of the usability of interactive software systems. Adv. Hum. Comput. Interact. **2016**, 1–16 (2016). https://doi.org/10.1155/2016/4089520
91. Nasir, M., Ikram, N., Jalil, Z.: Usability inspection: novice crowd inspectors versus expert. J. Syst. Softw. **183**, 111122 (2022). https://doi.org/10.1016/j.jss.2021.111122
92. Hassan, H.M., Galal-Edeen, G.H.: From usability to user experience. In: 2017 International Conference on Intelligent Informatics and Biomedical Sciences (ICIIBMS), Okinawa, pp. 216–222. IEEE (2017)

UX Calculator: An Online Tool to Support User Testing

Ruojun Wang$^{(\boxtimes)}$, Shang-Lin Chen , Chantal Labbé, Marc Fredette,
Amine Abdessemed, François Courtemanche, Constantinos K. Coursaris ,
Sylvain Sénécal , and Pierre-Majorique Léger

HEC Montréal, Tech3lab, Montréal, QC, Canada
{ruojun.wang,shang-lin.chen,chantal.labbe,marc.fredette,
amine.abdessemed,francois.courtemanche,constantinos.coursaris,
sylvain.senecal,pml}@hec.ca

Abstract. As the digital era is witnessing huge commercial success driven by design innovations focusing on usability as well as utility, businesses have also been positioning user experience (UX) research as the cornerstone of the competitiveness of their products and services. However, UX data analysis can be costly and demanding in terms of monetary and human resources, making it imperative to develop a cost-effective solution to assist UX evaluation. In this article, we present the design, development, and deployment process of the UX Calculator (uxcalc.web.app), a lightweight web-based tool that enables practitioners to run statistical tests tailored to the main analyses involved in a UX assessment. This tool allows designers to perform two-group comparisons and get robust conclusions about the UX performance without extra training in statistical programming. The interaction logic of this tool, together with the methodological considerations, practical implications, and future work for the tool's improvement are discussed in detail.

Keywords: Evaluation Methods and Techniques · User Experience · Usability Test · UX Performance · UX Calculator

1 Introduction

With the acceleration of enterprise digitalization, user experience (UX) is increasingly being recognized as an essential factor for the commercial success of digital products [1]. Despite its importance in assuring the optimal design of websites and interactive applications, the current UX evaluation practice is often conducted in an unclear and questionable manner. Compared with other aspects of the digital artefact's development process, the evaluation stage still suffers from inconsistency in paradigms, methodologies, and procedures, as well as a lack of objectiveness, partially due to the monetary and time costs involved [2]. In order to reduce costs, efforts have been made to develop solutions such as remote user testing [3] and semi-automatic usability evaluations [4]. However, these methods focus on streamlining data collection for UX evaluation, and the need for tools to assist UX professionals in analyzing the data gathered from usability tests remains.

A. Marcus et al. (Eds.): HCII 2023, LNCS 14032, pp. 101–111, 2023.
https://doi.org/10.1007/978-3-031-35702-2_7

Ideally, practitioners are expected to combine qualitative and quantitative methods in conducting UX evaluation. Even primarily qualitative usability tests can generate quantifiable outcomes, such as completion rates, task completion time, errors, psychometric data, and website traffic [5]. Therefore, to reach valid conclusions that can guide the iterative design process, proposing and performing suitable statistical tests is of vital importance. Open-source packages (e.g., R statistical programming package) and software platforms (e.g., SPSS, SAS, and Minitab) have been created to support with general statistical analysis, but practitioners often struggle to integrate these professional systems into their workflow. First, these tools do not place the emphasis on the use of methods designed specifically for small sample sizes, but in practice the sample size for most usability tests ranges from 8 to 20 participants, rendering parametric tests inappropriate. In fact, the debate about the sufficient sample size for UX evaluation is ongoing. On the one hand, UX experts with years of experience in this field have provided recommendations ranging from "4 ± 1" or "magic number 5" [6] to "10 ± 2" [7]. These values are estimations of the smallest sample required to identify a target proportion of problems based on empirical data. Although these discussions are not relevant to statistical tests, it does reveal the fact that extensive testing is not feasible in real-life scenarios. Most of the time, just like scholars, practitioners have limited resources including funding available for a project, implying they cannot recruit as many participants as they want. For example, in an analysis of 423 manuscripts published at a premier peer-reviewed conference, CHI, the most frequently reported sample size is 12 [8]. Such a small sample size is often not enough for the approximation of normality (i.e., the central limit theorem) to ensure the validity of parametric tests, meaning the most commonly used statistical tests (e.g., t-test) are not applicable. That, however, can exacerbate the second issue: currently available tools often require expertise in both programming and statistics. To produce valid statistical conclusions, UX professionals first need to master sophisticated statistical techniques to identify the appropriate tests based on their evaluation objective(s), sample size, and data types (i.e., required expertise in statistics). Even when they understand the need to perform rigorous statistics tests and have determined the test, UX experts may still lack the knowledge that enables them to choose specific statistics packages to run the appropriate statistical test (i.e., required expertise in programming and familiarity with the software environment). Moreover, the financial cost of professional analysis tools can be prohibitive. Considering the limited budget and pressured deadlines in practice, UX professionals need a solution that is more cost-effective compared to alternatives such as purchasing software licenses and self-learning complicated software.

Therefore, this article aims to present the UX Calculator (uxcalc.web.app), a lightweight web-based tool that allows professionals to run statistical tests tailored to the main statistical analyses involved in a UX assessment. Using this calculator, practitioners without prior training in statistical programming can easily compare two groups of observations and obtain straightforward conclusions about the UX performance. It is especially cost-effective if professionals would like to conduct a small-scale, formative user evaluation during their iterative design process.

This paper reports on the current state of our UX Calculator's design and outlines the plan for further evaluation and refinement of this tool. The next section presents the development process of the UX Calculator, as well as its working principle and the IT infrastructure involved. Section 3 describes the interaction logic between target users and this artefact and explains how it is connected to the real-world UX evaluation practice. Section 4 then presents rough statistics on the tool's usage. Finally, the last section of this article consists of an agenda of testing and improving the usability of this web-based analysis tool.

2 Approaches

To achieve the goal of this study, a user-centered design (UCD) approach was adopted. Accordingly, we started with the design scenarios, which are the tasks that the target user needs to perform in a specific context [9]. Through discussions with UX professionals, the major components of the user scenarios were identified (see Table 1). All these components can impact the choice of statistical tests. *Design stage* refers to the current phase of the development of a digital artefact, which usually implies the types of proposed UX evaluations: they may aim to find and fix usability problems (e.g., formative) or to describe the usability of an application (e.g., summative) [5]. At different design stages, designers' expectations and assumptions regarding the evaluation may differ, which can influence the choice of directionality and significance level used when performing statistical hypothesis tests. The *evaluation objective* is relevant to the usability test design. UX professionals can compare either between-subjects or within-subjects performance, implying a difference between paired or independent samples for statistical tests. *Metric* refers to the unit of measure to be compared in a UX study, and it can also impact the subsequent analysis. For example, parametric methods are not applied to ordinal data, such as Likert-scale measures.

Table 1. Main components of user scenario (UX professionals)

Component	Explanation
Design stage	The current stage of digital product development
Evaluation objective	The nature of the comparison is to be made
Metric	The unit of measure to be compared in a UX study

In this case, the UX Calculator is expected to execute the appropriate statistical test based on the users' disclosure regarding these components. In line with the above-mentioned components, we designed the user input block to collect the required information and data (details and interface screen captures are shown in Sect. 3). To ensure the statistical method embedded in this tool is compatible with most datasets, we chose Wilcoxon rank sum test (for two independent samples) and signed-rank test (for two paired samples) [10, 11] as the underlying algorithms of the comparison function. These are widely used nonparametric methods applicable to continuous or ordinal variables of any distribution, with small or large sample sizes. For a larger sample size (e.g., at least 25 in each group), the asymptotic p-value is calculated as an approximation of the exact value. The back-end development is finished in Python 3.0 with R package version 0.8–31 [12].

After the script passed the pilot test with sufficient user cases, we deployed a small HTTP server on a virtual machine hosted on the cloud and then launched the script to create a web application. This server receives an HTTP GET query that includes the user's input gathered on the application interface. This front-end facing application is built with the Angular framework and is small enough to be hosted on any machine including a Raspberry Pi.

3   Results

3.1   User Input

The first section of user input in the UX Calculator consists of four single-answer multiple-choice questions (see Fig. 1).

Evaluation Design. For the first question, users report the nature of the comparison to be made. Depending on the evaluation design, a UX study can produce paired measures or fully independent measures. Inter-participant (i.e., between-subjects) designs generate independent measures. That means each participant is associated with only a single measure. For example, a study may compare the completion time on the same interface between two groups of participants. On the other hand, intra-participant (i.e., within-subjects) designs lead to repeated measures, i.e., each participant is associated with at least two observations for a specific UX metric. For instance, researchers may plan to compare the completion time on two different interfaces with the same group of participants. Hence, to ensure the UX Calculator executes the appropriate statistical test, users need to specify their evaluation design.

UX Metric. Users then need to specify the unit of measure they would like to compare. The three main types of metrics generally involved in UX evaluation are time measurements, measures of success, and measurement scales.

Time measurements refer to reaction time or response time, defined as "the amount of time it takes for someone to make some sort of overt response" [13]. In UX research, such measurements reflect the behavioral result of participants' brain activity invoked by the designed digital artefact, namely, the stimulus. By way of example, the time taken to complete an assigned task with digital agents has been used by researchers to infer its performance in terms of UX design [14]. Since reaction time can theoretically take an infinite range of values, the data used for the UX Calculator is rounded to two decimal places for general practical considerations. In addition, the value of reaction time should be limited in the upper bound by the maximum time allowed for a task (i.e., when a participant fails to complete a task within a time limit). Note that the time also needs to be converted to values in seconds to make testing possible. For instance, a time period of 1-min 30-s should be converted to 90 s for the purposes of statistical analysis.

Task success is a binary variable with only two possible values (0 = Fail or 1 = Success). This measure of success can be viewed as indicating the accuracy of participants' behavioral responses. More specifically, this binary value refers to "whether an individual makes a correct response on a given experimental trial" [13]. However, on occasion, researchers may detect and plan to compare partial success in practice. Thus, the UX Calculator allows coding the results in three modalities (0 = Failure, 1 = Partial success, 2 = Success). Moreover, preference is also considered as a variation of task success. In general A/B testing, practitioners' objectives often involve comparing users' preferences between version A and version B of a digital artefact. Accordingly, preference can be modeled as a special form of success and assigned the value of 1 if the user prefers version A and of 0 otherwise. Just take an example: In a factorial evaluation design that aims to compare the preference towards two applications (A vs. B) between two groups of participants (Novice vs. Expert), the preference reported by each participant can be processed through 0/1 coding. If the statistical test shows this binary variable is significantly higher among experts, we will conclude that experts prefer version A more than novices.

Finally, the measurement scale is a pre-determined set of response options for a question. The options are continuous or discrete, ordinal values with upper and lower limits. One of the most common scales is the Likert scale, which contains a set of discrete gradations for each questionnaire item, typically five or seven levels between two poles. The levels can be later converted into numeric values for statistical comparisons to assess the users' emotions or perceptions during their interaction with IT artefact. Many typical measurement scales have long been used in the field of UX, such as the Customer Effort Score (CES) [15] and Self-Assessment Manikin (SAM) [16].

Significance Level. Users of the tool are also required to indicate the level of statistical significance desired (i.e., *the alpha*), which is the risk of rejecting the null hypothesis (i.e., concluding a significant difference exists between two sets of data) when there is no actual difference. Setting the significance level as 0.05 is a consensus within the scientific community. However, the overuse of such a threshold value has been receiving criticism from scholars in that the α value adopted should depend on the field of study, and the significant result at $\alpha = 0.05$ level does not guarantee substantive research or practical significance [17, 18]. Therefore, our users can choose either the conventional threshold of 0.05 or an acceptable value of 0.1, given that the latter may also produce insights during the exploratory UX assessment.

Directionality. Finally, users will choose between the one-tailed and two-tailed tests to answer the last question presented on the tool's interface. If they hypothesize that there is a difference between the two sets of data, without assuming the direction of this difference, a two-tailed test will be necessary. User profiling research provides an example: we might assume that there is a difference between the current customer and non-customer experience for a mobile application, while not knowing which experience will be better. A two-tailed test should be conducted to address this case. On the other hand, if we already have an assumption regarding whether this difference will be positive or negative, then a one-sided test is an appropriate choice. For the same scenario, one can reasonably hypothesize that existing customers should have a shorter response time than non-customers towards an application. In this case, a one-sided test is recommended to indicate the directionality (if A is greater than B, or B is greater than A).

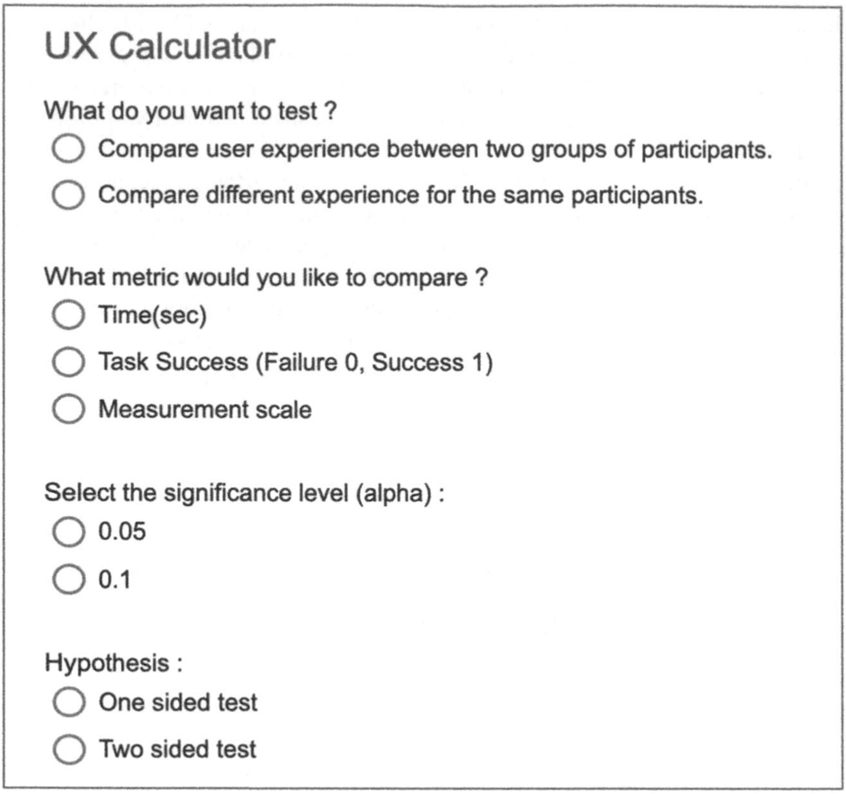

UX Calculator

What do you want to test ?
- ⃝ Compare user experience between two groups of participants.
- ⃝ Compare different experience for the same participants.

What metric would you like to compare ?
- ⃝ Time(sec)
- ⃝ Task Success (Failure 0, Success 1)
- ⃝ Measurement scale

Select the significance level (alpha) :
- ⃝ 0.05
- ⃝ 0.1

Hypothesis :
- ⃝ One sided test
- ⃝ Two sided test

Fig. 1. User input block of the UX Calculator (multiple-choice input fields)

The second section of input is two columns of text fields corresponding to the two groups of observations, as depicted in Fig. 2. When the web application launches (i.e., the web browser page loads), six fields will be shown in each column, which indicates the minimum sample size required to perform the comparison. Users can enter the observations either by typing them one-by-one or by copying and pasting an entire data column from other worksheets (e.g., MS Excel, Google Sheets). Buttons labeled " $+$ " and " $-$ " signs at the end of each column are used to adjust the number of observations that will be included in the statistical test. Users can therefore add or delete text fields to ensure the number of fields matches the number of observations in their samples.

For independent samples, the order of the values does not matter. That is, if users would like to compare a specific UX metric between two groups of participants, they can simply paste the values of the two groups without considering the order in the rows. On the contrary, if it is a paired sample test, the input values must stick to a particular order. In this vein, the observations taken from the same participant must be placed on the same row while filling the two text fields.

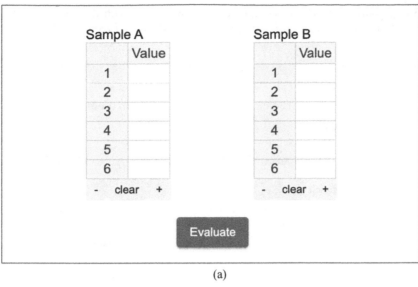

(a)

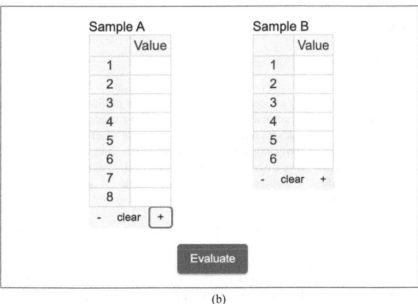

(b)

Fig. 2. User input block of the UX Calculator (text input fields) (a) user view with initial setting (b) user view with adjusted setting

3.2 System Output

After completing the two parts of data input, users can click the "evaluate" button. The UX Calculator will determine the suitable statistical test based on the requirements extracted from the user's input and automatically execute the analysis. As shown in

Fig. 3, a pop-up window will be presented on the screen, with the conclusion of the proposed test, p-value, and statistical method involved in this execution.

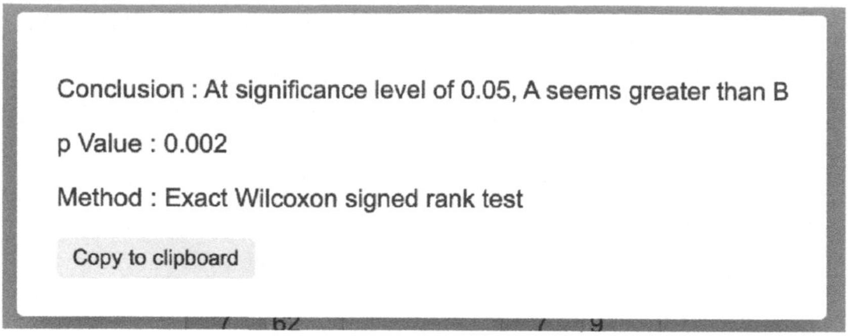

Conclusion : At significance level of 0.05, A seems greater than B

p Value : 0.002

Method : Exact Wilcoxon signed rank test

Copy to clipboard

Fig. 3. System output window of the UX Calculator

4 Discussion

4.1 Usage Statistics

The design, development, and deployment of the UX Calculator follow the user-centric paradigm. Since the tool was created by a UX research lab affiliated with a Canadian educational institution, its target users – UX designers and researchers - were actively involved in all stages of the design and development process. Users were able to recall their working scenarios, identify existing issues and articulate their expectations for this new tool. They participated in discussing and validating all design decisions, such as the inclusion of specific UX metrics and the interaction logic for data entry. These UX professionals also participated in the formative prototype test and the pilot test before the formal launch of the tool's final online version.

By providing a lightweight web interface that enables the execution of common statistical tests in UX evaluations, our work is expected to enhance the efficiency of practitioners in the workplace, as well as provide a valuable addition to traditional analysis platforms for the HCI community. This open-source tool is cost-free, meaning that its users do not need to be concerned with the purchase of any license. The calculator is designed to be web-based and able to automatically select the appropriate statistical comparison, saving users considerable time searching for appropriate statistical tests, reading user manuals, or learning programming languages.

Since September 2022, the UX Calculator has been available online and has been incorporated into an online UX training program on edX called UX Evaluation[1]. The back-end data from our server shows a total count of 951 user sessions since it was formally launched, including 419 unique users from 47 countries. As Fig. 4 depicted, the majority of our users visited this online tool from North America. Users from Canada

---

[1] https://www.edx.org/micromasters/hecmontrealx-ux-design-and-evaluation.

account for 63.2% of the total user count, followed by the share of those from the United States (5.7%). Colombia and France followed, each having a 3.8% share of the total unique users. Since its formal launch, we have seen robust and steady growth in usage over time. In summary, this tool has been intensively used for real-life UX evaluations and there is a steadily growing trend of its use. Hence, we conclude that the main design goal of the current stage of this project has been achieved.

Fig. 4. The geographical distribution of the users of the UX Calculator

4.2 Future Work

While the major design goals of this UX Calculator have been achieved, there is still room for further improvement. A small subset of users reported issues regarding the explainability of the current version. More specifically, users are informed of the executed statistical test (e.g., the exact Wilcoxon signed-rank test in Fig. 3), but the UX Calculator does not explain why the specific test was chosen. Thus, a more detailed explanation should be provided to link the users' objective (e.g., the nature of the comparison) and study design (e.g., sample size and adopted UX metrics) to the system's choice of the statistical test, rather than adopting a "black box" approach when presenting the calculation results. Moreover, the current calculator does not list other useful information that could be drawn from the statistical tests, such as the confidence interval. Therefore, making the UX Calculator more informative can be another direction for its refinement. However, adding these elements can lead to an increase in the complexity of the interface thus hindering users' navigation and comprehension of the tool. As a result, the emphasis of future work should be placed on improving the explainability of this tool while maintaining ease of use. The next step will be designing and developing variants of the UX Calculator, which encompass the proposed configuration mentioned above. We plan to conduct a within-subjects evaluation with current users to compare users' perceptions of the current and future versions. This formal test is expected to provide insights on how to balance the explainability and the simplicity of this tool as we iterate on the design of the UX Calculator.

References

1. Schrepp, M., Hinderks, A., Thomaschewski, J.: Construction of a benchmark for the user experience questionnaire (UEQ). Int. J. Interact. Multimedia Artif. Intell. 4(4), 40 (2017). https://doi.org/10.9781/ijimai.2017.445
2. Alves, R., Valente, P., Nunes, N.J.: The state of user experience evaluation practice. In: Proceedings of the 8th Nordic Conference on Human-Computer Interaction: Fun, Fast, Foundational, pp. 93–102 (2014). https://doi.org/10.1145/2639189.2641208
3. Burzacca, P., Paternò, F.: Remote usability evaluation of mobile web applications. In: Kurosu, M. (ed.) HCI 2013. LNCS, vol. 8004, pp. 241–248. Springer, Heidelberg (2013). https://doi.org/10.1007/978-3-642-39232-0_27
4. Federici, S., et al.: Heuristic evaluation of eGLU-box: a semi-automatic usability evaluation tool for public administrations. In: Kurosu, M. (ed.) HCII 2019. LNCS, vol. 11566, pp. 75–86. Springer, Cham (2019). https://doi.org/10.1007/978-3-030-22646-6_6
5. Sauro, J., Lewis, J.R.: Quantifying the User Experience: Practical Statistics for User Research. Morgan Kaufmann, Burlington (2016)
6. Nielsen, J.: Estimating the number of subjects needed for a thinking aloud test. Int. J. Hum. Comput. Stud. 41(3), 385–397 (1994)
7. Hwang, W., Salvendy, G.: Number of people required for usability evaluation: the 10±2 rule. Commun. ACM 53(5), 130–133 (2010). https://doi.org/10.1145/1735223.1735255
8. Caine, K.: Local standards for sample size at CHI. In: Proceedings of the 2016 CHI Conference on Human Factors in Computing Systems, pp. 981–992 (2016). https://doi.org/10.1145/2858036.2858498
9. Bodker, S.: Scenarios in user-centred design-setting the stage for reflection and action. In: Proceedings of the 32nd Annual Hawaii International Conference on Systems Sciences. HICSS-32. Abstracts and CD-ROM of Full Papers, vol. 3, pp. 3053. IEEE Computer Society (1999). https://doi.org/10.1109/hicss.1999.772892
10. Wilcoxon signed-rank test - Handbook of Biological Statistics. http://www.biostathandbook.com/wilcoxonsignedrank.html. Accessed 31 Oct 2022
11. Wilcoxon, F.: Individual comparisons by ranking methods. Breakthr. Stat., 196–202 (1992). https://doi.org/10.1007/978-1-4612-4380-9_16
12. Hothorn, T., Hornik, K.: exactRankTests: exact distributions for rank and permutation tests, R package version 0.8-31 (2019)
13. Newman, A.: Research Methods for Cognitive Neuroscience. SAGE (2019)
14. Holmes, S., Moorhead, A., Bond, R., Zheng, H., Coates, V., Mctear, M.: Usability testing of a healthcare chatbot: can we use conventional methods to assess conversational user interfaces? In: Proceedings of the 31st European Conference on Cognitive Ergonomics, pp. 207–214 (2019). https://doi.org/10.1145/3335082.3335094
15. Dixon, M., Freeman, K., Toman, N.: Stop trying to delight your customers. Harv. Bus. Rev. 88(7/8), 116–122 (2010)

16. Bradley, M.M., Lang, P.J.: Measuring emotion: the self-assessment manikin and the semantic differential. J. Behav. Ther. Exp. Psychiatry **25**(1), 49–59 (1994). https://doi.org/10.1016/0005-7916(94)90063-9
17. Amrhein, V., Greenland, S., McShane, B.: Scientists rise up against statistical significance. Nature **567**(7748), 305–307 (2019). https://doi.org/10.1038/d41586-019-00857-9
18. Carver, R.: The case against statistical significance testing. Harv. Educ. Rev. **48**(3), 378–399 (1978). https://doi.org/10.17763/haer.48.3.t490261645281841

Usability, User Experience
and Technology Acceptance Studies

Preliminary Usability Evaluation of UpSkill@Mgmt 4.0: A Tool to Promote Competency and Career Management in Industry 4.0

Tiago Bastos[1]([⊠]) [iD], Juliana Salvadorinho[1] [iD], and Leonor Teixeira[2] [iD]

[1] Department of Economics, Management, Industrial Engineering and Tourism, University of Aveiro, 3810-193 Aveiro, Portugal
{bastostiago99,juliana.salvadorinho}@ua.pt
[2] Department of Economics, Management, Industrial Engineering and Tourism, Institute of Electronics and Informatics Engineering of Aveiro / Intelligent Systems Associate Laboratory (LASI), University of Aveiro, 3810-193 Aveiro, Portugal
lteixeira@ua.pt

Abstract. Promoting personal development and learning is increasingly a concern for organizations in retaining employees in what is a volatile paradigm and so heavily impacted by technology. Thus, this concern must be managed in an easy and agile way, where digital tools can be important enablers of these characteristics. Allied with digital tools, specifically their innovative character, arises the need for validations to avoid errors in advanced stages of development. Usability studies are a very important technique for this type of evaluation, often used to understand whether platforms meet users' needs, and to evaluate and if possible, improve user experiences. In this regard, this paper aims to preliminarily assess the usability of an innovative tool, capturing some adjustments suggested by users, at the same time as perceiving the users' receptiveness to its use. The application showed that it was very well accepted by users and good contributions to improve the platform were suggested.

Keywords: Workforce engagement · Usability test · Co-Design

1 Introduction

The emergence of new technologies in the fourth industrial environment revolutionized companies' production processes [1–3]. Utopias such as "individual" products at the prices of mass-produced products have become closer realities and economic sustainability will clearly be fostered with this boost [4]. Contrariwise, social sustainability is exposed to some challenges [4], since task complexity is increasing, and employee skills are not keeping up. All this is generating inefficiencies and puts uncertainty in employees about what their role will be in the future [5]. Therefore, fostering personal development and learning is increasingly a reality that organizations must consider, and this is consistent with the strategy of the European Commission, which places a strong emphasis on the necessity of a skilled labor force to support the growth and competitiveness of European businesses [6]. Nevertheless, this concern must be managed in an easy and agile way, where digital tools can be important enablers of these characteristics. So, to try to take advantage of the benefits inherent to digital tools, a concept was created of an innovative tool capable of empowering employees, making them more capable of operating in the digital paradigm [5].

This concept, already presented in other studies, was created using the complementation of theoretical analyses, arising from literature review and human resource management documents, with practical validations resulting from a focus group with specialists in human resources management and information systems [7, 8].

Although experts in the field have validated the concept, due to the innovative nature of the solution and the need for acceptance by future users of the platform, it is essential to understand and validate the proposed prototype. Systems with new features can result in poor user experiences, so there is a need to apply a User Centered Design approach [9]. User experience is referred to as the user's perceptions and reactions because of using a system, product, or service [9, 10]. For software to benefit consumers and gain a competitive edge, user experience is crucial. The value of user experience techniques in the software development process is demonstrated by studies in the literature [10] and these elements may be evaluated using usability assessment techniques [11]. It should be noted that high usability is closely related to user acceptance and high usage of the system or program in reaching goals [12]. On the other hand, poor software usability can have a negative influence on a company and, frequently result in significant personal and financial costs to the firm and the services it provides [13, 14].

User testing is a common usability assessment technique that involves observing users engage with the system while doing scenario-based tasks. The advantage of usability testing is that it allows for the objective collection of input on usability, including user happiness and feedback on the interface and features being utilized [12]. Still included in the user testing process, post-test surveys are frequently used to gather subjective data [9].

In this scenario, the major objective of this paper is to make a preliminary validation of a previously studied concept for a tool, which intends to facilitate the management of individual competencies and simultaneously improve individual development plans, through usability tests. For this, a prototype of the tool was developed using the Adobe XD® software, adopting a co-design strategy, and preliminary usability tests were made to reduce the risk of future users not accepting the product.

This article is structured in the following way, first it begins with a theoretical contextualization, then it describes the methodology used in this work, then it communicates the results obtained, makes a brief discussion, and finally highlights some of the conclusions obtained.

2 Theoretical Background

2.1 Sustainability in I4.0: A Brief Context of One Challenge Faced by the Social Pillar

Today's markets are very different than they once were and customized products are the ones that buyers value the most [15]. The new technologies gave a boost and potentiated production more efficiently, which allows a cost reduction [16]. In the past, namely in the past industrial revolutions, sustainability was only about the economic pillar, so in this way Industry 4.0 (I4.0) is a very inviting paradigm. However, today, companies must update their production processes, focusing on benefits to both the environment and society while generating profit [17].

Many academics agree that I4.0 can offer numerous opportunities for sustainability, namely higher resource efficiency, waste reduction, and more favorable production environment for workers [18]. Concerning employees, the increased safety, the increased independence and self-determination, and the possibility of acquisition of new skills are good gains and drivers of great motivation within the new industrial paradigm [19]. To optimize employee well-being and system performance, it is important to pay attention on the area of human capital, which studies the perception of interactions between humans and other elements of the systems [20]. In the new industrial context arising from new technologies, it is essential to understand the changes in the duties and responsibilities of workers [21]. Increased work demands, new skill demands, and increased cognitive load, in the physical vs. cognitive load ratio, can contribute to stress and burnout. Frustration and unwillingness caused by the worry of being let go and having few options for work can also be seen as a point to consider [22]. The necessity to train the workforce is evident [23] and organizations can´t adopt the idea that machines will replace people. In spite of that, they must envision this challenge as a window of opportunity and people, actually, can have a crucial role in the digital transition, according to some studies [24].

Another vital point to consider in this digital paradigm is the high volatility which can lead to turnover by employees. A high turnover rate is a sign of potential losses for the company, including knowledge loss, gaps in the production process, the time and expense involved in replacing people, and investments in training new employees who will be added to the process [25]. According to the same authors [25], job satisfaction and turnover are linked, so it is important to formulate strategies that fill this problem. One of the strategies may be career development plans, which were proven to impact positively workforce engagement, accordingly to Lartey [26].

2.2 The Importance of User Experience: User Testing and Co-design Approaches

The study of major phenomena connected with interactive computer systems for human use and, their design, evaluation, and implementation are topics covered by the field of human-computer interaction. The system must be built with users and human needs must be in mind. It is supposed that a system can receive instructions and information from the user and provide information to the user using a user interface [27].

Offering good usability is no longer enough to succeed in today's competitive market. There are other products out there with comparable capability and usability for the majority of activities [28]. The ease of use of a software program depends on how user-friendly the interface is and how comfortable the user is with it. A product or service's ability to guarantee maximum user pleasure, efficiency, effectiveness, learnability, and simplicity of use for a variety of users is measured through the usability evaluation process, which looks at the minimal accomplishment degree of various usability aspects [13, 14]. Usability is the simplicity with which a client may use a product or service to achieve their objectives with the least amount of hassle and the greatest level of happiness [29].

User testing is a typical usability evaluation technique that involves watching people conduct scenario-based activities while interacting with the system. User behaviors and activities are observed using a range of approaches that can be classified as subjective (for example, perceived usefulness or satisfaction level) or objective (for example task completion time or success rate). At the end of the usability test, post-test questionnaires are typically used to acquire subjective metrics, such as levels of satisfaction or perceived usefulness [9].

Co-design, in the context of software development, may be characterized as a collaborative approach that draws on the shared creativity of software professionals and non-technical persons [30]. It can be considered as a subdiscipline of participatory design that may be included in the user-centered design process to ensure that end users can voice their desires for a product or service [31]. Prototyping can foster this strategy since it is used to test new goods to determine if they are operated and, simultaneously, it can be an effective approach to engage and promote creativity among participants in idea groups as visible in the work of Khanbhai et al. [32].

3   Goals and Methods

The main objective of this work is to understand and improve the usability of a tool that aims to help the management of employees' development plans and competencies. This concept, already presented in a previous paper [7], was obtained using a focus group and literature review. Section 4.1 briefly presents the concept accompanied by illustrations of the prototype that has undergone usability testing described in this study. In Sects. 3.1 and 3.2 the details of the test performed (protocol), and the sample used will be presented, respectively.

3.1   Usability Evaluation Protocol and Data Collection Tools

First, a brief presentation of the tool was made and, afterward, the users had a few minutes to interact with the tool. After the user felt sufficiently familiar with the tool, the usability test was started, which lasted about 15 min and consisted of a set of 9 tasks, described in Table 1. The tasks chosen were those that the authors of the concept and of the interface considered to be the most difficult. When completing the tasks, each user rated the ease felt (on a scale from 1–5, which 1 corresponding to very difficult and 5 to very easy). During the test, there was an observer who collected the following information: if the task was done well, if the task was done without asking for help, and if the task was done with the wrong paths. Besides this, the observer also rated, on a scale identical to the one used by the users, the ease observed in performing the task. At the end of the tasks, the sample of users completed a questionnaire where they rated some statements (described in Sect. 4.2) on a scale of 1–5, where 1 corresponds to strongly disagree and 5 to strongly agree. Regarding the system, general aspects of the platform, and specific aspects of the system, more related to the details of the interface, were evaluated. At the end, the users had a space to make comments and suggestions for changes to make the application more user-friendly.

Table 1. List of tasks performed in the test

Task	Description
1	See the digital passport module
2	Check your competencies
3	Indicate, in the system, two preferences for competencies to be developed
4	Consult your potential in the function
5	Consult the talent review and analyze it
6	Select the development plans dashboard. After entering, see the details of the jour fixed from 02/01/2022
7	Open the SWOT matrix (just click on it)
8	Simulate the addition of a new jour fixed (submit the form)
9	Check out the team plans

3.2 The Sample

To validate the tool concept, a prototype was built in Adobe XD® and 10 usability tests were conducted. Table 2 shows the details of the participants in the usability test. The chosen sample includes different areas such as: Industrial and Management Engineering (IME), Human Resources Management (HRM), Informatics and Tourism. It should be noted that the HR-People partner is the human resources (HR) contact closest to the people, and the HR-Business partner is another, more "administrative" HR function.

4 Results

4.1 Description of the Concept – Previous Work

This technological tool tries to respond to two major areas: skills management and individual/team career development. For the first area, the tool will allow employees to analyze their competencies (the proficiency that the manager assesses to his/her performance) and perceive what certain functions will need to execute in an ideal way. The possibility to insert preferences by what they want to develop and use and function

Table 2. Details from participants in the usability tests

Task	Age	Level of education	Professional activity	Time spent on the internet per day
1	20–30	Bachelor's degree	IME Intern and MSc student	10 h 30 min
2	20–30	Bachelor's degree	IME Intern and MSc student	12 h 00 min
3	31–40	Doctorate degree	Researcher/University Professor in the HRM area	10 h 00 min
4	20–30	Master's degree	Researcher in information systems for accessible tourism	4 h 00 min
5	20–30	Bachelor's degree	HR-People partner	3 h 00 min
6	31–40	High school	Shop Floor Operator	1 h 00 min
7	20–30	Bachelor's degree	HR Intern	3 h 00 min
8	20–30	High school	Shop Floor Operator	4 h 00 min
9	31–40	Bachelor's degree	HR-Business Partner	10 h 00 min
10	20–30	High school	Front-end developer	10 h 30 min

potential (the potential that a manager sees in a collaborator if he/she has in the right hierarchical level or has the capacity to assume more responsibility) are also contemplated features. Both supervisors and employees will have access to a wide range of indicators that will facilitate decision-making. This tool was reported in previous study [7] and during this, it was realized that it would be interesting to integrate another component to complement all the functionalities described in the cited work. In this context, and with this second purpose in mind, collaborators will have access to a set of questions to guide the Jour fixed (meetings between manager and employee to plan the individual development) that have coaching models in its core. Additionally, managers will have access to a dashboard identical to individual employees to track team goals, in a team development aspect.

To understand the usability and to allow better use of the opinions for improvements, we used the development of a prototype in Adobe XD®. This prototype, besides being useful to evaluate the system's usability, also stimulates creativity, improving users' brainstorming, and increasing the quality of their participation. Figure 1 a, b, and c represent 3 interfaces needed to accomplish some of the tasks described in the chapter below, more interfaces are visible in this study [7].

Fig. 1. (a) Interface for visualizing competencies; (b) Interface related to the potential of collaborator in the function; (c) Interface with the data from jour fixed

4.2   Prototype Validation – Usability Tests

The first result presented is the median of ease degree in performing the various tasks, this is visible in Fig. 2. Here the two visions were contemplated, the one felt by the user and the one perceived by the observer.

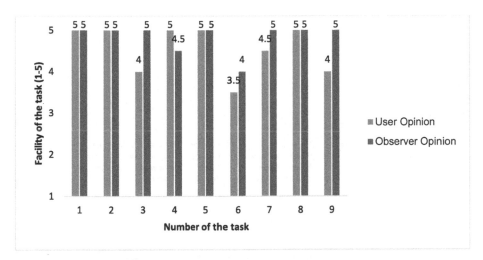

Fig. 2. The facility of the tasks from the user's perspective and the observer's perspective

To complete this analysis, the values of the percentage of users who completed the task with wrong paths (%WP), and to complement this, the percentage of users who completed the task with help requests (%H) are presented. Table 3 summarizes the results.

From the analysis of the table (Table 3), it can be concluded that tasks 4 and 6 were the most difficult. In the case of task 4, some of the terminology in the application led to confusion among users and therefore had a high %WP. In task 6, the terminology of the task guide did not allow a clear understanding and execution of the tasks without asking for help.

Table 3. Some indicators of user performance by the task

Task number	1	2	3	4	5	6	7	8	9
%WP	0	10	10	50	10	20	10	10	10
%H	0	0	20	0	0	50	0	0	30

As said, there was a post-task questionnaire and a set of sentences that asked users to give their opinion about the usability aspects of the system (i) and specific aspects of the system (ii). Figure 3 shows on the x-axis the statements for the goal (i) and for each, the median value of the users' answers. In the same way, Fig. 4 is presented the median response values for the second objective mentioned (ii).

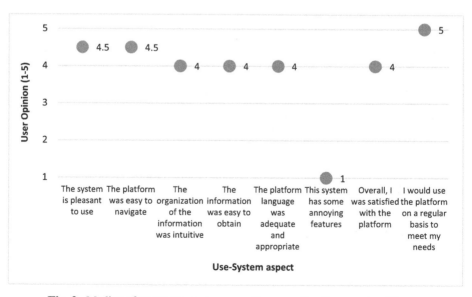

Fig. 3. Median of users' answers per question regarding the aspects of the use

Overall, the tasks were accomplished with relative ease, and the remaining indicators perceived by the observer scored well. As for the results of the questionnaire, the general opinion was good. In the free comments section, some users describe the platform as

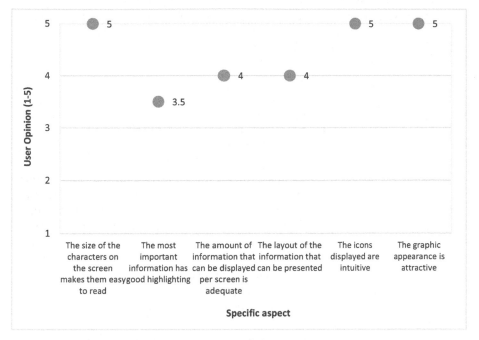

Fig. 4. Median of users' answers per question regarding the aspects of the system

"good looking" and "intuitive". However, one purpose of the free comments section was to highlight some adjustments to improve the platform. At the interface level, some points were mentioned and will be considered in future versions. The next sub-section, emphasizes the most important contributions that will be considered.

4.3   Some Inputs to Readjust the Interface Design: The Co-design Process

Such mentioned in the previous sub-section, some intervenors gave some proposals to improve the efficiency of the system, as well as the indicators above cited, showing the co-design process. In this regard the following adjustments have been highlighted:

- Create a bar to facilitate the perception of the possibility of side-scrolling in the table with the main date from the jour fixed present in the dashboard of individual development plans (the first version has only a table with information cut off).
- Decrease the amount of information on the Jour fixed page (visible in Fig. 1 (c)), dividing the page into smaller, more focused pages, so it would be unnecessary to run around to find information.
- On the interface visible in Fig. 1 (b), it was suggested to change the sub-menu in the sidebar, because it gets confusing to enter in "My potential" and then in "My potential in the function".
- It was also suggested to reduce the footer size because some intervenient highlighted that it was not proportional to the total size of the page.

- Add short explanatory texts to elucidate the purpose of certain concepts in the tool, for example, to understand what the purpose of the SWOT matrix in the tool is without having to wait for training or having to use manuals.

5 Discussion

The challenges that people face in the digital paradigm is a subject to be considered and that need attention by the researcher. The economic pillar of sustainability is no longer the only concern that deserves attention, and there is a need to value the social and environmental pillars [17].

Digital applications can be a facilitator for the transition of employees, moving them from workers with skill gaps, to highly skilled operators to operate in this digital environment. The UpSkill@Mgmt 4.0 application has a huge contribution to this issue as discussed in the paper [7]. This work had the great purpose of understanding the receptivity and usability of the tool, even though in a preliminary stage, to allow modifications to be made and a much more consolidated concept to be taken to final validation. Usability, as seen in the literature, has an extremely preponderant role to have good results in terms of acceptance by future users [13, 14, 29].

In this work the methodology adopted it to try to combine task evaluation techniques as discussed in the work of Altin Gumussoy [9] to try to understand subjective aspects. Adopting these visions, the study shows us the ease with those users perceived in the test.

The task with the most difficulties was 6, however this task was not the one with the most wrong paths, having a low percentage of users who completed the task without help. Here, two problems emerge, the first one related to the terminology of the questionnaire (it was different from the one used in the prototype), which can be mitigated with a preliminary questionnaire with one or two persons with the only objective of validate the language; and the other linked to the fact that these tasks were performed in interfaces with a lot of information. In this sense the step was correct, but then the information was difficult to obtain, highlighting the clear relation with the aspect mentioned in the interface improvements (reducing the information per page).

Looking at the task with the lowest percentage of users who completed it without making mistakes, one finds task 4, yet users rated this task the third highest in the ease ranking. This can be explained by the fact that they had unnecessary clicks due to inattention, not least because a large portion of them were able to complete the task (despite the errors) without any help. In tasks 3, 7 and 9 there is a large discrepancy between the degree of ease observed and the degree of ease that the users felt, which may lead to the conclusion that there was some insecurity and "luck" in solving the question, leading the observer to conclude that it was easily achieved, when in fact it was not. The issues that have the lowest value are related to the layout of the information.

In the chapter on the suggestions given by the people who participated in the test, the amount of suggestions given shows the role that prototyping has in stimulating the creativity of the participants, corroborating what the literature tells us [32]. The last two sentences of the Usage System aspects (Fig. 3), related to the usability of the platform for users' needs, show that the platform proves to be highly powerful in its major purpose.

6   Conclusion

The need for training inherent to the technological advances in the digital paradigm is quite visible. Besides the technical component, the affective component, most often translated by the engagement concept, is also highly leveraged by training. In this sense, tools can be facilitators of this process. The focus of the paper is to evaluate the usability of the prototype and at the same time analyze some inputs that could be made to increase the closeness between what is expected by the users and what is proposed by the tool. As can be seen in the literature, usability tests have a preponderant role in the validation of software, and for this reason, this technique was adopted in this work. In this aspect, it was seen that the tool was in general well accepted and in accordance with what was expected, having aspects very appreciated by the users. There was only one task that, due to its complexity, was not so well executed, even though it had a positive easiness level.

Concerning some improvements, the approach of other works that highlight prototyping as a means of enhancing creativity on the part of users was used, so the prototype not only mediated the testing but also contributed to the appearance of the proposed adjustments.

In terms of limitations, this work has limitations in the two proposed objectives, in the usability chapter, the chosen public could have been larger in number and with a lower level of education, and more tasks could have been done to see other difficulties. In terms of the co-design process, the number of people who participated in this study can also be seen as a limitation, as well as the fact that this process takes place at the same time as a usability test, so almost all recommendations are related to the activities done and especially with task 6 (the one that had more difficulty in execution).

Despite the limitations, this type of study, given its relative ease and the fact that it does not allocate too many costs, can be a good way to obtain preliminary validation and avoid following up the development of the platform with aspects that do not contribute positively to the application. For future work, there is a need to improve the entire prototype with the considerations that have been presented by users, and, finally, it is intended that the final application would be implemented in a real context (enterprise use case), to understand its viability.

Acknowledgement. The present study was developed in the scope of the Project Augmented Humanity [POCI-01-0247-FEDER-046103 e LISBOA-01-0247-FEDER-046103], financed by Portugal 2020, under the Competitiveness and Internationalization Operational Program, the Lisbon Regional Operational Program, and by the European Regional Development Fund.

References

1. Choi, T.M., Kumar, S., Yue, X., Chan, H.L.: Disruptive technologies and operations management in the industry 4.0 era and beyond. Prod. Oper. Manag. **31**(1), 9–31 (2022). https://doi.org/10.1111/poms.13622
2. Leesakul, N., Oostveen, A.M., Eimontaite, I., Wilson, M.L., Hyde, R.: Workplace 4.0: exploring the implications of technology adoption in digital manufacturing on a sustainable workforce. Sustainability **14**(6), 3311 (2022). https://doi.org/10.3390/su14063311

3. Tsaramirsis, G., et al.: A modern approach towards an industry 4.0 model: from driving technologies to management. J. Sens. **2022** (2022). https://doi.org/10.1155/2022/5023011

4. El Baz, J., Tiwari, S., Akenroye, T., Cherrafi, A., Derrouiche, R.: A framework of sustainability drivers and externalities for industry 4.0 technologies using the best-worst method. J. Clean. Prod. **344**, 130909 (2022). https://doi.org/10.1016/j.jclepro.2022.130909

5. Bastos, T., Salvadorinho, J., Vitória, A., Teixeira, L.: Competence management in industry 4.0: an innovative concept to support a Skill@Mgmt 4.0 tool (2022). https://ieomsociety.org/proceedings/2022orlando/151.pdf

6. Ciccarelli, M., Papetti, A., Germani, M., Leone, A., Rescio, G.: Human work sustainability tool. J. Manuf. Syst. **62**, 76–86 (2022). https://doi.org/10.1016/j.jmsy.2021.11.011

7. Bastos, T., Salvadorinho, J., Teixeira, L.: UpSkill@Mgmt 4.0 - a digital tool for competence management: conceptual model and a prototype. Int. J. Ind. Eng. Manag. (2022). https://doi.org/10.24867/IJIEM-2022-4-315

8. Salvadorinho, J., Vitória, A., Ferreira, C., Teixeira, L.: Designing an engagement's technological tool: user needs and motivations in a humanized way. In: Duffy, V.G. (eds.) HCII 2022. LNCS, vol. 13320, pp. 266–279. Springer, Cham (2022). https://doi.org/10.1007/978-3-031-06018-2_19

9. Altin Gumussoy, C., Pekpazar, A., Esengun, M., Bayraktaroglu, A.E., Ince, G.: Usability evaluation of tv interfaces: subjective evaluation vs. objective evaluation. Int. J. Hum. Comput. Interact. **38**(7), 661–679 (2022). https://doi.org/10.1080/10447318.2021.1960093

10. Guerino, G.C., et al.: User experience practices in software startups: a systematic mapping study. Adv. Hum. Comput. Interact. **2022** (2022). https://doi.org/10.1155/2022/9701739

11. Quiñones, D., Rusu, C., Rusu, V.: A methodology to develop usability/user experience heuristics. Comput. Stand. Interfaces **59**, 109–129 (2018). https://doi.org/10.1016/j.csi.2018.03.002

12. Kilis, B.M.H., et al.: Usability evaluation of the android operating system using use questionnaire. Int. J. **1**(2), 16–23 (2022). http://ijite.jredu.id/index.php/ijite/article/view/34. https://ijite.jredu.id/index.php/ijite/article/download/34/20

13. CossyLeon-Pereza, R., Gallardo-Vazqueza, B., Soaresb, M.: Usability test for a bank service website. In: Advances in Ergonomics In Design, Usability & Special Populations: Part II, p. 394 (2022)

14. Alhadreti, O.: A comparison of synchronous and asynchronous remote usability testing methods. Int. J. Hum. Comput. Interact. **38**(3), 289–297 (2022). https://doi.org/10.1080/10447318.2021.1938391

15. Jiang, Z., Yuan, S., Ma, J., Wang, Q.: The evolution of production scheduling from industry 3.0 through industry 4.0. Int. J. Prod. Res., 1–21 (2021)

16. Ing, T.S., Lee, T.C., Chan, S.W., Alipal, J., Hamid, N.A.: An overview of the rising challenges in implementing industry 4.0. Int. J. Supply Chain Manag. **8**(6), 1181–1188 (2019)

17. Kumar, V., Vrat, P., Shankar, R.: Factors influencing the implementation of industry 4.0 for sustainability in manufacturing. Glob. J. Flex. Syst. Manag. **23**, 453–478 (2022). https://doi.org/10.1007/s40171-022-00312-1

18. Brozzi, R., Forti, D., Rauch, E., Matt, D.T.: The advantages of industry 4.0 applications for sustainability: results from a sample of manufacturing companies. Sustainability **12**(9), 3647 (2020). https://doi.org/10.3390/su12093647

19. Molino, M., Cortese, C.G., Ghislieri, C.: The promotion of technology acceptance and work engagement in industry 4.0: from personal resources to information and training. Int. J. Environ. Res. Public Health **17**(7), 2438 (2020). https://doi.org/10.3390/ijerph17072438

20. Cimini, C., Lagorio, A., Pirola, F., Pinto, R.: Exploring human factors in logistics 4.0: empirical evidence from a case study. IFAC-PapersOnLine **52**(13), 2183–2188 (2019). https://doi.org/10.1016/j.ifacol.2019.11.529

21. Kadir, B.A., Broberg, O., da Conceicao, C.S.: Current research and future perspectives on human factors and ergonomics in industry 4.0. Comput. Ind. Eng. **137**, 106004 (2019)

22. Kadir, B.A., Broberg, O.: Human-centered design of work systems in the transition to industry 4.0. Appl. Ergon. **92**, 103334 (2021). https://doi.org/10.1016/j.apergo.2020.103334

23. Ligarski, M.J., Rożałowska, B., Kalinowski, K.: A study of the human factor in industry 4.0 based on the automotive industry. Energies **14**(20), 6833 (2021). https://doi.org/10.3390/en14206833

24. Koleva, N.: Conceptual framework to study the role of human factor in a digital manufacturing environment. Industry 4.0 **4**(2), 82–84 (2019)

25. Urrutia Pereira, G., de Lara Machado, W., Ziebell de Oliveira, M.: Organizational learning culture in industry 4.0: relationships with work engagement and turnover intention. Hum. Resour. Dev. Int., 1–21 (2021). https://doi.org/10.1080/13678868.2021.1976020

26. Lartey, F.M.: Impact of career planning, employee autonomy, and manager recognition on employee engagement. J. Hum. Resour. Sustain. Stud. **09**(02), 135–158 (2021). https://doi.org/10.4236/jhrss.2021.92010

27. Khairat, M.I.S.B., Priyadi, Y., Adrian, M.: Usability measurement in user interface design using heuristic evaluation severity rating (case study: mobile TA application based on MVVM). In: 2022 IEEE 12th Annual Computing and Communication Workshop and Conference, CCWC 2022, pp. 974–979 (2022). https://doi.org/10.1109/CCWC54503.2022.9720876

28. Kushendriawan, M.A., Santoso, H.B., Putra, P.O.H., Schrepp, M.: Evaluating user experience of a mobile health application 'Halodoc' using user experience questionnaire and usability testing. J. Sist. Inf. **17**(1), 58–71 (2021). https://doi.org/10.21609/jsi.v17i1.1063

29. Ahmad, N.A.N., Hussaini, M.: A Usability testing of a higher education mobile application among postgraduate and undergraduate students. Int. J. Interact. Mob. Technol. **15**(9), 88–102 (2021). https://doi.org/10.3991/ijim.v15i09.19943

30. Fox, S., et al.: Co-design of a smartphone app for people living with dementia by applying agile, iterative co-design principles: development and usability study. JMIR mHealth uHealth **10**(1), e24483 (2022). https://doi.org/10.2196/24483

31. Martin, A., et al.: A mobile phone intervention to improve obesity-related health behaviors of adolescents across Europe: iterative co-design and feasibility study. JMIR mHealth uHealth **8**(3), e14118 (2020). https://doi.org/10.2196/14118

32. Khanbhai, M., et al.: Enriching the value of patient experience feedback: web-based dashboard development using co-design and heuristic evaluation. JMIR Hum. Factors **9**(1), e27887 (2022). https://doi.org/10.2196/27887

Vibration Strength Comfort of Smartwatch in Notification Scene

Le Chang, Tao Qin, and Haining Wang[✉]

Hunan University, Changsha 410000, Hunan, China
{Clara,qin66,wanghn}@hnu.edu.cn

Abstract. Vibration is an emergent interaction method for information transmission in mobile devices, but there is still progress to be achieved for the vibration experience of smart watch devices, and few existing studies have concerned the relationship between vibration frequency and intensity. In this paper, we focused on the intensity and frequency of smartwatch vibration in notification scenarios. Twelve participants were recruited to experience smartwatch vibration with different initial vibration frequencies, then chose the comfortable intensity interval, and scored it by a subjective evaluation scale. Finally, based on the statistical analysis, in four groups of the most comfortable intensity intervals at different frequencies were conducted in this study, which could be used to improve the vibration experience design of smart watches.

Keywords: Vibration · Smart watch · Vibration frequency · Comfort

1 Introduction

Vibrotactile feedback is an emerging interactive method for information transmission in mobile devices, which has the potential to replace or supplement visual and auditory displays and is one of the most commonly used feedback effects by users. Devices that offer vibrotactile feedback have been shown to have a more positive effect on the quality, error rate, and satisfaction of user-defined operations compared to devices that lack feedback [1]. Additionally, such devices can effectively reduce operation time [2]. Studying vibrotactile feedback and understanding the user's threshold for hand vibration can lead to appropriate adjustment of vibration parameters, which can enhance the subjective comfort and satisfaction of handheld mobile device users [3].

Despite the potential benefits of vibrotactile feedback, current research on handheld mobile devices still faces some challenges. Specifically, the current focus of vibrotactile research is on vibration intensity, vibration feedback time, the interval between two vibrations, vibration frequency, vibration direction, device weight, detection threshold, perceived intensity, and the equal sensation curve [4–7]. However, establishing the vibrotactile threshold through subjective evaluations is challenging due to individual differences such as age [8], the stimulated body part [9], differences in vibration intensity and frequency, and the diversity of the real vibration environment [10].

Therefore, the purpose of this study is to establish the correlation between vibration intensity, frequency, and user comfort experience in fixed notification scenarios. The objective is to explore the most comfortable vibrotactile feedback effect. By achieving this objective, we can develop a better understanding of how vibrotactile feedback can be used to enhance the user experience of handheld mobile devices. This research can also contribute to the development of guidelines and standards for vibrotactile feedback design, which will be useful for designers and developers of handheld mobile devices.

2   Object and Motivation

This study aims to establish a correlation between vibration comfort and subjective comfort evaluation. To achieve this goal, we constructed a sensory evaluation system for vibration tactile sensation and corresponding objective definitions. We determined the vibration comfort interval of intelligent watches under four frequency notification scenarios and explored the relationship between vibration intensity, frequency, and different age groups. Our findings are intended to guide the design of vibration experience for watches and enhance the user's watch usage experience.

3   Experiment Method

3.1   Materials

Electronic Watch Vibration Device
In this experiment, a watch vibration device equipped with a vibration motor connected to a phone fitted with vibration adjustment software was used (see Fig. 1). The electronic wristwatch was adjustable in terms of its frequency and intensity parameters, and it was equipped with a 1.91-in. screen, making it suitable for individuals with varying hand sizes. To ensure optimal vibration transmission, participants were instructed to wear the watch uniformly on their left wrist, with no gaps between the watch and the skin. This allowed for clear and distinct perception of the vibrations.e anthropometric databases (Standardization, 2018). Participants were asked to wear a wig cap on their heads and over the ear to avoid hair disturbance. In addition, participants were asked to sit straight and look at a fixed point on the wall with his/her usual facial expression.

The RichTap software (Fig. 2), developed by the ACC TECHNOLOGY organization, offers the ability to adjust pre-defined vibration parameters, including vibration unit type, vibration intensity, vibration frequency, and vibration duration. For this experiment, only the long vibration unit type was utilized, with a fixed vibration duration of 200 ms. It is noteworthy that vibrations lasting over 200 ms may lead to discomfort [11]. The vibration state was maintained at a constant velocity.

Fig. 1. The vibrating device used in the experiment.

Fig. 2. The interface of the RichTap.

User Informed Consent

All subjects signed an informed consent form for participants drawn up before the experiment, covering the purpose of the study, the duration and procedure of the experiment, and confidentiality of information and data. Before the start of each experiment, the participant was required to prepare a signed consent form by the guild.

Rating Scale

At the outset of the study, each participant was provided with a comfort rating scale (Fig. 3). The notion of comfort was operationalized using a satisfaction rating scale that gauges the degree to which the tactile sensation induced by vibration is both comfortable and gratifying in the context of notifications. The measure takes into account the confluence of operational, psychological, and physical factors that contribute to the overall comfort of the vibration experience. Specifically, we employed a seven-point Richter scale (1 = "uncomfortable and unsatisfactory," 7 = "extremely comfortable and satisfactory") to quantify participants' subjective assessments of comfort .

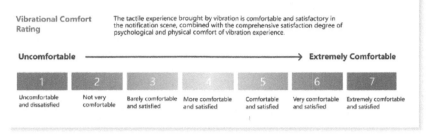

Fig. 3. The comfort rating scale includes a specific definition of comfort and the level of vibration comfort represented by each score.

3.2 Participants

A total of twelve female users were recruited for participation in this experiment. Their age ranges were 18 to 25 years old, 26 to 35 years old and four each in the 35 + age group (Mean $\approx$ 32.58). All of them have used the vibration function, are sensitive to the feeling of vibration, and can clearly express their feelings and emotions. Those with hand, shoulder and neck strain or disease will be excluded.

3.3 Questionnaire Design

The vibration comfort questionnaire (Fig. 4) was designed to measure users' emotional experiences of vibration comfort at different frequencies and intensities. To determine the range of comfortable vibration, subjects were asked to define their own range of comfortable intensity starting from a predetermined initial frequency. Three characteristic points (I1, I2, I3) were marked within the comfortable intensity range, and subjective comfort scores were obtained by adjusting the frequency values. Each participant was able to obtain experimental results of the (comfort-frequency-intensity) area for each initial frequency. The comfortable intensity ranges for all participants at the four frequencies were combined to obtain the overall (comfort-intensity) distribution characteristics for each fixed frequency, and further analysis was performed accordingly. In order to ensure the validity and efficiency of the experiment, the initial frequencies were based on the common motor frequencies of smart watches on the market (80 Hz, 130 Hz, 150 Hz, 170 Hz). Through pre-experimental testing, it was found that 130 Hz, 150 Hz, and 170 Hz were too close and the vibration differences were small. In order to obtain more diverse and unique data, it was finally decided to choose four initial frequencies of 80 Hz, 150 Hz, 250 Hz and 350 Hz. To facilitate the adjustment of frequency and intensity in the vibration software, the converted frequencies (0 Hz, 58 Hz, 97 Hz, 119 Hz) were marked in the questionnaire for the internal and external display values in the software.

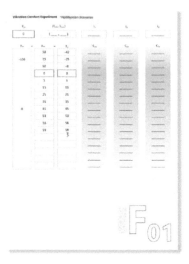

Fig. 4. The comfort questionnaire in the experiment.

3.4 Experimental Procedure

At four initial frequencies, participants were instructed to independently locate the optimal range of vibratory intensity that would elicit a comfortable sensation. This involved determining the values of the lower and upper endpoints of the range, as well as identifying the intensity value within the range that was perceived as most comfortable and denoting it as (I1, I2, I3). Subsequently, participants were directed to adjust the frequencies according to the three intensity values previously identified, namely the lower and upper endpoint values of the optimal range, as well as the most comfortable intensity value, based on the frequency adjustment table. Thereafter, participants were asked to rate their level of comfort using a standardized rating scale.

Determination of Fixed Frequency Comfort Intensity Range
Prior to the experiment, the experiment adjusted all vibration parameters to a standard state and set the vibration frequency to the initial frequency, F0, as indicated in the table. Subsequently, the frequency was fixed at F0, and participants were instructed to freely adjust the intensity to find their subjective comfort intensity range. The experimenter recorded the values of the two endpoints of the comfort intensity range as (Imin, Imax) and noted that I1 = Imin and I3 = Imax.

Determination of Comfort Intensity Characteristics
The participants are asked to determine the most comfortable intensity value within the comfort intensity range (Imin, Imax), which is I2. If the most comfortable intensity value is an endpoint of the range, Imin or Imax, then the midpoint of the range, I2, is used instead (if the midpoint is not an integer, the adjacent integer values are used and

the more comfortable one is chosen as I2). If the participants feel equally comfortable within the comfort intensity range, then the midpoint of the range is also used as I2.

Subjective Comfort Rating Session
Upon completion of the determination of the three characteristic values of comfort intensity (I1, I2, I3), the subjective comfort rating phase is initiated. With the frequency fixed at F0, the vibration intensity is first adjusted to the comfortable intensity characteristic value I1. Subsequently, the subjects are directed to adjust the frequency from above and below F0, according to the frequency adjustment table, and to experience vibration at each frequency while providing a subjective comfort rating, denoted as Cn. The boundary for vibration comfort at this intensity is considered to have been reached when the comfort rating falls to the lowest score of "1". Upon locating a boundary above and below in the frequency table, the measurement is terminated and the process is repeated for the comfort rating of I2 and I3, respectively.

Complete Four Sets of Experiments in Sequence
In the same procedure and test method, four frequencies of vibration comfort experiments were conducted in turn.

4 Results

Following the completion of the experiment, the data was initially collated and preprocessed using Microsoft Excel software. Subsequently, the IBM SPSS Statistics 26 (IBM Corp., Armonk, New York) tool was utilized to analyze the experimental data, with a homogeneity of variance test being conducted to ensure the validity of the results. Finally, independent sample t-tests were performed on the processed and validated data to determine whether any significant differences existed in the vibration comfort ratings among participants under four distinct frequencies. The ensuing analysis results are presented below.

4.1 Vibration Comfort Score at Each Frequency

Among the four frequency levels, the first step involves analyzing the comfort ratings of the vibrations, where a score of 5–7 is deemed as the threshold for a comfortable vibration rating. The distribution of comfortable vibration ratings across the four frequency levels is presented in the accompanying Fig. 5. Based on the data, it is evident that the maximum number of participants reported a comfortable vibration experience at a frequency level of 250 Hz, whereas the minimum number of participants reported such experiences at a frequency level of 350 Hz.

The present study investigated the mean and standard deviation of comfort ratings for varying vibration intensities across four distinct frequencies. After verifying homogeneity of variances, a one-way analysis of variance (ANOVA) was utilized to examine potential differences between frequencies. Results indicated a statistically significant difference among the four groups ($P < 0.05$), as evidenced by the data presented in the accompanying Table 1. Post-hoc multiple comparisons were subsequently conducted to

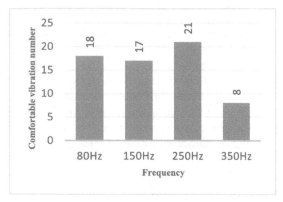

Fig. 5. The number of vibrations rated as comfortable at four frequencies, with levels 5–7 being considered comfortable and counted.

explore the significance of differences in comfort ratings across different frequencies (Table 2). Our findings suggest that 350 Hz is statistically significantly different from the comfortable vibration intensity between 80 Hz, 150 Hz and 250 Hz.

Table 1. ANOVA for comfort scores at each frequency.

Frequency	Mean	SD	F	Sig
80 Hz	4.31	1.489	5.334	0.002
150 Hz	4.39	1.46	-	-
250 Hz	4.67	1.394	-	-
350 Hz	3.36	1.552	-	-

Table 2. Post hoc multiple comparisons of differences in comfort scores for each frequency.

Frequency1	Frequency2	Average difference	Sig
80 Hz	150 Hz	−0.083	0.811
	250 Hz	−0.361	0.301
	350 Hz	.944[a]	0.007
150 Hz	250 Hz	−0.278	0.426
	350 Hz	1.028[a]	0.004
250 Hz	350 Hz	1.306[a]	0

[a]Is statistically significant at the 0.05 level.

To investigate the relationship between age and vibration comfort, we examined the comfort ratings of three distinct age groups across four different frequencies. We first conducted a test for homogeneity of variances, followed by a one-way analysis of variance (ANOVA) to assess the differences in vibration comfort between age groups (see Table 3). Our results indicated that there were statistically significant differences in vibration comfort ratings between age groups at 80 Hz, 250 Hz, and 350 Hz ($P < 0.05$).

Table 3. Analysis of variance for age difference.

Frequency	Age	Mean	SD	Sig.
80 Hz	18–25	5.250	0.622	0.002[a]
	26–35	4.417	1.443	
	>35	3.250	1.545	
150 Hz	18–25	5.083	1.084	0.077
	26–35	3.750	1.765	
	>35	4.333	1.231	
250 Hz	18–25	5.250	0.622	0[a]
	26–35	4.417	1.443	
	>35	3.250	1.545	
350 Hz	18–25	4.167	1.403	0.016[a]
	26–35	3.500	1.883	
	>35	2.417	0.669	

[a]Levene's test for homogeneity of variances was significant ($p < 0.05$).

Based on the calculation of mean differences, standard deviations, and significance of vibration comfort scores across different age groups, the results presented in the Table 4 indicate that there is a significant difference in vibration comfort scores for the four frequencies between young participants aged 18–25 and older participants over 35 years of age. These findings suggest that age is a significant factor in the evaluation of vibration comfort.

4.2 Comfortable Strength at Each Frequency

To begin with, a nonfactorial analysis of differences in intensity between the four groups of frequencies was performed to get Table 5, which was found to be significant between groups. Then, post hoc multiple comparisons of differences in comfort intensity values revealed significant differences between 150 Hz and 80 Hz, 250 Hz, and 350 Hz (Table 6).

Table 7 was obtained by analyzing the variance of age differences in comfort intensity across four frequencies, it was determined that significant differences in comfort intensity exist between individuals of different age groups at 150 Hz and 250 Hz ($p < 0.05$). Subsequently, age difference analysis of variance (ANOVA) was performed on three populations at 150 Hz and 250 Hz (Table 8), revealing that significant differences in

Table 4. Post hoc multiple comparisons of differences among the three age groups

Frequency	Age1	Age2	Sig.
80 Hz	18–25	26–35	0.118
		>35	0.001[a]
	26–35	> 35	0.032
250 Hz	18–25	26–35	0.579
		>35	0.000[a]
	26–35	>35	0.000[a]
350 Hz	18–25	26–35	0.255
		>35	0.005[a]
	26–35	>35	0.069

[a]Is statistically significant at the 0.05 level.

Table 5. ANOVA of comfort intensity at each frequency.

Frequency	Mean	SD	Sig.
80 Hz	62.222	15.004	0.011[a]
150 Hz	45.471	19.082	–
250 Hz	58.095	21.642	–
350 Hz	69.125	9.047	–

[a]The significance level of the difference between means is 0.05.

Table 6. Post hoc multiple comparisons of the differences in comfort intensity for each frequency.

Frequency1	Frequency2	Sig
80 Hz	150 Hz	0.008[a]
	250 Hz	0.480
	350 Hz	0.372
150 Hz	250 Hz	0.036[a]
	350 Hz	0.003[a]
250 Hz	350 Hz	0.147

[a]The significance level of the difference between means is 0.05.

comfort intensity exist between individuals aged 18 to 25 years and those older than 35 years at 150 Hz. Moreover, at 250 Hz, significant differences in comfort intensity were found between individuals older than 35 years and those aged 18 to 25 years and 26 to 35 years.

Table 7. Analysis of variance of age differences in comfort intensity at each frequency.

Frequency	Age	Mean	SD	Sig
80 Hz	18–25	57.636	10.939	0.172
	26–35	66.000	20.628	
	>35	78.000	11.314	
150 Hz	18–25	35.889	9.918	0[a]
	26–35	32.667	12.503	
	>35	70.400	8.678	
250 Hz	18–25	55.000	11.916	0.014[a]
	26–35	52.375	25.037	
	>35	98.000	2.828	
350 Hz	18–25	73	4.08248	0.254
	26–35	65.25	11.58663	

[a]The significance level of the difference between means is 0.05.

Table 8. Analysis of variance for age differences in comfort intensity.

Frequency	Age1	Age2	Sig
150 Hz	18–25	26–35	0.636
		>35	0[a]
	26–35	>35	0[a]
250 Hz	18–25	26–35	0.757
		>35	0.006[a]
	26–35	>35	0.005[a]

[a]Levene's test for homogeneity of variances was significant (p < 0.05).

Table 9 was generated by statistically computing the mean, standard deviation, and quartiles of each frequency's comfort rating score. Based on the distribution of comfort rating intensity values, the corresponding intensity values of the 25th (Q1) and 75th (Q3) percentiles of the comfort rating score were utilized to establish the comfort intensity range, which resulted in the production of the subsequent Fig. 6. At a frequency of 80 Hz, the optimal vibration intensity range for comfort was determined to be between (52,70); at a frequency of 150 Hz, it was between (29,62); at a frequency of 250 Hz, it was between (46,74); and at a frequency of 350 Hz, it was between (62,77).

After completing the experiments, we used a vibration measuring instrument (SV 103, SVANTEK, Poland) to measure the comfort vibration intensity. The measurement results were expressed as peak-to-peak vibration acceleration values in mm/s^2. We measured the comfort intensity intervals at each frequency using the device, and detailed the

Table 9. Statistical analysis of data on comfort intensity at each frequency.

Frequency	Mean	Median	SD	Min	Max	Q1	Q2	Q3
80 Hz	62.2222	59.5	15.0041	40	100	51.75	59.5	70
150 Hz	45.4706	45	19.0824	20	80	28.5	45	61.5
250 Hz	58.0952	52	21.6423	20	100	45.5	52	73.5
350 Hz	69.125	70.5	9.0465	53	80	62	70.5	76.75

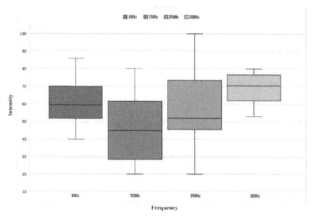

Fig. 6. The comfort intensity interval at four frequencies.

actual vibration acceleration and corresponding relationships in a table. These results will guide the subsequent vibration design of the smartwatch (Table 10).

Table 10. Four comfort intensity intervals with corresponding acceleration.

Frequency	Intensity1	P-P (mm/s^2)	Intensity2	P-P (mm/s^2)
80 Hz	52	2.2183	70	2.8804
150 Hz	29	0.8313	62	2.7898
250 Hz	46	1.0047	74	1.8655
350 Hz	62	1.0119	77	1.3293

5 Discussion

This study recruited three distinct age groups of participants: young adults aged 18–25, middle-aged adults aged 26–35, and older adults aged 35 and above, to examine the comfort of wristwatch vibration. By combining prevailing motor frequencies on the market with pre-experimental data, four initial frequencies were selected to assess the comfortable intensity values of four different frequencies and determine the comfortable vibration range. The experimental findings revealed significant differences in vibration comfort between young and older participants across all four frequencies. Accordingly, the study underscores the importance of accounting for age differences in the experience of vibration comfort and identifying a common comfortable vibration range for participants of different age groups.

Despite the considerable contributions of our experimental design, it is important to acknowledge certain limitations. First, the present study did not encompass a comprehensive range of vibration frequencies and intensities, and it is possible that additional comfort ranges were not explored. Second, the study was limited to female participants, which may preclude the identification of potential gender differences. Hence, future investigations should aim to recruit male participants to determine a more reliable vibration range for the general public. Additionally, given the growing popularity of smartwatches, expanding the age range of participants to include children may facilitate broader age appropriateness.

In conclusion, vibration feedback should not only serve as a means of attracting attention and conveying information, but also provide a discreet and pleasant experience for users. Our experiments represent a significant step towards bridging the gap between the physical parameters of vibration feedback and the subjective comfort experience of users. As such, the findings of this study provide valuable insights for the design of vibration feedback in smartwatches, thus enhancing the overall user experience.

References

1. Altinsoy, M.E., Merchel, S.: Audiotactile feedback design for touch screens. In: Altinsoy, M.E., Jekosch, U., Brewster, S. (eds.) HAID 2009. LNCS, vol. 5763, pp. 136–144. Springer, Heidelberg (2009). (in English). https://doi.org/10.1007/978-3-642-04076-4_15
2. Fukumoto, M., Sugimura, T.: Active click: tactile feedback for touch panels. In: CHI 2001 (2001)
3. Extended abstracts on human factors in computing systems, pp. 121–122 (2001)
4. Yao, H.-Y., Grant, D., Cruz, M.: Perceived vibration strength in mobile devices: the effect of weight and frequency. IEEE Trans. Haptics 3(1), 56–62 (2010). https://doi.org/10.1109/TOH.2009.37
5. Kaaresoja, T., Anttila, E., Hoggan, E.: The effect of tactile feedback latency in touchscreen interaction. In: World Haptics Conference, pp. 65–70 (2011)
6. Hwang, I., Seo, J., Kim, M., Choi, S.: Vibrotactile perceived intensity for mobile devices as a function of direction, amplitude, and frequency. IEEE Trans. Haptics 6(3), 352–362 (2013)
7. Ryu, J., Jung, J., Park, G., Choi, S.: Psychophysical model for vibrotactile rendering in mobile devices. Presence Teleoper. Virtual Environ. 19(4), 364–387 (2010)
8. Cholewiak, R.W., Collins, A.A.: Vibrotactile localization on the arm: effects of place, space, and age. Percept. Psychophys. 65, 1058–1077 (2003). https://doi.org/10.3758/BF03194834
9. Dim, N.K., Ren, X.: Investigation of suitable body parts for wearable vibration feedback in walking navigation. Int. J. Hum. Comput. Stud. 97, 34–44 (2017)

10. Hoggan, E., Brewster, S.A., Johnston, J.: Investigating the effectiveness of tactile feedback for mobile touchscreens. In: CHI 2008: Conference Proceedings of 26th Annual Chi Conference on Human Factors in Computing Systems, vols. 1 and 2, pp. 1573–1582 (2008). (in English)
11. Kaaresoja, T., Linjama, J.: Perception of short tactile pulses generated by a vibration motor in a mobile phone. In: First Joint Eurohaptics Conference and Symposium on Haptic Interfaces for Virtual Environment and Teleoperator Systems. World Haptics Conference, Pisa, Italy, pp. 471–472 (2005). https://doi.org/10.1109/WHC.2005.103

Evaluation of Usability and User Experience of Dishwasher Rack Design for Chinese Families

Dengyaxue Chen[1], Wei Wang[1(✉)], Xinyi Gao[1], Ying Ding[1], and Wengan Liang[2]

[1] Hunan University, Changsha 410082, China
wangwei1125@hnu.edu.cn
[2] Vatti Co., Ltd., Zhongshan, China

Abstract. Due to the differences between Chinese and Western cooking styles and the shape of tableware, western dishwasher racks face challenges in meeting the needs of Chinese kitchen tableware from easy placement to thorough cleaning. However, it needs related research for the Chinese market and product design. This paper presents a human-centered design research from ethnographic studies, usability testing sessions, to design validation based on the exploration of real user needs and experience characteristics for Chinese consumers. Design guides were proposed to enhance the perceived quality and promote the localization of domestic dishwasher rack products, which have been proven effective by A/B testing. The methods and findings in this paper could inspire the related design of home appliances.

Keywords: Usability evaluation · Dishwasher rack design · Design guides

1 Introduction

Given the demand for the new urban lifestyle, kitchen upgrades, and sterilization of tableware, dishwashers have been increasingly owned in China in recent years. However, they were invented and optimized based on Western preferences. Placing tableware is an important step when using a dishwasher, and the dishwasher rack is the primary interface between the user and the machine in this part. Currently, western dishwasher racks face challenges in meeting the needs of Chinese kitchen tableware from easy placement to thorough cleaning due to the differences between Chinese and Western cooking styles and the shape of tableware, such as chopsticks, noodle bowls and woks.

In Sweden, Delin [1] focused on the dishwasher door design to improve the user experience during using the product, which indicated the importance of partial design. Imai et al. [2] developed an algorithm to achieve the optimal tableware layout in racks to solve the problem of dishwasher loading in Japan. However, as an emerging product in the Chinese market, little research has been reported on designing dishwashers for Chinese consumers. Wang et al. [3] evaluated the samples in the Chinese market and pointed out that further research is still needed for the localization of domestic dishwashers. Thus motivated, this study aims to explore the real user needs and experience characteristics of dishwasher racks for Chinese consumers. It proposes design guides for dishwasher racks to improve the user experience and usability.

© The Author(s), under exclusive license to Springer Nature Switzerland AG 2023
A. Marcus et al. (Eds.): HCII 2023, LNCS 14032, pp. 141–156, 2023.
https://doi.org/10.1007/978-3-031-35702-2_10

2 Research Process

2.1 Study Design

Our design approach consists of four stages based on a human-centered design scheme [4] as shown in Fig. 1: A) conducting quick ethnographic studies and B) testing the usability of existing products comparatively to develop design guidelines, C) redesigning the target product based on the design guidelines and prototyping, and D) evaluating the effect of design changes from an A/B testing.

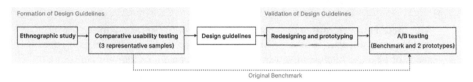

Fig. 1. The study approaches

2.2 Participants and Data Collection

All studies were carried out from October 2021 to September 2022. Our data comprised field notes from nine observed Chinese families, experimental records, think-aloud transcripts, semi-structured interviews, and posttest questionnaires from the comparative usability testing and A/B testing. Participants were recruited through questionnaires and social platforms with compensation.

3 Ethnographic Study

We visited nine families in four cities to find the real customer needs from their voices [5] and the characteristics of tableware in Chinese kitchens. The practical field study consisted of two parts: first, participants were asked to use the dishwasher as usual during the observation. This field experiment aimed to capture the typical context of use [5] and obvious operational issues. Second, a semi-structured interview was conducted to get straight feedback from customers. This part gathered a broad range of user needs and allowed users to quickly evaluate the designers' early ideas in the real context [6].

The findings of the ethnographic study shaped the basis of ideas for the initial design. Major issues were found that special tableware such as woks, pans, and teacups could not fit into the rack and difficulties existed in understanding the rack usage and planning a better organization of tableware in the compact rack. Moreover, we discovered the design potential of modular racks to accommodate various tableware types in Chinese kitchens.

4 Usability Testing for the Comparison of Existing Products

Since many operational problems were found in the ethnographic study, the usability testing focused on comparing product samples selected from the Chinese market. It was conducted in a usability laboratory to specify the limitations of current products and explore the factors that affect the comfort of the process of locating tableware.

4.1 Experiment Design and Participants

The usability experiment was designed to evaluate user performance and perceived usability with the selected dishwasher racks for a series of user tasks. For the apparatus, three types of racks with the same capacity were chosen from different brands based on the sales data in Chinese e-commerce platforms. Their brand labels were removed to avoid brand bias.

Before the experiment, the subjects were given operation videos to familiarize these racks and were encouraged to use the Think Aloud method [7] during the trial to express their feelings. When the test started, subjects needed to finish sequential tasks for each rack under observation and recorded conditions: A) open the dishwasher, B) place a specific number of tableware which in line with actual household use, and C) Close the dishwasher. The order of operating each rack between each subject was randomized to counterbalance the order effect. Immediately after the use test of each rack, subjects were asked to complete a post-test questionnaire to evaluate the usability, consisting of 5-point Likert scale questions. After the entire experiment, a short semi-structured interview was conducted as the post-hoc analysis. The main independent variable was based on the above within-subject experiment between three rack types (Fig. 2). These racks have different functional zones and layouts, limiting structures and components for different tableware types, and colors. Adjustment methods of structures are also different. Subjects need to rank the three dishwashers according to their overall impression and express their opinions.

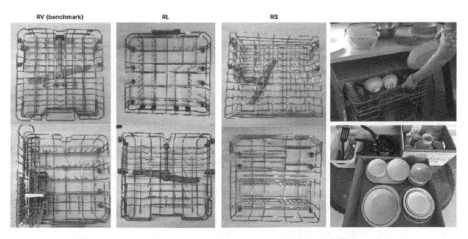

Fig. 2. Samples and environment in comparative usability testing

A total of 30 participants were involved in the evaluation (Female = 24, Male = 6, Age = 30.2 ± 12.4). Two user groups were compared to obtain a more comprehensive evaluation: expert users (n = 15) who own a dishwasher and use it frequently, and novices (n = 15) with no experience using a dishwasher. All participants have no previous experience with the test samples.

4.2 Evaluation Criteria and Data Analysis

Bailey [8] suggested that specific methods and metrics help to ensure that usability suggestions are data-driven and performance-based. In this test, quantitative and qualitative data were used to analyze the user experience of the dishwasher rack. Quantitative data consists of objective data reflecting task performance extracted from video recordings, and subjective data reflecting perceived usability collected from post-hoc questionnaires and evaluation ranking. Qualitative data was gathered from observation notes, TA transcripts, and interviews. As shown in Fig. 3, the evaluation criteria of the usability are divided into four dimensions according to product traits of dishwasher racks following the principle of ISO 9241-11 [9]:

- *Intelligibility*: Quickly understand the usage of the structure and components of the rack.
- *Functionality*: Correctly place the tableware.
- *Simplicity*: Quickly put the tableware in place.
- *Satisfaction*: The actual usage of the rack meets the users' needs and expectations.

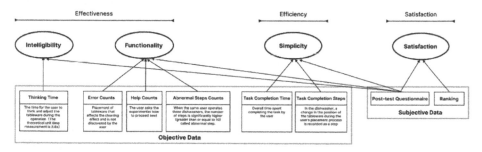

Fig. 3. Usability evaluation framework

Objective Data. The results of the metrics corresponding to each dimension were compared horizontally to explore the advantages and disadvantages of each rack. Next, the average thinking time was measured to evaluate *intelligibility*. The number of errors, help-seeking, and abnormal steps was summed over 30 subjects to account for *functionality*. Finally, the average task completion time and steps were measured to evaluate *simplicity*. The definition of each metric is explained in Fig. 3.

Subjective Data. The average score of the 5-point Likert scale and the total number of people corresponding to each ranking were also compared in the horizontal analysis to explore users' preferences. In addition, the average scores of each question were longitudinally compared to obtain areas that need to be improved for a single rack.

To ensure the questionnaire for evaluating dishwasher rack design is reliable and valid, the questions (Appendix 1) were adjusted along the four dimensions mentioned above based on the structure of the System Usability Scale [10]. Questions Q1 and Q9 were linked to *intelligibility*. Evaluation of *functionality* was done by questions Q2–Q8 and Q11–Q16. For the evaluation of *simplicity* and *satisfaction*, questions Q10 and Q17 were used.

Statistical Analysis. IBM SPSS Statistics 29 was used to analyze the dependent variables. A one-way repeated measures ANOVA was carried out to determine the significant differences among the three racks in comparative usability testing, followed by LSD post-hoc comparisons to determine the exact location of significant differences.

4.3 Results of the Experiment

Horizontal Analysis (Comparison Between Products). Overall, the RV rack received the best feedback in terms of user experience, followed by the RS rack. And the RL is the worst.

Intelligibility. The result indicated that the RS rack has the highest intelligibility, followed by the RV rack, and then the RL rack. As an objective measure of intelligibility, the longer the thinking time means the less indicative the design of the rack is and the harder it is for the user to understand. On the data of time that participants spent on their consideration during operation, the RL rack took the longest time (M = 342.47 ± 183.20 s), while the RV rack and the RS rack took a similar time (M = 297.88 ± 134.60

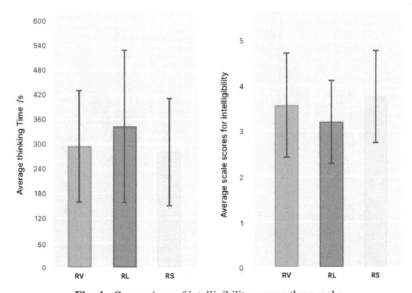

Fig. 4. Comparison of intelligibility among three racks.

s and M = 280.17 ± 131.00 s) (Fig. 4). Although we observed differences across the three brands, the results did not indicate significance (p = 0.168). It is consistent with objective performance that the subjective intelligibility of the RS rack is higher than the other two racks. The RS rack had the highest score (M = 3.78 ± 1.05) compared to the other two racks (M = 3.58 ± 1.15 and M = 3.2 ± 0.91). From the LSD post-hoc test results, the RS rack is much easier to understand than the RL rack (p = 0.007 < 0.01).

From the qualitative content, the rack with clear functional zones and layouts and limiting structures with simple semantics tend to receive a higher score in intelligibility. Users often need help recognizing the usage of unconventional limiting structures with indirect shapes related to the tableware. To our surprise, the rack color guide was not recognized.

Functionality. The results of objective data showed that the RL rack and the RV rack performed better, and the RS rack performed the worst. However, in terms of subjective functionality, the RV rack and the RS gained better feedback, while the RL rack was the worst.

As a measure of functionality, lower numbers of errors, help-seeking, and abnormal steps indicate higher product and service quality. In general, the RL rack achieved better functionality. On the data of the number of errors and help-seeking, all three racks had similar performance. But on the data of the number of abnormal steps, the RS rack (Sum = 7) had a higher number than the RV rack (Sum = 2) and the RL rack (Sum = 3) as shown in Fig. 5, which indicates that users repeatedly adjusted the position of tableware when using the RS rack.

Subjective data showed that the scores of the RS rack (M = 3.89 ± 0.74) and the RV rack (M = 4.06 ± 0.58) were higher than that of the RL rack (M = 3.66 ± 0.59). The results of repeated measures ANOVA showed significant differences (F (2) = 4.109, p < 0.05), and were found between the RV rack and the RL rack (p = 0.005 < 0.01). This

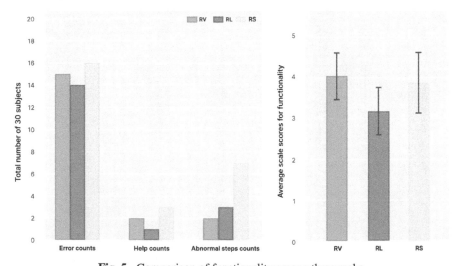

Fig. 5. Comparison of functionality among three racks.

means that users found the RV rack much easier to use than the RL rack when placing tableware.

From the qualitative content, the weaknesses in the functionality of these racks are 1) mismatching of rack design with Chinese tableware in terms of tableware shape and demand ratio, 2) decreased space utilization due to loose functional zones and layouts, and 3) insufficient height between upper and lower floors. In addition, 4) the adjustable function of the rack was unrecognized by users.

Simplicity. Overall, the RV rack has the best simplicity, followed by the RS rack, and then the RL rack. As a measure of simplicity, less time and fewer steps to complete the task mean a smoother operation process. On average, the RL rack yielded the longest task completion time (M = 527.27 ± 209.67 s) and the greatest completion steps (M = 47.67 ± 10.91) compared to the other two racks. Task completion time and steps of the RV rack were 462.90s (SD = 153.17) and 47.10 (SD = 7.93), and 451.77 s (SD = 157.55) and 47.67(SD = 10.91) for rack the RS rack. These data indicated that the tableware placing process was the most inconvenient when using the RL rack.

Consistent with objective performance, the RV rack has the best subjective simplicity, and the RL rack is the worst. The RV rack had the highest score (M = 3.80 ± 0.89) compared to the other two racks (M = 3.40 ± 1.25 and M = 3.07 ± 1.05). Furthermore, from the LSD post hoc test results, the RV rack is much smoother to use than the RL rack (p = 0.011 < 0.05).

From the qualitative content, less limiting structure and large space make the rack more inclusive and the tableware placement process smoother. Meanwhile, a better match between the limiting structure and tableware makes it faster for the user to locate the tableware (Fig. 6).

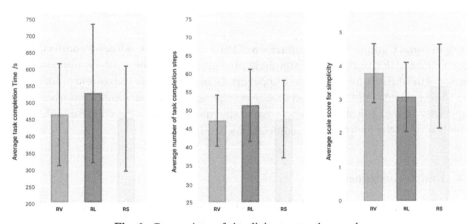

Fig. 6. Comparison of simplicity among three racks

Satisfaction. The results showed that the RV rack was rated the best, followed by the RS rack, and then the RL rack. As shown in Fig. 7, the RV rack had the highest satisfaction score (M = 3.70 ± 0.92) compared to the other two racks (M = 3.63 ± 1.00 and M =

3.27 ± 0.83). Furthermore, on the ranking data, the highest number of people ranked the RV rack in the first place (Sum = 14) compared to the other two racks (Sum = 11 and Sum = 2), meaning most users preferred the RV rack.

From the qualitative content, users prefer structures that indicate clear tableware placement directions. And they tend to place tableware most straightforwardly, without actively adjusting the structure. Hereby, the placement space, the degree of freedom of placement which depends on the number of the limiting structure, and the spacing and the orientation of limiting structures are the key factors that affect user satisfaction.

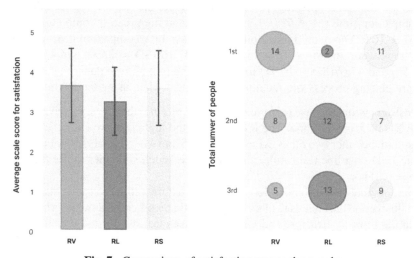

Fig. 7. Comparison of satisfaction among three racks

Longitudinal Comparison (Comparison of Different Aspects of Each Product). The results showed that intelligibility, simplicity, and user satisfaction are the common weaknesses of the three dishwasher racks (Appendix 2). In other words, the current products on the Chinese market did not yet meet the user requirements for an ideal dishwasher rack, especially in the indicative of structure and the matching with the Chinese tableware, which verified the findings in the ethnographic study.

4.4 Design Guidelines

From the user tests, we found that the usability problems are concentrated in the following four aspects: A) low indication of rack zoning and tableware placement, B) mismatching of the rack structure and component design with different tableware types, C) less inclusion of various tableware in most Chinese families, and D) decreased space utilization due to disorganized functional zones and layout. To solve these problems, we proposed new design guides for dishwasher rack design (Table 1) based on user placement habits and cognitive logic along the four dimensions of evaluation criteria.

Table 1. Design guidelines for dishwasher rack design.

Dimensions	Design guidelines
Intelligibility	Clear rack zones to help quickly identify the type of tableware to be placed
	Rich but uncomplicated styling semantics are needed to help users understand how tableware is placed
	Colors need to be used more holistically to increase the emotional characteristic of the rack
Functionality	Multiple functions of one structure to accommodate flexible placement for various tableware
	Reasonable arrangement of different types of tableware space ratio to avoid space waste
Simplicity	Rack lines need to be simple and smooth, in line with the visual principles
	Enhanced precision control of details, such as adjusting the space to make tableware positioning faster and more stable
Satisfaction	Give users tips on the starting position and direction of placement
	More accurate targeting of user placement behavior and the ratio of demand for tableware in different dining scenarios

5 Redesigning and Prototyping Based on the Design Guidelines

Design changes were conceptualized based on the ethnographic findings and design guides from the usability testing, which were applied in the two new prototypes (Fig. 8):

- PM: A improved rack called "Micro Innovation", was a detailed adjustment to the structure and components design of the benchmark. This prototype considered all design guidelines. Compared to the benchmark, it has re-planned the layout of functional zones according to the demand ratio and occupancy space of different tableware types, simplified the limiting structure's shape, and changed the chopstick basket into an adjustable chopstick tray to facilitate the direct placement of tableware by users. In addition, it has adjusted the spacing and tilt angle of the limiting structure according to Chinese tableware and attached the silicone cap to the structure to increase friction with the tableware, and each limiting structure could be folded to ensure placement flexibility. It also gave the user tips on placement through color and tableware markings.
- PS: A innovative rack called "Second Space", was a solution for the extension of the usage scenario of the dishwasher rack. Both upper and lower layers had two separate racks, which could be taken out and used on the dining table or by the sink to avoid bending over repeatedly. This prototype considered design guidelines for zones, color, details of limiting structure, and user placement behavior. Compared to the benchmark, it has modularized functional zones and layouts, used color more extensively to guide the location of tableware placement, and adjusted the spacing and tilt angle of the limiting structure as well. Besides, the limiting structure could be removed to ensure a direct placement of the tableware.

PM   PS

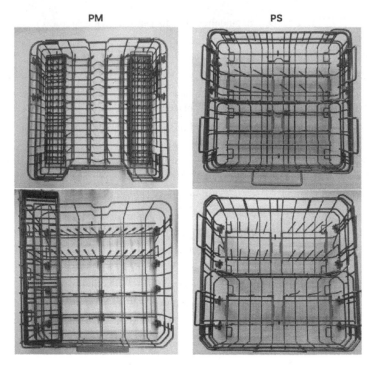

Fig. 8. Two new prototypes

6   A/B Testing

6.1   Experiment Design and Participants

To test new designs and verify design guidelines' validity, 15 participants (7 novices and 8 experts) were recruited (Female $= 11$, Male $= 4$, Age $= 30.0 \pm 7.7$). We compared the usability of the two new prototypes with the original rack benchmark following the same experimental procedure and evaluation scheme used in comparative usability testing.

Slightly differently, the task of operating the PS rack was modified since it was modular in structure. Users were asked to take the rack out to place tableware and put it back into the machine after filling it up. In addition, we added two new questionnaires to specify the users' preference strength between the two new prototypes and benchmark. Questions such as "Compared with the first set, I prefer the placement experience of the cups in the second set of rack" still used the 5-point Likert scale. The data from these questionnaires were not used for statistical analysis but for semi-structured interviews.

6.2   Evaluation Criteria and Data Analysis

For Objective Data, the same evaluation scheme was used. However, with one difference, the "Error counts" and "Help counts" metrics were deleted because we found very few critical errors in the trial. For subjective data, questions in the post-test questionnaire still followed four dimensions. However, to get more aesthetic and emotional responses from users [11] to two improved products, we added questions regarding color-material-finishing (CMF) and the intention to buy (Appendix 3). Additionally, an independent-samples t-test was used to analyze the effect of design iterations.

6.3 Results of the Experiment

The statistical analysis (Appendix 4) showed that the performance in all aspects of the usability of the PM rack improved significantly, especially in task completion steps ($p = 0.01 < 0.05$), subjective intelligibility ($p = 0.002 < 0.01$), subjective simplicity ($p = 0.05$), and satisfaction ($p = 0.012 < 0.05$). Perceived intelligibility and satisfaction of the PS rack also improved, although they did not indicate significant differences.

The reasons for the improved intelligibility are summarized below. The limiting structures in both new racks had simple shapes and the same alignment direction (i.e., only horizontal or longitudinal in the rack). And the interval between each limiting structure was adequate, making zones appear as blocks. Moreover, from the visual logic, the presence of the block could be emphasized by a dense grid-like pattern. However, the color guide was still not recognized in this test, indicating that the use of color needs to be further evaluated based on a larger data scale.

The reasons for the improved satisfaction are summarized below. Both prototypes adjusted the spacing and tilt angle of the limiting structure, resulting in more stable tableware placement and higher matching to Chinese tableware. The fitting with the tableware shape increased the space utilization of each zone. The reorganized function zones and layout according to the demand ratio and occupancy space of various tableware improved the space utilization of the entire rack. Furthermore, these two prototypes have their own design highlights. The PM rack provided clear functional zones for basic tableware and ensured freedom of placement for irregular tableware. The design point that could be taken out to place tableware made the PS rack friendly to users with bad backs.

7 Discussion

7.1 Principle Findings

This study improved dishwasher rack products effectively from a user-centered per-spective. Design guides for dishwasher racks were proposed by comparing the usability of existing products and locating factors that affect user experience, which provided a basis for designing the two new prototypes. Most usability problems were related to the low indication of the usage of the rack, mismatching with Chinese tableware char-acteristics, and tableware organization and layout in a compact rack. Judging from the results of the A/B testing, PM adopted all design guidelines to address these problems, significantly improving both task performance and perceived usability in all aspects. PS adopted the design guides for functional zones, color, details of limiting structure, and user placement habits, improving perceived intelligibility and satisfaction. From these two usability tests, the following design suggestions were summarized to improve the future dishwasher rack design for Chinese consumers:

- First, identify the demand ratio for various tableware in different families and dining scenes to determine the type and number of functional zones in the rack. Then, plan the layout of zones according to the space occupied by the corresponding tableware to avoid space waste.
- Second, the functional zones and limiting structures need to be highly indicative. For example, from the visual logic, an adequate interval between each limiting structure or a high-density grid structure tends to make the zones more obvious to help users locate tableware. Additionally, concise semantics or a clear association between the limiting structure shape and table shape tends to help users understand how tableware is placed.
- Third, during the experiment, stable tableware after being placed is an important criterion for users to judge whether the position is correct. Therefore, the limiting structure's spacing, height, and tilt angle must strongly match its corresponding tableware.
- Forth, multi-functionality and highly perceived adjustment of a single structure enable users to accommodate flexible placement for various tableware. And repeated use of single structures makes the physical interface [12] of the dishwasher rack neater.
- Last, give users tips on placement through signs, holistic colors, or additional structures like silicone caps to enable users to feel the product's thoughtfulness. Moreover, the CMF, interweave and even the thickness of the metal wire will affect the user's evaluation of the product's texture. For example, simple and smooth rack lines tend to receive better feedback.

The result of the field study showed that western-based simple structured dishwasher racks are no longer suitable because of the complexity of Chinese tableware. The tableware in Chinese kitchens has more bowls with deeper depth, fewer dishes, and much more special-shaped tableware such as pots and pans. Therefore, having rich and clear functional zones, designing compact loading layouts, and keeping appropriate freedom and flexibility are very important for dishwasher racks designed for Chinese kitchens.

7.2 Limitation

The results of the A/B testing indicated that our product iteration method and the improved prototype are meaningful. However, the improvement effect of the innovative prototype is not obvious based on three aspects:

- First, from the prototype design, the prototype used the same dimensions as the benchmark to fit into the original machine. But the space for placing tableware was reduced because of the wrapped structure of the prototype, which affected the user experience.
- Second, from the experiment design, since the prototype's target users and usage scenarios have typical characteristics, both recruitment of participants and task scenarios in usability testing for this rack should be more accurate to get the actual feedback from a narrower user base.

- Last, from the evaluation criteria, the original evaluation metrics may no longer be applicable due to the change in the functional traits of innovative products.

8 Conclusion

This paper presents an iterative usability study and redesign process to improve the user experience of the dishwasher rack. Design guides are proven effective in A/B testing, proposing to increase usability and promote the localization of dishwasher rack design to meet the real needs of Chinese families. Furthermore, the methods and findings in the paper could inspire related kitchen appliance design for the Chinese market.

Acknowledgments. This research was supported by the National Key Research and Development Program (2021YFF0900605), the Research Fund for Humanities and Social Sciences of the Ministry of Education (22YJA760082), the Science and Technology Innovation Program of Hunan Province (2022WZ1039), the National Foreign Cultural and Educational Experts Program of the Ministry of Science and Technology (G2022160013L), the Fundamental Research Funds for the Central Universities and Lushan Lab. We acknowledge Xin Shao in Vatti Co. Ltd., Aosha Long, Wenxuan Li, Fangli Song and MingQi Zhang in Hunan University, and the reviewers in HCII 2023.

Appendix 1: Questions for the Evaluation of Dishwasher Racks in the Comparative Usability Testing

Q1	It is easy to understand how tableware is arranged by looking at the structure	5 pt. Likert
Q2	I can use the structure of the rack to arrange chopsticks properly	5 pt. Likert
Q3	I can use the structure of the rack to arrange bowls properly	5 pt. Likert
Q4	I can use the structure of the rack to arrange dishes properly	5 pt. Likert
Q5	I can use the structure of the rack to arrange cups properly	5 pt. Likert
Q6	I can use the structure of the rack to arrange woks properly	5 pt. Likert
Q7	I can use the structure of the rack to arrange cooking tools (i.e., spoon) properly	5 pt. Likert
Q8	I can use the structure of the rack to arrange irregular tableware properly	5 pt. Likert
Q9	It is easy to understand how the different structures in the rack are used	5 pt. Likert
Q10	The process of placing the tableware is convenient	5 pt. Likert
Q11	The height between the upper and lower layers of the rack is appropriate	5 pt. Likert
Q12	There is enough room for chopsticks	5 pt. Likert
Q13	There is enough room for cups	5 pt. Likert
Q14	There is enough room for bowls	5 pt. Likert
Q15	There is enough room for dishes	5 pt. Likert

(continued)

(*continued*)

Q16	There is enough room for woks	5 pt. Likert
Q17	The experience of the overall placement process is satisfactory	5 pt. Likert

Appendix 2: Longitudinal Comparison of Three Racks

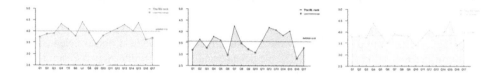

Appendix 3: Questions for the Evaluation of Dishwasher Racks in the A/B Testing

Q1	By observing the structure of the rack, I can easily understand the placement and partition of various tableware	5 pt. Likert
Q2	By observing the structure of the rack, I can easily understand the arrangement of various tableware	5 pt. Likert
Q3	I think the tableware placement process went smoothly	5 pt. Likert
Q4	I can arrange the tableware properly in the dishwasher rack	5 pt. Likert
Q5	I think there is enough space for tableware	5 pt. Likert
Q6	I think the material matching of the rack is beautiful	5 pt. Likert
Q7	I can put all the tableware on the rack very quickly	5 pt. Likert
Q8	I think the functional zones of this rack are reasonable	5 pt. Likert
Q9	I think the height of the upper and lower space of the rack is appropriate	5 pt. Likert
Q10	If I have the intention to use the rack, I am willing to buy this rack	5 pt. Likert

Appendix 4: The Results of the A/B Testing

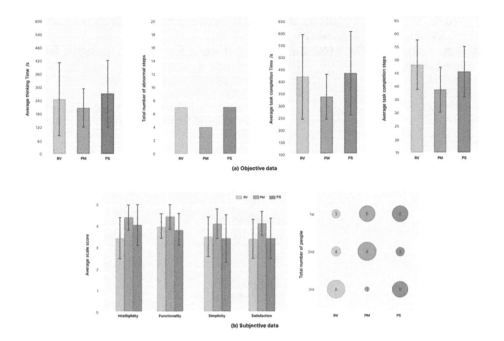

(a) Objective data

(b) Subjective data

References

1. Delin, A.: Enhancing the perceived quality of a dishwasher through user-centered design (2013)
2. Imai, K., Maeda, Y.: A user support system that optimizes dishwasher loading. In: 2017 IEEE 6th Global Conference on Consumer Electronics (GCCE), pp. 1–2. IEEE, October 2017. http://www.springer.com/lncs. Accessed 21 Nov 2016
3. Wang, Z., Luo, L., Zhao, C.: Research on dishwasher with user experience evaluation. In: Stephanidis, C. (ed.) HCI 2018. CCIS, vol. 850, pp. 309–315. Springer, Cham (2018). https://doi.org/10.1007/978-3-319-92270-6_45
4. Vredenberg, K., Isensee, S., Righi, C.: User-Centered Design: An Integrated Approach with Cdrom. Prentice Hall PTR (2001)
5. Otto, K.N.: Product design: techniques in reverse engineering and new product development (2003)
6. Wang, W., Bryan-Kinns, N., Sheridan, J.G.: On the role of in-situ making and evaluation in designing across cultures. CoDesign 16(3), 233–250 (2020)
7. Charters, E.: The use of think-aloud methods in qualitative research an introduction to think-aloud methods. Brock Educ. J. 12(2) (2003)
8. Bailey, R.W., Wolfson, C.A., Nall, J., Koyani, S.: Performance-based usability testing: metrics that have the greatest impact for improving a system's usability. In: Kurosu, M. (ed.) HCD 2009. LNCS, vol. 5619, pp. 3–12. Springer, Heidelberg (2009). https://doi.org/10.1007/978-3-642-02806-9_1

9. Iso, W.: 9241-11. Ergonomic requirements for office work with visual display terminals (VDTs). The international organization for standardization, vol. 45, no. 9 (1998)

10. Lewis, J.R.: The system usability scale: past, present, and future. Int. J. Hum. Comput. Interact. **34**(7), 577–590 (2018)

11. Thüring, M., Mahlke, S.: Usability, aesthetics and emotions in human–technology interaction. Int. J. Psychol. **42**(4), 253–264 (2007)

12. 王巍，杨逸景．智能产品时代的交互之变面向实体可触交互的设计刍议[J]．美术大观**414**(06), 129–133 (2022)

Research About Usability Improvement in Cursor Operation of 3D Configurator

Yugo Furuhash$^{(\boxtimes)}$ and Wonseok Yang

Shibaura Institute of Technology, Koto-ku, Tokyo 135-8548, Japan
yugof0887@gmail.com

Abstract. Automakers are accelerating their online sales strategies; augmented reality (AR) and three-dimensions (3D) configurators are being utilized to allow consumers to conveniently perceive information from multiple angles. However, since the user interface (UI) and posted content regarding, 3D configurators, on current e-commerce sites differ from manufacturer wise, many users who are not familiar with active information fail to use the said configurators. Therefore, examining the result of a past interview survey on the guide, cursor shape, and zoom function in the 3D configurator UI, we thought it necessary to clarify exactly how users are influenced by cursor manipulation in the 3D configurator, which is constantly manipulating the screen. For this purpose, we created a new questionnaire item with reference to the web usability scale (WUS) survey method, and conducted an experiment. Using the results of the experiment, we confirmed that the shape and rotation speed of the cursor influence the user when they are operating the cursor. In addition, we found that the optimal rotation speed differs depending on the method of rotation, and we are of the opinion that varying the speed will improve operability. Based on this research, we believe that ameliorating the shape and rotation speed of the cursor in 3D configurators will lead to a reduction in user stress and a positive user experience, thereby improving usability.

Keywords: 3D Configurator · UI usability · Cursor control · E-commerce

1 Introduction

Electric commerce (EC) businesses are trying to expand online sales of their products, from daily necessities in the apparel and food industry, to more expensive items such as "cars and houses," with a focus on goods sales [1]. With the sale of electric vehicles, many manufacturers in the automobile industry, including Tesla, are accelerating their online sales strategies by taking advantage of the features of various devices to make information recognizable from multiple perspectives [2]. However, the current automotive e-commerce business has not expanded because of its small market size compared to that of the apparel and food industries. Previously, while purchasing a car, consumers would gather information (through the Internet, commercials, magazines, etc.) and then visit a store to check the operation of the car via a test drive.

In reference to the above, the main purpose of e-commerce sites is to increase consumers' willingness to purchase a car by providing detailed information about that car

A. Marcus et al. (Eds.): HCII 2023, LNCS 14032, pp. 157–170, 2023.
https://doi.org/10.1007/978-3-031-35702-2_11

and customizing its exterior and interior; indeed, this increases potential consumers' interest in the car before they apply for a test drive. However, to expand online sales, it is necessary to convince consumers to purchase using the information posted on e-commerce sites, and so it is important to connect the Search to Action concept to the Attention, Interest, Search, Action, Share (AISAS) purchasing behavior model [3, 4]. Therefore, we believe that online sales can be accelerated by posting information that is more realistic for potential consumers researching products, and which allows them to judge information from multiple perspectives.

With the spread of AR and virtual reality, due to Digital Transformation (DX) and digitalization in the business field, two main information posting methods – namely passive information and active information – are used on automotive e-commerce websites [5]. Passive information is generally information that consumers want to derive from text, photos, videos, and so on. In contrast, active information employs 3D configurators and AR to manipulate the information presented to the user, thus making it an important tool for convincing users to purchase and for promoting online sales in future. Current automotive e-commerce websites allow users to customize tires, exteriors, and interiors on the screen, according to their preferences, and rather than just taking a test drive, those users/consumers can compare manufacturers from more diverse perspectives, such as size, color scheme, and operation, even online, without being bound by time or location. However, current AR and 3D configurators differ greatly in usage and presentation from one manufacturer to another, and many users who are not accustomed to active information are unfamiliar with 3D configurators [6]. These issues are a major cause of aggravation, because they mean that users cannot achieve their goals as quickly as they would like. Therefore, the current study considers usability improvement in cursor operation, which is closely related to the usability of 3D configurators.

2   Literature Review: User Perception of Information Manipulation

This study considers the improvement of usability by investigating how the interaction caused by manipulating the 3D configurator affects the user.

2.1   Information Processing Model in Interaction Operations

To understand the information processing model in interactions, we describe it from the perspective of human cognitive processes [7]. Human cognitive processes can be divided into three stages: sensation, perception, and cognition. Regarding the sensation stage, humans store, in their sensory memory, information obtained from the outside through the five senses, including vision and hearing [8]. Perception is the process of retrieving such information from the sensory memory and organizing/processing it so that it can be moved to the short-term memory where it is retained for tens of seconds. Cognition is the process of judging and interpreting perceived information using long-term memory. In addition, interpreting what is perceived by adding past experiences and memories to sensations and perceptions creates different interpretations depending on individual experiences, memories, and the environment [9].

The information-processing model in interaction relates to human cognitive processes and information-processing mechanisms [7, 10] (see Fig. 1). In a human–computer interaction situation, information received by humans is processed based on short-term and long-term memory through human cognitive processes, and, as a result, the information is manipulated by moving hands, fingers, etc. Information input from humans is transmitted to the computer through input devices, such as keyboards and mice, processed, and displayed on output devices, such as displays. This cycle of human perception allows humans to perceive their interactions with computers. Norman's Gulf Model uses the said cycle to consider cognition in interaction more thoroughly.

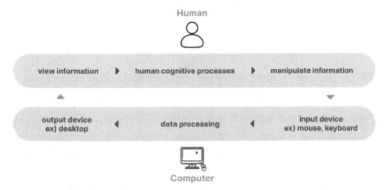

Fig. 1. Information processing model in interaction operations

2.2 Norman's Gulf Model by Perception of Information Manipulation

Norman's Gulf Model states that "there are two differently oriented gulfs between the psychological world of human needs and the physical world of actual task equipment use, and the interface is the bridge between these two gulfs [11]." Based on this, the cycle of bridging the gulf between humans and artificial systems is divided into seven stages: perception, interpretation, evaluation, intention, input selection, input execution, and execution by artifact; indeed, the cycle is represented in the figure below [12] (see Fig. 2). According to Norman's Gulf Model, inefficiencies, breakdowns, and other errors occur in the respective information processing cycles of humans and computers. These errors create a gulf between physical and psychological spaces, which interferes with the user's objectives. The gulf is between the execution when the user's information is transmitted to the system and the evaluation when the system transmits information to the user. Interaction design is important for easing the bridge between these two gulfs, and an appropriate display of interaction design can lead to improved user perception.

2.3 Improved Usability in the 3D Configurator

In a 3D configurator, the user perceives the information presented by the creator through interactions in which the former takes the initiative to manipulate the screen. Therefore,

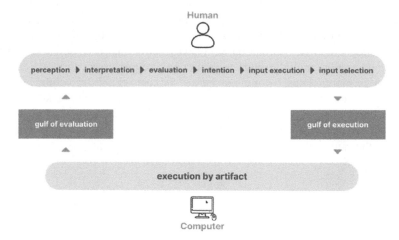

Fig. 2. Norman's Gulf Model by perception of information manipulation

we believe that the interface, which is the gulf between the physical and psychological spaces of the user and the system, should be made more navigable to improve operability when the user manipulates the screen, as advocated in Norman's Gulf Model [13, 14]. Therefore, to narrow the gulf between the psychological and physical worlds as much as possible, it is important to approach interaction design from the perspectives of both the physical aspect-based interaction design, such as mouse operation and sensation through the body, and cognitive aspect-based interaction design, such as UI and experience [15, 16, 17]. We believe that this would reduce user stress and improve usability [18] (Fig. 3).

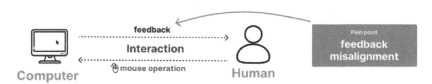

Fig. 3. Improved usability in the 3D configurator

3 Experiments on Cursor Manipulation

Based on a survey of the current status of automotive e-commerce sites, we believe that different UIs and functions can be a pain point for users who are not accustomed to active information. Therefore, as a preliminary study, we asked users to use four different UIs with different guides, cursor shapes, and zoom functions, and conducted an interview survey to gauge their impressions of these functions. As a result of the interview survey, we thought that it was necessary to consider the influence of the cursor operation on the user, especially regarding 3D configurators, which operate the screen, and we also felt that this would improve usability.

3.1 Methods

Experiment summary: To consider the influence of cursor operation on users
Target manufacturers: BMW, MINI, JUGER, HONDA
Number of subjects: 20 people
Experimental method: The students are given an assignment and asked to answer a questionnaire about their impressions (see Fig. 4)

- Conditions

1. Different factors such as cursor shape, rotation speed, and size.
2. Vehicle shape is SUV, color is the same color, and there are no guides, backgrounds, or other extraneous designs on the site (Fig. 5).

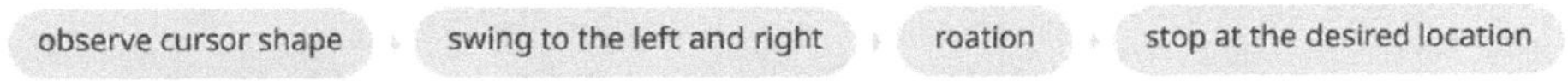

observe cursor shape
swing to the left and right
roation
stop at the desired location

Fig. 4. Tasks for experiments on cursor manipulation

automaker	MINI	BMW	JUGER	HONDA
logo				
cursor shape				
Cursor size	big	midium	midium	midium
Rotation speed	a little fast	slow	midium	fast
Trajectory length	long	short	midium	a little long
scroll auto	yes	yes	no	no

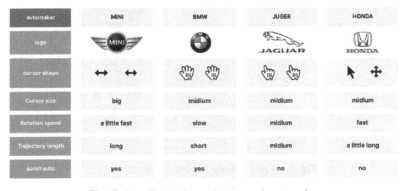

Fig. 5. Detailed information on each automaker

1) Characteristics of each automaker
   MINI: Scroll auto and high-speed rotation for easy operation.
   BMW: The shape of the cursor is suitable for rotation, and the rotation is slow,making operation intuitive.
   JUGER: The overall shape of the cursor and rotation speed are not distinctive and average, making it easy to compare with other companies.
   HONDA: Analyze the user's impression of the fast rotation speed and the action of returning to the sketch screen during rotation.
2) Evaluation item (Web Usability Scale)

   The Web Usability Evaluation Scale is a questionnaire evaluation method developed jointly by Fujitsu and IID to quantitatively evaluate Web usability. In total, 21 items related to Web usability were included in a 5-point scale, and seven evaluation factors generated from these questions were scored to evaluate Website usability. The

usability of a website was evaluated by scoring the seven evaluation factors generated from the questions [19]. Since the purpose of this study was to improve usability in cursor operation, five factors were set with reference to the Web Usability Scale.

Five evaluation factors and evaluation items of WUS
In this study, five axes of evaluation were selected based on the analysis method of the WUS survey: likability, operability, visibility, image, and reaction. Each of these was seen as being closely related to improving the usability of the cursor operation. The number of items selected was set to four for each evaluation axis, considering the respondent's workload in actual operational situations. Thus, the total number of items was five axes × four items = 20 items. A summary of the items is presented in the table below (see Fig. 6).

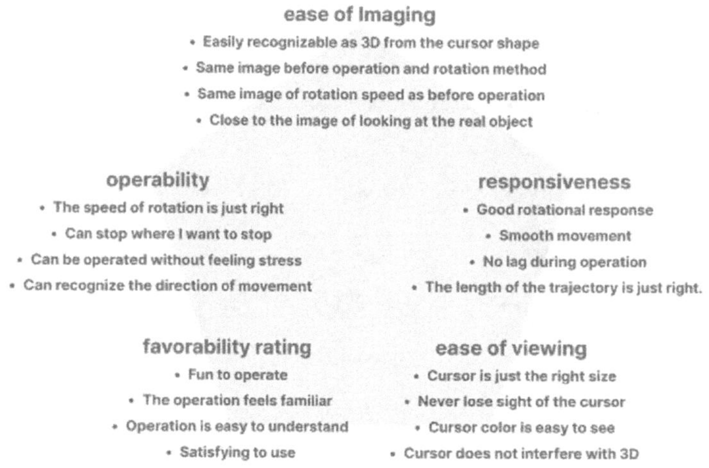

ease of Imaging
- Easily recognizable as 3D from the cursor shape
- Same image before operation and rotation method
- Same image of rotation speed as before operation
- Close to the image of looking at the real object

operability
- The speed of rotation is just right
- Can stop where I want to stop
- Can be operated without feeling stress
- Can recognize the direction of movement

responsiveness
- Good rotational response
- Smooth movement
- No lag during operation
- The length of the trajectory is just right.

favorability rating
- Fun to operate
- The operation feels familiar
- Operation is easy to understand
- Satisfying to use

ease of viewing
- Cursor is just the right size
- Never lose sight of the cursor
- Cursor color is easy to see
- Cursor does not interfere with 3D

Fig. 6. Web Usability Scale Evaluation items

3.2 Result

1) The characteristics of the manufacturer and the impact on the user
We asked each manufacturer to complete a questionnaire and considered the data in terms of the characteristics of those manufacturers and the impression of the cursor operation using mean graphs and principal component analysis. Principal components with an eigenvalue of 1.0 or greater and a cumulative contribution ratio of 60% or greater were extracted, and the items with the highest value in each impression were colored [20].

① Comparison of each manufacturer based on average graph
HONDA tended to underperform compared with other manufacturers in many categories, including the "image of the revolving method," "sense of realism," and "familiarity." Additionally, MINI tended to outperform other manufacturers in terms of

the "response to turnover" and "smoothness of movement." Since JUGER and BMW had the same factors other than cursor shape, and BMW was higher in the items of "not losing sight of the cursor," "cursor size," and "cursor shape is suitable for 3D," we believe that the cursor shape may have a better influence on the user at BMW (Fig. 7).

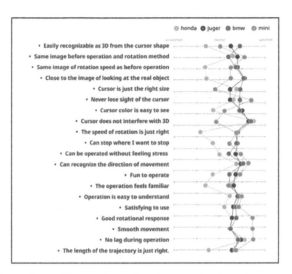

Fig. 7. Comparison of impressions of each automaker based on average graphs

② The impact on users based on principal component graphs

Based on the results of the principal component analysis, as shown below, principal component 1 was set as "intuitive and easy to understand," principal component 2 as "not responsive," principal component 3 as "easy to operate the cursor," and principal component 4 as "difficult to imagine the operation." The impressions of each manufacturer were then summarized, based on the principal component graphs, as follows.

- HONDA's "intuitive and easy-to-understand" factor was significantly lower than that of the other companies. The reason for this, as with the average graph, is thought to be the effect of returning to the sketch screen during the rotation operations, which is unique to HONDA.
- JUGER and BMW were found to be similar in almost all factors. The mean graph and the principal component analysis showed that the cursor shape was more likely to be recognized as 3D by the "liking" and "image" factors, with pointer, grab, and grabbing being more likely to be recognized than the cursors used in the normal operation of default and move.
- MINI had, by far, the lowest response factor for principal component 2, with many people perceiving it as having an excellent response. We believe that the scroll auto and rotation speeds are related to the response factor (Tables 1, 2, 3 and Fig. 8).

Table 1. Eigenvalue, contribution rate

No.	Eigenvalue	Contribution rate	Cumulative Contribution Ratio
1	6.089	30.445	30.445
2	2.620	13.101	43.546
3	1.790	8.950	52.495
4	1.563	7.767	60.262

Table 2. Principal component data

Evaluation items	Principal component1	Principal component2	Principal component3	Principal component4
Easily recognizable as 3D from the cursor shape	0.565	0.339	-0.362	-0.212
Same image before operation and rotation method	0.375	-0.171	-0.121	-0.571
Same image of rotation speed as before operation	0.645	0.068	-0.259	0.384
Close to the image of looking at the real object	0.510	0.447	-0.463	-0.160
Cursor is just the right size	0.216	0.441	0.682	0.226
Never lose sight of the cursor	0.352	-0.707	0.528	-0.033
Cursor color is easy to see	0.384	0.478	0.203	0.174
Cursor does not interfere with 3D	0.227	0.486	0.488	0.179
The speed of rotation is just right	0.759	0.137	-0.208	0.373
Can stop where I want to stop	0.563	0.317	-0.120	0.225
Can be operated without feeling stress	0.772	-0.122	-0.045	0.206
Can recognize the direction of movement	0.579	-0.120	0.230	-0.386
Fun to operate	0.721	-0.050	0.090	-0.314
Familiarity with the operation	0.585	0.358	-0.104	-0.266
Operation is easy to understand	0.543	-0.016	0.337	-0.413
Satisfying to use	0.803	-0.092	0.111	-0.118
Good rotational response	0.528	-0.621	0.170	0.205
Smooth movement	0.374	-0.695	0.007	0.147
No lag during operation	0.351	-0.698	0.078	0.060
The length of the trajectory is just right.	0.640	-0.131	-0.215	0.304

Table 3. Principal component list

Principal component	Principal component factors
Principal component1	Intuitive and easy to understand
Principal component2	Slow to respond
Principal component3	Easy operate cursor
Principal component4	Difficult to imagine the operation

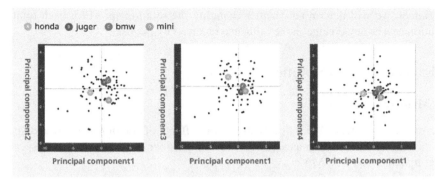

Fig. 8. Principal component graph

2) Analysis of variance for rotational speed and reaction

Based on the results of the mean graph and principal component analysis, a bivariate analysis was applied to determine if there were significant differences based on the p-value, since rotational speed may be a factor involved in the response. As a result of the analysis of variance, no significant differences were observed for rotational speed and response in this experiment. However, significant differences were found for rotation speed, image of rotation speed, actual rotation speed, feeling of realism, and familiarity; thereby indicating that a faster rotation speed has a positive impact on users regarding these four factors (Table 4).

Table 4. Relationship between rotational speed and user

Evaluation items	Significant difference
Same image of rotation speed as before operation	fast < slow p < 0.05
Close to the image of looking at the real object	fast < slow p < 0.05
The speed of rotation is just right	fast < slow p < 0.05
Familiarity with the operation	fast < slow p < 0.05
Good rotational response	n.s.

3.3 Discussion

First, analysis of the mean and principal component graphs showed that cursor shape is more likely to make users perceive the 3D configurator as pointer, grab, or grabbing, rather than default or move, based on the factors of liking and image. The results of the analysis of variance also illustrated a relationship between rotation speed and the image of the rotation method, actual rotation speed, realism, and familiarity, thus suggesting that rotation speed is a factor that influences cursor operation. Therefore, in the next experiment, we will determine whether changing the rotation speed for each rotation operation causes any change in the influence received by the user.

4   Experiments on Rotational Speed

4.1   Methods

Experimental summary: We will investigate the effects of rotation method and speed changes on the user and consider the optimal rotation speed.

Target manufacturer   MAZDA
Number of subjects: 20 people
Experimental method: The students are given an assignment and asked to answer a questionnaire about their impressions (see Fig. 9).
The rotation speed is adjusted by the DPI function (600, 1200, 1800 DPI) of the gaming mouse.

- About rotation method

① **swing left/right.** Rotation method used by the user for normal operation
② **Rotate.** Rotation method used by the user when viewing the entire automobile
③ **Stop where you want to stop.** Rotation method used to pinpoint where you want to see the car

Fig. 9. Experimental tasks on rotational speed

4.2   Results

1) Relationship between rotation speed and user influence
To clarify whether the impression of each of the two types of operation changed as the rotation speed changed, we conducted a bivariate analysis of the questionnaire results and colored the items with a p-value of 0.05 or less to indicate whether there were significant differences according to the p-value (Table 5).
2) The relationship between the method of rotation and the speed.

We averaged the items for which significant differences were observed and analyzed the relationship between the method of rotation and speed to determine whether the rotation method changed the optimal speed.

① "Swing left/right" rotation method

In terms of satisfaction, image of speed, and comfort, we believe that users tend to be most impressed with 1200DPI (Table 6).

Table 5. Impact of rotational speed on the user

Evaluation items	swing to the left and right	rotation	stop at the desired location
Feel stressed or not feel stressed	n.s.	p < 0.05	p < 0.05
Feel or not feel responsive	p < 0.01	p < 0.01	p < 0.01
Feel familiar or not	n.s.	p < 0.01	p < 0.05
Satisfied or not satisfied	P < 0.01	p < 0.01	p < 0.05
Same image of rotation speed or different image of rotation speed	p < 0.05	p < 0.01	p < 0.01
Feel real or not feel real	n.s.	n.s.	n.s.
The speed of rotation feels good or not good	p < 0.01	p < 0.01	p < 0.01
The motion feels smooth or not smooth	p < 0.01	p < 0.01	p < 0.01
I can stop where I want to stop			p < 0.05

Table 6. Average of "swing left and right

Evaluation items	600DPI	1200DPI	1800DPI
Feel or not feel responsive	2.65	3.85	4.25
Satisfied or not satisfied	2.90	4.15	4.05
Same image of rotation speed or different image of rotation speed	2.60	3.85	3.80
The speed of rotation feels good or not good	2.45	3.80	3.75
The motion feels smooth or not smooth	2.10	4.20	4.40

② "Rotation" rotation method

The overall impression of the "rotation" operation is that 1800 DPI is a good speed for the user. The slower the rotation speed, the more stressful it is for the user, and therefore, a high rotation speed is appropriate for the "rotation" operation (Table 7).

Table 7. Average of "rotation"

Evaluation items	600DPI	1200DPI	1800DPI
Feel stressed or not feel stressed	3.20	2.12	2.30
Feel or not feel responsive	2,45	3.80	4.40
Feel familiar or not	2.95	3.80	3.90
Satisfied or not satisfied	2.85	3.68	4.15
Same image of rotation speed or different image of rotation speed	2.40	3.90	4.10
The speed of rotation feels good or not good	2.40	3.95	4.20
The motion feels smooth or not smooth	2.50	3.79	4.45

③ "Stop where you want to stop" rotation method

In the "stop where you want to stop" operation, the slow rotation speed of 600DPI makes it easy to feel stress, and the fast rotation speed of 1800DPI makes it difficult to "stop where you want to stop". Therefore, we believe that 1200DPI, which has a high overall factor, will give a good impression to users (Table 8).

Table 8. Average of "stop where you want to stop"

Evaluation items	600DPI	1200DPI	1800DPI
Feel stressed or not feel stressed	3.30	2.10	2.60
Feel or not feel responsive	2.57	4.05	4.40
Feel familiar or not	2.95	3.89	3.35
Satisfied or not satisfied	2.80	3.75	3.40
Same image of rotation speed or different image of rotation speed	2.60	3.90	3.60
The speed of rotation feels good or not good	2.30	3.90	3.50
The motion feels smooth or not smooth	2.10	4.35	3.50
I can stop where I want to stop	3.35	4.40	3.15

4.3 Discussion

In this experiment, we tested how the rotational speed of the 3D configurator affects the user's impression of the 3D configurator. On average, the optimal speed differed depending on the rotation method, with 1,200 DPI suitable for "swing left/right" and "stop where you want to stop" motions, and 1,800 DPI suitable for "rotate." The speeds of 1,200 DPI and 1,800 DPI were found to be suitable for the "swing to the left and right" and "stop at the place where you want to stop" motions, respectively. This means that, when considering the use scenario of the 3D configurator, the "swing left/right" and "stop where you want to stop" motions are used in normal operations during the customization of the car, and so they should be able to be operated at the same speed. The "rotation" operation is often used to check the entire car or after customizing the car, and so it would be better to use different rotation speeds for the "rotation" operation and other operations. Therefore, we believe that the usability of the 3D configurator can be improved by employing different rotation speeds for "rotation" and other operations.

5 Conclusion

1) Experiments on cursor manipulation

   We conducted a survey of the UI of 3D configurators and carried out interviews regarding guides, cursors, and zoom to compare the UI functions of each e-commerce site. As a result, we conducted an experiment to explore the factors that affect cursor operation, since we had previously determined that users are more likely to recognize visual information by considering cursor operation in a 3D configurator, which is a constant screen operation. The experimental results showed that users were more likely to recognize the 3D configurator by changing the shape of the cursor to grab and grabbing based on the factors of liking and image. The results of the analysis of variance also illustrated that there is a relationship between the rotation speed and the image of the rotation method, actual rotation speed, realism, and familiarity.

2) Experiments on rotation speed

Since it was found that the rotation speed is one of the factors that affects cursor operation, we conducted experiments on the effects of changing the rotation method and speed. The three rotation methods were "shake left and right," "rotate," and "stop where you want to stop," which are thought to be employed during the use of the 3D configurator. In the experiment, the 3D configurator was operated at different rotation speeds (600, 1,200, and 1,800 DPI) using the DPI function of the gaming mouse for the three rotation methods. The results of the analysis first confirmed the influence of speed on the cursor operation. The optimal speed for "swinging left/right" and "stopping at the desired location" was 1,200 DPI, while the optimal rotation was 1800 DPI, depending on the rotation method. Based on these results, we believe that the usability of the 3D configurator can be improved by increasing the speed when performing the "rotation" operation.

6 Further Work

In this study, we investigated cursor manipulation in a 3D configurator from the viewpoint of perception of visual information. The study itself was limited to the shape and rotation speed of the 3D configurator's cursor, but the effects on the user's use of the 3D configurator are not limited to these factors; therefore, it is necessary to pay attention to other factors, such as background changes and camera angles. With the further development of digitization, information displays using 3D configurators are expected to expand not only to high-value products such as automobiles, but also to inexpensive products. Therefore, we believe that this research will provide the basis for expanding online sales of products that could only be sold through face-to-face avenues and information displays using images and videos.

References

1. Sometani, H., Ootuka, T., Mitsutomo, H.: Impact of E-commerce diffusion on consumer purchasing behavior. J. Jpn. Sect. Reg. Sci. Assoc. Int. **37**(2), 1157–1172 (2007)
2. Park, S.: Study on usability for fully online e-commerce business (2022)
3. Akai, Y.: Applications recent trends and applications of the business model for the user experience. Shonan Inst.Technol. J. **55**(1), 49–55 (2021)
4. Kondo, F.: The modeling of AISAS marketing process. Jpn. J. Syst. Dyn. **8**, 95–102 (2009)
5. BNN Co.: Interaction Design. BNN Co, Tokyo (2015)
6. Minzhe, Y., Zihao, H., Yuxiang, Y.: Creating a sustainable e-commerce environment: the impact of product configurator interaction design on consumer personalized customization experience. Int. J. Ind. Eng. Manag. **14**(23) (2019)
7. Nishida, T.: Understanding and Designing Interactions. Iwanami Bookstore, Tokyo (2005)

8. Inoue, K.: Textbook of Interface Design. Maruzen Publishing Co, Tokyo (2019)
9. Yamaoka, S., Okada, A., Tanaka, K., Mori, R., Yoshitake, R.: Basics of Design Engineering. Musashino Art University Press, Tokyo (2015)
10. Imai, R.: Cognitive Chemistry of Interaction, Shinyo Co, Tokyo (2018)
11. Donad, A.N.: The Design of Everyday Things. Shinyo Co. (1990)
12. Hori, M., Kato, T.: A modification of the cognitive walkthrough based on an extended model of human-computer interaction: its effectiveness in web usability evaluation. J. Inf. Process. Soc. Jpn. **48**(3), 1071–1084 (2007)
13. Dan, S.: Design for Interaction, 2nd edn. New Riders Press, San Francisco (2009)
14. Harada, S.: UI Design Essentials. Shoei Co. (2022)
15. Bortz, B., Peng, M., Polys, N., Hoegh, A.: Exploring the integrality and separability of the leap motion controller for direct manipulation 3D interaction. In: IEEE Symposium on 3D User Interfaces (3DUI), pp. 153–154 (2014)
16. Nakakoji, K.: Interaction design. Inf. Process. Soc. Jpn. **2004**(115), 1–3 (2004)
17. Dan, S.: Microinteractions. O'Reilly Media, Tokyo (2014)
18. Takeuchi, Y., Uesugi, S., Terada, K., Katagami, D.: Minimum design for interaction. J. Hum. Interface Soc. **15**(1), 1–14 (2013)
19. Nakagawa, K., Suda, T., Zenpo, H., Matsumoto, K.: The development of questionnaire for evaluating web usability. In: Proceedings of the Symposium on Human Interface, pp. 421–424 (2001)
20. Sakano, H.: Principal component analysis in pattern recognition. Proc. Inst. Stat. Math. **49**(1), 23–42 (2001)

The Effect of Time Lapse on the Halo Effect in the Subjective Evaluation of Digital Interfaces

Qilin Gu, Wenzhe Tang, and Chengqi Xue[✉]

School of Mechanical Engineering, Southeast University, Nanjing 211189, China
ipd_xcq@seu.edu.cn

Abstract. The halo effect is a cognitive error, but it is still unclear how the halo effect changes with time lapse in the subjective evaluation of digital interfaces. This paper presents a study which the halo effect diminishes with time lapse in the subjective evaluation of digital interfaces. To research the halo effect caused by visual aesthetics and usability, subjects learned about, studied, and used four web pages from two control groups for six tests over one week. The results showed that the halo effect caused by visual aesthetics was present before the start of use and decreased with time lapse, especially declining significantly on the third day. The effect of time lapse on the halo effect caused by usability was not found. These findings can optimize the subjective evaluation, lessen the blunder brought about by the radiance impact on the interface evaluation results, and further improve the accuracy of subjective evaluation.

Keywords: Halo effect · Time lapse · Digital interface · Usability · Aesthetics

1 Introduction

With the development of society, evaluation has penetrated into all aspects of social life and become a research hotspot in many disciplines such as social sciences, management sciences, and engineering fields, and the status of evaluation as a cross-cutting discipline has received more and more recognition and attention. Among them, subjective evaluation can compare different nature indicators in the most widely used in practical testing. For example, the scale method is a method of evaluating the subjects based on the hierarchical evaluation scale. This method is applicable regardless of whether the number of evaluated persons is large or small; Moreover, this method is more comprehensive and therefore the most widely used [1]. However, subjective evaluation is often influenced by the cognitive characteristics of users, which can produce a halo effect and lead to biased evaluation results [2–4].

In the digital age, the subjective evaluation method of digital interface mainly refers to the evaluation method of usability of digital interface based on subjective feelings and opinions. Some scholars have studied the influence of subjective evaluation in digital interfaces and found that visual aesthetics and usability are important factors affecting website evaluation [5]. Mahlke and Thuering found that in subjective evaluations of digital interfaces, the halo effect caused by visual aesthetics usually diminishes after

A. Marcus et al. (Eds.): HCII 2023, LNCS 14032, pp. 171–183, 2023.
https://doi.org/10.1007/978-3-031-35702-2_12

using the system [6]. But at present, there are fewer researches have been conducted on digital interfaces, and the effect of time lapse in digital interfaces on the halo effect is unclear.

Among the many factors affecting evaluation, time is an important variable that influences memory quality, emotional changes and judgment criteria. In evaluation, some studies have shown that the results of scale evaluations change over time. Daniel Kahneman 2004 proposed the Daily Reconstruction Method (DRM) to reduce recall errors by having subjects record the events of the previous day multiple times and having people rank the pleasure obtained from different activities over a period of time [7]. In the medical field, Anne Brédart found that patients' perceived satisfaction changes over time at six-week intervals by exploring the timing of assessing patient satisfaction assessments [8]. Existing studies have mainly focused on the time interval of scale evaluations, and there is a lack of research on time lapse, especially in the field of subjective evaluation of digital interfaces. It is beneficial to optimize the evaluation scale to study the changing trend of evaluation results caused by the time effect.

We aim to identify the time points at when the halo effect is diminished caused by usability and visual aesthetic respectively, and to provide valuable guidance for the evaluation time of subjective evaluation scales, to improve the accuracy and applicability of the scales.

2   Methodology

2.1   Materials

The experimental materials are two groups of web interfaces, the first group is Web A and Web B, which keep the same usability and distinguish high visual aesthetics from low visual aesthetics by color and layout, as shown in Fig. 1. The second group of interfaces is Web C and Web D, which keep the same visual aesthetics, and distinguish high usability from low usability by the presence or absence of a navigation bar, as shown in Fig. 2. The experimental materials were all designed and not used by users.

The experimental questionnaires were two questionnaires selected according to the measurement dimensions, Assessing dimension of perceived visual aesthetics of websites [9] shown in Appendix 1. And Perceived Usefulness and Ease of Use (PUEU) [10] shown in Appendix 2.

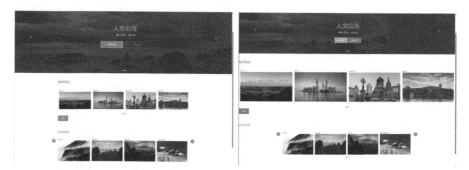

Fig. 1. Web interface with high and low visual aesthetics (left is high visual aesthetics & right is low visual aesthetics)

Fig. 2. High and low usability web interface (left image is low usability & right image is high usability)

2.2 Subjects

20 subjects were enrolled from the School of Mechanical Engineering in Southeast University. Subjects included 6 males and 6 females between the ages of 20 and 30 years (M = 24), all of whom were right handed and had normal vision or corrected vision. Subjects all had experience in using websites and all used computers to browse websites and fill out questionnaires in the experiment.

2.3 Experimental Equipment and Experimental Procedures

In this study, web interfaces were used as experimental materials. We evaluated the interface from the perspectives of usability and aesthetics, and explored the rule of halo effect changes with the time of the three stages before, during, and after use respectively under these two perspectives. The research process is shown in Fig. 3. The time point of the halo effect weakening was found by experiment. According to the obtained time points, we can get the appropriate evaluation time of the subjective evaluation scale to optimize the scale.

The experiments were conducted in a quiet environment with normal lighting conditions. The experimental equipment were laptop computers with screen size in the range of 13 to 17 in. The experiments were divided into two groups: Web A and Web B in the first group were filled out with a questionnaire to assess the visual aesthetics of the website; Web C and Web D in the second group were filled out with PUEU to measure subjective usability. Both groups were tested six times within a week. The six tests were carried out on the first, second, third, fifth and seventh days of using the interface, and on the first day including two tests, when the participant first saw the interface and when

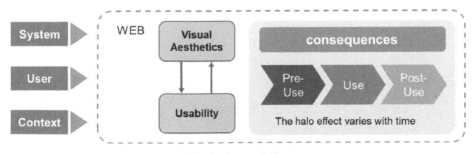

Fig. 3. Research flow

the participant freely interacted with the interface five minutes. To obtain the visual aesthetics ratings of A and B and the usability ratings of C and D at different time points. To ensure that users use the website during this week, experimental tasks were given to the subjects before every test. The experimental tasks mainly are understanding, learning about, and using the website:

1. Realize the layout and functions of the website: The first test made subjects watch a video introduction of the website; the second test was to make subjects explore the website freely for 5 min.
2. Learning the functions of the website: The third and fourth tests made the subjects click on the function buttons of the four websites.
3. Using the website independently: In the fifth and sixth tests, Subjects used the website independently to accomplish the goal setting.

Ultimately, the visual acsthetic evaluation data of Web A and Web B and the usability evaluation data of Web C and Web D within a week will be obtained through the two groups of experiments. The main purpose of this experiment is to investigate the effect of time lapse on the halo effect in the subjective evaluation of digital interfaces. Based on the analysis of users' evaluation data of visual aesthetics and usability of websites at different time points, the time points at which the halo effect due to usability and visual aesthetics diminishes are derived.

3 Results

3.1 Visual Aesthetics Data

Table 1 and Table 2 show the subjects' ratings of visual aesthetics for Web A and Web B. The "Items" column indicates the subscales of visual aesthetics. "First to sixth" indicates the number of tests. The data in the corresponding column indicate the mean value of the subitem for that time. The "Mean" column indicates the mean value of all subitems for that time, namely the mean value of visual aesthetics of this order. The "Median" column represents the median value of all subitems for that time, that is the overall level of visual aesthetics for the subitem.

Table 1. Web A Mean scores of Visual aesthetics (1 = unlikely, 7 = likely)

Items	First	Second	Third	Fourth	Fifth	Sixth
Original	4.500	4.583	4.769	4.615	4.583	4.500
Clean	5.700	5.167	5.308	5.462	4.833	5.071
Sophisticated	4.900	4.417	4.615	4.769	4.583	4.571
Clear	5.200	5.500	5.462	5.462	5.000	5.214
Fascinating	4.800	4.000	4.462	4.692	4.417	4.443
Pleasant	4.600	4.833	4.615	5.077	4.667	4.521
Creative	4.100	4.142	4.154	4.308	4.583	4.214
Symmetrical	5.400	6.000	5.769	5.692	5.333	4.898
Use special effects	4.100	5.167	4.862	4.615	4.083	4.357
Aesthetic	5.000	5.333	4.962	5.154	4.667	4.414
Mean	4.830	4.914	4.898	4.985	4.675	4.620
median	4.850	5.000	4.816	4.923	4.625	4.511

Table 2. Web B Mean scores of Visual aesthetics (1 = unlikely, 7 = likely)

Items	First	Second	Third	Fourth	Fifth	Sixth
Original	4.167	4.667	4.231	4.385	4.500	4.346
Clean	5.667	4.917	4.846	5.077	4.917	4.967
Sophisticated	4.500	4.750	4.921	4.846	4.417	4.643
Clear	5.250	5.417	5.167	5.077	4.667	4.429
Fascinating	3.333	3.833	4.277	4.231	4.250	4.241
Pleasant	4.167	4.500	4.531	4.615	4.417	4.462
Creative	3.583	3.750	4.241	4.231	4.250	4.183
Symmetrical	5.333	5.167	5.283	5.308	5.000	4.846
Use special effects	4.250	4.083	4.233	4.231	4.333	4.286
Aesthetic	4.167	4.417	4.628	4.846	4.500	4.684
Mean	4.442	4.550	4.636	4.685	4.525	4.509
median	4.208	4.583	4..579	4.731	4.458	4.446

The difference between the evaluation results of Web A and Web B was defined as the halo effect caused by visual aesthetics. By representing the evaluation results of the visual aesthetics of Web A and Web B in an area map, as shown in Fig. 4. As can be seen from the figure, it can be seen that the visual aesthetics of Web B is better than that of Web A, and both of the visual aesthetics showed a decreasing trend after the fourth test (i.e., the third day of using the website). As well as with the lapse of time, the difference in the visual aesthetic evaluation of the two websites gradually decreases and the two folds tend to be parallel.

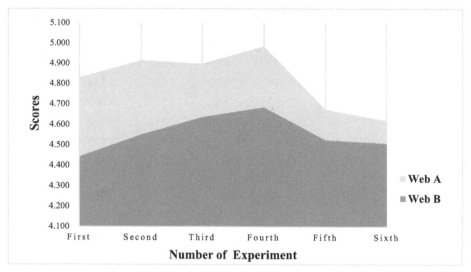

Fig. 4. Visual aesthetic evaluation results of web A and Web B with time lapse

3.2 Usability Data

Table 3 and Table 4 show the usability scores of subjects for Web C and Web D. The "Questions" column indicates the serial numbers of the usability test questions. "First to sixth" indicates the number of times the test was conducted. The data in the corresponding column presents the mean value of the subitem for that time. The "Mean" row indicates the mean value of all subitems for that time, and the mean value of usability for that time. The "Median" row indicates the median value of all subitems for that time, which is the overall level of usability for that time.

Table 3. Web C Mean scores of usability (1 = unlikely, 7 = likely)

Questions	First	Second	Third	Fourth	Fifth	Sixth
1	5.000	5.333	5.417	5.286	5.154	5.154
2	4.900	5.250	5.500	5.071	5.154	5.154
3	5.100	5.083	5.500	5.071	5.385	5.231
4	4.700	5.000	5.500	5.214	5.308	5.231
5	4.900	5.000	5.500	5.214	5.462	5.077
6	4.500	4.750	5.083	5.143	5.385	5.077
7	5.500	5.167	5.583	5.429	5.462	5.923
8	5.000	5.000	5.583	5.071	5.462	5.462
9	5.600	5.250	5.750	5.571	5.462	5.385
10	5.300	5.167	5.500	5.357	5.462	5.154
11	5.600	5.167	5.583	5.571	5.538	5.615
12	5.000	5.333	5.583	5.571	5.615	5.308
Mean	5.092	5.125	5.507	5.297	5.404	5.314
median	5.000	5.167	5.500	5.250	5.462	5.231

Table 4. Web D Mean scores of usability (1 = unlikely, 7 = likely)

Questions	First	Second	Third	Fourth	Fifth	Sixth
1	4.600	3.917	4.583	4.357	4.462	3.769
2	4.500	3.750	4.667	4.357	4.692	4.077
3	4.500	4.250	4.833	4.214	4.308	4.077
4	4.700	3.917	4.750	4.143	4.231	3.923
5	4.600	4.083	4.500	4.071	4.462	4.231
6	4.500	4.167	4.500	4.429	5.000	4.615
7	5.100	4.667	4.833	4.643	4.231	4.385
8	4.600	4.083	4.250	4.500	4.308	4.385
9	4.800	4.083	4.833	4.357	4.308	4.231
10	4.300	3.750	4.583	4.071	5.077	4.231
11	5.200	4.167	4.583	4.857	4.692	4.385
12	5.000	4.083	4.333	4.214	4.538	4.308
Mean	4.700	4.076	4.604	4.351	4.526	4.218
median	4.600	4.083	4.583	4.357	4.462	4.231

The difference between the evaluation results of Web C and Web D was defined as the halo effect caused by usability. By representing the evaluation results of the usability of Web C and Web D in an area map, as shown in Fig. 5. As can be seen from the figure, the usability of Web C is better than that of Web D, and the difference between the two evaluation results is smallest only at the first test (i.e., before using the website). With the time lapse, the usability evaluation results of the two websites showed the same trend and the difference remained stable in the remaining five tests.

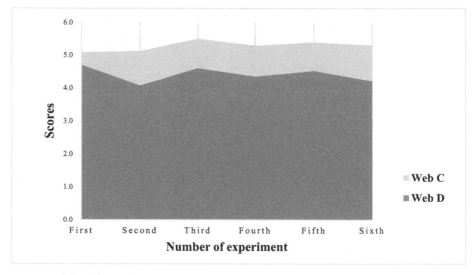

Fig. 5. Usability evaluation results of Web C and Web D with time lapse

3.3 The Halo Effect Data

The size of the difference value (D-value) between the control groups indicates the size of the halo effect. Table 5 shows the D-value in ratings between the control group pages. The Number of Experiment column indicates the number of tests, time lapse. The Visual aesthetics D-value column shows the difference in visual aesthetics ratings between Web A and Web B; the Usability D-value column shows the difference in usability ratings between Web C and Web D.

Table 5. Difference value of Visual aesthetics and Usability

Number of Experiment	Visual aesthetics D-value	Usability D-value
First	0.388	0.392
Second	0.364	1.049
Third	0.262	0.903
Fourth	0.300	0.946
Fifth	0.150	0.878
Sixth	0.111	1.096

The different results of the two control groups were represented by a line graph, as shown in Fig. 6. It can be seen from the figure that the evaluation difference value of visual aesthetics shows a slow decreasing trend over time; the difference value of usability is small in the first test, increases violently in the second test, and tends to stabilize with time lapse.

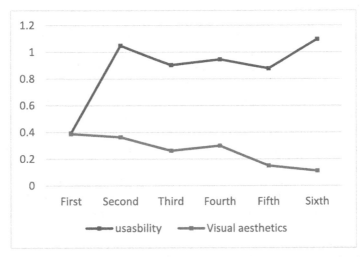

Fig. 6. Variation of the difference between the evaluation results of two groups of web pages with time lapse

4 Discussion

4.1 The Halo Effect Caused by Visual Aesthetics

The evaluation results of visual aesthetics showed that there was a large difference in the first three tests, and the difference results decreased over time and began to level off at a certain point in time. The halo effect caused by visual aesthetics decreases with time lapse. The Cronbach alpha of the visual aesthetics scores was 0.941 > 0.9, so the research data had reliability quality for further analysis. Through ANOVA, it was found that each evaluation subscale of temporal usability showed significant differences for all six tests (p = 0.019, 0.025, 0.011, 0.005, 0.006, 0.029, $\alpha = 0.05$, p < α). Therefore, time lapse has an impact on the halo effect caused by visual aesthetics, which is present before use and gradually decrease over time.

4.2 The Halo Effect Caused by Usability

The evaluation results of the usability showed that the difference value of the first test was small, and it increased sharply at the second test and subsequently stabilized. The Cronbach alpha of the usability evaluation scores was 0.959 > 0.9, thus the reliability quality of the study data was high enough to be used for further analysis. Through ANOVA, it was found that the questions with time lapse of usability questionnaire do not show the significance for all time points (p = 0.508, 1.000, 1.000, 0.999, 0999, 0.999, $\alpha = 0.05$, p > α), the evaluation results show consistency. Thus, the halo effect caused by usability may not change over time.

5   Conclusions

The purpose of this paper is to study the effect of time lapse on the halo effect in the subjective evaluation of digital interfaces. Two sets of web interfaces with different visual aesthetics and different usability were designed by changing the layout and color or function of the website. Time lapse was chosen to be tested at six time points within a week to collect evaluation scores over time. The experiment was conducted entirely through websites. Assessing the dimension of perceived visual aesthetics of websites and Perceived Usefulness and Ease of Use (PUEU) to measure subjective usability were chosen to collect the visual aesthetics and usability data of subjects of the four webs.

As expected, the halo effect caused by visual aesthetics appears before using the websites. Moreover, through analysis we found that the halo effect caused by visual aesthetics declined from the beginning and significantly decreased by the third day. Since the test period was only one week, we did not observe the point at which the halo effect disappeared. In addition, no effect of time on the halo effect caused by usability, and further research is needed.

For the subjective evaluation of digital interfaces, the error caused by the halo effect can be reduced by changing the test time. For the subjective evaluation related to visual beauty, the test time can be set on the third day of use or after. Our research provided an effective references and basis for the design and implementation of the subjective evaluation of digital interfaces.

Appendix 1 Assessing Dimensions of Perceived Visual Aesthetics of Web Sites

1. Original *

○unlikely   ○2   ○3   ○4   ○5   ○6   ○likely

2. Clean *

○unlikely   ○2   ○3   ○4   ○5   ○6   ○likely

3. Sophisticated *

○unlikely   ○2   ○3   ○4   ○5   ○6   ○likely

4. Clear *

○unlikely   ○2   ○3   ○4   ○5   ○6   ○likely

5. Fascinating *

○unlikely   ○2   ○3   ○4   ○5   ○6   ○likely

6. Pleasant *

○unlikely   ○2   ○3   ○4   ○5   ○6   ○likely

7. Creative *

○unlikely   ○2   ○3   ○4   ○5   ○6   ○likely

8. Symmetrical *

○unlikely   ○2   ○3   ○4   ○5   ○6   ○likely

9. Uses special effects *

○unlikely   ○2   ○3   ○4   ○5   ○6   ○likely

10. Aesthetic *

○unlikely   ○2   ○3   ○4   ○5   ○6   ○likely

Appendix 2 Perceived Usefulness and Ease of Use

1. Using the web in my job would enable me to accomplish tasks more quickly *
○unlikely   ○2   ○3   ○4   ○5   ○6   ○likely

2. Using the web would improve my job performance *
○unlikely   ○2   ○3   ○4   ○5   ○6   ○likely

3. Using the web in my job would increase my productivity *
○unlikely   ○2   ○3   ○4   ○5   ○6   ○likely

4. Using the web would enhance my effectiveness on the job *
○unlikely   ○2   ○3   ○4   ○5   ○6   ○likely

5. Using the web would make it easier to do my job *
○unlikely   ○2   ○3   ○4   ○5   ○6   ○likely

6. I would find the web useful in my job *
○unlikely   ○2   ○3   ○4   ○5   ○6   ○likely

7. Learning to operate the web would be easy for me *
○unlikely   ○2   ○3   ○4   ○5   ○6   ○likely

8. I would find it easy to get the web to do what I want it to do *
○unlikely   ○2   ○3   ○4   ○5   ○6   ○likely

9. My interaction with the web would be clear and understandable *
○unlikely   ○2   ○3   ○4   ○5   ○6   ○likely

10. I would find the web to be flexible to interact with *
○unlikely   ○2   ○3   ○4   ○5   ○6   ○likely

11. It would be easy for me to become skillful at using the web *
○unlikely   ○2   ○3   ○4   ○5   ○6   ○likely

12. I would find the web easy to use *
○unlikely   ○2   ○3   ○4   ○5   ○6   ○likely

References

1. Hartson, R., & Pyla, P.S. (2012). Chapter 12 – UX Evaluation Introduction
2. Bingham, & W., V.: Halo, invalid and valid. J. Appl. Psychol. **23**(2), 221–228 (1939)
3. Soper, D.S.: User interface design and the Halo effect: some preliminary evidence. In: Americas Conference on Information Systems (2014)
4. Soper, D.S., Piepkorn, F.: Halo Effect Contamination in Assessments of Web Interface Design. Open J. Inf. Syst. **5**, 1–23 (2018)
5. McDermid, S. (2019). The Halo Effect of Website Experience: Examining The Impact of Aesthetics and Usability Beyond The Page (Doctoral dissertation, Colorado State University)
6. Minge, M. , & M Thüring. (2018). Hedonic and pragmatic halo effects at early stages of user experience. International Journal of Human-Computer Studies, 109
7. Kahneman, D., Krueger, A.B., Schkade, D.A., Schwarz, N., Stone, A.A.: A survey method for characterizing daily life experience: the day reconstruction method. Science **306**(5702), 1776–1780 (2004)
8. Brédart, A., Razavi, D., Robertson, C., Brignone, S., Haes, J.C.J.M.D.: Timing of patient satisfaction assessment: effect on questionnaire acceptability, completeness of data, reliability and variability of scores. Patient Educ. Couns. **46**(2), 131–136 (2002)
9. Lavie, T., Tractinsky, N.: Assessing dimensions of perceived visual aesthetics of web sites. International Journal of Human - Computer Studies **60**(3), 269–298 (2004)
10. Davis, F.D.: Perceived usefulness, perceived ease of use, and user acceptance of information technology. MIS Q. **13**(3), 319–340 (1989)

The Usability Assessment of Meta Quest2 and Recommendations for Improving

Yuanning Han, Yijing Zhang$^{(\boxtimes)}$, and Marcelo M. Soares

Southern University of Science and Technology, Shenzhen 518055, People's Republic of China
12010843@mail.sustech.edu.cn

Abstract. With the development of Virtual Reality (VR) technology in recent years, the VR market is expanding rapidly, from the commercial side to the user side gradually. VR headset devices have begun to popularize. This study focusses on Meta Quest2, a mainstream VR headset device, to analyze its usability by using the Leventhal and Barnes' usability model and conducting qualitative research. Based on the analysis, this study compares Meta Quest2 with another VR headset Pico 4 and gives recommendations for future improvement.

Keywords: Virtual Reality · VR Headset · Usability

1 Introduction

The user group of virtual reality (VR) headsets has expanded due to the development of technology that has made the VR headset more acceptable and accessible. Compared with regular screen display technology, virtual reality technology is more immersive, which gives it an advance to popularize. International Data Corporation has predicted that the sale of VR headsets will continue to expand in the next several years [1]. The VR headset is not only designed for personal entertainment purposes but also for professional use ranging from education to rehabilitation treatment. The usability of VR devices is worth being concerned with, providing users with a better experience and supporting wearing activities for an expanded time. The Meta Quest 2 (formerly Oculus) has become one of the most popular VR headsets on the market by perfectly balancing its comfort with the price. However, it still has many aspects that can be improved.

This research mainly focuses on analyzing the usability of the Meta Quest 2 by conducting user research base on the usability model by Leventhal and Barnes [2]. We also compare the Meta Quest 2 with Pico 4, a new VR headset by ByteDance, to propose directions for future development.

2   Research Method

The research mainly focusses on qualitative methods to analyze the usability of Meta Quest2. The evaluation experiment can be divided into four parts: holistic evaluation, product evaluation, interface evaluation and comparison of similar products.

In the first part, analyze the user interfaces of Meta Quest2, then we made a task analysis and a usability inspection to have a preliminary understanding about the usability of Meta Quest2. In the third part, we focus on the physical product. Based on the understanding, we set a specific task and do the user test. We got the information from observation and posttest interview. In the fourth part, we evaluate the interface by using a property checklist and conducting think-aloud protocols and interview with users. In the last part, we compare Meta Quest2 with another VR headset Pico 4 to compare the usability pros and cons.

2.1   Analyzing the User Interfaces of Meta Quest2

First, we analyzed the relationship between the inputs and outputs of the Meta Quest2 physical interface (VR headset as well as the handle). Then, we analyze the input and output in the activity of setting the guardian - a task that users have to do every time they want to use Meta Quest2. Besides, we analyzed the user interface structure and information hierarchy design of Meta Quest2's main interface. This analysis will give us a basic understanding of the Meta Quest2 interface.

2.2   Holistic Evaluation Using Task Analysis and Usability Inspection

In the early stage of the research, by analyzing the user input and output of Meta Quest2, we compiled the user interface it contains and the corresponding operation methods and corresponding functions. This gave us a general understanding of the design. Based on the information, we selected a common activity of using Meta Quest2, turning on the machine and playing Beat Saber, as our typical task, and performed a task analysis. By combining the demonstrations of three actors, we refined the model for the task analysis and selected some of the key steps to be applied to the second part of the user test afterwards.

Based on our understanding of Meta Quest2, we raised some usability issues with the product through the usability inspection and paid more attention to these parts in the subsequent user testing and interviews.

2.3   Physical Product Evaluation Using User Testing and Interview

In the second part, we focused on the physical interface of Meta Quest2, including the headset and the controllers. Based on the previous analysis of the task, we further refined our task: to turn on the device independently, complete a series of settings (including setting the guardian, setting the volume, etc.), and open Beat Saber game application. Through five user tests, we tried to find common problems with the physical interface of Meta Quest2 and combined this with post-test semi-structured user interviews to dig further into these problems and user thoughts. Questions asked in the interviews included: Are you clear about the physical button placement and functionality? Did you have any problems during the task that affected your efficiency a lot? What made you feel that it was convenient for you to operate? Was there anything good about your experience? Anything that was not good?

2.4 Software Interface Evaluation Using Property Checklist, Think-Aloud Protocols and Interview

In the third section, we focus more on the usability of software interface as seen by the user within the headset screen.

1. Recommendations for GUIs: Based on Sofia Fröjdman's research [3] on the user experience of virtual reality graphical user interface, we refer to several of its recommendations for GUIs: "Place the UI so it is comfortable to interact with; Place visual feedback to selections within the immediate interaction area; Keep information dense areas interaction-free; Use dwell times of various lengths. Avoid using time-limited information; Never force users to interpret information in movement; Use standards and affordances." And we use these recommendations to evaluate the GUI of Meta Quest2.
2. Combine GUI results with checklist: We combined the results of the evaluation with the property checklist from a website called Testmatick to check the usability of the software interface.
3. System evaluation by expert and non-expert users: In addition, we used think-aloud protocols. Invite users who have never used VR to explore Meta Quest2 on their own, and monitoring the user interface in real time through the Meta Quest app sync streaming from our phones. We also invited an experienced user to conduct semi-structured user interviews, allowing us to evaluate usability from different perspectives. The user's frequency of use was about twice a week for six months. In the interview, we focused on the following key questions: What affects your efficiency when you have a specific task or a goal? Do you think there is something that makes your action more convenient, comfortable or effective?

2.5 A Subsection Sample

We compared the Meta Quest2 and Pico 4 by collecting information and comments about their usability on the internet. The experiment was divided into two parts: the physical user interface and the software user interface.

3   Research Result and Analysis

3.1   Result of User Interfaces Analysis

First, we analyzed the user's input and corresponding output on the physical interface of the Meta Quest2 headset (Fig. 1). Next, we analyzed the user's inputs and corresponding outputs on the physical interface of the Meta Quest2's two companion controllers (Fig. 2). Then, we analyzed the user input and the system output in the task of set the guardian (Fig. 3). Finally, we analyzed the hierarchy of the main interface within the Meta Quest2 system (Fig. 4).

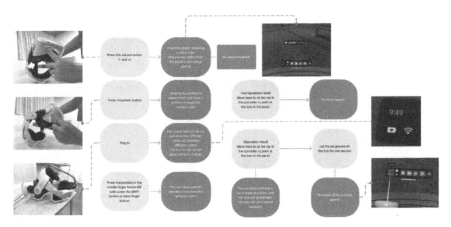

Fig. 1. Result of Meta Quest2 headset user interface analysis

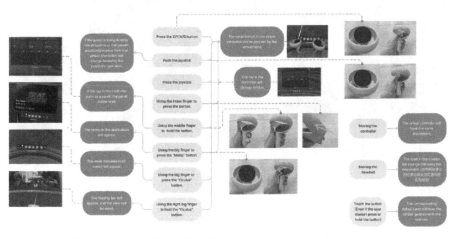

Fig. 2. Result of Meta Quest2 controllers' user interface analysis

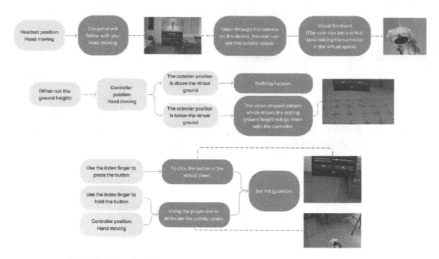

Fig. 3. Result of input and output analysis in set the guardians

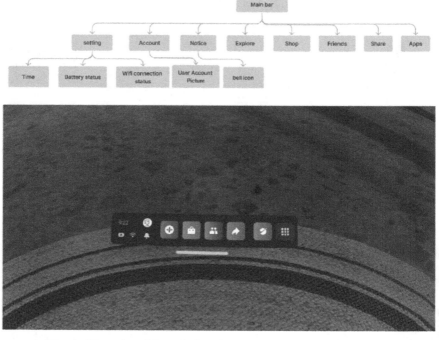

Fig. 4. Hierarchy of the main interface within the Meta Quest2 system.

3.2   Result of Task Analysis and Usability Inspection

The setup of this task starts from turning on the machine and end to turning on Beat Saber (Fig. 5). And from the Usability inspection, we found some issues of Meta Quest2.

These issues include improper center of gravity of the headset, fixed lens prescription, bad heat dissipation system, and lack of adequate using guidelines.

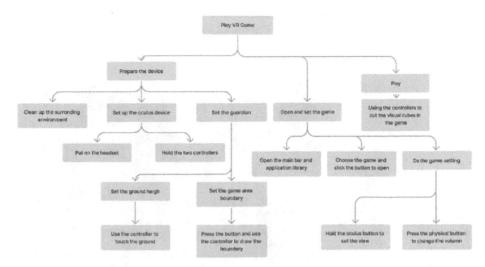

Fig. 5. Result of task analysis

3.3 Result of User Testing and Post-test Interview

In the user test, we recruited five users, all of whom were students of Southern University of Science and Technology with an average age of 20 years old. Because the task was not complicated, and there were not many buttons to use during the process, after proper guidance, all test users were able to complete the task successfully, but there were some typical problems during this process. When adjusting the sound volume, only one person chose to use the physical button to adjust it, while the others chose to adjust the volume in the software, and in the subsequent user interviews, the test users were not clear about the direction of increase or decrease of the physical button volume adjustment. Three of them started using with their left and right hand-controllers reversed.

In user interviews, test users reported that the buttons on the controller were difficult to remember, but there were corresponding virtual controllers in the screen for reference. Some of the test users said that they tried some other buttons, but their functions were not very clear, and there was no response or feedback when they pressed. At the same time, the five testers are all nearsighted, four of them said that wearing glasses to use is very uncomfortable. Three of the five people said they felt that the headset was not tight, and felt the headset had been falling down during the testing.

3.4 Result of Property Checklist, Think-Aloud Protocols and Interview

Using the user interface checklist from testmatick, combined with the seven recommendations from Sofia Fröjdman's study, we evaluated the usability of Meta Quest2's software interface. Overall, its usability is good, with a uniform style and a relatively clear logic. However, there still are several problems. First, some icons and functions do not match well, such as the share button on the main menu corresponding to the screen casting, taking photo and recording functions (Fig. 6). Second, it lacks a quick access function to return to the home page. Third, it lacks some guideline for the novice users while using the software.

Fig. 6. The current user interface of sharing function

We recruited users with no experience using VR to find problems in usability through the think-aloud protocols. During testing, users can independently set up the guardian with Meta Quest2 its own guidelines (Fig. 7). Also, through text and icon information, users were able to basically understand the functionality and logical structure within the system. During this process, users encountered more problems with the physical user interface. When users wanted to click on the icons, they did not know which button in the controller to use. And when users thought they had pressed a button but did not press it completely, they could not get timely feedback and assumed that there was a problem with the device. In addition, because they are not familiar with the way of wearing the headset, it is difficult for them to find the right support position, so the headset often moves in use, affecting the use experience. And after wearing it for about 15min, they will feel uncomfortable with the pressure on the face and need to take it off to rest.

In the user interview, we asked a user with six months of experience using Meta Quest2 through a semi-structured interview to assist in assessing the usability of the software interface. In terms of bad experiences, the user stated that he could not get enough guidance and feedback, and many times he would not know how to operate,

Fig. 7. Setting the guardian

such as exiting the application. And he would not get any feedback when pressing some buttons that did not currently correspond to a function, so he would not be able to know that he had pressed an invalid button. In terms of good experience, he likes the virtual controller is displayed in the screen, which helps him to greatly reduce the difficulty of remembering button positions.

3.5 Result of Comparison

In terms of the physical user interface, the Pico 4 does a better job of making the headset part usable. Excluding the straps and rear structure on the headset, the Meta Quest2 weighs 470 g in the front display area, compared to 295 g for the Pico 4 [4]. The main reason for this is that the Pico 4 separates the battery section and places it behind the head. This shifts the entire product's center of gravity backwards, reducing the potential of headset sliding downward. In terms of the controller, there is little difference in usability between the two, but based on user feedback, the Meta Quest2's controller design is more ergonomic.

In terms of software interface, Meta Quest2 is significantly better than Pico 4. Meta Quest2 has a more uniform color scheme and icon design, and does a relatively better job of guiding novice users. Meta Quest2 also makes the user less information-loaded by darkening the background content when displaying multiple layers of content. However, for the common recording function, Pico 4 adds a physical button to open it, while Meta Quest2 can only be opened in the software interface. And the function is under the sharing function, which is not user-friendly.

4 Discussion

Since the user base of Meta Quest2 in mainland China is small and most of them are short-term users, our usability evaluation studies use qualitative methods, lacking some quantitative studies, and the results are more subjective. If we could combine some quantitative data, we would be able to conduct further analysis and get more valuable conclusions.

At the same time, in our experimental program, we tested the physical user interface and the user interface within the software separately, but in this, many usability issues were affected by the combination of both, which gave us some problems in data collection and recording and result processing, and some overall tests were missing in the global evaluation section to help refine the later separate testing program.

5 Conclusion

Meta Quest2, as one of the leading devices in the mainstream VR market, has a good overall performance in terms of usability, but there are still somethings that need improvement. We make the following recommendations based on the research and analysis.

First, improve the structure of the headset by dispersing the weight of the headset. It can consider adopting a separated structure. In our research, many usability problems, such as fatigue, headset slippage, and uncomfortable wearing are caused by the improper center of gravity of the headset. We can consider separating the headset and shifting some modules such as the battery to other locations to reduce the weight-bearing burden at the front. At the same time, you can consider changing the contour of the force area. It can provide a custom mask, which can be adapted to different facial contours of the population, and also reduce the device leakage of light.

Second, more feedback should be given to users at the right time. Give users more guidelines on common functions and new functions, and consider adding some interactive videos for guiding. At the same time, feedback can be given appropriately to some invalid operations of users, such as pop-up hints when users press buttons that do not contain functions, so that users can realize that his operations are invalid.

In addition, consider changing the location of the function for taking photos and recording. In our research, we found that taking photos and recording is one of the function commonly used by users, but in the current design, this function is within the sharing function, which increases the operation cost for users. It can make it to be a common function that can be opened quickly on the main menu or add physical button to allow users to use this function more easily.

References

1. IDC - AR & VR Headsets Market Share. (n.d.). IDC: The Premier Global Market Intelligence Company. https://www.idc.com/promo/arvr
2. Leventhal, L., Barnes, J.: Usability Engineering: Process, Products and Examples. Pearson Education Inc., New Jersey (2008)

3. Fröjdman, S.: User experience guidelines for design of virtual reality graphical user interfaces controlled by head orientation input (2016)
4. Heaney, D.: Pico 4 Specs & Features vs Quest 2: Weight, Resolution, Field of View, Passthrough & More.UploadVR, 19 October 2022. https://uploadvr.com/pico-4-vs-quest-2-specs-features/

Interacting with an Algorithm: The Influence of Experience and Individual Differences

Krista Harris[1]([⊠]), Gene Alarcon[2], Sarah Jessup[3], Jacob Noblick[1], and Scott Meyers[1]

[1] General Dynamics Information Technology, Dayton, OH 45431, USA
Krista.Harris@gdit.com
[2] Air Force Research Laboratory, Wright-Patterson AFB, Dayton, OH 45433, USA
[3] Consortium of Research Universities, Washington, DC 20036, USA

Abstract. Prior research has defined algorithm aversion as the decision to not rely on an algorithm and prefer human forecasts instead [9]. Algorithm aversion is a growing and necessary area of study, especially because algorithms often outperform human forecasters. Although research in this area has increased, the phenomenon is still prevalent and impactful. The purpose of the current study is to utilize a forecasting task to examine factors influencing algorithm aversion, specifically individual difference variables and experience with the algorithm. Our results demonstrated desirability of control and perfect automation schemas influenced both algorithm use and reliance intentions. Furthermore, experience with the algorithm, such as previous interactions and prior accuracy perceptions explain variance beyond the personality variables. These findings suggest that the relationship between algorithm aversion and personality is a fruitful area of research and experience with the algorithm is an important component of algorithm interactions. Finally, we discuss limitations of the current study along with practical implications of our findings.

Keywords: Algorithm Aversion · User Interaction · Trust in Automation

1 Introduction

With the continued increase in research surrounding machine learning and its uses in decision-making, human computer interaction is inevitable and a prominent area of interest. Algorithms coupled with machine learning have been found to outperform human decision-making in a wide variety of forecasting domains such as medical diagnosing [8], employee performance [16], and academic performance [9]. Grove and colleagues [14] meta-analyzed 136 studies and found that algorithms outperformed human forecasters by 10% on average. Based on the results of the research in this field, one might assume that because algorithms often outperform humans, people would choose to use algorithms in their decision-making. However, that is often not the case. Coined by Dietvorst and colleagues [9], algorithm aversion is the tendency to prefer human forecasts over forecasts produced by algorithms. The purpose of the current study was to utilize a forecasting task to predict college GPA and examine how reliance behaviors and reliance intentions are influenced by individual differences and model experience.

© The Author(s), under exclusive license to Springer Nature Switzerland AG 2023
A. Marcus et al. (Eds.): HCII 2023, LNCS 14032, pp. 194–207, 2023.
https://doi.org/10.1007/978-3-031-35702-2_14

1.1 Algorithm Aversion Within Forecasting Tasks

The Merriam-Webster Dictionary [31] defines algorithm as "a step-by-step procedure for solving a problem or accomplishing some end," and states that it is often used when referring to machines or computers. In a recent review article on algorithm aversion, Mahmud et al. [27] stated that the addition of machine learning and artificial intelligence (AI) has enabled algorithms to continually learn and find trends to make better decisions. The authors go on to say in some instances these algorithms make decisions independently, although more often, they are used as a decision aid and can be chosen to be relied upon or ignored. Dietvorst et al. [9] showed that people tend to choose human forecasters over algorithms, demonstrating algorithm aversion, even though algorithms are often superior decision-makers. Interestingly, people were found to be more tolerant of mistakes made by humans compared to algorithms, even when the mistakes made by the algorithm were smaller than the mistakes made by the human [9]. Some researchers suggest that people are more likely to choose to do the task themselves, compared to using the algorithm because of overconfidence in their own abilities [12] along with an underestimation of the ability of the algorithm [7, 24]. However, Filiz and colleagues [12] found that over time and given feedback, participants were more likely to recognize the limitations of human forecasting as compared to the algorithm's forecasting, and that the learning process significantly reduced algorithm aversion. This finding conflicts with Dietvorst and colleagues' [9] finding demonstrating that participants would continue choosing to not use the algorithm even after seeing it outperform human forecasts. Therefore, more research is needed to examine how experience with an algorithm can impact algorithm aversion.

Although there have been strides taken to examine the factors that influence algorithm aversion, and even reduce it, the phenomenon is still prevalent and impactful. The current study hopes to help expand the literature and shed light on factors that influence algorithm aversion and use. The first goal of the present research is to add to the support that shows that algorithms outperform humans in a forecasting task.

H1: The model will perform significantly better than the participants.

1.2 Algorithm Aversion and Trust

When people are deciding whether to use a human or a statistical algorithm for a forecasting task, they will typically rely on the human forecaster (i.e., algorithm aversion) [9]. Dietvorst et al. [10] extended this definition stating, "people are reluctant to use superior algorithms that they know to be imperfect..." (p. 1156), emphasizing participant knowledge and experience regarding the algorithm. This suggests that after seeing a forecasting algorithm make a mistake, people are less likely to continue to interact with the algorithm.

This extended definition aligns with Lee and See's [18] model of trust in automation, in which trust is an iterative process that changes based on interaction experience (as well as other factors), which forms a feedback loop that informs subsequent interactions. The authors define trust as "the attitude that an agent will help achieve an individual's goals in a situation characterized by uncertainty and vulnerability" (p. 54). Beliefs shape one's trust, which then influences reliance intentions (i.e., the willingness to rely on another), which in turn influence reliance behaviors (i.e., the observable act of reliance). Lee and See also highlight that individual differences such as personality are important for initial interactions, because they influence a trustor's trust before other information is known about the trustee. Therefore, the examination of the trust process with algorithm aversion, and the variables that impact it, is an important and necessary area of study.

Individual Differences. Research has shown that individual differences can be strongly related to algorithm aversion. Prior to experience with the algorithm, theory suggests that people high on the perfect automation schema (PAS) will have high expectations for automation performance [32]. Then, after interacting with the automation and seeing it err, they will more likely abandon it. The former describes the facet of the PAS, high expectations (HE), whereas the latter describes all-or-none thinking (AN). Therefore, it makes sense that those who score higher in HE would be more likely to expect the model performance to be high and rely on it initially. This aligns with previous research regarding trust and the influence of personality traits on initial interactions [18].

A major finding in the algorithm aversion literature is the impact of confidence on algorithm use. Those who are more knowledgeable [23] and more confident in their abilities [36] are more likely to use their own decisions and have less confidence in the algorithm. This aligns with Lee and Moray [18], who found that those with high confidence in themselves, along with low trust in automation, were more likely to rely on their own abilities rather than the automation. In a similar vein of research, Lewandowsky et al. [20] indicated that participants trusted in automation when they were low in self-confidence and could not rely on their own judgments. Logg et al. [23] demonstrated that experts in a given area, or those who have increased knowledge, were less likely to rely on the algorithm compared to those who were less knowledgeable. However, those higher in online confidence, or algorithm confidence, had higher levels of confidence in the algorithm and therefore used it more often [34]. Therefore, the amount of confidence an individual has in themselves, and their knowledge of the domain, impacts their algorithm reliance. Specifically, those who are more confident and knowledgeable in the task are more likely to use their own forecasting estimates, while those lower in confidence and knowledge would be more likely to use the algorithm's estimates.

Another variable found to be significant in algorithm use was desire for control. Those high in the desire to control are described as assertive, decisive, and active, whereas those low in the desire to control are seen as nonassertive, passive, and may prefer to let others make decisions for them [6]. Based on this description, it is intuitive to believe that those with a higher desirability of control would be more likely to use their own forecasting estimates, and those lower would be more likely to adhere to the algorithm. Prior research has demonstrated this effect [11, 35]. In fact, Dzindolet and colleagues [11] suggested that individuals want to keep control in their decision-making and therefore make their own decisions instead of relying on automation. Other research has shown that those who are higher in internal locus or control, or have the belief that they have control over their own lives, were more algorithm averse [35]. Based on these above reviewed variables, we propose that reliance on the model and intentions to rely on the model will be predicted by said variables

H2: Initial reliance behaviors will be positively related to high expectations and negatively related to confidence, knowledge, and desirability of control.

H3 Initial reliance intentions will be positively related to high expectations and negatively related to confidence, knowledge, and desirability of control.

Experience with the Algorithm. Participant forecasts tend to be less successful than the model's forecasts, but participants often tend to still use their own forecasts over an algorithm. However, research has found that with continued use with an algorithm, in as little as 10 rounds many subjects will realize that their forecasts are suboptimal [12]. In their study, they found that after 5 rounds of forecasting, about 27% of the decisions were for the algorithm, but after 10 rounds that jumped to almost 45% for the algorithm. Other researchers have suggested that training people on how to use algorithms or even just having hands-on experience with them can lessen aversion [34]. This aligns with the results demonstrating that a lack of familiarity may be a contributing factor to aversion [21].

Other studies have shown that algorithm performance plays an important role with participant interaction. Researchers have shown that those who are higher in perfect automation schema perceptions (people who have high expectations for automation performance and low forgiveness if they fail) [13, 33] and see the algorithm make a mistake, are less likely to continue using the algorithm [26]. Additionally, research has shown that as algorithm performance deteriorates, the algorithm is penalized to a greater degree than human advisors [5]. Others have found that algorithm aversion is lessened when participants see that it outperforms the human [4] or when the participant understands how the algorithm performs [7]. Based on the literature review of familiarity and experience, we propose that reliance behaviors and intentions are predicted by experience beyond the previously hypothesized individual difference variables.

H4: Reliance behaviors for the second set of rounds (rounds 6–10) will be predicted by previous experience variables over and above individual difference variables.

H5: Reliance for the second set of rounds (rounds 6–10) will be predicted by previous experience variables over and above individual difference variables.

1.3 Current Study

Previous studies have explored the construct of algorithm aversion and factors that influence aversion; however, the results are often mixed and contradictory. For example, Dietvorst and colleagues [9] found that with increased experience with an algorithm, after seeing an algorithm err, participants are less likely to use the algorithm. However, other research has shown that with increased use, participants are more likely to use an algorithm because they realize their own forecasts are suboptimal [12]. Therefore, additional research on algorithm aversion, and the influence of variables such as initial high expectations and experience with the algorithm is needed. In particular, the current study focuses on aspects of the user such as schemas, prior knowledge, and preference for control. The purpose of the current study was to explore how reliance behaviors and reliance intentions are influenced by individual differences and model experience.

2 Method

2.1 Participants

Participants were recruited online (N = 321) via Amazon Mechanical Turk (MTurk). Eligible participants were required to be at least 18 years of age or older and reside in the United States. Of the participants, 55.5% identified as male, 76.6% were Caucasian/white, and the average age was 39 years old (SD = 11.15). To facilitate data collection, we utilized the platform CloudResearch [22], which interfaces with MTurk. We restricted availability of the task only to MTurk workers who had completed a minimum of 100 human intelligence tasks (HITs) and had a minimum approval rate of 95% for their past HITs. This research was approved by the Air Force Research Laboratory Intuitional Review Board. Each participant received $6.00 as payment, plus whatever bonus money they were able to earn throughout the task (see below).

2.2 Task

The current research consisted of a subset of data from a larger data collection. The task utilized in the current study was an adapted version developed by Dietvorst and colleagues [9]. Participants were asked to roleplay as a college academic advisor predicting future academic performance of first-year college students, based on the following six parameters: 1) first year GPA, 2) age, 3) study time per week, 4) free time per week, 5) gender, and 6) involvement in extracurricular activities. The study consisted of 15 practice rounds, in which no money was at stake. In the task sessions, participants as well as a statistical model predicted 10 students' second year GPA. The model's forecasts were predetermined and did not vary between participants in each condition. The total number of accurate estimates made in each of the two task sessions (either by the participant or the model) was used to calculate the bonus amount. Participants could earn a bonus of $1.00 for every round that was correctly predicted during the two task sessions, which each had five rounds, for a total bonus of $10.00.

2.3 Measures

Desirability of Control. Participants desire for control was assessed with the 20-item Desirability of Control (DoC) scale [6]. The response scale ranged from 1 (Strongly disagree) to 7 (Strongly agree), and four items were reverse scored. The scale had adequate reliability ($\alpha = .84$).

Pre-knowledge GPA. To assess participants' knowledge of GPA prior to the experimental task, they were asked to rate how knowledgeable they felt about college academic performance, which was a single-item measure, on a scale from 1 (Not at all knowledgeable) to 5 (Very knowledgeable).

Perfect Automation Schema. Participants responded to 8 items from the updated Perfect Automation Schema (uPAS) scale [13]. Responses were rated on a 1 (Strongly disagree) to 5 (Strongly agree) response scale. This measure includes two subscales: high expectations (HE) and all-or-none thinking (AN), with four items measuring each sub facet. The scale had adequate reliabilities (α high expectations $= .84$; α all-or-none thinking $= .87$).

Reliance Intentions. We used Lyons and Guznov's [25] 10-item scale to assess participant's willingness to rely on the statistical model. Participants rated items on a 1 (Strongly disagree) to 7 (Strongly agree) response scale, with an option for "No Opinion/Not Applicable." Two items were reverse scored. The scale had adequate reliability (α Pre-Task $= .86$; α Post Rounds 1–5 $= .93$).

Task Confidence. To access participants' confidence in the task prior to the experimental task, they were asked a single item to rate how confident they felt in performing the task, which was on a scale from 1 (Not at all confident) to 5 (Very confident).

Perceived Accuracy in Self and Model. Participants rated their perceived accuracy towards their estimates and the model's estimates with the item, "How much confidence do you have in [your/the statistical model's] estimates for the [first/last] 5 estimates?" on a 1 (None) to 5 (A lot) response scale modified from Dietvorst et al. [9].

Reliance Behaviors. Reliance behaviors were measured by asking participants if they would like to use the model's estimates or their own estimates to determine their bonus amounts, later referred to as "Use" and "Don't Use," respectively.

2.4 Procedure

Participants were randomly assigned to one of 12 conditions, which was a factorial combination of 3 (model experience) × 2 (framing) × 2 (risk). As the factors are not the focus of the current paper, they were not explored in the analyses of the current paper. After providing consent, participants were asked to respond to items from the DoC and uPAS scales, as well as the Pre-knowledge item. Participants were provided with a brief explanation about statistical models in forecasting, their role in the task, and the parameters both they and the model would use to make their forecasts. Afterwards, participants were quizzed on this information, which served as a knowledge check. Participants completed 15 practice rounds of forecasting, which varied in model experience based on condition. Afterwards, participants completed the first reliance intentions measure. Next, participants rated their self-confidence in performing the task (task confidence) and made their selection for whether to use their own or the model's estimations (reliance behavior) for determining their bonus compensation during the first five rounds (session 1). Participants provided estimates for all rounds regardless of which option they selected. After each forecast, participants were asked which prediction they thought was more accurate: their own or the one made by the model. After session 1, they were asked to estimate the number of rounds they thought they accurately predicted as well as the number of rounds they thought the model correctly predicted (within 20% of the actual value). Then participants were asked to rate their perceived accuracy in themselves and the model's forecasts. Next, their or the model's performance was displayed, which was dependent on their choice to determine bonus amounts. For the final five rounds (session 2), which were conducted in the same manner as the first five, participants decided whether to utilize their own predictions or those of the model. Following the completion of all forecasts, the participants again completed the reliance intentions items before completing a demographic questionnaire. The study concluded with a display of their bonus amount earned and participants were compensated through MTurk.

3 Results

First, t-tests were run to determine the differences between human and model performance. The results indicated the model performed significantly better than the participants in both the first five and last five rounds ($t(320) = -20.39, p < .01$ for rounds 1–5; $t(320) = -9.49, p < .01$ for rounds 6–10). We were also interested to see if reliance behaviors increased with continued forecasting. We found that after the practice rounds, for rounds 1–5, 62% of the of participants relied on the model. Then after, for rounds 6–10, 69% of the decisions were for the model.

Next, we conducted a multiple logistic regression and found that the first five reliance behaviors were significantly predicted by the individual difference variables of reliance intentions (RI), task-confidence, and high expectations (HE). We did not find significance for knowledge in the task (pre-knowledge), DoC, or all-or-none thinking (AN.) Overall, the regression for rounds 1–5 accounted for 20% of the variance. See Table 1 for the full results.

Additionally, when running the same individual difference variables for the second set of rounds, only RI and DoC were significant. Examining experience with the model (via previous interaction, perceived accuracy in the model after rounds 1–5, and perceived accuracy in self after rounds 1–5) in step 2 for rounds 6–10 reliance behaviors, rounds 1–5 experience was found to predict over and above the individual difference variables ($\chi^2 = 35.20; p < .01$), accounting for 10% of the variance. See Table 2 for the full results.

Table 1. Logistic Regression Predicting Reliance Behaviors at Rounds 1–5.

Predictors	b	OR
Reliance Intentions	-1.44**	0.38
Desirability of Control	0.10	1.00
High Expectations	-0.58*	0.90
All-or-None Thinking	-0.37	0.95
Pre-knowledge	0.40	1.19
Task Confidence	0.75**	1.49

Note. $N = 321$. *$p < .05$; **$p < .01$. Use model estimates = 0. Use self-estimates = 1. LR test = 49.68**; Nagelkerke's $R^2 = 0.20$.

Table 2. Hierarchical Logistic Regression Predicting Reliance Behaviors at Rounds 6–10.

Predictors	b	OR	LR test	Nag R^2	ΔR^2
Step 1			133.92**	0.48	
Reliance Intentions	-3.12**	0.11			
Desirability of Control	-0.78*	0.97			
High Expectations	0.61	1.12			
All-or-None Thinking	-0.34	0.95			
Pre-knowledge	0.58	1.28			
Task Confidence	0.48	1.29			
Step 2			169.12**	0.58	0.10**
Reliance Intentions	-2.84**	0.13			
Desirability of Control	-0.93*	0.97			
High Expectations	0.79	1.15			
All-or-None Thinking	-0.20	0.97			
Pre-knowledge	0.28	1.13			
Task Confidence	-0.12	0.93			
Accuracy in the model	0.02	1.01			
Accuracy in the self	0.96*	1.78			
Previous RB	1.64**	5.00			

*Note. N = 321. *p < .05; **p < .01* Previous RB = Reliance Behavior for first 5 rounds. LR test = Likelihood Ratio Test. Nag R^2 = Nagelkerke's R^2. Use model estimates = 0; Use self-estimates = 1.

We also performed multiple linear regressions along with hierarchical multiple linear regressions to examine predictors of reliance intentions (RI) at rounds 1–5 and 6–10. For rounds 1–5 RI, the individual difference variables DoC, HE, and task-confidence were significant and explained 29% of the variance (Table 3). As with reliance behaviors, knowledge in the task and AN were not significant at any point.

Examining those same predictors for rounds 6–10 RI only HE and task-confidence were significant and accounted for 14% of the variance in RI. Adding in rounds 1–5 model experience at step 2 showed that previous RI, perceived accuracy in model, and perceived accuracy in self predicted RI for rounds 6–10 over and above the individual difference variables ($\Delta R^2 = 0.34$, $p < .01$). See Table 4 for detailed results.

Table 3. Linear Regression Analysis Predicting Reliance Intentions for Rounds 1–5.

Predictors	b	β
Desirability of Control	-0.01*	-0.14
High Expectations	0.12**	0.43
All-or-None Thinking	-0.00	-0.01
Pre-knowledge	0.01	0.02
Task Confidence	0.20**	0.23

*Note. N = 321. *p < .05; **p < .01. R^2 = 0.29.*

Table 4. Hierarchical Linear Regression Analyses Predicting Reliance Intentions for Rounds 6–10.

Predictors	b	β	R^2	ΔR^2
Step 1			0.14**	
Desirability of Control	-0.00	-0.07		
High Expectations	0.11**	0.33		
All-or-None Thinking	-0.0	-0.02		
Pre-knowledge	-0.03	-0.04		
Task Confidence	0.11*	0.12		
Step 2			0.48**	0.34**
Desirability of Control	0.00	0.03		
High Expectations	0.00	0.01		
All-or-None Thinking	-0.01	-0.03		
Pre-knowledge	-0.03	-0.04		
Task Confidence	-0.07	-0.07		
Accuracy in the model	0.33**	0.26		
Accuracy in the self	-0.14*	-0.12		
Previous RI	0.66**	0.58		

*Note. N = 321. *p < .05; **p < .01. Previous RI = Initial Reliance Intentions.*

Along with the above results, we also performed exploratory analyses examining how individual difference variables and experience predicted a change in reliance behaviors between rounds. Therefore, we examined the predictors of a change in behavior from rounds 1–5 to rounds 6–10 (1 = switched from self to model estimates, 0 = no change, -1 = switched from model to self estimates) by subjecting data to a combination of hierarchical multiple regressions and discriminant analyses. Hierarchical multiple regressions found that accuracy variables (perceived accuracy in self: $\beta = 0.07$, $p = .02$; perceived accuracy in model: $\beta = -0.06$, $p = .05$) predicted change in reliance behaviors over and above the individual difference variables of HE, AN, DoC, and task confidence ($\Delta R^2 = 0.02$, $p = .02$). Next, we conducted discriminant analyses to predict membership to the aforementioned groups. The variables of interest significantly predicted the change in reliance behaviors (Wilks' $\lambda = 0.88$, $F(2, 318) = 2.85$, $p < .01$). The classification results found that the selected variables correctly predicted change in reliance behaviors 78.2% of the time.

4 Discussion

The purpose of this study was to examine factors influencing algorithm aversion, specifically the individual differences that influence algorithm aversion. We found desirability of control and perfect automation schemas influenced both use and reliance intentions. Additionally, task confidence also predicted use in our models. Prior knowledge of the domain was not related to any criterion in the current study. Results indicate the relationship of algorithm aversion and individual differences are more complex than previously thought.

4.1 Performance

The predetermined forecasts of the algorithm were more accurate than participants in both task rounds, which is consistent with the literature regarding better model performance in a variety of tasks, including forecasting [9, 12] The continued evidence for models outperforming humans is important for algorithm aversion research because individuals often continue to choose their own suboptimal estimates [9]. Indeed, a key finding from the trust in automation literature is that performance of the automated system is the most salient aspect of trust development [15, 17, 28]. Therefore, it is imperative that developers ensure that the performance of the algorithm is transparent to its users so that trust can be better calibrated during interactions, but more importantly is the idea that the user actually perceives these differences and uses the system.

4.2 Desirability of Control

Desirability of control (DoC) was a significant predictor of reliance behaviors for rounds 6–10 indicating individuals higher in DoC were less likely to use the algorithm's decisions. Similarly, DoC was shown to have a negative relationship with initial reliance intentions for the first five rounds. Individuals that have a high DoC will be less likely to use the algorithm no matter the accuracy because they have a high need for control. This may be linked to several different mechanisms such as being less willing to trust systems or wanting to do the task to avoid boredom. Either way, DoC predicted significant variance in both reliance intentions and behaviors in the current study.

4.3 Perfect Automation Schema

The PAS is composed of the facets of high expectations (HE) and all or none thinking. All or none thinking (AN) was not significant for any of our outcome variables in the current study, but HE was related to both reliance behaviors and reliance intentions. These findings align with prior research on PAS, which demonstrated the importance of HE in relation to automation trust, but not AN [25]. The facet of HE was an important predictor for initial reliance intentions and reliance behaviors at both decision points. However, HE was not a significant predictor of decision to use the algorithm for rounds 6–10. A potential reason for this could be that HE is anticipatory, in which people have high expectations for automation performance [33]. Therefore, those higher in HE would be more likely to expect the model performance to be high and use it initially. However, after interacting with the model, the participants would have more information to rely on and use to make subsequent decisions. Individual difference variables such as personality traits are predictive of trust intentions and behaviors during initial interactions [19]. However, as the trustor gains more information about the trustee, the foci of trust shifts from the trustor to the trustee [1]. Participants with HE who chose the model and saw it err could use this information to adapt behaviors as indicated by previous studies [9, 26].

In addition, HE no longer significantly predicted reliance intentions with the addition of model experience nor was HE a significant predictor in criteria in rounds 6–10. It stands to reason that HE is not a prominent predictor after initial rounds, even though it was found significant for round two intentions. This can be shown by its lack of significance after adding in more important predictors and in predictions of later decision processes (i.e., rounds 6–10). This aligns with previous research regarding trust and the influence of personality traits on initial interactions [19] along with the theory underpinning the PAS and how HE is related to propensity to trust technology [33], which is also related to initial perceptions of trust but not later perceptions [32, 33].

4.4 Experience

Previous Experience. The importance of participants' previous experience with the model regarding trust outcomes was highlighted in this study. Participants who exhibited initial reliance behaviors were more likely to exhibit subsequent reliance behaviors. The same held true for reliance intentions. These findings highlight the reciprocal nature of these trust variables over time and suggest the presence of additional feedback loops in the trust model where variables other than outcomes of risk-taking influence subsequent trust variables [29]. This is also supported by information processing approaches that suggest trustors will use previous experience with the trustee (i.e., model) to base their trustworthiness perceptions and reliance intentions [2, 29, 30].

Perceived Accuracy in Self and the Model. Other significant experience variables were perceived accuracy in the self and perceived accuracy in the model. These variables predicted trust outcomes in different ways depending on the referent. Participants that perceived their decisions as more accurate were less likely to use report reliance intentions in the model. Interestingly, participants that had higher perceived self accuracy were more likely to use the model for both rounds 1–5 and rounds 6–10. It may be participants felt more confidence in being able to accurately assess the model due to their ability to perform the task. In other words, if the model deviated from performing well, the participants may have felt able to change their decision later because they can accurately per-form the task and thus accurately monitor the decisions of the algorithm. The findings for reliance intentions are unsurprising as past research has emphasized self-accuracy and shown its mediating effect of trust on reliance [18, 19]. Lee & Moray [18] found similar results where operators with high self-confidence and low trust in the system tended to rely more on manual controls.

Taken together, participant experience including initial reliance intentions, reliance behaviors, and participant accuracy perceptions (self/model) largely explain differences in trust outcomes. As an example, previous reliance intentions and both types of partic-ipant accuracy accounted for slightly under half of the variance in reliance intentions. The current study demonstrates the importance of experience with the model in pre-dicting continued trust and use of the model. This suggests that even though individual difference variables are important when initially interacting with a model, the choices someone makes and how they perceive the performance of both themselves and the model are more important regarding subsequent interactions. As stated previously, this aligns with previous research examining the iterative trust process and the feedback loops that inform future behaviors [2, 29, 30].

4.5 Implications

Our study has implications regarding algorithm use for users and those implementing algorithms in their work. First, our study gives insight into individual difference variables that influence algorithm use or disuse. Our findings suggest the importance of high expectations (a facet of the perfect automation schema) and desirability of control such that algorithm aversion may not be just an aversion to algorithms but rather a want for control and management of expectations. Additionally, we note that several other aspects of the user played a role in the decision process such as previous experience and perceived self-accuracy. This illustrates that algorithm aversion may be more complex than previously thought. We note the complexity trying to determine GPA scores from the data in the current environment which may not be the easiest task as presented by Dietvorst et al. [9]. Indeed, their target samples were generally undergraduate students, which may not have understood regression predictions especially in the design format presented in their study and ours.

4.6 Limitations and Future Directions

This study is not without limitations. The first limitation deals with data collection and the data used for creating the algorithm. Although MTurk allows access to a wide range of potential participants, there are known issues with using online participants, including an increased chance of misunderstanding instructions, participant distractedness, and increased levels of stress from hassles [3]. The use of bots are also possible. This study took measures to curb the likelihood of bots, but the techniques used to evade countermeasures are always developing. As for the data used, the GPA data used in our task was not GPA data from real students but simulated data. Using real GPA data could increase the effects and generalizability of our results because we can be more confident in the scope of the GPA scores along with participant knowledge of how the scores were calculated.

An additional limitation to this study was that participants were not shown the performance results of the alternate agent (model or themselves). For example, participants who chose to use their own estimates weren't told how often the model was correct (and vice versa), and thus a comparison between model-use and disuse could not be made. Filiz et al. [12] found that providing feedback to participants after each round of forecasts led to decreases in algorithm aversion. Not allowing participants to see either the model or their own performance may have influenced results. However, we note that participants did receive feedback in the current study after five rounds, thus being a half-way in between [9, 12].

4.7 Conclusion

This study sought to examine the factors that influence algorithm aversion and extend Dietvorst and colleagues' [9] research by examining individual difference variables and model experience as potential predictors of reliance behaviors. Additionally, we examined the effect of model experience on self-reported reliance intentions (i.e., trust) of the model, which was not measured by Dievorst and colleagues. Overall, our findings suggest that the relationship between personality and algorithm aversion is more complex than previously thought and that experience with the model is an important component of this process. We demonstrated that not only did individual difference variables predict algorithm trust and use, but that subsequent trust behaviors are informed by previous task interactions, as posited by prior trust research [2, 29, 30].

Distribution Statement A. Approved for public release: RHABWCleared 2/21/23; RH-23-124083.

References

1. Alarcon, G.M., Capiola, A., Pfahler, M.D.: The role of human personality on trust in human-robot interaction. In: Nam, C.S., Lyons, J.B. (eds.) Trust in Human-Robot Interaction, pp. 159–178 (2021)
2. Alarcon, G.M., Lyons, J.B., Christenson, J.C., Bowers, M.A., Klosterman, S.L., Capiola, A.: The role of propensity to trust and the five factor model across the trust process. J. Res. Pers. **75**, 69–82 (2018)
3. Al-Salom, P., Miller, C.J.: The problem with online data collection: predicting invalid responding with undergraduate samples. Curr. Psychol. **38**, 1258–1264 (2019)
4. Bigman, Y.E., Gray, K.: People are averse to machines making moral decisions. Cognition **181**, 21–34 (2018)
5. Boegart, E., Schecter, A., Watson, R.T.: Humans rely more on algorithms than social influence as a task becomes more difficult. Sci. Rep. **11**(8028) (2021)
6. Burger, J.M., Cooper, H.M.: The desirability of control. Motiv. Emot. **3**, 381–393 (1979)
7. Castelo, N., Bos, M.W., Lehmann, D.R.: Task-dependent algorithm aversion. Am. Mark. Assoc. **56**(5), 809–825 (2019)
8. Dawes, R., Faust, D., Meehl, P.: Clinical versus actuarial judgement. Science **243**(4899), 1688–1694 (1989)
9. Dietvorst, B.J., Simmons, J.P., Massey, C.: Algorithm aversion: people erroneously avoid algorithms after seeing them err. J. Exp. Psychol. Gen. **144**(1), 114–126 (2015)
10. Dietvorst, B.J., Simmons, J.P., Massey, C.: Overcoming algorithm aversion: people will use imperfect algorithms if they can (even slightly) modify them. Manag. Sci. **64**(3), 1155–1170 (2018)
11. Dzindolet, M.T., Pierce, L.G., Beck, H.P., Dawe, L.A.: The perceived utility of human and automated aids in a visual detection task. Hum. Factors **44**(1), 79–94 (2002)
12. Filiz, I., Judek, J.R., Lorenz, M., Spiwoks, M.: Reducing algorithm aversion through experience. J. Behav. Exp. Financ. **31** (2021)
13. Gibson, A.M., Capiola, A., Alarcon, G.M., Lee, M.A., Jessup, S.A., Hamdan, I.A.: Construction and validation of an updated perfect automation schema (uPAS) scale. Theor. Issues Ergon. Sci. 1–26 (2022)
14. Grove, W.M., Zald, D.H., Lebow, B.S., Snitz, B.E., Nelson, C.: Clinical versus mechanical prediction: a meta-analysis. Psychol. Assess. **12**(1), 19–30 (2000)
15. Hancock, P.A., Billings, D.R., Schaefer, K.E., Chen, J.Y.C., de Visser, E.J., Parasuraman, R.: A meta-analysis of factors affecting trust in human-robot interaction. Hum. Factors **53**(5), 517–527 (2011)
16. Highhouse, S.: Stubborn reliance on intuition and subjectivity in employee selection. Ind. Organ. Psychol. **1**, 333–342 (2008)
17. Hoff, K.A., Bashir, M.: Trust in automation: integrating empirical evidence on factors that influence trust. Hum. Factors **57**(3), 407–434 (2015)

18. Lee, J.D., Moray, N.: Trust, self-confidence, and operators' adaption to automation. Int. J. Hum. Comput. Stud. **40**(1), 153–184 (1994)
19. Lee, J.D., See, K.A.: Trust in automation: designing for appropriate reliance. Hum. Factors **46**(1), 50–80 (2004)
20. Lewandowsky, S., Mundy, M., Tan, G.P.A.: The dynamics of trust: comparing humans to automation. J. Exp. Psychol. Appl. **6**(2), 104–123 (2000)
21. Lim, J.S., O'Connor, M.: Judgemental forecasting with interactive forecasting support systems. Decis. Support Syst. **16**(4), 339–357 (1996)
22. Litman, L., Robinson, J., Abberbock, T.: TurkPrime.com: a versatile crowdsourcing data acquisition platform for the behavioral sciences. Behav. Res. Methods **49**(2), 433–442 (2016). https://doi.org/10.3758/s13428-016-0727-z
23. Logg, J.M., Minson, J.A., Moore, D.A.: Algorithm appreciation: people prefer algorithmic to human judgement. Organ. Behav. Hum. Decis. Process. **151**, 90–103 (2019)
24. Longoni, C., Bonezzi, A., Morewedge, C.K.: Resistance to medical artificial intelligence. J. Consum. Res. **46**, 629–650 (2019)
25. Lyons, J.B., Guznov, S.Y.: Individual differences in human-machine trust: a multi-study look at the perfect automation schema. Theor. Issues Ergon. Sci. **20**(4), 440–458 (2018)
26. Madhavan, P., Wiegmann, D.A.: Effects of information source, pedigree, and reliability on operator interaction with decision support systems. Hum. Factors **49**(5), 773–785 (2007)
27. Mahmud, H., Islam, A.N., Ahmed, S.I., Smolander, K.: What influences algorithmic decision-making? A systematic literature review on algorithm aversion. Technol. Forecast. Soc. Chang. **175**, 1–26 (2022)
28. Malle, B.F., Ullman, D.: A multidimensional conception and measure of human-robot trust. In: Nam, C.S., Lyons, J.B. (eds.) Trust in Human-Robot Interaction, pp. 3–25 (2021)
29. Mayer, R.C., Davis, J.H., Schoorman, F.D.: An integrative model of organizational trust. Acad. Manag. Rev. **20**(3), 709–734 (1995)
30. McKnight, D.H., Cummings, L.L., Chervany, N.L.: Initial trust formation in new organizational relationships. Acad. Manag. Rev. **23**(3), 473–490 (1998)
31. Merriam-Webster. Algorithm. https://www.merriam-webster.com/dictionary/algorithm. Accessed 25 Jan 2023
32. Merritt, S.M., Ilgen, D.R.: Not all trust is created equal: dispositional and history-based trust in human-automation interactions. Hum. Factors **50**(2), 194–210 (2008)
33. Merritt, S.M., Unnerstall, J.L., Lee, D., Huber, K.: Measuring individual differences in the perfect automation schema. Hum. Factors **57**(5), 740–753 (2015)
34. Önkal, D., Gönül, M.S., De Baets, S.: Trusting Forecasts. Futures Foresight Sci. **1**, e19 (2019)
35. Shaffer, M.A., Kraimer, M.L., Chen, Y.P., Bolino, M.C.: Choices, challenges, and career consequences of global work experiences: a review and future agenda. J. Manag. **38**(4), 1282–1327 (2012)
36. Sieck, W.R., Arkes, H.R.: The recalcitrance of overconfidence and its contribution to decision aid neglect. J. Behav. Decis. Mak. **18**, 29–53 (2005)

Usability Study on the User Interface Design of Ride-hailing Applications

Yi-Hung Hsu(✉) and Chien-Hsiung Chen

Department of Design, National Taiwan University of Science and Technology,
No.43, Keelung Rd., Sec. 4, Da'an Dist, Taipei City 106335, Taiwan
cchen@mail.ntust.edu.tw

Abstract. It is increasingly common for modern people to use Ride-Hailing services. The Ride-Hailing platform needs to design applications (Apps) that meet users' needs in a limited display area. Providing an excellent interactive experience is the goal of the Ride-Hailing service platform's continuous efforts. This study selected three representative ride-hailing service platforms, i.e., Uber, Lyft, and Gojek, and designed five operational tasks according to the commonly used functions of users, namely setting the destination, modifying personnel information, setting payment methods, finding past ride records, and adjusting setting parameters. This study adopted MODAO to make the experiment model, and the experimental equipment is iPhone X. This study invited 30 participants for the experiment via convenience sampling method. Except for finding the past ride records, the operation tasks' results significantly differed from other tasks. There was no significant difference in the System Usability Scale (SUS) results. Uber is 66.75, Lyft is 60.25, and Gojek is 62.75. Combining post-experiment interviews, observation methods, and quantitative results, the following results are drawn:

(1) If the Ride-Hailing Apps page area is over the device display zone, this page has to add "Signifiers" for users to help them understand all page information.
(2) Pages and information settings unrelated to Ride-Hailing Apps can be integrated into a single modular tab or a module tab with the collapsible panel.
(3) The Ride-Hailing Apps should supply switch models without advertisement. In this model, users can directly interact with the Ride-Hailing Apps and receive no bother.
(4) Frequently used functions should be set on the main page or sub-page. The extended advertising page and food delivery service page can be used as an App or an independent interface so that users can quickly identify the page and service items they are using, avoid operational errors, and generate misunderstandings.
(5) Select an avatar or personnel display zone that can modify or update photos and personnel information in the personnel setting option. The Apps do not need to set the next layer for this operation.

Keywords: Interface usability · System usability scale (SUS) · Usability evaluation · Interaction design · Ride-Hailing application

© The Author(s), under exclusive license to Springer Nature Switzerland AG 2023
A. Marcus et al. (Eds.): HCII 2023, LNCS 14032, pp. 208–216, 2023.
https://doi.org/10.1007/978-3-031-35702-2_15

1   Introduction

Due to the rise of the sharing economy, online Ride-Hailing services, such as Uber and Lyft, have become more popular, challenging the traditional taxi-hailing business model by matching taxi drivers and passengers [5]. Uber and Lyft are international Ride-Hailing application platforms. Gojek was launched in 2015. In Southeast Asian countries, people generally use Grab and Gojek. Ride-Hailing applications can help solve traffic problems like traffic congestion and exhaust emissions [7]. How to design Ride-Hailing services by User-Centered Design (UCD) for an interaction designer is a challenge. UCD is a design process that ensures the users' needs are met so that a product can be used by users to achieve their goals and be able to provide them with an enjoyable experience [8]. Usability assessment is an essential step in the user-centered design process of any interactive system, be it software, a website, or any information and communication technology or service. The goal of usability evaluation is to evaluate the effectiveness of the system (i.e., the degree to which the performance of the system meets its design tasks) and efficiency (i.e., how many resources, such as time or energy, are required to use the system to complete the tasks of the system design) [9]. There exist four perspectives affecting interface usability: (1) usability can be measured from product ergonomics; (2) User psychology perspectives; (3) User and product interactions; (4) Usability must be tailored to the characteristics of the users according to whom [2]. When designing a Ride-Hailing App, the designer and researcher need to understand human capabilities and limitations. In particular, cognitive and perceptual abilities are relevant to design. Humans have severe limitations in information processing and other tasks such as decision-making searching, and the fields of cognitive psychology and economics provide theoretical and practical context for these problems [12]. The Ride-Hailing service application is a very convenient tool. Most of the user interface is a single main screen, which provides functional links through different images or buttons. A single user interface cannot integrate all functions. It must be designed according to user habits and mental models. Provide an appropriate number and hierarchy of links on the page, and the interaction between the user and the interface relies on visual search and navigation. Visual search is a common human-computer interaction task. The visual search process is to receive and input external information. The form of pre-entered information affects the efficiency of the user's access to page information and interaction with the interface, influenced by factors such as page layout, font size, color combinations, graphic icons, and display modes [10]. Based on the literature, Ride-Hailing is becoming more and more commonly used around the world. Some Ride-Hailing applications provide exclusive functions and services in response to localization. Ride-Hailing applications need to take into account users' visual cues, cognitive load, and other factors. Therefore, we should conduct usability research on the current Ride-Hailing applications to find out the parts that need to be improved. This study conducts usability research on representative Ride-Hailing applications and discusses with and find out what needs to be corrected for reference by relevant practitioners.

2   Related Work

This study used MODAO to make the simulated interfaces of three Ride-Hailing applications and design five operation tasks: setting the destination, modifying personnel information, setting payment methods, finding past ride records, and adjusting setting parameters. For each Ride-Hailing application sample, the user must pre-set the login information, so the steps of login in and filling in the data are omitted. Since some samples do not provide the Chinese language option, all the experimental interfaces are set to English. The three Ride-Hailing samples are shown in Table 1.

Table 1. The three Ride-Hailing samples for the experiment.

Sample image			
APP type	Sample 1: Uber	Sample 2: Lyft	Sample 3: Gojek

3   Experimental Tasks

The setting positions of different user interfaces for each operation task are explained as follows:

Task1: Setting the destination.

Uber: Enter the destination in the search window on the main page or swipe the page to use past ride records to click on the destination directly. (first layer)

Lyft: Search for destinations in the main page's search window at the bottom left or use records to set destinations. (first layer)

Gojek: Users can search for destinations on the search window at the top of the main page, or users can click on the car type and then click on the frequently used destinations based on past ride records. (first or second layer)

   Task2: Modifying personnel information.

Uber: Click the account option at the bottom right of the main page, and the personal information page will appear. (second layer)

Lyft: A second layer of the function bar will appear on the main page of the function symbol after clicking. The upper part is the personal data area; click the photo area to upload photos, click view profile, and then click "Edit" on the upper right to update personal information. (fourth layer)

Gojek: On the upper right corner of the main page, click on the personal avatar, and then click the pen tool next to the personal information to modify the personal information. (third layer)

Task3: Setting payment methods.

Uber: On the personal information page, there is a wallet icon. Users can click to set. (second layer)

Lyft: On the main page of the function symbol, after clicking, the second-level function column will appear. There is a "payment" option in the function area. (third layer)

Gojek: On the upper right corner of the main page, click on the user profile picture, and then there will be "payment methods" in the tool below. User can set the payment method. (third layer)

Task4: Finding past ride records.

Uber: Users can use the usage records displayed at the bottom of the main page or click the "Activity" icon at the bottom of the page to display the records. (first or second layer)

Lyft: "Recent record" icon is located at the bottom of the main page. Users also can click the function symbol of the main page. There is "Ride history" in the functional area. (third layer)

Gojek: On the main screen, click on the "Orders" icon on the lower toolbar to display the "history" page. (second layer)

Task5: Adjusting setting parameters.

Uber: Click on the personal information page on the main page, and there will be a setting icon on the personal information page. (third layer)

Lyft: On the main page of the function symbol, after clicking, the second layer of the function bar will appear. There will be a "settings" option under the function area. (third layer)

Gojek: On the upper right corner of the main page, click on the personal profile picture, and there will be a "Manage account" option in the tool below. Users can lick to modify. (third layer)

The five operational tasks and purposes are shown in Table 2.

Table 2. Five operation tasks and their proposes

Task	Content	Proposes
1	Setting the destination	The Ride-Hailing applications' most polar function
2	Modifying personnel information	The registrant's information
3	Setting payment methods	The Ride-Hailing applications accept payment using several platforms
4	Finding past ride records	Sometimes users will rely on consumption history records to check whether the distance and charges are reasonable
5	Adjusting setting parameters	Users can adjust the functions according to their needs

4 Methods

A usability experiment is usually based on the following steps. (1) The definition of the test objectives, (2) the qualification and recruitment of tests participants, (3) the selection of tasks participants will have to realize, (4) the creation and description of the task scenarios, (5) the choice of the measures that will be made as well as the way data will be recorded, (6) the preparation of the test materials and of the test environment (the usability laboratory), (7) the choice of the tester and the design of the test protocol perse (instructions, design protocol, etc.) (8) the design and/or the selection of satisfaction questionnaires, the data analysis procedures, (9) finally the presentation and communication of the test results [2]. According to the literature mentioned above, the experimental procedure is as follows: A total of 30 participants ($M = 19.7$; $SD = 2.54$), 8 males and 22 females, aged 18 to 29, were selected by convenience sampling. The experimental equipment was an iPhone X 5.8". The procedure was described as follows: before the experiment started, the participants were informed of the experimental procedure, and then the experiment started. The participants followed the instructions to perform five operational tasks, and the time taken to complete each task was recorded during the experiment. Interviews were conducted with some of the participants, and interactions between the participants and the interface were observed during the experiment.

5 Results and Discussions

5.1 Results

The Results of Task Completion Time. In the results section pertinent to task completion time, four of the five tasks were found to be significant by the one-way ANOVA, namely Task 1, Task 2, Task 3, and Task 5. That is, the one-way ANOVA result of Task 1 revealed a significant difference amount the three Apps ($F = 7.26$, $P = 0.003^* < 0.05$). Among them, participants task performance of Uber ($M = 11.86$, $SD = 4.20$) is better than Lyft ($M = 27.11$; $SD = 14.92$) and Gojek ($M = 23.51$; $SD = 4.71$). In addition, the one-way ANOVA result of Task 2 illustrated significant difference amount the three Apps (F = 5.05, P = 0.014* < 0.05). More specifically, participants' task performance of Uber (M = 11.91, SD = 11.29) and Gojek (M = 13.31; SD = 19.07) was better than Lyft (M = 37.35, SD = 26.90). For Task 3, the results were significantly different (F = 4.92, P = 0.0015* < 0.05). Participants' task performance of Uber (M = 11.21, SD = 13.49) and Lyft (M = 5.26, SD = 2.58) was better than Gojek (M = 25.41; SD = 21.99). There was no significant difference among the results of Task 4 (F = 0.479, P = 0.624 > 0.05). In Task 5, the results were significantly different (F = 9.275, P = 0.001* < 0.05). Participants' task performance of Uber (M = 4.20, SD = 1.60) and Lyft (M = 11.14, SD = 9.17) better than Gojek (M = 19.18; SD = 9.76). The results generated from the one-way ANOVA of all five tasks are shown in Table 3.

Table 3. The one-way ANOVA results of all five tasks (in second)

	Uber M(SD)	Lyft M(SD)	Gojek M(SD)	F	P	Post Hoc (LSD)
Task1	11.86 (4.20)	27.11 (14.92)	23.51 (4.71)	7.26	0.003*	Lyft = Gojek > Uber
Task2	11.91 (11.29)	37.35 (26.90)	13.31 (19.07)	5.05	0.014*	Lyft > Uber = Gojek
Task3	11.21 (13.49)	5.26 (2.58)	25.41 (21.99)	4.92	0.015*	Gojek > Uber = Lyft
Task4	8.86 (2.80)	32.65 (88.69)	20.62 (41.49)	0.479	0.624	
Task5	4.20 (1.60)	11.14 (9.17)	19.18 (9.76)	9.275	0.001*	Gojek > Uber = Lyft

* Significantly different at $\alpha = 0.05$ level (* P < 0.05)

The System Usability Scale (SUS) Result. The SUS is a fast and low-cost scale with a total of ten questions using the 5-point Likert scale. There are five positive questions and five negative questions, and the score ranges from 0 to 100 [6]. The SUS items have been developed according to the three usability criteria defined by ISO 9241–11: (1) The ability of users to complete tasks using the system, and the quality of the output of those tasks (i.e., effectiveness), (2) the level of resource consumed in performing tasks (i.e., efficiency), and (3) the users' subjective reactions using the system (i.e., satisfaction) [4].

In the SUS, there was no significant difference in the results of the one-way ANOVA, with mean values of 66.75 for Uber, 60.25 for Lyft, and 62.75 for Gojek. In past research, the SUS score of the Gojek application for novice users is below 64, and the score from the expert users is higher and above average is 69 [11]. The participants viewed the usability of all three Apps at the marginal level [1]. Descriptive statistics and One-way ANOVA of SUS are shown in Table4. The SUS scale results of the three experimental samples are shown in Fig. 1

Table 4. Descriptive statistics and One-way ANOVA of SUS.

	Uber M(SD)	Lyft M(SD)	Gojek M(SD)	F	P
SUS	66.75	60.25	62.75	0.346	0.711
	(14.19)	(21.58)	(16.30)		

* Significantly different at $\alpha = 0.05$ level (* P < 0.05).

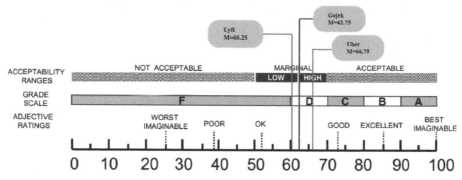

Fig. 1. The 3 sample's SUS results with acceptability ranges.

5.2 Discussions

5.3 The Pros and Cons of Interface Analysis

In terms of Uber's Interface, participants often comment positively on Uber's user interface design, and the functional classification is precise. However, the information on the payment setting page is, at most, the display range of a single page on the mobile phone, and the participant needs to swipe the page to the bottom unless the participant is exploring or needs to operate the App. In addition to looking for a particular function, it will not deliberately slide the page to the bottom. In addition, Uber will install food delivery options in a part of the operation process and user interface to bury the food delivery service on the ride page. It needs to be solved for users of the Ride-Hailing function. An independent function page should be provided to avoid the need to close or switch to the Ride-Hailing process when the Ride-Hailing service is needed quickly. Compared with previous studies, samples compared Pathao, Obhai, and Uber. Young and middle-aged people had better use of efficiency and error management for Uber. Women also had higher satisfaction with Uber, but language lack of options is the App's most significant problem [3]. When setting the destination, it provides a variety of setting methods, such as text input, past ride records, and location on the map. It can provide all forms of the destination setting for users on the same interface, which is better among all samples.

Lyft's Interface: The participants feel that the page is simple, the operation is intuitive, and the car-calling function can be completed on the bottom's main screen of the toolbar icon. Fees and other functions are all concentrated in the toolbar in the upper left corner, and users can search for them when the user needs them, which is friendly to the participants. However, the function of modifying personal information could be better designed. The method of changing personal data is to separate the part of the unique avatar from the amount of editing personal text data. When editing personal data, it needs to select the fourth level before it can find it. This design is not suitable for the participants. If it causes trouble, the participant should distinguish between the avatar and text areas. Click the avatar area to upload and modify the avatar photo, and click the text area to directly display the personal information, which can be changed instantly without adding a layer and designing an "Edit" text modification link.

Gojek's Interface: It is a ubiquitous Ride-Hailing application in Indonesia. In past research, the SUS test result for novices was 64.38, and that for experienced users was 69.68, which is close to the result of 62.75. This study adopted no user experience as the experimental participants [11]. Provide up to six services on the main screen, which is too much information. In addition to Ride-Hailing, the car types provide unique locomotive options and other functions such as luggage storage. However, more options are likely to be needed for users who only use the Ride-Hailing function. In past studies, local users were used as participants. There are no such problems, and it is a relatively bad experience for the participants who have no experience in using it. The chat function is set in the work bar at the bottom of the main screen to facilitate the interaction between the hired driver and the passengers. In the payment function, participants can set it under the personal information area and display "Payment Methods" in the text list menu. The participant needs to explore many times to find this function. The "$" symbol or an image is a better design than a text display. Gojet also provides many methods. The GoPay coins launched by Gojek appear at the top, and on the page's bottom are the cash payment options. It should be the primary promotion of its digital payment platform. In the "Adjusting setting parameters" section, the participants preferred the graphic design and were less fond of the text list menu.

Common issues for all user interfaces: Many participants mentioned that in the past user experience, Ride-Hailing Apps needed to provide more multi-language conversion, especially when using Ride-Hailing software in different countries. It was often impossible to locate the destination due to input method problems and display the user's language version.

6 Conclusion

1. If the Ride-Hailing Apps page area is over the device display zone, this page has to add "Signifiers" [6] for users to help them understand all page information.
2. Pages and information settings unrelated to Ride-Hailing Apps can be integrated into a single modular tab or a module tab with the collapsible panel.
3. The Ride-Hailing Apps should supply switch models without advertisement. In this model, users can directly interact with the Ride-Hailing Apps and receive no bother.
4. Frequently used functions should be set on the main page or sub-page. The extended advertising page and food delivery service page can be used as an App or an independent user interface so that users can quickly identify the page and service items they are using, avoid operational errors, and generate misunderstandings.

5. Select an avatar or personnel display zone that can modify or update photos and personnel information on the personnel setting option. The Apps do not need to set the next layer for this operation.

References

1. Bangor, A., Kortum, P., Miller, J.: Determining what individual SUS scores mean: adding an adjective rating scale. J. Usability Stud. **4**(3), 114–123 (2009)
2. Bastien, Christian, J.M.: Usability testing: a review of some methodological and technical aspects of the method. Int J. Med. Inform. **79**(4), e18–e23 (2010)
3. Bevan, N., Macleod, M.: Usability measurement in context. Behav. Inform. Technol. **13**(1–2), 132–145 (1994)
4. Borsci, S., Federici, S., Lauriola, M.: On the dimensionality of the system usability scale: a test of alternative measurement models. Cogn. Process. **10**(3), 193–197 (2009)
5. Jiang, S., Chen, L.,Mislove, A., Wilson, C.: Ridesharing competition and accessibility: Evidence from Uber, Lyft, and Taxi. Proceedings of the 2018 World Wide Web Conference, pp. 863–872 (2018)
6. Brooke, J.: SUS: A "quick and dirty' usability. Usability evaluation in industry, p. 189 (1996)
7. Inostroza, R., Rusu, C., Roncagliolo, S., Rusu, V., Collazos, C.A.: Developing SMASH: a set of SMArtphone's uSability Heuristics. Comput. Stand. Interfaces **43**, 40–52 (2016)
8. International Standards Organisation: ISO 13407: Human-centred design processes for interactive systems. ISO, Geneva (1999)
9. Iso, W. 9241–11. Ergonomic requirements for office work with visual display terminals (VDTs). The international organization for standardization 45.9 (1998)
10. Tseng, F.-Y., et al.: Effects of display modality on critical battlefield e-map search performance, Behaviour & Information Technology, vol. 32.9, pp. 888–901 (2013)
11. Sara, C.D., Nurwulan, N.R.: Comparative Usability Evaluation of Novice and Expert Gojek Users. In: 6th International Conference on Sustainable Information Engineering and Technology 2021, pp. 16–22 (2021)
12. Schneiderman, Ben., Designing the user interface: strategies for effective human-computer. Interaction, vol. 3 (1998)

The False Utopia of VR Gaming: The Mind and Body Under VR Video Games

Shuo Liu[✉]

Beijing City University, No. 269 Bei Si Huan Zhong Lu, Hai Dian District, Beijing, China
liushuo20182018@163.com

Abstract. The proliferation of virtual reality (VR) video games has revolutionised the gaming industry and is expected to have at least 20% growth in the next couple of years. The success of VR games urged different game developer to focus on the development of VR technology and thus lead to a rapid advancement of the technology. While the technology of VR is being improved and become widely distributed, it is high time to look at how the players would be affected by immersing in VR games. The essay argues that VR games affect not only the body but also the mind of players, lead to a rise in new ethical issues that requires an alternative way to look VR video games, and eventually affect the relationship between players and the reality. This essay will investigate the psychological and physical impacts from long term immersion of VR games, then the essay will discuss how such impacts change the perception of players' themselves and the real world that leads to a series of ethical issues. This essay will concluded by say that no form of media are entirely free of agenda, neither is VR which seemingly blurred the sense of human being and create an illusion of utopia.

Keywords: VR Games · Psychological · Ethical Issues

1 Introduction

When PlayStation, one of the largest game developer in the market, launched Project Morpheus[1] and started to invest on developing virtual reality (VR) technology in gaming, the media were uncertain, let alone underwhelmed, about the future of VR in entertainment. Kain (2014) wrote an article on Forbes, and expressed his concerns on the development of VR in gaming: "Perhaps anti-social isn't even the right word—unsocial, detached, isolated…VR encourages a new kind of selfishness." But when the first Playstation VR headset was released in 2016 and created a huge success in the market, the concerns raised by critics are soon forgotten as PlayStation VR has revolutionised the whole gaming experience for the players and the market of gaming industry. As in

---

[1] The codename "Project Morpheus" was later renamed to "PlayStation VR" in 2015. Such change indicates the shift in how the developer perceived VR technology: Morpheus is a name derived from the Greek myth and represent a god who controls sleep and dreams. By replacing dreams with reality, PlayStation seemed to assure the players that they are experiencing an alternative reality instead of a false one.

© The Author(s), under exclusive license to Springer Nature Switzerland AG 2023
A. Marcus et al. (Eds.): HCII 2023, LNCS 14032, pp. 217–226, 2023.
https://doi.org/10.1007/978-3-031-35702-2_16

March 2019, more than 4.2 million PlayStation VR was sold globally. And according to "Virtual Reality Gaming Market: Global Industry Trends, Share, Size, Growth, Opportunity and Forecast 2018–2023", the global VR gaming market has gained a value of US$8.2 Billion in 2017, and is expected to have a 26% growth by 2023 (2018). Looking at the thrive of VR games in recent years, it is high time for us to look at the problems created by the proliferation of VR games, as well as its impact on the thriving consumer society that play a huge role in controlling the public. This essay choses to focus on the ethical issues brought by VR games, and in what ways VR technology can influence the relationship between the players and outside world. It is argued that VR games affect not only the body but also the mind of players, lead to a rise in new ethical issues that requires the a new way of understanding VR video games, and eventually affect the relationship between players and the reality.

To address this issue, this essay will first briefly locate the term VR historically and explain its application in the gaming industry. The first part will provide a definition of VR and offer a glimpse on the VR game industry. Then the essay will then move on to the bodily impacts from long immersion to VR games, and then move on to the ethical issues that question the moral value of VR games. Gamer's experience, in terms of psychologically and physically being, would be closely analysed to illustrate the ethical problems of VR games. Finally, the conclusion of the essay will direct the readers to rethink the relationship between players and game developers. This research is aimed to emphasise that no form of media are entirely free of agenda, neither is VR which seemingly blurred the sense of human being and create an illusion of utopia.

2   Definition of Virtual Reality

Although the use of VR in entertainment may seem to popularised only in recent years, the concept of VR appeared long beforehand. The concept of virtual reality first appeared in 1960, when Ivan Sutherland describe the technology as a window for users to perceive, respond and act realistically in the virtual world (Sutherland 1965). Sutherland create the first Helmet-Mounted Display, one may call it the early prototype of today's VR glasses, and tried to connect man to machine by projecting two images through the helmet instead of one stereoscopic view (Bouvier 2009). It is only until 1980s, when computer science become democratised and become part of everyone's daily life, that the development of VR had a breakthrough.

To cope with the development of VR technology, scholars attempted to define the complicated concept of VR throughout the 1990s. According to Ellis, virtual reality is a "interactive, virtual image displays enhanced by special processing and by non-visual display modalities, such as auditory and haptic, to convince users that they are immersed in a synthetic space" (1991). Gignate, who shared a similar view with Ellis, focused on the factor of immersion. Gignate defined VR as "The illusion of participation in a synthetic environment rather than external observation of such an environment. VR relies on a 3D, stereoscopic headtracker displays, hand/body tracking and binaural sound. VR is an immersive, multi-sensory experience" (1993). In Burdea et Coiffet's view, VR does not only concerns with immersion or interactive, but also the imagination of people, in which contribute to the level of immersion. Although academia still have not agreed on a single definition on the term VR, they shared similar views and agreed on the importance of immersion, stimulation of the real world and interaction with the virtual environment. Combining the definitions mentioned above, this essay will define VR as a virtual environment where people can interact with the computer by using an avatar to create a sense of immersion.

3 Application of VR in Gaming and VR Games Studies

In today's society, VR technology has became something that can be applied in various field, namely architectural design (Song et al. 2017), education (Englund et al. 2016), medical purposes (Gallagher et al. 2005), psychological treatment (Botella et al. 2017) and of course gaming. It is through gaming that VR technology started to proliferate in the public and infiltrated people's ordinary lives. VR in video games usually works with a special head-mounted display (HMD)[2], a headset that shows visual effect right in front of the players, and project a "computer-simulated reality", where the player immerses into a fictive 3D world (Roettl and Terlutter 2018). The virtual world projected by the HMD are far more realistic than that of 2D or 3D technologies, as players can interact with and in the game and is sheltered from the outside world once they put on the headset (Roettl and Terlutter 2018). Such high level of immersion gives the players a sense of false reality when they are given the chance to experience the game as if they are actually in the setting of the game.

Despite of the commercial and financial success of VR games, academies started to express concerns over the problems aroused by the VR games. For example, scholars including Kade (2015) and Adam et al. (2018) suggested the game developer should be regulated through a code of ethical condition in order to protect the well-being and privacy of the players. Although these research offers a seemingly clear set of rules of what the game developer should or should not do, these research overlooked the relationship between the ethical problems and the psychological and physical influences on the player. The bodily impacts play a huge role in explaining and addressing the ethical issue created by the VR games. In this case, the next part of this essay will firstly address actual bodily changes from these VR games, and then move on to discuss the ethical issues behind this changes.

4 Long-Term Immersion: The Psychological and Physical Impacts

According to James Paul Gee (2003), the "real identity", the identity of the gamer in the real world, and the "virtual identity", the identity in the game, are mediated by "projective identity", the interface between the real and virtual. Our "projective identity" is important, as it helps us to perceive the world differently while we are playing or not playing the video games. And yet, VR technology intentionally blurred our "projective identity" and made the video game "transparent". "Transparent" is a term suggested by Bolter and Grusin (2003) that used to describe how the media become ideological

---

[2] PlayStation VR, Google Cardboard, Oculus Rift, and Samsung Gear VR are examples of head-mounted display.

by encouraging people to forget that the media (in this case, the game) are standing between the player and reality. The more transparent the game is, the less the players will be aware of the fact that they are being mediated. As such, the transparency of VR games usually leads to a series of issues that affect mental and physical state of the players. The following parts will therefore focus on how the player's mind and body would react after they expose themselves to VR games for a considerable long period of time.

Long term exposure to VR games can leads to serious psychological problems that increase the vulnerability of the player when they are apprehending the real world. It is common sense that long exposure to ordinary video games can lead to addiction. But the effects brought by VR games are far worse than just addiction. As VR games aimed at stimulating an illusion of one can control the virtual self through the machine, VR technology must imitate the movement of the players and have the virtual character move in a similarly that the player does. As such, the brain is tricked and the players would though they have a full control in the virtual world but in reality all of their movement are being mediated by technology. According to Metzinger and Hildt (2013), long term immersion to VR games can cause "manipulation of agency" (2013). Psychologically speaking, players usually feel detached to the real world after they finish playing the VR game. When writing about his experience in playing Tilt Brush, a VR game developed by Google in 2016, van Schneider captured the essence of what the players would feel returning to the reality after playing the game:

"What stays is a strange feeling of sadness and disappointment when participating in the real world, usually on the same day... The sky seems less colorful and it just feels like I'm missing the 'magic' (for the lack of a better word). ... I feel deeply disturbed and often end up just sitting there, staring at a wall" (van Schneider 2016).

What van Schneider describe is less of a psychological disorder, but more of a sense of detachment. Another example of feeling detached to reality is written by Lee Vermeulen, a video game developer who tried Valve's SteamVR system as a part of his daily job:

"I understood that the demo was over, but it was [as] if a lower level part of my mind couldn't exactly be sure. It gave me a very weird existential dread of my entire situation, and the only way I could get rid of that feeling was to walk around or touch things around me" (Vermeulen 2014).

Both Vermeulen and van Schneider described symptoms that are similar to Derealisation Disorder, a dissociative disorder that a person external world as unreal. As Madary and Metzinger suggested in their report on influences of VR Games (2016), Derealisation Disorder is caused by the damaged neural mechanisms after long period of manipulating our sense of agency. The neural mechanisms are responsible for creating the feeling of reality, and assisting the body to have immediate contact with the world (Madary and Metzinger 2016). While it is uncertain whether Vermeulen or van Schneider actually suffer from the disorder, their experiences shed light on the psychological consequences of long term immersion to VR games. Both Vermeulen and van Schneider spend more only an hour on the VR games, and yet the consequences of longer exposure could be a lot more serious to younger players who have less self control than that of an adult. The longer the time spent on VR, the more our neural mechanisms will be damaged.

In this case, what might feel as the sense of detachment could develop into a serious psychological disorder if one immerse into VR games for longer than he or she should.

Losing one's sense of agency in a long period of time could also harm the physical body and leads to various kind of disorientation. On one hand, some VR game players would experience slight discomfort including motion sickness or headache during the start of the game. On the other hand, it is also common among players that they experience discomfort after playing the games, and have problems adapting to the reality afterwards. A player named jkendt1989 was seeking help from Oculus Community Forum, a place where players exchange information on various VR games developed by Oculus, and explained how he or she felt the hands are being disconnect from the body after playing the VR game:

"When I look at my hands, I feel like they're not really my hands, like they're the Rift hands. Even when looking at my monitor I get the exact feeling like I'm looking my monitor in Big Screen. Like it's in VR and it's in 3d almost. The weirdest disconnect is with my hands. Even typing this I feel like my arms aren't there and it's just my hands moving." ("I feel like I'm in VR when I'm not…", 2017).

One player named Zenbane later on commented on the same post saying that they have similar experience with the eyes losing focus when he or she are waking u on the next day:

"On at least 3 different occasions when waking up from a full nights sleep… before my eyes would open, it was as if they were trying to find their focus; similar to a camera lens moving in/out until it finds the clear sweet spot. My eyes were shut but the physical feeling was generating from my actual eyeballs." ("I feel like I'm in VR when I'm not…", 2017).

What both players are experiencing is actually a common problem among the VR games player called Depersonalisation, a disorder that makes a person experience a sense of unreality of their own body (Madary and Metzinger 2016). Such disorder happened when a person's neural mechanisms are being damaged, and consequently leads to disconnection between the physical body to the real world. It is not that the players believe what happened in the VR games are real, but their bodies are being tricked to adapted to virtual environment so effectively that they forget how to perceive the reality normally.

Some players would argued that such sense of detachment is only temporary, as Oculus players often used the term "Virgin Rifting" to describe those who are still experiencing sickness or sense of detachment after playing the game (I feel like I'm in VR when I'm not…, 2017). However, the psychological and physical changes after experiencing VR games should not be overlooked, as they are actually a signal of changing perceptions of one's self and the world. VR games are capable of changing the way players relate themselves to the world and people around them, in which might causes the player to behave abnormally in various social occasion. This is where the ethics of VR games should be questioned. As such, the following part will focus on how the VR games can manipulate our mentality in which changes the players' perception of self and the world.

5 Ethical Concerns: Changing Perceptions of Self and World

The application of VR technologies in gaming changes the way people think, behave, and communicate, in which affects how people relate themselves to the world. It no longer concerns about being detached from the society but a change in mind that affect our daily lives. This concept is studied by McLuhan, who developed an elaborated and in-depth study in how media mediated almost every aspects of our lives in Understanding Media: The Extension of Man (1965). McLuhan believes that every extensions of ourselves, including different form of media that facilitate different actions, can affect "the whole psychic and social complex" (1965). In this sense, VR technologies in gaming also possess the ability to influence the players' perception of self and outside world, in ways that are different from traditional video games that concerns about console games, PC games or even arcade games. The following parts of the essay will focus on the ethical questions of how VR games manipulate the players' mind, behaviour and their ways to identify themselves.

To begin with, the plasticity of human mind makes the players vulnerable to the virtual reality presented by the VR games. According to modern experimental psychology, human mind is considered as plastic, something that can be shaped and reshaped depending on the change of context (Madary and Metzinger 2016). As human are trained to adapted to new environment through changing one's behaviour, the continuous shaping of our mind could cause a series of behavioural change if one is exposed to a distinctively new environment for a long period of time. The way that humans are sensitive to context are proven by Milgram's famous obedience experiments (1974), Asch's conformity experiments (1951), as well as the infamous Stanford Prison Experiment (1973). While these experiments documented a drastic change from the participants by changing their physical context, it is still relevant to our discussion of VR games. Due to the rapid development of advanced technology, behavioural change no longer limited to the changing of physical reality. The immersion to virtual reality that is drastically different from our ordinary lives, for example a violent game like GTA VR, is already capable of shifting our behaviour without the players even noticing. More specifically, it is the players' subject experience in the VR game that influence the players' mind and possibly changes their behaviour. As Heeter (1992) and Metzinger (2003) argued, the sense of being in the virtual world are developed not only from sensory input and output or the ability to change the virtual environment, but is also about the level of interactivity in the VR games. Being identify as a real person in the virtual world, in this sense, increases the chance of the players' being subjected to behavioural change (in both reality or virtual reality) as their brain already perceived the virtual world as real.

Once the mind of the players are reshaped to adapt the virtual world, the way they behave outside the gaming world might changed in consequence due to the questionable content of the games. Virtual reality is a technology that can modify the function of our brain by manipulating the player's "unit of identification" (Metzinger 2013). Psychologists have been attempting to use VR technologies in treating certain mental illness including anxiety, depression and even addiction and substance abuse, as VR is proven to be capable of correcting certain behaviour by regular exposure to VR (Jerdan et al 2018). If use in a correct way, VR could be beneficial to users. However, the major problem in VR gaming is that they usually allows the players to explore some grey areas that are morally questionable. One of the most popular video game, Resident Evil, has launched its latest versions named Resident Evil 7 (RE7) that can be played with a VR headset in 2016. RE7 is a "survival horror" game played from a first-person perspective, and is rated PEGI rating of 18 due to its extreme violence and sensitive languages. Similar to the previous version, this game includes numerous scenarios that requires the players to attack violently with weapon, as well as experiencing death, blood and gore repetitively throughout the game. And yet, by applying VR technology to the game has changed the way the players view violence in video games. By having a group of twenty adults playing RE7 in VR condition and flat screen condition, Wilson and McGil found out that the VR version increase the "perceptions of both enacting and receiving violence" (2018). People were feeling a lot uncomfortable in playing the VR version than the 2D one, and the gaming experience almost turned into realism when the players are attacking in the VR version of RE7 (Wilson and McGil 2018).

Such behavioural change can be explained by the direct manipulation of the Unit of Identification (UI) from being exposed to VR for too long. UI, as Metzinger termed it, is a phenomenal unit of identification, determinate representational content that contributes to phenomenal self model (2003). As mentioned in the above section, the Unit of Identification in our brain can be tricked and generated an illusion of embodiment in the virtual world. In Wilson and McGil's experiment, players were experiencing murder in a first hand bases and they are holding the game console as if the actual weapon. In other words, even though the players are aware that they are controlling the character on screen, but the VR technologies can confuse their brain and cause an illusion of they are actually participating inside the game. The fact that the players are given a chance to enact violence in a game with high resemblance to reality is dangerous, as high exposure to violent video game increase physiological arousal and propensity to aggression (Anderson and Bushman 2001). In fact, Hempe and Doan indicated that violent video game player are more likely to suffer from gamer rage, in which usually ended up abusing their child as a mean to relief their anger (2013). Parents could go as far to kill their child with game controller (NBC News 2008) or kill their child simply because the player was interrupted by the crying of their child (Golgowski 2012). If the participants from Wilson and McGil's experiment were disturbed by enacting the violence themselves, we can only imagine the immense impact on the well-being of children or teenagers when they immerse to such violent virtual world for far too long.

A part form violent or aggressive behaviour, behavioural change including neglecting physical body and environment is also common among VR games players. Similar to other forms of media, VR is only a technology that attempts to enhance human interaction in the virtual world. And every mediating tool comes with certain consequences. Just as social media platforms including Facebook and Instagram are gradually replacing actual social interactions with virtual ones, VR games are replacing our sensory mechanism and movement with VR technologies. Consequently, our bodies might fail to pick up on certain bodily cues that contribute to our social communication through unconscious entrainment Frith and Frith 2007). This is no longer about confusing the real with the virtual, but is about the ability of functioning in daily lives. The worse case scenario would be the normalisation of losing embodied signalling for social interaction, in which leads to losing the sense of modalities in reality (Madary and Metzinger 2016). In this sense, human mind would be slowly degraded through the intensive exposure to advanced sensory effects, and forces our mind to ignore the our physical context, if not worst, the physical body.

6 Conclusion

At first glance, applying VR to gaming certainly enhance the gaming experience through intense visual and audio effect. And yet, if we step back and consider the psychological and physical impacts, VR is certainly a double-edged sword. First of all, long term immersion to VR games can damaged the mental and physical well being of the player. Not only can VR games increase the vulnerability of the player when they are apprehending the real world, staying in virtual reality for far too long can also leads to various kind of disorientation that harm the physical body. The sense of detachment, in this case, occurs not only in the mind but also the body of the players. Such transformation of the mind and body of the play would then leads to the ethical concerns of VR games, as the transformation indicates the perception of self and world of the players are changing along the way. The plasticity of human mind makes the players adapt to the virtual world so effectively that it is possible for them to forget how to interact or behave in face-to-face social context. They may go as far to behave violently or aggressively due to long exposure to violent VR game, causing social disturbances.

This essay may sound like promoting what Jones and Hafner termed as "technological dystopianism", believing that digital technology are undoubtedly destroying our ability to communicate or interact in a meaningful way (2012). However, the essay is attempting to provide an alternative view on VR that are different from the grand narrative of VR's extraordinary experience. VR technologies in gaming is not necessary bad, as it does enhances gaming experience and provide an alternative form of entertainment to the public. And yet, the major problem of VR games is that the transparency of this particular medium makes us difficult to question its morality. The mind and body of the players are being tricked into believing that they are experiencing "truth" instead of "versions of reality" (Jones and Hafner 2012). Let us be remained that VR is a complicated technologies that seemingly blurred the sense of human being, and somehow create an illusion of utopia for players inside the gaming world.

References

3delement.com. Lee Vermeulen » VR and Steam days (2014). http://www.3delement.com/?p=332
Adams, D., Bah, A., Barwulor, C., Musaby, N., Pitkin, K., Redmiles, E.M.: Ethics emerging: the story of privacy and security perceptions in virtual reality. In: Fourteenth Symposium on Usable Privacy and Security (SOUPS 2018). USENIX Association (2018)
Anderson, C., Bushman, B.: Effects of violent video games on aggressive behavior, aggressive cognition, aggressive affect, physiological arousal, and prosocial behavior: a meta-analytic review of the scientific literature. Psychol. Sci. 12, 353–359 (2001). https://doi.org/10.1111/1467-9280.00366
Asch, S.: Effects of group pressure upon the modification and distortion of judgment. In: Guetzkow, H. (ed.) Groups, Leadership and Men: Research in Human Relations, pp. 177–190. Carnegie Press, Oxford (1951)

Baudrillard, J.: Selected Writings. Stanford University Press, Stanford (1988)

Bolter, J., Grusin, R.: Remediation. MIT Press, Cambridge (2003)

Baofu, P.: The Future of Post-human Mass Media, p. 11. Cambridge Scholars Pub., Newcastle Upon Tyne (2009)

Ellis, S.: Nature and origins of virtual environments: a bibliographical essay. Comput. Syst. Eng. 2(4), 321–347 (1991). http://www.sciencedirect.com/science/article/pii095605219190001L

Englund, C., Olofsson, A., Price, L.: Teaching with technology in higher education: understanding conceptual change and development in practice. High. Educ. Res. Dev. 36(1), 73–87 (2016)

Erik, K.: Sony's 'Project Morpheus' VR headset and the uncertain future of virtual reality (2014). https://www.forbes.com/sites/erikkain/2014/03/19/sonys-project-morpheus-vr-headset-and-the-uncertain-future-of-virtual-reality/#6804a65436cb

Frith, C., Frith, U.: Social cognition in humans. Curr. Biol. 17(16), R724–R732 (2007)

Gallagher, A., et al.: Virtual reality simulation for the operating room. Ann. Surg. 241(2), 364–372 (2005)

Gee, J.: What Video Games have to Teach Us About Learning and Literacy. Palgrave Macmillan (2003)

Gigante M.A.: Virtual reality: definitions, history and applications. Virtual Real. Syst. 3–14 (1993)

Haney, C., Banks, W., Zimbardo, P.: Study of prisoners and guards in a simulated prison. Nav. Res. Rev. 9, 1–17 (1973)

Jerdan, S., Grindle, M., van Woerden, H., Kamel Boulos, M.: Head-mounted virtual reality and mental health: critical review of current research. JMIR Serious Games 6(3), e14 (2018)

Jones, R., Hafner, C.: Understanding Digital Literacies. Routledge, London [i.e. Abingdon, Oxon] (2012)

Kade, D.: Ethics of virtual reality applications in computer game production. Philosophies 1(1), 73–86 (2015)

Madary, M., Metzinger, T.: Recommendations for good scientific practice and the consumers of VR-technology. Front. Robot. AI 3 (2016). https://www.frontiersin.org/articles/10.3389/frobt.2016.00003/full

McLuhan, M.: Understanding Media; The Extension of Man. McGraw-Hill Book Company, New York (1965)

Melanie Hempe, M., Doan: Gamer Rage & Child Abuse: A Growing Problem Deserving Our Attention | Moving to Learn. Movingtolearn.ca. http://movingtolearn.ca/2013/gamer-rage-child-abuse-a-growing-problem-deserving-our-attention

Metzinger, T.: Being No One. The Self-Model Theory of Subjectivity. MIT Press, Cambridge (2003)

Metzinger, T.: The myth of cognitive agency: subpersonal thinking as a cyclically recurring loss of mental autonomy. Front. Psychol. 4 (2013)

Milgram, S.: Obedience to Authority. An Experimental View. Tavistock, London (1974)

msnbc.com: Police: Baby killed with video game controller (2008). http://www.nbcnews.com/id/24026486/ns/us_news-crime_and_courts/t/police-baby-killed-video-game-controller/#.XKvUrLaVbdf

Nina, G.: Father killed three-month-old daughter when her crying interrupted his video game. Mail Online (2012). https://www.dailymail.co.uk/news/article-2096010/Father-killed-month-old-daughter-crying-interrupted-video-game.html

Oculus: I feel like I'm in VR when I'm not (2017). https://forums.oculusvr.com/community/discussion/53287/i-feel-like-im-in-vr-when-im-not

PlayStation.Blog: PlayStation VR: The Next Wave of Games Coming in Spring and Summer 2019 (2019). https://blog.us.playstation.com/2019/03/25/playstation-vr-the-next-wave-of-games-coming-in-spring-and-summer-2019/

Researchandmarkets.com: Virtual Reality Gaming Market: Global Industry Trends, Share, Size, Growth, Opportunity and Forecast 2018–2023 (2018). https://www.researchandmarkets.com/research/gz85x5/global_virtual?w=5

Roettl, J., Terlutter, R.: The same video game in 2D, 3D or virtual reality – how does technology impact game evaluation and brand placements?. PLOS One **13**(7), e0200724 (2018). https://doi.org/10.1371/journal.pone.0200724

Tiltbrush.com: Tilt Brush by Google (2016). https://www.tiltbrush.com

Tiffin, J., Nobuyoshi T.: Paradigm for the third millennium. Hyperreality **1** (2005)

Van Schneider, T.: The Post Virtual Reality Sadness. Medium (2005). https://medium.com/desk-of-van-schneider/the-post-virtual-reality-sadness-fb4a1ccacae4

Wilson, G., McGill, M.: Violent video games in virtual reality : re-evaluating the impact and rating of interactive experiences. In: CHI PLAY '18 Proceedings of the 2018 Annual Symposium on Computer-Human Interaction in Play, pp. 535–548. ACM, New York (2018)

Research About Influence of Information Presentation in UI on Scanability

Kanta Matsumoto[✉] and Wonseok Yang

Shibaura Institute of Technology, 3-7-5, Toyosu, Koto-Ku, Tokyo 108-8548, Japan
ma2.kanchan46@gmail.com

Abstract. Although self-ordering is convenient, people tend to feel uneasy when using it. For example, they cite issues such as "I am not sure if I can operate the system well" and "I feel rushed because there are people waiting in line behind me." Therefore, it is necessary to alleviate this psychological burden. This study aims to address this problem with scanability (quick and easy to understand) and clarifies the high scanability of UI. In this study, we first identified the issues of self-order UI by observing users. Next, we surveyed the existing self-orders and summarized their UI elements. Finally, we created a UI sample and examined the impact of the UI design on scanability. Furthermore, we determined the scanability of the product photo size, text size, text color, and margins by measuring the selection time and number of errors. Additionally, while scanability was less likely to affect the perceived time, it was more likely to affect the perception quality.

Keywords: Scanability · Self-ordering systems · Psychological Influences

1 Introduction

The installation of touch-monitor-based terminals, known as self-ordering, has been increasing in various countries, especially in franchised restaurants. In South Korea, the introduction of this technology has especially increased in fast-food restaurants, and the number of self-ordering units installed in restaurants has increased from 5,479 in 2019 to 21,335 in 2021, a four-fold increase [1]. The main reasons for this increase include the coronavirus pandemic, which has increased the demand for contactless devices, the ability to streamline operations [2], and the ability to meet inbound demand by changing the display language. Furthermore, the increasing demand for self-ordering in regions with rising labor costs is expected to accelerate its adoption. However, self-ordering is likely associated with resistance and anxiety. For example, in some cases, payments can be made at both self-ordering and manned cash registers; however, many people avoid self-ordering and use manned cash registers instead. The main reasons for this are: "I am not sure if I can operate it properly because the UI differs from store to store," and "I feel rushed because there are people waiting in line behind me while I am operating it." Thus, the operation of self-ordering is prone to psychological burdens such as anxiety and impatience. Consequently, not only is the user unable to fully think about the product he or she wants to buy, but errors due to impatience are also a major pain point in the user's service experience.

© The Author(s), under exclusive license to Springer Nature Switzerland AG 2023
A. Marcus et al. (Eds.): HCII 2023, LNCS 14032, pp. 227–238, 2023.
https://doi.org/10.1007/978-3-031-35702-2_17

Ohno's research shows that when users first encounter a UI, they read each area of the UI for only 200 ms–500 ms [3]. Therefore, it is believed that scanability (ease of understanding at a quick glance) is important for making users feel that they can operate the system successfully. However, there is currently a lack of research on the scanability of touch-monitor-type UIs, such as self-ordering.

For these reasons, we felt the need to conduct research on UI that reduces the psychological burden by clarifying the impact of the method of presenting information in self-ordering on scanability. Therefore, this study aimed to clarify the impact of different information presentations on self-ordering and scanability.

2 Literature Review

2.1 Self-ordering

Kiosks are touch monitor-based terminals installed in stores and public facilities. Typical examples of kiosks include self-checkouts, semi-self-registers, and self-ordering [4]. In general, they are classified according to the differences in operating procedures, as shown in Fig. 1. Kiosk terminals are often associated with uncertainty in use because they are installed in public places [5, 6]. However, self-ordering is a long and time-consuming operating procedure. Moreover, many of the places where it is installed are restaurants, which tend to be crowded; thus, it is considered relatively easy for users to experience discomfort. Therefore, this study deals with self-ordering, which is particularly in need of further improvement.

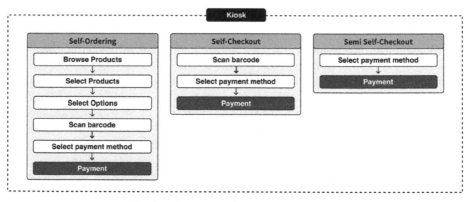

Fig. 1. Kiosks classification and procedures

2.2 Efficacy of Scanability

According to Ohno, users spend approximately 200 ms–500 ms gazing at each area of a screen. In other words, users skip many areas of the screen [3]. Therefore, it is important to present information that is easy for users to understand. In this study, we define scanability as the understandability of this short period. (Fig. 2) Jacob Nielsen et al. clarified the impact of scanability on usability by rephrasing the writing into simple words or changing it to bullet points. The result was a 124% improvement in scanability, with improvements in task time, number of errors, and time required [7]. This indicates that scanability is important for usability. Yamazaki et al. found that the psychological burden of time limits reduces performance in accuracy and time required. However, a decline in performance can be mitigated when a task is easy to understand [8]. Therefore, scanability is expected to reduce performance degradation.

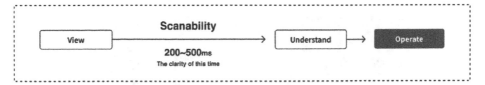

Fig. 2. Definition of Scanability

2.3 Improved Usability Through Scanability

There are many possible components of scanability; however, typical examples include color, shape, and layout. For example, when layouts are close together or similar, as in the Gestalt principle, they can convey the structure intuitively to the user because they are easily recognized as a single cohesive unit [9–11]. It is also possible to increase visibility and convey the importance of information intuitively by creating a difference in brightness and saturation between the figure and ground [12]. Readability can also be improved by changing the size, thickness, color, and line spacing of text [13–16]. Additionally, scanability can be increased by designing mental models, such as an F-shaped layout [17] or a familiar UI to suit the user's reading style [18].

3   Research and Results

In order to determine the effect of different information presentation in self-ordering on scanability, the study followed the flow shown in Fig. 3.

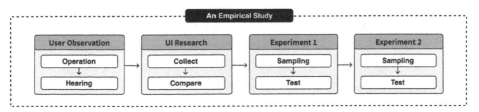

Fig. 3. The flow chart of empirical study

3.1 Observation of Users Using Self-ordering

The use of self-ordering can be accompanied by psychological burdens such as impatience and anxiety. The causes are not only due to the incomprehensibility of the UI, but also to the in-store environment and the context of use. To investigate such causes, we observed the operation of a self-ordering system installed in a store.

Method. Eleven college students were asked to order their favorite food and observed as they did so. The subjects were fitted with a camera on their heads as shown in Fig. 4, and their vision and sound were recorded.

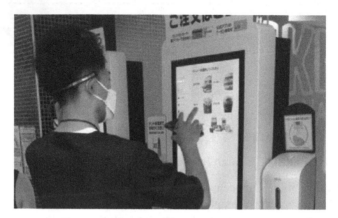

Fig. 4. Using a camera to observe operations

Thoughts during the operation were recorded by the thought-speech method [19] and the questions in Table 1. We then compiled them into a customer journey map [20] and analyzed them, focusing on the pain points.

Table 1. Questions about user status and thoughts

No.	Question
Q1	Have you ever used McDonald's?
Q2	Have you ever used self-ordering?
Q3	How did you choose what to buy?
Q4	Were you able to operate it successfully?
Q5	Did you feel uneasy during the operation?

Results. Ten out of eleven respondents were concerned about the people in line behind them during the operation and felt a sense of urgency to finish quickly. Additionally, those who had not thought about the products they wanted to buy in advance tended to feel rushed because they started thinking about it after seeing the UI. They also felt anxious that if they had difficulty understanding the UI at a quick glance, it would take too long and cause trouble. Specifically, they felt uneasy due to the following difficult to understand UI.

1) When product photos are similar, it is difficult to find what they are looking for.
2) When the text is difficult to read, it takes time to read the text.
3) If there is a lot of scrolling, it takes time to see everything.

3.2 Comparative Study of Self-ordering UI

To verify the scanability of the self-ordering UI, it is necessary to organize the elements in the UI that may affect scanability. In addition, by comparing UIs, it is expected to discover trends by store type and surrounding environment, as well as problems caused by scanability. Therefore, we conducted a survey of existing self-ordering UIs.

Method. Eight self-ordering installed in Japanese stores and seven in Korean stores were surveyed. The detailed survey subjects are as follows.

1) Those installed in restaurants
2) Those with functions for product selection, purchase, and payment
3) Vertical touch monitors of about 20 inches

We then compared their UIs in terms of design elements such as color and shape. Since most of the screens used in self-ordering are menu screens, the comparison was made for menu screens (Fig. 5).

Fig. 5. Example of self-ordering

Results The results of the survey revealed the following.

1) The number of columns of product cards was found to exist from 2–5 columns.
2) Easily distinguishable pictures like ice cream are displayed in 3–4 columns and smaller.
3) Photos that are difficult to distinguish, such as hamburgers, are displayed larger with 2–3 columns.
   Other findings include the following
4) Black is the most common text color, but peach is present in 20% of the price texts.
5) UI without a border on the product card accounts for 60% (Tables 2, 3, 4 and 5).

Table 2. Number of product card columns

Number of product card columns	2	3	4	5	Others
Percentage	20%	33%	27%	7%	13%

Table 3. Text color

Text color	Black	White	Pink	Others
Product name text	80%	13%	7%	0%
Price text	47%	13%	20%	20%

Table 4. Color around the product card

Product card color	None	Black	Gray	Others
Product Card Background	3%	7%	13%	7%
Product Card Border	60%	13%	20%	7%

Table 5. Direction

Direction	Vertical	Horizontal	Others
Photo and product name alignment	50%	50%	50%
Scroll	27%	20%	53%

3.3   Experiment 1: Testing the Effect of Product Card Size on Scanability

From the survey in Sect. 3.2, we were able to identify several factors that could influence scanability, such as the color and layout of the product cards. Among them, the size of the product cards varied from one self-ordering to another. This is considered to be a factor significantly related to scanability, as studies have shown that different sizes of text change visibility [15]. In addition, the study in Sect. 3.1 shows that anxiety is caused by the large amount of time required. From this, we considered that scanability should be evaluated in terms of time required. Based on the above, a sample was created and validated to determine the effect of the size of the product card on the selection time.

Method. As shown in Fig. 6, three samples were created with different sizes of product cards, depending on the number of rows of product cards. Note that if the length of the sample is too long to be seen off the screen, as in the two-column sample in Fig. 6, the sample can be scrolled to view it. Based on these samples, we gave them a task such as "Please buy a Big Mac" and measured their selection time. The task was specifically to select the fourth, eighth, and twelfth items, counting according to Z's law, for every two, three, and four columns. In order to avoid the influence of differences in experience in the use of self-ordering, an exercise was conducted at the beginning of the study. This experiment was conducted with 10 college students (Fig. 7).

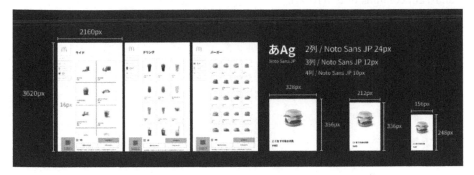

Fig. 6. Sample with different number of columns

Fig. 7. Task overview

Experiment Environment. The experimental environment was as shown in Fig. 8, as the survey in Sect. 3.2 showed that many self-ordering were operated in a standing position. In addition, a monitor that can be operated by touching it with a finger was used as in the existing self-ordering system.

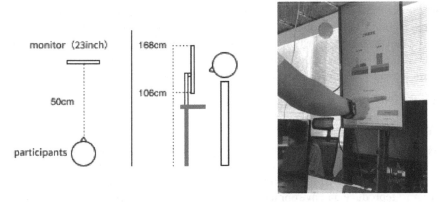

Fig. 8. Test environment of Experiment 1

Results. The results of the survey revealed the following.

1) The fewer the number of columns, the shorter the time required (except for the 8th and 12th columns of two rows).
2) When there was scrolling, the time required was very long.
3) Comparing columns 3–4, column 3 was 0.5 s faster (Fig. 9).

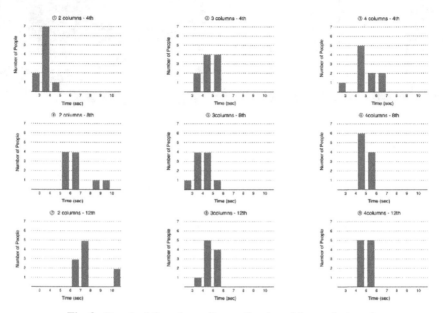

Fig. 9. Required time depending on the size of the product card

3.4 Experiment 2: Testing the Effect of Margins on Scanability

From the experiment in Sect. 3.3, it was found that the larger the product card, the shorter the time required, but the longer the time required increases when scrolling occurs. This suggests that the product card should be displayed as large as possible without scrolling. However, if the margins of the product card are made too large and lost, it may become difficult to read. Therefore, we examined the effect of margins on scanability.

Method. Post-experiment interviews revealed that in the experimental method of Sect. 3.3, users only searched for the products of the task and did not read each product carefully. Therefore, the results of Sect. 3.3 were only a reproduction of the case where users search for the product they are looking for. However, the results of Sect. 3.1 indicate that anxiety is more likely to occur when the product is undecided. Therefore, it is desirable to verify scanability in the state where the product is undecided. Therefore, in order to reproduce an environment in which the user reads the product carefully, we created a mistake-finding task. Specifically, we created a sample of three columns of cards based on different margins as shown in Fig. 10 and arranged them on a 65-in. monitor as shown in Fig. 11. Then, the participants were asked to change the picture or name of one of these three products and perform a mistake-finding task. This was done with two different types of mistakes: middle, and bottom. Selection time and the number of errors (the number of times a mistake was missed) were then measured. The experiment was also conducted with 20 college students.

Fig. 10. Samples of different margins

Fig. 11. Test environment of Experiment 2

Results. The results of the survey revealed the following.

1) There was little trend in selection time for different margins.
2) Comparing text took more time than comparing photos.
3) There were few errors in the medium margin size for both photos and text (Tables 6 and 7).

Table 6. Table captions should be placed above the tables.

question	Small & Middle	Small & Bottom	Medium & Middle	Medium & Bottom	Big & Middle	Big & Bottom
photo	12.2	7.32	9.82	9,93	7.21	7,84
character	13.46	16.32	14.13	12.32	12.21	12.42

Table 7. Number of errors due to different margins

question	Small & Middle	Small & Bottom	Medium & Middle	Medium & Bottom	Big & Middle	Big & Bottom
photo	1.25	0.25	0.00	0.08	0.42	1.33
character	0.86	0.86	0.00	0.00	1.00	0.57

3.5 Experiment 2: Testing the Effect of Text Color on Scanability

From the experiment in Sect. 3.4, it was found that the time required for letters is likely to take longer. Therefore, the scanability of the letters is a factor that is likely to affect the time required. From previous studies, we know that changing the color can improve the visibility. Therefore, we examined the effect of character color on scanability.

Method. The experimental method was the same as in Sect. 3.4. However, in this experiment, the font color was changed instead of the margin size. The experiment was also conducted on 20 college students (Fig. 12).

Fig. 12. Samples of different text colors

Results. The results of the survey revealed the following.

1) The number of errors in black was higher, and the number of errors in brown and peach were higher.
2) There was no significant trend in the selection time for different margins.
3) There was no trend between the number of errors and the selection time (Table 8).

Table 8. Selection time and number of errors for different margins

question	Small & Middle	Small & Bottom	Medium & Middle	Medium & Bottom	Big & Middle	Big & Bottom
Time	9.82	13.20	24.38	15.95	24.69	9.82
Error	0.00	0.29	1.86	0.14	0.71	0.00

4 Conclusion

1. The Psychological Impact of scanability

    By perceiving that scanability is poor and the selection time is likely to take longer, it is thought that users are impatient because it is likely to take longer. Therefore, scanability may reduce the user's psychological burden.

2. Importance of photo size

    One possible factor contributing to the trend shown in Sect. 3.2 is the possibility that items that are easy to distinguish by appearance, such as ice cream, can be displayed smaller, but items that are similar in appearance, such as hamburger, are difficult to recognize unless they are displayed larger. If so, items that are similar in appearance may also decrease in scanability as the number of columns of product cards increases. As a result, users may be more likely to feel uneasy or impatient.

3. Should be as large as possible.

    Because the selection time decreases with the number of columns, it is expected that the larger the pictures and text displayed, the higher the scanability. However, because scrolling requires a large amount of selection time, scrolling may significantly lower scanability. Therefore, scanability can be maximized by displaying the information as large as possible within a range where scrolling does not occur. However, because the number of errors increased when the margin was lost due to the excessive size of the display, it is thought that scanability can be increased by providing appropriate margins (24px in this experiment).

4. Scanability Factors

    Because the selection time decreases with the number of columns, it is expected that the larger the pictures and text displayed, the higher the scanability. However, because scrolling requires a large selection time, the presence of scrolling may significantly lower scanability. Additionally, medium margins (24px) and black text (#000000) were considered to have high scanability because the number of errors was low. Contrastingly, small (24px) and large (64px) margins and brown (#D08900) and peach (#CD003E) text colors were considered to have low scanability.

5. Scanability and error count

    Although scanability is unlikely to affect the selection time, it may affect the error count. Brown and peach colors are considered to have low scanability because of their high error rates; however, they were found to have little impact on the time required to scan. These results suggest that scanability does not have a large impact on selection time, but it does affect the error count significantly.

5 Future Consideration

Scanability may be affected not only by margins and text color but also by background color and the type of photo; therefore, several more samples should be created and experimented with. In addition to increasing the scanability of self-ordering, methods such as improving the store environment may be effective in achieving the goal of reducing the psychological burden of self-ordering. Further research on these factors is also required.

References

1. Investigation of the use of kiosks (unmanned information terminals). https://www.kca.go.kr/smartconsumer/board/download.do?menukey=7301&fno=10036497&bid=00000146&did=1003409523. Accessed 19 Jan 2023
2. National Supermarket Association of Japan, 2019nenji-tokei. http://www.super.or.jp/wp-content/uploads/2019/10/2019nenji-tokei.pdf. Accessed 19 Jan 2023
3. Ohno, T.: Where you look while you navigate the web? – Eye mark analysis of WWW, ITE Technical Report, vol. 24, no. 38, pp. 31–36 (2000)
4. Kurahashi, M., Morimoto, C.: Future development of self-checkout. In: JASMIN National Research Presentation Conference 2019 Autumn, pp. 175–178 (2019)
5. Ueda, K.: How passenger decides check-in option at the airport: self-service technology adoption model in passenger process. Simul. Gaming **24**(2), 1–15 (2017)
6. Hukuiti, A.: Direct observation of purchasing behavior in a cinema complex in Japan: age group analyses. Kandai Psychol. Rep. **11**, 39–47 (2020)
7. Nielsen Norman Group. https://www.nngroup.com/articles/how-users-read-on-the-web/. Accessed 19 Jan 2023
8. Yamazaki, T., Karashima, M.: The influence of time constraints on the performance in decision making task. Japan. J. Ergon. **39**(3), 123–130 (2003)
9. Spahr, T., Lehmkuhle, W.: Cognitive science & information processing. SAIENSU-SHA, Tokyo (1999)
10. Kitano, T., Kikuchi, M.: Gestalt factors in binocular vision. ITE Tech. Rep. **33**(17), 69–72 (2009)
11. William, L., Kritina, H.: Design Rule Index, BNN, Tokyo (2015)
12. Mitsui, N., Mitsui, H.: Shikisai design gaku (color design studies), Rikuyosha (2009)
13. Akutsu, H.: Character legibility 1: character size and legibility evaluation. Japan. J. Sens. Eval. **12**(2), 94–101 (2008)
14. Endo, A.: Engineering research on visibility evaluation of display character in LCD. Res. Rep. Kumamoto Natl. Coll. Technol. **6**, 13–19 (2015)
15. Arase, M.: Hensyu design nyumon (Introduction to Editorial Design), Media pal, Tokyo (2007)
16. Akutsu, H.: Character legibility 2: legibility and reading speed. Japan. J. Sens. Eval. **14**(1), 26–33 (2010)
17. Nielsen Norman Group. https://www.nngroup.com/articles/f-shaped-pattern-reading-web-content/. Accessed 19 Jan 2023
18. Indi, Y.: Mental Model. Maruzen Publishing, Tokyo (2014)
19. Matsunaga, S.: Methodology in experiments using think-aloud methods for the purpose of exploring writing processes. Kumamoto Univ. Stud. Soc. Cult. Sci. **9**, 249–260 (2011)
20. Ando, M.: UX design no kyokasyo (UX Design Textbook). Maruzen Publishing, Tokyo (2016)

Usability of Cloud Computing in Educational Communities of Practice: A Case Study of for Youth for Life Tool (FYFL)

Justus Nyamweya Nyagwencha[✉]

United States International University-Africa, P.O. Box 14634-00800, Nairobi, Kenya
jnyagwencha@usiu.ac.ke

Abstract. This research paper reports the experimental process and empirical usability information of a collaborative tool or system that addresses issues related to managing community of practice groups. The initial part of research considers security, technophobia and limited computer skills as main factors limiting collaboration among members of a community of practice. This research strives to provide and validate a secure, extensible and flexible computer supportive collaborative work (CSCW) tool that is easy to use and learn. The research proposes a computational framework that can manage and limit fictitious memberships within groups. The empirical usability study among potential users, validates that users can access information and collaborate effectively through a cloud tool, For Youth For Life (FYFL. The expert responses also validate the cloud tool as well. Our major contribution is the proposed group management model, universal quadrant model (UQM) aimed at mitigating insider threat within virtual groups and is validated through a simulation. The model is implemented based on a Tree structure with a theoretical run time of $O(n\log_4 n)$ with a high theoretical significant performance compared to the base case of $O(n)$. The adoption and success of the cloud tool and its value as a secure and ease to use, was heavily supported on its usability acceptance test by likely users in line with computer supportive collaborative work theory and human computer interaction research. The final usability acceptance test and the effective user evaluation acceptance tests results indicate that the cloud tool is easy to use and learn.

Keywords: Programming · User interface · Usability · WebOS (web operating system) · Communities of Practice · Computer Collaborative Work · Secure · Access information · Technophobia · Online Collaboration · For Youth for Life (FYFL) · Cloud

1 Introduction

Engaging community of practice members especially a broad youth audience across this country and internationally is a tremendous challenge in today's online environment. Current and developing communication technologies offer fast paced online environments through which they can engage in entertainment, online games, social networking, knowledge searches, and other experiences.

© The Author(s), under exclusive license to Springer Nature Switzerland AG 2023
A. Marcus et al. (Eds.): HCII 2023, LNCS 14032, pp. 239–257, 2023.
https://doi.org/10.1007/978-3-031-35702-2_18

The online learning environment is largely informal in nature in that the user explores at their initiative in a self-directed manner. It can also be formal in nature as a more deliberately directed experience with established objectives generally related to obtaining certification of some sort or a degree. Another approach combines aspects of informal and formal learning in what is known as non-formal learning with some crossover. Non-formal learning, which also includes experiential learning, for youth is the predominate form of learning in organizations such as 4-H Youth Development, scouting, and other venues that target a youth audience. Many internet sites provide learning for youth through one approach or the other.

The research explores how to provide content to the public in formal, informal, and non-formal methods through a collaborative online tool that is easy to use and learn. This is in line with CSCW (computer supportive collaborative work) the mission of land grant universities and the U.S. Department of Agriculture (USDA). The exploration and its success is pegged on a more recent concept of e-extension that seeks for a means of extending knowledge and information in a more focused manner from the land grant university system (LGU), the Cooperative Extension Service (CES), and to some degree the U.S. Department of Agriculture (USDA) to the American public through a common online means. By engaging Communities of Practice (CoPs) online, content to its clientele or communities can be provided in a secure and user-friendly manner.

To achieve our main objective, a CSCW cloud tool was selected and evaluated as an effective secure online tool for sharing best practices. The study investigated and focused on usability and security issues that affect online environments. The evaluation was to ensure that the tool met minimum online usability standards and had robust security to safeguard member privacy. The process utilized HCI techniques and design guidelines gathered feedback on how to improve the initial system from usability experts, K-12 teachers, 4-H members who were nominated as the initial user test population. The survey responses provided valuable input for re-designing user interfaces and re-affirmed security concerns as a major issue among novice computer users. However, issues concerning security and how it relates to Human Computer Interaction (HCI) will not be addressed in detail in this research.

In addition to HCI principles, the other goals of this research were to examine the issue of providing a collaborative tool to support communities of practice members engaged in informal learning online and propose a group management model for emerging groups by combing an informal learning and spatial locality theories. We relied on CSCW usability evaluation acceptance test approach necessary to effectively provide an environment feasible to accommodate and support novice users. The work resulted into a FYFL cloud tool to support communities and a model to foster and manage emerging groups relying on literature reviews on collaborative theory and online group principals. Our recommendation is a first attempt supported by empirical usability and acceptance tests data from focus groups on online collaboration and information learning.

The research 's main objective is to valuate and validate a tool or framework that can be used to encourage sharing of best practices within a community of practice to steadily benefit and enhance member's career aspirations through CSCW as witnessed in the code-re-use within the software development industry [5]. The research will validate the need to incorporate a tool to support virtual communities to share and re-use of best practices and take advantage of the numerous benefits offered by the CSCW tools. This work will be validated through surveys about the FYFL cloud and a virtual community that has been developed in our HCI lab in collaboration with the Alabama e-extension department. The research findings are aimed at highlighting the following benefits of collaborating through the secure CSWC tools verses traditional methods. These benefits include:

1. Possibility to Communicate Effectively.
   There is a high a possibility for members of a community of practice to learn how to communicate effectively, by reaching out to each other and building trust and understanding through friendships by seeking common ground [5, 6].
2. Motivation to Collaborate
   Members of community of practice groups will build a sense of responsibility by feeling obligated to the group and will take responsibility for the group. In due course they will learn to be responsible and become team players with the skills necessary to succeed in today's world [5, 6].
3. Secure and Efficient Access to Information
   Members of community of practice will access information and other resources easily without the restriction of time and place, unlike the prevalent face-to–face collaboration system. In addition, the permanency of records on shared practices, the independence of time and place to access information will allow members (e.g. students, teachers, and 4-H members) to learn and complete the tasks at hand remotely. This will also eliminate the fear of starting from scratch when the need for a practice arises and encourage members to focus on the task at hand [5, 6].

   Thus, the study aimed to encourage and promote the informal learning through a new environment for collaboration among groups of CoP. We hope to accomplish this goal by focusing on the usability of the tool because a previous survey conducted among the K-12 teacher population in the initial stages of this study, concluded that teachers will utilize the prototype tool only with improved usability. To ascertain the usability of the selected tool, a broad array of questions to be answered by the experimental participants were created to gather data for the research through a survey. The survey required a user to identify themselves as a novice or having advanced computer skills for the purpose of assessing the usability level of the tool and its impact on subjects in order to achieve our main objectives.

   Therefore, the original 5 main goals of the study are:

a. Select an appropriate secure tool for CoP to share best practice for available utilizing an expert inspection and feedback report.
b. Reconfigure the secure tool to accommodate the user group in accordance to software engineering principles.
c. Come up with a minimalist tutorial for the redesigned tool
d. Conduct a usability and acceptance test with the test group before deploying the tool
e. Introduce new and enhance technical skills of novice computer users.

   To achieve our objectives, the study was broken into three phases as outlined below to gather requirements, create a prototype and conduct a comprehensive evaluation of the system. During evaluation, subjects were given a minimalist tutorial to utilize to perform a series of tasks and at the end of the list of tasks they completed a detailed survey questionnaire to provide feedback on their experiences with the system.

Therefore, the research utilizes a cloud tool (FYFL) and focus groups to validate a CSCW tool in relation to 1) sharing and re-use of best practices, 2) justify the usability of the selected collaborative tool (FYFL) and the effects on novice users.

2 Literature Review

A lot of research is focused in the area of CSCW (computer supportive collaborative work) after researchers from various academic disciplines realized that computers should be designed according to the user's needs and that various technological designs and efforts can greatly benefit from the input of others in the areas of cognitive science and humanities. This has led to a new theory and branch of computer science CSCW and user centered design.

The usage of the term CSCW inside various academic fields and fortiori across the fields is wide [3]. Beside the wide range of usage of the term, this research will focus and include specific tasks which will require member participants to converge to a shared understanding of CSCW among members of communities of practice for the purposes of collecting data, analyzing, and evaluating it to ascertain the impact on subjects. The study chooses to utilize a cloud-based tool to support communities of practice in a method that is user friendly, secure, efficient, effective, and ease of use compared to most social CSCW networks systems. This work is inspired by the appeal of FaceBook and its ease of use. The motivation is to create an environment that will support a large community of practice in virtual space. The environment will encourage K-12 teachers and 4-H members to share and re-use best practices in the initial phase.

CSWC is an area of study with numerous unexplored benefits for a cross section of the population groups [2, 3]. For example, through CSWC K-12 teachers can be encouraged to share and re-use best practices as a community of practice (to emulate) the business industry which has highly benefited from sharing best practices through collaboration (e.g. the software development industry that successfully utilizes code-re-use during software development through collaboration).

2.1 CSCW to Mold Communities

The term computer supported cooperative work (CSCW) was first coined by Irene Greif and Paul M. Cashman in 1984 at a workshop attended by individuals interested in using technology to support people in their work [5]. In 1987, Dr. Charles Findley presented the concept of collaborative learning-work; "how collaborative activities and their coordination can be supported by means of computer systems" [6]. Through many authors consider CSCW and groupware to be the same, they are different. Groupware refers to computer-based systems; CSCW is the study of tools and techniques of groupware as well as their psychological, social, and organizational effects. Wilson (1991) expresses the difference between these two concepts: "CSCW is a generic term, which combines the understanding of the way people work in groups with the enabling technologies of computer networking, and associated hardware, software, services and techniques" [4].

CSCW is a design-oriented academic field bringing together social psychologists, sociologists, and computer scientists, among others. Despite the variety of disciplines, CSCW is an identifiable research field focused on understanding characteristics of interdependent group work with the objective of designing adequate computer-based technology to support such cooperative work.

There are three CSCW core dimensions of cooperative work that have been discovered over the years by researchers:

i. **Awareness:** Refers to individuals working together need to be able to gain some level of shared knowledge about each other's activities [7].

ii. **Articulation work**: Refers to cooperating individuals must somehow be able to partition work into units, divide it amongst themselves, and after the work is performed, reintegrate it [8, 9].

iii. **Appropriation (or tailorability):** refers how an individual or group adapts a technology to their own particular situation [7]; the technology may be appropriated in a manner completely unintended by the designers [10].

These concepts have largely been derived through the analysis of systems designed by researchers in the CSCW community, or through studies of existing systems (e.g. Wikipedia). CSCW researchers that design and build systems try to address core concepts in novel ways. However, the complexity of the domain makes it difficult to produce conclusive results; the success of CSCW systems are often so contingent on the peculiarities of the social context that it is hard to generalize. Consequently, CSCW systems that are based on the design of successful ones may fail to be appropriated in other seemingly similar contexts for a variety of reasons that are nearly impossible to identify a priori [11]. CSCW researcher Mark Ackerman calls this "divide between what we know, what we must support socially, and what we can support technically", the socio-technical gap and describes CSCW's main research agenda to be "exploring, understanding, and hopefully ameliorating" this gap [12].

In order to implement CSCW effectively, Mark Ackman's social technical divide must be addressed. The gap of what technology can support from a social context introduces the challenge of "how we can replicate the social events virtually?" Bridging this gap will ensure that CSCW tools are effective in satisfying the need they are designed to mitigate/solve. To address the social – technology divide Morgan Kaufmann uses a Time/Space matrix and divides CSCWs into groups; same time- same place, different times – same place, different time different space and different time – different space. The matrix is intended to be a replica of real life social situations that CSCWs designers will have to address when creating/refining CSCWs. The Time/Space Groupware Matrix shown below courtesy of Morgan Kaufmann publishers outlines the different ways people collaborate [12].

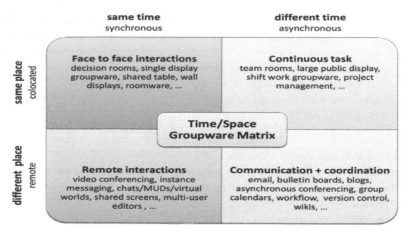

Fig. 2.1. Computer Supported Collaborative Work Matrix. (Source: Johansen, R. 1988 "Group-ware: Computer Support for Business Teams" The Free Press.)

Both time and space facets are bipolar (i.e. same time or different time and same lace different place perspective). Thus the time space groupware matrix has online communities divided into four categories:

Same Time, Same Place – Synchronous Co-located: Characterized with face to face interactions in decision rooms, single displays, groupware, shared table, wall displays, room ware etc.[12].

Same Place, Different Time – Asynchronous: A major collaboration between a group working on continuous tasks through tea rooms, large public displays, shift work groupware, project management etc.[12].

Different Place, Same Time – Asynchronous Remote: Remote interactions accomplished through video conferencing, instant messaging, charts/MUDs/virtual worlds, shared screens, multi-user editors etc. [12].

Different Place, Same Time – Asynchronous-Remote: Communication, coordination, e-mail, bulletin boards, blogs, asynchronous conferencing, group calendars, workflow, version control, wikis [12].

The CSCW paradigm provides a framework of what we know we can support socially but the social technical mapping still remains the main problem. Many of the researchers in this area are looking for ways to bridge the disparity between the social need and the capability to support the need technically from a computer science perspective [13].

Communities can be formed to support almost any activity. This creates a need for CSCW in a multitude of areas that need to be supported through computer collaborative work. In real life, there are some sorts of community supportive computer-based collaborative service being used by major commercial, social and academic activities in the world today. IBM uses the use the term social computing to describe the field of computer collaborative work. This is an attempt to infuse social convention in opposition to the technological characteristics that are associated with computer systems and software (i.e. the use of e-mail for maintaining social relationships, instant messaging for daily micro-coordination at one's workplace, or weblogs as a community building tool instead of the programming aspects of the e-mail or blog). The outlined tools have been successfully implemented and accepted by many users as a way of social life. Likewise many educational and commercial institutions are in the forefront of advancing their services using CSCW tools. Some of the major services offered to clients include online degrees and online banking services by most major banks in the commercial service sector. Many social forums have been implemented to serve communities. The forums are an intended meeting "spot" for individuals to gather and socialize. In the academic world, systems are utilized as pedagogical agents to enhance teaching and sharing knowledge (e.g. blackboard, WebCT and Moodle) [13]. The general public has many forums to support social interaction for example FaceBook, yahoo chart and Twitter. Our goal to leverage FaceBook in providing a cloud system where members of a community of practice will spend time and contribute to the knowledge of peers as well as learn from others in a user friendly and secure manner through social networking on a community practices.

2.2 Users and User Experiences with CSCW Systems

A study conducted by Social Networking Teaching Tools: A Computer Supported Collaborative Interactive Learning Social Networking Environment for K-12 in the spring 2010 surveyed 33 teachers in North Carolina city schools with different backgrounds and levels of education using a forum based prototype system. The surveyed group filled the usability survey to express their experiences of the system. The results were encouraging since 70% of those surveyed felt that a forum type virtual tool will be good for K-12 education and expressed confidence in using the proposed tool to teach if it were available. To confirm and validate the preliminary results, this study extends the previous study and focuses on providing a secure and user friendly social computing environment for a community of practice to collaborate, learn and share best practices. The proposed system will require the three to entangle to safeguard the privacy of the community members while online. For the success of the system, the user's opinion will weigh heavily on the adoption through the usability acceptance of the system. In this study, users evaluated the system, gave their opinions and suggestions for improvement. The opinions were incorporated into future designs as changes to improve usability of the system. To ascertain improvements usability surveys based were conducted on the enhanced system and its results published as part of the contribution of this research.

3   The Approach to the Research

This study has identified K-12 teachers and 4-H club members as the initial subgroups. The main criterion for choosing members to participate in the study is a voluntarily acceptance of teachers and schools to participate by willingly subscribing to use the FYFL cloud tool to collaborate and share best practices. Participants provided a feedback on its usability, efficiency and suitability for collaboration purposes (Fig. 3.1).

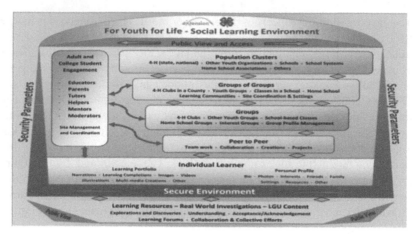

Fig. 3.1. The Initial For Youth, For Life theory – The Envisioned Secure Social Learning Environment Copyright © 2009 Auburn University, Alabama Cooperative Extension System

3.1 Phase I: Requirements

Requirements were gathered in phase I of the study to assemble the building blocks for the system. A thorough scenario based usability, security inspection and analysis approach ensued on the existing tools/software to identify the best suited tool to support the gathered requirements.

3.2 Phase II: Prototyping

Guided by the requirements, the team selected two suitable tools and modified them for evaluation. The resulting tool received a prototype step through scenario based usability, security inspection and analysis from the experts group. The modifications were necessary before testing with the potential users in line with CSCW guidelines. The requirements served as foundation for an iterative design and development work for the desirable community of practice tool in Phase III.

3.3 Phase III: Testing and Comprehensive Evaluation

A comprehensive analytical and empirical analysis gauges the success of the collaborative tool to support informal learning among CoP groups. The process included a comparative expert security and usability inspection of the selected and modified tool, usability and acceptance survey test of the FYFL by potential users, and a detailed qualitative and quantitative analysis of results from study. The expert evaluation stages were meant to produce results leading to the answers to the research questions while potential user's data served as a guideline for measures to be taken to improve the overall usability and acceptance of the cloud tool (Fig. 3.2).

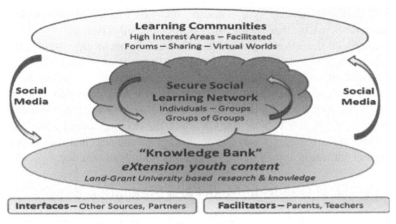

Fig. 3.2. The Refined For Youth, For Life theory – The revised and improved Social Learning Environment theory Copyright © 2010 Auburn University, Alabama Cooperative Extension System

Thus, the study adopted a cloud environment to leverage existing tendencies of human social nature and utilized it to enhance a collaborative environment based on the expert recommendation after reviewing more than a dozen tools. We anticipated that the participants of this work will have improved efficacy of their computer literacy, improved educational performance and more intrinsic motivation to spend more time concentrated on efforts that promote scientific content materials at the end of the study. In the second phase of the study, participants will work together as teams in a community of practice (e.g. student and teacher teams) that will utilize and contribute to this sharing and learning environment [1].The usability and acceptability results of this study support the creation of an environment that supports communities of practice in creating and sharing more content materials in a virtual community in a cloud environment as outlined in Fig. 2.1.Our hope was that this method of resource presentation will increase the usage of educational materials and applications among community of practice members in line with HCI and CSCW research. The environment will support improved use of materials within the virtual community leveraging the ease of use and popularity of other social networking environment such as FaceBook with enhanced security.

3.4 Phase IV: Group Management Problem

Managing 4-H members spread across wide region i.e. a state is challenging and poses an insider threat problem for users. To alleviate this problem, a formal model to manage this complexity is required to allow administrators to effectively navigate and locate resources within the system. For example, it is easy for an individual to moderate 100 members in a group, but intractable to navigate if the groups grows and surpasses 10,000 members within a spatial locality. To moderate a topic or a discussion among thousands of members by a single administrator is not solved through the currently available method. The model is effective in managing registered members through an appointed group leader. But, it is overwhelming for one administrator if the member's population exceeds a certain threshold (P), since the current system doesn't focus on monitoring and moderation of members activities in case there is an influx of member subscription.

Our analysis on the current solution reveals that it is intractable, static and lists all members in a single list without associating them to groups automatically. The model is 100% dependent on the administrator to create and assign registered members to specific groups/various groups manually. This method is recommended for possible for managing groups with a small number of users i.e. $N < = 1000$ but is intractable and inefficient for a bigger N (i.e. $N > 10000$). Thus, the existing model does not support self-purporting and sustaining groups important for the success a collaborative tool to foster informal education among members of communities of practice.

4   The Universal Quadrant Model and Simulation Results

To overcome the $N > 10000$ limitation imposed on our earlier solution, we initially suggested solution for managing groups of groups. The solution involves listing/creating regions based on the political boundaries and alignments in the United States. The four regions (North East, South, Midwest and West), being the cornerstone and further delaminate the rest into states followed by counties. This is a practical solution, however it has it has it discrepancies. For example, some counties may not have clubs and will lead to dummy clubs without members and could affect the search process when N- is greater. Thus, it makes it an inefficient solution for a group problem. On the other hand, the formation of groups and management of posts is entirely depended on an administrator who should assign then manually an impractical task for an $N > 10000$ especially even considering having many administrators. Doing business this way, will slow the group formation process as well limit sharing of information on the cloud forum. Therefore, this is not an optimal solution for the group problem. It has a color coded interface; but doesn't automate the process or aid in the process of creating self-purporting and sustaining groups. It is an intractable solution with an influx with members joining various groups. The final UQM solution is inspired by the four regions analogy illustrated in Fig. 4.1. The figure is a color-coded map of the four regions of the United States of America (USA) in tandem with the four-quadrant analogy. We base the conceptual prototype of the existing membership and group model supported by a data structure list with O(n) run time representing the envisioned UQM quadrants; the west, central, east and south regions translated to Fig. 4.2 in the proposed UQM group model.

Our solution the UQM (universal Quadrant Model) improves the current model by providing a way to alleviating the fictitious membership's problem and promoting self-purporting and sustaining groups. The model allows vetting of memberships by associating applicants with spatial locality groups as well provides a graphical interface for easy management of those groups.

We propose a Quadrant Universal Model algorithm to address the problem. The algorithm will in addition address the membership anonymity problem, perpetuate new manageable groups within a spatial locality and associate it with the original group once a certain membership threshold is reached within a specific quadrant or region. Managing individuals, groups, and groups of groups geographically (globally) in a less costly, manageable, predictable manner is NP-complete problem without an exact solution. However, the proposed set theory quadrant universal model (QUM) simplifies

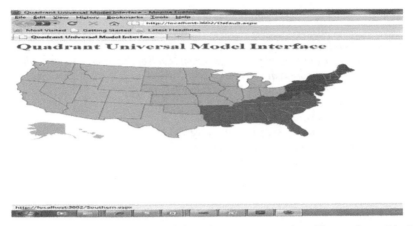

Fig. 4.1. Conceptual color coded simulated quadrants representative of four regions of the Unites States of America (USA) i.e. North (Orange), West (Green), South (Maroon) and the East (Blue). (Color figure online)

the management of individuals, groups, and groups of groups spatially and overcomes overlapping of memberships within groups.

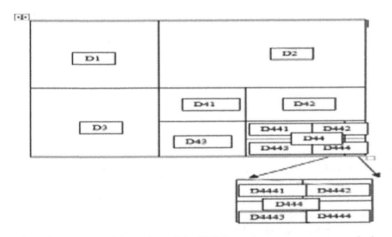

Fig. 4.2. This is an illustration of the UQM creating new groups recursively.

UQM is a recursive, nondeterministic, backtracking algorithm that finds all solutions to number of quadrants needed to be represented by spatial locality groups based on the population. The goal is to select a subset of the quadrants and classify them based on geographical location and population density or count. This is meant to ease moderation and elicit training alerts of moderators when need arises (Table 4.1).

Compared to the initial method, UQM is recursive, segmenting and self-managing with $O(n\log 4n)$ run time compared to the initial solution's $O(n)$ run time. Thus, implementing UQM presents highly significantly run time gain theoretically.

Table 4.1. Proposed UQM algorithm is a Tree structure with O(nlog$_4$n) run time.

Algorithm UQM functions as follows:
1. *If the quadrant Q is empty, the problem is solved; terminate successfully.*
2. *Otherwise choose a quadrant (Q) NW, SW, NE or NW (deterministically).*
3. *Read P, total 4H members P, P-4H members population*
4. *IF P < threshold*
5. *Include quadrant in the partial solution.*
6. *For each quadrant such that P > threshold,*
   Divide quadrant into NWi, SWi, NEi, SEii = 1
7. *Repeat recursively on the reduced quadrant Q.*

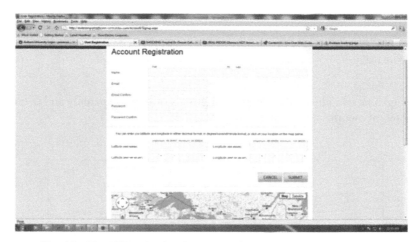

Fig. 4.3. The UQM simulated User Interface account registration page.

The extended Universal Quadrant Model implements and defines a user interface for group creation and group management. The simulation which is an extension of the theoretical model provides a login and registration user interfaces shown in Fig. 4.3 and Fig. 4.4 respectively. The UQM login and registration prototype pages are a direct representation of Fig. 4.2 in the UQM model simulation, a color-coded group interface for users and managers to visually locate, view, monitor membership group status and determine those ready to split.

Having such information at a glance will aid in the process of identifying a leader for the newly created groups. We believe that the color-coded user interface, is an improvement on the previous solution which did not have a means of issuing a warning to managers on the size of groups in question.

Figure 4.3, the account registration page uses Google maps for users to sign up and identify themselves in relation to a spatial locality of individuals by entering the latitude and longitude coordinates in the database of the current address and club. Figure 4.4, the account login page allow users to login and engage in various collaborative activities. Figure 4.5.A and Fig. 4.5.B displays UQM's simulated groups in virtual space, being the

Fig. 4.4. The UQM simulated User Interface account login page

final result of the UQM model which allocates groups in line with the UQM fundamental principles. Figure 4.2 locality principle provides user information which is fundamental in determining which group to be assigned. The process is automated and helps in creating groups as well as maintains accuracy for members since potential members will be vetted a member of their local club limiting the number of false accounts significantly.

The QUM supports the Table-Insert and Table-Delete. The Table-Insert inserts onto the table an item that occupies a single slot space for one item. Table delete can be thought of as a removing an item from the table.

5 The Usability Study Results

Most tools eligible for sharing information among members of communities of practice (i.e. K-12 teachers and 4-H club members) rely on direct manipulation of text to create, edit, post and share with other members as revealed by the expert survey information. On the other hand, the majority of the do not have the capability/means to control and monitor post as well regulate the groups, making new posts from members a must see for all members once posted. This extends the usability features for public social networks of sharing with moderation, a dangerous trend of bullying which resulted in loss of lives in past which should be negated in this case. The loss of lives attributed to social network sites is a down side also of social computing and is as a result of lack of screening for information before going public, thus making it visible for all members at an instance. The loss of life problem should be addressed and solved to avoid further losses. On the other hand, the potential collaboration tools require advanced technical skills (e.g. a bit of programming skills) that can be a learning curve for some of the self-reported novice users, which are the bulk of K-12 and 4-H community of practice members. This skills requirement is attributed to decreased motivation to participate in the sharing of best practices. Thus, it is our hope that the analysis of human studies data focusing on user tasks and acceptance test with potential users of the selected FYFL "cloud"

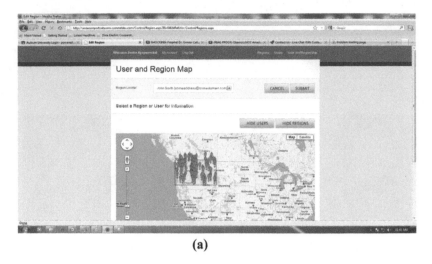

(a)

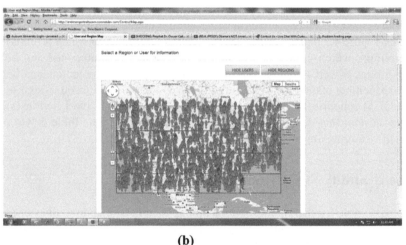

(b)

Fig. 4.5. A. Illustrates the UQM simulation of a single group for the organization and management of self-sustaining and purporting online groups B. Illustrates the new model (UQM) current user groups displayed on a Google map with group leaders displayed in red. (Color figure online)

environment's will validate the usability, cyber-trust, and security to motivate 4-H club members to participate, share and re-use best practices utilizing the cloud based FYFL tool.

5.1   System Support of Usability

The study's main aim is to answer the question, does the usability of this new tool promote or hinder collaboration among 4-H club members in performing creations, editing, commenting, and re-using best practices among themselves? (Fig. 5.1)

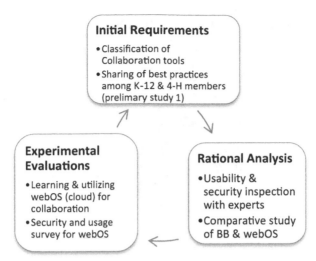

Fig. 5.1. Illustrates the system research, evaluation and analysis process

5.2 Experimental Procedure

The research experiment is paper based and web based. The subjects who have agreed to participate online will be sent a link and through e-mail or on site with the details of the study in order for them to complete it at the own convenience. The main study was conducted through a series of workshops and those who have agreed to participate were given details and be required to complete most of the study at the end of the workshop. Before taking part in the study participants were provided with an IRB form to inform them of their rights. The IRB also consents that their participation is purely voluntary and that they can withdraw from the study at any time without any giving any reason. The experiment process had four sections which include: (1) Signing consent form (2) Pre-questionnaire, (2) Visiting the www.4Y4L.org cloud and performing assigned tasks, and (3) Post-questionnaires.

5.3 Usability Results

In order to collect data for our study, we installed, redesigned, and configured, the FYFL cloud collaborative environment for participants to perform various tasks to provide feedback on its usability. The webOS cloud was acquired through an agreement between Stoneware and the E-extension program in collaboration with the Auburn University Computer Science and Software Engineering HCI lab for testing and evaluation.

Participant Background. In the usability evaluation process, we collected and measured several user characteristics in the background survey feedback form. The shown pie chart data stems from self-reported responses from participants and it shows the frequency of responses for each category.

The occupation is a categorical variable but, was found out the majority of our participants were e-extension teachers, however, this demographics data helps the researcher to disaggregate this group into agents, 4-H administrators, extension specialist and other.

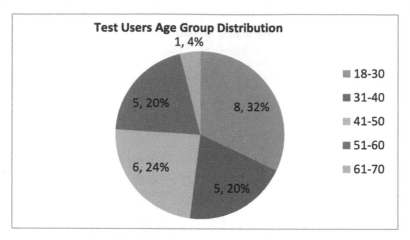

Fig. 5.2. FYFL cloud user tests distribution chart

In this study we began with summaries of participant responses as raw counts and created frequency bar charts to identify the categories (see Fig. 5.3). The shown histogram (Fig. 5.3) stems from self-reported responses from participants and it shows the frequency responses in that category.

We utilized bar charts to provide an easy way to visualize information by breaking data into various categories. Wirth respect to gender preferences, we broke data by male/female but did not ascertain any significant difference or trend by comparing responses. In addition we collected and reported the demographics of the participants so that our results are not gender biased. Figure 5.2 shows that there were more men than women who participated in the study, however we still hold our results accurate because we did not pinpoint any anomaly on the responses during gender based data analysis as depicted in by Fig. 5.4.

The background survey responses from participants on occupation and level of education responses were used to assign four groups, the extension specialists, teachers, administrators and other. We categorized users based on age group; the level of education; residency- number of years they have been working for the 4-H group, and computer experience in years ending with the results summarized Table 5.1. However, it is interesting to note that sub-categories of education level-years of experience with the 4-H group and the number of years they have been using computers are two different measures respectively; the former is a knowledge base while the later is Information Technology experience.

Task Performance and Satisfaction. This study identifies two data categories from a usability stand point: the objective data concerning user performance (times and errors, inventory of behaviors), and a subjective data concerning their attitudes and reactions (the ratings and comments they make during or after their interactions with the system) that are self-reported.

In this study, the performance and behavior rating results for the FYFL cloud usability study are summarized in Tables 5.1. As far as performance in performing the FYFL

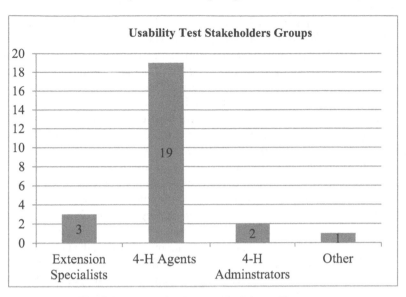

Fig. 5.3. FYFL cloud Categorical data self-reports.

cloud tasks, we reported task time with means and standard deviations as a measure of variability as shown in Table 5.1. Table 5.1 also shows how we recorded errors as counts and recorded an average frequency across all users was reported. Our decision to report an error count instead of categorizing them into groups was as a result of a trending threshold for error identification with less than four errors doesn't qualify for a common theme error grouping. In this study, the error was below a research assumed grouping threshold and was treated as a count for data reporting purposes.

Table 5.1. Summary of time, standard deviations and errors for the cloud test tasks ($N = 25$)

	FYFL Cloud Tasks	Mean	STD	Errors
1	Post an Announcement	8.55	(6.93)	0.64
2	Updating Calendar and group size simulation	5.45	(3.80)	0.36
3	Uploading a document	6.18	(4.21)	0.71
4	Uploading a photo	6.00	(3.92)	0.46
	Combined Total	26.18	(18.87)	2.18

6 Conclusion

The adoption and success of an informal educational cloud tool depends entirely on its security and usability. Computer supportive collaborative work and human computer interaction theories provide usability acceptance test knowledge that can support the effective user evaluation and acceptance tests of collaborative tools. However, the formulation of an effective and efficient acceptance testing process is made difficult by the plethora of design theories and models that outline how support a novice user in understanding and using a collaborative tool to share best practices without compromising its security. The premise of this research was that user acceptance test and expert analysis can provide a mechanism for identifying a suitable secure CSCW tool that is understandable and easy to use for a novice user. We base the practicality of this approach to the previous research efforts in using human studies and expert feedback to test the suitability of software products before deployment.

Initially our efforts were focused on identifying a viable tool for communities of practice to share best practices but later ventured into defining a model to aid in managing groups of groups that emerge within the online community while protecting the integrity of the community. The security analysis expert survey selected the FYFL cloud tool among other potential candidates and it been validated through an acceptance usability survey data from potential users. On group of group management, the universal quadrant model will be incorporated once it's fully tested by refining the existing cloud tool (manual) group management feature to create an environment that supports self-purporting and sustaining groups for both development and design users within the cloud.

The contribution of this research is beneficial to computer supportive collaborative work (CSCW) design, human computer interaction research, online group theory research, green computing and informal learning research, and usability studies research. Our major contribution is we also propose a group management model universal quadrant model (UQM) aimed at mitigating insider threat within virtual groups and validate it through a simulation. The adoption and success of the cloud tool and its value as a secure and ease to use was heavily supported on its usability acceptance by likely users inline with computer supportive collaborative work theory and human computer interaction research. The final usability acceptance test and the effective user evaluation acceptance tests results indicate that the cloud tool to easy to use and learn.

Acknowledgments. Our special thanks to Auburn University vice president for research for funding this project and encouraging us to pursue it beyond Auburn.

References

1. Cain, C., Seals, C., Nyagwencha, J.: Social networking teaching tools: a computer supported collaborative interactive learning social networking environment for K-12. In: Proceedings of World Conference on E-Learning in Corporate, Government, Healthcare, and Higher Education 2010 (pp. 1612–1617). Chesapeake, VA: AACE (2010)
2. Grudin, J.: Computer-Supported cooperative work: history and focus. IEEE Comput. 19–26 (1994)
3. Nworie, J., Haughton, N.: Good intetions unanticipated effects: the unintended consequences of the application of technology in teaching and learning environments. TechTrends, 52–58 (2008)
4. Maryam, A.: Computer-mediated collaborative learning: an empirical evaluation MIS Q. **18**(2), 159–174 (1992)

5. Dourish, P., Bellotti, V.: Awareness and coordination in shared workspaces. In: Proceedings of the 1992 ACM Conference on Computer-supported Cooperative WORKCC. ACM Press New York, NY, USA. pp. 107–114 (1992)
6. Schmidt, K., Bannon, L.: Taking CSCW seriously. Comput. Support. Coop. Work 1(1), 7–40 (1992)
7. MacKay, W.E.: Patterns of sharing customizable software. In: Proceedings of the 1990 ACM Conference on Computer-supported Cooperative Work. ACM Press New York, NY, USA. pp. 209–221 (1991)http://portal.acm.org/citation.cfm?id=99332.99356&type=series
8. Grudin, J.: Why CSCW applications fail: problems in the design and evaluation of organization of organizational interfaces. In: Proceedings of the 1988 ACM conference on Computer-supported cooperative work. ACM Press New York, NY, USA, pp. 85–93 (1988)
9. Ackerman, M.: The Intellectual Challenge of CSCW: the gap between social requirements and technical feasibility. Hum.-Comput. Interact., pp. 179–203 (2000)
10. Goodsell, A., Maher, M., Tinto, V., Smith, B.B., MacGregor, J.: "What is collaborative learning?" National Center on Postsecondary Teaching, Learning, and Assessment at Pennsylvania State University (1992)
11. Findley, C.A.: Collaborative learning-work. Presentation at the Pacific Telecommunications Council 1989 Conference, January 15–20, Honolulu, Hawaii (1989)
12. Mitnik, R., Recabarren, M., Nussbaum, M., Soto, A.: Collaborative robotic instruction: a graph teaching experience. Comput. Educ. 53(2), 330–342 (2009)
13. Baecker, R.M., Others: Readings in human-computer interaction: toward the year 2000. Morgan Kaufmann Publishers (1995)

Personality Traits Inference in the Hybrid Foraging Search Task

Yunxian Pan(iD) and Jie Xu$^{(\boxtimes)}$ (iD)

Zhejiang University, Hangzhou, China
xujie0987@zju.edu.cn

Abstract. Techniques to predict participants' personality traits in real-time are not yet developed or well-studied. The objective of the current study was to explore the use of gaze and behavioral metrics and machine learning techniques in a hybrid foraging search task to infer an individual's personality traits to enable personalized interaction. We recruited and collected data from 40 university student participants in a hybrid foraging search task experiment. Specifically, the metrics were extracted from different time window sizes (5s, 10s, 15s, and 20s), which referred to the length of time before the participant stopped searching the current screen. Hierarchical clustering analysis was performed on the personality traits scores to group the participants into three groups, namely neuroticism (47.50%), conscientiousness (25.00%), and agreeableness (27.50%). Machine learning models were trained using the eye-gaze and behavioral metrics as inputs and personality trait groups as labels using well-known algorithms (including random forest (RF), support vector machine (SVM), k- nearest neighbor (kNN), and artificial neural network (ANN)). The results from the machine learning modeling showed that the prediction accuracy increased as the window size increased in general. The highest prediction accuracy (83%) was achieved with the kNN algorithm with a 15s time window. Combining eye-gaze and behavioral metrics as input features usually resulted in a better-performing model compared to using eye-gaze metrics alone (up to 10% improvement in accuracy). The current results can be to implement this approach in a brief game-like activity to infer a user's personality traits to enable subsequent intelligent user interface adaptations.

Keywords: Personality traits · Eye-tracking · Visual search task · Machine learning

1 Introduction

In psychology, personality traits are defined as the stable behavioral characteristics that an individual shows across different situations. Research has shown that personality traits can predict behaviors and outcomes on the individual, interpersonal, and institutional levels [1], including human-computer interaction (HCI) scenarios [2]. Knowledge of an individual's personality traits allows us to predict his/her preferences and behavioral tendencies in different contexts and environments [3, 4], which can be useful for personalized recommender systems [5] and services [6].

A. Marcus et al. (Eds.): HCII 2023, LNCS 14032, pp. 258–269, 2023.
https://doi.org/10.1007/978-3-031-35702-2_19

The traditional method of measuring personality traits is to require participants to finish paper or electronic questionnaires, with participants self-report a series of questions to obtain their corresponding personality trait scores. For instance, the Big Five personality traits are typically measured by various validated versions of questionnaires (e.g., [7, 8]). However, in HCI applications, questionnaire-based data can be difficult to obtain due to logistical issues; furthermore, the results can be deceptive due to people's tendency to show a socially acceptable or desirable appearance [9]. Alternative approaches to measuring personality traits have been proposed. For example, recent studies have used online social data and logs from mobile devices to infer user personality traits [10]. Gao et al. [11] showed that it was feasible to infer personality traits using call and messaging logs in phones. While promising, the above approach has the disadvantage of time lagging – one must collect data for an extended period of time (usually months, e.g., [11]) before making accurate inferences. Therefore, some studies have explored the use of neural-physiological data in short-term tasks to infer personality traits. Recently, research has been done on the use of regression or machine learning for personality prediction with eye gaze (e.g., [12, 13]), galvanic skin response (GSR) (e.g., [14–16]), and electroencephalogram (EEG) (e.g., [17–19]). For instance, using eye-gaze metrics as input features, Hong et al. [13] developed a random forest classifier for personality traits inference in a daily walking activity (10 min). Li and Hu et al. [18] proposed and implemented an EEG-based personality assessment method in emotional words viewing tasks (5 min). These studies suggested that the proposed methods serve as promising alternatives to traditional personality questionnaires.

Given these promising results, we aimed to explore personality trait inference using eye-tracking and behavioral metrics with a brief visual search task. In this research, we extracted participants' relevant eye-gaze and behavioral metrics in the hybrid foraging visual search task to predict participants' personality traits. Specifically, this study predicted participants' task performance and infers participants' personality traits by using well-known machine learning techniques. Furthermore, we might be able to implement these results fast enough to be applied to real-time systems.

1.1 Personality Trait in Visual Search

Humans with different personality traits have different behavioral styles [20]. For example, humans with high conscientiousness usually shows high self-discipline, methodical, and conscientious behavior style, while those with low conscientiousness tend to show more impulsive, easygoing, and flexible behavior style [21]. In previous research on cognitive processes, researchers found that personality traits also influence perception and attention. For example, high anxious humans take longer to pay attention to fear-related stimuli than low anxious ones, and they have difficulty disengaging their attention from fear-related stimuli [22]. Research in the visual search paradigm also supported this conclusion [23]. Those findings provided further evidence for the impact of personality traits on perception and attentional processes and suggested that personality traits are correlated with behaviors in visual search tasks [24, 25].

Studies have pointed out that personality traits are potential predictors of visual search performance. A study found that personality traits can effectively predict visual search performance with regression models [26]. Brown et al. [27] used machine learning to predict participants' personality traits based on their visual search behavior data and found that participants could be classified as neuroticism and extraversion with 67% accuracy. A review and analysis of 65 studies [28] also found a relationship between the Big Five personality traits and performance motivation. Research showed that neuroticism and conscientiousness were the best predictors of performance motivation.

Previous research has shown that some personality traits are correlated with performance in visual search tasks. For example, introverts may be better at visual search than extroverts [29]. Therefore, individual differences can be a factor to consider in the selection of specialized personnel for occupations that rely heavily on visual searches, such as airport baggage inspection [30, 31] or radiology [32, 33]. Recently, studies have found that personality traits correlated with visual search performance in the US Transportation Security Administration [34]. Among the Big Five personality traits (neuroticism, extroversion, openness, agreeableness, and conscientiousness), conscientiousness was significantly associated with visual search accuracy. These findings supported that a searcher's personality traits influence their visual search performance.

1.2 Personality Trait and Eye-Gaze Pattern

In our daily social interactions, we often understand and predict others' behavior and emotion through their eye-gaze pattern [37]. Studies have shown that there was a correlation between personality traits and eye-gaze patterns, and humans with similar personality traits tend to exhibit similar eye-gaze patterns [13]. As a result, this direction is now being explored by emerging research, which suggested that our eye-gaze patterns were partially mediated by personality traits [39, 40].

Recent studies have used machine learning to predict personality traits using eye-gaze metrics as input features [41–43]. For example, Al-Samarraie et al. [44] explored the feasibility of participants' eye-gaze patterns to predict personality traits in a visual presentation task. Based on these results, they inferred the participants' individual visual preferences. They further found that individuals with high scores on specific personality traits showed unique eye-gaze patterns when focusing on regions of interest [45]. Al-Samarraie et al. [12] also investigated the impact of personality traits (conscientiousness, agreeableness, and extraversion) on participants' information-seeking behavior, and found that eye-gaze patterns could predict participants' personality traits in online information-seeking tasks. Hoppe et al. [13] collected eye-gaze metrics from participants during daily tasks, and their results also revealed that eye-gaze metrics can be used as a predictor of personality traits. These findings provided evidence for how to predict an individual's personality traits during visual searching.

1.3 The Current Study

The above-mentioned studies will motivate us to further investigate how eye-gaze patterns are effective in inferring and predicting personality traits. This study attempted to predict participants' personality traits by using their eye-gaze patterns with a brief visual search task. The distribution of eye-gaze may vary depending on the personality traits of the participants. The purpose of this study is to answer the following research questions (RQs):

- RQ1: Are participants' personality traits correlated with eye-gaze and behavioral metrics?
- RQ2: Can eye-gaze and behavior metrics predict participants' personality traits in a hybrid foraging visual search task?

The main objective of this study was to gain insight into (a) the effect of eye-gaze metrics (including saccade amplitude, saccade velocity, saccade peak velocity, fixation duration, fixation count, and pupil size) in explaining the search behavior of participants on hybrid foraging searches, and (b) the feasibility of developing models based on these data to predict personality traits online. The current results can be used to guide the development of personality profiles with visual search tasks.

2   Method

2.1   Participants

Forty university students were recruited from a large public university in East China through a campus-wide job-posting network (20 males and 20 females; Mage = 22.98 years, SDage = 2.47; all had normal or corrected-to-normal vision). Power analysis was conducted in G*Power software to guide the choice of sample size before data collection. The study protocol was approved by the Institutional Review Board (IRB) at the institution.

2.2   Task and Setting

In the hybrid foraging visual search task (Wolfe et al., 2016), the participants were required to search for multiple types of multiple target items among multiple nontarget items as quickly and as accurately as possible (see Fig. 1). In this study, participants were asked to remember four different memory set sizes (8, 16, 32, and 64 items). Then they searched those target items in 60, 75, 90, and 105 items of visual set size, which included 20–30% of target items. The experimental program was developed using Unity 3D with C#. The program's background color was light gray (RGB = 128, 128, 128). All items were set up to 75 × 75 px (field of view (FOV) $\approx 2.0° \times 2.0°$).

We employed the EyeLink 1000 Plus eye-tracking system (SR Research, Ottawa, Canada) with a sampling rate of 1000 Hz to record the eye-tracking data. A stimulus was presented on a 25-inch monitor (1920 × 1080 px) attached to the desktop PC connected with the EyeLink system (Intel Core i5–4570 S 2.9 GHz) via an internet cable. The participants were seated 60 cm from the monitor (FOV $\approx 37.7° \times 24.5°$) and used a chin support.

We collected the behavior and eye-gaze metrics. In behavior metrics, the click time, which was the interval between the moment when the participant clicked an item and the next item (millisecond), and the click distance, which was the distance between the point when the participant clicked an item and the next item (px), were collected. Eye-gaze metrics collected included saccade amplitude (degree), saccade velocity (degree/s), saccade peak velocity (degree/s), average fixation duration (millisecond), fixation counts, and pupil size.

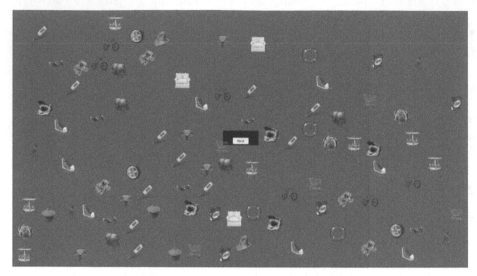

Fig. 1. A sample searching screen in the task.

2.3 Procedure

Participants were asked to self-report the 60 items of the NEO Five-Factor Inventory (NEO–FFI; [8]). The NEO–FFI can reliably and effectively assess the Big Five personality factors: openness, conscientiousness, extraversion, agreeableness, and neuroticism. The Five Factor Model of personality (also known as the Big Five), first proposed by Goldberg's [46], not only enable powerful and parsimonious descriptions of personality traits but also has been used extensively in research across different fields.

The experiment includes two tasks: a memory task and a search task. In the memory task, participants were asked to memorize the set of target items (8-, 16-, 32-, 64-item). During the memorization stage, participants viewed each item for three seconds. After that, they had to finish a recognition memory test. Only when the accuracy of recognition reached over 90%, they were allowed to continue to the search task. If they failed the recognition test, they would come back to the memorization stage. In the search task, participants were asked to click target items with the goal of collecting 100 points in the practice stage and 1000 points in the experimental stage. When participants clicked a target item, they would get two points. If not, they would get minus one point. Participants could freely click on the "next" button to go to a new patch to search.

2.4 Data Processing and Analysis

We first excluded some invalid trials which lost gaze data (including 0.14% of the total number of data points). The statistical analysis was conducted using R [47] with tidyr [48] and caret [49] packages. Eye-gaze metric screening and cleaning procedures were conducted using the automated analysis software—Data Viewer (SR Research, Ottawa, Canada). We set a series of time window sizes (5s, 10s, 15s, and 20s) to analyze eye-gaze metrics.

NEO–FFI measured five personality traits for each participant. We calculated the mean and standard deviation (SD) of the five personality trait dimensions for each participant and label the score as "medium" when the score was within half SD of the mean. Scores outside this range were labeled as "low" or "high". We then performed a hierarchical clustering analysis to group participants based on their personality scores. The cluster analysis results yielded a three-cluster solution. Then combined with the above three tags ("high", "medium" and "low"), we labeled the dimension with the highest number of "high" tags of the first cluster as the name of the first cluster. And the second and third clusters were also labeled in the same way. The resultant first group consisted of 19 (47.50%) participants with a high neuroticism score, the second group consisted of 10 (25.00%) participants with a high conscientiousness score, and the third group consisted of 11 (27.50%) participants with a high agreeableness score.

For the first research question (RQ1), a correlation analysis was used to measure the main effect of the correlated personality traits on eye-gaze and behavioral metrics within three groups of personality traits. The following eye-gaze metrics were used in this study: fixation counts, average fixation duration, saccade amplitude, saccade velocity, saccade peak velocity, and pupil size. For the second research question (RQ2), we used machine learning algorithms to classify the participants' personality traits from the eye-gaze metrics, including random forest (RF), support vector machine (SVM), k- nearest neighbor (kNN), and artificial neural network (ANN).

3 Results

3.1 Correlation Results

Correlations between personality traits and eye-gaze and behavioral metrics are shown in Table 1. In visual search tasks, conscientiousness, agreeableness, and neuroticism were correlated with fixation counts, fixation duration, saccade amplitude, and average pupil size. Conscientiousness and neuroticism were correlated with click time, and neuroticism and extraversion were correlated with click distance. Openness was not significantly correlated with average pupil size and saccadic parameters, while agreeableness and neuroticism were not significantly correlated with saccade peak velocity. Moreover, conscientiousness was not significantly correlated with saccade velocity.

Table 1. Correlation results for personality traits and eye-gaze and behavioral metrics.

Personality traits	Saccade amplitude	Saccade velocity	Saccade peak velocity	Fixation duration	Fixation counts	Pupil size	Click distance	Click time
Neuroticism	0.06**	0.14**	0.00	-0.16**	0.09**	0.11**	0.14**	0.06**
Extraversion	0.12**	0.05**	0.32**	0.04**	-0.04*	0.07**	0.04**	0.01
Openness	0.01	-0.04*	0.10**	-0.08**	0.07**	0.03	0.00	0.01
Agreeableness	0.04*	0.05**	-0.01	0.19**	-0.09**	0.12**	0.01	0.02
Conscientiousness	-0.05**	-0.01	-0.11**	0.23**	-0.10**	-0.07**	0.00	-0.04**

3.2 Predicting Personality Traits

Predicting Personality Traits Only Using Eye-gaze Metrics. In general, the bigger the t_{window} value, the higher the classification accuracy with only eye-gaze metrics, regardless of the algorithm used. When the t_{window} was set to 15 s or 20 s, all four algorithms were more accurate than with other values of *twindow* (see Fig. 2). The SVM performed better than the other algorithms in *twindow* = 20 s. It achieved over 79% accuracy in classifying personality traits.

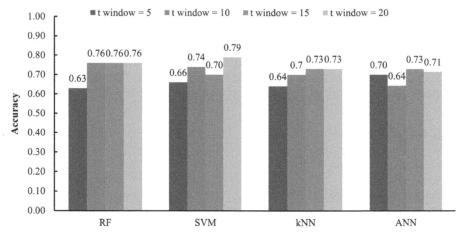

Fig. 2. Accuracy in classifying personality traits with different window size (t_{window}) values and different input features only using the eye-gaze metrics.

Predicting Personality Traits Using both the Eye-gaze and Behavioral Metrics. The trend of classification accuracy with fusion features was the same as that with only eye-gaze metrics. When the *twindow* was set to 15 s, the kNN performed better than the other algorithms (see Fig. 3). It achieved over 83% accuracy in classifying personality traits. In the majority of cases, combining eye-gaze and behavioral metrics as features usually resulted in a better-performing model compared to using eye-gaze metrics alone (up to 10% improvement in accuracy), suggesting that multimodal features could improve prediction performance compared to unimodal features. This study contributes to the accumulating evidence that gaze and behavioral metrics could be useful for personality traits inference.

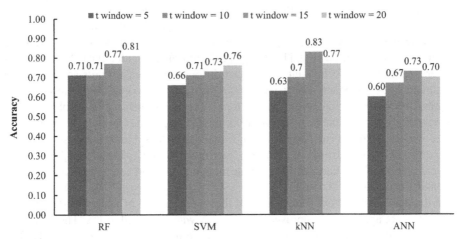

Fig. 3. Accuracy in classifying personality traits with different window size (t_{window}) values and different input features using both the eye-gaze and behavioral metrics.

4   Discussions

In the current study, the results from statistical analyses showed that scores of conscientiousness, agreeableness, and neuroticism were significantly correlated with fixation count, fixation duration, saccade amplitude, and pupil size; scores of conscientiousness and neuroticism were correlated with click time and distance. The results from the machine learning modeling showed that the prediction accuracy increased as the window size increased in general (see Fig. 2 and Fig. 3). The highest prediction accuracy (83%) was achieved with the kNN algorithm with a 15s time window. Combining eye-gaze and behavioral metrics as input features generally led to better-performing classifiers than using eye-gaze metrics alone (up to 10% improvement in accuracy), indicating that multimodal features may be more effective at making predictions than unimodal features. This work contributes to the growing body of evidence revealing that behavioral and gaze metrics can be used to infer personality traits.

Visual information is one of the important sources of information we obtain from our surroundings. Our brains have more than 30 regions dedicated to visual processing [35]. Our eye movements are a fundamental behavior that, in addition to revealing important cognitive characteristics, can also indicate emotional, and social characteristics [36]. Studies have shown that there was a correlation between personality traits and eye-gaze patterns, and humans with similar personality traits tend to exhibit similar eye-gaze patterns [4]. For example, optimists spend less time examining negative emotional stimuli than pessimists [38]. People with high openness spend longer looking at abstract pictures [36], while perceptually curious people prefer to look at pictures of natural scenes [39]. In our study, we found that different personality traits were significantly associated with different eye-gaze patterns. Our result suggested that eye-gaze patterns were partially mediated by personality traits, which is consistent with recent studies.

Some studies have revealed connections between personality traits and eye-gaze patterns by using machine learning [41–43]. By analyzing the eye-gaze patterns of participants, Al-Samarraie et al. [12, 44, 45] inferred the individual visual preferences and personality traits. Their results found that different personality traits are associated with unique eye-gaze patterns when it comes to gazing in areas of interest. Among them, eye-gaze patterns predicted the personality traits (conscientiousness, agreeableness, and extraversion) of participants in online information-seeking tasks. Our study also collected eye-gaze metrics from participants during a visual search task. Our results also validated the findings of Al-Samarraie et al., that eye-gaze metrics could be used as a predictor of personality traits. These findings may provide more guidance on how to predict individual personality traits in visual search.

In the current study, our results showed that the accuracy of personality traits prediction was not appreciably improved after t_{window} was increased to 15s. The larger the t_{window}, the more computational resources might require to process the gaze data. The results suggested that the time window (e.g., 15 s) of gaze data was sufficient to predict the personality traits in a visual task. Moreover, we also found that fusion features both gaze and behavioral metrics could better predict personality traits compared with using only eye-gaze metrics. This is consistent with the results of previous studies [50]. In future research, we should explore how to improve the identification and prediction of personality traits in real-world settings, for instance, visual search behavior during daily Internet use scenarios. Second, future research should explore the use of multimodal input data to improve personality traits prediction, such as models of gaze data and electroencephalography (EEG), models of eye-gaze and galvanic skin metrics, and so on.

5   Conclusions

This study showed that participants' personality traits were correlated with their eye-gaze and behavioral metrics in a hybrid foraging visual search task. We found that the distribution of eye-gaze and behavioral metrics related to the personality traits of the participants. Moreover, machine learning models based on fusion features from both gaze and behavioral metrics could better predict personality traits. This study contributes to the accumulating evidence that gaze and behavioral metrics can be useful for personality trait prediction. This technology enables the artificial intelligence system to customize the user's visual search settings.

Acknowledgment. This work was supported by the National Natural Science Foundation of China (Grant No. T2192931).

References

1. Ozer, D.J., Benet-Martinez, V.: Personality and the prediction of consequential outcomes. Annu. Rev. Psychol. **57**, 401 (2006)
2. Bachrach, Y., Kosinski, M., Graepel, T., Kohli, P., Stillwell, D.: Personality and patterns of Facebook usage. In: Proceedings of the 4th Annual ACM Web Science Conference, pp. 24–32 (2012)
3. Neuberg, S.L., Newsom, J.T.: Personal need for structure: individual differences in the desire for simpler structure. J. Pers. Soc. Psychol. **65**(1), 113 (1993)
4. Perlman, S.B., Morris, J.P., Vander Wyk, B.C., Green, S.R., Doyle, J.L., Pelphrey, K.A.: Individual differences in personality predict how people look at faces. PLoS ONE **4**(6), e5952 (2009)
5. Lambiotte, R., Kosinski, M.: Tracking the digital footprints of personality. Proc. IEEE **102**(12), 1934–1939 (2014)
6. Kosinski, M., Bachrach, Y., Kohli, P., Stillwell, D., Graepel, T.: Manifestations of user personality in website choice and behaviour on online social networks. Mach. Learn. **95**(3), 357–380 (2013). https://doi.org/10.1007/s10994-013-5415-y
7. Goldberg, L.R.: The structure of phenotypic personality traits. Am. Psychol. **48**(1), 26 (1993)
8. Costa, P.T., McCrae, R.R.: Neo personality inventory-revised (NEO PI-R). Odessa, FL: Psychological Assessment Resources (1992)
9. Han, S., Huang, H., Tang, Y.: Knowledge of words: an interpretable approach for personality recognition from social media. Knowl.-Based Syst. **194**, 105550 (2020)
10. Al Marouf, A., Hasan, M.K., Mahmud, H.: Comparative analysis of feature selection algorithms for computational personality prediction from social media. IEEE Trans. Comput. Soc. Syst. **7**(3), 587–599 (2020)
11. Gao, N., Shao, W., Salim, F.D.: Predicting personality traits from physical activity intensity. Computer **52**(7), 47–56 (2019)
12. Al-Samarraie, H., Eldenfria, A., Dawoud, H.: The impact of personality traits on users' information-seeking behavior. Inf. Process. Manage. **53**(1), 237–247 (2017)
13. Hoppe, S., Loetscher, T., Morey, S.A., Bulling, A.: Eye movements during everyday behavior predict personality traits. Front. Hum. Neurosci. **12**, 105 (2018)
14. Butt, A.R., Arsalan, A., Majid, M.: Multimodal personality trait recognition using wearable sensors in response to public speaking. IEEE Sens. J. **20**(12), 6532–6541 (2020)
15. Wache, J.: The secret language of our body: affect and personality recognition using physiological signals. In: Proceedings of the 16th International Conference on Multimodal Interaction, pp. 389–393 (2014)
16. Wache, J., Subramanian, R., Abadi, M. K., Vieriu, R. L., Sebe, N., Winkler, S.: Implicit user-centric personality recognition based on physiological responses to emotional videos. In: Proceedings of the 2015 ACM on International Conference on Multimodal Interaction, 239–246 (2015)
17. Bhardwaj, H., Tomar, P., Sakalle, A., Bhardwaj, A.: Classification of extraversion and introversion personality trait using electroencephalogram signals. In: Solanki, A., Sharma, S.K., Tarar, S., Tomar, P., Sharma, S., Nayyar, A. (eds.) AIS2C2 2021. CCIS, vol. 1434, pp. 31–39. Springer, Cham (2021). https://doi.org/10.1007/978-3-030-82322-1_3
18. Li, W., et al.: Quantitative personality predictions from a brief EEG recording. IEEE Trans. Affect. Comput. (2022)
19. Zhao, G., Ge, Y., Shen, B., Wei, X., Wang, H.: Emotion analysis for personality inference from EEG signals. IEEE Trans. Affect. Comput. **9**(3), 362–371 (2017)
20. Kazdin, A.E. (ed.).: Encyclopedia of Psychology, vol. 1–8. Washington, DC: American Psychological Association (2000)

21. Hogan, J., Ones, D.S.: Conscientiousness and integrity at work. In: Handbook of Personality Psychology. Academic Press, 849–870 (1997)
22. Rosario, P., María del, C.E., César Á.: On the relationship between attention and personality: covert visual orienting of attention in anxiety and impulsivity. Personality Individ. Differ. **36**(6), 1471–1481 (2004)
23. Öhman, A., Flykt, A., Esteves, F.: Emotion drives attention: detecting the snake in the grass. J. Exp. Psychol. Gen. **130**(3), 466–478 (2001)
24. Hickey, C., Chelazzi, L., Theeuwes, J.: Reward guides vision when it's your thing: trait reward-seeking in reward-mediated visual priming. PLoS ONE **5**(11), e14087 (2010)
25. Hickey, C., Peelen, M.V.: Neural mechanisms of incentive salience in naturalistic human vision. Neuron **85**(3), 512–518 (2015)
26. Peltier, C., Becker, M.W.: Individual differences predict low prevalence visual search performance. Cogn. Res.: Principles Implications **2**(1), 1–11 (2017). https://doi.org/10.1186/s41235-016-0042-3
27. Brown, E.T., et al.: Finding waldo: learning about users from their interactions. IEEE Trans. Visual Comput. Graphics **20**(12), 1663–1672 (2014)
28. Judge, T.A., Ilies, R.: Relationship of personality to performance motivation: a meta-analytic review. J. Appl. Psychol. **87**(4), 797–807 (2002)
29. Sen, A.N.I.M.A., Goel, N.: Functional relation between personality types and some impirically derived TSD parameters in a visual searching task. Psychol. Stud. **26**, 23–27 (1981)
30. Biggs, A.T., Mitroff, S.R.: Improving the efficacy of security screening tasks: a review of visual search challenges and ways to mitigate their adverse effects. Appl. Cogn. Psychol. **29**(1), 142–148 (2015)
31. Mitroff, S.R., Biggs, A.T., Cain, M.S.: Multiple-target visual search errors: overview and implications for airport security. Policy Insights Behav. Brain Sci. **2**(1), 121–128 (2015)
32. Krupinski, E.A.: Current perspectives in medical image perception. Atten. Percept. Psychophys. **72**(5), 1205–1217 (2010)
33. Krupinski, E.A.: Improving patient care through medical image perception research. Policy Insights Behav. Brain Sci. **2**(1), 74–80 (2015)
34. Biggs, A.T., Clark, K., Mitroff, S.R.: Who should be searching? Differences in personality can affect visual search accuracy. Personality Individ. Differ. **116**, 353–358 (2017)
35. Felleman, D.J., Van Essen, D.C.: Distributed hierarchical processing in the primate cerebral cortex. Cerebral Cortex (New York) **1**(1), 1–47 (1991)
36. Rauthmann, J.F., Seubert, C.T., Sachse, P., Furtner, M.R.: Eyes as windows to the soul: gazing behavior is related to personality. J. Res. Pers. **46**(2), 147–156 (2012)
37. Emery, N.J.: The eyes have it: the neuroethology, function and evolution of social gaze. Neurosci. Biobehav. Rev. **24**, 581–604 (2000)
38. Isaacowitz, D.M.: The gaze of the optimist. Pers. Soc. Psychol. Bull. **31**, 407–415 (2005)
39. Risko, E.F., Anderson, N.C., Lanthier, S., Kingstone, A.: Curious eyes: Individual differences in personality predict eye movement behavior in scene-viewing. Cognition **122**, 86–90 (2012)
40. Baranes, A., Oudeyer, P.Y., Gottlieb, J.: Eye movements reveal epistemic curiosity in human observers. Vis. Res. **117**, 81–90 (2015)
41. Bulling, A., Zander, T.O.: Cognition-aware computing. IEEE Perv. Comput. **13**, 80–83 (2014)
42. Bixler, R., D'Mello, S.: Automatic gaze-based user-independent detection of mind wandering during computerized reading. User Model. User-Adap. Inter. **26**(1), 33–68 (2015). https://doi.org/10.1007/s11257-015-9167-1
43. Hoppe, S., Loetscher, T., Morey, S., Bulling, A.: Recognition of curiosity using eye movement analysis. In: Proceedings of the 2017 ACM International Joint Conference on Pervasive and Ubiquitous Computing (UbiComp 2015) (Osaka), 185–188 (2015)

44. Al-Samarraie, H., Sarsam, S.M., Alzahrani, A.I., Alalwan, N., Masood, M.: The role of personality characteristics in informing our preference for visual presentation: an eye movement study. J. Ambient Intell. Smart Environ. **8**(6), 709–719 (2016)
45. Al-Samarraie, H., Sarsam, S.M., Alzahrani, A.I., Alalwan, N.: Personality and individual differences: the potential of using preferences for visual stimuli to predict the Big Five traits. Cogn. Technol. Work **20**(3), 337–349 (2018). https://doi.org/10.1007/s10111-018-0470-6
46. Goldberg, L.R.: The development of markers for the Big-Five factor structure. Psychol. Assess. **4**(1), 26–42 (1992)
47. R Core Team. R: A language and environment for statistical computing. R Foundation for Statistical Computing, Vienna, Austria. https://www.r-project.org/ (2019)
48. Wickham, H., Henry, L., RStudio.: Tidyr: easily Tidy Data with "Spread" and "Gather" Functions. https://cran.r-project.org/package=tidyr (2019)
49. Kuhn, M.: Building predictive models in R using the caret package. J. Stat. Softw. **28**(1), 1–26 (2008)
50. Ge, X., Pan, Y., Wang, S., Qian, L., Yuan, J., Jie, X., Y., Qian: Improving intention detection in single-trial classification through fusion of EEG and eye-tracker data. IEEE Trans. Hum.-Mach. Syst. **53**(1), 132–141 (2023). https://doi.org/10.1109/THMS.2022.3225633

Perception of the Vibration Intensity of Smartwatches in the Notification Scene

Tao Qin, Le Chang, and Haining Wang[✉]

Hunan University, Changsha 410082, China
haining1872@qq.com

Abstract. Existing smartwatches often use vibration for reminders and feedback, especially in the notification scene. In the notification scene, the intensity of the vibration directly affects whether the user can receive the notification. Therefore, establishing the relationship between notification vibration and user perception is essential to improve the efficiency of notifications and user experience. In the literature, while some studies have examined the relationship between vibration and perceptions of mobile phones, no connection has been established between vibration intensity and vibration perceptions of watches, particularly in the context of notifications. In this paper, intensity perceptions of various vibration intensities at three common watch frequencies are studied. Ten adult subjects (5 males and 5 females) were recruited and asked to wear experimental watches and evaluate the vibration perceptions using to a Likert scale. Our research results include the perceived differences in vibration intensity at three frequencies and the corresponding appropriate intensity range values. These findings can provide guidance for designing notification vibrations in smartwatches.

Keywords: Smartwatch · Vibration · Vibration intensity · Intensity perception

1 Introduce

Due to the product characteristics of smartwatches requiring wearable use, vibration is widely applied as a tactile feedback interaction method in their operation and feedback, particularly in notification scenarios. In notification scenarios, the vibration intensity of a smartwatch directly determines the level of notification perception by the user. Therefore, establishing the relationship between the vibration intensity of a watch product and the user's perception is of great significance for improving the efficiency of watch notifications and providing a good user experience. Currently, there are many related studies on vibration experience, and the addition of vibration can improve user experience and improve user cognition of the device, enabling users to better understand message behavior [1–3]. During the process of receiving vibration, user perception is often influenced by different parameters. For example, I. Hwang et al. studied various factors that may affect vibration perception intensity [4], including vibration frequency, amplitude, duration, and other factors. The change in intensity has a significant impact on the user experience, as Tan et al. found that vibration intensity can enhance the level of user experience on mobile phones [5], while Christian Schönauer et al. found that users tend to overestimate vibration intensity [6]. Similarly, vibration frequency also affects the level of perception. In another article by Hwang I, it was found that frequencies below 100Hz give rise to a stronger perception intensity [7]. In addition to the above studies, some scholars have also conducted research on vibration perception for specific populations. For example, Liu SF et al. studied the differences in vibration perception between elderly and young people and proposed vibration schemes that may have better perception for the elderly [8]. However, in current vibration experience research, most studies focus on vibration research for mobile devices, such as smartphones, or on vibration type design. There is a lack of research on vibration perception for smartwatches, particularly in specific scenarios such as notification scenarios, which is an important vibration application scenario that still lacks related research. Therefore, this study takes notification scenarios as the vibration research scenario to investigate the problem of vibration intensity perception by users on smartwatches and provide appropriate intensity ranges under different frequencies.

This study aimed to investigate differences in vibration intensity perception among users of smartwatches at three distinct frequencies (80 Hz, 145 Hz, and 235 Hz). Ten participants (5 males and 5 females) with an average age of 24.1 years were recruited for the vibration perception experiment. Subjective evaluations of vibration intensity were collected from the participants using a 7-point scale. Participants used a specific adjustment program and experimental phone to experience vibrations in a set notification scenario. The experiment collected rating data for subsequent analysis. The expected research outcomes include differences in vibration intensity perception across the three frequencies and appropriate intensity value ranges for each corresponding frequency.

2 Methods

2.1 Participants

Ten undergraduate students from Hunan University in China were recruited to participate in the study. The participants included five males and five females with a minimum age of 22, a maximum age of 27, and an average age of 24.1 years. All participants had no hand-related diseases, functional impairments, or vibration disorders, and they all had right-hand dominance. Additionally, the recruited participants had previous experience using wearable devices and passed the screening for the vibration perception task in the recruitment questionnaire, indicating good sensitivity to vibrations.

2.2 Materials

Vibration Apparatus
The vibration apparatus comprised an adjustable vibration program for a mobile phone and a smartwatch prototype equipped with a vibration motor, which was used to simulate the real-world scenario of smartwatch users receiving notification vibrations. The first device was the RichTap adjustable vibration program developed by ACC TECHNOLOGY (Fig. 1). The RichTap program could adjust predefined vibration parameters,

including vibration unit type, vibration intensity, vibration frequency, vibration duration, and specific internal parameters of the vibration unit, to design various vibration effects with ease. For this study, only one vibration unit set to the long vibration type was used in the experiment, and it was adjusted to a fixed vibration duration of 200 ms.

Fig. 1. RichTap application interface.

The second device was a smartwatch prototype embedded with a vibration motor (Fig. 2). To fully simulate the experience of using a smartwatch vibration, we connected the vibration motor fixed on the watch prototype to the experimental mobile phone equipped with the adjustable program through copper wires. This method enabled the vibration occurrence of the watch to be remotely controlled via the RichTap application. The vibration motor on the watch was secured and sealed with hot melt adhesive. During the experiment, participants were required to wear the modified watch prototype on their right wrists and adjust the watch band according to their wrist size until it was stable and comfortable. As this experiment aimed to investigate the vibration perception of smartwatches in notification scenarios, there was no specific posture requirement for participants wearing the watch; and they were instructed to maintain natural and common postures to match the real-world use of smartwatches.

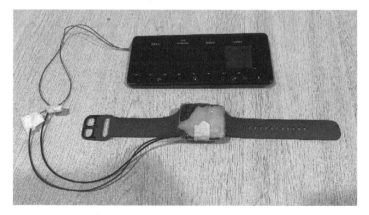

Fig. 2. Vibration smartwatch prototype.

Intensity Perception Scale

The experiment employed a self-designed seven-level intensity perception rating scale to collect data, as shown in Fig. 3. The scale rating instruction was "The extent to which the vibration characteristics in notification scenarios provide feedback, the perceptibility and perceptiveness of vibration effects or textures, and whether they capture your attention." Descriptions for scores of 1 and 7 in the scale are as follows: "Almost Imperceptible" and "Extremely Perceptible". Additionally, in the scale's rating instructions, a vibration intensity of 4–5 points was considered appropriate for vibration notification strength, and this rating data will be used to calculate the corresponding intensity value in the subsequent data analysis. Participants in the experiment were required to perform the intensity perception rating after experiencing the vibration at least three times.

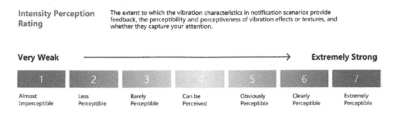

Fig. 3. Intensity perception scale.

2.3 Procedures

All experimental studies were conducted in the laboratory of Hunan University. Participants signed informed consent forms and provided basic information before participating in the experiment. Three sets of experiments were conducted at different vibration frequencies: 80Hz, 145Hz, and 235Hz. The vibration intensity was adjusted in increments of 10, from intensity level 10 to 100, for a total of 10 adjustments per experiment. Thus, each complete experiment included at least $3 \times 10 = 30$ vibration experiences and corresponding ratings.

Prior to the formal experiment, participants were led by experimenters to become familiar with the software and to complete a vibration task (without rating) to ensure that they fully understood the purpose, process, and complete vibration sensation. During the formal experiment, participants completed the three sets of vibration intensity experiences in the order specified in the experimental table. In each score, participants were required to complete at least three full vibration experiences before rating them according to the scale. If a participant had any ambiguity or needed to modify their previous rating, they were allowed to re-experience and modify their rating in a timely manner. After completing a set of vibration tasks, participants were required to rest for at least 5 min to ensure the sensitivity of their hand vibration perception. Each experiment lasted approximately 35 min. Part of the experimental process is shown in Fig. 4.

The rating data during the experiment were recorded on paper by experimenters and then uploaded to a computer for subsequent analysis. It should be noted that the vibration intensity values used in the experiment were program-set values and did not represent the

Fig. 4. Left: Adjusting vibration parameters in RichTap; Right: Intensity perception rating scale and questionnaire.

actual vibration amplitude. Therefore, after the experiment, the vibration intensity was measured using a vibration measuring instrument (SV 103, SVANTEK, Poland), and the measurement results were expressed in vibration acceleration peak-to-peak value in mm/s^2. The relationship between the measured actual vibration acceleration and corresponding intensity levels is detailed in Table 1.

Table 1. Peak-to-peak vibration acceleration in each frequency.

Intensity	P-P (mm/s^2)		
	80Hz	145Hz	235Hz
10	0.512	0.546	0.535
20	0.971	1.091	0.708
30	1.381	1.553	0.921
40	1.827	3.130	1.421
50	2.137	4.149	1.685
60	2.524	5.162	2.256
70	2.880	5.612	3.101
80	3.256	6.107	3.807
90	3.551	7.480	4.337
100	3.665	8.448	

3 Result

3.1 Perceived Score of Each Frequency Intensity

The rating data for each frequency are presented in Table 2, including the mean and standard deviation. Additionally, rating-intensity profiles were plotted for different frequencies, as shown in Fig. 5.

Table 2. Vibration intensity perception score of each frequency.

Intensity	Frequency	Mean (M)	Standard Deviation (SD)
10	80Hz	1.700	0.823
	145Hz	1.500	0.707
	235Hz	1.400	0.699
20	80Hz	2.200	1.135
	145Hz	3.300	1.059
	235Hz	2.600	1.350
30	80Hz	2.900	1.197
	145Hz	4.700	1.252
	235Hz	3.500	1.354
40	80Hz	3.900	0.876
	145Hz	5.900	1.101
	235Hz	5.000	1.333
50	80Hz	4.900	1.101
	145Hz	6.500	0.850
	235Hz	5.900	1.197
60	80Hz	5.800	0.919
	145Hz	6.800	0.422
	235Hz	6.500	0.972
70	80Hz	6.500	0.707
	145Hz	6.900	0.316
	235Hz	6.600	0.699
80	80Hz	6.800	0.422
	145Hz	7.000	0.000
	235Hz	6.900	0.316

(*continued*)

Table 2. (*continued*)

Intensity	Frequency	Mean (M)	Standard Deviation (SD)
90	80Hz	7.000	0.000
	145Hz	7.000	0.000
	235Hz	7.000	0.000
100	80Hz	7.000	0.000
	145Hz	7.000	0.000
	235Hz	7.000	0.000

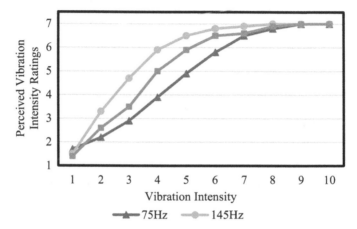

Fig. 5. Distribution of perceived vibration intensity ratings.

As revealed by the curve distributions in Fig. 5, there are differences in the perceived intensity of vibration across different frequencies. Overall, the perceived intensities of vibration across the three frequencies were ranked as 145 Hz > 80 Hz > 235 Hz. Furthermore, Fig. 1 also shows the differences in perceived intensity ratings at different intensities. The rating curves appear to be dispersed in the middle intensity range (e.g. 30–60), while they exhibit a clustering tendency in the lower and higher intensity ranges (e.g. 10–20, 70–100). One-factor ANOVA is required to explore the differences in perceived intensity across different intensities.

After verifying the homogeneity of variances using a statistical test (Table 3), one-way ANOVA was conducted on the rating data for different frequencies. Post hoc multiple comparisons were performed on the intensity rating data that showed significant differences ($P < 0.05$) to determine the specific differences among the three frequencies, which are presented in Table 4 and Table 5. Since the vibration perception ratings for intensity levels 90 and 100 were both 7 for all three frequencies, the analysis of differences between these two intensity levels was omitted.

The data in Table 4 and Table 5 show that there was at least one significant difference between the three frequencies for intensity levels 30–60. Specifically, the differences between each frequency for these intensity levels were as follows: (1) at intensity level 30, there was a significant difference between 145Hz and 80Hz as well as between 145Hz and 235Hz, and it can be concluded from Fig. 5 that the perceived intensity of vibration at 145Hz was significantly higher than that of the other two frequencies at intensity level 30; (2) at intensity level 40, there was a significant difference between 80Hz and both 145Hz and 235Hz, and it can be concluded from Fig. 5 that the perceived intensity of vibration at 145Hz and 235Hz was significantly higher than that of 80Hz; (3) at intensity level 50, there was a significant difference between 80Hz and both 145Hz and 235Hz, and it can be concluded from Fig. 5 that the perceived intensity of vibration at 145Hz and 235Hz was significantly higher than that of 80Hz; (4) at intensity level 60, there was a significant difference between 80Hz and 145Hz, and it can be concluded from Fig. 5 that the perceived intensity of vibration at 145Hz was significantly higher than that of 80Hz.

In summary, the perceived intensity of vibration at 145Hz was highest when the intensity levels were between 20 and 80, and it was significantly higher than the other experimental frequencies at intensity level 30. The perceived intensity of vibration at 80Hz was the lowest among the three experimental frequencies.

Table 3. Variance homogeneity test at different intensities.

Intensity	Levene	Df1	Df2	Sig.
10	0.417	2	27	0.663
20	0.309	2	27	0.737
30	0.176	2	27	0.84
40	0.553	2	27	0.581
50	2.077	2	27	0.145
60	3.221	2	27	0.056
70	5.295	2	27	0.011*
80	6.031	2	27	0.007*

[*] Levene's test for homogeneity of variances was significant ($p < 0.05$).

4 Comfort Intensity Range of Each Frequency

To calculate the comfortable vibration intensity values corresponding to different perceptual ratings at each frequency, it is necessary to conduct curve fitting analysis on the rating data. Firstly, a Pearson correlation analysis was performed on the vibration intensity and perceptual ratings at each frequency, and the specific data are listed in Table 6. Significant correlations were found between the perceptual ratings and vibration intensity at all frequencies, as shown in Table 7, and regression analysis was subsequently conducted on the rating data.

Table 4. Significance of differences in vibration intensity perception scores.

Intensity	Df2	Sig.
10	0.420	0.661
20	2.197	0.131
30	5.214	0.012*
40	8.015	0.002*
50	5.822	0.008*
60	4.017	0.030*
70	1.194	0.319
80	1.080	0.354

* is statistically significant at the 0.05 level.

Table 5. Post hoc multiple comparisons for vibration intensity perception ratings.

Intensity	Frequency 1	Frequency 2	Sig.
30	80Hz	145Hz	0.004 *
		235Hz	0.300
	145Hz	235Hz	0.044 *
40	80Hz	145Hz	0.000 *
		235Hz	0.037 *
	145Hz	235Hz	0.083
50	80Hz	145Hz	0.002 *
		235Hz	0.044 *
	145Hz	235Hz	0.216
60	80Hz	145Hz	0.010 *
		235Hz	0.064
	145Hz	235Hz	0.415

* The significance level of the difference between means is 0.05.

The results of the curve regression analysis are presented in Table 7 and Fig. 6, with the relevant data listed. The fitted functions were all statistically significant. The fitting results for 80Hz, 145Hz, and 235Hz explained 98.9%, 99.9%, and 96.7% of the rating data, respectively, and the fitting coefficients were significantly different at the 0.05 level.

We calculated the corresponding intensity values for the perceived ratings of 4 and 5 at three different frequencies, and the results were presented in Table 8. Due to the adjustment unit for vibration intensity being an integer in RichTap software, the fitted vibration intensity was rounded to the nearest integer before actual vibration measurements were conducted, and the results were recorded in Table 8. Based on the data in

Table 6. Correlation analysis between ratings and vibration Intensity.

Frequencies	Pearson correlation	Sig. (two-tailed)
80Hz	0.995**	0.000
145Hz	0.867**	0.001
235Hz	0.930**	0.000

** In 0.01 level (two-tailed), the correlation was significant.

Table 7. Regression analysis results of rating curves.

Frequency	Unstandardized coefficient			t	p	F	R^2
		B	Standard error				
80Hz	Constant	0.740	0.149	4.980	0.001	726.369	0.989
	B	0.065	0.002	26.951	0.000		
145Hz	Constant	-1.057	0.154	-6.873	0.000	1739.606	0.999
	B1	0.282	0.012	24.429	0.000		
	B2	-0.003	0.000	-13.696	0.000		
	B3	$1.245E^{-5}$	0.000	8.736	0.000		
235Hz	Constant	-5.218	0.695	-7.503	0.000	233.671	0.967
	Ln(B)	2.743	0.179	15.286	0.000		

Table 8, the suitable ranges of vibration intensity and the difference in values for the three frequencies were determined as follows: (1) 80Hz: intensity range of 50–66, a difference of 13 intensity units; (2) 145Hz: intensity range of 23–30, a difference of 7 intensity units; and (3) 235Hz: intensity range of 29–41, a difference of 12 units.

According to the analysis above and the fitted rating curves in Fig. 6, we found that: (1) 145Hz had the lowest suitable intensity value and the smallest range among the three frequencies; (2) the suitable intensity value at 235Hz was less than 50, and the range of values was lower than 50; and (3) the suitable range of intensity values for 80Hz was similar to that of 235Hz, with the value being greater than 50.

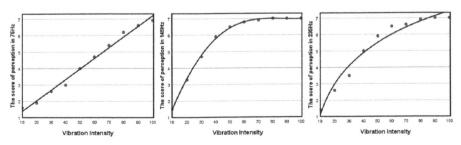

Fig. 6. Curves of rating for three frequencies.

Table 8. Appropriate vibration intensity range at each frequency.

Frequency	Perceived rating	Fitted vibration intensity	RichTap intensity value	P-P (mm/s^2)
80Hz	4	50.153	50	2.137
	5	65.538	66	2.742
145Hz	4	23.039	23	0.550
	5	29.712	30	0.898
235Hz	4	28.805	29	0.696
	5	41.476	41	0.932

5 Gender Differences

Table 9. Gender difference analysis results at the three frequencies.

Intensity	Frequency	Mean (M)		Standard Deviation (SD)		Sig.
		Male	Female	Male	Female	
10	80Hz	2.000	1.400	1.000	0.548	0.273
	145Hz	1.800	1.200	0.837	0.447	0.195
	235Hz	1.600	1.200	0.894	0.447	0.397
20	80Hz	2.800	1.600	1.304	0.548	0.094
	145Hz	3.800	2.800	1.095	0.837	0.143
	235Hz	3.000	2.200	1.414	1.304	0.380
30	80Hz	3.400	2.400	1.342	0.894	0.203
	145Hz	5.000	4.400	1.581	0.894	0.481
	235Hz	4.000	3.000	1.414	1.225	0.266
40	80Hz	4.000	3.800	1.000	0.837	0.740
	145Hz	6.000	5.800	1.000	1.304	0.792
	235Hz	5.400	4.600	1.140	1.517	0.373
50	80Hz	5.400	4.400	1.342	0.548	0.161
	145Hz	6.600	6.400	0.894	0.894	0.733
	235Hz	6.200	5.600	1.095	1.342	0.461

(*continued*)

Table 9. (*continued*)

Intensity	Frequency	Mean (M)		Standard Deviation (SD)		Sig.
		Male	Female	Male	Female	
60	80Hz	6.200	5.400	1.095	0.548	0.182
	145Hz	6.800	6.800	0.447	0.447	1.000
	235Hz	6.800	6.200	0.447	1.304	0.359
70	80Hz	6.800	6.200	0.447	0.837	0.195
	145Hz	6.800	7.000	0.447	0.000	0.347
	235Hz	6.800	6.400	0.447	0.894	0.397
80	80Hz	6.800	6.800	0.447	0.447	1.000
	145Hz	7.000	7.000	0.000[a]	0.000[a]	
	235Hz	7.000	6.800	0.000	0.447	0.347

a. Since the standard deviation of both groups is 0, t-value cannot be calculated.

To control for variables, a gender difference analysis was conducted assuming no significant differences in vibration intensity perception between males and females. According to the independent sample t-test analysis results in Table 9, the p-values for males and females at each intensity level were all greater than 0.05, indicating that the hypothesis cannot be rejected from a statistical standpoint. Therefore, it can be concluded that there is no gender difference in vibration intensity perception at the three frequencies. Since all the ratings at 90 and 100 were 7, gender differences analysis for these two intensity levels were omitted.

6 Discussion

Our experimental objective was to investigate the differences in vibration intensity perception at three different frequencies and provide appropriate vibration intensity ranges for each frequency based on rating data. The main findings of our study revealed that the vibration perception level was most apparent at a frequency of 145Hz, which could meet the vibration requirements at lower intensity settings. The appropriate moderate vibration intensity range for this frequency was 23–30.

In terms of the differences in vibration intensity perception at different frequencies, we found that the most significant difference was observed at a fixed intensity level for 145Hz, followed by 235Hz and then 80Hz. Similar findings were reported by S. Kasaei et al. [9], who found that vibrations at frequencies above 250Hz were weakly perceived, which limited their study. However, Hwang I's research [7] found that frequencies below 100Hz were perceived more strongly than those above 100Hz. It was speculated that the inconsistency of the vibration generator caused the differences. The vibrations in our study were controlled by RichTap software, and the same intensity level did not correspond to the same amplitude for different frequencies, as shown in Table 2. In Hwang I's study, the amplitude was given and the differences in perception at different frequencies were compared. Further research is needed to determine the specific differences that cause these inconsistencies.

Furthermore, we fitted the intensity-rating curve and calculated the appropriate intensity values for ratings of 4–5 according to the user perception rating scale. Table 8 shows the appropriate intensity value ranges for each frequency. From the perspective of value, the appropriate intensity values for 145Hz were the lowest, followed by 235Hz and then 80Hz. However, the intensity values were all below 70% of the maximum intensity, and particularly, the intensity values for 145Hz and 235Hz were below 50%. From the perspective of the difference between the upper and lower limits, the appropriate range for 145Hz was the narrowest, followed by 235Hz and then 80Hz, which both had wider ranges. Both aspects indirectly confirmed the trend of differences in intensity perception at different frequencies. In Christian Schönauer et al.'s study [6], it was mentioned that users tend to overestimate the intensity of vibration and perceive it as too strong. This finding was similar to the results of our study, in which the comfortable intensity values for each frequency were relatively low.

We did not find significant gender differences in our research analysis, which may be related to the different frequency values used. Burström L et al. found significant gender differences in vibration perception thresholds at 31.5Hz, but not at 125Hz [10]. In the future, it may be necessary to expand the frequency range or sample size for further research.

7 Conclusion

This study investigates the perception of vibration intensity at different frequencies in notification scenarios, using subjective rating methods. Based on intensity-rating data, the appropriate range of intensity values for each frequency was determined by fitting curves. The results show that, among the three experimental frequencies, vibration perception was strongest at 145Hz, with the smallest appropriate range of intensity values. Although gender differences were analyzed, no significant differences were found. It is speculated that this may be due to differences in frequency parameter selection, which requires further research and analysis.

Based on the above conclusions, when designing vibration feedback in notification scenarios, frequencies around 145Hz should be given priority as they can satisfy the vibration perception requirements with relatively low intensity. However, the range of intensity values should also be considered to avoid ineffective feedback due to vibrations that are either too weak or too strong.

Since the recruited participants were all undergraduates at Hunan University, with ages under 30, further research and analysis with a larger sample size may be necessary for other age groups. Additionally, due to limitations such as equipment and time, only a small number of frequencies and intensities were studied. Future work could focus on a wider range of frequencies or other relevant vibration factors to further explore this area.

References

1. Henderson, J., Avery, J., Grisoni, L., Lank, E.: Leveraging distal vibrotactile feedback for target acquisition. In: Proceedings of the 2019 CHI Conference on Human Factors in Computing Systems. ACM, New York, NY, USA, pp. 1–11 (2019). https://doi.org/10.1145/329 0605.3300715
2. Hachisu, T., Suzuki, K.: Representing interpersonal touch directions by tactile apparent motion using smart bracelets. IEEE Trans. Haptics 12(3), 327–338 (2019)
3. Zhao, S., Israr, A., Fenner, M., Klatzky, R.L.: Intermanual apparent tactile motion and its extension to 3D interactions. IEEE Trans. Haptics 10(4), 555–566 (2017)
4. Hwang, I., Seo, J., Kim, M., Choi, S.: Vibrotactile perceived intensity for mobile devices as a function of direction, amplitude, and frequency. IEEE Trans. Haptics 6(3), 352–362 (2013)
5. Tan, J., Ge, Y., Sun, X., Zhang, Y., Liu, Y.: User experience of tactile feedback on a smartphone: effects of vibration intensity, times and interval. In: Rau, P.-L. (ed.) HCII 2019. LNCS, vol. 11576, pp. 397–406. Springer, Cham (2019). https://doi.org/10.1007/978-3-030-22577-3_29
6. Schönauer, C., Mossel, A., Zaiţi, I.-A., Vatavu, R.-D.: Touch, movement and vibration: user perception of vibrotactile feedback for touch and mid-air gestures. In: Abascal, J., Barbosa, S., Fetter, M., Gross, T., Palanque, P., Winckler, M. (eds.) INTERACT 2015. LNCS, vol. 9299, pp. 165–172. Springer, Cham (2015). https://doi.org/10.1007/978-3-319-22723-8_14
7. Hwang, I., Seo, J., Kim, M., Choi, S.: Vibrotactile perceived intensity for mobile devices as a function of direction, amplitude, and frequency. IEEE Trans. Haptics. Jul-Sep; 6(3), 352–362 (2013). https://doi.org/10.1109/TOH.2013.2. PMID: 24808331
8. Liu, S.-F., Yang, Y.-T., Chang, C.-F., Lin, P.-Y., Cheng, H.-S.: A study on haptic feedback awareness of senior citizens. In: Zhou, J., Salvendy, G. (eds.) ITAP 2018. LNCS, vol. 10926, pp. 315–324. Springer, Cham (2018). https://doi.org/10.1007/978-3-319-92034-4_24
9. Kasaei, S., Levesque, V.: Effect of vibration frequency mismatch on apparent tactile motion. In: 2022 IEEE Haptics Symposium (HAPTICS), Santa Barbara, CA, USA, pp. 1-62022https:// doi.org/10.1109/HAPTICS52432.2022.9765602
10. Burström, L., Lundström, R., Hagberg, M., Nilsson, T.: Vibrotactile perception and effects of short-term exposure to hand-arm vibration. Ann Occup Hyg. 53(5), 539–547 (2009). https:// doi.org/10.1093/annhyg/mep027. Epub 2009 Apr 29 PMID: 19403839

Evaluating Interface Layouts for Conditionally Automated Vehicle Messages

Manuela Quaresma$^{(\boxtimes)}$ (ID), Isabela Motta(ID), Gabriel Martins(ID), and Clara Gavinho

LEUI | Laboratory of Ergodesign and Usability of Interfaces, PUC-Rio | Pontifical Catholic University of Rio de Janeiro, Rio de Janeiro, Brazil
mquaresma@puc-rio.br

Abstract. Appropriate interface design is essential for drivers' understanding of automated driving systems states, especially for systems that present complex information such as conditionally automated vehicles. To explore adequate interface design solutions, this study aimed to assess the effects of two different interface layouts (side-by-side symbols and overlapping symbols) on drivers' comprehension of five system messages. To this end, we conducted an online comprehension testing which was answered by licensed drivers. We observed no significant differences in the effects of the layout on participants' comprehension of the messages. However, qualitative data showed that respondents may not completely understand the functioning of conditionally automated vehicles, since drivers could comprehend failure or take over request messages but struggled to recognize the "unavailable" and "available" states. Our main contribution is a discussion on observed interface design issues that may be explored in future research.

Keywords: Interface Design · Comprehension Testing · Conditionally Automated Vehicles

1 Introduction

The development of automated vehicles has been under the spotlight in the automotive industry, noticeably evolving over the years, as demonstrated by manufacturers such as Tesla [44] and Waymo [17]. Currently, vehicles embedded with automated driving systems (ADS) of automation levels 1 and 2 [42] are already available for purchase and driving on roadways. Such vehicles combine advanced driving assistance systems (ADAS) to support the driving task and relieve its resulting mental workload on drivers. Aiming to advance these products even further, manufacturers have been focusing on developing level 3 (L3) ADS, which differ from their predecessors by not only controlling the vehicle's lateral and longitudinal movement, but also by sparing the driver from actively monitoring the system within pre-established operational design domains [20, 42].

Despite ADSs' potential benefits for relieving the driving task's physical and cognitive demands, utilizing an L3 ADS changes the task's nature [45], requiring the driver

A. Marcus et al. (Eds.): HCII 2023, LNCS 14032, pp. 284–303, 2023.
https://doi.org/10.1007/978-3-031-35702-2_21

to perform a series of new interactions that bring novel issues. For instance, Parasuraman et al. [33] suggested that by relinquishing physical control of a task (e.g. driving) the human operator assumes a new role inside the task, acting as a system workflow supervisor. Considering the misunderstanding of the system's status may lead to several issues, and bring safety implications to the task environment [32].

To mitigate such issues, the literature [15, 28, 29, 39] have shown that presenting comprehensible, effective visual information aids drivers in taking over the vehicle's control and understanding the system's general functioning [2, 12, 23]. Similarly, policies proposed by NHTSA [27] recommend that conditionally automated vehicle (L3) systems should clearly present their main states through five indicators (messages): 1) System Unavailable for automated driving (i.e., unavailable), 2) Functioning Properly (i.e., available), 3) System Engaged in automated driving mode (i.e., activated), 4) Failure in the ADS' functioning (i.e., failing), 5) Takeover Request (TOR).

The first message, System Unavailable, informs the driver that the system is not ready to be used and cannot be turned on. The message which informs that the system is Functioning Properly states the opposite, indicating that the automation is ready to be turned on without any trouble. System Engaged follows that message, notifying the driver that they are no longer in charge of the driving task once the system has taken over. Campbell et al. [4] name these three messages as the system activation or on/off status, defining those states as an indication to the driver regarding which automation mode is currently active, if at all. When provided, this information supports the driver's awareness of the current automation mode. The Failure in ADS' functioning indicates that part of the system has malfunctioned or that it is no longer functioning properly, thus the importance of alerting the drivers that they might have to intervene in case the system finds itself unable to fix the problem or work in those conditions. The Takeover Request is a follow-up after the occurrence of a system failure [42], in which the system expects a response by the user to take control of the driving tasks and perform them to achieve a minimal risk condition.

To offer guidance on how to display such essential information, an increasing body of literature indicates recommendations to present ADS states to drivers on Human-Machine Interfaces (HMI). Naujoks et al. [29] suggested several guidelines for automated vehicles' HMIs, built upon existing design guidelines for manual driving [1, 5, 9, 18, 22, 26, 43], but which apply to the automated driving context. In a similar manner, Boelhouwer et al. [3] systematically reviewed the literature and commercially available HMIs and developed a taxonomy describing different ways to present ADSs messages.

Nevertheless, the implementation of a new visual language in a pioneering technology that changes the driving task brings issues that still challenge the state of the art of human factors in vehicular automation. As indicated by Perrier et al. [36], although there is a certain degree of symbol standardization for some ADAS, such as lane-keeping assistance or adaptive cruise control systems, different manufacturers still exhibit variations in the application of these visual elements. Thus, ADSs still lack uniformity in the presentation of status information on HMIs. Studies in the literature [34–37, 40, 41] have also suggested that drivers have varied expectations about how a system's functioning should be represented. Richardson et al. [41] evidenced this tendency by evaluating HMIs' icons and identifying low levels of symbol comprehension accuracy. Considering

HMIs' importance for reacquiring situation awareness [13], eventual flaws in human-machine communication may lead drivers to misunderstand system states [38], and, consequently, compromise their safety.

Considering the aforementioned issues, it is still necessary to create strategies to facilitate drivers' proper comprehension of ADS states, extending the tactics presented in the literature. A possible approach may lay in how information can be grouped on the HMI. In his works on the usability and product design field, Norman [31] argues that the physical form of an object alone may offer clues for users about its functioning and usage, through the employment of affordances: "the quality or property of an object that defines its possible uses or makes clear how it can or should be used" [16, p. 127]. The concept of affordances is a widely applied tool in the field of digital interfaces to develop self-explanatory interfaces and improve a products' usability. Hoober and Berkman [19] suggest that sequential menus (or carrousels) should be used to indicate the progression in smartphone apps' interfaces, aiding users in understanding the app's functioning. Also, within the concept of proximity (one of Gestalt principles of perception; Lidwell et al., [24]), perception of information evolution becomes more evident when some symbols icons are arranged side by side.

The use of information grouping on vehicles' HMIs is also recommended by the literature on embedded interfaces. Graphic elements should be grouped according to the functions they represent [43], for example, in separated boxes of windows [7]. Campbell et al. [7] argue that grouping icons improves users' capacity to perceive such elements as a group of similar messages or commands, providing clues about the system's functioning and leveraging the icons' comprehensibility. Likewise, Naujoks et al. [29] suggest that grouping should be used to communicate state transitions, mitigating dispersion of drivers' gaze to different parts of the vehicle.

Considering NHTSA's [27] recommendations, the five ADS states may be understood in a sequential manner, starting from the least (System Unavailable) to the most (System Activated) automated state, closing a complete cycle as the system requires the driver's intervention (TOR). Therefore, we hypothesized that presenting HMIs' elements sequentially, through a side-by-side layout, may leverage drivers' understanding of ADSs' states since such visual disposition might communicate the sequential process of an L3 ADS functioning. To evaluate the before-mentioned proposal, this study aimed to assess the applicability of visual elements' layout on HMIs' as a tool to aid drivers' comprehension of ADSs.

2 Materials and Methods

To address the aforementioned questions, we conducted an online information comprehension test based on Campbell et al. [6] and ISO [21]. We aimed to understand the effects of an HMI's layout on drivers' comprehension of the five messages proposed by NHTSA [27] to portray an ADS's operating states.

2.1 Participants

Owning a drivers' license was established as a participation requirement to ensure that respondents had some familiarity with automotive symbols and passenger vehicles' interfaces, and therefore avoid learning effects on the results. The study had a total of 63 respondents (28 female). Participants were recruited through social media and chat apps, as well as specific passenger vehicles' discussion groups. They were prompted with a brief description of the study's purpose and the form's link with the term of consent, and no compensation was promised nor given to respondents.

2.2 Design

The online test was entirely developed and maintained on the Eval&Go software (eva-landgo.com). We chose the online form tool due to its capacity to receive a large number of responses and its remote nature, as the COVID-19 pandemic hinders in-person testing. In the form, we presented the five main ADS messages (System Unavailable, System Available, System Activated, System Failure, and Takeover Request) through symbols applied on instrument clusters' images.

The independent variable was the placement of the symbols - developed to represent each message - presented on an HMI in two layouts conditions: side-by-side symbols layout and overlapping symbols layout. Additionally, we measured the dependent variable - the messages' comprehensibility - through open-ended questions. The two independent variable conditions were chosen based on the principles of proximity and sequencing in grouping information, and we hypothesized that side-by-side layout would generate better understanding. The technique followed a between-subject design, in which half the sample was assigned to the side-by-side symbols layout condition (31), and the other half to the overlapping symbols layout condition (32), in a counterbalanced way.

2.3 Test Materials

We created five symbols to represent each of the five ADS (L3) messages described previously (Fig. 1). To aid this process, we reviewed symbols used in commercially available ADAS, as well as research on symbols for ADS [36, 40, 41]. In addition, we followed the literature's design guidelines [4, 21, 29, 43] to color the symbols: white for status information, green for indicating proper system functioning, yellow for warnings and preventive information, and red for high-urgency messages.

Fig. 1. The symbols developed for the study with their respective meanings/messages.

To aid participants' immersion in the test, we applied the symbols to a simulated instrument cluster (Fig. 2), presenting essential informational elements: speedometer, tachometer, odometer, temperature and fuel gauges, and a central area representing the vehicle and the road (as can be observed in some vehicles equipped with L2 ADSs).

Moreover, we dedicated the inferior central area to display and highlight the symbols representing the ADS states, which participants were to analyze.

We created the simulated HMIs (Table 1) to present symbols in two layouts: displaying all symbols sequentially (side-by-side symbols layout) and displaying one symbol at a time (overlapping symbols layout). The layouts intended to measure the symbols' grouping impact on participants' comprehension of the ADS's information and determine their efficiency in helping the driver perceive system state changes.

Fig. 2. Simulated instrument cluster used in the test.

Table 1. Symbol's layouts and messages.

Message	Layout	Image
System Unavailable	Side-by-side	
	Overlapping	
System Available	Side-by-side	
	Overlapping	
System Activated	Side-by-side	

(continued)

Table 1. (*continued*)

Message	Layout	Image
	Overlapping	
System Failing	Side-by-side	
	Overlapping	
Takeover Request	Side-by-side	
	Overlapping	

2.4 Online Form Structure

The online form comprised four sections: 1) an introduction, with a consent term and requiring confirmation that the respondent owned a drivers' license, 2) the test's instructions, 3) the comprehension test itself, and 4) demographic data collection.

In the instructions section, we presented a brief textual explanation introducing an overview about automated vehicles and exposing the five ADS information to be presented. We added such directions to minimize errors caused by participants' potential lack of familiarity with ADSs. For similar reasons, we also presented a short explanation of commonly employed colors on in-vehicle interfaces. Furthermore, we displayed a preview of the simulated instrument cluster highlighting the area in which symbols would be presented to clarify to which messages the open-ended questions were referring. Finally, we presented the symbols (in black and white) that were to be displayed in the test, allowing participants to glance at all the symbols from the start, thereby avoiding potential learning effects between the proposed layouts.

In the third section, the simulated instrument cluster displaying the five ADS information was presented randomly, one by one, to avoid order presentation bias, with each symbol being displayed only once. All the participants answered three questions about each of the images. No limitations were established for participants' response time since we were evaluating their comprehension and interpretations of ADS messages rather than how quickly such information would be recognized. The first question asked participants to describe their understanding of the system message being displayed. The second question required participants to rate their degree of confidence in their answer to the previous question on a 5-point scale (from very low to very high). We added this question to assess whether the conditions (layouts) would elicit differences in participants' confidence levels in their understanding of the messages. Finally, the third question asked the respondents to indicate which visual elements they used to interpret the presented information to allow a qualitative analysis on which elements influence drivers' understandings of the messages.

The form's last section collected demographic data (age, gender, years of driving experience, education level), the participant's affinity with technology, and ADAS usage. These questions aimed to check possible correlations between the participants' characteristics and their responses.

2.5 Data Analysis

The analysis of the responses reflecting the participants' interpretation of the information was based on the ratings scales suggested by Campbell et al. [6] to assess the comprehensibility of automotive safety symbols. First, five researchers individually assigned a score to all responses per symbol/message following the criteria suggested by the authors (Table 2). Next, the researchers collectively discussed disagreements and revised the scores. Thereafter, the responses were categorized into four categories of combined comprehension scores (high, low, no comprehension, and critical confusion [6], which were posteriorly used for the quantitative analyses.

Table 2. Rating scales for categorizing and scoring subject responses to the icons [6].

Combined Score	Score	Description
High	1	The response matches the intended meaning of the icon exactly
	2	The response captures all major informational elements of the intended meaning of the icon, but is missing one or more minor informational elements
Low	3	The response captures some of the intended meaning of the icon, but it is missing one or more major informational elements
	4	The response does not match the intended meaning of the icon, but it captures some major or minor informational elements
None	5	The response does not match the intended meaning of the icon, but it is somewhat relevant
	6	Participant's response is in no way relevant to the intended meaning of the icon
	7	Participant indicated he/she did not understand the icon
	8	No answer
Critical confusing	9	For safety-critical icons, identify the number and percentage of critical confusions or errors. Critical confusions or errors reflect responses that indicate that the subject perceived the message to convey a potentially unsafe action

The data was preprocessed in Matlab 2018 (Mathworks) and statistically analyzed in SPSS V26 software (IBM Corp.). Homogeneity tests were performed among the sample subjects to check for the presence of potential contaminants due to the between-subject structure. The combined comprehension scores were treated as a categorical value, where the probabilities of a response being assigned to each of the four categories of comprehension were treated as mutually exclusive independent events. Kolmogorov Smirnov tests attested to normality in the confidence data for each of the responses. For statistical tests, a significance criterion of 5% (alpha = 0.05) was used.

Furthermore, to identify and analyze the visual elements mentioned by participants as influential for their understanding of the information, we made an affinity diagram [25] on the collaborative platform Miro (Miro.com). For each of the five messages, we reviewed the responses and categorized them according to the element type used for interpretation (color, symbol, interface, etc.) and the message's interpretation (i.e., what was understood from the image in terms of system states). As we reviewed responses in light of the reported visual elements utilized to achieve interpretations, this process not only aided in identifying relevant elements and interpretation types but also favored the recognition of relationships between these two variables.

3 Results and Discussion

3.1 Data Uniformity Analysis

As described above, we first looked for disparities in participants' profiles among the two respondent groups, which could have been caused by the random selection of participants for such a between-subject structured test. Using the layouts as independent variables (i.e., side-by-side, overlapping) we measured the categorical variables (i.e., age range, affinity to technology) through chi-squared tests, while the continuous variables (i.e., number of in-vehicles interfaces utilized, driving experience) were measured through t-tests.

The results showed that the age distribution of the participants seems to be evenly balanced across the test's conditions, as there was no significant effect of grouping structure on participant's age ($X2$ (4, $N = 63$) = 1.044, $p = 0.904$). The sample seems to be evenly distributed between younger (18–40 years old) and older respondents (41-year-old or above) for both the side-by-side symbols layout condition (45.2% younger drivers) and for the overlapping symbols layout condition (44.7% younger drivers). This even distribution of drivers' age is also reflected on their driving experience, as the T-test results showed no significant effect of the independent variable (T (61) = 0.5185, p = 0.607) on how many years drivers hold their driving license (side-by-side M = 22.84, SD = 14.81; overlapping M = 20.97, SD = 13.769).

When it comes to participant's affinity with technology, chi-squared tests showed no significant differences in participants' early-adoption behaviour of technologies ($X2$ (2, $N = 63$) = 3.5191, $p = 0.176$). Most participants (67.7% side-by-side symbols layout, 87.5% overlapping symbols layout) identify themselves as average technology users, who are willing to try out new technology as soon as it is commercially available. The T-test results also showed no significant effect of the independent variable on the number of IVIS/ADAS used by drivers (T (61) = 0.315, p = 0.754). Respondents on the side-by-side symbols layout condition seem to have experience with an average of

6.161 systems (SD = 3.569), while the participants on the overlapping symbol layout condition seem to have experience with an average of 5.906 systems (SD = 0.501).

3.2 Combined Comprehension Score Analysis

To measure the effects of the layouts on participants' comprehension of the ADS information displayed on the HMI, we conducted chi-squared tests for each of the five status messages presented. For each message, we considered the proportion of the combined comprehension scores (high, low, no comprehension, critical confusion) as the dependent variable, while the layout conditions (side-by-side, overlapping) were used as the independent variables for the tests. The table below (table 3) shows the chi-squared tests' results, and Fig. 3 graphically illustrates the combination of all five messages' proportion of combined comprehension scores for the two conditions.

Table 3. Statistical results of the Chi-Squared tests.

		Unavailable	Available	Activated	Failing	TOR
Chi-Squared Statistics	X2	0.939	0.530	3.04	2.404	4.057
	df	2	2	2	2	2
	P	0.625	0.767	0.219	0.301	0.225
Combined Comprehension Score Proportion	Percentage Side-by-Side Symbols Layout					
	High	16.1%	12.9%	64.5%	80.6%	87.1%
	Low	19.4%	68.1%	25.8%	19.4%	3.2%
	None	64.5%	29.0%	9.7%	0%	3.2%
	Crit. Conf	0.0%	0.0%	0.0%	0.0%	6.5%
	Percentage Overlapping Symbols Layout					
	High	9.4%	12.5%	81.2%	81.3%	90.6%
	Low	15.6%	50.0%	9.4%	12.5%	9.4%
	None	75.0%	37.5%	9.4%	6.3%	0.0%
	Crit. Conf	0.0%	0.0%	0.0%	0.0%	0.0%

As can be seen below (Fig. 3), there was no significant effect of the layout on the comprehension level for any of the messages. Such results contradict our initial hypothesis that presenting information through a sequential order would serve as an affordance to communicate the ADS's functioning – as generally observed in the literature on HMI design [10, 30].

Nevertheless, as reported on Fig. 3, about half of the participants (47.7%, 45.0%) showed low comprehension levels of the symbols displayed for both conditions. This result suggests that, generally, symbols indicating automated system status are not yet clear for the average population. Regardless of the expected underwhelming performance of the overall symbols, it seems like the intended affordances were not evident enough, or not informative enough to interfere with participants' comprehensibility.

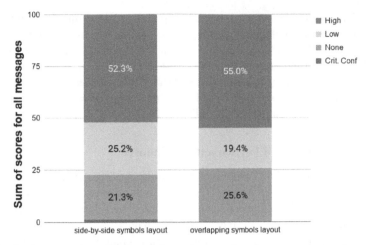

Fig. 3. Aggregated scores of participants' comprehension across the two layouts.

To check if the distribution of the combined comprehension score was unbalanced across the different messages of this study, a new Chi-squared test was conducted, using information type (automation available, automation unavailable, automation activated, automation failing, takeover requests) as the independent variable.

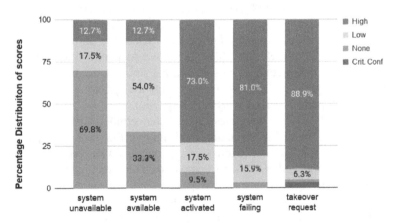

Fig. 4. Aggregated scores of participants' comprehension across the five messages.

The results of the test found a significant effect of information type on the participants' combined comprehension score ($X2$ (5, $N = 63$) = 202.645, $p < 0.001$). The figure above (Fig. 4) showed that the sample probability for a participant to score a "High" score on the questions of questionnaire is much lower for both the the "Automation Unavailable" (12.7%) and "Automation Available" (12.7%) when compared to the other three messages (Automation Activated 73.0%, Automation Failing = 81%, Takeover Request = 88.9%).

The level of confidence on participants' response was evaluated by a 2x5 ANOVA, measuring the effect of both layout conditions across the five information types on the respondents' level of confidence on their responses. The results showed no significant effect of neither information type ($F(1, 63) = 0.002$, p-0.996,, $\eta^2 = 0.01$) nor layout condition ($F(1, 63) = 0.120$, $p = 0.731$. $\eta^2 = 0.02$), where the mean degree of confidence was considerably high for both side-by-side symbol layout ($M = 3.621$, $SD = 0.21$) and overlapping symbols layout ($M = 3.72$, $SD = 0.217$).

3.3 Qualitative Analysis of Participants' Responses

To further explore participants' interpretations of the ADS messages and the rationales behind them, we qualitatively analyzed answers to the two open-ended questions. For both layouts, participants reached their interpretation by relying on elements such as colors and symbols' visual cues (e.g., usage of "hands" or "steering wheel") and by comparing the five symbols. However, the comparison strategy was more evident for the side-by-side symbols layout condition, which was expected since such a layout favored comparisons. Participants from both conditions also used other indicators on the simulated instrument cluster (e.g., speedometer, headlamp symbol) to draw conclusions about the ADS, comparing such indicators to the ADS's symbols. Furthermore, the responses frequently mentioned known commercially available ADAS symbols (e.g., Tesla Autopilot) and other traffic or technology-related products (e.g., the traffic light's color code) when reasoning about their interpretation of ADS states.

The System Failing and TOR messages had the most accurate recognition rates among the five information, followed by the System Activated message, which also presented reasonable recognition rates. On the other hand, few participants recognized the intended meaning for the System Unavailable and Available messages, having the most varied range of interpretations. In some cases, similar meanings were attributed to these two messages, which was also observed for the system available and system activated messages (both perceived as System Engaged).

Rather than HMIs' layout, responses showed that symbols and colors were more influential for the message's interpretation, highlighting that such cues play a major role in comprehending information. Moreover, we identified that precise interpretations tended to consider fewer HMI's elements compared to incorrect judgments. For example, responses that diverged from the messages' intended meaning tended to rely on other elements displayed on the instrument cluster (e.g., speedometer) rather than the ADS's symbols to reach conclusions. Oppositely, participants reported using the ADS-related elements (especially symbols and colors) more frequently when analyzing the information with higher comprehension accuracy levels (System Activated, Failure, and TOR).

Examining the overall interpretations of ADS states, we identified an expressive struggle from the participants to understand the operating characteristics of L3 ADSs. On occasions, some responses (from both layout conditions) even displayed understandings that were opposite to the messages' intended meaning. For example, a participant expressed the belief that the ADS would be engaged in automation continuously and without restrictions, and since there was no warning or alert indicating malfunctions, they interpreted the System Unavailable message as "working under normal conditions".

It seems that many respondents believed that the vehicle could be engaged in automated driving uninterruptedly, misunderstanding the conditional nature of L3 systems, which might not be available at all times. Such a tendency has already been reported by Carsten and Martens [8] and is in line with Dixon's [11] concept of "autonowashing": a general perception by people that automated vehicles are, in the current state of development, capable of doing more than they actually can, due to media and marketing descriptions of such vehicles. Nonetheless, our results also indicate that some drivers may underestimate such systems' capacity, conceptualizing them as L1/L2 ADSs. Some respondents compared the presented ADS with commercially available systems such as CC/ACC (even employing the "autopilot" term), suggesting the influence of an existing mental model of interaction with these types of systems.

Another less frequent issue identified in the responses was the misconception that the HMI would present possible driver/ system actions instead of system status. The presence or absence of the hands on the wheel caused a polarity in participants' perceptions: while the steering wheel with no hands was related to automated driving, the hands-on-the-wheel symbol was related to manual driving. For example, some participants understood that the gray steering wheel symbol (System Unavailable) indicated that the steering wheel was disabled for manual driving, therefore interpreting the system as activated. Similarly, for the red hands-on-the-wheel symbol, two participants interpreted the symbols as representing that the driver had taken over the steering wheel and that the ADS was deactivated. In such cases, respondents seemed to have overlooked the red color as an alert of imminent danger, and consequently did not perceive the TOR (critical confusion). Furthermore, some participants displayed an even more literal interpretation, reporting that the steering wheel referred to the vehicle's steering wheel itself (similarly to a lane-keeping assistant, for example) instead of the ADS.

Considering the disparity in the comprehension rates among messages, we conducted an individual analysis to uncover issues and misunderstandings around each information. We present such results in the next section.

3.4 Qualitative Analysis of Participants' Responses for Each Message

Our goal in performing a qualitative analysis was to understand how each of the participants interpreted the system messages displayed to them, especially regarding what confused them and led them to believe that the information was different. To analyze each of the categories, we created subgroups considering their responses to each particular message (Fig. 5). It was clear that the System Unavailable and System Available are the messages where the category with the biggest percentage of respondents is not correct.

Firstly, few respondents interpreted the System Unavailable message according to its intended meaning for both layouts, resulting in varied interpretations for such information (Fig. 6). A frequently reported perception was that the system was turned off and the vehicle was in manual control. Although this interpretation is very close to the message's intended meaning, it seemed that respondents did not understand that the system would not be available to engage in automated driving. Contrarily, several participants thought that the ADS was activated, arguing that the absence of warnings on HMI indicated proper functioning of the HMI. This interpretation was often accompanied by high

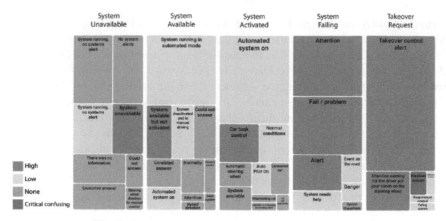

Fig. 5. Responses' categories for each message group.

reported confidence levels, suggesting that respondents had a strong expectation that the HMI would only show messages in case of malfunction or to require driver actions. We believe that the previously mentioned struggle to understand the ADS' functioning may have been determinant for these interpretations.

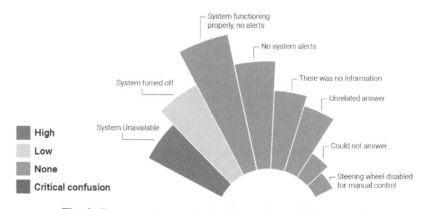

Fig. 6. Responses' categories for System Unavailable message.

Nonetheless, we observed that the absence of color on symbols' design also impacted responses, independently of the interpretation. As the symbol used for System Unavailable was equal in shape to the System Available symbol, changing only the colors from gray (Disabled) to white, the lack of a specific symbol for such information might have suggested the absence of information, especially for the side-by-side condition in which all symbols were sequentially presented in gray. For example, one participant from this condition mentioned that they thought the system was turned off by comparing the symbols, but argued that there should be a specific icon to communicate such information. On the other hand, the color similarities in the four aligned Disabled symbols also caused the perception that no information was being displayed, which was understood as normal functioning. Reinforcing that the absence of an illuminated tell-tale may be inadequate to represent the system's unavailability, we identified that some participants searched for the message's meaning in other instrument cluster elements (e.g., speedometer, fuel gauge).

Similar to the previous information, few respondents correctly interpreted the System Available message, presenting the biggest number of different interpretations among messages (Fig. 7). The correct recognition of this information was frequently related to the white color applied to the symbol. However, about half of respondents from both conditions understood the message as System Activated and working, a discrete but significant misconception as the automation is not yet engaged in this case. Participants who had this perception relied on the absence of other seemingly relevant visual cues and on similarities between the white symbol and other HMI elements (e.g., odometer, speedometer, etc.). Other interpretations for this message include: system deactivated and in manual driving, system inoperative, attention alert, TOR, and people who felt unable to answer about the message.

Considering such results, we believe that, just as it is challenging for drivers to understand the possibility that ADS may be unavailable, the idea of a system that is available but not engaged may be hard to conceptualize. Moreover, using the steering wheel symbol in a neutral color and without any other elements/symbols may not be the best way to convey some message about ADS.

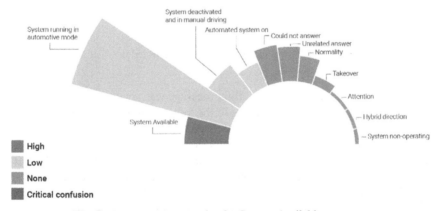

Fig. 7. Responses' categories for System Available message.

In the System Activated message most respondents understood the intended message (Fig. 8), mainly due to the green color employed and the on/off symbol attached to the steering wheel. However, some participants considered the on/off symbol as a switch symbol, and were uncertain about the message's meaning when they tried to compare it to the white symbol (System Activated). In this sense, some respondents also interpreted that the ADS was ready to be turned on, i.e., the ADS was available for activation. One respondent interpreted that the steering wheel could be literally turned on (perhaps in an LKA proposition).

Specifically for some other respondents' whose interpretations were "vehicle turned on" or "normal and safe conditions", the mindset remained that the vehicle would be in automated driving at all times (like an L4/L5) and that the green color conveyed a safe, normal ADS operation status. Most respondents with this mindset were confident in their answers. As mentioned previously, this result reinforces the existence of difficulty in conveying that there are different automation levels for vehicles. There is still a big challenge for HMI design teams in communicating safety and hazards information in automated vehicles. Users may have difficulty understanding when they are dealing with an L3, L4, or L5 ADS and consequently may not know how to correctly perform their role in the human-ADS relationship.

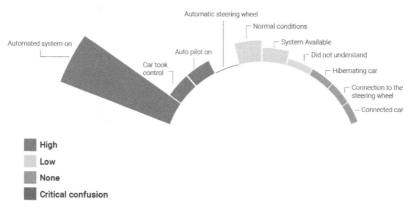

Fig. 8. Responses' categories System Activated message.

As mentioned earlier, the System Failing message was very well recognized by the study respondents (Fig. 9), especially due to the yellow color and the warning symbol attached to the steering wheel. Respondents were confident in associating the symbol with messages such as warning, attention, failure, or ADS malfunction, regardless of the layout. Those who indicated that the ADS was failing or operating with limitations frequently reported relying on the warning symbol to interpret the message, and some made analogies between the symbol and traffic lights' yellow color. Even for incorrect interpretations, almost all responses showed the understanding that a problem or malfunctioning was occurring. For example, some responses indicated a more literal reading of the icon, stating that the driver should pay attention to the steering wheel specifically rather than the automated driving altogether. Other inadequate interpretations included the need to help the system, some abstract danger or concrete obstacle on the road, and the ADS's unavailability (which was mentioned by only one respondent). Therefore, considering such high comprehension rates, using the warning symbol and the yellow color along the steering wheel symbol is a potential design recommendation conveying ADSs' malfunctions.

Finally, despite being a novelty in the driving context and a strong feature of L3 ADSs (which are not yet commercialized), the TOR message was the most accurately understood by respondents in both conditions (Fig. 10). Similar to how the visual elements

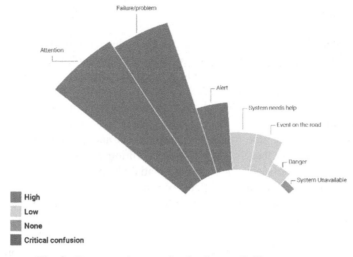

Fig. 9. Responses' categories for System Failing message.

were analyzed in the System Failing message, the respondents relied on the hands-on-the-wheel wheel symbol and the color red to interpret TORs. For this message, the red color was the key element that communicated the urgency (as an expected stereotype) that the driver should immediately take over the vehicle's control. However, as observed in other messages, some participants took the literal approach in understanding that the driver should put their hands on the steering wheel, but not necessarily to resume manual control. This type of understanding resembles hands-on-the-wheel alerts in L2 ADSs' HMIs, which requires drivers to touch the wheel to remain in the action-decision loop mentioned in Sect. 1. Notwithstanding, as many respondents understood the information as a TOR, there is strong potential for such a symbol to be used for TOR in combination with labels, voice message, and other auditory and/or haptic cues as a multimodal message, as already pointed out in the literature [4, 29].

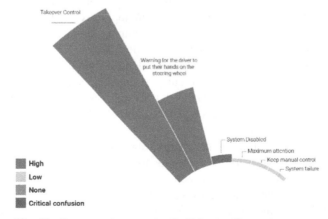

Fig. 10. Responses' categories for Takeover Request message.

4 Conclusion

Appropriate interface design is essential for drivers' understanding of automated driving systems (ADS) states, especially for systems that present complex information such as conditionally automated vehicles. To explore information presentation strategies, this study aimed to assess the effects of HMIs' layouts on drivers' comprehension of L3 ADS states. To this end, we conducted a comprehension test through an online form, in which participants interpreted five messages presented on a simulated instrument cluster on two conditions: side-by-side symbols layout and overlapping symbols layout. We had hypothesized that the side-by-side condition would facilitate participants' comprehension of the messages due to the sequential nature of its layout.

The results showed no significant effects of layouts on respondents' comprehension of the ADS messages, contradicting our hypothesis. Such results may be due to the side-by-side symbols layout not conveying an information sequence (as was expected), and thus being ineffective to communicate transitions in system states. Rather, we identified that symbols and colors seem to be strongly influential for drivers' interpretations of ADS messages, mitigating potential effects of the HMI's layout when such elements are present and adequately displayed. Our results echoed guidelines offered by the literature for the application of colors, especially for yellow and red, showing a strong association between these colors and their meanings. As for the symbols, we observed that the warning symbol was effective in representing failures in the ADS and, as already discussed in the literature, the hands-on-the-wheel symbol successfully conveyed TORs. Nevertheless, qualitative analyses showed that drivers frequently took literal readings when interpreting symbols. Therefore, designers should carefully choose symbols to apply to HMIs, assessing all possible interpretations, as misconceptions could lead to critical confusion errors.

Furthermore, despite the symbols and colors' efficiency in communicating ADS information, we identified that participants struggled to understand the ADS's states. The System Available and System Unavailable messages had the lowest comprehension levels. Such results may be due to the use of the same symbol with different colors (gray, representing a "disabled" color, and white) to represent the system status. Nonetheless, it is probable that drivers did not understand the restrictions in L3 ADSs' functioning, possibly due to unfamiliarity with different automation levels. Thus, we consider that determining how to communicate differences in automation levels of ADS through an HMI is a challenge that is yet to be addressed by designers.

The main contribution of this study was the identification that people have different interpretations about the information presented by an ADS, possibly caused by unfamiliarity with the system's operation. Thus, we observed that principles of proximity and sequencing of information are not enough to have an effect on the understanding of L3 ADSs' group of information.

This study had some limitations. Firstly, due to the remote nature of the tool employed, we were not able to uncover participants' comprehension or reasoning beyond their written answers. Moreover, as respondents only viewed static images in our low-fidelity simulation, the sense of progression and state transition of a real driving experience (which could have impacted their comprehension of the ADSs' states) might have been minimized.

Acknowledgments. This study was financed in part by the Coordenação de Aperfeiçoamento de Pessoal de Nível Superior - Brasil (CAPES) - Finance Code 001, Conselho Nacional de Desenvolvimento Científico e Tecnológico (CNPq), and Fundação Carlos Chagas Filho de Amparo à Pesquisa do Estado do Rio de Janeiro (FAPERJ). The authors would also like to thank Rafael Cirino Gonçalves for his contribution in this study.

References

1. Alliance Automobile Manufactures.: Statement of principles, criteria and verification procedures on driver interactions with advanced in-vehicle information and communication systems (2006). http://www.umich.edu/~driving/publications/PGCRCChapter24DRAFT.pdf%5Cn%5Cn

2. Beller, J., Heesen, M., Vollrath, M.: Improving the driver-automation interaction: an approach using automation uncertainty. Hum. Fact. **55**(6) (2013). https://doi.org/10.1177/0018720813482327

3. Boelhouwer, A., van Dijk, J., Martens, M.H.: Turmoil behind the automated wheel. In: Krömker, H. (ed.) HCII 2019. LNCS, vol. 11596, pp. 3–25. Springer, Cham (2019). https://doi.org/10.1007/978-3-030-22666-4_1

4. Campbell, J.L., et al.: Human factors design principles for level 2 and level 3 automated driving concepts (Report No. DOT HS 812 555). Highway Traffic Safety Administration, National Department of Transportation, (August) (2018)

5. Campbell, et al.: Human factors design guidance for driver-vehicle interfaces (Report No. DOT HS 812 360). Washington, D.C (2016)

6. Campbell, J.L., Hoffmeister, D.H., Kiefer, R.J., Selke, D.J., Green, P., Richman, J.B.: Comprehension testing of active safety symbols. In: SAE Technical Papers, (March 2004) (2004). https://doi.org/10.4271/2004-01-0450

7. Campbell, J.L., Richman, J.B., Carney, C., Lee, J.D.: In-vehicle display icons and other information elements. Transp. I , 238 (2004). https://doi.org/10.1037/e664642007-001

8. Carsten, O., Martens, M.H.: How can humans understand their automated cars? HMI principles, problems and solutions. Cogn. Technol. Work **21**(1), 3–20 (2018). https://doi.org/10.1007/s10111-018-0484-0

9. Commission of the European Communities. Commission Recommendation of 26 May 2008 on safe and efficient in-vehicle information and communication systems: update of the European Statement of Principles on human-machine interface. Official J. Eur. Union (2008). http://data.europa.eu/eli/reco/2008/653/oj

10. De Souza, C. S., Prates, R. O., Carey, T.: Missing and declining affordances: are these appropriate concepts? J. Brazilian Comput. Soc. 7(1) (2000). https://doi.org/10.1590/s0104-65002000000200004

11. Dixon, L.: Autonowashing: the greenwashing of vehicle automation. Transp. Res. Interdisc. Perspect. **5**, 100113 (2020). https://doi.org/10.1016/j.trip.2020.100113

12. Dziennus, M., Kelsch, J., Schieben, A.: Ambient light based interaction concept for an integrative driver assistance system – a driving simulator study. In: Proceeding of the Human Factors and Ergonomics Society Europe Chapter 2015 Annual Conferences, pp. 171–182 (2016). http://elib.dlr.de/99076/

13. Endsley, M.R.: Toward a theory of situation awareness in dynamic systems. Hum. Fact.: J. Hum. Fact. Ergon. Soc. **37**(1), 32–64 (1995). https://doi.org/10.1518/001872095779049543

14. Endsley, M.R., Kiris, E.O.: The out-of-the-loop performance problem and level of control in automation. Hum. Fact.: J. Hum. Fact. Ergon. Soc. **37**(2), 381–394 (1995). https://doi.org/10.1518/001872095779064555

15. Forster, Y., Naujoks, F., Neukum, A.: Your turn or my turn? Design of a human-machine interface for conditional automation. In: Proceedings of the 8th International Conference on Automotive User Interfaces and Interactive Vehicular Applications, 253–260. New York, NY, USA: Association for Computing Machinery (2016). https://doi.org/10.1145/3003715.300 5463

16. Gibson, J.J.: The ecological approach to visual perception. In:The Ecological Approach to Visual Perception. Psychology Press (1979)

17. Google.inc.: Waymo (2021). Retrieved November 9, 2021, from https://waymo.com/

18. Green, P., Levison, W., Paelke, G., Serafin, C.: Suggested Human Factors Design Guidelines for Driver Information Systems. Technical Report FHWA-RD-94–087. (Vol. 1993) (1994)

19. Hoober, S., Berkman, E.: Designing Mobile Interfaces. O'Reilly Media (2011)

20. International Organization for Standardization. Road vehicles — Human performance and state in the context of automated driving, p. 24 (2020)

21. International Organization for Standardization. ISO 9186–1: Graphical symbols — Test methods — Part 1: Method for testing comprehensibility p. 26 (2014)

22. JAMA: Guideline for in-vehicle display systems - version 3.0. In: Jama (vol. 1). Tokyo (2004). http://www.jama-english.jp/release/release/2005/In-vehicle_Display_GuidelineVer3.pdf

23. Körber, M., Prasch, L., Bengler, K.: Why do i have to drive now? Post HOC explanations of takeover requests. Hum. Factors 60(3), 305–323 (2018). https://doi.org/10.1177/001872081 7747730

24. Lidwell, W., Holden, K., Butler, J.: Universal Principles of Design: 125 ways to enhance usability, influence perception, increase appeal, make beter design decisions, and teach through design. In: Universal Principles of Design: 125 Ways to Enhance Usability, Influence Perception, Increase Appeal, Make Beter Design Decisions, and Teach Through Design (2010)

25. Marsh, S.: User research: a practical guide to designing better products and services. Kogan Page, London (2018)

26. National Highway Traffic Safety Administration. Visual-manual NHTSA driver distraction guidelines for in-vehicle electronic devices. In: Docket No. NHTSA-2010–0053 (2013)

27. National Highway Traffic Safety Administration. Federal automated vehicles policy: accelerating the next revolution in roadway safety. In: U.S. Department of Transportation. Washington, D.C (2016). 12507-091216-v9

28. Naujoks, F., Forster, Y., Wiedemann, K., Neukum, A.: A human-machine interface for cooperative highly automated driving. Adv. Intell. Syst. Comput. 484, 585–595 (2017). https://doi.org/10.1007/978-3-319-41682-3_4

29. Naujoks, F., Wiedemann, K., Schömig, N., Hergeth, S., Keinath, A.: Towards guidelines and verification methods for automated vehicle HMIs. Transps. Res. F: Traffic Psychol. Behav. 60, 121–136 (2019). https://doi.org/10.1016/j.trf.2018.10.012

30. Nielsen, J.: Heuristic evaluation. In: Nielsen, J., Mack, R., (Eds.), Usability Inspection Methods. New York: John Wiley & Sons (1994)

31. Norman, D.A.: The Design of Everyday Things. Basic Books, New York (2013)

32. Parasuraman, R., Riley, V.: Humans and automssssation: use, misuse, disuse, abuse. Hum. Fact. 39(2) (1997). https://doi.org/10.1518/001872097778543886

33. Parasuraman, R., Sheridan, T. B., Wickens, C. D.: A model for types and levels of human interaction with automation. IEEE Trans. Syst. Man Cybernet. Part A: Syst. Hum. 30(3) (2000). https://doi.org/10.1109/3468.844354

34. Pauzié, A., Ferhat, L., Tattegrain, H.: Innovative human machine interaction for automatised car: analysis of drivers needs for recommended design. In: Proceedings of the 26th ITS World Congress. Singapore: ITS Singapore (2019)

35. Perrier, M.J.R., Louw, T., Gonçalves, R.C., Carsten, O.: Applying participatory design to symbols for SAE level 2 automated driving systems. In: Proceedings of the 11th International Conference on Automotive User Interfaces and Interactive Vehicular Applications: Adjunct Proceedings, 238–242. New York, NY, USA: ACM (2019). https://doi.org/10.1145/3349263.3351512

36. Perrier, M.J.R., Louw, T.L., Carsten, O.: User-centred design evaluation of symbols for adaptive cruise control (ACC) and lane-keeping assistance (LKA). Cogn. Technol. Work (2021). https://doi.org/10.1007/s10111-021-00673-0]

37. Quaresma, M., Motta, I.: Co-Creation workshop for interface design - designing innovative HMI for automated vehicles. Revista ErgodesignHCI, 7(Especial), 24–35 (2019). https://doi.org/10.22570/ergodesignhci.v7iEspecial.1305

38. Reason, J.: Human Error. Cambridge University Press (1990). https://doi.org/10.1017/CBO9781139062367

39. Richardson, N.T., Lehmer, C., Lienkamp, M., Michel, B.: Conceptual design and evaluation of a human machine interface for highly automated truck driving. In: 2018 IEEE Intelligent Vehicles Symposium (IV), 2018-June(Iv), 2072–2077. IEEE (2018). https://doi.org/10.1109/IVS.2018.8500520

40. Richardson, J., Revell, K., Kim, J., Stanton, N. A.: Signs symbols & displays in automated vehicles: a focus group study. Adv. Intell. Syst. Comput. 1131 AISC, 980–985 (2020). https://doi.org/10.1007/978-3-030-39512-4_149

41. Richardson, J., Revell, K.M.A., Kim, J., Stanton, N.A.: The iconography of vehicle automation – a focus group study. In: Designing Interaction and Interfaces for Automated Vehicles, pp. 211–227. First edition. Boca Raton, FL : CRC Press/Taylor & Francis Group, LLC, 2021. CRC Press (2021). https://doi.org/10.1201/9781003050841-14

42. Society of Automobile Engineers: Taxonomy and definitions for terms related to driving automation systems for on-road motor vehicles J3016. In: SAE International, vol. J3016. Warrendale (2021). https://doi.org/10.4271/J3016_202104

43. Stevens, A., Quimby, A., Board, A., Kersloot, T., Burns, P.: Design guidelines for safety of in-vehicle information systems. Wokingham (2002). https://trl.co.uk/sites/default/files/PA3721-01.pdf

44. Tesla: Tesla Model S. Retrieved January 4, 2021 (2021). https://www.tesla.com/models?redirect=no

45. Xu, W.: From automation to autonomy and autonomous vehicles. Interactions **28**(1), 48–53 (2021). https://doi.org/10.1145/3434580

Acceptance of Autonomous Electric Vehicles as a Collective Passenger Transport: The Case of Portugal

Francisco Rebelo[1,2] , Ana Faria[3], João Costa[3], Ricardo Dias[3],
Elisângela Vilar[1,2(✉)] , and Paulo Noriega[1,2]

[1] CIAUD, Research Centre for Architecture, Urbanism and Design,
Lisbon School of Architecture, Universidade de Lisboa, Lisbon, Portugal
`fsrebelo@fa.ulisboa.pt`, {`ebpvilar,pnoriega`}`@edu.ulisboa.pt`
[2] ITI/LARSyS, Universidade de Lisboa, Lisbon, Portugal
[3] Lisbon School of Architecture, Universidade de Lisboa, Lisbon, Portugal

Abstract. Even with some exemplars of autonomous shuttles that perform simple paths already being available to be used by the general population, with the rising popularity of autonomous vehicles, it is important to understand whether the population is willing to use such transport in multi-lane highways. Thus, this study investigates the acceptance of autonomous collective vehicles as a viable choice for public transportation. For this, the Autonomous Vehicle Acceptance Model (AVAM) was translated into Portuguese, adapted, and launched as an online questionnaire. Since autonomous vehicles are rare in Portugal, we hypothesised that people would be reticent to this type of technology as a type of public transportation. One hundred fifty-seven valid answers from the Portuguese population were collected and analysed. The results were very similar in all demographic and social contexts. Two main factors resulted from data analysis: Behavioural Intention and Cost-benefit. Behavioural Intention is responsible for 42.4% of the variance and consists of Performance Expectancy, Social Influence, Facilitating Conditions, Attitude, Self-Efficacy, and Behavioural Intention. Cost-Benefit is responsible for 16.9% of the variance and comprises Effort Expectancy, Anxiety and Perceived Safety. From people who usually use public transportation to people who are accustomed to driving, most respondents favour adopting such vehicles in today's public transportation. However, they know that the necessary infrastructures do not exist.

Keywords: Autonomous Vehicle Acceptance Model · Autonomous Public Transportation · User Acceptance · User Experience · Interaction Design

1 Introduction

Research demonstrates how transportation is and will continue to be a critical factor for societal development, especially regarding the Economy, Environment, and Society itself [1]. However, the modern introduction of autonomous vehicles in everyday life represents a paradigm shift in the making for the last hundred years [2, 3].

A. Marcus et al. (Eds.): HCII 2023, LNCS 14032, pp. 304–316, 2023.
https://doi.org/10.1007/978-3-031-35702-2_22

Although there are still many challenges to be addressed regarding existing infrastructures, ethical implications [2], and, especially when it comes to acceptance by consumers, predictions have been made that autonomous vehicles (also named robotic or self-driving) may, in the next few years, become a generally available method of transportation [4–6]. Various technologies, including Artificial Intelligence, self-driving navigation systems, onboard sensors, vehicle-to-vehicle communication, and vehicle-to-infrastructure communication systems, enable this rapid advancement. These new technologies would allow cars to navigate correctly from point A to point B while avoiding collisions without requiring direct human input [2].

Some research also couples together the trends of vehicle automatization with the de-privatisation of the car, hence opening the possibility that increased levels of automatization may lead to a decrease in overall vehicle ownership [7]. It is known that the world's vehicle population is responsible for many ecological issues and is highly inefficient. Estimations show that cars are used less than 5% of their total lifetime and are a direct hazard to human life in accidents [8]. In this sense, it seems like shared autonomous vehicles, whether in the shape of "aTaxis", public transports or shuttles, may be a crucial part of a future where metropolitan areas are more efficient and ecologically friendly [5, 9, 10].

With the imminent arrival of the fourth industrial revolution, marked by technologies such as Artificial Intelligence and, of course, Automated Transportation, it is highly relevant to continue researching the relationship between users and Autonomous Vehicles. Will humans accept this new solution? How receptive will consumers be to a product that cuts the necessity to drive? Not just in a general sense but also to understand what specific characteristics of this relationship represent more serious concerns to people. The results from these studies may be crucial to conducting design efforts that will culminate in a more well-accepted product by the general public.

In this context, this paper presents a study investigating user acceptance of shared electric autonomous vehicles (SAV), more concretely the case for shuttle transportation, in the Portuguese market. Furthermore, the study intends to investigate what factors impact user intent most. The taxonomy used to determine levels of autonomy comes from SAE [11].

1.1 Previous Studies on Automated Vehicle User Acceptance

In a 2014 study that connects the concepts of User Acceptance and User Experience regarding Automated Transportation, Rödel and colleagues [12] found an inverse correlation between User Acceptance of Automated Vehicles and their levels of autonomy (based on the National Highway Traffic Safety Administration scale (NHSTA)). Interestingly, they also found that this correlation is non-linear because the 2000's car (NHSTA Level 1) has the highest overall ratings across past and future models. The results show that, although the respondent's attitudes towards using the systems in scenarios of NHSTA Levels 3 and 5 are not high, their behavioural intent of use is still positive, i.e., people still intend to use them if they are available. It was also concluded that having previous experience with these vehicles positively influenced user acceptance. This might mean that, like many other technologies, autonomous vehicles will go through different product life cycle phases [13], where after a slow Initial Trajectory

Stage where early adopters pioneer usage, there is a Rapid Growth in adoption, leading to mass use.

There are, however, other factors than the automation level that can influence User Acceptance. Yuen and colleagues [6] used the Unified Theory of Acceptance and Use of Technology 2 (UTAUT2) and the Theory of Planned Behaviour (TPB) to analyse the different dimensions that influenced the intention to use Shared Autonomous Vehicles (SAV). They concluded that users' perception of adequate infrastructures and good organisational and governmental support (defined in their study as Facilitating Conditions that influence Perceived Behavioural Control) are major influencers of User Adoption of SAVs. However, they also state that their research is limited to Da Nang, Vietnam's geographical area and may not be extrapolatable to other regions of the globe.

It is also important to point out some of the concerns that users raise when considering the possibility of autonomous vehicles. Many users worry about issues such as technical security and data privacy, the vehicles not performing as well as human drivers and robotic vehicles moving while unoccupied [14, 15]. This becomes increasingly relevant to our study as, in a 2014 research on English-speaking countries (USA, UK, and Australia), Schoettle and Sivak [14] found that, on average, 45,9% of all respondents are very concerned with "Public transportation such as buses that are completely self-driving", being that none of the three countries recorded averages below 44% on this particular item.

1.2 Autonomous Vehicles Acceptance Model (AVAM)

As mentioned, multiple authors contributed to the literature on Autonomous Vehicles User Acceptance (e.g., [2, 5, 6, 12, 15–17]). Many of these studies based their methodology on questionnaires. However, many do not establish their research on validated, formal models [17], making them hard to compare against other literature. Other authors use these formal models, approaching the issue from different perspectives.

The Autonomous Vehicles Acceptance Model - AVAM was proposed by Hewitt and colleagues in 2019 [17]. According to the authors, this model intends to unify the efforts in measuring the acceptance of autonomous vehicles, combining elements from other models related to technology acceptance and car acceptance with levels of autonomy.

According to Hewitt and colleagues [17], the AVAM model combines and adapts two user acceptance models for generic technologies, the UTAUT [18] and the CTAM [19]. Thus, the AVAM model comprises nine factors, eight factors from UTAUT (i.e., Performance Expectancy, Effort Expectancy, Attitude Towards Technology, Social Influence, Facilitating conditions, Self-Efficacy, Anxiety and Behavioural Intention) and the Perceived Safety factor from CTAM. From these, the authors developed a 26-item questionnaire and autonomy scenarios. Figure 1 shows the constructs adapted from UTAUT and CTAM by Hewitt and colleagues [17] to be used for the AVAM model.

The questionnaire comprises 26 items, collected from a 7 points Likert-type scale. Additionally, there is a question related to the control type users expect to have for vehicles with different levels of autonomy, collected from a 5 points Likert-type scale.

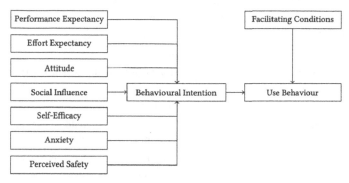

Fig. 1. The constructs adapted from UTAUT and CTAM models and used by Hewitt and colleagues [17] for the AVAM model. Figure retrieve from Hewitt and colleagues [17].

2 Methodology

This study intends to investigate the users' acceptance towards Level 5 [11] autonomous electric vehicles as a means of collective passenger transport. A questionnaire was developed to assess the degree of acceptance of such vehicles in Portugal by adapting the AVAM - Autonomous Vehicle Acceptance Model [17]. This model was chosen because it is specifically dedicated to autonomous vehicles, using factors of previously certified models (i.e., UTAUT and CTAM) to assess behavioural intention accurately. Thus, the AVAM questionnaire was adapted and translated into Portuguese. A small video was produced to present participants with the electric autonomous collective transport the questionnaire referred to and was shown to them before they answered the questions.

2.1 The Questionnaire

For the present study, an adapted version of the AVAM model was considered to decrease the application time, as an online application protocol would be used. The number of questions for each factor of the model (i.e., Performance Expectancy, Effort Expectancy, Attitude Towards Technology, Social Influence, Facilitating Conditions, Self-Efficacy, Anxiety, Behavioural Intention and Perceived Safety) was reduced from three to two.

Thus, to adapt the AVAM questionnaire, all questions were carefully analysed to select the most suitable to the current study's objectives. The questions were translated into Portuguese, and a pilot test was made to verify if the translations were well understood or caused any doubts to the public. All the respondents thought the questionnaire was clear. After the translation check, the questions were mixed to produce the final version of the questionnaire that was the same for all respondents.

To collect the answers from the 18 items of the questionnaire, a 7 points Likert-type scale was used, varying from 1 - "Strongly Disagree" to 7 - "Totally Agree".

Two questions about the use of public transportation and the frequency of driving were added to understand the respondents' driving habits. Additionally, demographic questions were inserted at the end of the questionnaire. Table 1 shows the factors and the questions related to them. The number before each question represents its order in the final questionnaire. The questionnaire was made using the Google Forms® platform and distributed online.

Table 1. Questions by factors and their order in the questionnaire

Factors	Question number	Question
Performance Expectancy	2	Using the vehicle would enable me to reach my destination cost-efficiently
	5	Using the vehicle would enable me to reach my destination safely
Effort Expectancy	1	I would find the vehicle easy to use
	6	It would be easy for me to learn to use the vehicle
Social Influence	3	I would feel more inclined to use the vehicle if it was widely used by others
	6	I would prefer to use the vehicle with other passengers in the vehicle as well
Facilitating Conditions	4	I have the knowledge necessary to use the vehicle
	8	The vehicle and infrastructure necessary to use the vehicle are practically feasible
Attitude	9	The vehicle would make driving more interesting
	14	Using the vehicle would be fun
Self-Efficacy	10	I could reach my destination using the vehicle if I had just the built-in instruction for assistance
	15	I could reach my destination using the vehicle if I had no assistance
Anxiety	11	The vehicle would be somewhat frightening to me
	16	I am afraid that I would not understand the vehicle
Behavioural Intention	12	Given that I had access to the vehicle, I predict that I would use it
	17	If the vehicle becomes available to me, I plan to obtain and use it
Perceived Safety	13	I believe that using the vehicle would be dangerous
	18	I would feel safe while using the vehicle
Driving Habits	19	Do you usually drive?
	20	Do you use public transportation?

2.2 Interaction Scenario - Presentation Video

A presentation video was developed to introduce shared autonomous vehicles to the respondents. The video was designed mainly considering two points: illustrate the use of Level 5 [11] collective autonomous electric vehicles in urban contexts and clarify the benefits, such as a reduction in urban traffic density and pollution, as well as the inconveniences, for example, the creation of new infrastructures they could have.

Thus, the video was created using free images and online videos, separated by black screens with explicative texts and calm background music. The video (Fig. 2) starts inviting users to think about the future, following a presentation of images of city traffic and the new reality of having electric vehicles. The video continues introducing the concept of shared autonomous vehicles, presenting some images of existing testing models. After this, some practical points are shown, such as a speed limit of 50 km/h and circulation allowed only in circumscribed areas, such as campuses, industrial facilities, and airports, or in pre-defined and exclusive lanes into cities. The expected need to develop new infrastructures to accommodate this type of vehicle is also presented. The video can be seen at https://www.youtube.com/watch?v=Z5YYZjXud7U.

Fig. 2. An example of a sequence from the video presented to the respondents. The entire video can be seen at https://www.youtube.com/watch?v=Z5YYZjXud7U.

2.3 Survey Protocol

An online application protocol was used. For this, the adapted questionnaire was made on the Google Forms® platform and shared through personal contacts or private groups on social media networks. The online questionnaire comprises three main parts. First, participants are asked to watch the presentation video. After this, they have an introductory text explaining the study's objectives and asking for their participation agreement. They were allowed to move forward to answer the questions only after their acceptance.

The entire form can be seen on:

https://docs.google.com/forms/d/e/1FAIpQLScy5LfprQqIjd1O15YiCu7LifZGR1 yKRIwTa-DG3L-7vxPsfg/viewform?usp=sf_link.

2.4 The Sample

There were collected 157 valid questionnaires. All respondents live in Portugal (exclusion criteria). From the 157 participants who completed the questionnaire, 69.8% were women (n = 108), 29.3% were men (n = 46), 1.3% were non-binary (2), and 0.6% preferred not to respond (n = 1), with ages varying from 16 to 80 years old. The last two questions (made to understand the context of the participants' driving habits) evaluated that 76.4% of the participants (n = 120) usually drive, and 58% (n = 91) use public transportation.

3 Results and Discussion

The data from the 157 valid questionnaires was analysed considering a descriptive statistic. Table 2 shows the percentages of scores for each factor (N = 157). The results are averaged for the items of each construct. Percentages are presented for average values minor or equal to 3, value 4, and greater or equal to 5; from the scale, 1 strongly disagree, and 7 totally agree. The two questions on the factor Anxiety (i.e., questions 11 and 16) and question 13 of the factor Perceived Safety were inverted, meaning that small values represent high anxiety and perceived safety.

In Table 2, the first column represents discordance, response 4 is the neutral response that does not agree or disagree with the sentence, and responses greater than 5 are considered concordance.

Table 2. Percentages of scores for each construct (n = 157), averaged for the items of each group, Scale Average, and Standard Deviation

Factors	Responses ≤ 3 (%)	Responses = 4 (%)	Responses ≥ 5 (%)	Scale Avg. (min = 1, max = 7)	Std. Dev.
1. Performance Expectancy (PE)	2.5	19.1	78.3	**5.6**	**1.1**
2. Effort Expectancy (EE)	1.9	10.2	87.9	**6.0**	**1.0**
3. Social Influence (SI)	5.7	19.1	75.2	**5.5**	**1.3**
4. Facilitating Conditions (FC)	28.0	40.8	31.2	**4.1**	**1.4**
5. Attitude (AT)	7.6	25.5	66.9	**5.1**	**1.4**

(continued)

Table 2. (*continued*)

Factors	Responses ≤ 3 (%)	Responses = 4 (%)	Responses ≥ 5 (%)	Scale Avg. (min = 1, max = 7)	Std. Dev.
6. Self-Efficacy (SE)	3.2	15.9	80.9	**5.6**	**1.2**
7. Anxiety (AX)	20.4	28.0	51.6	**4.7**	**1.6**
8. Behavioural Intention (BI)	7.0	14.6	78.3	**5.6**	**1.4**
9. Perceived Safety (PS)	3.2	26.8	70.1	**5.3**	**1.2**
Average %	**8.8**	**22.2**	**68.9**	**5.3**	
Std. Deviation	**9.1**	**9.1**	**17.5**		

Thus, when data from Table 2 is analysed considering the study's primary objective (i.e., to investigate user acceptance of shared autonomous vehicles), and the main variables that affect the acceptability, a tendency to the right that is, answers greater than 5 (68.9%). The factors with a more positive influence are Effort Expectancy (87.9%), Self-Efficacy (80.9%), Behavioural Intention (78.3%), Performance Expectancy (78.3%), Social Influence (75.2%) and Perceived Safety (70.1%), all of them with a percentage of positive answers higher than 70%. Considering the Facilitating conditions factor, participants present a neutral response (40.8%), with a slight tendency to the right. Anxiety, which can influence the adaptation and use of new technologies, is one of the first concerns when acceptance is studied [20]. For this study, Anxiety seems to positively influence the acceptance, with 51.6% (we highlight that anxiety has an inverted value, representing that half of the participants disagreed with the statement "The vehicle would be somewhat frightening to me" and "I am afraid that I would not understand the vehicle"). Thus, even with some negative remarks, we verify that the scale average for all constructs stayed in the positive range. (see Fig. 3).

Considering each question by the factor, separately, for the factor of Performance Expectancy, the results show that 80,9% of the participants believe that using the vehicle would enable them to reach their destination cost-efficiently, and 81.6% say that it would allow them to reach their destination safely. In Effort Expectancy, 89.9% of the respondents find the product easy to use, and 89.1% would find easy to learn how to use it. As for Social Influence, 83.5% affirm they would feel more inclined to use the vehicle if others widely used it, and 65.6% would prefer to use the vehicle with other passengers in the vehicle as well. Addressing the Facilitating Conditions, 46.4% declare having the knowledge necessary to use the vehicle, and only 33.8% believe that the vehicle and infrastructure required to use the vehicle are practically feasible. The results for Attitude show that 66.3% of participants believe the vehicle would make driving more interesting, and 72% think that using the vehicle would be fun.

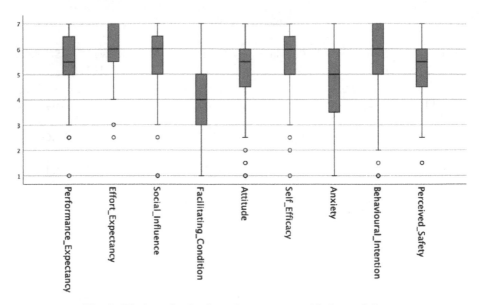

Fig. 3. The box plot for the scale average considering each factor.

For Self-Efficacy, 79.6% of the respondents say they could reach their destination using the vehicle if it had just the built-in instruction for assistance and 77.7% could reach their destination using the vehicle if they had no assistance. As for Anxiety, only 23% of the participants consider the product somewhat frightening, and 35% would be afraid of not understanding the vehicle.

Analysing Behavioural Intention, 77.7% affirm that given access to the vehicle, they predict that they would use it, and 86.7% agree that if the vehicle becomes available, they plan to obtain and use it.

To conclude, for the factor Perceived Safety, 71.4% of the respondents don't consider the vehicle dangerous, and 81.5% say they would feel safe while using the vehicle. Cronbach's alpha was applied to measure the reliability or internal consistency of the 18 items questionnaire. For the used questionnaire, Cronbach's alpha is 0.852. A value higher than 0.8 indicates excellent internal consistency [21]. This sample's high level of consistency shows that the questionnaire is reliable and accurately measures the variable of interest.

A factorial analysis was performed to identify the minimum number of factors representing the relationships between the various questionnaire items. The Keyser-Meyer-Olkin test had a value of 0.784, revealing that the analysis of the main components is meritorious. Table 3 shows the factor matrix after varimax rotation. Factor extraction determined two factors. The first factor is responsible for 42.4% of the variance and consists of Performance Expectancy, Social Influence, Facilitating Conditions, Attitude, Self-Efficacy, and Behavioural Intention. These variables relate to the user's perception of how this new technology can be pleasant, the functional aspects involved in using it, and the user's intention to use a shared autonomous vehicle. Hewitt and colleagues

Table 3. Factor matrix after varimax rotation

	Factor 1	Factor 2
1. Performance Expectancy (PE)	**0,675**	0,499
2. Effort Expectancy (EE)	0,544	**0,586**
3. Social Influence (SI)	**0,647**	0,017
4. Facilitating Conditions (FC)	**0,621**	−0,015
5. Attitude (AT)	**0,747**	−0,036
6. Self-Efficacy (SE)	**0,605**	0,376
7. Anxiety (AX)	−0,207	**0,866**
8. Behavioural Intention (BI)	**0,640**	0,475
9. Perceived Safety (PS)	0,154	**0,822**

[17] already considered these constructs as components of behavioural intention in their model. Thus, this first factor will be called Behavioural Intention.

The second factor, responsible for 16.9% of the variance, comprises Effort Expectancy, Anxiety and Perceived Safety. These variables are more related to users' perception of the cost-benefit relationship, mainly considering safety and effort in understanding and learning this new technology. Thus, this factor is called Cost-Benefit. These results indicate that prior attention should be given to the Behavioural Intention factor as the constructs that this factor represents most influence user acceptance of shared autonomous vehicles.

Regarding the demographic differences, gender does not appear to be a factor of consideration for the acceptance of shared autonomous vehicles, with the female sample averaging 5.3 overall acceptance and the male sample averaging 5.2 overall acceptance. Men and women seem to present the same concerns, specifically agreeing that the Facilitating Conditions are one of the factors with the lowest score (mean = 4.0 in men and mean = 4.1 in women). Both genders agree that these vehicles will be easy to learn and use (mean = 6.0 in the male and female sample for the Effort Expectations factor). The most significant difference stands in Behavioural Intention, with females averaging 5.8 and males 5.2. Gender differences were only observed for the factor Anxiety. According to the Mann-Whitney Test, for the construct Anxiety, there is a marginal difference ($U = 1900$; $z = -2.317$; $p = 0.021$) - remembering that the scale was inverted for this variable, so high values mean less anxiety (male: mean = 5.14, median = 5.25, stdev = 1.57, and female: mean = 4.53, median = 4.5 and stdev = 1.53).

In terms of the relationship between usually driving and accepting shared autonomous vehicles, results show that people who usually drive have a higher mean value for the factor Behavioural Intention (mean = 5.7 for drivers and 5.4 for non-drivers), as well as for the factor Effort Expectations (mean = 6.1 for drivers and 5.9 for non-drivers). In agreement with the remaining analysis, the main results show that public transportation usage does not influence users' acceptance of shared autonomous vehicles, with very similar mean values for all questions. Both public transportation users and non-users think that the facilitating conditions are below ideal (mean $= 4.1$ for users and 4.0 for non-users).

4 Conclusion

Overall, results show a favourable acceptance towards Level 5 [11] shared autonomous vehicles as a means of collective passenger transport. This conclusion is supported by the calculated means, being over 75% in factors such as Performance Expectancy, Effort Expectancy, Self-Efficacy, Behavioural Intention, and Perceived Safety. This result predicts that respondents would use the product, believe they would feel safe using it, and think it would be easy to use and learn. Moreover, we found that demographic variables such as age and gender are not determinant factors of user acceptance for shared autonomous vehicles.

Even though a good acceptance is perceived, some dichotomies were found when comparing the responses to some questions. For example, most of the respondents believe that the product is easy to use (89,9%) and learn (89,1%), but not even half consider knowing necessary to use it (46,4%). It could occur because even though participants perceive the technology as easy to use, they are not confident about their level of knowledge about it yet.

The primary constraint for implementing this type of vehicle in Portugal was observed in the factor Facilitating Conditions. Respondents think the infrastructures available are ready for this new form of collective urban vehicles, and many would fear (as previously disclaimed) not having the knowledge necessary to use the vehicle.

As for the practical implications of our results, we believe there are two main points to touch upon:

- The strong opinions regarding infrastructures and knowledge regarding the functioning of the vehicles (both factors of the Facilitating Conditions construct) indicate that the adoption of these vehicles will depend on a shift that is both systematic in the way cities are organised and the means available to accommodate shared autonomous vehicles, but also intellectual, as educating the users on how to take advantage of the system will also be crucial.
- While Behavioural Intention is above average for all the studied segments, we also find that anxiety levels are not as low as they should be to implement such a solution. It will likely be the responsibility of designers to design a system (including the vehicles and all surrounding infrastructures) that reduces the feeling of anxiety and intimidation facing automatic vehicles.

As a drawback of the study, we highlight the lack of neutral distribution regarding demographics such as age and gender and the limited number of the total sample. Also, this study should be expanded to cover a higher range of countries. Finally, although quantitative studies are a good starting point for studying such a complex subject, complementing it with qualitative research could be a plus to a better understanding of users' acceptance.

Overall, we emphasise how Portuguese users seem to be ready for the eventual arrival of this new disruptive technology, but not without their reservations. We hope this data can contribute to companies, specifically designers, engineers, and marketers, in developing strategies to overcome some pointed constraints, focusing on the main factors that could prevent people from using shared autonomous vehicles.

Acknowledgement. National funds finance this work through FCT - Fundação para a Ciência e a Tecnologia, I.P., under the Strategic Project with the references UIDB/04008/2020 and UIDP/04008/2020 and ITI-LARSyS FCT Pluriannual fundings 2020- 2023 (UIDB/50009/2020).

References

1. Mosaberpanah, M.A., Khales, S.D.: The role of transportation in sustainable development. In: ICSDEC 2012: Developing the Frontier of Sustainable Design, Engineering, and Construction - Proceedings of the 2012 International Conference on Sustainable Design and Construction, pp. 441–448 (2013). https://doi.org/10.1061/9780784412688.053
2. Adnan, N., Md Nordin, S., bin Bahruddin, M.A., Ali, M.: How trust can drive forward the user acceptance to the technology? In-vehicle technology for autonomous vehicle. Transp. Res. Part A Policy Pract. **118**(Part A), 819–836 (2018). https://doi.org/10.1016/j.tra.2018.10.019
3. Skeete, J.P.: Level 5 autonomy: the new face of disruption in road transport. Technol. Forecast. Soc. Chang. **134**, 22–34 (2018). https://doi.org/10.1016/J.TECHFORE.2018.05.003
4. Litman, T.: Autonomous vehicle implementation predictions implications for transport planning (2023)
5. Wang, S., Jiang, Z., Noland, R.B., Mondschein, A.S.: Attitudes towards privately-owned and shared autonomous vehicles. Transp. Res. Part F Traff. Psychol. Behav. **72**, 297–306 (2020). https://doi.org/10.1016/j.trf.2020.05.014
6. Yuen, K.F., Huyen, D.T.K., Wang, X., Qi, G.: Factors influencing the adoption of shared autonomous vehicles. Int. J. Environ. Res. Publ. Health **17**(13) (2020). https://doi.org/10.3390/ijerph17134868
7. Menon, N., Barbour, N., Zhang, Y., Pinjari, A.R., Mannering, F.: Shared autonomous vehicles and their potential impacts on household vehicle ownership: an exploratory empirical assessment. Int. J. Sustain. Transp. **13**(2), 111–122 (2019). https://doi.org/10.1080/15568318.2018.1443178
8. Burghout, W., Rigole, P.-J. J.: Impacts of shared autonomous taxis in a metropolitan area prediction and scenario-based traffic management (POST) view project Hybrid microscopic-mesoscopic traffic simulation view project. In: He Proceedings of the 94th Annual Meeting of the Transportation Research Board, pp. 1–13 (2015). https://www.researchgate.net/publication/298346251
9. Bagloee, S.A., Tavana, M., Asadi, M., Oliver, T.: Autonomous vehicles: challenges, opportunities, and future implications for transportation policies. J. Mod. Transp. **24**(4), 284–303 (2016). https://doi.org/10.1007/s40534-016-0117-3
10. Krueger, R., Rashidi, T.H., Rose, J.M.: Preferences for shared autonomous vehicles. Transp. Res. Part C Emerg. Technol. **69**, 343–355 (2016). https://doi.org/10.1016/j.trc.2016.06.015
11. SAE International: SURFACE VEHICLE RECOMMENDED PRACTICE Taxonomy and Definitions for Terms Related to Driving Automation Systems for On-Road Motor Vehicles (2021). https://www.sae.org/standards/content/j3016_202104/
12. Rödel, C., Stadler, S., Meschtscherjakov, A., Tscheligi, M.: Towards autonomous cars: the effect of autonomy levels on acceptance and user experience. In: Proceedings of the 6th International Conference on Automotive User Interfaces and Interactive Vehicular Applications, pp. 1–8 (2014). https://doi.org/10.1145/2667317.2667330

13. Day, G.S.: The product life cycle: analysis and applications issues. J. Mark. **45**(4), 60–67 (1981). https://doi.org/10.1177/002224298104500408
14. Schoettle, B., Sivak, M.: A survey of public opinion about autonomous and self-driving vehicles in the U.S., the U.K., and Australia (2014)
15. Kyriakidis, M., Happee, R., de Winter, J.C.F.: Public opinion on automated driving: results of an international questionnaire among 5000 respondents. Transp. Res. F: Traff. Psychol. Behav. **32**, 127–140 (2015). https://doi.org/10.1016/J.TRF.2015.04.014
16. Golbabaei, F., Yigitcanlar, T., Paz, A., Bunker, J.: Individual predictors of autonomous vehicle public acceptance and intention to use: a systematic review of the literature. J. Open Innov. Technol. Market Complex. **6**, 106 (2020). https://doi.org/10.3390/JOITMC6040106
17. Hewitt, C., Politis, I., Amanatidis, T., Sarkar, A.: Assessing public perception of self-driving cars: the autonomous vehicle acceptance model. In: Proceedings of the 24th International Conference on Intelligent User Interfaces, pp. 518–527 (2019). https://doi.org/10.1145/330 1275.3302268
18. Venkatesh, V., Morris, M.G., Davis, G.B., Davis, F.D.: User acceptance of information technology: Toward a unified view. MIS Q. Manag. Inf. Syst. **27**(3), 425–478 (2003). https://doi.org/10.2307/30036540
19. Osswald, S., Wurhofer, D., Trösterer, S., Beck, E., Tscheligi, M.: Predicting information technology usage in the car: towards a car technology acceptance model. AutomotiveUI 2012 - 4th International Conference on Automotive User Interfaces and Interactive Vehicular Applications, In-Cooperation with ACM SIGCHI - Proceedings, pp. 51–58 (2012). https://doi.org/10.1145/2390256.2390264
20. Dönmez-Turan, A., Kır, M.: User anxiety as an external variable of technology acceptance model: A meta-analytic study. Procedia Comput. Sci. **158**, 715–724 (2019). https://doi.org/10.1016/j.procs.2019.09.107
21. Cortina, J.M.: What is coefficient alpha? An examination of theory and applications. J. Appl. Psychol. **78**(1), 98–104 (1993). https://doi.org/10.1037/0021-9010.78.1.98

Physiological Analysis of Spectator Engagement in Counter Strike: Global Offensive

Eulerson Rodrigues[1,3](✉) (iD), Ernesto Filgueiras[1,2,3] (iD), João Valente[2,4,5] (iD),
and Leonor Godinho[4] (iD)

[1] University of Beira Interior, Covilhã, Portugal
eulerson.pedro@gmail.com
[2] Research Centre for Architecture, Urbanism and Design, CIAUD, Lisbon School of
Architecture, Universidade de Lisboa, Lisbon, Portugal
[3] Communication Laboratory – LabCom, University of Beira Interior, Covilhã, Portugal
[4] BrainAnswer – Neuroscience in your hands, Castelo Branco, Portugal
[5] Polytechnic Institute of Castelo Branco, Castelo Branco, Portugal

Abstract. This study aims to explore the use of biosensors to capture the emotional responses spectators while watching competitive Counter Strike: Global Offensive matches. The focus was on the heart rate variability (HRV) indices of the participants (n = 20) and self-report emotions using the PrEmo scale to identify variations in the subject's states such as relaxation, mental stress, frustration, anger, joy, sadness, and fear, as well as activation of sympathetic and vagal activities. The results showed that it was possible to determine the most engaging rounds of analyzed matches by analyzing the heart rate variability, which can have a significant impact on the way the broadcasts are made. This study emphasizes the importance of using biosensors for future studies in eSports spectators, and a comparative analysis with other related studies is necessary to better identify emotions felt by the spectators. The self-reports showed that pleasant emotions increased during the videos, and there were variations between the videos, indicating that different situations within the same game can arouse different degrees of satisfaction in viewers. The use of these technologies can provide valuable information to game designers and developers, as well as offer potential therapeutic applications in the field of gamification. The results of this study can serve as a guide for future eSports projects, taking into consideration the different needs and preferences of players and spectators.

Keywords: eSports · CS:GO · spectatorship · biosensors · emotional engagement

1 Introduction

This study builds upon our previous research conducted in 2021 [1], which examined the role of spectators in the world of competitive video games (eSports) and proposed the development of a protocol for guiding and measuring the behavioral and emotional responses of spectators during competitive matches. The objective of this study is to present the evolution of the protocol and initial test results.

1.1 Related Studies

To comprehend the emotional responses of media viewers, we need to understand how existing emotion measurement tools work. For this study, we used neuroreality as an example, which is a science based on alternative realities [2, 3]. Such realities described by neuroreality studies are supported by computational technologies and use connections with the human brain and adaptations of the system according to the user's biology. That is, the system adapts according to the needs and responses of those who use it.

Another related science is cognitive load theory, described by a psychological construct which is responsible for clarifying resources such as memories, attention, perception, knowledge representation, reasoning and creativity in problem solving [4]. According to the theory, the use of these resources is directed to solving problems and designing adequate responses to the environment in which the individual finds himself. The justification for these scientific areas in our study is due to the use of biofeedback to aid in the development of several areas of digital games, including level design, narrative, mechanics, and transmission elements that can be changed according to the user's emotional state, whether while playing or spectating a game.

The connection between the human brain and the external world through computer systems is called BCI (Brain-Computer Interface) [5]. Among the various uses of BCI, we highlight researching, mapping, assisting, increasing, or repairing human cognitive and sensorimotor functions from biological signals. Such interfaces can be invasive (when they require some type of implant) or non-invasive (when they use external equipment, such as electrodes or other devices to capture the physiological signal) and depend on the cognitive connections of the users [2].

1.2 Spectatorship Engagement

To better understand spectators, we need to understand how they behave at events and encourage players and teams. At eSports events, it is not uncommon to see hundreds of fans wearing team shirts, waving scarves, flags or any other item that remind others which teams they are supporting [6].

During the match, the concentration of spectators is intense, with a reduction in the use of smartphones and food consumption during moments of tension. Besides that, in moments of agitation, it is possible to see the fans screaming, whether for support or disapproval, jumping and talking excitedly among themselves [7].

To understand the depth of connection between people and products, we can use the definition of engagement to understand how viewers and consumers react to experiences with game content. Engagement is the responsible for generating profit, communicating with the public, and creating value [8]. Our consumption choices are directly related to patterns and memories allocated in our brain. Even if unconsciously, we receive sensory, emotional, and cognitive inputs and engage, or not, with what is proposed to us, joining attention and emotional impact [9] (Fig. 1).

Fig. 1. Spodek arena in Katowice Poland during the event IEM Katowice 2019 CS:GO Major. Source: author.

1.3 Studying Emotions

During our research, we found some methods that can be used for emotional recognition. For this study, we focus on the of use biosensors, which are devices with a non-invasive methodology and certain mobility, as is the case of the BItalino (Fig. 2).

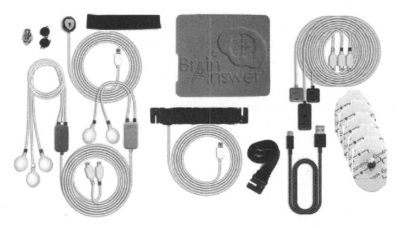

Fig. 2. BrainAnswer Bitalino kit and possible connections.

The interpretation of the signals can be done in several ways, but we highlight the heart rate variability (HRV) which is used to monitor emotions and emotional disturbances, such as happiness, fear, anger, and sadness. HRV is considered an effective tool for measuring and monitoring emotional response, with wide applicability [10].

HRV can be captured through electrocardiography, which tracks the electrical activity generated by the heart. The use of this tool is generally aimed at cardiac variations during exercises and physical activities, in addition to situations of emotional stress and physical fatigue [11]. The device captures the heart rhythm through three electrodes that are connected to the subject's skin in the chest region. A low heart rate variability can indicate a state of relaxation, while a high variability can indicate a state of frustration or mental stress of the subject [12].

The use of biosensors in digital games offers various opportunities for both commercial and research purposes. For example, in a medical context, biosensors can be used to monitor the emotional state of patients through levels, visual and sound stimuli. This approach enhances the acceptability of the tool by making it more engaging, by incorporating elements of gamification and entertainment. Furthermore, the advancement of technology has enabled seamless communication between players and game designers, thereby increasing the importance of user experience and further expanding the scope of its application.

2 Methodology

The main goal of the analysis is to determine if it is possible to gather information about the physiological state of spectators during competitive Counter-Strike: Global Offensive (CS:GO) matches and identify any emotional changes they may experience. This might be done by using biosensors and the BrainAnswer platform to measure physiological responses and self-reports from the participants.

This study focuses on observing spectators of eSports because they play a crucial role in the success of the industry. Viewers are responsible for moving thousands of dollars around the world, whether through donations for streams, purchase of merchandising and purchase of virtual and digital tickets, among others [13]. The audience provides energy and support to the competition and is crucial to the success of the games, which are considered the most interactive media today.

Additionally, collecting data from players would also require their active participation and consent, as the use of biosensors can raise privacy concerns. In the case of spectators, they can be observed passively without necessarily interfering with their experience. Thus, collecting data from spectators is less intrusive and less complex than from players. However, the findings from observing spectators may not fully reflect the experience of the players, as the physiological responses of the spectators may not necessarily be directly related to the players' actions.

2.1 BrainAnser Platform

Among the platform's features, we highlight the (a) study manager, which organizes one or more studies according to the user's preferences, the (b) data synchronization, which allows the collected data to be automatically stored in a database, the (c) previewer, which allows making comments and markings on certain data points, and (d) reports, which are capable of exporting all the information of a study. BrainAnswer also allows the creation of protocols that can include (among others) images, videos, questionnaires, biosensor collection, video collection and eye tracking.

From the audiovisual stimuli present in video games even in different graphic complexities (for example, 2D, 3D and VR) it is possible to measure and map the psychophysiological responses of players and spectators, whose emotional changes are captured using biosensors during interaction with the BrainAnswer platform. Focusing on the analysis of physiological responses and self-reports, we try to propose a guideline for eSports projects that may be applied to different types of users (players and spectators).

2.2 Picking an eSport

The eSport chosen for this study was Counter Strike: Global Offensive (or simply CS:GO, Valve) due to its match format being formed by rounds, which would facilitate a direct comparison between different match moments compared to other eSports where the match is played in running time, like DOTA 2 (Valve) or League of Legends (Riot Games).

In a competitive CS:GO match, up to 30 rounds are played (disregarding overtime) and the first team to win 16 rounds is declared winner. CS:GO consists of two teams of 5 players each, fighting for different objectives at certain times of the game. The team marked as Counter-Terrorists (or CTs) are responsible for defending the bomb targets (bombsites) on the maps. The Terrorists (Ts) are responsible for detonating the bomb in these same objectives. The victory condition in a round is met if:

- The Terrorists eliminate the entire Counter-Terrorist team (Ts win).
- Counter-Terrorists eliminate the entire Terrorist team before the bomb is planted on the objective (CTs win).
- The Terrorists plant the bomb on the objective, and a successful detonation occurs (the bomb is automatically detonated after 40 s, Ts win).
- Counter-Terrorists defuse the bomb within 40 s (CTs win).
- Terrorists fail to plant the bomb within the round time (1:55 min, CTs win).

For greater fairness between the teams involved in the dispute, the sides are switched after round 15. That is: if a team plays as a Terrorist from round 1 to 15, it will play as a Counter-Terrorist from round 16, where the economy is reset.

In order not to use videos of matches with an average duration of 45 min, we started to focus on videos with a duration of 6 to 7 min, for greater control by the platform and comfort of the participants. However, some rules were followed for selecting the rounds that entered the cuts, namely:

- Matches are during the same tournament (IEM Katowice 2019).
- Matches take place on the same game map (Inferno).
- All videos have 3 rounds in their entirety, each VA of a specific round.

- All videos have English narration.

Rounds where a team wins or loses the match were not included, to avoid any influence of the outcome of the match.

To compose our Protocol Videos (PV) used in BrainAnswer, rounds 1, 8 and 15 were selected. The choice of these rounds was based on the format of competitive CS:GO matches where up to 30 rounds are played, and the first team to win 16 rounds is declared the winner.

Round 1 was chosen because it is the most "democratic" round of all, where all players start with limited resources ($800 and a pistol per player) and still don't have access to weapons with greater firepower.

Round 8 was chosen because it is an intermediate round in the dispute and has a slightly developed economy (teams receive different amounts based on their performance in the previous round).

Round 15 was selected because it was the last of the first half of the match and the game's economy was well developed. As the match can end in any round from the 16th, no round from the second half of the match (16th onwards) was selected.

2.3   Creating the Protocol

While using biosensors, the current condition of the individual is extremely important [4], so it was necessary to add a breathing exercise (reducing the level of initial stress) and a form (self-report) where the individuals detail their emotional state. Self-report forms use the PrEmo scale as a guide for interpreting the emotional state of individuals.

The PrEmo scale uses fourteen emotions, seven of which are pleasant and seven are unpleasant, (desire, pleasant surprise, inspiration, amusement, admiration, satisfaction, fascination), and seven are unpleasant (indignation, contempt, disgust, unpleasant surprise, dissatisfaction, disappointment, and boredom). The biggest advantage of this scale is related to the use of images instead of words, which can avoid problems related to the language of the participants (Fig. 3).

Fig. 3. PrEmo figures. First line represents pleasant emotions, and second line represents unpleasant emotions.

The protocol used in this study contains an initial form, where the subjects make a self-report about how they felt at that exact moment, a breathing exercise to reduce stress, three alternate videos containing cuts from matches of a CS:GO, and a self-report form (three in total), which uses the PrEmo scale with intensity levels (0 – not feeling at all, 1 – minimum intensity, 2 – low intensity, 3 – high intensity, 4 – maximum intensity) (Fig. 4).

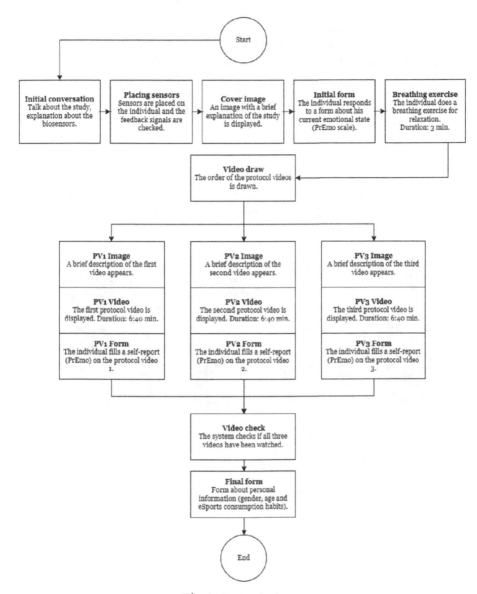

Fig. 4. Protocol scheme.

To create the protocol, we needed some object of analysis that contained moments characterized as possible triggers for the emotional variation of the spectators. With that in mind, we chose to select videos from highly commercially relevant professional championships [7], from their importance within the eSports scenario, to the value of the total prize pool.

Once the data is collected, we use a comparative methodology to identify variations and important moments that may be indicative of something important. The raw analysis of the collected signals is not enough to bring us relevant information, so direct comparisons will be made between rounds and matches, in search of statistically relevant variations based on heart rate variability (HRV), to determine the existence of emotional engagement with the objects of study (protocol videos and their content).

The sets of images from the protocol videos + protocol video + form from the protocol video (total 3 sets) are part of random group A. This means that the display order is drawn among the 3 sets each time a test is performed.

2.4 Collected Bio Signals

The ECG sensor is placed at three points on the chest to capture the individual's heartbeat. However, for our analysis, it is more interesting to observe the participant's heart rate, with the aim of identifying large variations by relating them to the moments of each protocol video (Fig. 5).

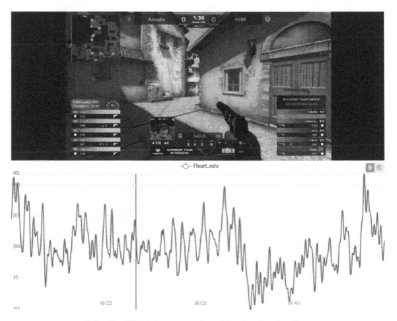

Fig. 5. ECG data sample with visual stimulus.

To determine the existence of emotional engagement with the objects of study (protocol videos and their content), we used the statistically relevant variations between the heart rate signals collected during the tests. Heart rate variability (HRV) is a term that describes many metrics and analysis techniques, including time domain, frequency domain, and nonlinear analysis. Through an adaptation of a study on HRV indices [10], we set up a table with descriptions of some of the indices that can be extracted from the data, along with their relationship with studies of emotions [14–16] (Table 1).

Table 1. HRV indices and their connections.

HRV index	Description	Connections with emotions
HR MEAN	Provides information about the functioning of the nervous control over cardiac activity and the heart's responsiveness	Relaxation, mental stress, frustration, and anger
HR MIN		
HR MAX		
SDNN	Standard deviation of RR intervals	Correlated with LF; Joy/Sadness
RMSSD	Square root of the mean squared differences of successive RR intervals	Correlated with HF; Emotional stress
PNN50	Proportion of differences between successive RR intervals longer than 50ms	Correlated with HF; Joy/fear
LF	Low frequency power	Reflects activity of the sympathetic and vagal nerves, mainly sympathetic activity
HF	High frequency power	Reflects vagal activity

These indices help us understand how the individuals' bodies behaved during the tests. The vagal nerve is one of the main components of the parasympathetic nervous system, which controls the body's automatic or involuntary actions. Meanwhile, the sympathetic nervous system stimulates actions that allow the body to respond to stressful situations.

Despite this, there is still much uncertainty regarding the interpretation of signals, especially those related to heart rate variability. However, there is some literature on the subject, which assign low heart rate variability to situations of relaxation, as opposed to situations of mental stress and frustration with high variability [12]. Higher levels of SDNN, MEAN HR and LF/HF are found in happy conditions, compared to low levels in sadness conditions, while the RMSSD index increases in situations of emotional stress [10, 16]. Anger may also be associated with an increase in MEAN HR, compared to relaxed individuals [15].

Therefore, when comparing the averages of the participants' signals during the tests, we focused on finding index variations that could help us to relate to the emotions that were reported in the forms. These indices are maximum (HR MAX), average (HR MEAN) and minimum (HR MIN) heart rate, SDNN, SDSD, RMSSD and PNN50.

3 Results

Three comparisons were made: (A) the most general comparison is between matches, not counting a specific round, (B) between different rounds of the same match and (C) between the same rounds in different matches. as described in the following figure (Fig. 6):

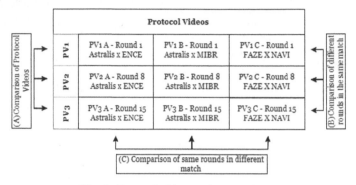

Fig. 6. Protocol videos and comparisons.

3.1 Comparison Between Protocol Videos

This analysis shows the participant group's physiological responses to the videos (PV1; PV2; PV3;) Among the indices analyzed, no statistically significant difference was found. Our objective in this analysis is not to define the emotional state of the participants by reading the data, but rather to find variations between the different objects of analysis. With this, we noticed that there is no significant difference between the matches in general, although we can find several differences when analyzing specific rounds (Table 2).

Table 2. Comparison between protocol videos

HRV index	PV1	PV2	PV3	PV1 – PV2	PV1 – PV3	PV2 – PV3
HR MEAN	63: 80: 97	62: 79: 96	62: 78: 94			
HR MIN	48: 64: 80	44: 64: 84	45: 62: 79			
HR MAX	83:98:113	82:100:118	83:99:115			
SDNN	32: 49: 66	27: 50: 73	31: 50: 69			
RMSSD	15: 27: 39	17: 32: 47	21: 34: 47			
SDSD	9: 17: 25	9: 19: 29	11: 20: 29			
PNN50	-5631: 4500: 14631	-2029: 8100: 18229	-897: 9300: 19497			

3.2 Comparison of Same Rounds in Different Matches

Among the first set (Table 3), which was composed by different round 1, we believe it is possible to describe the first round of the match between NAVI x FAZE as the most emotionally engaging, as it involves more statistically relevant variations of physiological signals. This round shows a high-level skill move, where a player gets five kills from the opposing team, thus guaranteeing the round victory for his team and showing that this type of move can activate physiological responses in spectators.

Table 3. Comparison of rounds 1 in different matches

HRV index	(1) Astralis vs. ENCE	(2) Astralis vs. MIBR	(3) FAZE vs. NaVi	(1) – (2)	(1) – (3)	(2) – (3)
HR MEAN	65: 82: 99	65: 82: 99	62: 79: 96	-	-	Variation
HR MIN	53: 71: 89	51: 69: 87	52: 70: 88	-	-	-
HR MAX	79: 95: 111	77: 94:111	78: 93:108	-	-	-
SDNN	23: 45: 67	23: 41: 59	28: 44: 60	-	-	-
RMSSD	11: 25: 39	8: 22: 36	12: 25: 38	-	-	-
SDSD	5: 15: 25	6: 15: 24	7: 15: 23	-	Variation	-
PNN50	-6: 4: 15	-9: 4: 16	-5: 4: 14	-	Variation	-

The self-report results show high levels of joy and hope, in addition to lower levels in all pleasant emotions. In the unpleasant part of the scale, we noticed the presence of sadness, shame, and dissatisfaction, although at a low level.

We were unable to determine which round is more engaging among the round set 8 (Table 4). Data shows that this set maintain a constancy in the physiological variations of the spectators, that is: they are not extremely engaging, but they might have been somehow attractive. According to the reports, all pleasant emotions were reported, in addition to sadness and shame.

Table 4. Comparison of rounds 8 in different matches

HRV index	(1) Astralis vs. ENCE	(2) Astralis vs. MIBR	(3) FAZE vs. NaVi	(1) – (2)	(1) – (3)	(2) – (3)
HR MEAN	61: 78: 95	61: 78: 95	62: 79: 96	Variation	-	-
HR MIN	50: 68: 86	50: 69: 88	46: 66: 86	-	-	-
HR MAX	81: 97:113	77: 94:111	79: 96:113	-	-	-
SDNN	15: 40: 65	20: 44: 68	20: 42: 64	-	-	-
RMSSD	13: 28: 43	16: 30: 44	10: 25: 40	-	-	-
SDSD	7: 17: 27	13: 22: 31	5: 17: 29	-	-	-
PNN50	-4: 6: 16	-3: 8: 19	-3: 7: 17	-	-	-

By being involved in two statistically relevant physiological variations (Table 5), round 15 of the match between MIBR x Astralis appears to be more engaging than the other rounds 15. This round also had major twists, such as recovery of the defense and defusing the bomb. When we think of round 15 as the outcome of the first part, we believe that it is necessary to dedicate more attention to this specific round.

Table 5. Comparison of rounds 15 in different matches

HRV index	(1) Astralis vs. ENCE	(2) Astralis vs. MIBR	(3) FAZE vs. NaVi	(1) – (2)	(1) – (3)	(2) – (3)
HR MEAN	62: 78: 94	64: 80: 96	62: 79: 96	Variation	-	Variation
HR MIN	46: 65: 84	50: 66: 82	49: 66: 83	Variation	-	-
HR MAX	79: 94:109	81: 97:113	77: 94:111	-	-	-
SDNN	30: 48: 66	22: 41: 60	22: 45: 68	-	-	-
RMSSD	19: 32: 45	18: 30: 42	15: 31: 47	-	-	-
SDSD	13: 22: 31	10: 18: 26	5: 17: 29	-	-	-
PNN50	-4: 7: 17	-3: 7: 17	-2: 8: 19	-	-	-

This set appears to have the highest average of pleasant emotions among all the forms, with emphasis on joy and hope at high levels, and admiration, fascination and attraction also appearing in stronger levels than pride and satisfaction.

3.3 Comparison of Different Rounds in the Same Match

In the match between Astralis x ENCE (Table 6), we noticed differences in maximum heart rate when comparing round 1 to round 8, and when comparing round 1 to round 15. This indicates that round 1 differs from rounds 8 and 15, which are similar to each

Table 6. Comparison of rounds 1, 8 and 15 in Astralis x ENCE.

HRV index	(1) Round 1	(2) Round 8	(3) Round 15	(1) – (2)	(1) – (3)	(2) – (3)
HR MEAN	65: 82: 99	60: 77: 94	62: 78: 94	-	-	-
HR MIN	53: 71: 89	51: 69: 87	48: 66: 84	-	-	-
HR MAX	79: 95: 111	75: 92: 109	73: 89: 105	Variation	Strong Variation	-
SDNN	23: 45: 67	19: 42: 65	25: 44: 63	-	-	-
RMSSD	11: 25: 39	14: 29: 44	18: 31: 44	-	-	-
SDSD	5: 15: 25	9: 19: 29	12: 20: 28	-	-	-
PNN50	-6: 4: 15	-2: 9: 19	-4: 7: 17	-	-	-

other. We also noticed that rounds might bring, for example, relaxation to individuals demonstrated by peaks (such as HR MAX) in the collected data.

The match between Astralis x MIBR (Table 7) stands out for containing several relevant variations in the heart rate variability (HRV) indices, in comparison between rounds 1 and 8, in addition to variations when comparing rounds 8 and 15. We might say that in terms of emotional engagement, the round 8 differs from rounds 1 and 15 in this match. Round 8 has averages farther than the other rounds in three HRV indices, showing that it may be less engaging.

Table 7. Comparison of rounds 1, 8 and 15 in Astralis x MIBR.

HRV index	(1) Round 1	(2) Round 8	(3) Round 15	(1) – (2)	(1) – (3)	(2) – (3)
HR MEAN	64: 81: 98	61: 78: 95	64: 80: 96	-	-	-
HR MIN	51: 67: 83	50: 69: 88	49: 65: 81	Variation	-	-
HR MAX	81: 97: 113	78: 94: 110	81: 97: 113	-	-	-
SDNN	22: 39: 56	21: 46: 71	27: 46: 65	-	-	-
RMSSD	10: 23: 36	21: 36: 51	18: 30: 42	Strong Variation	-	Variation
SDSD	7: 15: 23	13: 23: 33	10: 18: 26	Strong Variation	-	Variation
PNN50	-7: 4: 15	-2: 10: 21	-3: 7: 18	Strong Variation	-	-

The rounds of the match between NAVI and FAZE (Table 8) show only a variation in heart rate variability indices between rounds 1 and 15, revealing similarities between rounds 1 and 8, and 8 and 15, and with that, highlighting 8 as the most engaging. This match did not demonstrate many physiological variations, showing a constancy in the emotional engagement of the spectators.

Table 8. Comparison of rounds 1, 8 and 15 in NAVI X FAZE.

HRV index	(1) Round 1	(2) Round 8	(3) Round 15	(1) – (2)	(1) – (3)	(2) – (3)
HR MEAN	63: 79: 95	62: 79: 96	61: 78: 95	-	-	-
HR MIN	48: 66: 84	46: 66: 86	49: 66: 83	-	-	-
HR MAX	80: 94: 108	79: 96: 113	78: 94: 110	-	-	-
SDNN	31: 48: 65	20: 42: 64	24: 47: 70	-	-	-
RMSSD	16: 28: 40	10: 25: 40	16: 32: 48	-	-	-
SDSD	11: 19: 27	5: 17: 29	5: 17: 29	-	-	-
PNN50	-2: 7: 16	-3: 7: 17	-3: 8: 18	-	Variation	-

Emotions on Self-reports. Regarding emotions throughout the test, happiness is more expressed in rounds 1 and rounds 15, although it was also present in the initial form and in rounds 8. There is a variation in happiness throughout the tests, especially when we compare the level of happiness of the rounds 1 and rounds 15 with the initial form and rounds 8.

Joy and hope appeared more in the reports of rounds 1 and rounds 15, in addition to showing an increase when we compare the initial form and rounds 8. That is: joy increased after watching the videos, but it was not possible to identify which of the videos is the biggest influencer of this emotion. Pride appears in all rounds, but in low volume and with low variation.

Admiration is also noted in rounds 1 and round 15, but with the same as in the initial form. Satisfaction is present in all rounds, although satisfaction in the initial form was level 3, showing a slight drop. Apparently, the tension of match moments can lead players to reduce satisfaction.

Fascination starts at a high level in the initial reports and fluctuates mid-levels in the rounds, indicating that the protocol videos should not be related to any increase of this emotion. Attraction shows an increase when we make a direct comparison between rounds 1 and 8 and rounds 15, showing that rounds 8 can be considered less attractive, possibly because they are in the middle of the first part of the match.

In the unpleasant part of the scale, the emotions sadness, fear, shame, contempt, boredom, and disgust are not present in all forms. Only dissatisfaction figured prominently among the negative emotions. Even so, during rounds 8, dissatisfaction showed a slight drop, when compared to the initial form.

4 Conclusion

This study helped us understand that there is a relationship between events/moments of the match and the spectators' physiological response (identified through statistically relevant changes in heart rate variability), which directly influences emotional engagement. The use of this information can help game developers in handling game design, expanding the user experience, both for players and spectators.

Our objective in this study was not to define the emotional state of the participants by reading the data, but rather to find variations between the different objects of analysis. With that, we realize that there is no significant difference between the games in general, although we can find several differences when analyzing specific rounds.

It is possible to identify several variations in the physiological responses of spectators throughout competitive CS:GO matches. We identified statistically significant variations in the participants' heart rate variability (HRV) indices. These variations may indicate in the subject states of, for example: relaxation, mental stress, frustration, anger, joy, sadness and fear, as well as activation of sympathetic activity (responsible in the body for responding to stress and emergency situations) and vagal activity (responsible for controlling non-conscious actions).

Although it is not possible to determine which video arouses reactions directly related to emotions such as happiness or sadness, we were happy to see that it is possible to identify variations to the point of determining which excerpts (among the 9 cuts of the videos) were most engaging, through variability analysis of the heart rate found in the subjects, data that are already widely used in studies related to emotions and well-being.

The indications mentioned above can be extremely important for CS:GO viewers, as they can have a direct influence on the way the broadcasts are made, depending on the objective established by the companies responsible for broadcasting the competitions. Viewers may lose interest, for example, in an entertainment-focused broadcast that causes mental stress or excessive relaxation. Thus, we emphasize the results of this study as fundamental for future analyzes of studies of eSports spectators.

Studies related to biosensors have been more frequent, and therefore new more powerful and accurate tools should be available in the future. A comparative analysis is necessary, where the collected data are confronted with other studies related to emotions, in search of an identification of signals that can better represent the emotions felt by the spectators, and not only the identification of variations, as was our case.

Self-reports helped us to notice that pleasant emotions such as joy and hope increased during the videos compared to the beginning of the test. It was also possible to detect variations between the videos, revealing that different situations within the same game can arouse different degrees of satisfaction in viewers.

5   Limitations

We could not further analyze the collected data. This is due to the difficulty in correlating the physiological signals and the emotions produced at the moment of the signal. This limitation is recognized by the scientific community and has increasingly evolved over time, as technology and neuroscience understand the relationships between bio signals and emotions.

It is difficult to discuss whether such variations indicate pleasant or unpleasant emotions from the point of view of the digital game. That's why we focus on determining the engagement of events, rather than the detailed emotion. Another point to highlight was the lack of experience with biosensors and their equipment, something that was worked on throughout the study, but there is still a lot to learn, especially when deciding which sensors will be used in the research and justifying their use. Use, which can save time and costs.

References

1. Rodrigues, E., Filgueiras, E., Valente, J.: Behavioral analysis of esports spectators: a research proposal. In: Soares, M.M., Rosenzweig, E., Marcus, A. (eds.) Design, User Experience, and Usability: Design for Contemporary Technological Environments. HCII 2021. Lecture Notes in Computer Science, vol. 12781, pp. 371–383. Springer, Cham (2021). https://doi.org/10.1007/978-3-030-78227-6_27
2. de França, A. C. P., Villarouco, V.: Brain reality gaming: concepts, advances and current challenges. In: Ahram, T., Falcão, C. (eds.) Advances in Usability, User Experience, Wearable and Assistive Technology. AHFE 2020. Advances in Intelligent Systems and Computing, vol. 1217, pp. 611–618. Springer, Cham (2020). https://doi.org/10.1007/978-3-030-51828-8_80
3. Dworak, W. S.: Biofeedback e Resposta Emocional em Game Design (Master's dissertation)

4. Buchwald, M., Kupiński, S., Bykowski, A., Marcinkowska, J., Ratajczyk, D., Jukiewicz, M.: Electrodermal activity as a measure of cognitive load: a methodological approach. In: 2019 Signal Processing: Algorithms, Architectures, Arrangements, and Applications (SPA), pp. 175–179. IEEE (2019)
5. Zhang, D., Gao, X., Gao, S., Engel, A. K., Maye, A.: An independent brain-computer interface based on covert shifts of non-spatial visual attention. In: 2009 Annual International Conference of the IEEE Engineering in Medicine and Biology Society, pp. 539–542. IEEE (2009)
6. Brenda, H. K.: Spectating the rift: a study into esports spectatorship. Em eSports Yearbook **16**, 9–35 (2015)
7. Rodrigues, E.P.F.: Desporto e Videojogos (Master's dissertation)
8. Broersma, M.: Audience engagement. Int. Encyclopedia J. Stud. 1–6 (2019)
9. Marci, C.D.: A biologically based measure of emotional engagement: context matters. J. Advert. Res. **46**(4), 381–387 (2006)
10. Zhu, J., Ji, L., Liu, C.: Heart rate variability monitoring for emotion and disorders of emotion. Physiol. Meas. **40**(6), 064004 (2019)
11. Hughes, A., Jorda, S.: Applications of biological and physiological signals in commercial video gaming and game research: a review. Front. Comput. Sci. **3**, 557608 (2021)
12. Haag, A., Goronzy, S., Schaich, P., Williams, J.: Emotion recognition using bio-sensors: first steps towards an automatic system. In: André, E., Dybkjær, L., Minker, W., Heisterkamp, P. (eds.) Affective Dialogue Systems. ADS 2004. Lecture Notes in Computer Science, vol. 3068, pp. 36–48. Springer, Berlin, Heidelberg (2004). https://doi.org/10.1007/978-3-540-248 42-2_4
13. Rodrigues, E., Filgueiras, E.: eSports: how do video game aspects define competitive gaming streams and spectatorship. In: Marcus, A., Rosenzweig, E. (eds.) Design, User Experience, and Usability. Design for Contemporary Interactive Environments. HCII 2020. Lecture Notes in Computer Science, vol. 12201, pp. 506-516. Springer, Cham (2020). https://doi.org/10.1007/978-3-030-49760-6_36
14. Kakaria, S., Bigné, E., Catrambone, V., Valenza, G.: Heart rate variability in marketing research: a systematic review and methodological perspectives. Psychol. Mark. **40**(1), 190–208 (2023)
15. Rumpa, L. D., Toding, A., Jefriyanto, W., Sapulette, R. O.: Heart Rate Variability (HRV) during anger emotion stimulation: features for affective. IOP Conf. Ser. Mater. Sci. Eng. **1088**(1), 012103 (2021). IOP Publishing (2021)
16. Shi, H., et al.: Differences of heart rate variability between happiness and sadness emotion states: a pilot study. J. Med. Biol. Eng. **37**, 527–539 (2017)

Multimodal Gaze-Based Interaction in Cars: Are Mid-Air Gestures with Haptic Feedback Safer Than Buttons?

Oleg Spakov, Hanna Venesvirta, Jani Lylykangas, Ahmed Farooq[✉], Roope Raisamo, and Veikko Surakka

Faculty of Information Technology and Communication Sciences, Tampere University, Tampere, Finland
{jani.lylykangas,Ahmed.Farooq}@tuni.fi

Abstract. We studied two interaction techniques to perform secondary tasks in a driving simulator environment with the focus on driving safety. In both techniques, the participants ($N = 20$) used gaze pointing to select virtual task buttons. Toggling the controls was achieved by either mid-air gestures with haptic feedback or physical buttons located on the steering wheel. To evaluate each technique, we compared several measures, such as mean task times, pedestrian detections, lane deviations, and task complexity ratings.

The results showed that both techniques allowed operation without severely compromising driving safety. However, interaction using gestures was rated as more complex, caused more fatigue and frustration, and pedestrians were noticed with longer delays than using physical buttons. The results suggest that gaze pointing accuracy was not always sufficient, while mid-air gestures require more robust algorithms before they can offer functionality comparable to interaction with physical buttons.

Keywords: multimodal gaze-based interaction · mid-air gestures · ultrasonic haptic feedback · in-vehicle interaction

1 Introduction

The recent decade has marked a new era in car manufacturing by bringing unconventional information presentation and interaction techniques available to drivers and passengers of top car models. Some of these new technologies, such as the head-up displays (HUDs), are fast becoming an essential tool even in mid-range vehicles (e.g., [23]). Today they are available for any car as a separate piece of hardware that may be connected to the CAN bus (e.g., via OBD-2 connection that is a standard one for cars manufactured after mid of 2000th) and / or the driver's phone (see [28] for examples).

In-car interaction has traditionally taken a conservative approach, but this is changing quickly as several research prototypes and commercial systems have been constructed with speech commands [26, 43] given to car's services, mainly to the infotainment service, or with hand gestures (e.g., [16]). Some of these techniques may be currently

© The Author(s), under exclusive license to Springer Nature Switzerland AG 2023
A. Marcus et al. (Eds.): HCII 2023, LNCS 14032, pp. 333–352, 2023.
https://doi.org/10.1007/978-3-031-35702-2_24

found in only a few car models (e.g., Cadillac CT6, BMW 5, VW Golf; see [40]), but there exist additional devices on the market that offer, for example, scroll playlist displayed on a HUD, or to request a navigator to show the route by voice command.

As the amount and complexity of information available to driver's increases with the development of infotainment systems, the need for new cockpit designs and interaction methods is increasing. In order to avoid overloading the driver's attention with new solutions, one way has been to reduce the amount of information presented. For example, only driving-critical information (speed, fuel level, warning signs, etc.) is displayed all the time. Non-critical information, such as navigation routes, fuel consumption, etc., is shown as auxiliary information, and drivers need to explicitly navigate between menus to bring them into view. Traditionally, scrolling functionality has been available with button(s) located either close to the display or to the steering column through the right or left stalks. However, in a few recent car models these buttons are located on a steering wheel itself [31].

Most of the basic in-car devices, such as heater and air conditioner, still require the use of physical controls, with each button / handle / switch / knob usually dedicated strictly to one function: for example, a 3-state up-down button to open / close a side window, a 4-state switch to start / stop windshield wipers, or a knob to adjust sound volume, albeit music players may be more flexible. While the controls located in proximity to the steering wheel are easy to operate with hands remaining on the wheel and gaze directed to the traffic, controls located further away may not be that convenient. Indeed, any action that requires finding a control located anywhere else than next to the steering wheel requires prolonged glancing away from the road, in many cases longer than identified in NHTSA [45]. This can cause issues with driving safety.

Recently, mid-air hand gestures were proposed to replace some of the above-mentioned functionality with simple hand gestures that would not require visual attention [33]. It is expected that a driver, after activating a certain device like a music player, will be able to control the functionality of the device without paying visual attention to it. However, drivers still need to concentrate on the action mentally by coordinating their gestures and assessing the results. In general, any action not connected to the driver's primary task requires a certain attention shift away from the traffic. The question at hand is whether such a shift may compromise driving safety.

This study aimed to compare driver's behavior while operating on a selected list of functionalities when interacting with either mid-air gestures or button presses. We were especially interested in investigating the functionality of mid-air gestures from the perspective of driving safety related factors.

2   Related Work

There are several studies devoted to interacting with car systems using gaze [5, 35]. Drivers could control in-vehicle information system (IVIS) either using only gaze (with dwell-time used for activation) or using gaze for pointing and touch or button press to activate a command. In another study touch input was replaced with finger pointing [6]. These studies, however, lack details regarding the interaction method and thus, conclusions about the interaction methods cannot be made. Dobbelstein et al. [9] proposed that gaze direction could be utilized to recognize the interface to be interacted with using a single rotary control knob. The authors, however, did not report the results of their study. Lux et al. [27] built a prototype system where the driver could select a user interface element in a driving simulator by using either gaze or buttons. The paper, however, lacks details of implementation of the selection by gaze.

Kern et al. [22] aimed to replace touch and speech with gaze when operating a touchscreen display in cars. Items focused by gaze stayed focused even when the gaze moved away, and selection was implemented with a button on the steering wheel. Authors report that deviation from the lane and error rate in gaze condition was higher than in voice or touch conditions, thus the use of gaze compromised the driving safety and the fluency of the interaction.

The majority of studies on using new interaction methods, such as gaze and gestures, have been conducted in laboratory conditions. As an exception, Trösterer et al. [42] discussed issues using eye tracking to interact with IVIS in a real car. The authors acknowledge Smart Eye Pro eye tracker for its robustness, but they suggest that even this system should be used preferably on a very smooth road and only when the sky is cloudy. Another example is a work by Kang et al. [20] where gaze was used to determine the object of interest located outside of a car. Here, the gaze tracking was not found to be very reliable.

In sum, some studies have tested the idea of using gaze as a means for interaction in in-vehicle context. However, gaze alone may be insufficient for reliable interaction or even a safe option in this context, as the use of gaze-only input would require prolonged glancing off the road. Thus, another modality is needed to complement gaze. As most of the operations traditionally have been done by hand (e.g., utilizing button presses), the use of hand gestures could potentially be functional in combination with gaze tracking. By enabling hand gestures for interaction, it would be possible to utilize even wide surface areas in a reach of arm for input, and at the same time still stick to somewhat familiar hand-based operation that is known in the context.

Besides Biswas et al. [6], hand gestures as a selection technique used while driving have been studied in few other papers. For example, Ohn-Bar and Trivedi [33] discuss issues and pitfalls when building a system for using hand gesture recognition in cars. The authors demonstrated the system that recognized gestures based on computer vision system they developed. Similar systems were built earlier by [2, 11, 44].

Roider et al. [38] used Leap Motion device to recognize mid-air gestures, however the paper has no explanation of the gesture recognition algorithm. In their study, selections were made by pointing to objects displayed on a screen and then tapping in the air with the index finger to select it. The gesture method was compared against selection by gaze and by voice. The study was continued by utilizing gaze direction to increase accuracy of pointing gestures [37]. May et al. [29] found that pointing gestures were much slower than direct touch when making selections from a menu. At the same time, they were safer and did not require prolonged gazing off the road. Another comparison between touch and mid-air gestures revealed that driver's deviations from the lane in Lane Change Test were comparable when using both methods [25]. Mid-air pointing gestures were employed also in autonomous driving scenarios [39]. In this study, as well as in [34], gestures were combined with voice.

A similar study to [38] was conducted by Angelini et al. [3], where gestures were not performed in the air but on the surface of steering wheel. Authors reported that such gestures were comparable with voice and touch modalities in terms of perceived usability, subjective workload, and emotional response. There are more studies on using gestures on a steering wheel surface (e.g., [10, 32] showing that gestures are safe to use while driving, as long as both hands stay on the steering wheel.

As follows from this overview, the use of mid-air gestures while driving is still under-studied. An early discussion about using gestures in cars is available in [1]. May et al. [30] collected a set of gestures that could be used for interaction in cars. The set consisted of grab, palm display, swipe down with either index finder, two fingers, or open palm, point down, and hold gestures. Shakeri et al. [40] studied swipe, "V", and circular gestures, but their aim was to compare several types of feedback that could be used to support these mid-air gestures. They found that non-visual feedback can reduce visual distraction when operating with in-car mid-air gestures. Cabreira and Hwang [8] noted that swipe gestures implemented in Leap Motion SDK are not well suited for elderly drivers. Shakeri et al. [41] studied the impact of ultrasonic haptic feedback on the time the eyes were off the-road and found that this type of feedback was superior to visual feedback for in-vehicle interaction. Graichen et al. [15] used six various mid-air gestures (basic and complex) to compare against touch. They found that those drivers who used gestures for interaction did not show a decrease in driving behavior quality, whereas for drivers who used touch interaction the quality of behavior did decrease. Kim et al. [24] studied in-car interaction with two input methods combined from a set of five (touch, mid-air gesture, voice, gaze, button) and found that combinations including mid-air gestures resulted in more deviations from a lane and extended the duration of the secondary task.

Usability and comfortability have been the main concerns in most of the studies dedicated to these new in-car interaction and information presentation methods. Surprisingly, the safety issues related to the driver attention have been addressed rather rarely, even though safety-related indicators are the most crucial ones for any technology that is aimed to be utilized in human-operated machines with risk on an accident. Similarly, it is not clear how these new interaction methods perform when compared against more traditional methods that are based on operating with hardware buttons, knobs, and so forth: the existing studies provide contradictory conclusions and focus mainly on other new interaction methods.

The present aim was to combine gaze pointing with either buttons operated with a right-hand thumb or by mid-air gestures with haptic feedback operated with right hand, and to study especially driving safety together with subjective preferences while selecting and manipulating in-car devices.

3   Methods

3.1   Participants

Twenty voluntary participants (15 males and 5 females) took part in the study (23–59 years, mean age = 40 years). The criteria for the participants were: 1) no need to wear eyeglasses while driving a car due to a head-mounted eye-tracker used in the study;

2) no indication of simulator sickness; 3) righthandedness due to hardware setup with hand gesture recognition device located on the right; and 4) driving experience of at least 2 years on a weekly basis.

3.2 Equipment

Driving Simulator

The experiment took place in a laboratory equipped with the driving simulator made by Creanex. The simulator allows driving in a virtual city and in countryside. It outputs a video to three projectors that takes about 160° of a driver's visual span. The simulator steering wheel column had two stalks, one on each side: gear shifter on the right and turn signal/headlights switch on the left. During the study the transmission was set to automatic, whereas the seat was adjustable as in a regular car.

The maximum driving speed was limited to 90 km/h. Participants were driving on a country road in the countryside where the simulator's API allowed pedestrians walking along both sides of the road. The pedestrians included either a male or a female figure dressed in grey clothes, walking in either direction at a speed of 1 m/s on either side of the road. These pedestrians served as attention-demanding objects and there was no other traffic on the road. In addition to the pedestrians, only speed limit traffic signs were visible along the side of the road at a few locations.

Fig. 1. Modified Creanex in-car interface with six device icons: left window, contact list, headlights, audio, heater, and air conditioning. The AprilTags serve for eye-tracking purposes. Red rectangles in the view taken from the Pupil Labs Core world camera visualize the seven "surfaces" (a.k.a. AOIs) used for gaze interaction.

The Creanex simulator output view was slightly modified for this experiment. The digital speed and gear displays were moved from the original location at the bottom to the location slightly below of the center of the screen, thus serving as a HUD (see Fig. 1).

The default Creanex in-car view of the frontal panel was removed. Instead, we placed five icons representing the following in-car devices (see Fig. 1, from left to right): 1) multimedia display with a list of contacts, 2) headlights, 3) audio-system's volume, 4) heater, and 5) air conditioning. The sixth icon was placed on the left window to represent this window as a device that was an object of interaction.

Each interactive device had four states. Three devices on the right side (audio, heater, air conditioning) had about similar states: off, minimum, moderate, and maximum. The headlights were in one of the following states: off, low-beam, fog lights, and high-beam. The list of contacts contained four names (Anthony, Laura, John, and Mary), and each name was represented with its first letter. The left window had a closed state and three opened states: slightly, moderately, and widely opened.

Eye Tracking
We used the head-mounted Pupil Labs Core eye tracker (30 Hz) equipped with two eye-cameras to estimate driver's gaze direction. Its Pupil Capture software allows creating "surfaces" (i.e., areas of interest) using AprilTags/36h11 in the view form the world camera that is further used to create links between user's gaze and real objects.

Hand-Tracking and Ultrasound Haptic Feedback
Mid-air gestures were recognized using data produced by a Leap Motion hand-tracking device. It was assembled into a single unit together with Ultrahaptic STRATOS device equipped with 256 ultrasonic actuators that was capable of creating a touchless haptic sensation on the palm of the hand (see Fig. 2. Left). The unit was located close to the driver's right hand and slightly below the seat level, approximately where the manual gear shifter would be in passenger cars, as shown in Fig. 2, right.

Fig. 2. Leap Motion and Ultrahaptics devices with visualized sensation of a "wall" created with the ultrasound skin stimulation (left) and driving environment with the interaction devices: steering wheel with buttons (circled in red) (middle) and gesture recognition area (right).

Buttons
We used the DinoFire presentation device that was acting as a keyboard with "page up" and "page down" buttons. The device was attached to the steering wheel as shown in Fig. 2, middle. The pilot tests confirmed the buttons were easy to reach and could be operated blindly with the driver's thumb.

3.3   Interaction Design

Selecting In-Car Devices

To interact with an in-car device and change its state, a driver had to first activate them by gaze. For this purpose, we created three surfaces in Pupil Capture application: 1) left-window surface spanning over the right part of the left window, 2) windshield surface spanning over most of the windshield, and 3) cockpit surface located below the windshield (see the screenshot from the tracker's world camera shown on Fig. 1). Our experiment software divided the cockpit surface into five equal parts to identify which in-car device located on the front panel was in focus. This operation was based on the gaze point location relative to the surface, as reported by Pupil Capture software.

Drivers were instructed to gaze at the road while driving (see Fig. 3a). To select a device, a driver first had to glance at its icon. After 120 ms of gaze pointing the icon became "focused", as shown in Fig. 3b. If needed, the driver could change the focus to another icon by gazing at it for another 120 ms or more.

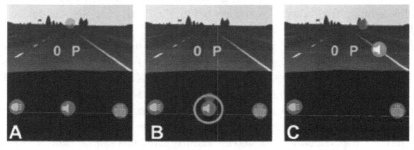

Fig. 3. Device selection by gaze: (a) a driver is looking at the road; (b) driver glances at a device icon and the device becomes "focused", which is visualized with the orange circle; (c) driver glances back to the road and the device becomes "selected": it moves to the HUD. The red spot representing the gaze point is shown in the figure for visualization purposes.

The focused icon became selected only after the driver glanced back at the road. The selected icon was relocated from its initial position to the HUD and was shown on the right from the gear indicator (see Fig. 3.c). Therefore, it was easy to inspect which device was selected and what its state was at any time.

The device stayed selected for four seconds and then became unselected automatically (the icon disappeared from the HUD and returned to its initial position) unless the driver started changing its state. Also, the device became unselected automatically within two seconds after the driver's hand left the gesture detection area, or after the last button was pressed: these two incidents meant that the selection of the device state was ready. The exact deselection timings were obtained empirically from pilot tests.

Changing Device State

There were two interaction methods to change the state of the device: either with buttons attached to the steering wheel, or with horizontal sliding hand gestures over the Ultra-haptic STRATOS device. All in-car devices had four states indexed from 1 to 4, and the extreme states (the first and the last) had only one direction of allowed change, thus the states were not cycled in a loop. Each state index had its own note that was played as audio feedback when the state with that index was selected; the state with the lowest index had the lowest tone.

In "buttons" condition the buttons attached to the steering wheel were used to change the state of the activated device. Pressing "up" button increased the index of the device state by one and pressing "down" button decreased it. The note of the new state was played upon pressing a button, and if no button presses were made for two seconds, then the task ended automatically and voice feedback "Completed!" was played.

In "gestures" condition a simple back-forth sliding gesture detector consumed data from the Leap Motion device. The location of the gesture recognition area above the hand tracking device was fixed and limited in horizontal dimension by the size of Ultrahaptics device. Drivers could find the gesture area blindly with the help of ultrasonic haptic feedback resembling a "wall" that was activated above the center of the STRATOS device (see Fig. 2, left). The device-wide "wall" was sensible in the range between 10 and 25 cm above the device surface. We instructed the participants to position their palm so that the haptic feedback was sensible at about the distal palmar crease (roughly ¾ of the palm counting from a wrist to fingers) before they start changing the device state. The device state change procedure is described next.

Step 1. The haptic "wall" appeared upon the hand approaching the tracking sensor. Gesture recognition was enabled, and a short sound feedback was given after the hand speed dropped below 7 mm/s. Hand position at this moment was memorized as a reference representing the current device state (see Fig. 4, marker "X").

Step 2. The device state was changing as the driver moved the right hand along the Leap Motion's Z axis (toward/backward from the screen). Each device state change interrupted the haptic feedback for 400 ms and triggered this state's audio feedback.

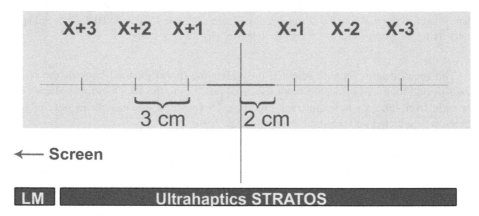

Fig. 4. Mid-air sliding gesture spatial model. After the hand stops moving at location X, this location further represents the device current state index, and gesture recognition starts. The locations that represent device states are located at 3 cm distance from each other. The current state spans 4 cm.

The spatial distance D between states was 3 cm. The change in device state occurred when the hand crossed the boundary between the states. This boundary was always located at the distance of 0.65D from the current state spatial center, i.e., 2 cm. Thus, the effective spatial size of a state was 4 cm as shown in red in Fig. 4. The inter-state distance D was selected so that the haptic feedback would be sensible by the driver even when changing the device state index from one extremum to another that required a movement of 8 cm (e.g., in the task to change heater state from "off" to "maximum").

Step 3. Gesture recognition was deactivated, and audio feedback was played if the hand motion speed exceeded 50 mm/second, or the driver moved the hand away from the motion sensor. The task ended automatically and voice feedback "Completed!" was played if no actions were taken during the following two seconds.

3.4 Procedure

The purpose of the study together with participant's rights and data privacy statement was introduced to the participants upon arriving at the driving laboratory. Each participant filled out the written consent, simulator sickness questionnaire (SSQ, [21]), and background information forms. The participant was seated into the simulator's seat which was adjusted if needed. Subsequently, the participant was asked to familiarize themselves with the steering wheel, gear shifter, pedals, and stalks on the steering column of the simulator. We also asked the participant to drive for a few minutes to ensure they did not experience any simulator sickness.

If the participant felt well, we continued the training by spawning 8–10 pedestrians and teaching the participant to flash the high beam (pull the high beam stalk toward the wheel) as soon as a pedestrian was noticed. The participant was explained that the primary task was, besides reacting to pedestrians, to drive straight and to obey speed limits indicated by traffic signs. After this practice, we collected the SSQ for a second time. We also trained the participant to fill in the NASA Task Load Index (NASA-TLX) questionnaire [18] regarding the complexity of this practice session. The weighting phase of the rating scales was omitted in accordance with [17].

We then set Pupil Core eye tracker and calibrated it using the printed-marker calibration method: the marker was shown in five locations. The calibration was repeated as many times as needed until the gaze point was located on or close to any of the frontal panel icons when we asked the participants to glance at it. Then the participant was taught to select a device by eye gaze using the procedure described above.

After the participant confirmed high competence in device selection by gaze, we taught them to change the device state with either hand gestures or buttons. We demonstrated a table of icons of all six in-car devices in each of the four states and let the participant spend some time for memorizing the order of icons.

The participant was then asked to perform a sample task instructed via a synthesized prerecorded message (e.g., "Open left window widely"). At least eight tasks were completed by each participant in "gestures" condition until we recognized the participant's high competence in using this interaction method. We used 2–3 practicing tasks when training the participant to change the selected device state with buttons.

Finally, we reminded the participants about their primary driving task and noted that the secondary task (device state change) will be provided as a prerecorded synthesized voice message generated by the PC.

Then the first session began. The order of the interaction methods was counterbalanced between the participants. They completed 12 device manipulation tasks. Each task started 20 s after the previous was finished, except the tasks #5 and #9 which started in 1 min. Within each task, one pedestrian was spawned 180 m in front of the car in three seconds after the task instruction was given. The delay was selected so that the pedestrian was likely noticed when manipulating the device state, and not when selecting the device. One pedestrian was also spawned during non-task driving, in eight seconds after a task was completed. Three additional pedestrians were spawned every 15 s during the long non-task driving intervals. Thus, there were 29 pedestrians spawned during one session.

After the first session was completed, the participant filled in the SSQ and NASA-TLX forms. At this point the participant could take a short break if needed. Then the second session began in which the participant was changing the selected device state using the other interaction method. At the end of the second session the SSQ and NASA-TLX forms were filled once again.

The experiment ended with a questionnaire consisting of five questions (preferred interaction method, difficulty keeping the lane, difficulty noticing pedestrians while completing tasks, ability to notice pedestrians, and ability to stay attentive) that the participant answered in own words. Also, they were encouraged to express any comments regarding this experiment. The participant received a movie ticket when leaving the laboratory. The study was evaluated by the local university ethics committee.

3.5 Logged Data

We logged events generated by gaze tracker (focused to the road or to an in-car device icon, or gaze moved away from any of these), hand tracker (hand entered / left the gesture area, gesture recognition started / finished), device controller (activation / deactivation and changes in the state), task controller (task started / ended), pedestrian controller (pedestrian spawning, noticed by the participant, and passing unnoticed), and car system (car speed, distance from the start point, and offset from the road center).

3.6 Data Processing and Analysis

Data Processing
We grouped all data according to the condition (gestures and buttons) and computed the following values from the logged data: 1) pedestrian noticing ratio as the number of noticed pedestrians to the number of pedestrians displayed during driving; 2) time taken to notice a pedestrian after it was spawned; 3) device selection time and device manipulation time as intervals between the instruction was given, a device was selected, and the final device state was set; 4) task error rate as a ratio between the number of tasks completed with incorrect device state and the number of tasks; 5) standard deviation of

the car offset from the lane center; and 6) the ratio of time the participants were gazing off the road during device manipulation task.

Given that participants were driving at approximately same speed in both conditions (78.6 ± 4.5 km/h in gestures condition and 79.7 ± 4.3 km/h in buttons condition, the difference was not statistically significant), we consider that time taken to notice a pedestrian in this study can be treated as a valid indicator of attention to the road.

Data Filtering and Statistical Analysis

Few participants experienced issues with eye tracking accuracy and in some trials repeatedly selected an undesired device several times before they were able to select the desired one. In approximately 13% of 240 trials (roughly equally in both conditions) participants initially selected the wrong device; however, not all these selections were due to issues in eye tracking. In 3.7% of all trials (equally in both conditions) the participants manipulated the wrong device. Most of these events occurred due to participants confusing the icons. In a couple of cases connected with issues in eye tracking the participants received oral instruction from the supervisor: "just select anything and change its state: this way you continue the experiment".

An increased delay in selecting an in-car device after the audio instruction was given served as the indicator of eye tracking issues, and we filtered out all cases when it took more than 4 s to select the expected device. This way, 15.4% of 240 trials were removed from the analysis (about equally in both conditions).

Statistical analyses were performed using the Friedman and the Wilcoxon signed ranks tests. Bonferroni correction was used for post hoc pairwise comparisons when needed.

4 Results

4.1 Driving Attention

The mean pedestrian noticing ratio was 94.1% in "gestures" condition, 95.7% in "buttons" condition, and 98.2% while driving without a selection task (see Fig. 5, left), the differences were not statistically significant. During interaction tasks the mean time to notice a pedestrian was 4.9 s in "gestures" condition and 4.2 s in "buttons" condition (see Fig. 5, right), while during non-task driving the mean time was 3.4 s.

The Friedman test showed a statistically significant effect of interaction condition for pedestrian notice time ($\chi2 = 12.3$, $p < .001$). Post-hoc pairwise comparisons showed that the pedestrian notice time was significantly shorter in the baseline condition than in "gestures" ($Z = -2.73$, $p < .01$) and "buttons" ($Z = -2.27$, $p < .05$) conditions. The difference between "gestures" and "buttons" conditions was not statistically significant.

More than half of pedestrians (51.8%) in "gestures" condition were noticed after the device manipulation had finished, 28.9% pedestrians were noticed while changing device state, and 12.4% pedestrians were noticed earlier (before, during, or after selecting a device by gaze). In "buttons" condition, 78.4% of pedestrians were noticed after the interaction was finished, 4.6% pedestrians were noticed while changing device state, and 9.6% pedestrians were noticed earlier. We indexed all stages from 1 to 5 and computed the average interaction stage index at which pedestrians were noticed. The Wilcoxon test revealed these average indexes of interaction stage were significantly different between the conditions (Z = −2.85, p < .01): pedestrians were indeed noticed at a later interaction stage in "buttons" condition as compared to "gestures" condition.

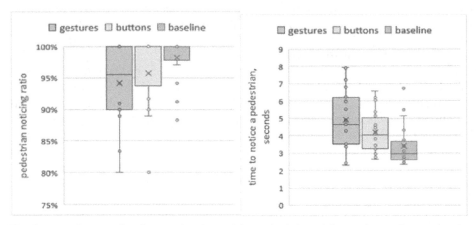

Fig. 5. Attention to pedestrians: pedestrian noticing ratio (left) and time took to notice a pedestrian (right).

Mean standard deviation of the car offset from the lane center was 0.245 m in "gestures" condition, 0.205 m in "buttons" condition, and 0.237 m in the baseline condition (see Fig. 6, left). The condition was not recognized as a factor influencing this measurement. The condition was an important factor for the ratio of time participants were gazing off the road ($\chi 2 = 82.3$, p < .001). However, during device manipulation tasks these times did not differ significantly (13.3% in "gestures" and 15.4% in "buttons" conditions), while in the baseline condition it was significantly lower, only 1.5% (Z = − 3.9, p < .001 for both pairwise comparisons). Figure 6, right, shows the reversed values of this metric, i.e. the time ratio with gaze kept on the road.

There were 11 events when participants were gazing off the road for longer than 2 s during tasks (5 in "gestures" condition and 6 in "buttons" conditions); this is specified as safety-violation event in the NHTSA guidelines [45]. Eight of these events were recorded from one participant who was experiencing issues with gaze tracking accuracy. The rest 3 events were recorded from the other 3 participants.

4.2 Interaction

The difference in mean device selection time (the time spent to activate a device using eye gaze) between the interaction conditions (3.3 s "gestures" condition and 2.9 s in "buttons" condition) was not statistically significant. In "buttons" condition the participants started changing the state of the selected device significantly faster than in "gesture" condition (1.5 and 3.0 s, correspondingly; Z = −3.9, p < .001). The total mean device manipulation time was 6.7 s in "gestures" condition, and 3.3 s in "buttons" condition (see Fig. 7, left); the difference was statistically significant (Z = −3.9, p < .001).

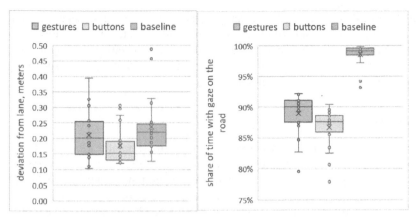

Fig. 6. Attention to the road during task completion: deviation from the lane (left), and time ratio with gaze kept on the road (right).

The complete sliding gesture duration expressed as the interval between the time the system was ready to make a gesture and the time the hand started to move away back to the steering wheel was 4.5 s. We computed this parameter separately for trials when device state was changed from one extreme value to another one, and for all other trials. Mean values were 3.8 s and 5.2 s, respectively, and the difference was statistically significant ($Z = -2.09$, $p < .05$). Mean task error rate was 19.3% in "gestures" condition and 17.4% in "buttons" condition (see Fig. 7, right). This difference was not statistically significant.

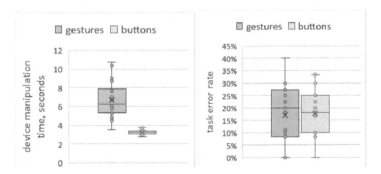

Fig. 7. Device manipulation time (left) and task errors (right).

Half of the tasks required participants to set one of the two extreme device states, while the other half required to set a state from the middle of the range (of 4 states). In the latter case, participants could overshoot the target state while manipulating a device. Indeed, in the "gestures" condition the participants overshot the target state in 45% of the tasks when the required state was from the middle of the range. In "buttons" condition they did it only in 20% of attempts.

Because of this, we computed mean device manipulation times separately for trials with inner target states and with outer (extreme) target states. In "gestures" condition these were 5.3 and 7.1 s, respectively, this difference was statistically significant ($Z = -2.67$, $p < .01$). In "buttons" condition these were 3.26 and 3.25 s, respectively, this difference was not statistically significant.

4.3 Simulator Sickness

None of the participants reported feelings related to simulator sickness. To analyze the SSQ data according to recommendations given in [21], the scales were grouped into "nausea", "oculomotor", and "disorientation" symptom clusters. Following this the cumulative scores for each of them were calculated. Wilcoxon signed ranks tests did not show significant differences between the interaction conditions in any symptom cluster. We further analyzed each separate SSQ rating scale. The Wilcoxon tests did not reveal any statistically significant differences between the conditions in any of the rating scales.

4.4 NASA-TLX Ratings

Figure 8, left, shows the mean raw scores $\pm$ SEM of the NASA-TLX subscales. Wilcoxon signed ranks tests showed that "gestures" condition involved significantly more physical demand and frustration than "buttons" condition ($Z = -2.89$, $p < .01$, and $Z = -2.53$, $p < .05$, respectively). Performance was rated significantly lower in "gestures" condition compared to "buttons" condition ($Z = -2.19$, $p < .05$). Ratings of mental demand, temporal demand and effort did not differ between the "gestures" and "buttons" conditions in terms of statistical significance.

The overall workload score computed as the unweighted average of the subscales (raw TLX, refer to [17]) was only insignificantly higher in "gestures" than in "buttons" condition (52.8 and 44.7, see Fig. 8, right).

4.5 Results from the End Questionnaire

Participants' subjective experiences collected with the end questionnaire regarding driving and interaction are reported in Fig. 9. Some participants noted in their comments that the haptic feedback was useful. However, when asked about the changes in feedback pattern when a device state was changing (short break in the feedback), nobody could recall noticing such a change. Some of the participants noted that in the "gestures" condition it was sometimes hard to fix the selected state: the state could unintentionally change when they removed their hand back to the wheel. They suggested that the system was somewhat too sensitive and wider hand movements could solve this issue. Two participants who preferred gestures over buttons reported that they liked to change several states (from one extreme to another) in one quick hand slide rather than pressing a button three times.

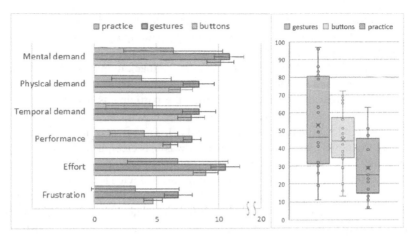

Fig. 8. Mean task workload ratings (± SEM error bars) (left) and the overall raw scores (right) of the NASA-TLX questionnaire. The 1–20 rating scales vary from "very low" to "very high" except for the Performance scale that varies from "perfect" to "failure".

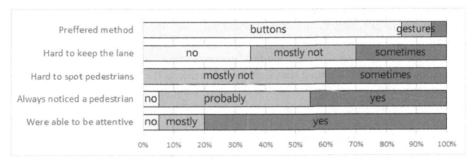

Fig. 9. Subjective experiences of driving and interaction.

5 Discussion

The results showed that mid-air gestures used for interacting with in-car devices did not distract driver's visual attention from the road more than buttons located on the steering wheel. This was evidenced by the fact that only a few gaze-of-the-road events longer than 2 s were recorded in both experimental conditions. Also, the pedestrian noticing ratio was approximately the same in both conditions. However, during "gesture" condition, pedestrians were noted with longer delays while conducting the manipulation task than when using physical buttons. This was visible also from the results where the pedestrians were noticed in different stages of the interaction tasks.

Further, the deviations from the lane were significantly larger in "gestures" condition than in the "buttons" condition. This is in line with the study by Kim et al. [24] which found that mid-air gestures may cause larger deviations from lane than other input techniques. In contrast, Roider et al. [38] found no difference in deviations when comparing gesture, speech, and gaze input.

On the other hand, gaze was less distracted from the road when using gestures. We hypothesize that this difference occurred due to participants inspecting their thumb location on the buttons in the first trial(s). The participants did not have to verify their hand position in "gestures" condition as, firstly, haptic feedback helped to place the hand to the correct location, and secondly, glancing to the gesture location would have required more prominent gaze shift from the road, thus the participants avoided it. Also, this observation suggests that haptic feedback was indeed useful in gesture initiation phase to find the gesture location blindly in line with [12]. The effect of haptic feedback on a palm during the device manipulation, however, was less clear, as participants reported not noticing it. This issue requires more attention in future studies.

When eye tracking accuracy was not compromised, device icon selection procedure was fast and reliable as only a short glance off the road was required. The current study, however, was conducted in a laboratory condition, whereas earlier attempts to conduct similar research in a car faced notable issues regarding the eye tracking robustness [20, 42]. With such technological issues solved, gaze pointing may serve as a convenient means to change an object of interaction without touching surfaces, thus substituting the speech input [24] or supplementing it [5] in multimodal in-car interfaces.

The simulator sickness was not affecting the ability to operate on both primary and secondary tasks. However, time was a significant factor for eye strain and fatigue. Similar observations are generally common for studies with high mental demand and attention required (for example, see [36]).

It took more time to complete the task using gestures than using buttons, but the number of erroneously selected states did not depend on the interaction method. Participants left errors uncorrected mostly due to confusing the icons, but in few cases the reason was eye tracking inaccuracy.

Interaction using gestures was rated as more complex, it caused more frustration, and was considered as physically more demanding by the participants. In earlier studies (e.g., [14]), mid-air gestures were found to cause no higher workload than touch interaction. In the current study, participants rated their own performance lower when using gestures, and this may cause that they favored physical buttons over the gestures in their end questionnaire responses. We propose that making the gesture recognition algorithm less sensitive may improve the interaction robustness and experience, which in turn may increase the driving safety by more attentiveness and less lane deviation, among other factors.

For mid-air gestural interaction to become functional in driving context there are several things to be considered besides the algorithm robustness. One is the location of the technology for imaging / tracking drivers' gestures. Locations closer to the steering column might require less time to initiate a gesture as well as less physical effort. Another thing is the interaction scenario. Using gestures for manipulating other than discrete 4-state in-car devices should also be tested in future studies. We propose that mid-air gestures might function better for operating infotainment systems. Devices with continuous scales, like sound volume, are among the first candidates to explore. Finally, other than horizontal swipe gestures (terminology according to [40]) may be more suitable for certain tasks: for example, a side window could be manipulated by a vertical swipe gesture.

6 Conclusions

We compared interaction with in-car devices using gaze activation combined with selection by either buttons on the steering wheel or mid-air sliding gesture to be completed approximately in the location where a gear shifter is located in passenger cars. We found that both selection techniques allowed operating in-car devices blindly without compromising driving safety significantly. From our results we can conclude that mid-air gestural interaction functions nearly as well compared to interaction with buttons. Thus, it has potential as a means of interaction. Mid-air interaction can and needs to be developed in many respects like improved algorithms, location, and of course the actual interaction scenario requires careful consideration: there may be additional use scenarios where drivers may utilize mid-air gestures with higher efficiency than buttons.

Acknowledgements. This research was carried out as part of the Adaptive Multimodal In-Vehicle Interaction project (AMICI), which was funded by Business Finland (grant 1316/31/2021).

References

1. Alpern, M., Minardo, K.: Developing a car gesture interface for use as a secondary task. In: CHI 2003 Extended Abstracts on Human Factors in Computing Systems (CHI EA 2003), pp. 932–933. ACM (2003). https://doi.org/10.1145/765891.766078
2. Althoff, F., Lindl, R., Walchshäusl, L.: Robust multimodal hand and head gesture recognition for controlling automotive infotainment systems, In: Proceedings of Fahrer im 21. Jahrhundert: der Mensch als Fahrer und seine Interaktion mit dem Fahrzeug, VDI-Gesellschaft Fahrzeug- und Verkehrstechnik, pp. 187–206 (2005)
3. Angelini, L., et al.: A comparison of three interaction modalities in the car: gestures, voice and touch. In: Actes de la 28ième conference francophone sur l'Interaction Homme-Machine (IHM 2016). ACM. (2016). https://doi.org/10.1145/3004107.3004118
4. Berg, F. J., Bennett, T. J., Davis, A. C., Riefe, R. K., Dybalski, R. H., Phillips, T. M.: Vehicle information system with steering wheel controller. U.S. Patent Application No. US11/239,876 (2006)
5. Biswas, P., Langdon, P.: Multimodal intelligent eye-gaze tracking system. Int. J. Hum. Comput. Interact. **31**(4), 277–294 (2015). https://doi.org/10.1080/10447318.2014.1001301
6. Biswas, P., Twist, S., Godsill, S.: Intelligent finger movement controlled interface for automotive environment. In: Proceedings of the 31st British Computer Society Human Computer Interaction Conference (HCI 2017), Lynne Hall, Tom Flint, Suzy O'Hara, and Phil Turner (eds.) 31, BCS Learning & Development Ltd., Swindon, UK, Article 25, p. 5 (2017). https://doi.org/10.14236/ewic/HCI2017.25
7. Boström, A., Ramström, F.: Head-up display for enhanced user experience, Ms Thesis, Chalmers University of Technology, Sweden (2014). SSN: 1651–4769
8. Cabreira, A. T., Hwang, F.: Movement characteristics and effects of gui design on how older adults swipe in mid-air. In: Proceedings of the 20th International ACM SIGACCESS Conference on Computers and Accessibility (ASSETS 2018), pp. 420–422. ACM (2018). https://doi.org/10.1145/3234695.3241014
9. Dobbelstein, D., Walch, M., Köll, A., Şahin, Ö., Hartmann, T., Rukzio, E.: Reducing in-vehicle interaction complexity: gaze-based mapping of a rotary knob to multiple interfaces. In: Proceedings of the 15th International Conference on Mobile and Ubiquitous Multimedia (MUM 2016), pp. 311–313. ACM (2016). https://doi.org/10.1145/3012709.3016064

10. Döring, T., et al.: Gestural interaction on the steering wheel: reducing the visual demand. In: Proceedings of the SIGCHI Conference on Human Factors in Computing Systems (CHI 2011), pp. 483–492. ACM (2011). https://doi.org/10.1145/1978942.1979010
11. Endres, C., Schwartz, T., Müller, C.A.: Geremin: 2D microgestures for drivers based on electric field sensing. In Proceedings of the 16th International Conference on Intelligent user interfaces (IUI 2011), pp. 327–330. ACM (2011). https://doi.org/10.1145/1943403.1943457
12. Freeman, E., Vo, D.-B., Brewster, S.: HaptiGlow: helping users position their hands for better mid-air gestures and ultrasound haptic feedback. In: 2019 IEEE World Haptics Conference (WHC), pp. 289–294 (2019). https://doi.org/10.1109/WHC.2019.8816092
13. Gable, T. M., May, K. R., Walker, B. N.: Applying popular usability heuristics to gesture interaction in the vehicle. In: Adjunct Proceedings of the 6th International Conference on Automotive User Interfaces and Interactive Vehicular Applications (AutomotiveUI 2014), pp. 1–7. ACM (2014). https://doi.org/10.1145/2667239.2667298
14. Graichen, L., Graichen, M., Krems, J.F.: Evaluation of gesture-based in-vehicle interaction: user experience and the potential to reduce driver distraction. Hum. Factors **61**(5), 774–792 (2019). https://doi.org/10.1177/001872081882425
15. Graichen, L., Graichen, M., Krems, J.F.: Effects of gesture-based interaction on driving behavior: a driving simulator study using the projection-based vehicle-in-the-loop. Hum. Factors: J. Hum. Factors and Ergon. Soc. **64**(2), 1–19 (2020). https://doi.org/10.1177/0018720820943284
16. Guttag, K. M., Simpson, D., Michalczuk, P., Madsen, J., Baik, D., Rahimi, A.: Compact heads-up display system. U.S. Patent Application No. 14/806,530 (2016)
17. Hart, S. G.: NASA-task load index (NASA-TLX); 20 years later. In: Proceedings of the Human Factors and Ergonomics Society Annual Meeting, 50(9), Los Angeles, Sage publications, pp. 904–908. (2006). https://doi.org/10.1177/154193120605000909
18. Hart, S. G., Staveland, L. E.: Development of NASA-TLX (Task Load Index): results of empirical and theoretical research. In: Hancock, P.A., Meshkati, N. (eds.) Advances in psychology, 52, Amsterdam, North Holland Press, pp. 139–183 (1988). https://doi.org/10.1016/S0166-4115(08)62386-9
19. Hu, Z., et al.: A literature review of the research on interaction mode of self-driving cars. In: Marcus, A., Wang, W. (eds.) Design, User Experience, and Usability. Application Domains. Lecture Notes in Computer Science, vol. 11585, pp. 29–40. Springer, Cham (2019). https://doi.org/10.1007/978-3-030-23538-3_3
20. Kang, S., Kim, B., Han, S., Kim, H.: Do you see what I see: towards a gaze-based surroundings query processing system. In: Proceedings of the 7th International Conference on Automotive User Interfaces and Interactive Vehicular Applications (AutomotiveUI 2015), pp. 93–100. ACM (2015). https://doi.org/10.1145/2799250.2799285
21. Kennedy, R.S., Lane, N.E., Berbaum, K.S., Lilienthal, M.G.: Simulator sickness questionnaire: an enhanced method for quantifying simulator sickness. Int. J. Aviat. Psychol., Taylor & Francis **3**(3), 203–220 (1993). https://doi.org/10.1207/s15327108ijap0303_3
22. Kern, S., Mahr, A., Castronovo, S., Schmidt, A., Müller, C.: Making use of drivers' glances onto the screen for explicit gaze-based interaction. In: Proceedings of the 2nd International Conference on Automotive User Interfaces and Interactive Vehicular Applications (AutomotiveUI 2010), pp. 110–116. ACM (2010). https://doi.org/10.1145/1969773.1969792
23. Khedkar, S. B., Kasav, S. M., Mahajan, S. M.: Head up display techniques in cars. Int. J. Eng. Sci. Innov. Technol. **4**(2), 119–124 (2015). ISSN: 2319–5967
24. Kim, M., Seong, E., Jwa, Y., Lee, J., Kim, S.: A cascaded multimodal natural user interface to reduce driver distraction. In: IEEE Access vol. 8, pp. 112969–112984. IEEE (2020). https://doi.org/10.1109/ACCESS.2020.3002775

25. Kopinski, T., Eberwein, J., Geisler, S., Handmann, U.: Touch versus mid-air gesture interfaces in road scenarios-measuring driver performance degradation. In: 2016 IEEE 19th International Conference on Intelligent Transportation Systems (ITSC), pp. 661–666. IEEE, (2016). https://doi.org/10.1109/ITSC.2016.7795624

26. Lee, J.D., Caven, B., Haake, S., Brown, T.L.: Speech-based interaction with in-vehicle computers: the effect of speech-based e-mail on drivers' attention to the roadway. J. Hum. Factors Ergon. Soc. **43**(4), 631–640 (2001). https://doi.org/10.1518/001872001775870340

27. Lux, B., Schmidl, D., Eibl, M., Hinterleitner, B., Böhm, P., Isemann, D.: Efficiency and user experience of gaze interaction in an automotive environment. In: Harris, D. (ed.) Engineering Psychology and Cognitive Ergonomics. Lecture Notes in Computer Science (Lecture Notes in Artificial Intelligence), vol. 10906, pp. 429–444. Springer, Cham (2018). https://doi.org/10.1007/978-3-319-91122-9_35

28. Maroto, M., Caño, E., González, P., Villegas, D.: Head-up Displays (HUD) in driving. ArXiv, abs/1803.08383 (2018)

29. May, K.R., Gable, T.M., Walker, B.N.: A multimodal air gesture interface for in vehicle menu navigation. In: Adjunct Proceedings of the 6th International Conference on Automotive User Interfaces and Interactive Vehicular Applications (AutomotiveUI 2014), pp. 1–6. ACM (2014). https://doi.org/10.1145/2667239.2667280

30. May, K.R., Gable, T.M., Walker, B.N.: Designing an in-vehicle air gesture set using elicitation methods. In: Proceedings of the 9th International Conference on Automotive User Interfaces and Interactive Vehicular Applications (AutomotiveUI 2017), pp. 74–83. ACM (2017). https://doi.org/10.1145/3122986.3123015

31. Meschtscherjakov, A.: The steering wheel: a design space exploration. In: Meixner, G., Müller, C. (eds.) Automotive User Interfaces. Human–Computer Interaction Series, pp. 349–373. Springer, Cham (2017). https://doi.org/10.1007/978-3-319-49448-7_13

32. Meschtscherjakov, A., Wilfinger, D., Murer, M., Osswald, S., Tscheligi, M.: Hands-on-the-wheel: exploring the design space on the back side of a steering wheel. In: Aarts, E., de Ruyter, B., Markopoulos, P., van Loenen, E., Wichert, R., Schouten, B., Terken, J., Van Kranenburg, R., Den Ouden, E., O'Hare, G. (eds.) Ambient Intelligence, pp. 299–314. Springer International Publishing, Cham (2014). https://doi.org/10.1007/978-3-319-14112-1_24

33. Ohn-Bar, E., Trivedi, M.M.: Hand gesture recognition in real time for automotive interfaces: a multimodal vision-based approach and evaluations. IEEE Trans. Intell. Transp. Syst. **15**(6), 2368–2377 (2014). https://doi.org/10.1109/TITS.2014.2337331

34. Pfleging, B., Schneegass, S., Schmidt, A.: Multimodal interaction in the car: combining speech and gestures on the steering wheel. In: Proceedings of the 4th International Conference on Automotive User Interfaces and Interactive Vehicular Applications (AutomotiveUI 2012), pp. 155–162. ACM (2012). https://doi.org/10.1145/2390256.2390282

35. Poitschke, T., Laquai, F., Stamboliev, S., Rigoll, G.: Gaze-based interaction on multiple displays in an automotive environment. In: 2011 IEEE International Conference on Systems, Man, and Cybernetics, Anchorage, AK, pp. 543–548. IEEE (2011). https://doi.org/10.1109/ICSMC.2011.6083740

36. Reinhard, R., et al.: The best way to assess visually induced motion sickness in a fixed-base driving simulator. Transp. Res. Part F: Traffic Psychol. Behav. **48**, 74–88 (2017). https://doi.org/10.1016/j.trf.2017.05.005

37. Roider, F., Gross, T.: I see your point: integrating gaze to enhance pointing gesture accuracy while driving. In: Proceedings of the 10th International Conference on Automotive User Interfaces and Interactive Vehicular Applications (AutomotiveUI 2018), pp. 351–358. ACM (2018). https://doi.org/10.1145/3239060.3239084

38. Roider, F., Rümelin, S., Pfleging, B., Gross, T.: The effects of situational demands on gaze, speech and gesture input in the vehicle. In: Proceedings of the 9th International Conference

on Automotive User Interfaces and Interactive Vehicular Applications (AutomotiveUI 2017), pp. 94–102. ACM (2017). https://doi.org/10.1145/3122986.3122999

39. Sauras-Perez, P., Gil, A., Gill, J. S., Pisu, P., Taiber, J.: VoGe: a voice and gesture system for interacting with autonomous cars. In WCX™ 17 SAE World Congress Experience (2017). https://doi.org/10.4271/2017-01-0068

40. Shakeri, G., Williamson, J. H., Brewster, S.: Novel multimodal feedback techniques for in-car mid-air gesture interaction. In: Proceedings of the 9th International Conference on Automotive User Interfaces and Interactive Vehicular Applications (AutomotiveUI 2017), pp. 84–93. ACM (2017). https://doi.org/10.1145/3122986.3123011

41. Shakeri, G., Williamson, J. H., Brewster, S.: May the force be with you: ultrasound haptic feedback for mid-air gesture interaction in cars. In: Proceedings of the 10th International Conference on Automotive User Interfaces and Interactive Vehicular Applications (AutomotiveUI 2018), pp. 1–10. ACM (2018). https://doi.org/10.1145/3239060.3239081

42. Trösterer, S., Meschtscherjakov, A., Wilfinger, D., Tscheligi, M.: Eye tracking in the car: challenges in a dual-task scenario on a test track. In: Adjunct Proceedings of the 6th International Conference on Automotive User Interfaces and Interactive Vehicular Applications (AutomotiveUI 2014), pp. 1–6. ACM (2014). https://doi.org/10.1145/2667239.2667277

43. Zhang, C., Zhu, A.: Research on application of interaction design in head-up display on automobile. In: Proceedings of the 2nd International Conference on Information Technologies and Electrical Engineering (ICITEE-2019), Article 113, pp. 1–6. ACM (2019). https://doi.org/10.1145/3386415.3387060

44. Zobl, M., Nieschulz, R., Geiger, M., Lang, M., Rigoll, G.: Gesture components for natural interaction with in-car devices. In: Camurri, A., Volpe, G. (eds.) Gesture-Based Communication in Human-Computer Interaction. Lecture Notes in Computer Science (Lecture Notes in Artificial Intelligence), vol. 2915, pp. 448–459. Springer, Heidelberg (2004). https://doi.org/10.1007/978-3-540-24598-8_41

45. Young, R.A.: Evaluation of the total eyes-off-road time glance criterion in the nhtsa visual-manual guidelines. Transp. Res. Rec.: J. Transp. Res. Board **2602**(1), 1–9 (2016). https://doi.org/10.3141/2602-01

A Study of Intergenerational Empathy Based on a Survey of Text Communication Characteristics

Mirai Takatama and Wonseok Yang[✉]

Shibaura Institute of Technology, Koto-Ku, Tokyo 135-8548, Japan
md22052@shibaura-it.ac.jp

Abstract. The development of ICT and smart devices has made communication between people more online centric. However, online communication, which has been activated more than face-to-face communication due to COVID-19, has many problems. This study aims to clarify the differences in perceptions and characteristics between older and younger generations to prevent the deterioration of the relationship between the younger generations and the older generation in their 40s or older due to differences in perceptions of communication due to generational differences, and to prevent the decline in empathy caused by the lack of understanding of younger words and culture by the older generation. We focused on the problem that "words complemented by non-verbal elements such as facial expressions and hand gestures in face-to-face communication are difficult to be understood by others online due to text-only communication," and that "different generations have different perceptions of text communication." We have conducted a survey of both, capturing changes in communication over time and the characteristics of each generation, and found that these problems occur especially in public environments where hierarchical relationships are emphasized, such as workplaces and schools. We believe that we can improve online communication tools that allow both parties to express themselves without worrying about the other party and to continue a fast-paced conversation online, and that we can utilize the appropriate use of non-verbal expressions to avoid ambiguity in language to increase empathy.

Keywords: Communication design · Kansei · Personal relations

1 Introduction

This study aims to identify gaps in text communication between younger and older generations and to help improve communication tools that can help both parties build positive relationships.

The global development and spread of the Internet since the 1990s have transformed the means of text-based communication from letters and faxes to online, real-time communication using email and chat [1, 2]. (Fig. 1).

In 1987, a number display function was added to pagers to enable one-way communication via text on mobile terminals for the first time in Japan. In 1997, SMS became

A. Marcus et al. (Eds.): HCII 2023, LNCS 14032, pp. 353–368, 2023.
https://doi.org/10.1007/978-3-031-35702-2_25

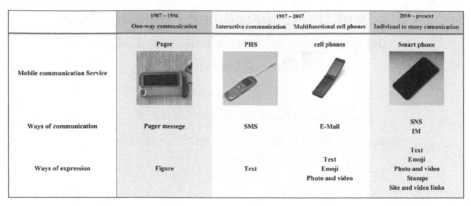

	1987~1996 One-way communication	1997~2007 Interactive communication Multifunctional cell phones	2008~present Indivisual to many comunication
Mobile communication Service	Pager	PHS cell phones	Smart phone
Ways of communication	Pager messege	SMS E-Mail	SNS IM
Ways of expression	Figure	Text Text Emoji Photo and video	Text Emoji Photo and video Stamps Site and video links

Fig. 1. Development and diffusion trends of mobile communication services and associated communication services

the first text communication that could be sent and received. In 1999, e-mail became available with the launch of internet access services from cell phone companies. By this time, the frequency of SMS or e-mail use had increased significantly compared with phone calls in terms of cell phone usage, and young people who had discovered the ease of text communication through pagers shifted from calling to texting as a means of communication on their cell phones [3, 4]. In 2008, with the release of iPhone3G, the first iPhone device in Japan, social networking services that could convey information on an individual-to-many basis, such as instant messengers, Facebook, and Twitter, which had previously been used on personal computers, became popular. As a result, text-based communication shifted from the e-mail format to chat-style message applications. In 2010, Internet use from smartphones surpassed that of PCs, and a wide range of people who had not used ICT daily now had more opportunities to participate in online communication. Furthermore, by 2020, COVID-19 had led to a rapid increase in the number of companies introducing remote work and schools adopting online classes, making online communication indispensable in various aspects of daily life [5].

Thus, while we are now able to exchange words easily, even when we are not face-to-face, online communication is associated with multiple challenges arising from disagreements in interpretation owing to the wording of words [6]. Specifically, we focused on the problem that "words that were complemented by non-verbal elements such as facial expressions and hand gestures in face-to-face conversations are difficult to be understood by others online because they are text-only" and that "perceptions of text communication differ by generation. The messages sent by humans consist of 55% facial expressions and gestures, 38% tone of voice, and 7% content of speech. However, more than 90% of the information is lost in text communication, where the facial expressions, gestures, and tone of voice of the other party are unknown, compared to face-to-face conversation. While non-face-to-face communication is increasing, "it is difficult to ask questions or consult casually during telework or online classes."

The most common problem that has occurred while using SNSs is that "what I said was received by others in a way that was different from my intention (misunderstanding)"

[6]. It has the advantage of allowing people to converse at their own tempo, regardless of time or place, but also poses many problems.

In addition, young people who have been familiar with the Internet since birth perceive online communication as valuable as face-to-face conversations. For them, online communication is a way of getting closer to others.

Phone calls, e-mails, and SMS are the main means of communication for older generations [3]. They have met the Internet environment in adulthood and beyond, and thus, value face-to-face communication. They also perceive the online world as different from the real world, as SNS and instant messengers are used among traditional friends and acquaintances, and not for extending friendships.

As text communication developed, "Younger Words" which are popular among young people from their late teens to around their 30s and contain many ambiguous expressions with elements of word play, and "Typed Words," which are words visualized by "typing" on a keyboard, also developed [7]. However, as such a language is only understood among young people, the older generation may not be able to understand what young people are trying to convey. We suspect that young people are frustrated that the older generation does not understand them and that they communicate with others out of concern and without expressing themselves to the older generation, which makes their own culture, such as the youth language, more closed and less acceptable to the other generations.

Empathy is necessary for people to feel comfortable communicating. To prevent the deterioration of the relationship between the two generations due to poor communication, and to prevent the decline in empathy resulting from the elderly's lack of understanding of the language of the young, we will investigate the touch points between the two and how a better relationship between the young and the elderly can be created.

2   Current Survey of Online Communication

We conducted a survey of previous research on text communication and a literature review to identify differences in writing characteristics between the older and younger generations.

2.1   Survey of Previous Research on Text Communication

When we communicate with others, we take care to maintain a good relationship and facilitate smooth conversation.

Brown, P and Levinson, S (1987), in their " Politeness: Some Universals in Language Usage " describe that when we communicate with someone, our linguistic representation reflects our intimacy and relationship with the other person [8]. Politeness is the consideration of maintaining an appropriate or good impression of others through one's words and actions, and it is defined as "positive face," or the desire to be admired or liked by others, and "negative face," which is the desire to distance oneself from others and not to be involved.

We use these two needs differently, depending on the other party, and these needs also affect the verbal expressions we use. In text communication, both letters and symbols are important, and they are used differently depending on the other party. The following two descriptions of linguistic representations are described.

1. One of the characteristics of Japanese is the use of honorifics. We decided whether to use honorifics based on the following three factors [9]: "Hierarchical" in relation to the use of honorifics toward those who are higher than us in the social group; "inside" and "outside" relationships, which involve the use of the word to someone who is not close to you, regardless of their position in the group; and "occasions" related to use in formal or public situations when one feels "obliged" to use it.

2. As communication media has changed and technology has developed, "Younger Words" have also developed. Furthermore, "Typed Words" have also developed. The proliferation of mobile communication services has created pressure for highly synchronized communication. Moreover, immediacy became one value of online connections that were monitored for 24 h a day. Synchronicity has given rise to words of ambiguity to maintain flat, frictionless relationships, while immediacy has given rise to words such as abbreviations to indicate the speed of response, making younger words more symbolic and manifest in the language.

Harada, N (2004), regarding emoticons, one of a group of symbols, states that "the use of emoticons in text communication is based on the 'tacit understanding' and mutual 'recognition' of the sender and receiver, and communication is established through the empathy of both parties" [11]. Emoticons are new symbols created by young people who are not good communicators as a way of self-expression in Internet society. The consideration and politeness strategies seen in the use of face marks are a new way of self-expression for Japanese people who do not like the thoughtfulness and assertiveness of young people. As young people's words such as "Typed Words" are also a type of symbol, we consider young people's words to be applicable to this description.

In contrast to the diffusion and development of information and communication technologies, the use of communication media by the elderly is low. The disparity in usage with the younger generation causes the isolation of the elderly, and social networks are limited. The psychological damage caused by the decline in physical function and changes in the living environment is significant, and "aging awareness" is a strong stressor for the elderly. Hasizume, A and Siitsuka, H (2010) stated that enhanced communication is also essential to stabilize the mental state, and that mutual social support with intimate partners is necessary to prevent isolation of the elderly in their sensitivity communication [12].

2.2 Differences Between Characteristics of Older and Younger Generations

Sentences produced by older generations tend to be long, with many line breaks and punctuation marks. This is because e-mail, which can send up to 2,000 characters, was the primary means of text communication in 1999 when those in the older generation were young. In addition, when exchanging e-mails, they use punctuation and line breaks to convey things at once to complete a story in a single message and to make it easier for the other party to understand. These days, "Ojisan syntax" and "Obasan syntax," as shown in Fig. 2, have become a hot topic among young people.

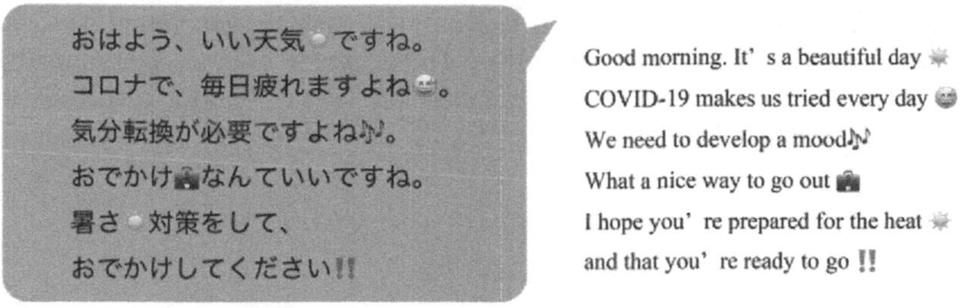

おはよう、いい天気　ですね。
コロナで、毎日疲れますよね　。
気分転換が必要ですよね♪。
おでかけ　なんていいですね。
暑さ　対策をして、
おでかけしてください‼

Good morning. It's a beautiful day ☀
COVID-19 makes us tried every day 😵
We need to develop a mood♪
What a nice way to go out 🧳
I hope you're prepared for the heat ☀
and that you're ready to go ‼

Fig. 2. "Ojisan syntax" "Obasan syntax" examples

These are sentences with many emojis and katakana, and are characterized by long messages and punctuation [13].

This style can be attributed to the influence of the "decoration mail" function that was popular when they were young, in which pictures and animated images were pasted.

Young people also use emojis, but as they do not use them to this extent, they are easily perceived as uncomfortable and shunned by the younger generation. Conversely, sentences produced by the younger generation are short and similar to spoken language. If a message is likely to be long, they tend to send short sentences in small pieces, and rarely use punctuation [14, 15].

Therefore, messages written by young people tend to be in "Typed Words," a casual spoken style, rather than written words [7, 16]. Because their goal is "conversation" rather than "communicating requirements," text communication is similar to the feeling of having a face-to-face conversation, with countless short, word-like text conversations taking place online [4].

Thus, for the older generation, online communication is a simplified version of "exchanging letters," while for younger generation, it is a "conversation" that sometimes ceases but continues endlessly. Furthermore, older generations in their 40s and older are more likely to feel that the national language is "disorganized" in response to the youth's unique language, and the linguistic representation is also a barrier [17].

The chat culture of digitally native young people will become the mainstream in text communications in the future [18]. The older generation also needs to reduce the gap in their perception of text communication and increase their "empathy" so that they can respond to changing times.

To this end, it is necessary to know how the younger generation changes its language and consideration toward the older generation, what the criterion factors are, and what impression the older generation and the recipients of these changes have of them.

3   Research Method

3.1   Preparation of Sample Texts for Experiments

In our investigation, we drew on Brown, P and Levinson, S (1987), "Politeness: Some Universals in Language Usage" [7]. We investigated how the degree of the Face Threatening Act (FTA), which violates important politeness in communication, changes the language spoken and the considerations given by the younger generation when initiating a conversation with the older generation. The degree of FTA is determined by two factors: the social distance between the speaker and listener, and the relative power of the speaker and listener. Higher and lower degrees of FTA are determined from Fig. 3.

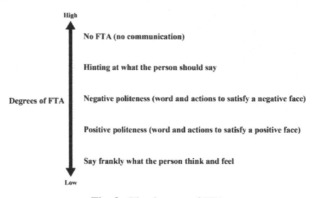

Fig. 3. The degrees of FTA

In this survey, we would like to clarify the differences in wording and attitudes that vary depending on the relationship and degree of intimacy when the younger generation comes in contact with the older generation, as well as the differences in impressions of the recipient, the older generation, and the younger generation. For this purpose, a literature survey was used as a reference for sentences to be presented to the subjects. Typically, people use honorifics when addressing someone older than themselves. However, depending on the relationship, people may use casual language when the other party is older but close to them or when honorifics and casual talk may be mixed. Arita. Y (2008) states that honorifics are used not only in upper-subordinate relationships, but also in "inside" and "outside" relationships [9]. In recent years, people have been moving away from using honorifics as the upper limit relationship to using honorifics among equals, depending on their roles and closeness to each other. In addition, when people use honorifics to communicate with someone close to them, it may be considered "unfriendly," and they may speak with a mixture of tame-mouthed expressions in a friendly manner. Therefore, we believe that young people's speech to older generations can be categorized into honorific sentences based on the standards of hierarchical relationships, honorific sentences based on the standards of internal/external relationship, sentences with a mixture of honorifics and casual talk, and sentences with casual talk. We categorized the sample sentences presented in the survey into five types: honorific sentences with punctuation, honorific sentences with exclamation marks, honorific sentences with emojis, sentences with a mixture of honorific and casual talk, and sentences with casual talk. (Table 1) Punctuated honorific sentences have the highest degree of FTA, whereas sentences with casual talk have the lowest degree of FTA.

Table 1. Text sent by young people to each subject

Wording expressions of sentences to be sent	Sentence	Sentence Content
Punctuated honorific Sentences	お世話になっております。 この間はありがとうございました。 もしよろしければ〇〇に一緒に行きたいのですが、〇日のご都合はいかがでしょうか？ ご連絡いただけますと幸いです。	How's it going? Thank you for the other day. If you don't mind, I would like to go to XX with you. How about your availability on X date? I look forward to your reply.
Honorific sentences with exclamation marks	お世話になっております！ この間はありがとうございました。 もしよろしければ〇〇に一緒に行きたいのですが、〇日のご都合はいかがでしょうか？ ご連絡いただけますと幸いです。	Hello! Thank you for the other day. If you don't mind, I would like to go to XX with you. How about your availability on X date? I look forward to your reply!
Honorific sentences with emojis	お世話になっております！ この間はありがとうございました😭 もしよろしければ〇〇に一緒に行きたいのですが、〇日のご都合はいかがでしょうか？ ご連絡いただけますと幸いです🙏	Hello! Thank you for the other day😭 If you don't mind, I would like to go to XX with you. How about your availability on X date? I look forward to your reply😭
sentences with a mixture of honorifics and casual talk	こんにちは！ この間はありがとう😭 ねね、〇〇行きたいんですけど〇日って空いてたりします？ 大丈夫だったら教えてほしい！😄	Hello! Thank you for the other day😭 Hey, I want to go to XX. Are you free on X Day? Let me if you're free then! □
Sentence with casual talk	やっほ！ この間はありがとう😭 ねね、〇〇行きたいんだけどわんちゃん〇日って空いてたりしない？大丈夫そ？😄	Hi! Thank you for the other day😭 Hey, I want to go to XX. Are you available on X Day? OK? □

3.2 Survey Items

From the previous research survey, two assumptions can be made: the closer the relationship and the higher the intimacy of the sender, the lower the degree of FTA of the sent text; and the sender, the youth generation, is more intimate with those who can express themselves using emojis and younger words. Based on this, the relationship between the sender's relationship to the linguistic representation and the elements influenced by it by the receiver's sender is as follows. (Fig. 4).

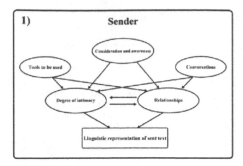 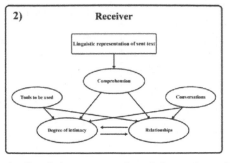

Fig. 4. Relationship between factors involved in the linguistic representation of the sender and receiver

Referring to Fig. 4, we formulated the following hypotheses to fulfil the objectives of this study and to determine the survey questions.

1. Sender (The younger generation).

- The more the awareness is similar to self-expression, the higher the intimacy and the closer the relationship.
- The more private the tools are, the higher the intimacy and the closer the relationship.
- The more the content of the conversation is similar to self-disclosure, the higher the level of intimacy and the closer the relationship.
- The higher the assessment of intimacy and future friendship, the more sentences with exclamation points and emojis are sent, even if the sentences use the same honorifics.

2. Receiver (The older generation)

- The wording of the sent text influences the level of understanding.
- Degree of understanding, tools used, content of conversation, and intimacy affect the relationship.
- Comprehension, tools used, content of the conversation, and intimacy affect the degree of rapport.
- Even if young people sent using the same honorifics, sentences with exclamation points and emojis are rated higher in terms of intimacy and future friendship.

We obtained three basic pieces of information from the responders: age, gender, and the communication tools they commonly used daily. As shown in Fig. 4, we considered it essential to survey young people as senders on their tools, their position and detailed relationship with the other person, their closeness density, the content of their conversations, and what they keep in mind when contacting the other person. We then added to the items an evaluation of whether they wanted to be closer than they are now, rather than their current closeness density, as we thought this might also affect linguistic representation and considerations. We also thought it necessary to investigate the understanding of the language spoken by young people only by the older generation, so we added it to the common items for the two generations and surveyed eight items.

1. The tools to be used on the appropriate subject for each sentence
2. What position the subject holds for them

3. Relationship to the subject
4. Density of intimacy with the subject
5. The content of your conversations with the subject
6. What they try to do when contacting the subject
7. How would they like to get to know the subject better?
8. Understanding of the target's language (only for the older generation)

Based on the above, we conducted a survey of two generations as outlined below.

- Survey of the younger generation

Survey outline: Survey on the relationship with and awareness of the target when contacting the older generation.
Survey target: younger generation in their teens and 20s.
Number of subjects: 93.
Survey items: ① to ⑦ above.

- Survey of the older generation

Outline of the survey: Survey on the difference in relationship and impression with the target sent by the younger generation when contacting them.
Survey target: older generation in their 40s to 50s.
Number of subjects: 31.
Survey items: ① to ⑧ above.

4   Research Content and Result

4.1   Results and Analysis of a Survey of the Younger Generation

We conducted a nonparametric test of the four hypotheses on 93 subjects from the survey of the youth generation to see if they hold true. The results showed significant differences at $p < 0.01$ for all hypotheses. (Tables 2 and 3).

Table 2. Significant differences on hypotheses in the youth generation

Items	Degree of intimacy	Proximity of relationship
Consideration	$p < 0.01$	$p < 0.01$
Tools	$p < 0.01$	$p < 0.01$
Conversation	$p < 0.01$	$p < 0.01$
Intimacy		$p < 0.01$
Relationship	$p < 0.01$	

The assumption that "the closer the relationship and the higher the degree of intimacy, the lower the degree of FTA in the sent text" is also valid, as significant differences were found at $p < 0.01$.

About 80% of the subjects who sent sentences using honorifics were company or school related, and it was found that the higher the degree of intimacy and evaluation of

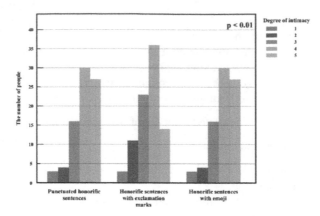

Fig. 5. Comparison of degrees of intimacy when sending sentences using honorifics

Table 3. The relationship between the presence/absence of symbol groups and the evaluation of intimacy among the younger generation

Items	Presence or absence of symbol group
The degree of intimacy	$p < 0.01$
Evaluation of future friendships	$p < 0.01$

future friendship, the more likely the subjects tended to send sent sentences with emoji rather than sent sentences with punctuation marks. (Fig. 5) (Table 3).

As for whether they want to get along better now, significant differences were confirmed at $p < 0.01$ for the language used in the sent text, tools, relationship with the subject, intimacy, content of the conversation, and what they try to do, indicating that all factors are involved.

4.2 Results and Analysis of a Survey of the Older Generation

We conducted nonparametric tests of four hypotheses on the older generation, using data from a survey of 31 older adults. (Tables 4, 5, and 6).

Table 4. Significant differences on hypotheses in the older generation

Items	Linguistic representation of the text
Degree of comprehension	$p < 0.01$

Table 5. Significant differences on hypotheses in the older generation

Items	Degree of intimacy	Proximity of relationship
Degree of comprehension	p < 0.01	p < 0.01
Tools	p < 0.01	p < 0.01
Conversation	p < 0.01	p < 0.01
Intimacy		p < 0.01
Relationship	p < 0.01	

Since the three hypotheses for the older generation were significantly different at p < 0.01, we can say the following three things.

- The lower the degree of FTA in the sent text, the lower their level of understanding.
- The lower their level of understanding, the more private the tool is, the closer the story is to self-disclosure, the closer the intimacy, the closer the relationship.
- The lower their understanding, the more private the tool is, the closer the talk is to self-disclosure, the closer the relationship is.

In addition, there were no significant differences in the degree of intimacy, evaluation of future friendships and the presence of exclamation points and emojis in the subjects who received texts using the honorifics in Hypothesis 4, contrary to the younger generation. (Fig. 6).

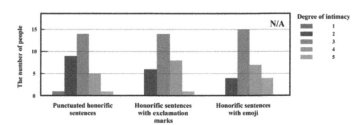

Fig. 6. Comparison of intimacy when sent sentences using honorifics

Table 6. The relationship between the presence/absence of symbol groups and the evaluation of intimacy among the older generation

Items	Presence or absence of symbol group
The degree of intimacy	N/A
Evaluation of future friendships	N/A

And their assessment of whether they want to get along better with the other person now involves tools, relationships, intimacy, and understanding.

5   Conclusion

5.1   Key Characteristics and Differences Identified from the Survey of the Two Generations

The results revealed that the sending youth generation depends heavily on relationality and closeness in its linguistic representation, while the receiving older generation depends heavily on relationality and closeness in its understanding of the messages. The older generation's ability to understand the target youth's verbal expressions depends on the closeness of the relationship between the two. For both generations, there was a deep connection between the relationship and intimacy with the subject. The younger generations are interrelated in terms of relationships and intimacy. They are also interrelated in terms of tools, conversational content, and awareness. The older generation is also interrelated in terms of intimacy and relationship. In addition, they are related to tools and conversation content.

On the other hand, there were two points of differences in perception between the younger and older generations.

1. There is a difference in the relationship between relationship and intimacy when consideration does not work. When the youth actively self-discloses using emojis and younger words, intimacy does not depend on the closeness of the relationship. (Fig. 7) However, their evaluation of future friendships and their linguistic representations depend on the closeness of the relationship. (Fig. 8) On the other hand, when the older generation cannot understand the language used by the youth because of the youth's self-disclosure, the closeness and evaluation of future friendships depend on the closeness of the relationship. (Figs. 7, and 8).

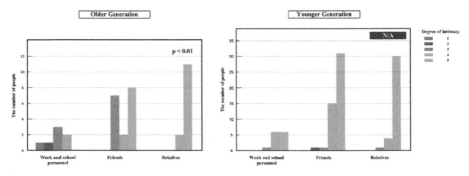

Fig. 7. Relationships and intimacy in two generations of self-disclosure by the young generation.

This is because the older generation has the perception that in a hierarchical environment, "young people should use the right words and be considerate," and they are more willing to be friends than they are now because they have a distance that is appropriate for their relationship with the other person. In our view, this may make it difficult for them to get along with others. In public relationships, the older generation perceives honorifics

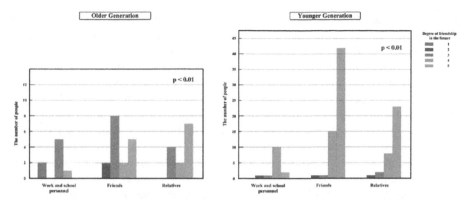

Fig. 8. Relationships between relationships and future friendship ratings in two generations when the young generation self-discloses.

as appropriate language to use regardless of intimacy and that consideration should be given. In contrast, the younger generation tends to use verbal expressions if intimacy is high, and they tend to self-disclose rather than give consideration. There was a difference in the perception of verbal expression and consideration between the two generations. We speculated that empathy can be enhanced by eliminating the discrepancy between verbal expressions and the perceptions of consideration.

2. It is a difference in perception of symbols such as exclamation marks and emojis. The younger generation tends to perceive sentences with exclamation marks and emojis as more intimate than those with punctuation alone, even in official relationships where honorifics are used, and they would like to be closer than they are now. However, the older generation did not feel that the presence of exclamation points or emojis had any effect on their assessment of intimacy or future friendships. This means that the older generation places more importance on the text itself rather than exclamation marks or emojis. However, the older generations also use emojis. Harada, N (2004) states that "The use of emojis in text communication is based on the "tacit understanding" of the sender and receiver and their mutual "understanding," and communication is established based on the empathy of both parties. We believe that because this theory is not based on two generations, a gap in perception occurs and empathy is low.

5.2 Summary of Considerations

Thus, we have confirmed that there are differences in text communication between the younger and older generations, especially gaps in official relationships, such as bosses and subordinates, teachers, and students. Considering the above, to enhance mutual intimacy, it is necessary to reduce ambiguous expressions common in young people's language and symbols, such as pictograms, whose meanings change depending on the generation, into expressions that can be commonly understood by both parties, and to bring their perceptions in line with each other.

In public environments such as workplaces and schools, a culture of seniority persists. In a "Survey on Attitudes toward Workplace Relations" conducted by Cybozu, Inc.

Among seniors aged 55–64, approximately 76% of the respondents thought that they would like people in the workplace to talk to them more casually, and the largest number of respondents raised "good relationships with others, regardless of age" as a requirement for those around them in the workplace [19]. However, many people do not like situations such as "my rule of thumb is not understood," "subordinates/juniors do not treat me with respect," and "participation in youth teams is for those under 30 years of age." These people responded that mutual understanding and discussion would be good for reducing bad feelings, and they expected that doing so would improve their work performance. As an increasing number of companies are making their employees work remotely, we believe that it is difficult to achieve mutual understanding using existing online communication tools. Therefore, based on the differences in the characteristics of the two generations obtained in this study, we believe that work performance will improve if the relationship between the two generations in the workplace is improved by moving the distance between them from the official, fixed-distance relationship to a closer relationship. Given that both generations share the same finding that tools affect their assessment of intimacy and future friendships, we speculate that creating new communication tools in public settings, such as the workplace, may help to shorten relationships.

6 Discussion

This study aimed to clarify the differences in perceptions and characteristics and prevent the deterioration of the relationship between the younger and older generations in their 40s or older due to differences in perceptions of communication caused by generational differences. It also aimed to prevent the decline in empathy caused by the lack of understanding of youth language and culture by the older generation. Through a literature review and questionnaire survey, we found that text communication has changed over time, with each generation has different perceptions and places different emphases on different factors. Gaps tend to occur in hierarchical relationships in public environments such as workplaces and schools. The new communication style formed by the digital native youth generation is difficult for earlier generations to understand. However, the form of communication has always changed with changes in ICT. Furthermore, with the spread of the Internet, human relationships have switched from a closed vertical society to an open horizontal society. We believe that we need to pursue how relationships should be formed in a public environment in which hierarchical relationships persist in a vertical society. Yoshioka, Y (2004) states that young people in their teens to thirties are positively politeness-oriented, placing importance on having fun in everyday conversation, whereas people in their forties and older are negatively politeness-oriented, placing importance on speaking correctly. He states that their communication styles are completely different [20]. Usami, M (1999) argues that the trend of increasing emphasis on positive politeness, especially among the younger generation, will become a major trend in interpersonal communication and politeness among Japanese people in the future [21].

Based on the results of this survey, we believe that we can improve communication tools to improve the relationship between both parties so that the older generation is not left behind and isolated in this current trend, and the younger generation can communicate their opinions without hesitation. We also believe that ambiguous expressions common in young people's language and groups of symbols, such as pictograms, whose meanings change from generation to generation, can be reduced to expressions that can be commonly understood by both parties. In doing so, the ambiguous parts of language can be utilized appropriately in non-verbal expressions by matching their perceptions.

References

1. Ministry of Internal Affairs and Communications.: Information & Telecommunications White Paper 2019, Part 1, Special Feature: The Evolving Digital Economy and Beyond: Society 5.0. https://www.soumu.go.jp/johotsusintokei/whitepaper/ja/r01/pdf/01honpen.pdf. Accessed 5 Jan 2023
2. Ministry of Internal Affairs and Communications, Information and Communications Bureau, Information Policy Division, Economic Research Office.: Research study on the impact of digitalization on the way we live and work in 2018. https://www.soumu.go.jp/johotsusinto kei/linkdata/r01_02_houkoku.pdf. Accessed 5 Jan 2023
3. Ministry of Internal Affairs and Communications.: White Paper on Telecommunications, pp. 25–29 (2000)
4. Murakami, N.: Transformation of communication by using smartphone(top): was SNS changing the sensibility of young people. In: Studies in humanities and communication, vol.2, pp. 22–29 (2018)
5. Ministry of Internal Affairs and Communications, Information and Communications Bureau, Information Policy Division, Economic Research Office.: Report on the Results of Contracted Research on Trends in Research and Development of the Latest Information Technology and Digital Applications in Japan and Abroad (2022)
6. Ministry of Internal Affairs and Communications, Global ICT Strategy Bureau, Information Policy Division, Economic Research Office.: Research Report on People's Attitudes Toward New ICT Services and Technologies for Solving Social Problems 2015. https://www.soumu.go.jp/johotsusintokei/linkdata/h27_06_houkoku.pdf. Accessed 19 Dec 2022
7. Kim, Y.: 'Youth and Typed Languages' in modern Japanese -A focus on word formation methods that are influenced by media changes and techno dependence, In: Comparative Japanese Studies 2018, vol. 44, pp. 225–274 (2018)
8. Brown, P., Levinson, S.: Politeness: Some Universals in Language Usage. Cambridge University Press, Cambridge (1987)
9. Arita, Y.: A Case Study: Japanese University Students' Usage of Polite Expressions. http://hdl.handle.net/11470/479 (2008)
10. Waki, T.: An essay on university student' s lifeworld: from the point of view of slang. J. Faculty Hum. Cult. Sci. Fukuyama Univ. **17**, 41–55 (2014)
11. Harada, N.: The role of "face marks" in promoting smooth communication and expressing consideration and politeness in Japanese. J. Instit. Lang. Cult. **8**, 205–224 (2004)
12. Hashizume, A., Shiitsuka, H.: The ageing society and Kansei communication. In: Advances in Intelligent Decision Technologies, pp. 607–615 (2010)
13. Suzuki, T.: Are you familiar with the "Ojisan syntax"? https://project.nikkeibp.co.jp/pc/atcl/19/08/28/00031/081000085/. Accessed 12 Dec 2022
14. Yoshihara, M.: Generation Z Attitude Survey In: Nikkei Trendy, October 2022 issue, pp. 36 (2022)
15. Net Marketing, Inc..: Research on the actual usage of matching apps by Generation Z and the situation of love and marriage activities. https://prtimes.jp/main/html/rd/p/000000114.000004974.html. Accessed 19 Dec 2022

16. Suzuki. T.: Typed Words for young people who only use "Ri" for "Ryoukai". https://project. nikkeibp.co.jp/pc/atcl/19/08/28/00031/081000086/. Accessed 12 Dec 2022
17. Agency for Cultural Affairs, Japanese Language Division.: Public Opinion Survey on Japanese Language in 2019. https://www.bunka.go.jp/tokei_hakusho_shuppan/tokeichosa/ kokugo_yoronchosa/pdf/92892882_01.pdf. Accessed 21 Dec 2022
18. Nishihara, Y.: That's not how you get your message across! The New Normal of Business Communication. Nikkei Business Publications, Inc (2022)
19. Cybozu, Inc.: Attitude Survey on Workplace Relations. https://prtimes.jp/main/html/rd/p/000 000184.000027677.html. Accessed 18 Jan 2023
20. Yoshioka, Y.: Regional and generational variation of politeness observed in communication consciousness and honorific behavior: Comparison of native speakers from metropolitan areas and Osaka. Jap. J. Lang. Soc. **7**(1), 92–104 (2004)
21. Usami, M.: Discourse Politeness in Japanese Conversation: Some Implications for a Universal Theory of Politeness. Doctoral dissertation. Hituzi Syobo (1999)

Usability Assessment of Nintendo Switch

Zilu Tang$^{(\boxtimes)}$, Hongyi Hu, and Marcelo M. Soares

School of Design, Southern University of Science and Technology, Shenzhen 518055,
Guangdong, People's Republic of China
{12011539,11912308}@mail.sustech.edu.cn

Abstract. A game is a structured form of play, usually undertaken for entertainment or fun, and sometimes used as an educational tool. With the development of modern technology, except for traditional games, people also play video games on different platforms. One of the most famous game consoles is Nintendo Switch. Because of its portability and sociability, Nintendo Switch rapidly spread among game lovers all over the world. This research is carried out with the main and specific functions of Nintendo Switch, which is measured through a series of tasks, compared with another popular game console – Xbox from Microsoft. In this research, there are users divided novice, occasional and experts, to ensure that the experimental results are authentic and credible. And this research was described as a summary usability assessment. Through a variety of usability evaluation methods, some shortcomings of the Nintendo Switch are found, and proposals with possible solutions are given.

Keywords: Usability · Game console

1 Introduction

Handheld game consoles have been a popular form of entertainment for decades. From the early Game Boy to the more recent Nintendo Switch, these portable devices allow people to play their favorite games on the go. The Nintendo Switch is a video game console developed by Nintendo, released in 2017. It is a hybrid console, which means it can be played both as a home console and as a portable device. The Nintendo Switch (See Fig. 1 below) can be used in three modes: TV mode, tabletop mode, and handheld mode. The Switch features a 6.2-inch touchscreen display, motion controls, and detachable controllers called Joy-Cons [1]. The detachable Joy-Cons provide more possibilities for playing the Nintendo Switch. One controller or two, vertical or sideways, attached to the console or separate – players can play multiple ways, depending on the game. An example of this is the game Ring Fit Adventure. Players can attach the Joy-Cons to the Ring-Con and use the motion sensors in the Joy-Cons to enjoy fun exercise gameplay experiences (See Fig. 2). Also, players can share Joy-Cons with their friends.

When connected to the dock, an OTG adapter, or a charger with sufficient power, it can output to other displays through HDMI. It is powered by a custom Tegra processor and has 32 GB of internal storage, which can be expanded with microSD cards. The

A. Marcus et al. (Eds.): HCII 2023, LNCS 14032, pp. 369–385, 2023.
https://doi.org/10.1007/978-3-031-35702-2_26

Fig. 1. Nintendo Switch (https://www.nintendo.com/store/products/nintendo-switch-neon-blue-neon-red-joy-con-117972/) (Color figure online)

Fig. 2. Player who is playing Ring Fit Adventure (https://www.nintendo.com/switch/system/)

Switch is home to a wide variety of games, including first-party exclusives like The Legend of Zelda: Breath of the Wild, Super Mario Odyssey, and Animal Crossing: New Horizons, as well as third-party titles like Fortnite and Minecraft. It has become a popular console for both casual and hardcore gamers. According to official data from Nintendo, as of now, the game "Mario Kart 8 Deluxe" has sold 48.41 million copies, making it the best-selling game produced by Nintendo [2]. As a racing party game, this demonstrates how popular the Nintendo Switch is worldwide.

Usability is a measure of how well a specific user in a specific context can use a product/design to achieve a defined goal effectively, efficiently, and satisfactorily [3]. In the context of video game consoles, usability can refer to various aspects of the user experience, including the user interface, controller design, and overall functionality. A console with high usability is easy to understand and use, has a user-friendly interface, and provides a seamless experience for the user. On the other hand, a console with low usability may be difficult to navigate, have confusing controls, or have other issues that make it frustrating or cumbersome to use. Usability is an important consideration for any product, as it can impact the user's satisfaction and the overall success of the product.

In this paper, we will introduce some of the investigations we conducted and the results we obtained to discuss the usability of the Nintendo Switch and make recommendations for improving it.

2 Methodology

To analyze the usability of Nintendo Switch, we chose: (1) Field observation, (2) Task analysis, and (3) the Leventhal and Barnes' usability model. These methods will be introduced below.

2.1 Field Observation

Field research encompasses a broad set of qualitative data collection techniques taking place in "the field" or natural, non-laboratory settings [4]. Field observation is a research method in which the researcher observes and records the behavior, interactions, and characteristics of a group or individuals in their natural environment. In the context of usability, field observation can be used to study how people use a product or system in real-world settings. Field observations can be conducted in a variety of ways, such as through direct observation, video recording, and notes. Field observations can provide valuable insights into how people use a product and can help identify issues or challenges that may not be apparent in controlled laboratory settings. Field observations can be useful for evaluating the usability of a product or system and for identifying areas for improvement.

In the test, we asked the users to finish these tasks:

1. Adjust the brightness of the screen.
2. Delete the pictures in the album.
3. Open a game and play.

By analyzing the reactions of users - including actions, language, etc. - as they completed the above tasks, we can understand their experience using the Nintendo Switch.

2.2 Task Analysis

Task analysis is an observation method that divides goals into smaller subtasks [5]. In the context of usability, task analysis is used to identify the steps and actions required to complete a task using a particular product or system. By understanding the components of a task, designers can identify potential problem areas and design solutions to improve the usability of a product. Task analysis can be conducted through various methods, such as interviews, observations, and user testing. It is an important tool for understanding and improving the usability of a product or system.

2.3   Leventhal and Barnes's Usability Model

Leventhal and Barnes' usability model is a framework for evaluating the usability of a product or system [6]. It includes six components: ease of learning, ease of relearning, ease of use, task match, flexibility, and user satisfaction. Ease of learning refers to the initial learning curve for using the product. A product with high ease of learning is easy for users to understand and use from the beginning. Ease of relearning refers to the ease with which a user can remember how to use the product after a period has passed. A product with high ease of relearning is easy for users to remember how to use even if they have not used it in a while. Ease of use refers to the overall ease with which a user can use the product to achieve their goals. A product with high ease of use is simple and straightforward to use. Task match refers to the degree to which the product's features and functions are aligned with the needs and goals of the user. A product with high task match is well-suited to the tasks and goals of the user. Flexibility refers to the range of tasks and goals that the product can support. A product with high flexibility can support a wide range of tasks and goals. User satisfaction refers to the overall satisfaction of the user with the product. A product with high user satisfaction is enjoyable and pleasurable to use.

3   Results

In our research, we selected five users who had never used the Nintendo Switch before and presented them with a series of tasks to complete. By observing their reactions and comments while using the Nintendo Switch for the first time and completing some tasks and conducting a brief interview to understand their user experience with the Nintendo Switch, we used this as a basis for analyzing the usability.

Among the participants in our study, there were two women over the age of 40 (Participant A and B), one man over the age of 40 (Participant C), and one male (age 21) and one female college undergraduate (age 20), respectively, Participant D and E. Participant C, D, and E use different kinds of electronic equipment more often, so they are more familiar with electronic equipment than participant A and B.

Before starting to finish the tasks, we found that participant A and B didn't know how to turn on the Nintendo Switch, and just pressed all the buttons on the front of Nintendo Switch. But participants C, D and E were successful to find the power switch on the sides of Nintendo Switch.

3.1   Field Observation

The results of the required tasks are described below.

Task 1: Adjust the brightness.   In the Nintendo Switch, there are two ways to complete the task of adjusting the screen brightness. The first is to go to the "Settings" page, find the "Screen Brightness" option, and adjust the brightness by adjusting the position of the slider. In this page, there is also a hint of the second adjustment method - that is, pressing and holding the home button will pop up a quick settings window (See Fig. 3).

Fig. 3. The "setting" icon on the homepage

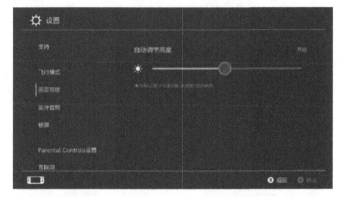

Fig. 4. The "screen brightness" page, and there is a hint for shortcut under the adjusting part

Fig. 5. The popping-up shortcut page out of the setting page, for the users to easily adjust the brightness when playing games

The observation results in the tasks is described in the table below (Table 1).

Table 1. The Result of Finishing Task 1: Adjusting the Brightness of the Screen

Participant	Gender	Age	Method 1: Adjust the brightness in the setting page	Method 2: the shortcut
A	Female	40+	Doesn't know where to adjust the brightness and needs the guidance of the researchers in every step but ignore the guidance on the screen. Can't recognize the icon of "setting"	Didn't see the hint for the shortcut
B	Female	40+	Doesn't know where to adjust the brightness and needs the guidance of the researchers in every step but ignore the guidance on the screen. Can't recognize the icon of "setting"	Didn't see the hint for the shortcut
C	Male	40+	Know where the setting page is. Just spend some time exploring how to move the cursor	Didn't see the hint for the shortcut
D	Male	20	Know where the setting page is. And can easily finish the task	Saw the hint for the shortcut
E	Female	20	Know where the setting page is. And can easily finish the task	Didn't see the hint for the shortcut

From the table, we can see that people who is familiar with electronic equipment can easily finish this task through the first method: adjusting the brightness in the setting page. But for users who are not that familiar with the electronic equipment, the guidance in Nintendo Switch is not clear for them to understand.

For the shortcut method, only participant D saw the hint for the shortcut. This indicates that the hint is not clear enough for the users to see.

Task 2: Delete the Pictures in the Album. In the album of Nintendo Switch, like on any other pages in Nintendo Switch, there are hints for the users. To delete the pictures, users should press "X" on the Joy-con and get into the selecting page. The information of the space of the Nintendo Switch will pop up.

On the selecting page, after selecting the pictures or videos he or she wants to delete, the user can press "A" on the Joy-con or "delete" on the screen to delete the selected ones (See Fig. 6).

When the cursor is on a picture, press " +" on Joy-con, the picture can be enlarged for the users to check.

Fig. 6. Select the pictures or videos when deleting them

And the result of finishing this task is described in the Table 2 below.

Table 2. The Result of Finishing Task 2: Delete Pictures in the Album

Participant	Gender	Age	Actions	Feedback
A	Female	40+	Need guidance from the researchers	N/A
B	Female	40+	Need guidance from the researchers	N/A
C	Male	40+	Can finish the task with the guidance at the button of the screen	N/A
D	Male	20	Can finish the task with the guidance at the button of the screen	The pop-up page of the information of the space of the Nintendo Switch and the SD Card is nonsense
E	Female	20	Can finish the task with the guidance at the button of the screen	The pop-up page of the information of the space of the Nintendo Switch and the SD Card is nonsense

From above we know that the guidance is clear for people who is familiar with electronic equipment. And participant D and E didn't understand why there is the page for the information of the space of the Nintendo Switch and SD card. Meanwhile, participant D said that he can only check the pictures by press " +" and then go back. It's a little bit troublesome for him to check the pictures by these steps.

Task 3: Open a Game and Play. To play a game on Nintendo Switch, users just choose the game and choose the account (See Fig. 7).

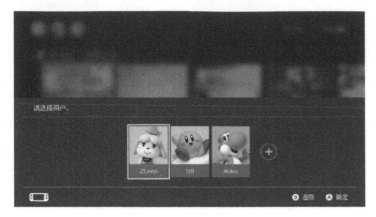

Fig. 7. Choose an Account for playing the Game

The result of the observation is in Table 3, below:

Table 3. The Result of Task 3: Open a Game and Play

Participant	Gender	Age	Actions
A	Female	40+	Knows how to choose the game after doing task 1 and 2, but directly choose the "add account" button when choosing the account
B	Female	40+	Knows how to choose the game after doing task 1 and 2
C	Male	40+	Knows how to choose the game
D	Male	20	Knows how to choose the game
E	Female	20	Knows how to choose the game

From above, we know that it's easy for them to complete this task. Participant A and B also learned how to finish this task by the previous tasks. But at the choosing account page, they may first hesitate. Because in most situation, users do not need to choose an account for the game like this.

3.2 Task Analysis

The tasks we chose for the participants are: (1) Adjust the brightness, (2) Delete the pictures in the album, and (3) Open a game and play. These tasks will be analyzed below.

Task 1: Adjust the Brightness.
Step1: Start a narrative description of the task. This task is about how users adjust the brightness of the screen of Nintendo Switch. For the users, it is possible that they adjust

the brightness of the screen when they are playing games, connecting Nintendo Switch with big screens, or just exploring.

Step2: Look at several scenarios describing specific tasks. From the observation of the participants in our field research and the observation of other users of Nintendo Switch, we found that there are scenarios below:

Scenario 1: A father, who is an engineer, wants to adjust brightness when he tries to play it at midnight.

Scenario 2: A teenager, who has just received her first Switch as a present, wants to adjust brightness when she is going through all the functions of Switch.

Scenario 3: A university student, who is playing Switch on a big screen connected to the console, wants to adjust brightness as the day goes dark.

Scenario 4: A university student, who wants to play Switch when the dorm light is off, wants to make the screen dimmer.

Step 3: For each scenario, build an informal use case diagram (See Fig. 8, 9, 10, 11).

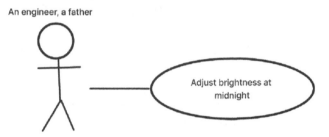

Fig. 8. Case Diagram for Scenario 1 of Task: Adjust the Brightness

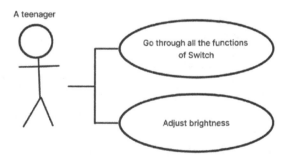

Fig. 9. Case Diagram for Scenario 2 of Task: Adjust the Brightness

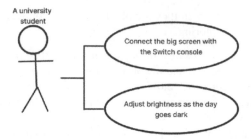

Fig. 10. Case Diagram for Scenario 3 of Task: Adjust the Brightness

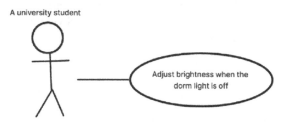

Fig. 11. Case Diagram for Scenario 4 of Task: Adjust the Brightness

Step 4: Extract primary entities.

In these cases, the actors of the task are the users. And the things are the joysticks, fingers, home button, setting icon and the screen.

Step 5: Form a high-level use case diagram (See Fig. 12).

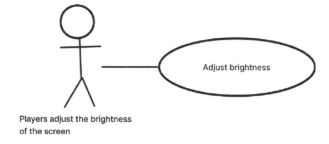

Fig. 12. High-level Use Case Diagram for Task: Adjust the Brightness

Step 6: Perform hierarchical task decomposition (See Fig. 13).

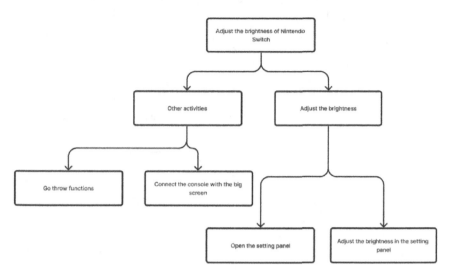

Fig. 13. Hierarchical Task Decomposition for Task: Adjust the Brightness

Task 2: Delete the pictures in the album. In the Nintendo Switch, users can take screenshots by pressing the camera button on the Joy-con. And the screenshots will be automatically saved in the album of Nintendo Switch. Users can go through, share and delete the photos and videos in the album.

Step1: Start a narrative description of the task. This task is about the process of deleting pictures in Nintendo Switch.

Step2: Look at several scenarios describing specific tasks. From the observation of the participants in our field research and the observation of other users of Nintendo Switch, we found that there are scenarios below:

Scenario 1: A university student, who thinks the space of Nintendo Switch and SD card is not enough, deletes many pictures which are took long time ago.

Scenario 2: A university student, who also thinks the space of Nintendo Switch and SD card is not enough, selects pictures which she regards as precious, and deletes other pictures.

Step3: For each scenario, build an informal use case diagram (See Fig. 14, 15).

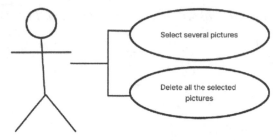

Fig. 14. Use Case Diagram for Scenario 1 of Task: Delete the Pictures in the Album

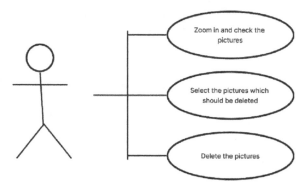

Fig. 15. Use Case Diagram for Scenario 2 of Task: Delete the Pictures in the Album

Step4: Extract primary entities. In these cases, the actors of the task are the users. And the things are the joysticks, fingers, pictures, buttons on Joy-con and the screen.

Step 5: Form a high-level use case diagram (See Fig. 16).

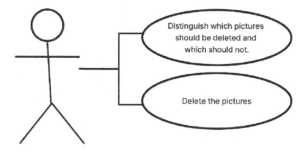

Fig. 16. High-level Use Case Diagram for Task: Delete the Pictures in the Album

Step 6: Perform hierarchical task decomposition (See Fig. 17).

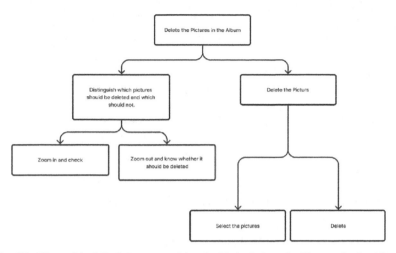

Fig. 17. Hierarchical Task Decomposition for Task: Delete the Pictures in the Album

Task 3: Open a game and play. In Nintendo Switch, users can have many accounts. Before start playing a game, users should first select the account. Different account has different archive. Interestingly, in game *Animal Crossing: New Horizons*, different accounts on the same Nintendo Switch will be on the same island but can build their own architectures and meet their own animal friends.

Step1: Start a narrative description of the task. This task is about how users select and play a game in Nintendo Switch. For the users, after selecting the game, they should also select the account or add a new account.

Step2: Look at several scenarios describing specific tasks.

Scenario 1: A university student, who plays Nintendo Switch every day, familiarly press the button "A" twice and play the game.

Scenario 2: A university student, who has the Nintendo Switch for the first day, select the game and add new account for the new Nintendo Switch.

Step3: For each scenario, build an informal use case diagram (See Fig. 18, 19).

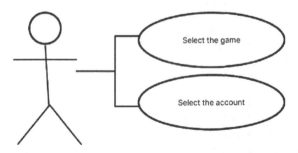

Fig. 18. Use Case Diagram for Scenario 1 of Task: Open a Game and Play

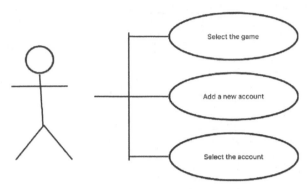

Fig. 19. Use Case Diagram for Scenario 2 of Task: Open a Game and Play

Step4: Extract primary entities. In these cases, the actors of the task are the users. And the things are the joysticks, fingers, cover of the game, and the screen.

Step 5: Form a high-level use case diagram (See Fig. 20).

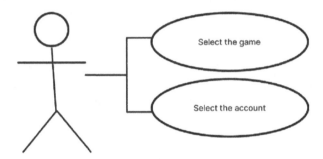

Fig. 20. High-level Use Case Diagram for Task: Open a Game and Play

Step 6: Perform hierarchical task decomposition (See Fig. 21).

3.3   Leventhal and Barnes's Usability Model

After doing the field observation and task analysis, we summarize the usability assessment of the Nintendo Switch by Leventhal and Barnes's Usability Model. After summarizing, we asked the participants some questions about the six aspects of assessment and got the results below.

Ease of Learning. In the field observation, we found that for the new users, there are clear instruction about which button refers to which operation on the interface of Nintendo Switch. But it's small for some new users to see. And some instructions, like the shortcut for adjusting the brightness, are in a color which is not conspicuous.

Ease of Relearning. We found that the button "A" on Nintendo Switch and Xbox both refers to "Confirm". Therefore, for a new user of Nintendo Switch who has used other

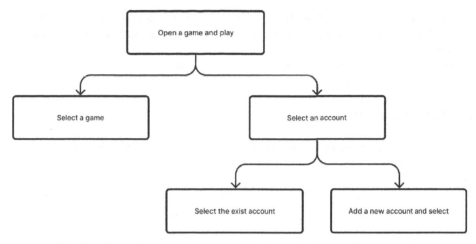

Fig. 21. Hierarchical Task Decomposition for Task: Open a Game and Play

consoles, e.g., Xbox, it will be easy for he or she to understand the buttons on Nintendo Switch.

Ease of Use. In the field observation, we found that it is easy for the users who are familiar with electronic products to use Nintendo Switch. But for users who are not familiar with electronic products – especially the products with joysticks, it will take some time for them to understand how the joystick works.

Task Match. When being given the three tasks, all the new users know what to do next and their thoughts are right.

Flexibility. To adjust the brightness of the screen of Nintendo Switch, the users can go into the setting page or use the shortcut. On the homepage, it is convenient for the users to go into the setting page and do some detailed settings. But when playing games, the shortcut is more convenient. Nintendo Switch gives users the choice.

User Satisfaction. Nintendo Switch is a kind of game console. Users can play games on it. And it also provides many functions to improve the game experience, for example, users can connect Nintendo Switch with bigger screen to play.

4   Limitations and Discussions

Due to time and Covid-19 restrictions, our study only collected results from 5 participants, which is a small sample size. Moreover, three of them are middle-aged, while the main user group of the Nintendo Switch is still young people in their 20s, so the collected samples are not very representative.

Discussions that require further research are listed below:

1. Look for more young users to observe and interview, including whether they have played on other consoles besides the Nintendo Switch and their frequency of playing console games.

2. Interview or survey some Nintendo Switch players to understand their level of under-standing of some features in the Nintendo Switch and any areas they find inconvenient to use.
3. Investigate and use some of Nintendo Switch's competitors such as PlayStation or Xbox and compare and analyze with the usability models.

5   Recommendations

From our observation, interview and our own experience, we believe there are some areas where the Nintendo Switch can be improved. These recommendations for improvement are as follows:

1. Make the hints clearer. For example, the hint for the shortcut of adjusting the brightness is grey, which is not that clear on the black background.

2. Give the users a chance to adjust the font size in the setting page, because sometimes the guidance is too small for users to see.

3. Add two gears to different Joy-Cons. One for brightness adjustment, another for volume adjustment. In this case, the adjustment for brightness and volume will be more convenient. Also, when connect Nintendo Switch with other facilities, it will be convenient to adjust volume and brightness just by the Joy-Cons (See Fig. 22).

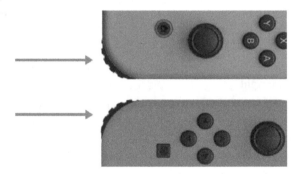

Fig. 22. Gears for brightness and volume adjustment on Joy-Cons

4. When deleting pictures, change the pop-up page of information of the space of Nintendo Switch and the SD card to a preview interface for the images. When an image is chosen, the preview would change (See Fig. 23).

Fig. 23. The preview interface for the selected image

6 Conclusions

The great success of the Nintendo Switch is not a coincidence, as it does extremely well in many aspects of user experience. It is recommended for users familiar with electronic products, its guidance for newcomers is very clear helping them quickly to accomplish their goals. Similarly, for many portable game console manufacturers and designers, the Nintendo Switch is undoubtedly a product worth learning from. However, it does have some areas that need improvement. We have also identified some through user research.

From the research above, we found that ease of learning, ease of relearning, flexibility and user satisfaction is a good characteristic of Nintendo Switch. But task match and ease of use need more improvement.

References

1. Nintendo Store page. https://www.nintendo.com/store/products/nintendo-switch-neon-blue-neon-red-joy-con-117972/. Accessed 2 Feb 2023
2. Nintendo IR information. https://www.nintendo.co.jp/ir/finance/software/index.html. Accessed 8 Nov 2022
3. What is Usability? International Design Foundation, Literature Page. https://www.interaction-design.org/literature/topics/usability. Accessed 3 Feb 2023
4. Vankatesh, S. A. Gang leader for a day: a rogue sociologist takes to the streets. Penguin (2008)
5. What Is Task Analysis? Definition, How To and Examples. Indeed Career Development page. https://www.indeed.com/career-advice/career-development/task-analysis. Accessed 2 Feb 2023
6. Leventhal, L., Barnes, J.: Usability Engineering: Process. Products and Examples. Pearson Education Inc, New Jersey (2008)

Relation Between Different UI Information Representation Methods and User Cognition

Yuki Uwajima[✉] and Wonseok Yang

Shibaura Institute of Technology, Koto-Ku, Tokyo 135-8548, Japan
uwaji4021@gmail.com

Abstract. This paper focuses on services with unique information expressions that differ from existing content services against the background of distributing a large amount of video content and differentiating them from similar services in the market, as well as the impact of differences in information expressions on user recognition and user load. In this study, research was conducted on mobile applications of existing over-the-top (OTT) services. First, we investigated the user's operational process in OTT services and found that visual and cognitive aspects of thumbnails were responsible for actions taken. Next, to clarify the influence of thumbnails on cognition and load in information representation, we conducted an experiment using a sample of thumbnails broken down into their constituent elements. The results showed that thumbnails could alter the impression made on users by focusing on the combination and arrangement of the elements. We also confirmed the influences of user gender, preferences, and differences in experience on genre judgment. In OTT services, changing thumbnail components according to user characteristics may induce interest and attention, leading to continued use of the service.

Keywords: Over-the-Top · Thumbnail · User Interface

1 Introduction

With the development of information and communications technology (ICT) and smart devices, it has become easier to provide a variety of information content to customers, and OTT services based on subscription systems have attracted attention. OTT services offer a unique user interface (UI) that differs from existing content (that presents a series of information in a linear fashion) to distribute a vast amount of video content and differentiate themselves from similar services in the market. Such UI has a greater direct impact on a user's overall understanding and operation of service content than mere operability. Therefore, we believe that the UI of OTT services, which is characterized by a large amount of information on a single screen, can increase the number of user choices and complicate the information being visualized and perceived, thus making information processing more difficult and placing a burden on user understanding and operation. In services that handle a large amount of content, users evaluate, select, and share information, which is an active, user-driven consumption behavior; thus, the ongoing relationship between the customer and the company will affect profits. Therefore, companies such as Amazon and Netflix, which offer member-centric services such as subscriptions, require enduring customer-oriented engagement to profit [1]. As the representation of information in content and services is the gateway between the user, company, and service, the existence of a UI that considers usability through accurate information perception in service use is a very important factor in maintaining customer relationships. Studies on user perception and load have mainly focused on the usability of websites. However, there are few studies on the analysis of UI consisting of specialized thumbnail-like objects, such as those used by OTT services, and the relationship between information representation and perception in mobile devices. In the case of services that handle a huge amount of visual content (e.g., movies and dramas), which are the focus of this study, it is possible to improve usability by designing a UI that use operations that have become habitual in other services or that follow already formed mental models, rather than making users perceive complex information in an unfamiliar way. We believe that intuitive decisions and operations by users can be realized. In addition, simplifying the overall operation of a service and improving the ease of recognizing its visual information may reduce the burden incurred by users. Based on the above, this study aimed to clarify the effects of different information representations in UI for information transfer and service differentiation of the content of OTT services on user cognition and load.

2 Literature: Information Representation and User Cognition and Load

This This research deals with information representation in a graphical user interface (GUI), which plays an important role as the boundary between the user and computer by objectifying information in the form of color, sound, language, and gestures that can be viewed and manipulated by directly touching what is projected on the liquid crystal display (LCD) [2–4].

2.1 Human Processing Processes for Information Representation

The representation of information in a UI is manipulated through sensory, perceptual, and cognitive information processing (Fig. 1). In sensation, information input to the eyes and other receptors is efficiently processed by transmitting the information to the sensory memory of the brain, followed by the processing and enhancing of the information [5]. Perception selects and combines multiple types of visual information to generate output representations for decision-making and action [6]. We also find meaning and value in actively received visual information based on our past memories and desires [5, 7]. This concept is called affordance, and changes depending on the recipient and the way it is communicated [8]. In the field of design, constraints on affordances intentionally limit user choices [9]. In cognition, information processing is divided into processing based on input information and processing based on past information stored in the long-term memory [5]. The information processing in this case varies depending on the emotions influenced by the surrounding environment [10]. It is closely related to concept-driven processing in the representation of information on the UI. The more similar a past operating experience or mental model is to the current operating experience, the easier it is to recall, understand, and operate [11, 12].

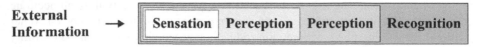

Fig. 1. Human cognitive processes for external information

2.2 The Information Foraging Theory

Information foraging theory is based on a series of behavioral mechanisms that wild animals use to gather food, such as selecting a feeding ground, finding food, acquiring it, and eating it, and is applied to our behavior when we gather information to give it significance [13]. This theory is valid when it contains information that we can interpret for objects with which we have no experience and is used to predict human processes in searching for information in the external world [14]. The most important concept in information foraging theory is "information scent". Information scent encompasses the subjective values and costs of obtaining information based on perceptual cues [15]. We estimate how much useful information can be obtained in our surroundings, and after seeking information, we compare the actual results to our prediction. When we have exhausted the information, we move on to another source. To be an efficient information forager, it is important to accurately perceive information. In the information foraging theory, the optimal feeding ground model is an information processing flow that focuses on how to choose a feeding ground (Fig. 2). Operations in OTT services involve browsing while foraging for information. Therefore, this study investigated user operations in OTT services from the perspective of information foraging theory.

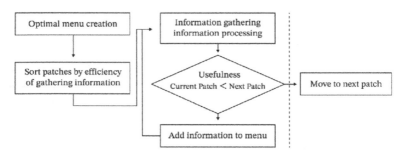

Fig. 2. Optimal feeding field model in the information foraging theory

2.3 The Information Foraging Theory

Cognitive load theory (CLT) presents a model that describes various aspects of load associated with learning experiences for the purpose of constructing cognitive schemas.

The construction of this cognitive schema occurs in working memory, which has a limited capacity. The causes of cognitive load can be broadly classified into three categories: intrinsic, external, and close [16]. From the perspectives of CLT and information processing, we show the relationship between learning experiences and cognitive load based on UI manipulation. The simpler the information representation, the easier it is to understand, and the easier the operational procedure, the smaller the cognitive load [17]. At the product development scale, these three burdens can be reduced by considering "function determination", "design", and "user cognitive process assistance" (Fig. 3).

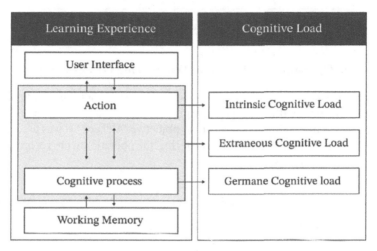

Fig. 3. Relationship between learning experience and cognitive load.

3   Method

First, a survey was conducted on the information representation and operation of OTT services, followed by an experiment focusing on thumbnails. The main flow of the survey is as follows (Fig. 4).

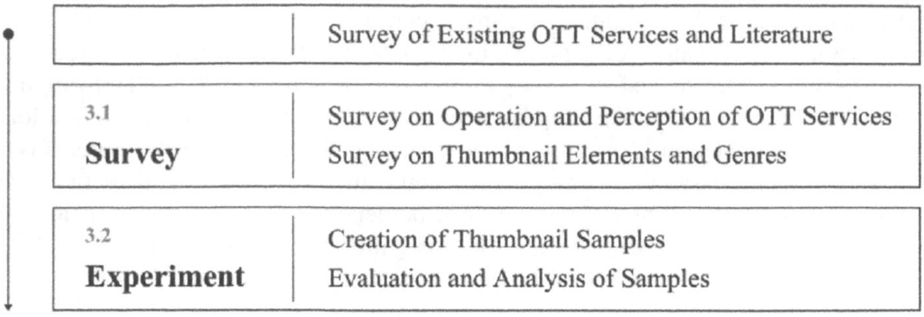

	Survey of Existing OTT Services and Literature
3.1 **Survey**	Survey on Operation and Perception of OTT Services Survey on Thumbnail Elements and Genres
3.2 **Experiment**	Creation of Thumbnail Samples Evaluation and Analysis of Samples

Fig. 4. Main flow of investigation and experiment.

3.1 Survey on Operation and Cognition When Using OTT Services

We conducted a walk-through evaluation of the Netflix smartphone application, in which 20 men and 20 women Netflix students were given the task of browsing until they found a movie they wanted to watch when they had no objective. A checklist was used during the observation, and pain points and emotions during the operation were recorded through post-observation interviews.

3.2 Investigation of the Relationship Between Thumbnail Components and Genre

In order to clarify the thumbnail components that users use to judge genres from thumb-nails, we conducted a questionnaire survey using the KJ method, using 30 thumbnails of those available on Netflix as cards. The study population consisted of three college students who had experience using OTT services. The survey was conducted using the following procedure.

1. Grouping the thumbnail cards
2. Naming the classified groups
3. Enumeration of thumbnail elements as reasons for steps 1 and 2

Next, in order to clarify the influence of the thumbnail factors on the judgment of genre for each group and to confirm individual differences, we used the design of experiment method to create 48 samples, 8 samples for each of the 6 groups, from L8's (25) direct-row table, using the top 5 factors that were frequently mentioned for each group obtained from the previous survey as factors [18]. The thumbnail samples created are shown below (Fig. 5). A questionnaire regarding the samples was then administered for evaluation and analysis. In the questionnaire, 8 samples were presented to those who had experience using OTT services for evaluation, and they were asked to select one sample that gave the strongest impression of the group name.

Group Name

Love Romance

Group Name

Horror

Group Name

Human

Group Name

SF

Group Name

Action

Group Name

Comedy

Fig. 5. Sample thumbnails created for each of the six genres.

4 Results and Discussion

4.1 Survey Results on OTT Service Use

Based on the information foraging theory and the results of the walkthrough study, we present a graphical representation of the user's operation process (Fig. 6). The user's operation on Netflix is similar to the optimal feeding ground model, with the genre row as a patch. The user repeatedly collects and processes thumbnail information and semantic information of details on-screen, leading to the viewing of the content. Thumbnails emit information in the patch and play an important role in assisting the user's movement through the patch and transition to the detail screens. Thumbnails in UI are widgets that influence the search experience in a general visualization format for video content [19]. Based on the above, we believe that by focusing on the information representation in thumbnails in the UI of OTT services and clarifying their relationship with user cognition, it may be possible to simplify overall service operations and improve the ease of recognizing visual information, thereby reducing user's cognitive load.

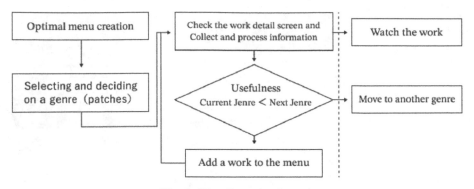

Fig. 6. User Operation Process

4.2 Survey Results on Thumbnails and Genres

The 30 thumbnails used in the KJ method were classified into six categories: "Love Romance," "Horror," "Human," "Science Fiction," "Action," and "Comedy." In addition, a total of 180 thumbnail elements were listed. Comparing each group, it became clear that there were differences in the elements that were mentioned frequently, and that elements had characteristics for each group. In addition, thumbnail elements could be classified into three elements: "Person," "Text," and "Background." These results suggest that thumbnails can be divided by component and that users pay attention to each element in the thumbnails and use them to determine the genre. Next, we conducted a one-way ANOVA using the questionnaire results and the experimental design table and organized the results into four categories: overall, male, female, and genre-preferring viewers, using the influence of each element in the thumbnails on users' genre judgments as the main effect value. The higher the main effect value, the greater the influence of that element on the user's genre choice. The results and discussion for each genre are presented below.

Love Romance. The results of the one-way ANOVA for "Love Romance" are shown in Table 1.

- The main effect size was higher for poses related to Love Romance because they are easy to accept at a glance, such as a men and a women facing each other.
- The fact that the thumbnails are composed of a men and a women also contributes to the judgment of the genre.
- Men tend to judge genres by looking at the person only, while women tend to judge genres by looking at both the person and the title.
- The inclusion of the two elements "Person: Relationship" and "Person: Pose" has a very strong influence on the judgment of genre in Love Romance. This is because the relationship between characters is the main point of the story in works classified as Love Romance.

Horror. The results of the one-way ANOVA for "Horror" are shown in Table 2.

- The main effect value of the element "Person: Facial Expression N/A" was higher because the fear of not being able to see the face matched the image of "Horror".

Table 1. Love Romance Results.

Factors and Levels	Love Romance			
	All	Men	Women	Preference
Person: Relationship	18.2	17.5	17.3	16.8
Person: Pose	19.2	17.5	19.2	14.8
Text: Meaning	14.2	11.8	15.4	12.8
Text: Font	13.2	8.0	17.3	16.8
Background: Color	13.2	9.9	15.4	12.8

- The main effect of text on women's genre judgments was considered to be small, since men focused on the thumbnails as a whole and women focused on the people and backgrounds.
- It is clear that those who prefer to watch horror movies and dramas do not pay attention to the element "Text: Meaning". We believe that this result is due to the fact that many famous horror movies have titles that have nothing to do with Horror at all (e.g., HOPE, Midsummer, Ring).

Table 2. Horror Results.

Factors and Levels	Horror			
	All	Men	Women	Preference
Person: Facial Expression N/A	15.25	10.8	18.3	17.9
Background: Decoration	8.25	8.0	7.7	3.6
Background: Brightness	8.75	7.1	9.6	6.0
Text: Font	3.25	5.2	1.0	8.3
Text: Meaning	4.75	7.1	1.9	−6.0

Human. The results of the one-way ANOVA for "Human" are shown in Table 3.

- In this thumbnail, the element "Background: Landscape" is used to express the presence or absence of the element by changing the screen ratio of the background by adjusting the size of the human figure. In addition, since the genre "Human" is a story centered on people, the main effect value would be higher if the element "Background: Landscape" was omitted and the people were displayed in a larger size.
- In the genre "Human" the development is basically more serious than humorous. In this thumbnail, "Person: Facial Expression" is expressed with a smiling face, so "Person: Facial Expression N/A", in which the face of the person is hidden, is considered to have a higher main effect value.

- The main effect values of each element in the genre "Human" were low and varied in all categories due to the lack of a clear level for each element.

Table 3. Human Results.

Factors and Levels	Human			
	All	Men	Women	Preference
Person: Pose	9.75	12.7	5.8	4.5
Text: Meaning	5.75	7.1	3.8	4.5
Background: Landscape N/A	3.75	8.0	−1.0	0.0
Person: Facial Expression N/A	6.75	11.8	1.0	2.3
Text: Font N/A	11.25	12.7	8.7	9.1

SF. The results of the one-way ANOVA for "SF" are shown in Table 4.

- In this thumbnail, the element "Text: Meaning" is titled "The Earth". Since the definition of "SF" can be interpreted and received in various ways, it was not possible to set a clear standard for how the element should be expressed. However, the name of the text is related to the universe, which is one of the interpretations of "SF", making it an easily accepted element with a particularly high main-effect value.
- Since all categories in Group 4 "SF" had similar results, we believe that the influence of individual differences on genre judgments is minimal.

Table 4. SF Results.

Factors and Levels	SF			
	All	Men	Women	Preference
Background: Landscape	1.25	4.2	−1.9	4.4
Text: Meaning	16.25	14.6	16.3	19.1
Person: Personally N/A	1.25	4.2	−1.9	4.4
Person: Not Including N/A	1.25	4.2	−1.9	4.4
Text: Font N/A	1.25	1.4	1.0	1.5

Action. The results of the one-way ANOVA for "Action" are shown in Table 5.

- In this thumbnail, the element "Text: meaning" is expressed as "Wild Guard". An action movie is an action play, in which fighting and battle scenes are important. Therefore, we believe that the recognition of the words "Wild" and "Guard", which are related to action movies, may have made it easier for respondents to accept that the movie is an action movie.

- Men and women tend to prefer action movies more than women. Therefore, we believe that women are making judgments based on explicit elements such as "Text: Meaning" without focusing on the characters.

Table 5. Action Results.

Factors and Levels	Action			
	All	Men	Women	Preference
Text: Font	10.75	10.8	9.6	9.5
Person: Facial Expression N/A	4.75	7.1	1.9	7.8
Background: Decoration N/A	4.25	4.2	3.8	3.4
Person: Personally	6.25	9.9	1.9	10.3
Text: Meaning	12.75	10.8	13.5	13.8

Comedy. The results of the one-way ANOVA for "Comedy" are shown in Table 6.

- In this thumbnail, the element "Text: Meaning" is expressed as "Happy Day". Since comedy is interpreted as a work that contains humor, we believe that the recognition of the word "Happy" and other related words may have made it easier to accept it as a comedy.
- In this thumbnail, the element "Text: Meaning" is expressed as "Happy Day". Since comedy is interpreted as a work that contains humor, we believe that the recognition of the word "Happy" and other related words may have made it easier to accept it as a comedy.
- We assume that people who like to watch comedic movies and dramas make comprehensive judgments by looking at various elements in the thumbnails, given that the main effect values seem to vary.

Table 6. Comedy Results.

Factors and Levels	Comedy			
	All	Men	Women	Preference
Text: Meaning	8.75	8.0	8.7	6.9
Person: Facial Expression	7.75	9.9	4.8	8.3
Text: Color N/A	2.25	0.5	3.8	4.2
Person: Pose	4.75	7.1	1.9	0.0
Person: Clothing	3.25	3.3	2.9	−1.4

5 Conclusion

The purpose of this study was to clarify the impact of differences in information representation in the UI for information transmission and service differentiation of content in
OTT services on user cognition. After understanding the logical background of a user's
cognitive load owing to UI informatization and changes in information representation
in information-providing services, we conducted a survey and experiment focusing on
thumbnails from the UI of OTT services.

From the experiment, we confirmed the influence of user gender, preference, and
experience on genre judgment in each genre. In the case of group 3, "Human," where
there was no clear on how to express the elements when the sample was created, we
found variation in the results. In addition, since the sample was created using elements
obtained from the KJ method survey, some elements moved in the negative direction
when all elements should have moved in the positive direction.

As a difference between men and women, it was found that men tended to judge
genres based on the overall impression of the thumbnail from Groups 2 "Horror" and
4 "Science Fiction," while women tended to judge genres by looking at specific and
clear elements such as the element "Title: Meaning." It was also found that the more
people preferred to view content of a specific genre, the more they judged the genre
by examining various elements in the thumbnail. Even if the thumbnails were intended
to represent the same genre, the impressions made on the users differed significantly
depending on the elemental composition.

Thus, we could clarify the impact of differences in information representation in
thumbnails on user perceptions from the perspective of thumbnail elements. Recently,
artwork visual analysis (AVA) have captured still images of scenes that are suitable as
thumbnails in video images. By associating the results of the combinations of thumbnail
elements obtained in this study, thumbnail compositions tailored to user characteristics
can be used in the UI. We believe that this will simplify the overall operation of the
service, improve the ease of recognizing visual information, and reduce the burden on
users.

6 Further Work

A limitation of this study was that it was limited to thumbnails consisting of image and
text information for UI information representation. However, because the information
that users see when using services is not limited, it is necessary to focus on cognition
throughout service use. In addition, when examining individual differences among users,
this survey only categorized users by genre preference rather than gender. It is necessary
to clarify user variables by asking about other factors such as the time of day they operated
the service or the surrounding environment. With the acceleration of digital marketing,
the number of similar, competing OTT services will increase. To differentiate themselves
from competing services, it is essential that companies create a unique selling proposition
(USP) for information expression in their interfaces that connect the user to their service.
We believe that a UI that considers user recognition is key to improving the usability of
a service.

References

1. Behera, R.K., Gunasekaran, A., Gupta, S., Kamboj, S., Bala, P.K.: Personalized digital marketing recommender engine. J. Retail. Consum. Serv. **53**(6) (2020)
2. Suwa, M.: Visual displays as stimuli to cognitive processes. J. Visual. Soc. Japan **19**(72), 13–17 (1999)
3. Ueno, M., Fujii, K.: Object-Oriented UI design. Gijutsu-Hyoron Co, Tokyo (2020)
4. Inoue, K.: Textbook of Interface Design. Maruzen Publishing Co, Tokyo (2013)
5. Yamaoka, T., Okada, A., Tanaka, K., Mori, R., Yoshitake, R.: Basics of Design Ergonomics. MUSABI Social Management Co, Tokyo (2015)
6. Dresp-Langley, B.: Principles of perceptual grouping: implications for image-guided surgery. Front. Psychol. 6 (2015)
7. Gibson, J.J.: The Senses Considered as Perceptual Systems. University of Tokyo Press, Tokyo (2011)
8. Nakajima, Y., Nojima, E.: Information and Human Sciences. Asakura Publishing Co, Tokyo (2008)
9. Norman, D.A.: The Design of Everyday Things. Shinyosya Co, Tokyo (1990)
10. Norman, D.A., Ortony, A., Revelle, W.: Affect and Proto-Affect in Effective Functioning. Oxford University Press (2005)
11. Doi, T., Tominaga, S., Yamaoka, T., NIshizaki, Y.: The Elements for Structuring the Mental Model in Operation of User Interfaces. BULLETIN OF JSSD **58**(5), 53–62 (2012)
12. Oota, N., Tsuzuki, T.: ICT and Information Behavioral Psychology. Kitaojisyobou Co, Kyoto (2017)
13. Ookawa, H.: Support for User's Behavior Based on Optimal Foraging Theory for Reuse of Products. Graduate School Research Annual Report (44) (2014)
14. Kawazoe, A., Shinohara, T.: Interfaces for Information seeking on the Web. J. Inf. Sci. Technol. Assoc. **68**(11), 548–554 (2018)
15. Chi, E.H., Pirolli, P., Chen, K.: Using information scent to model user information needs and actions and the Web. CHI **3**(1), 490–497 (2001)
16. Klepsch, M., Seufert, T.: Understanding instructional design effects by differentiated measurement of intrinsic, extraneous, and germane cognitive load. Instr. Sci. **48**(1), 45–77 (2020). https://doi.org/10.1007/s11251-020-09502-9
17. Sato, S.: The effects of the number of alternatives and the need for cognitive closure on decision making process. Toyo University Graduate School Bull. **47**, 177–189 (2010)
18. Sato, R., Tamura, R.: Study on thumbnail images and titles selected by viewers in YouTuber's videos. Int. J. Affect. Eng. **18**(1), 139–145 (2019)
19. Liu, W., Mei, T., Zhang, Y., Che, C., Luo, J.: Multi-task deep visual-semantic, embedding for video thumbnail selection. In: IEEE Conference on Computer Vision and Pattern Recognition, 3707–3715 (2015)
20. Medium I AVA: The. Art and Science of Image Discovery at Netflix. https://netflixtechblog.com/ava-the-art-and-science-of-image-discovery-at-netflix-a442f163af6. Accessed 08 Jan 2023

The Differences of Human-Computer Interaction on Smart Home Between the Young and the Elderly Users

Qin Wang and Huimei Lin[✉]

School of Design, South China University of Technology,
Guangzhou 510006, People's Republic of China
202220156090@mail.scut.edu.cn

Abstract. A semi-structured survey was conducted to investigate the differences between the young and elderly users' human-computer interaction on smart home. Fifteen young users and fifteen elderly users participated in the study, and the questionnaires and interviews were analyzed via NVivo software. It shows that there are obvious different types of smart home used by the young and elderly respectively. Meanwhile, the young mainly learn to operate smart products by themselves, while the most elderly need help from others. Since the common interactive methods are touch screen and button control, both the young and the elderly prefer voice control. And the elderly still attach great importance to button control, for there are some deficiencies in voice control. When using smart products, both the young and the elderly value security and usability, and the former pay special attention to privacy. Both user groups have higher satisfaction with the smart home. In the human-computer interaction of smart home in the future, voice control should be given priority to improve the accuracy and intelligence of speech recognition. And the button control should be retained in design for the elderly.

Keywords: Smart Home · Human-computer Interaction · Age Difference

1 Introduction

The rapid growth of the elderly population over 60 is a common phenomenon in the world today. "Aging-in-place" has become a trend in the lives of the elderly[1]. With the development of the Internet and digital intelligence, smart home can accurately identify users and rapidly provide the corresponding response, bringing a lot of convenience to users, thus it is widely accepted. There have been researches on smart home from the perspectives of safety, stability and reliability[2]. At present, the development of smart home is mainly driven by technology, and the design research concerning user demand is insufficient.

Different age groups have different demand for smart home. Research shows that smart home users are mostly young people, and there are some barriers for the elderly, and the latter reject smart home products because they are complicated[3, 4]. So it is of necessity to change the human-computer interaction mode of smart home accordingly

A. Marcus et al. (Eds.): HCII 2023, LNCS 14032, pp. 398–407, 2023.
https://doi.org/10.1007/978-3-031-35702-2_28

to improve the satisfaction of users of different ages. On the basis of the user-centered design, the study explores the different interaction modes of smart home that are suitable for users of different ages.

Smart home refers to the wide application of wireless network and sensing technologies in furniture and household appliances[2]. Smart home consists of interconnected hardware and software, which can identify activities and detect environment[5]. Products in smart home are divided into three categories: entertainment, function assistance and health[6]. The division of smart home is adapted from this classification. Since sports are dynamic, the division belongs to recreation. Therefore, smart home products are divided into three categories: sports entertainment, life services, health and safety. Sports and entertainment include sports mirrors, smart speakers, projections or displays, etc. Home services include curtains, door locks, lighting, sweeping robots, etc. Health and safety include weight scales, air purifiers, smart medicine boxes, etc. In the pre-survey, users pointed that large home appliances such as TVs, air conditioners, refrigerators and washing machines were purchased independently, so they were not included in the scope of smart home research.

2 Literature Review

The differences in operating smart devices should be taken into account when exploring human-computer interaction of smart home. Satisfaction has a great influence on users' behavioral intention [7]. Compatibility, perceived ease of use, along with perceived usefulness play a great role on purchase intention of smart home [8]. Simple and uncomplicated design should be adopted, for the elderly usually share some common characteristics, such as cognitive decline, slower learning, and decreased enthusiasm for technology. Voice control can meet the demand of the elderly to make up for cognitive decline and overcome loneliness [9]. The elderly are more likely to buy smart home than the young, and the young are more concerned about the risk of personal privacy data leakage [10]. According to the research on the design characteristics of the sliding component of smart home, the direction of the sliding block is not significantly different among users of different ages, but the track color and button size of the sliding block show obvious differences [11].

Grounded Theory, a qualitative analysis approach, is used for systematic analysis of text and picture data and transformation into conceptual framework. And the transcriptions is an important part of the grounded theory that classifies data by code. NVivo, a qualitative analysis software, is highly capable of analyzing the text of interview. It manages text materials in the form of nodes, and finds the internal correlation of data through coding. Grounded theory has been applied to design research. Combining NVivo and AHP, this paper explores the factors, barriers and drivers of technology adoption decision of construction company [12]. In a qualitative analysis of the professional values of design researchers, NVivo software proved to be effective [13].

3   Research Method

A semi-structured survey is chosen to collect data to study the human-computer inter-action of smart home. The paper tends to reveal the experience and attitude of the users, explain the reasons for the answers to the questions, and understand the preferences and dislikes of users through the semi-structured questionnaire. NVivo, which can conduct qualitative analysis of the text, import the text into the software for analysis, and compare the different views of the elderly and that of the young users on the human-computer interaction of smart home.

The outline of the interview was formulated by the researchers, and a simple pre-survey was carried out to determine the questions of the interview, including several open-minded questions. The main questionnaire was divided into three parts: the basic situation of using smart home, interaction mode and satisfaction (see appendix). The survey was conducted in January 2023. Each user who orally agreed or signed a consent form participated in the interview survey and received a reward of 30 RMB.

The research objects were divided into two groups: the young and the elderly users, with a total of 30 participants. There were15 elderly users, including 9 females and 6 males, among whom 13 were aged 60–75 years old and 1 was over 80. There were 15 young users, 7 females and 8 males, ranging in age from 19–25 years old. Due to distance or non-contact requirements and private reasons of elderly users, face-to-face, telephone, Wechat voice or filling in interview questionnaires were voluntarily selected by the interviewees. After permitting recorded, the interview was transcribed into words. Because some dialects or oral repetition appeared in the interview, the researcher sorted the text and then analyzed with NVivo11 software.

4   Results

4.1   Smart Home Product Categories

Figure 1 shows that elderly prefer smart products of life services to those of health and safety as well as sports and entertainment. Figure 2 shows there is no significant difference in the application of the various smart home products among the young users. What's more, the young generally know more about those of health and safety as well as sports and entertainment.

Considering that most of the elderly users interviewed live at home, life services smart products are mentioned more often than the young. However, most of the young users interviewed are students living in school dormitories with fixed facilities, so they pay limited attention to the smart home of life services. In addition, some users list more types of smart products while others only present a general idea of the smart home, so the detailed comparison between the elderly and the young users is not made.

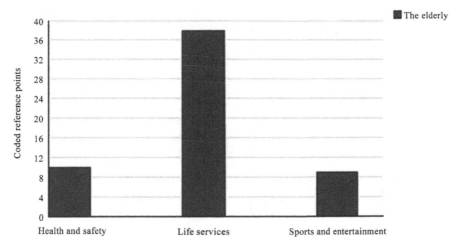

Fig. 1. Smart home product categories used by the elderly users.

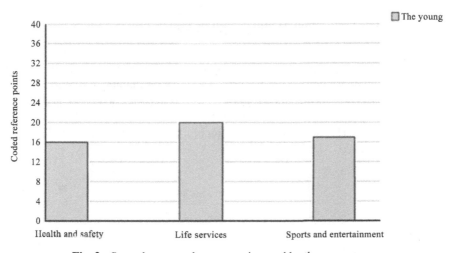

Fig. 2. Smart home product categories used by the young users.

4.2 Smart Home Operation Assistance

Figure 3 reveals that most elderly users need help from others when first using smart home products, and only a small number of them can learn by themselves. In general, the elderly are more dependent on others, but they can operate independently after getting familiar with them. While the young mainly learn on their own, such as studying online tutorials and reading the manual themselves in order to get a grasp of smart home products.

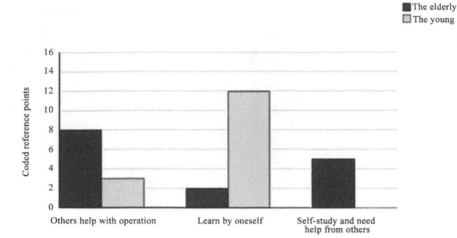

Fig. 3. Smart home operation assistance.

4.3 Smart Home Interaction Modes

As shown in Fig. 4, there are eight different interactive modes of smart home, including button control, touch screen input, facial recognition, mobile APP control, gesture control, voice control, fingerprint recognition and somatosensory interaction. Button control is most commonly used by the elderly users, followed by touch screen input and voice control. While the young prefer voice control, followed by button control and touch screen input. No elderly users refer to facial recognition, and the young are less likely to use gesture control.

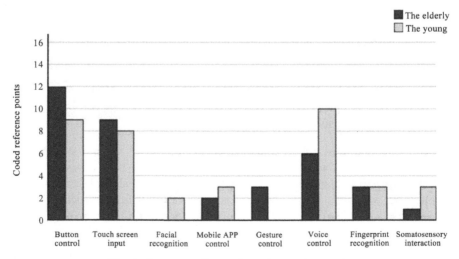

Fig. 4. Summary of smart home interaction modes.

Figure 5 indicates that the elderly users hold that the operation mode of smart home products is generally in line with their psychological expectation, but it is not necessarily the case for many young users. It illustrates that young users have more idea about the expectation and judgment of smart home products.

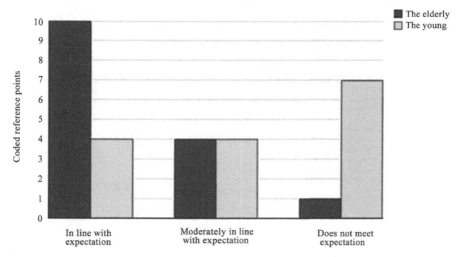

Fig. 5. Users' psychological expectation of the operation mode.

Figure 6 shows the user's assumption of different interactions in the home life. Voice control is the most popular choice by both the young and elderly, followed by button control.

The elderly find voice control easy, convenient and full of fun. Young users have more description in details. The voice intelligent product can provide psychological companionship and diversified output. Since it can be operated remotely, one does not have to go close to the product for the man-machine interface. Compared with gesture control, the steps and requirements of the operation do not need to be memorized in voice control. Both the young and elderly mention the disadvantages of voice control, mainly in two aspects. First, the fault tolerance of speech recognition is poor. If the pronunciation is not correct, the speaker will not respond; Second, the accuracy of speech recognition is not sufficient. If there is a dialect or non-standard Mandarin, it will lead to a wrong recognition instruction.

Button control is preferred by both the elderly and young users for its simplicity, ease and accuracy. Some elderly users indicate that other interaction methods are more complicated, and button control is more reliable; but others state button control is less convenient than voice control. While the young believe that the design should be simple without many buttons, and the buttons of remote control are often out of work.

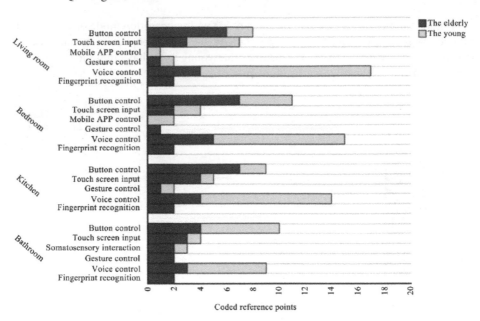

Fig. 6. The user's assumption of different interactions in the home life.

4.4 The Choice of Smart Products

Figure 7 shows that when it comes to using smart products, both the elderly and the young users attach more importance to usability, security, price and stability.

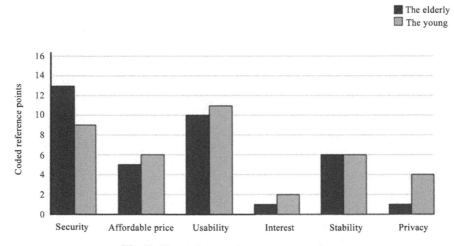

Fig. 7. Users' focus points on smart products.

However, the elderly pay more attention to security and less to interest, while the young attach more importance to privacy. Among the diversified operation modes, such as mobile APP, fingerprint recognition and facial recognition to control smart home products, data reading or the camera will probably bring about personal privacy issues.

4.5 Satisfaction

Figure 8 shows that the elderly users are highly satisfied with smart home operation. According to the survey, owing to the speech recognition failure in voice control, some young users are not satisfied.

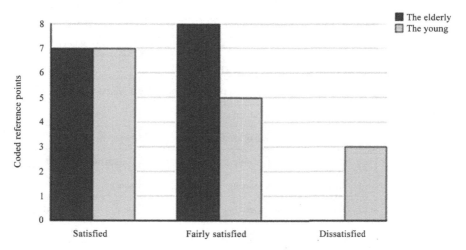

Fig. 8. Overall satisfaction with smart home operation.

5 Conclusion

Both the young and elderly users have high acceptance of smart home, but there are obvious differences between both user groups on human-computer interaction of smart home. The elderly have great expectation for smart living services due to physical decline, and most of them need help from others at the very beginning. While the young are good at self-learning, they mainly can learn to operate on their own. In terms of interaction mode, voice interaction has been accepted by both user groups, and the elderly still attach great importance to button operation. For the elderly smart products, traditional button control should be retained. Voice recognition is easy to operate, but it is not accurate enough. In the future, the accuracy of data processing and sensitivity of response should be rapidly improved, service objects be highly distinguished, product types be widely expanded, and voice control be given priority.

Appendix

Appendix: Survey Outline

Basic Information	1.	What are the smart home products that you currently mainly use or know about?
	2.	What do you mainly do by using the smart home products? How often do you use the smart home products?
	3.	How many years have you used smart home products? Will you continue to buy other smart home products in the future?
	4.	Do you need help when you first use smart home products? Do you use the smart home products all on your own?
Interaction Mode	5.	What is your common operation mode of intelligent products?
	6.	What are the motions in the intelligent home products you use? What difficulties have you encountered in the course of operation?
	7.	Does the current operation mode of smart home products meet your psychological expectations?
	8.	In different places (kitchen, living room, bedroom, toilet, etc.), which interactive way do you prefer to control the smart home? And why?
	9.	What do you value more about the smart home products? (Security, interest, privacy, affordability, availability, system stability)
User Satisfaction	10.	Are you satisfied with the current smart home products? What are you satisfied with smart home products? What are you not satisfied with smart home products?
End	11.	What other problems have you encountered? Thank you for your participation!

References

1. Jo, T.H., Ma, J.H., Cha, S.H.: Elderly perception on the internet of things-based integrated smart-home system. Sensors **21**(4), 1284 (2021)
2. Ma, J., Shangguan, X., Zhang, Y.: IoT security review: a case study of IIoT, IoV, and smart home. Wirel. Commun. Mobile Comput. 2022 (2022)

3. Zhou, C., Dai, Y., Huang, T., Zhao, H., Kaner, J.: An empirical study on the influence of smart home interface design on the interaction performance of the elderly. Int. J. Environ. Res. Public Health **19**(15), 9105 (2022)
4. Pal, D., Funilkul, S., Charoenkitkarn, N., Kanthamanon, P.: Internet-of-things and smart homes for elderly healthcare: An end user perspective. IEEE Access **6**, 10483–10496 (2018)
5. Chimamiwa, G., Giaretta, A., Alirezaie, M., Pecora, F., Loutfi, A.: Are smart homes adequate for older adults with dementia? Sensors **22**(11), 4254 (2022)
6. He, F., Wu, Y., Yang, J., Chen, K., Xie, J., et al.: Chinese adult segmentation according to health skills and analysis of their use for smart home: A cross-sectional national survey. BMC Health Serv. Res. **22**(1), 760 (2022)
7. Pal, D., Funilkul, S., Vanijja, V., Papasratorn, B.: Analyzing the elderly users' adoption of smart-home services. IEEE access **6**, 51238–51252 (2018)
8. Shin, J., Park, Y., Lee, D.: Who will be smart home users? An analysis of adoption and diffusion of smart homes. Technol. Forecast. Soc. Chang. **134**, 246–253 (2018)
9. Oliveira, J.D., Engelmann, D.C., Kniest, D., Vieira, R., Bordini, R.H.: Multi-agent interaction to assist visually-impaired and elderly people. Int. J. Environ. Res. Public Health **19**(15), 8945 (2022)
10. Korneeva, E., Olinder, N., Strielkowski, W.: Consumer attitudes to the smart home technologies and the internet of things (IoT). Energies **14**(23), 7913 (2021)
11. Yu, N., Ouyang, Z., Wang, H.: Study on smart home interface design characteristics considering the influence of age difference: focusing on sliders. Front. Psychol. 901 (2022)
12. Sepasgozar, S.M., Davis, S.: Construction technology adoption cube: An investigation on process, factors, barriers, drivers and decision makers using NVivo and AHP analysis. Buildings **8**(6), 74 (2018)
13. Maher, C., Hadfield, M., Hutchings, M., De Eyto, A.: Ensuring rigor in qualitative data analysis: A design research approach to coding combining NVivo with traditional material methods. Int. J. Qual. Methods **17**(1), 1–13 (2018)

Exploring Factors Influencing Community Consensus Building of Web3 Decentralized Apps

Ming-Hui Wen$^{(\boxtimes)}$, Cing-Yu Huang , Ying-Chen Chen , and I.-Ching Lin

National Taipei University of Business, Taipei City 100025, Taiwan (R.O.C.)
mura22331031@gmail.com

Abstract. Web3 (third generation of the World Wide Web) applications, such as Decentralized Finance (DeFi), Non-fungible token (NFT), Metaverse, etc., have created a new type of social interaction and agglomerated the Web3 community group members' consensus to help Web3 projects create opportunities for success. The consensus factors discussed in the real-world community previously cannot be directly applied to the topic of consensus in the Web3 community due to a different composition and structure of the community. The purpose of this study is to explore the factors that influence Web3 community consensus. By interviewing five users of the Web3 community, we collect data about their participation, motivation, behavior and interactive experience in the community, and summarize the collected qualitative data with Grounded Theory. The result of this pilot research found that the two factors that can dominate the formation of community consensus are "transparency" and "tangible rewards".

Keywords: Web3 · Social Interaction · Community Consensus

1 Introduction

The development of the Internet has progressed from the information economy in the past Web1.0 to the platform economy led by social enterprises such as Facebook and Twitter forming the current Web2.0 dominated by social networks. Web2.0 allows users to not be limited to browsing content, but also upload content to the Internet; interact and share with family, friends or other interested users; establish links to the user-centered community group network. Compared with Web2.0, Web3 uses a decentralized network architecture to provide a new type of community interaction to connect users.

Web3 is based on blockchain network technology. Blockchain is a decentralized point-to-point data storage system established by cryptography. Computing nodes are composed of user owned computers and other computing devices (e.g., mobile phones, servers). Crypto wallets act as identities in the Web3 network and connect users with other users forming the decentralized network. Applications on the decentralized network called Decentralized Applications (DApps). Web3 App applications include Cryptocurrency, Non-Fungible Token (NFT), Game Finance (Gamefi), Metaverse, etc. [1]. Decentralized Applications (DApps) users organize a community and manage community projects and funds through technologies such as blockchain smart contracts and governance tokens, forming a Decentralized Autonomous Organization (DAO).

A. Marcus et al. (Eds.): HCII 2023, LNCS 14032, pp. 408–420, 2023.
https://doi.org/10.1007/978-3-031-35702-2_29

People obtain the right to participate and vote in a DAO by obtaining or purchasing governance tokens. Members may own varying numbers of governance tokens resulting in members having different community identities (e.g., project operators, community owners, general participants, etc.), governance power, and interests. DAOs can configure the community vault through Tokenomics and provide a reward mechanism to community members for positive contributions. The reward mechanism encourages community members to participate and enhances members' recognition and identification of the community which strengthens the contribution behavior of users forming a healthy community [2].

A successful community allows members' contributions to be recognized by other community members giving people the sense of belonging and the motivation to continue participating in and developing the community [3]. In a traditional community, members share the same beliefs, values, and knowledge with each other. Members develop common behaviors and form a sense of community [4]. However, as a community expands, considering how to connect members' opinions and concerns becomes necessary. Through joint decision-making, such as voting and negotiation, members can reach mutual agreement easily. The two most well-known "decision-making rules" are: (1) consensus; (2) majority vote. Integrating the agreement of a group of people into the decision generally results in better, smarter, and more "co-intelligent" decisions that serve a group well into the future [5].

To summarize, Web3 applications are community-led DApps that rely on the consensus of a community. Vitalik Buterin, the founder of Ethereum, also believes that a decentralized community is a "digital consensus space" [6]. Therefore, the cohesion of community consensus will play an important role in the success of Web3 applications. To bring success to the community-led Web3 application, Web3 services should gather people in a community-driven way to develop the community with a community-first operation pattern.

The factors that form the consensus of a Web3 community are very important. However, the research on the factors focused mainly on the discussion of the entity organization community [7, 8], not in the context of Web3. Therefore, the research findings cannot be applied directly to a Web3 community because the background and context of a Web3 community and a traditional community are very different.

The purpose of this study is to explore the factors that build up and influence the consensus of a Web3 community. In order to obtain those factors, we interviewed Web3 community members regarding their experience in participating in the community. We also utilized the Grounded Theory to analyze the community's relationship with those factors. We then identified key factors that influenced the development of the Web3 community consensus. The factors found in this study are expected to serve as a reference for a Web3 community to build consensus.

2 Literature Review

2.1 Web3 and Decentralized Community

The first generation of the Internet (hereinafter referred to as Web1.0) refers to the first stage of the development of the World Wide Web, between 1991 to 2004. In Web1.0, there were few content creators, most of the information sources came from enterprises and organizations, and most users were only consumers of content [9]. Users could only browse the information and the overall web page is also presented in a static manner. Web 1.0 was only a tool to disseminate information. From a technical point, development in Web 1.0 focused on information presentation rather than creation. The second generation of the Internet (hereinafter referred to as Web2.0) interfaced with the Internet as a platform, and content could be generated and created by users [10]. Web 2.0 development created user-centered engagement through Web applications which promoted information cooperation and collaborative exchange between people on the Internet, thus generating a large amount of user-generated content (UGC).

Unlike the centralized authority of Web1.0 and Web2.0, Web3 is a decentralized network based on blockchain technology, allowing users to own their personal data and establish transparent network transactions. The earliest application of blockchain technology is cryptocurrency (e.g., Bitcoin, Ethereum) which has driven the prosperity and development of Decentralized Finance. After cryptocurrency, applications such as NFT and GameFi were developed. These applications allowed users to purchase and hold Governance Tokens to form a DAO (Decentralized Autonomous Organization). DAOs are decentralized communities that enable community members to participate in community governance and explore the community's common interests. DAOs operate through the execution of smart contracts, votes through governance token holders, or automatic management procedures (e.g., joint management of funds, project operation mechanism). As the scale of Web3 applications expands, these kinds of internet products begin to operate in a community-driven model. Community-driven is a mode of operation in which community groups make the decisions and action together [11]. Treating participants as partners to help promote the community growth, form community organizations, and strengthen consensus by actively involving beneficiaries in the project design, management, and implementation. The purpose of governance is to establish and develop a healthy community. Therefore, creating a thriving community is one of the critical factors affecting the success of Web3 service projects.

2.2 Community Consensus

In society, people have become interdependent and connected due to communication and interaction. The concept of "community" extends from interpersonal communication and originates from organizations and groups with homogeneous communication. With the popularization of the internet, people can communicate through the internet and fulfill their need for communication. The internet allows people to escape the restrictions of time and place and often leads to people gathering in the network world to create a "virtual community." A virtual community is a social network formed in cyberspace when many people share enough affection to sustain an open discussion over an extended period [12].

Members of virtual communities gather by their own interests, interpersonal relationships, imagination, and interest needs [13]. People's interactions in community organizations can be divided into three typical types of capital: "economic capital", "social capital" and "cultural capital" [14], among which "economic capital" is the economic foundation of the community, which represents the economic development of the community and it is an important factor in the development of the community [7, 8]. "Social capital" is related to what kind of value that a person can get from his own relationship. And social capital has a strong multiplier effect, because it establishes the premise of mutual recognition between people, and provides them the relationship crowned with symbolic meaning exchange, and maintains community assurance by the actions and behaviors [14]. Finally, "cultural capital" enables a person to control social life, get in touch with groups and express identity. It is closely related to a person's thinking, personality, and habitual ways [14]. Therefore, it takes a long time to infer the cultural capital of group identity value., but the impact is also long-term and lasting.

Mole et al. [15] have proposed a community hexagon including precisely tailored content, identification with the brand, awareness of other like minded users, ability to interact with others on website, opportunity to shape the development of website, mutual benefits of participation. In the process of community participation, people interact with community members according to their own needs, and explore opportunities for community growth and common interests. Since most communities establish communication relationships based on specific interests and issues, they support people to exchange information and share ideas and content to achieve the purpose of communication. The community can form a high degree of interaction that people need through "precisely tailored content", and cooperate with the rationality, diversity and management effectiveness of the content to form a highly connected structural organization [16].

"Identification with the brand", people are more willing to stay in the community and participate in community activities in order to gain a sense of belonging, and make contributions to build self-esteem and gain recognition from other community members [3]. Members of the community will also share the same beliefs, values, and knowledge sharing with each other, so they are willing to follow the norms to conduct interpersonal interactions, and show common behaviors [4], and develop "awareness of other like minded users" with other community members. Members have the feeling of like-mindedness."As a member of the community, people must have the "ability to interact with others on a website" People also need access to, and desire to share power. They want to partici- pate in the making of decisions that shape their well-being. They want freedom to articulate their views and perceive a right to receive and transmit information [17]. Members of the community also learn from each other in the interaction, so they establish a sense of belonging and give commitment [18]. Beamish (1995) [19] argued that the relationship between community members and the community is a kind of belonging or affiliation, and the community is a place where members share knowledge assets with each other. Development "Have the opportunity to develop with the community". The connecting of the community enables people to benefit from the results as the community develops, and to share benefits with community members [20].

3   Research Method

The purpose of this paper is to explore the factors that build up and influence the consensus in a Web3 community. We interviewed five Web3 community users to obtain their experience of participating in the Web3 community. We further utilized the Grounded Theory to summarize and analyze the oral data obtained from the interviewees. Last, we extracted those factors that affect Web3 community consensus and calculated their importance.

3.1   Interviewees and In-Depth Interviews

From August 2 to August 28, 2022, through Taiwanese local Web3 communities,including Discord of NFT project, Facebook communities, etc., an online recruitment campaign was launched to recruit Web3 users to conduct interviews regarding user experience and behaviors regarding Web3 community consensus. Five Web3 community users, including project owners, community moderators, and general community members, participated in the interview. Each interviewee has one or more of the aforementioned community identity and experience. Research team conducted online interviews with individual respondents for about 60–90 min. The researchers inquired about the participants' experiences in the Web3 community and recorded their response.

The interview begins with an introduction of the purposes of the research. The interviewer then explains the importance of users' interactions in a Web3 community and why building up consensus is a key factor in developing the community. Interviewees are further asked to share their motivations in participating in the Web3 project, their feelings of interaction in the community, and their experience of participating in activities in the community. Interviewees also share how they communicate within a group of friends, what is their experience of joint governance and their experience of building up consensus in the community.

3.2   Grounded Theory and Interview Data Analysis

The interview data belong to the "non-technical literature" in the grounded theory. The paper summarizes and analyzes the interview data through the grounded theory, examines and analyzes the interview content provided by the five interviewees, and based on the analysis of the open coding of the grounded theory, through code summarizes and connects the arguments and thought from the interviewees, and analyzes the key factors of the similar content, systematically transforms the written description of the oral data into the upper-level factor variables, and then obtain factors of Web3 consensus.

The process of open coding mainly includes such as decomposing data, conceptualizing data, and recombining concepts into another definition. To name, classify and conceptualize each phenomenon, and then ask questions or define them in depth for the classified phenomena. This study will code the verbatim transcripts of the interviews, and use the number of mentions of each code to understand the various types of users on each code and the importance of each factor. The following is a detailed introduction to the coding process of the consensus factors "fairness" coding in this study:

Interviewee A: Which governance method in the community do you think is better for protecting your own rights?

- Voting method does not use DC robots, it is more accurate to use a snapshot to vote. (male, 21–30, general currency holders)

Interviewee B: What do you think are the characteristics of your project?

- Has a perfect voting system. DAO has no management and maintains fairness through the management organization. (male, 21–30, general currency holder, MOD, Advisor)

Interviewee C: What do you think of the current operating conditions of SocialFi?

- DAO does not divide the proportion, and it should be one person, one vote. Current institutional relationships lead to inaccurate voting results. (male, 21–30, general currency holder)

The coding of the "fairness" factor is completed through the recording method of reproduction of the original sound. The "fairness" factor was mentioned 9 times in the in-depth interviews, accounting for 4.545% of the total 198 codes. The topics include speeches on one's own rights, decision-making system, and management related content. The paper summarizes this topic into the "fairness" factor item through technical literature support, and defines this factor as the user's ability to feel power equality in the decision-making of the community.

4   Research Results

Grounded theory coded and extracted factors from the oral data of the five interviewees using open coding analysis techniques, a total of 198 codes were obtained, which were distributed among the ten consensus-forming factors "Active (N = 17, 8.59%)", "Transparency (N = 44, 22.22%)", "Attention (N = 11, 5.56%)", "Fairness (N = 9, 4.55%)", "Regulation (N = 10, 5.05%)", "Affinity (N = 22, 11.11%)", "Dependence (N = 2, 1.01%)", "Glory (N = 4, 2.02%)", "Spiritual Satisfaction (N = 19, 9.60%)", " Tangible Reward (N = 60, 30.30%)", the analysis process and results of each factor and its open coding are as follows:

The First Factor is "ACtive (N = 17, 8.59%)". Which means that users are affected by the atmosphere of community members and the enthusiasm of discussions to make decisions in the community, for example:

- The project owners organize various forms of activities to allow community members to know the project and other members in the community (Interviewee NO.4: female, 21–30, has participated in the community identity: general currency holder.)
- The project owners actively provide decision-making content, so that users can participate in the results of the project schedule. (Interviewee NO.1: male, 21–30, has

participated in the community identity: project owners, general currency holder, MOD)

The Second Factor is "TRansparency (N = 44, 22.22%)". Which is used to indicate that users have mastered the information publicly disclosed by the project owners to influence decision-making in the community. For example:

- The project owners publicly discloses team information, so that users have the idea that the project owners will not run away (Interviewee No. 4: female, 21–30, has participated in the community identity: general currency holder.)
- The project owners provide a reasonable roadmap schedule, allowing users to have expectations and expectations for future planning. (Interviewee No. 4: female, 21–30, has participated in the community status: general currency holder.)
- The project owners provides the content of the white paper, so that users have a certain degree of familiarity with the project (Interviewee No. 1: male, 21–30, participated in the community identity: project owners, general currency holder, MOD)
- The project owners regularly explain the progress of the team to the community members, so that users can be respected and know the current situation of the team. (Interviewee No. 4: female, 21–30, has participated in the community status: general currency holder.)

The Third Factor is "ATtention (N = 11, 5.56%)". Which means that users can see the positive actions of the project owners community and promote the community, which affects the decision-making in the community. For example:

- The project owners continue to operate their own team project promotion, so that community members can see the positive attitude of the project and the ambition to expand the community. (Interviewee No. 1: male, 21–30, has participated in the community identity: project owners, general currency holder, MOD)
- The project owners will make changes in future planning, so that users can agree to feel respected. (Interviewee No. 3: male, 21–30 years old, has participated in community status: general currency holder, MOD, Advisor.)

The Fourth Factor is "FAirness (N = 9, 4.55%)". Which means that users can feel the equality of power in the community and influence the decision-making in the community. For example:

- Every time the project owners draws a lottery or calculates the probability, it will be live broadcasted and made public, so that users can know that the project owners have no default possibility. (Interviewee No. 5: male, 21–30, has participated in the community status: general currency holder.)

The Fifth Factor is "REgularity (N = 10, 5.05%)". Which is used to indicate that users' decision-making in the community is influenced by the regular update information of the project owners and the community. For example:

• The project owners provide a fixed and good management method, so that users can feel at ease in community activities. (Interviewee No. 5: male, 21–30, has participated in the community status: general currency holder.)

The Sixth Factor is "AFfinity (N = 22, 11.11%)". Which is used to indicate that users influence decision-making in the community because they match the values and concepts with the project owners and community members. For example:

• Believe in intrinsic value: interact and communicate with people in the community, and support each other to grow. (Interviewee No. 1: male, 21–30, has participated in the community identity: project owners, general currency holder, MOD)
• The project owners expounds the concept and ideal of the community, and resonates with the community holders. (Interviewee No. 1: male, 21–30, has participated in the community identity: project owners, general currency holder, MOD)
• The project owners support multiple languages, so that users can easily communicate with those who share the same language. (Interviewee No. 3: male, 21–30 years old, has participated in community status: general currency holder, MOD, Advisor.)
• The project owners patiently respond to various questions, so that users can feel the intentions of the project. (Interviewee No. 1: male, 21–30, has participated in the community identity: project owners, general currency holder, MOD)
• The project owners provide communication opportunities in different areas of interest, allowing community members to find suitable people for them to get along with. (Interviewee No. 1: male, 21–30, has participated in the community identity: project owners, general currency holder, MOD)
• The application mechanism of the project owners is in line with reasonable settings, so that users can agree with the application. (Interviewee No. 4: female, 21–30, has participated in the community status: general currency holder.)

The Seventh Factor is "dependence (N = 2, 1.01%)". Which is used to indicate that users' decision-making in the community is influenced by the special benefits and functions provided by the project owners. For example:

• The project owners provide functions so that users can like to operate and play notifications (Interviewee No. 3: male, 21–30, participated in the community identity: general currency holder, MOD, Advisor.)

The Eighth Factor is "Glory (N = 4, 2.02%)". Which is used to indicate that users have the opportunity to show themselves in the community and are respected and respected in the community, which affects the decision-making in the community. For example:

• The project owners provide a way to express themselves, so that community members have the opportunity to show their talents and reveal themselves. (Interviewee No.

1: male, 21–30, has participated in the community identity: project owners, general currency holder, MOD)

The Ninth Factor is "Spiritual Satisfaction (N = 19, 9.60%)". Which is used to indicate that users gain a sense of belonging in the community, that is, feel the friendliness of community members and get fun when participating in community activities. Decision making in the community. For example:

• The project owners provide community members with various information, so that people in the community can satisfy their feedback in the community. (Interviewee No. 1: male, 21–30, has participated in the community identity: project owners, general currency holder, MOD)
• The project owners invite different KOLs to share in the group, so that users can have the opportunity to communicate with each other through the community channels. (Interviewee No. 1: male, 21–30, has participated in the community identity: project owners, general currency holder, MOD)
• The project owners provide novel, creative, and interesting interactive ways, so that community members can relax in it without pressure. (Interviewee No. 4: female, 21–30, has participated in the community status: general currency holder.)
• The project owners provide a variety of teaching, so that users can lower the threshold of entry operation. (Interviewee No. 5: male, 21–30, has participated in the community status: general currency holder.)

The Tenth Factor is "Material Satisfaction (N = 60, 30.30%)". Which is used to indicate that users influence decision-making in the community through material interests such as wealth, information exchange, expected benefits and experience. For example:

• The project owners provide NEFT-enabled applications, allowing users to benefit from substantial help. (Interviewee No. 1: male, 21–30, has participated in the community identity: project owners, general currency holder, MOD)
• The project owners provide a lottery or airdrop, so that community participants have the motivation to participate in obtaining items. (Interviewee No. 5: male, 21–30, has participated in the community status: general currency holder.)
• The project owners provide task rewards, allowing users to be driven by fun and rewards. (Interviewee No. 5: male, 21–30, has participated in the community status: general currency holder.)
• The project owners provide physical surroundings, so that community members can obtain substantially commemorative items. (Interviewee No. 1: male, 21–30, has participated in the community identity: project owners, general currency holder, MOD)

5 Conclusion

The purpose of this paper is to explore the possible factor combination for the design of community consensus that will help building up the Web3 community. Our result found that two major factors: "tangible reward" and "transparency" are critical factors in building up and influencing the Web3 community consensus.

"Tangible reward" represents community members' expectations to obtain substantial personal benefits from the community. In a Web3 community, project owners can utilize the token economic model (i.e., tokenomics) of the DAO as available resources to configure the community's group funds and distribute rewards based on each member's contributions. A group of people with common interests and desires build virtual communities [13]. Technology has created unique opportunities for these communities to be expanded and developed [20]. However, there are still challenges to the development. Web3 communities rely on the development of blockchain technology, extending from Bitcoin and other encrypted currency assets. Web3 communities continue to develop various projects based on Web3 services, such as decentralized finance (DeFi), Non-fungible token (NFT), and Game Finance (GameFi), etc. Focusing on applications related to financial themes provides diverse economic investment benefits and rewards driving mechanisms. The potential benefit through holding the same digital asset investment exists. However, the motivation for users to participate in these Web3 services is still mainly based on expected returns of investments. Therefore, when people cannot obtain their expected return from Web3 decentralized applications, their interest in Web3 formation of community consensus decreases.

"Transparency" represents transparent communication, which is the basis for building community trust. This factor shows that an open and transparent community is more likely to influence the cohesion of community members' consensus. The decentralized autonomous organization is also the Web3 community, which can be publicly disclosed through white papers and other available information to achieve the purpose of information transparency. This finding echoes past research that trust itself is social capital embedded in a person or social network [21]. Both trust and altruism are considered as types of social capital embedded. In a virtual community, members were not familiar with each other previously, thus community trust is required for successful interaction and knowledge sharing to take place [22, 23]. Therefore, trust is believed to be the cornerstone of community building. Web3 community is built upon the openness, transparency and anonymization technology of the blockchain. Whether the community members can fully grasp and bear the risks brought by the community or the Web3 project itself is also related to the members' trust in the community trust itself is also an important predictor of risk-taking behavior [24]. The community can improve the openness and transparency of communication between the community and its members through transparency, high-frequency updates, and more efficient dialogue mechanisms, so as to enhance their trust as a community for group consensus cohesion.

This study found that the initial reason for people to enter the community is to pursue interests, find a sense of belonging and trust in the community are the reasons why a member is staying in the community. A sense of belonging and trust are developed through the interaction with other members in the community. This study focused on discussing community consensus behavior such as influencing people's willingness to gather and take action. A community that is transparent, open and credible, and a community that enables its members to have substantial benefit opportunities are critical in the development of consensus. The developers of Web3 projects can make good use of the characteristics of the decentralized community of the blockchain to create open and transparent communication among community members. At the same time, through the development of a reasonable token economic model, the developer can build a transparent and open consensus community.

In terms of application, the results of this study have two major applications in the design of community experience by community participants through the consensus design features of the Web3 community. First, the results of this study can be used in the application of information. The operator can provide community participants with different tangible rewards by regulating the design features related to material interests in the community, such as: Whitepaper, Tokenomics and other hierarchical controls. Such an economic model design can be regarded as a production resource. Community participants can not only use their own invested assets to obtain dividends, but can also have greater psychological ownership in the community [2]. In addition, it is also possible to design community consensus by manipulating the symmetry of information available to internal participants in the community and external observers. In terms of the application of available resources, the community operation team of the project owners can control the available resources by manipulating the "disclosure" or "disclosure" of resources, so that it can form a community guidance model in different situations, and then regulate the community participation of community participants. Group consensus.

From the perspective of community management and planning, this study proposes some practical practices for reference by Web3 community operators, companies, and enterprise teams. First of all, the community consensus factors explored in this research can help Web3 community operating units formulate planning guidelines for different factors for community planning to stimulate the formation of consensus that satisfies different community participants. At the same time, the feedback provided by the interviewers can also be used as a community operator to understand the composition of different consensus factors.

The quality of the Web3 community is not just a one-way creation of the project owners It requires two-way feedback from investment participants. Through planning, building and strengthening community consensus, a highly cohesive community is established, and community-driven and community-first thinking are constructed as guidelines for community development, through clear common goals with the same direction.

Compared with the two significant factors, the remaining eight factors are less likely to have an impact on community consensus among community participants. Therefore, this study suggests that in order to design a Web3 community that is likely to generate community consensus, it is necessary to increase the design of these two factors that significantly affect community consensus.

By manipulating the community consensus factors, the Web3 project community operation teams can go through their own inspection and adjustment before making it public. The operation team can use the community consensus framework discussed in this research to evaluate the consensus level of the community. To do so, the Web3 community manager only needs to find suitable interviewees and let them measure and evaluate the consensus factors when interacting with the community. Finally, the content concept proposed by the community consensus model helps the operation team of the same Web3 project community to adjust and control the planning. Finally, by developing a community around the consensus of the community, it can also stimulate the community operators to examine themselves. The community operators themselves are alert to the communities they create, and can also provide useful information for the community operation team advice.

Although the community consensus model proposed in this research has identified two factors that significantly affect community consensus, from a practical point of view, we cannot arbitrarily combine these two significant community consensus factors designed to maximize or only plan the two factors to operate the community. Although the other eight factors were not discussed in depth in this study, all factors can be examined more comprehensively through a large-scale survey in future research. Factors that affect the consensus of the community may also affect the community participants' perception or the sense of trust and experience that the community values.

If a community loses its perception, users in the community will not be willing to visit and become participants. Not only will the life cycle of the community be shortened, but the Web3 project owners will also face operational challenges. From the perspective of the community operation of the Web3 project owners, if the community consensus factors can be found out, the quadrant for community planning and guidance can be raised to a higher level. Based on the framework proposed in this study, future research can also propose the principle of predictive consensus and judgment use, which will have the opportunity to achieve a balance in community operation and planning.

Because this study is based on Web3 to discuss community issues, the structure of the community will change with the display of different technical levels and individual behaviors, The best way is to actually combine the community consensus factor framework through community planning and operation: Follow the community consensus factors explored in the paper and design the community from the perspective of the Web3 project owners.

References

1. Kovacova, M., Horak, J., Higgins, M.: Behavioral analytics, immersive technologies, and machine vision algorithms in the Web3-powered Metaverse world. Linguist. Philos. Invest. **21**, 57–72 (2022)
2. Liu, Z., Li, Y., Min, Q., Chang, M.: User incentive mechanism in blockchain-based online community: an empirical study of steemit. Inf. Manag. **59**(7), 103596 (2022)
3. Kim, A.J.: Community Building on the Web: Secret Strategies for Successful Online Communities. Peachpit Press (2006)
4. Pitta, D.A., Fowler, D.: Internet community forums: an untapped resource for consumer marketers. J. Consum. Mark. **22**, 265–274 (2005)
5. Bressen, T.: Consensus decision making. The change handbook: the definitive resource on today's best methods for engaging whole systems **495**, 212–217 (2007)
6. Buterin, V.: A next-generation smart contract and decentralized application platform. white paper **3**(37), 2–1 (2014)

7. Flora, C.B., Flora, J.L., Spears, J.D., Swanson, L.E.: Rural Communities: Legacy and Change. Westview Press, Boulder (1992)
8. Cavaye, J.: Understanding Community Development.Cavaye Community Development (2006)
9. .Cormode, G., Krishnamurthy, B.: Key differences between Web 1.0 and Web 2.0. First Monday 13(6) (2008)
10. O'Reilly, T.: What Is Web2.0: Design Patterns and Business Models for the Next Generation of Software. Oreilly (2005)
11. Braden, S., Mayo, M.: Culture, community development and representation. Commun. Dev. J. 34(3), 191–204 (1999)
12. Rheingold, H.: The Virtual Community: Homesteading on the Electronic Frontier, revised edition. MIT press (2000)
13. Hagel, J.: Net gain: expanding markets through virtual communities. J. Interact. Mark. 13(1), 55–65 (1999)
14. Bourdieu, P.: The forms of capital (1986). https://home.iitk.ac.in/~amman/soc748/bourdieu_forms_of_capital.pdf
15. Mole, C., Mulcahy, M., O'Donnell, K., Gupta, A.: Making real sense of virtual communities. PricewaterhouseCoopers Report (1999)
16. Kowch, E., Schwier, R.: Considerations in the construction of technology-based virtual learning communities. Can. J. Educ. Commun. 26(1), 1–12 (1997)
17. Jayaweera, N.: Rethinking Development Communication in The Asian Mass Communication (1989). https://www.worldcat.org/zh-tw/title/rethinking-development-communication/oclc/220641864
18. Wenger, E., McDermott, R.A., Snyder, W.: Cultivating Communities of Practice: A Guide to Managing Knowledge. Harvard Business Press (2002)
19. Beamish, A.: Communities on-line: Community-based computer networks, Doctoral dissertation, Massachusetts Institute of Technology (1995)
20. Vesely, P., Bloom, L., Sherlock, J.: Key elements of building online community: comparing faculty and student perceptions. MERLOT J. Online Learn. Teach. 3(3), 234–246 (2007)
21. Granovetter, M.: Economic-action and social-structure: the problem of embeddedness. Am. J. Sociol. 91(3), 481–510 (1985)
22. Hsu, C.L., Lin, J.C.C.: Acceptance of blog usage: the roles of technology acceptance, social influence and knowledge sharing motivation. Inf. Manag. 45(1), 65–74 (2008)
23. Ridings, C.M., Gefen, D., Arinze, B.: Some antecedents and effects of trust in virtual communities. J. Strat. Inf. Syst. 11(3/4), 271–295 (2002)
24. Serva, M.A., Fuller, M.A., Mayer, R.C.: The reciprocal nature of trust: a longitudinal study of interacting teams. J. Organ. Behav. 26, 625–648 (2005)

The Effects of Primary Output Design of True Wireless Earbuds on the Wearing Comfort

Yan Yan📖, Kexiang Liu, Rui Jiang, and Haining Wang(✉)

Hunan University, Changsha 410000, Hunan, China
{111kx001,jiangrui175,wanghn}@hnu.edu.cn

Abstract. The study aimed to examine the impact of primary output opening angle on subjective comfort perception of earbuds. 32 participants were selected for the study, and their external ear models were used to determine the spatial relationship between their ears and half-in-ear earphones. Based on this information, 5 prototypes of earphones were designed, each with a different angle for the primary output opening. 34 participants then wore and evaluated these prototypes for 20 min while performing static and dynamic tasks. Techniques such as reverse engineering, virtual fit, and deviation analysis were utilized to assess the gap and interference between the ear and earphones. The results showed that changing the primary output opening angle of half-in-ear earphones did not significantly affect subjective comfort perception. Objective variables such as the mean and maximum values of interference were found to be correlated with subjective comfort perception. The study concluded that higher levels of interference between the ear and earphone lead to decreased comfort perception. This research provides valuable insights for the design and development of future half-in-ear earphones.

Keywords: Wearing Comfort · Primary Output Dimensions of True Wireless Earbuds · Virtual fit and deviation analysis

1 Introduction

The market for ear-worn wearable devices has experienced growth since 2020. Due to varying ear shapes and sizes, users often report discomfort or even pain when wearing earphones for extended periods of time. Additionally, earphones can sometimes slip out of place during activities like jogging or walking. As a result, it is important to provide consumers with earphones that are comfortable and fit well, taking into account the unique geometry of each individual's ears [1]. Studies on the user experience research of ear-related products have shown that comfort is a significant factor in overall customer satisfaction [2]. End-user data from Amazon.com product reviews reveals that comfort and sound quality are the top priorities for customers when buying earbuds [3]. In the development of ear-worn wearables such as headsets and Bluetooth communication devices, comfort is a critical issue that often causes many concepts to be rejected at later stages [4]. Therefore, it is essential to prioritize comfort as a key factor in the design of earphones.

A. Marcus et al. (Eds.): HCII 2023, LNCS 14032, pp. 421–435, 2023.
https://doi.org/10.1007/978-3-031-35702-2_30

To enhance the comfort of ear-worn devices, the key design properties are ear anthropometric diameter, shape, and materials [5]. In the research of Song [6], the anthropometric factors of ears were analysed to identify elements that influence the comfort of using wireless earbuds. It is believed that anthropometric parameters relevant to the product's characteristics are crucial components in ensuring a comfortable fit through ergonomically designed products [7, 8].

Ear anatomy consists of cartilage covered with skin and arranged in a pattern of various elevations and depressions [9]. Generally, the external ear is composed of three main parts: the pinna, the concha, and the external auditory canal. The shape of the external auditory canal is not a straight course but passes upward in an anterior direction from the external opening. Then, it turns slightly posteriorly, still passes upward, and finally turns again in an anterior direction with a slight descent. When it comes to designing earphones, only the external two-thirds of the external auditory canal are in contact with the product, making the biological structures and components a complex challenge for ergonomic design [10].

Previous anthropometric studies on the ear have employed a variety of methods to measure the external ear, including traditional measurement, 2D photogrammetry, and 3D scanning [11]. Non-contact 3D scanning was revealed to be the most accurate, reliable, and efficient method [11]. For ergonomic design, the virtual fitting is frequently used [12] and deviation analysis tools are always applied in ergonomics assessment [12, 13]. In several studies, recommendations for the design of earphones were based on the expertise of designers and ergonomists [5, 8, 14, 15], or were derived from Quality Function Deployment (QFD) methods carried out by experts in ear-related product design and ergonomics [16]. Very few studies have combined user preference data with product characteristics to cater to a specific target market demographic.

In this research, it is hypothesized that the design of the primary output opening of earbuds has a correlation with subjective comfort perception. The hypothesis is verified using virtual fit and deviation analysis. The spatial relationship between the external auditory canal and the primary output opening of earbuds is obtained through virtual fit analysis, and the designs of the primary output opening are then modified accordingly. The comfort perception of different prototypes is evaluated through subjective assessment, virtual fit and deviation analysis. The hypothesis posits the following:

(1) The prototype with the primary output opening perfectly aligned with the ear canal entrance will receive the highest positive feedback regarding comfort perception.
(2) Variations in the design of the primary output opening will result in significant variations in subjective comfort evaluations.
(3) Comfort perception can be partially predicted using objective variables calculated by the virtual fit and deviation analysis method.

2 Survey 1: The Spatial Relationship Between the Ear Canal Entrance Plane and Primary Output Opening Plane of AirPods 2

2.1 Participants

The initial survey of this study was conducted across various locations in China, lasting for a duration of two months in 2020. A total of 32 young adults (14 males and 18 females) were selected as participants who met the inclusion criteria of being users of True Wireless Stereo Earbuds (TWS Earbuds), being over 18 years of age, and having a specific size of concha length and concha width. The study received approval from the ethics review committee at the School of Design at Hunan University of China.

2.2 Data Collection and Processing

The purpose of this study was to examine the spatial relationship between the TWS earbuds and the ears. The investigation employed reverse engineering, virtual fit, and deviation analysis technique to achieve this objective.

Data Collection

Auricle Scanning. Artec Spider^{tm} (Palo alto, CA, USA) 3D scanner was used for scanning the 3D shape of external ear without external auditory canal. The posture position and scanning techniques meet the requirements of ISO 20685-1:2018 3-D scanning methodologies for internationally compatible anthropometric databases (Standardization, 2018). Participants were asked to wear a wig cap on their heads and over the ear to avoid hair disturbance. In addition, participants were asked to sit straight and look at a fixed point on the wall with his/her usual facial expression.

External Auditory Canal Scanning. 3Shape phoenix (Copenhagen, Denmark) in-ear scanner was used for scanning the 3D shape of the concha and the external auditory canal of the external ear.

Intermediate Scanning of the Participant Wearing the Prototypes. Scanning the external ear with AirPods 2 by Artec Spider 3D scanner.

Data Processing

Ear Model Meshing. Models of the external ear were then exported to Artec Studio 12 (Palo alto, CA, USA) for further processing, including noise elimination, global registration, sharp fusion, mesh simplification & hole filling, mesh smoothing, texture mapping, and coordinate system unification.

Ear Model Alignment. Aligning external auditory canal model and external ear model with reference points by Geomagic Studio 12® (rock Hill, SC, USA) initially. And then, these two models were imported into Meshlab (Paolo Cignoni, Italy) and aligned by the iterative closet point (ICP) method, including choosing reference points in Geomagic Studio 12, relative position alignment, aligning with the ICP method in Meshlab, sharp fusion and feature smoothing in Artec Studio 12. The ICP method is used in merging the 3D point cloud of ear impression with a head model in the research of Zhang [18].

Ear Meshes Alignment. AirPods 2 was digitized using an industrial optical scanner (ATOS Core-80; GOM GmbH; 0.02 m point spacing, 0.008 mm per single scan). The meshes of AirPods 2, ear meshes, and intermediate meshes, were then aligned by Meshlab and Artec Studio 12. The alignment process was split into two stages, including aligning the AirPods 2 with intermediate meshes, and aligning ear meshes with intermediate meshes. After the two-stage alignment process has been completed, the intermediate meshes were removed, and ear meshes and earphone meshes were aligned accurately.

2.3   Landmarks and Dimensions

The ear models of the 32 participants were aligned with the AirPods 2 model using Geomagic Wrap 2017. Four landmarks (superior entrance, inferior entrance, anterior entrance, and posterior entrance) of the ear canal entrance were captured, and the relationship between the primary output opening plane and the horizontal plane of the true wireless earbuds was established.

2.4   Results and Discussion

The geometric center of four landmarks was analyzed and calculated independently. The results of the virtual fit analysis of 32 participants showed that the angle, α, between plane 2 and plane 4, is 15.698°, and the angle, β, between plane 1 and 3 is 23.586°. The relative positioning of the planes and angles can be seen in Fig. 1.

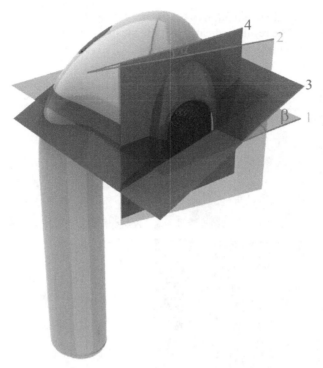

Fig. 1. Spatial relationships between two planes of ear and two planes of earbuds. (Plane 1: the horizontal plane of TWS earbuds; Plane 2: the primary output opening plane of TWS earbuds; Plane 3: the plane which goes through the minor axis of ear canal entrance and is vertical to the ear canal entrance plane.; Plane 4: the ear canal entrance plane. α: Angle between the plane 2 and plane 4; β: Angle between the plane 1 and plane 3)

3 Survey 2: Dimensions of the Primary Output Opening Plane of TWS Earbuds and Comfort Perception

3.1 Reconstruction of AirPods 2 Model

As the original scanned model of AirPods 2 cannot be edited or modified smoothly, a NURBS surface reconstruction of the model was performed using Autodesk Alias AutoStudio 2020 as a reference to the scanned model. The reconstruction process began with a sphere that had 144 control points. The control points were then adjusted, scaled, and rotated to fit the surface of the body. The "Project" and "Trim surface" tools were utilized to project lines onto the surface of the body and eliminate any redundant surface areas. Subsequently, the tube portion was constructed using the "Align" tool and connected to the body portion through the "Square" and "Birail gen two surface" tools to ensure smooth integration.

The surface of the body portion of the earbuds was determined to be continuous according to the G3 criterion and evaluated using the "zebra" constellation line, as shown in Fig. 2, which demonstrated the continuity of the surface. Both the reconstructed model and the original model were input into Geomagic Studio 12® (rock Hill, SC, USA) for deviation analysis. The results indicated that the mean distance between the two models was less than 0.08 mm (Fig. 2d).

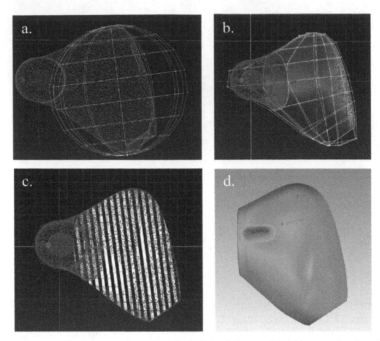

Fig. 2. The process of reconstruction of AirPods 2 (a. Sphere with 144 control points; b. Reconstructed NURBS surface of body portion of earbuds; c. "zebra" line of body portion of earbuds; d. The deviation analysis between the reconstructed model and the original model.)

3.2 Prototypes

Based on the spatial relationships between two planes of ear and the two planes of earbuds demonstrated in Survey 1, five prototypes were modified and 3D-printed. The reconstructed NURBS model of the AirPods 2 was utilized as a basis, and the control points of the primary output opening were adjusted through movement, scaling, and rotation to align with each respective prototype. The "transform CV-prop mod" tool was employed to link the ambient points and allow for proportional movement when modifying the control points of the primary output opening.

Prototype 0 was designed to be identical to the AirPods 2 and serves as a reference for comparison. Prototype 1 features plane 2 parallel to plane 4. Prototype 2 has plane 1 parallel to plane 3. The primary output opening plane of Prototype 3 is parallel to the ear canal entrance plane. Prototype 4 has the primary output opening plane coincident with the ear canal entrance plane. These five prototypes are illustrated in Fig. 3. The weight of each prototype was controlled to be approximately 4 ± 0.03 g.

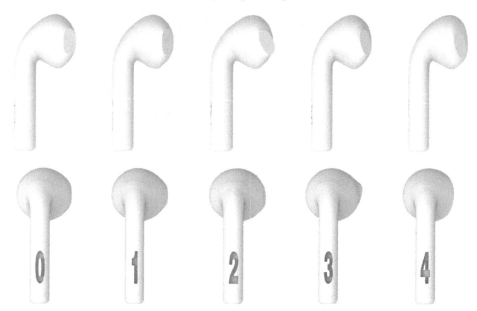

Fig. 3. The physical model of five prototypes (P0–4)

3.3 Participants

The second survey in this study was carried out at Hunan University, involving a sample of 34 young adults (16 males and 18 females). The study was approved by the Ethical Review Committee in the School of Design at Hunan University in China. The inclusion criteria were the same as those described in Sect. 2.1.

3.4 Qualitative Survey

Demographic Questionnaire and Traditional Anthropometric Measurements. Participants were requested to fill out a self-administered demographic questionnaire, which included questions about gender, age, nationality, and hometown. Additionally, traditional anthropometric measurements were performed.

Experiment Process
During the experiment, participants were randomly assign five prototypes. Each prototype was evaluated for a duration of 20 min. The evaluation process for each prototype was consistent with the procedures outlined in previous research [19].

After the 20-min evaluation period, participants were asked to complete a modified Borg scale (Table 1), which assess their sense of discomfort (0 is nothing at all, without discomfort feeling, 10 is extremely strong (almost max) discomfort feeling), sense of pressure, sense of stability, sense of volume as well as the sense of pressure of external auditory canal (Fig. 4). Participants were given a five-minute break between evaluations of each prototype.

Table 1. Modified Borg scale

Modified Borg CR10 scale	
Score	Level of exertion
0	Nothing at all
0.5	Extremely weak (just noticeable)
1	Very, very weak
2	Very weak
3	Weak (light)
4	Somewhat weak
5	Moderate
6	Somewhat strong
7	Strong (heavy)
8	Very strong
9	Very, very strong
10	Extremely strong (almost max)

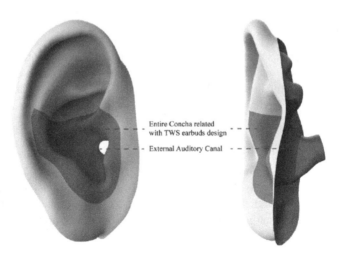

Fig. 4. Entire Concha related with TWS earbuds design and external auditory canal

3.5   Objective Data Collection and Processing

Data collection and processing procedure consists of three main steps: external ear scanning and processing, partitioning of the ear region, and alignment of the ear and earbuds meshes. The procedures for external ear scanning and processing, and ear meshes alignment, are consistent with those outlined in Sect. 2.2.

In this study, the modification was limited to the primary output opening of the earbuds. Hence, the external auditory canal was studied independently. The partitioning of the external auditory canal was performed using Geomagic Studio 12, based on anatomical landmarks and curvature of the users' ears as described in the anatomy of the ear [9, 20]. This is illustrated in Fig. 4.

3.6 Deviation Analysis

The improved deviation analysis algorithm [19] was utilized for performing deviation analysis on five earphone prototypes with all participants. Minimum (Min), maximum (Max), mean, and standard deviation (SD) value of deviation analysis results was calculated.

3.7 Results

The analysis was a fully with-in subjects design, in which different earbud prototypes (P0, P1, P2, P3, P4) were evaluated. (1) A descriptive analysis was conducted to describe the subjective discomfort score and objective deviation analysis variables between the ear and earbuds. (2) Given that the subjective discomfort score did not conform to a normal distribution, Spearman analyses were performed to examine the correlation between the subjective discomfort score and objective variables between the ear and different earbud prototypes.

Overall Subjective Discomfort Score of Five Prototypes

Table 2 presents the descriptive statistics of the overall subjective discomfort scores. Out of the five prototypes, prototype 2 recorded the lowest overall subjective discomfort score, with a value of 1.382 (SD = 1.420). Prototype 4 had a mean overall subjective discomfort score of 1.426 (SD = 1.088), followed by prototypes 0 and 1, with scores of 1.471 ± 1.387 and 1.485 ± 1.640 respectively. Conversely, prototype 3 was identified

Table 2. The descriptive statistics of overall subjective discomfort score and objective variables of five prototypes.

Prototypes		Discomfort	Sense of volume	Sense of stability	Sense of pressure
P0	Mean	1.471	1.5	1.353	1.485
	SD	1.387	1.775	1.786	1.357
P1	Mean	1.485	1.544	1.515	1.544
	SD	1.64	1.607	2.119	1.658
P2	Mean	1.382	1.794	1.544	1.853
	SD	1.42	1.415	2.024	1.449
P3	Mean	1.691	1.926	1.603	1.868
	SD	1.61	1.629	1.77	1.657
P4	Mean	1.426	1.618	1.838	1.765
	SD	1.088	1.745	2.014	1.468

as the most uncomfortable prototype, with a score of 1.691 ± 1.610. In terms of sense of volume, stability, and pressure, prototypes 0 and 1 recorded lower scores compared to prototype 2.

The independent t-test analysis was conducted to compare five different prototypes, as shown in Table 3. The results indicated that there was no statistically significant difference in subjective discomfort scores between the two prototypes.

Table 3. Results of independent sample t-test for subjective discomfort scores between five different prototypes.

Dependent Variable	Mean	SD	t	p
P0–P1	−0.0147	1.4115	−0.061	0.952
P0–P2	0.0882	1.3733	0.375	0.710
P0–P3	−0.2206	1.3382	−0.961	0.343
P0–P4	0.0441	1.1830	0.217	0.829
P1–P2	0.1029	1.2418	0.483	0.632
P1–P3	−0.2059	1.1489	−1.045	0.304
P1–P4	0.0588	1.4289	0.240	0.812
P2–P3	−0.3088	1.2793	−1.408	0.169
P2–P4	−0.0441	1.0827	−0.238	0.814
P3–P4	0.2647	1.2507	1.234	0.226

A bivariate correlation analysis was conducted to examine the relationship between overall comfort and three overall variables (sense of pressure, volume and stability), as well as the sense of pressure on the external auditory canal (Table 4). The results indicated that there was a significant correlation between overall comfort and overall sense of volume (0.764, $p < 0.01$) and overall sense of pressure (0.749, $p < 0.01$). Meanwhile, the correlation between overall comfort and overall sense of stability was weak (0.331, $p < 0.01$). Additionally, the sense of pressure on the external auditory canal was weakly correlated with overall comfort (0.392, $p < 0.01$), but not correlated with the overall sense of stability. These findings suggest that the sense of pressure on the external auditory canal is not related to the sense of stability.

Additionally, a bivariate correlation analysis was performed on all prototypes to determine the relationship between overall subjective discomfort scores (overall comfort, overall sense of volume, and overall sense of pressure) and the overall objective variables, including maximum value of interference (I-Max), mean value of interference (I-Mean), standard deviation of interference (I-SD), standard deviation of gap (G-SD), and overall mean value (A-Mean), which are shown in Table 5.

The results illustrate a negative correlation between overall comfort and I-Mean (−0.267, $p < 0.01$) and A-Mean (−0.196, $p < 0.05$). Additionally, there is a negative correlation between overall sense of volume and I-Mean (−0.244, $p < 0.01$) and A-Mean (−0.255, $p < 0.01$), as well as a positively correlation with I-SD (0.176, $p <$

Table 4. Coefficient of spearman correlation between overall subjective discomfort score.

Variables		Discomfort	Sense of volume	Sense of stability	Sense of pressure	Sense of pressure on external auditory canal
Overall comfort	Spearman Correlation	1.000				
	Sig.(2-tailed)					
Overall sense of volume	Spearman Correlation	.764**	1.000			
	Sig.(2-tailed)	0.000				
Overall sense of stability	Spearman Correlation	.331**	.153*	1.000		
	Sig.(2-tailed)	0.000	0.047			
Overall sense of pressure	Spearman Correlation	.749**	.738**	.302**	1.000	
	Sig.(2-tailed)	0.000	0.000	0.000		
sense of pressure on external auditory canal	Spearman Correlation	.392**	.431**	0.112	.496**	1.000
	Sig.(2-tailed)	0.000	0.000	0.147	0.000	

**. Correlation is significant at the 0.01 level.
*. Correlation is significant at the 0.05 level

0.05). Furthermore, overall sense of stability is positively correlated with I-Max (0.155, $p < 0.05$) and G-SD (0.163, $p < 0.05$). Finally, the results show a negative correlation between overall sense of pressure and A-Mean (-0.233, $p < 0.01$).

Table 5. Coefficient of spearman correlation between overall subjective discomfort scores and the overall objective variables.

Variables		Overall comfort	Overall sense of volume	Overall sense of stability	Overall sense of pressure
I-Max	Spearman Correlation	-0.030	-0.089	.155*	-0.022
	Sig.(2-tailed)	0.699	0.250	0.046	0.782
I-Mean	Spearman Correlation	$-.267**$	$-.244**$	0.018	-0.122
	Sig.(2-tailed)	0.000	0.002	0.819	0.116

(*continued*)

Table 5. *(continued)*

Variables		Overall comfort	Overall sense of volume	Overall sense of stability	Overall sense of pressure
I-SD	Spearman Correlation	0.139	.176*	−0.115	0.082
	Sig.(2-tailed)	0.074	0.023	0.138	0.295
G-SD	Spearman Correlation	−0.014	−0.052	.163*	−0.089
	Sig.(2-tailed)	0.854	0.498	0.033	0.247
A-Mean	Spearman Correlation	−.196*	−.255**	0.125	−.233**
	Sig.(2-tailed)	0.010	0.001	0.105	0.002

**. Correlation is significant at the 0.01 level.
*. Correlation is significant at the 0.05 level.

3.8 Discussion

Among the five different prototypes, prototype 2 was assessed as the most comfortable one in terms of overall subjective discomfort score. The analysis showed that there was no statistical difference between prototypes 0 to 4. This suggests that changes to the primary output opening of half-in-ear earbuds do not significantly impact comfort perception. The findings of this research indicate that modifying the angle of the primary output opening of half-in-ear earbuds does not result in a significant difference in comfort perception.

Furthermore, the results indicate that overall sense of volume and overall sense of pressure are significantly correlated with overall comfort. However, sense of stability is not significantly correlated with overall comfort. Additionally, the prototype with the lightest feeling of pressure on the external auditory canal does not necessarily result in the best comfort experience. The results suggest that the sense of pressure on the external auditory canal may not accurately reflect the overall pressure on the ear. There remains a gap in understanding the relationship between different comfort indicators and the overall and regional evaluation of earbud comfort.

The relationship between subjective discomfort scores and objective variables was explored using a spearman correlation analysis, both for the overall ear and the external auditory canal. The results indicate that objective variables that indicate the overlapping volume between the earbuds and ear can predict subjective discomfort scores and the scores for three indicators: sense of volume, sense of pressure, and sense of stability, to some extent. Additionally, the I-Mean of the overall ear and external auditory canal is significantly correlated with overall comfort, suggesting that reducing the interference between the ear/external auditory canal and the earbuds can increase comfort assessment. The A-Mean of the overall ear and external auditory canal is correlated with overall sense of pressure, both in terms of the overall assessment and on a regional level. For overall sense of stability, I-Max and G-SD are correlated with it, suggesting that the earbuds are more likely to remain stable in the ear when there are fewer distinct overlapping areas between the earbuds and ear.

4 General Discussion

The subjective assessment of AirPods 2, as per internet evaluations, is deemed superior to other half-in-ear earbuds available for purchase. A virtual fit analysis was performed to investigate the spatial relationship between the ear and the AirPods 2. The results indicated that the primary output opening plane of the AirPods 2 was not parallel with the ear canal entrance plane. An anthropometric analysis of 32 participants' ears, combined with a physical fit analysis of the AirPods 2, revealed that the primary output opening of the AirPods 2 was angled towards the posterior ear auditory canal entrance, with a horizontal angle of $15.698°$ between the primary output opening plane of the earbuds and the open plane of the external auditory canal. The long axis of the primary output opening of the earbuds was rotated clockwise by $23.586°$ with respect to the long axis of the ear canal entrance plane. A second survey found no significant differences between five prototypes in overall subjective comfort scores. Overall, the modification of the primary output opening of the earbuds in this study had no marked impact on comfort perception. As such, perfect alignment of the primary output opening of the earbuds with the ear canal entrance is not deemed necessary to attain positive feedback regarding comfort.

In this study, the overlapping areas between earbuds and ears were quantified through 3D scanning and an improved deviation algorithm to explore the impact of such overlapping on the wearing comfort of earphones. The correlation between comfort perception and deviation analysis variables was found to be weak. This can be attributed to three main factors. Firstly, the shape difference between earbuds is relatively minimal, making it challenging to accurately discriminate and assess shape subjectively. Secondly, individuals have varying levels of pressure pain sensitivity in the ear. Lastly, the biological structure and components of the ear, including fat, cartilage, and skeleton, are extremely diverse and complex, leading to differing mechanical deformations even with similar deviation analysis results, thus affecting comfort perception. Moreover, it is believed that material, weight, the center of gravity of earbuds, user behavior, and all contact areas in the ear are crucial design factors that affect the comfort of wearing wireless earbuds [6]. These factors should be taken into consideration in future subjective comfort evaluations of earbuds.

5 Conclusion

This study focused on the design of the primary output opening of half-in-ear earbuds, which plays a crucial role in determining wearing comfort [3]. Both subjective and objective measures were used to evaluate the comfort perception of the earbuds. The results showed that:

(1) There is no need to align the primary output opening of earbuds perfectly with the ear canal entrance in order to achieve positive feedback on comfort perception.

(2) Modifications of the primary output opening angle of the earbuds did not significantly impact comfort perception.

(3) The deviation analysis variables, which indicate the overlapping volume between the earbuds and ear, were found to be weakly correlated with the subjective discomfort scores, with three indicators (sense of volume, sense of pressure, and sense of stability) having some predictability. Additionally, overall comfort was found to decrease as the I-Mean value of the overall ear and external auditory canal increased.

This study aimed to evaluate the effect of the design of the primary output opening on the wearing comfort of half-in-ear earbuds. The virtual fit analysis and deviation analysis methods were utilized to assess this relationship. For future research, it is recommended to modify the primary output opening of half-in-ear earbuds at different angles, and include participants from a wide range of demographic backgrounds. The results and approach of this study provide a useful foundation for further studies in both the field of wearing comfort and the design of half-in-ear earphones.

References

1. Lu, P., Tsao, L., Yu, C., Ma, L.: Survey of ear anthropometry for young college students in China and its implications for ear-related product design. Hum. Factors Ergon. Manuf. (2020). https://doi.org/10.1002/hfm.20871
2. Choi, K., Ban, K., Choe, J., Jung, E.S.: A framework for affective quality of ear-related product design. Jpn. J. Ergon. **51**, S426–S429 (2015). https://doi.org/10.5100/jje.51.s426
3. Ferguson, T., Greene, M., Repetti, F., Lewis, K., Behdad, S.: Combining anthropometric data and consumer review content to inform design for human variabilty. In: Proceedings of the ASME 2015 International Design Engineering Technical Conferences & Computers and Information in Engineering Conference (2015). https://doi.org/10.1115/DETC2015-47640
4. Stavrakos, S.K., Ahmed-Kristensen, S.: Assessment of anthropometric methods in headset design. In: Proceedings of International Design Conference, DESIGN. DS 70, pp. 1123–1132 (2012)
5. Chiu, H.P., Chiang, H.Y., Liu, C.H., Wang, M.H., Chiou, W.K.: Surveying the comfort perception of the ergonomic design of bluetooth earphones. Work **49**, 235–243 (2014). https://doi.org/10.3233/WOR-131723
6. Song, H., Shin, G.W., Yoon, Y., Bahn, S.: The effects of ear dimensions and product attributes on the wearing comfort of wireless earphones. Appl. Sci. (Switz.) **10**, 1–15 (2020). https://doi.org/10.3390/app10248890
7. Fan, H., et al.: Anthropometric characteristics and product categorization of Chinese auricles for ergonomic design. Int. J. Ind. Ergon. **69**, 118–141 (2019). https://doi.org/10.1016/j.ergon.2018.11.002
8. Liu, B.S.: Incorporating anthropometry into design of ear-related products. Appl. Ergon. **39**, 115–121 (2008). https://doi.org/10.1016/j.apergo.2006.12.005
9. Drake, R.L., Vogl, A.W., Mitchell, A.W.M.: Gray's Basic Anatomy, 2nd edn. (2018)
10. Fu, F., Luximon, Y.: A systematic review on ear anthropometry and its industrial design applications. Hum. Factors Ergon. Manuf. **30**, 1–19 (2019)
11. Fu, F., Luximon, Y.: A systematic review on ear anthropometry and its industrial design applications. Hum. Factors Ergon. Manuf. Serv. Ind. **30**, 176–194 (2020). https://doi.org/10.1002/hfm.20832

12. Lee, W., et al.: Measurement and application of 3D ear images for earphone design. In: Proceedings of the Human Factors and Ergonomics Society, pp. 1052–1056 (2016). https://doi.org/10.1177/1541931213601244

13. Ellena, T., Subic, A., Mustafa, H., Pang, T.Y.: The helmet fit index - an intelligent tool for fit assessment and design customisation. Appl. Ergon. **55**, 194–207 (2016). https://doi.org/10.1016/j.apergo.2016.02.008

14. Jung, H.S., Jung, H.S.: Surveying the dimensions and characteristics of Korean ears for the ergonomic design of ear-related products. Int. J. Ind. Ergon. **31**, 361–373 (2003). https://doi.org/10.1016/S0169-8141(02)00237-8

15. Mououdi, M.A., Akbari, J., Mohammadi Khoshoei, M.: Measuring the external ear for hearing protection device design. Ergon. Des. **26**, 4–8 (2018). https://doi.org/10.1177/1064804617731177

16. Ban, K., Jung, E.S.: Ear shape categorization for ergonomic product design. Int. J. Ind. Ergon. (2020). https://doi.org/10.1016/j.ergon.2020.102962

17. Standardization, international organization for: ISO 20685–1:2018 3-D scanning methodologies for internationally compatible anthropometric databases—Part 1: Evaluation protocol for body dimensions extracted from 3-D body scans (2018)

18. Zhang, M., Ball, R., Martin, N.J., Luximon, Y.: Merging the point clouds of the head and ear by using the iterative closest point method. Int. J. Digit. Hum. **1**, 305 (2016). https://doi.org/10.1504/ijdh.2016.10000732

19. Yan, Y., Liu, Y., Wang, H.: An earphone fit deviation analysis algorithm. Sci. Rep. **13**, 1084 (2023). https://doi.org/10.1038/s41598-023-27794-y

20. Griffin, M.F., Premakumar, Y., Seifalian, A.M., Szarko, M., Butler, P.E.M.: Biomechanical characterisation of the human auricular cartilages; implications for tissue engineering. Ann. Biomed. Eng. **44**(12), 3460–3467 (2016). https://doi.org/10.1007/s10439-016-1688-1

Effects of Image Size and Position on Text Legibility of Foldable Smartphones

Ke Zeng, Qiannan Deng, and Haining Wang$^{(\boxtimes)}$

School of Design, Hunan University, Changsha 410082, China
haining1872@qq.com

Abstract. Foldable smartphones have been newly developed by the cell phone industry and are growing in the global market. The goal of this study was to investigate the effects of image size and position on the text readability of foldable smartphones. Eight participants were recruited to complete text comprehension tasks and provide user preferences on a foldable smartphone. Four test conditions, consisting of two image sizes and two positions, were studied. The results of this study suggest that the position of the images significantly affect the legibility of text on foldable smartphones. The combinations of size and position used should vary by situation. The results of this study provide useful information for display factors and interface design on foldable smartphones, which should help improve text reading efficiency and decrease visual fatigue for users of foldable smartphones.

Keywords: Text Legibility · Foldable Smartphones · User interface evaluation

1 Introduction

As basic communication needs were met, the demand for mobile phones began to grow steadily, prompting new iterations of technology. To meet the demand for higher multimedia displays, the new generation of mobile phones relied on screen technology to reduce the size of the handset. In this context, the foldable smartphone was born. With a fixed size, a larger screen is achieved through new technologies and designs. When unfolded, the proportions of the screen on a foldable smartphone are different to a conventional smartphone, and the user's grip and reading habits are therefore different. However, much of the software on foldable smartphones is still adapted in the traditional way, making the experience less than ideal. It is therefore a matter of concern that the experience of browsing software on a foldable smartphone should be improved.

Current research in screen reading usability has focused on text readability, content recall, user satisfaction and visual fatigue [1]. Studies using text reading tasks and visual search tasks are a common way to determine readability. The two dependent variables, reading speed and reading comprehension, are more commonly studied in relation to the effect of electronic devices on text readability [2].

When assessing the readability of text, researchers often use typographical changes, such as adjusting the font or font size, to determine the factors that affect a reader's ability to perceive visual form [3]. Studies have generally found that font has a greater

© The Author(s), under exclusive license to Springer Nature Switzerland AG 2023
A. Marcus et al. (Eds.): HCII 2023, LNCS 14032, pp. 436–446, 2023.
https://doi.org/10.1007/978-3-031-35702-2_31

effect on reading. For example, [4] compared the effects of two fonts on text legibility using a reading comprehension task. The effect of font size on reading, however, remains controversial. [5] argued that subjective measures are more sensitive to changes in readability than objective measures.

Many studies have investigated font, character size and line spacing, with [6] concluding that only character size had a significant effect on comprehension scores. However, [7] found no significant effect of character size on reading performance, which may be due to the fact that their subjects were free to adjust their viewing distance in real-life situations and that there were differences in the difficulty of the reading material selected in the experiment. However, there is experimental data showing that larger characters are easier to recognise than smaller ones [8]. The results of [9] confirmed the above, with eye-tracked data showing that small font size was the primary cause of visual fatigue. This confirms that the font size should correspond to a different appropriate size when the paragraph length of the text varies.

In addition to font and font size, research has generally found that text orientation and screen size [10] have an impact on search time. In order to improve reading comprehension, attention or cognitive load, [11] argued that the type of text display for mobile reading on small screens should be adapted to the reading context.

New ideas in the design of screen usability experiments have emerged in recent years. For example, user satisfaction has been compared to typography parameters using tactile interaction data [12]. Studies have confirmed that blue light [13], illumination and brightness [14] correlate with screen usability. [2] compared readability differences between paper and tablet computers. A small number of studies have also focused on the influence of text and video ads on each other [15].

Usability of screen reading is therefore an issue. There is currently a wealth of research on text readability in the areas of paper-based text and traditional mobile phones.

2 Research Purpose

Foldable smartphones differ from traditional mobile phones in that the larger screen brings a different software experience, and factors such as images and videos also affect the presentation of text content on the screen, a situation that is particularly noticeable in social media software for foldable smartphones. Therefore, this study sets up experiments to measure the effect of image placement and size on text readability based on the foldable social media reading scenario. By comparing the number of typos detected, reading speed and subjective preference, it was determined which typography had the best reading effect.

3 Methodology

3.1 Participants

A total of 8 participants (5 male, 3 female, aged 21–23 years) were recruited to take part in the experiment. Participants were recruited via a published questionnaire and had experience of using social software on a mobile phone or tablet PC. Among them, 3 participants had used social software on a foldable smartphone. All participants had normal vision and no other eye diseases. They had passed the reading and cognitive tests and signed an informed consent form.

3.2 Apparatus

An OPPO Find N was used as a device to display the reading content. The physical dimensions of this device are 132.6 × 73 × 15.9 mm and it weighs approximately 275 g. The device has both an internal and an external screen, and when open the device has a screen size of 7.1 inches and a screen resolution of 1792 × 1920 pixels. In this study, the device is used in the unfolded state to display reading material. The user can choose a comfortable viewing distance, and once the distance has been determined, the reading position must be maintained throughout the experiment.

The background color of each group of materials was white and the font color was black. Each participant's screen brightness, contrast and ambient light intensity were always maintained. The experiment was conducted on the Figma mirror (https://www.figma.com), which is installed in the mobile phone and allows participants to record clicks on the misspelled words they find.

3.3 Experiment Design

In this study, the combination of image position and size was used as the independent variable, reading time, correct task completion rate and oculomotor physiological data as the objective dependent variables, and reading ease, aesthetic preference and task difficulty rating as the subjective dependent variables. During the experiment, participants were required to read four sets of material using a foldable smartphone. Before the experiment began, participants were informed of the task: to find misspelled words in each group of reading material. Participants performed the reading task at a normal reading speed, clicking on the misspelled words to mark them as they were read. At the end, a subjective questionnaire with a short preference statement was completed.

3.4 Materials

4*12 tweets were selected from the images on the front page of Weibo and from the text messages. The content of each tweet was slightly modified to achieve the same length, and each final tweet message contained 65 Chinese characters and an image associated with the text content. Each of the 12 tweets was formed into a complete set of reading material, and a total of four different sets of reading material were obtained. The arrangement and size of the images differed between each set of reading material.

Figure 1 shows the specific form of distribution of images and text, where the images in the first and third groups were no wider than 1384 pixels and no longer than 1250 pixels, and the images in the second and fourth groups were no wider than 1038 pixels and no longer than 938 pixels. The images in the first and second groups are placed above and below the text, and the images in the third and fourth groups are placed to the left and right of the text. In the material, the text content always follows below the associated images in order to explore the relationship between the size and position of the images and the readability of the text in social software displayed on a flip phone.

Fig. 1. Four sets of reading material and layout.

For each set of reading materials, the font used in the article is Chinese 12-point bold. One point (pt.) is 1/72 of an inch, and the actual size of the 12-point font. Each piece of reading material contained ten typos, namely homophone typos, lookalike typos, and misspellings [16].

3.5 Procedure

After signing the informed consent form, participants entered the laboratory for the start of the experiment. Each participant was required to complete 4*2 sets of tasks. Task 1 required the participant to read the material through a foldable smartphone in its unfolded state and check for typos in the material. When the participant was ready, the experiment began, and time was recorded. The flip phone displayed a combination of images and text messages from the social networking platform. When a typo was found, the participant had to click on its location on the screen. The clicked typos turned red. (see Fig. 2).

Fig. 2. Forms of marking misspelled words in reading material.

The red marks were used to assess the participants' recognition of the typos. After the participant had read through the material, the end time of the experiment was recorded. Participants were then asked to complete Task 2. Task 2 consisted of five multiple-choice questions (see Fig. 3) to test whether the participant could recall the picture information associated with the text. Each multiple-choice question contained four different picture options.

Q1:Please recall that the image corresponding to the text "南怀瑾老先生曾经说过：脾气倔强、越硬的人，越是较劲的人命越不好。要学水，上善若水，最上等的善人像水一样的柔软，利万物而不染，而不辞。" is:

A   B   C   D

Fig. 3. Examples of question formats for Task 2.

The participants were then asked to subjectively rate the layout of the pages in a short interview. For both tasks, they were asked to rate the level of difficulty, level of physical and mental fatigue, level of information retention, and aesthetic preference for typography. Reading time was measured by recording the time at the beginning and end of the experiment. Participants were told that they had to read continuously (no skipping) in order to find typos by reading and understanding the content of the text. Reading time, the time spent looking for typos, was therefore used as a criterion to assess the speed and difficulty of completing the task, and as a further measure of the quality of the typography. The number of typos found was used to assess the readability of the text. After completing each task, participants were given a five-minute break before moving on to the next set of material.

After completing the four sets of tasks, participants chose the most acceptable of the four different sets of typographic styles. The total duration of the experiment was about one hour.

3.6 Data Analysis

Statistical analysis of all data was performed using SPSS software. Participants' level of task difficulty, level of physical and mental fatigue, level of memory for information, and aesthetic preference for typography were recorded using the Likert 1–10 scale. Higher scores were associated with less fatigue, higher levels of information retention and greater preference for typography. The readability of the text increased with the number of typos participants identified. The shorter the reading time recorded, the more efficient the reading of that layout. Multiple-way ANOVA was used to process the data.

4 Results

The results of the experimental data are presented as four outcomes: task completion (number of typos identified, picture recall), task load (task difficulty, fatigue), reading time and aesthetic appeal. A Multiple-way ANOVA test was used, with significance set at $P < 0.05$.

4.1 Task Completion

Table 1. Number of typos identified of participants.

Variable	Typography		M	SD	Image size (P)	Image location (P)	Image size & Image location (P)
number of typos identified	Big picture	Left-right alignment	8.63	1.69	0.15	0.38	0.49
		Top-down structure	7.63	1.41			
	Small picture	Left-right alignment	7.25	2.05			
		Top-down structure	7.12	1.88			

A two-way ANOVA was used to analyze the number of typos found by participants, with image size and position as influencing factors, and the results are shown in Table 1. A higher number of typos found indicates better readability, with more typos found in both the left and right layout than in the top and bottom layout, however the main effects of image position and size are not statistically significant for finding typos (all $p > 0.05$).

Table 2 lists the M and SD of picture recall for image size and location Two-factor repeated-measure ANOVAs were conducted on picture recall.

Table 2. Picture recall of participants.

Variable	Typography		M	SD	Image size (P)	Image location (P)	Image size & Image location (P)
Picture recall	Big picture	Left-right alignment	4.50	0.93	0.84	0.84	0.84
		Top-down structure	4.50	1.07			
	Small picture	Left-right alignment	4.63	0.52			
		Top-down structure	4.50	0.76			

4.2 Task Load

Table 3 shows the M and SD of task load for different typesetting methods, including the two dimensions of task difficulty and fatigue.

The results show that the main effect of the picture location variable is statistically significant only for the difficulty of retrieving picture information ($p < 0.01$). The difficulty of picture recall is significantly higher for the left-right orientation (M = 3.88, SD = 1.46) than for the top-bottom orientation (M = 2.13, SD = 1.46) in the case of large-sized pictures, and in the case of small-sized pictures.

Table 3. Task load (scores with the Likert 1–10 scale) of participants.

Variable	Typography		M	SD	Image size (P)	Image location (P)	Image size & Image location (P)
Difficulty in finding typos	Big picture	Left-right alignment	3.75	2.05	0.86	0.46	0.73
		Top-down structure	4.50	2.07			
	Small picture	Left-right alignment	4.13	1.72			

(*continued*)

Table 3. (*continued*)

Variable	Typography		M	SD	Image size (P)	Image location (P)	Image size & Image location (P)
		Top-down structure	4.38	2.20			
Difficulty in recalling picture information	Big picture	Left-right alignment	3.88	1.46	0.81	0.01**	0.47
		Top-down structure	2.13	1.46			
	Small picture	Left-right alignment	3.63	1.60			
		Top-down structure	2.63	1.30			
Fatigue	Big picture	Left-right alignment	3.37	2.20	0.86	0.85	0.86
		Top-down structure	3.13	1.80			
	Small picture	Left-right alignment	3.13	1.96			
		Top-down structure	3.13	1.73			

**. Correlation is significant at the 0.01 level.
*. Correlation is significant at the 0.05 level

4.3 Reading Time and Aesthetic Appeal

Table 4. Reading time of participants.

Variable	Typography		M	SD	Image size (P)	Image location (P)	Image size & Image location (P)
Reading time	Big picture	Left-right alignment	164.45	46.32	0.75	0.93	0.44
		Top-down structure	175.28	43.21			
	Small picture	Left-right alignment	181.72	37.94			
		Top-down structure	168.05	46.96			

Table 5. Aesthetic appeal of participants.

Variable	Typography		M	SD	Image size (P)	Image location (P)	Image size & Image location (P)
Aesthetic appeal	Big picture	Left-right alignment	4.38	2.33	0.16	1.00	0.21
		Top-down structure	5.25	1.58			
	Small picture	Left-right alignment	4.25	2.31			
		Top-down structure	3.38	1.41			

Tables 4 and 5 show the M and SD for reading time and aesthetic appeal under different typographies, for which a two-way repeated measures ANOVA was performed. The results show that the main effects of image position and size are not statistically significant for either reading time or aesthetic appeal (all $p > 0.05$).

5 Discussion

The aim of this study was to explore the effect of graphic layout style on readability in a social media scenario, and the results showed that there was no significant difference in the effect of image size on subjective and objective factors. The ease of finding the typo itself and the different reading materials may also have had an impact on the time taken to find and read the typo. The level of user recall of the correspondence between text and images was significantly correlated with the location of the images, with participants' subjective difficulty in remembering the correspondence being significantly higher when the images were on either side of the text than when the images were at the top and bottom of the text.

This may be because the difference in size and proportions between foldable smartphones and traditional phones allows for a new typographic approach to images. While the position of text and images on conventional phones is often limited by the size of the phone, the larger size of foldable smartphones offers the possibility of a left-right layout for images and text. However, a better way to read the layout is not to fill the screen directly. When the image is below the text, the text and image are in the same vertical orientation and the image and text are read in a relatively natural way; when the image is to the right of the text, the reading order of the image and text changes and the user must choose whether to look at the image or the text first, with the eye jumping from left to right and up and down.

At the same time, users' reading preferences for text and images have an impact on aesthetic appeal and fatigue. Users who prefer to read images prefer a left-right layout of text and images. At the same time, users who paid attention to textual information preferred images to be placed below the text. This partially confirms our research on the position of images. Users who pay attention to images want them to have a higher priority on a larger screen. On a page, they tend to focus on the content of the image before reading the text, and the left-right layout is more in line with their reading habits. Future research can incorporate devices such as eye-tracking to study users' eye jumps and eye dwell times during reading, and suggest more comfortable typography.

Also, this study only looked at social media software with 65 characters. For software with less or more text content, the layout of the page will need to be changed, with the placement and proportion of text and images determined by their priority.

Therefore, the use of social media software should be adapted to the user's reading habits and the positioning of the software itself, and the layout of the software should be different from that of text-based media.

6 Conclusion

In this study, eight students from the School of Design and Arts were selected to conduct a study on the readability of foldable screen phones. They completed a reading task with four different combinations of picture and text. The study compared the effect of different image sizes and positions on readability. The results showed that the size of the images had little effect on readability, while the position of the images had a significant effect on the user's recall of the images. Therefore, the position of images and text should be carefully considered when designing the typography of foldable smartphones.

Furthermore, user reading preferences indicate that users who tend to read images prefer left-right typography, while those who prefer text information prefer top-down typography. This suggests that the priority of images and text influences the typography in different software for foldable smartphones, and the results of this study could inform the software layout design for subsequent foldable smartphones.

References

1. Li, J., et al.: Effects of different interaction modes on fatigue and reading effectiveness with mobile phones. Int. J. Ind. Ergon. **85**, 103189 (2021)
2. Čerepinko, D., Keček, D., Periša, M.: Text readability and legibility on iPad with comparison to paper and computer screen **24**(4), 1197–1201 (2017)
3. Bloodsworth, J.G.: Legibility of Print (1993)
4. Hojjati, N. and B. Muniandy: The effects of font type and spacing of text for online readability and performance. Contemp. Educ. Technol. **5**(2). 161–174 (2014)
5. Huang, D.-L., P.-L.P. Rau, and Y. Liu: Effects of font size, display resolution and task type on reading Chinese fonts from mobile devices. Int. J. Ind. Ergon. **39**(1), 81–89 (2009)
6. Chan, A.H.S., Lee, P.S.K.: Effect of display factors on Chinese reading times, comprehension scores and preferences. Behav. Inf. Technol. **24**, 81–91 (2005)
7. Huang, S.-M., Li, W.-J.: Format effects of traditional Chinese character size and font style on reading performance when using smartphones. In: 2017 International Conference on Applied System Innovation (ICASI). IEEE (2017)
8. Dobres, J., et al.: The effects of visual crowding, text size, and positional uncertainty on text legibility at a glance. Appl. Ergon. **70**, 240–246 (2018)

9. Lin, H., Wu, F.-G., Cheng, Y.-Y.: Legibility and visual fatigue affected by text direction, screen size and character size on color LCD e-reader. Displays **34**, 49–58 (2013)
10. Jiang, L., Chen, Y.-H.: Menu design on small display user interfaces: measuring the influence of menu type, number of preview items, and menu breadth on navigation efficiency. Int. J. Hum.–Comput. Interact. **38**(7), 631–645 (2022)
11. Chen, C.-M., Lin, Y.-J.: Effects of different text display types on reading comprehension, sustained attention and cognitive load in mobile reading contexts. Interact. Learn. Environ. **24**, 553–571 (2016)
12. Wang, J., et al.: Evaluating user satisfaction with typography designs via mining touch interaction data in mobile reading. In: Proceedings of the 2018 CHI Conference on Human Factors in Computing Systems (2018)
13. Tu, Y., et al.: 17.2: invited paper: influence of blue light from smartphone on visual fatigue. In: SID Symposium Digest of Technical Papers. Wiley Online Library (2021)
14. Benedetto, S., et al.: Effects of luminance and illuminance on visual fatigue and arousal during digital reading. Comput. Hum. Behav. **41**, 112–119 (2014)
15. Jankowski, J., et al.: Integrating text with video and 3D graphics: the effects of text drawing styles on text readability. In: Proceedings of the SIGCHI Conference on Human Factors in Computing Systems (2010)
16. Huang, S.-M., Li, W.-J., Tung, S.-C.: An effect of white space on traditional Chinese text-reading on smartphones. Appl. Syst. Innov. **1**(3), 24 (2018)

Effects of Virtual Map Visual Presentations and Gender Differences on Wayfinding Using Touchscreen Electronic Guides

Weimin Zhai and Chien-Hsiung Chen(✉)

Department of Design, National Taiwan University of Science and Technology, Taipei 106, Taiwan

zokeay@hnu.edu.cn

Abstract. The interactive touchscreen electronic guide plays a significant role in the commercial services of large shopping malls, providing an excellent interactive experience for users. This study aims to investigate the factors of virtual map visual presentation and gender differences on users' wayfinding performance with interactive touchscreen electronic guide devices. The research variables were the types of virtual map visual presentations (i.e., top view maps and perspective view maps) and gender (i.e., males and females). A total of 40 participants were invited to take part in the experiment via convenience sampling methods. This experiment is a 2×2 between-subjects design. Participants needed to complete three wayfinding tasks and fill out questionnaires regarding the effortlessness and preference. In addition, the NASA Task Load Index (NASA-TLX) questionnaire was also adopted. The generated results are as follows: (1) Gender differences exist in the task performance of the interactive touchscreen electronic guides. (2) Different virtual map visual presentation types affect participants' subjective evaluations. (3) There is a significant interaction effect between the virtual map visual presentation and gender on wayfinding task performance, i.e., male participants performed better than female participants in the perspective view maps. In contrast, female participants performed better than male participants in the top view maps. (4) The degree of effortlessness of the perspective view maps was significantly higher than that of the top view maps.

Keywords: Virtual map visual presentation · Touchscreen electronic guide · Gender difference · Wayfinding · User experience

1 Introduction

It is commonly easier to get lost indoors than outdoors (Brunner-Friedrich and Radoczky 2005). For consumers, it is challenging to find the target location in large shopping malls (Kim et al. 2020), and the hassle of wayfinding can directly affect their shopping experience and even bring negative emotions (Chebat et al. 2005). Therefore, consumers' guidance and orientation in commercial spaces are significant issues (Kutnicki 2018). In the past, visual guidance signage provided great convenience for wayfinding behavior

© The Author(s), under exclusive license to Springer Nature Switzerland AG 2023
A. Marcus et al. (Eds.): HCII 2023, LNCS 14032, pp. 447–459, 2023.
https://doi.org/10.1007/978-3-031-35702-2_32

in indoor spaces. Today, interactive touchscreen electronic guides can provide a way for consumers to find their way in commercial spaces (Wright et al. 2010), and greatly enhance the user's wayfinding performance (Tüzün et al. 2016). It is well known that interactive touchscreen electronic guides allow consumers to easily access information through fingertip clicks alone without relying on any other device, which is highly attractive to consumers (Benko et al. 2006). In recent years, touch screens have been widely used in retail environments (Tüzün et al. 2016) and are becoming more popular for consumers to deliver information (Nicholas et al. 2006).

Generally speaking, Interactive touchscreen electronic guides can provide consumers with functions such as "store searching," "facility searching," "parking payment & car searching," "promotion activities," etc. (Li et al. 2021). Wayfinding is the most frequently used operation among all functions (Tüzün et al. 2016). The touchscreen electronic guide is controlled directly by the user's fingers and is easy to use for most people (Wang 2014). However, interface problems can also reduce the user experience (Tüzün et al. 2016), so this study focuses on the impact of the interface design on wayfinding using interactive touchscreen electronic guides.

Wayfinding is the process by which a person determines the correct route from their current location and identifies the destination they have reached (Peponis et al. 1990). For example, in shopping space wayfinding, maps are the primary tool for shoppers in the shopping center wayfinding process (Dogu and Erkip 2000). In the past, it was also found that 2D maps (i.e., top views) could improve the user's ability to see the target's location and gain a better perception of the location (Lu and Peponis 2014), thus better extracting information from the map (Laakso et al. 2003). However, it has been found that users need more cognitive load in cognitive processing to perceive the matching relationship between 2D maps and real space (Goodman et al. 2003). In contrast, 3D maps (i.e., perspective view maps) can easily facilitate users to match virtual space information to real physical space and generate a positive user experience (Oulasvirta et al. 2007). In addition, 3D maps can quickly improve novice users' cognitive abilities in unfamiliar environments (Plesa and Cartwright 2008). Johnson et al. (1995) also highlighted that 3D maps could help users recall more information and have easier access to information about positioning in terms of cognitive processing of space. However, Popelka and Doležalová (2015) found no significant differences in eye-movement metrics between 2D and 3D maps in a visual search task. It has even been suggested that too much map information in 3D maps can reduce user performance in wayfinding compared to 2D maps (Zheng 2020). In addition, Lei et al. (2016) concluded that 3D maps produce clustered gaze with longer durations and smaller sweeps, which is responsible for the lower efficiency of users in acquiring detailed information.

Gender differences are also considered essential in user interface design (Hubona and Shirah 2008). In wayfinding research, many past studies have supported the significant impact of gender differences on wayfinding strategies (Bosco et al. 2007; Lawton 1994). Many earlier studies generally concluded that males outperformed females in wayfinding (Malinowski and Gillespie 2001; Silverman et al. 2000). In addition, Lawton and Kallai (2002) found that females spent more time finding the goal and generated more anxiety. This increased anxiety led to more errors (Hund and Minarik 2006). In contrast, males were more confident in their wayfinding performance (Harrell et al. 2000). However, Lin et al. (2012) found no conclusive evidence to support the hypothesis that males perform better than females in a pathfinding task in a virtual environment. Therefore, this study's primary purpose was to investigate the effect of the type of map visual presentation on gender by manipulating the interactive touchscreen electronic guide to enhance users' wayfinding performance and cater to their subjective preferences.

2 Method

In this study, a 2 × 2 between-subject design was employed in the experiment, in which the two independent variables were "virtual map visual presentations" and "gender difference." The two levels of the virtual map visual presentations are top view maps and perspective view maps, and the two levels of gender difference are males and females. The following is the research framework of this study (see Fig. 1).

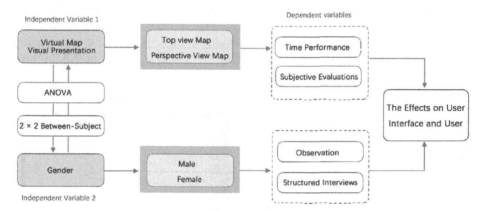

Fig. 1. The research framework of this study.

2.1 Participants

This study invited 40 participants (i.e., 20 males and 20 females) in the range of 18 to 30 years old to interact with different touchscreen electronic guides via the convenience sampling method. The education level is above the bachelor's degree. They have experience in using touchscreen electronic guides. All participants had standard or corrected-to-normal vision and were all right-handed. Each participant could complete the experiment independently. The participants agreed to participate and signed the consent form. They all fully understood the experimental tasks and questionnaires. The experiment duration was approximately 25 min, and the participants were paid approximately US$7 (about 200 NTD) for participating.

2.2   Materials and Apparatus

The experimental prototypes were created with Proto.io. Illustrator was used for graphic design and drawing in this experimental design. The experimental prototypes were designed to simulate the touchscreen electronic guide devices. The experiment is equipped with an IOS 32-inch touchscreen with 3840 × 2160 pixels 69 ppi and an aspect ratio of 16:9. The experimental site is a laboratory free from noise and external interference.

2.3   Experimental Design and Procedure

The prototypes of this experiment are shown in Fig. 2. Before the experiment, participants were informed of the research purpose. Then participants were asked to complete a questionnaire and consent form with basic information about their individuals. Screen recording software recorded each participant's task completion time for further analysis. Each participant needs to find the target landmark by clicking on the touch screen display as required by the experimental task (see Fig. 3). After completing all the tasks, participants were required to fill out a questionnaire of subjective evaluations (including the degree of effortlessness, the degree of subjective preference, and the NASA Task

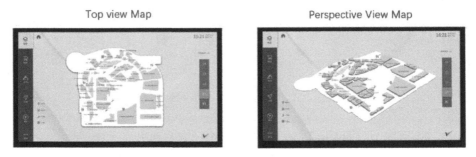

Fig. 2.   The prototype of this experiment.

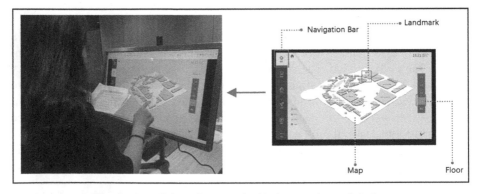

Fig. 3.   A participant interacted with the experimental device.

LoadIndex (NASA-TLX) questionnaire). A semi-structured interview was conducted at the end of the experiment.

In addition, three tasks of this experiment were determined (including visual search and information comparison tasks). A simulation of one of the most frequently used touchscreen electronic guides of the shopping mall in Taiwan was used to help participants take part in the experiment. This participants were all National Taiwan University of Science and Technology students. In addition, the controlled variables were the same environmental settings with stable WiFi speeds (Table 1).

Table 1. Experimental task designs of this study.

Task number	Descriptions
Task 1	Find your current location on Level L1 and find your way to Michaelkors on Level L1
Task 2	Find your way around the L1 floor from the brand Michael kors to the brand Dior
Task 3	Find your way from TIFFANY&CO on L1 to AIMER on L3

3   Results

A between-subject design was conducted for further statistical analysis in this study. The collected data regarding the main effects of the information layout, dynamic presentation of advertising, and their interaction effects on participants' task completion time (i.e., in seconds), as well as subjective evaluations were analyzed using the SPSS software.

3.1   Analysis of Task Completion Time

The results generated from the between-subject design of the task 1 completion time are shown in Table 2. It revealed no significant difference in the main effect of the virtual map visual presentation ($F_{(1, 26)} = 0.33$, $p = 0.856 > 0.05$; $\eta^2 = 0.01$). However, there was a significant difference in the main effect of the gender differences ($F_{(1, 26)} = 13.72$, $p = 0.001 < 0.05$; $\eta^2 = 0.28$). This means that the task completion time of the males (M = 15.30, SD = 4.04) were significantly shorter than that of the females (M = 20.46, SD = 5.20). Besides, there existed a significant interaction effect between the virtual map visual presentation and the gender differences ($F_{(1, 26)} = 6.44$, $p = 0.016 < 0.05$; $\eta^2 = 0.15$). Figure 4 illustrates that the task completion time of the perspective view maps (M = 13.41, SD = 2.43) was significantly faster than that of the top view maps (M = 17.20, SD = 4.53) when males operated the task. In contrast, the task completion time of the top view maps (M = 18.82, SD = 5.10) was significantly faster than that of the perspective view maps (M = 22.10, SD = 5.02) when females operated the task.

Table 2. The two-way analysis of variance (ANOVA) of each task regarding participants' task completion time.

	Source	SS	df	MS	F	p	η^2	LSD test
Task 1	virtual map visual presentation	0.65	1	0.65	0.33	0.856	0.00	
	gender difference	266.15	1	266.15	13.72	0.001*	0.28	Male < Female
	virtual map visual presentation × gender difference	124.96	1	124.96	6.44	0.016*	0.15	
Task 2	virtual map visual presentation	18.08	1	18.08	0.63	0.431	0.02	
	gender difference	90.33	1	90.33	3.17	0.084	0.08	
	virtual map visual presentation × gender difference	10.87	1	10.87	0.38	0.541	0.01	
Task 3	virtual map visual presentation	19.10	1	19.10	1.27	0.267	0.03	
	gender difference	87.44	1	87.44	5.82	0.021*	0.14	Male < Female
	virtual map visual presentation × gender difference	7.31	1	7.31	0.49	0.490	0.01	

* Significantly different at the $\alpha = 0.05$ level (* $p < 0.05$);
** Significantly different at the $\alpha = 0.01$ level (* $p < 0.01$)

The results generated from the between-subject design of the task 2 completion time are shown in Table 2. It revealed no significant difference in the main effect of the virtual map visual presentation ($F_{(1, 26)} = 0.63$, $p = 0.431 > 0.05$; $\eta^2 = 0.02$). Besides, there was also no significant difference in the main effect of the gender differences ($F_{(1, 26)} = 3.17$, $p = 0.084 > 0.05$; $\eta^2 = 0.08$). There also existed no significant interaction effect between the virtual map visual presentation and the gender differences ($F_{(1, 26)} = 0.38$, $p = 0.541 > 0.05$; $\eta^2 = 0.01$).

The results generated from the between-subject design of the task 3 completion time are shown in Table 2. It revealed no significant difference in the main effect of the virtual map visual presentation ($F_{(1, 26)} = 1.27$, $p = 0.267 > 0.05$; $\eta^2 = 0.03$). However, there was a significant difference in the main effect of the gender differences ($F_{(1, 26)} = 5.82$, $p = 0.021 < 0.05$; $\eta^2 = 0.14$). This means that the task completion time of the males (M = 22.17, SD = 2.82) were significantly shorter than that of the females (M = 25.12, SD = 4.68). There existed no significant interaction effect between the virtual map visual presentation and the gender differences ($F_{(1, 26)} = 0.49$, $p = 0.490 > 0.05$; $\eta^2 = 0.01$).

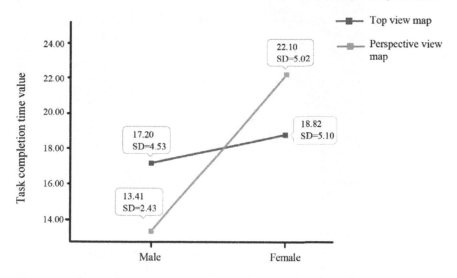

Fig. 4. The interaction diagram of the "virtual map visual presentation" and the "gender difference" regarding the completion time of task 1.

3.2 Analysis of Subjective Evaluations

According to the 7-point Likert scale (i.e., 1: least agree, 7: most agree) used for the questionnaire of subjective evaluations, the results of participants' responses after completing the assigned tasks were collected for further statistical analysis. The results of the between-subject two-way ANOVA regarding participants' subjective evaluations are provided in Table 3.

Table 3. The two-way analysis of variance (ANOVA) of participants' subjective evaluations.

	Source	SS	df	MS	F	p	η^2	LSD test
The degree of effortlessness	virtual map visual presentation	16.90	1	16.90	17.19	0.000*	0.32	Top view map < Perspective view map
	gender difference	2.50	1	2.50	2.54	0.12	0.07	
	virtual map visual presentation × gender difference	3.60	1	3.60	3.66	0.064	0.09	

(*continued*)

Table 3. (*continued*)

	Source	SS	df	MS	F	p	η^2	LSD test
The degree of subjective preference	virtual map visual presentation	3.03	1	3.03	4.41	0.043*	0.11	Top view map < Perspective view map
	gender difference	0.03	1	0.03	0.04	0.850	0.00	
	virtual map visual presentation × gender difference	7.23	1	7.23	10.53	0.003*	0.23	
The degree of physical demand	virtual map visual presentation	0.10	1	0.10	0.11	0.738	0.00	
	gender difference	1.60	1	1.60	1.81	0.187	0.05	
	virtual map visual presentation × gender difference	4.90	1	4.90	5.55	0.024*	0.13	

* Significantly different at the $\alpha = 0.05$ level (* p < 0.05);
** Significantly different at the $\alpha = 0.01$ level (* p < 0.01)

The results generated from the between-subject two-way ANOVA in terms of the degree of effortlessness are shown in Table 3. It revealed a significant difference in the main effect of the virtual map visual presentation ($F_{(1, 26)} = 17.19$, p = 0.000 < 0.05; $\eta^2 = 0.32$). This means that the degree of effortlessness of the perspective view maps (M = 5.85, SD = 0.88) was significantly higher than that of the top view maps (M = 4.55, SD = 1.19). However, there was no significant difference in the main effect of the gender differences ($F_{(1, 26)} = 2.54$, p = 0.120 > 0.05; $\eta^2 = 0.07$). There also existed no significant interaction effect between the perspective view maps and the gender differences ($F_{(1, 26)} = 3.66$, p = 0.064 > 0.05; $\eta^2 = 0.09$).

The results generated from the between-subject two-way ANOVA in terms of the degree of subjective preference are shown in Table 3. It revealed a significant difference in the main effect of the virtual map visual presentation ($F_{(1, 26)} = 4.41$, p = 0.043 < 0.05; $\eta^2 = 0.11$). This means that the degree of subjective preference of the perspective view map (M = 5.50, SD = 0.76) was significantly higher than that of the top view maps (M = 4.95, SD = 1.05). However, there was no significant difference in the main effect of the gender differences ($F_{(1, 26)} = 0.04$, p = 0.850 > 0.05; $\eta^2 = 0.00$). There existed a significant interaction effect between the perspective view maps and the gender differences ($F_{(1, 26)} = 10.53$, p = 0.003 < 0.05; $\eta^2 = 0.23$). Figure 5 illustrates that the degree of subjective preference of the perspective view maps (M = 5.90, SD = 0.57) was significantly higher than that of the top view maps (M = 4.50, SD = 1.27) when males operated the task. In contrast, the degree of subjective preference the top view maps (M = 5.40, SD = 0.52) was significantly higher than that of the perspective view maps (M = 5.10, SD = 0.74) when females operated the task.

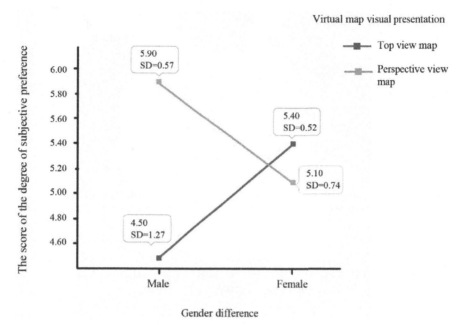

Fig. 5. The interaction diagram of the "virtual map visual presentation" and the "gender difference" regarding the degree of subjective preference.

The results generated from the between-subject two-way ANOVA in terms of the degree of physical demand are shown in Table 3. It revealed no significant difference in the main effect of the virtual map visual presentation ($F_{(1, 26)} = 0.11$, p = 0.738 > 0.05; $\eta^2 = 0.00$). Besides, there was also no significant difference in the main effect of the gender differences ($F_{(1, 26)} = 1.81$, p = 0.187 > 0.05; $\eta^2 = 0.05$). However, there also existed a significant interaction effect between the perspective view maps and the gender differences ($F_{(1, 26)} = 5.55$, p = 0.024 < 0.05; $\eta^2 = 0.13$). Figure 6 illustrates that the degree of physical demand of the perspective view maps (M = 1.60, SD = 0.70) was significantly lower than that of the top view maps (M = 2.40, SD = 1.43) when males operated the task. In contrast, the degree of physical demand of the top view maps (M = 1.30, SD = 0.48) was significantly lower than that of the perspective view maps (M = 1.90, SD = 0.88) when females operated the task.

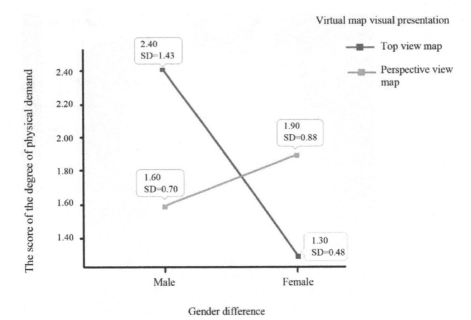

Fig. 6. The interaction diagram of the "virtual map visual presentation" and the "gender difference" regarding the degree of physical demand.

4   Discussions

According to the results shown by the tasks, male participants operated faster performance than female participants in Task 1 and Task 3; the results are consistent with previous research that males outperform females in virtual environments for wayfinding (Van Gerven et al. 2012). Furthermore, in task 3, we found an interaction effect between virtual map visual presentation and gender difference, i.e., when male participants manipulated the task, task completion time for the perspective map was significantly faster than for the overhead map, and conversely, when female participants manipulated the task, task completion time for the overhead map was significantly faster than for the perspective map, a possible reason for this is that female participants are more likely than male participants to focus their visual attention on landmarks during wayfinding (Saucier et al. 2002). In particular, female participants pay more visual attention to landmarks than male participants during 2D maps (Liao and Dong 2017), so female participants have a significant advantage in visual search regarding the 2D map. On the contrary, male participants pay more attention to 3D map landmarks than female participants regarding 3D maps (Liao et al., 2021).

In the analysis of subjective evaluations, we found that 3D map was more advantageous than 2D maps in terms of the degree of effortlessness and subjective preference, probably because 3D maps increase the dimensionality of the map, enrich its features, and help users form spatial structures and cognitive maps (Zheng and Hsu 2021). On the contrary, translating 2D maps into an egocentric physical world may require a significant cognitive load when participants comprehend the maps (Goodman et al. 2003).

Furthermore, there was an interaction effect between virtual map visual presentation and gender difference in terms of the degree of subjective preference and the degree of physical demand, i.e., male participants had a better preference and lower physical demand for perspective maps. Conversely, females had a higher preference and lower physical demand for 2D maps. It is known that the 2D electronic map viewing mode is characterized by a broader peripheral view and is more suitable for searching over a larger area. In contrast, the 3D map viewing mode shows a more focused vision and produces information that is easier to see in detail (Lei et al. 2003). In addition, females have a more extraordinary ability than males to perceive and feel their surroundings when processing map information (Seegmiller and Epperson 1987), i.e., females perceive greater telepresence than males. This may explain the difference between females' and males' subjective evaluation about the different types of virtual map visual presentations in terms of the degree of subjective preference and the degree of physical demand.

5 Conclusions

This study examined the combined effects of virtual map visual presentation and gender difference on participants' task performance and subjective evaluations. Based on the experimental results, more concrete evidence is provided for the touchscreen electronic guide interfaces. Several specific design recommendations for the user interface contributed by this study are listed as follows:

1. Gender differences exist in the task performance of the interactive touchscreen
2. electronic guides.
3. Different virtual map visual presentation types affect users' subjective evaluations.
4. There is a significant interaction effect between the virtual map visual presentation and gender on wayfinding task performance, i.e., male participants performed better than female participants in the perspective view maps. In contrast, female participants performed better than male participants in the top view maps.
5. The degree of effortlessness of the perspective view maps was significantly higher than that of the top view maps.

This study's findings can contribute to the research on the user interface design of touchscreen electronic guides. It is also recommended that designers consider adding more visual design variables or even multimodal design to help expand the touchscreen electronic guide interface research. These design features of the user interface are worth of further investigation.

Funding. This research study received no external funding.

Conflicts of Interest. The authors declare no conflict of interest.
    Consent to Participate: Informed consent was obtained from all participants.
    The authors would like to acknowledge.

References

Benko, H., Wilson, A. D., Baudisch, P.: Precise selection techniques for multi-touch screens. In: Proceedings of the SIGCHI Conference on Human Factors in Computing Systems, pp. 1263–1272 (2006)

Bosco, A., Longoni, A., Vecchi, T.: Gender effects in spatial orientation: cognitive profiles and mental strategies. Appl. Cogn. Psychol. **18**(5), 519–532 (2004)

Brunner-Friedrich, B., Radoczky, V.: Active landmarks in indoor environments. In: VISUAL, pp. 203–215 (2005)

Chebat, J., Gélinas-Chebat, C., Therrien, K.: Lost in a mall, the effects of gender, familiarity with the shopping mall and the shopping values on shoppers' wayfinding processes. J. Bus. Res. **58**(11), 1590–1598 (2005)

Dogu, U., Erkip, F.: Spatial factors affecting wayfinding and orientation. Environ. Behav. **32**(6), 731–755 (2000)

Goodman, J., Brewster, S.A., Gray, P.: How can we best use landmarks to support older people in navigation? Behav. Inf. Technol. **24**(1), 3–20 (2005)

Harrell, W.A., Bowlby, J.W., Hall-Hoffarth, D.: Directing wayfinders with maps: the effects of gender, age, route complexity, and familiarity with the environment. J. Soc. Psychol. **140**(2), 169–178 (2000)

Hubona, G.S., Shirah, G.W.: The paleolithic stone age effect? Gender differences performing specific computer-generated spatial tasks. Int. J. Technol. Hum. Interact. (IJTHI) **2**(2), 24–48 (2006)

Hund, A.M., Minarik, J.L.: Getting from here to there: Spatial anxiety, wayfinding strategies, direction type, and wayfinding efficiency. Spat. Cogn. Comput. **6**(3), 179–201 (2006)

Johnson, J.T., Verdi, M.P., Kealy, W.A., Stock, W.A., Haygood, R.C.: Map perspective and the learning of text. Contemp. Educ. Psychol. **20**(4), 457–463 (1995)

Kim, Y., Baek, S., Bae, Y., Oh, R., Choi, J.: Evaluation of the effective cognition area (ECA) of signage systems with backlighting under Smoke Conditions. Sust. (Basel Switz.) **14**(7), 4057 (2022)

Kutnicki, S.: Wayfinding media and neutralizing control at the shopping mall. Crit. Stud. Media Commun. **35**(5), 401–419 (2018)

Laakso, K., Gjesdal, O., Sulebak, J.R.: Tourist information and navigation support by using 3D maps displayed on mobile devices. In: Mobile HCI workshop on HCI in mobile guide, Udine, Italy, pp. 34–39 (2003)

Lawton, C.A.: Gender differences in way-finding strategies: relationship to spatial ability and spatial anxiety. Sex Roles **30**, 765–779 (1994)

Lawton, C.A., Kallai, J.: Gender differences in wayfinding strategies and anxiety about wayfinding: a cross-cultural comparison. Sex Roles **47**, 389–401 (2002)

Lei, T.-C., Wu, S.-C., Chao, C.-W., Lee, S.-H.: Evaluating differences in spatial visual attention in wayfinding strategy when using 2D and 3D electronic maps. GeoJournal **81**(2), 153–167 (2014). https://doi.org/10.1007/s10708-014-9605-3

Li, Y., Wu, Q., Zhang, Y.: Choice of behavior model in new retail: usability testing of intelligent shopping terminals functional framework. In: Rebelo, F. (ed.) AHFE 2021. LNNS, vol. 261, pp. 554–563. Springer, Cham (2021). https://doi.org/10.1007/978-3-030-79760-7_66

Liao, H., Dong, W.: An exploratory study investigating gender effects on using 3D maps for spatial orientation in wayfinding. ISPRS Int. J. Geo Inf. **6**(3), 60 (2017)

Liao, H., Dong, W., Peng, C., Liu, H.: Exploring differences of visual attention in pedestrian navigation when using 2D maps and 3D geo-browsers. Cartogr. Geogr. Inf. Sci. **44**(6), 474–490 (2017)

Lin, C.T., et al.: Gender differences in wayfinding in virtual environments with global or local landmarks. J. Environ. Psychol. **32**(2), 89–96 (2012)

Lu, Y., Peponis, J.: Exhibition Visitors are Sensitive to Patterns of Display Covisibility. Environ. Plan. B, Plan. Des. **41**(1), 53–68 (2014)

Malinowski, J.C., Gillespie, W.T.: Individual differences in performance on a large-scale, real-world wayfinding task. J. Environ. Psychol. **21**(1), 73–82 (2001)

Nicholas, D., Huntington, P., Williams, P.: Establishing metrics for the evaluation of touch screen kiosks. J. Inf. Sci. **27**(2), 61–71 (2001)

Oulasvirta, A., Nurminen, A., Nivala, A.M.: Interacting with 3D and 2D mobile maps: an exploratory study. Helsinki Institute for Information Technology April 11 (2007)

Peponis, J., Zimring, C., Choi, Y.K.: Finding the building in wayfinding. Environ. Behav. **22**(5), 555–590 (1990)

Plesa, M.A., Cartwright, W.: Evaluating the effectiveness of non-realistic 3D maps for navigation with mobile devices. In: Map-Based Mobile Services: Design, Interaction and Usability, pp. 80–104 (2008)

Popelka, S., Doležalová, J.: Non-photorealistic 3D visualization in city maps: an eye-tracking study. Mod. Trends Cartography: Selected Papers CARTOCON **2014**, 357–367 (2015)

Saucier, D.M., Green, S.M., Leason, J., MacFadden, A., Bell, S., Elias, L.J.: Are sex differences in navigation caused by sexually dimorphic strategies or by differences in the ability to use the strategies? Behav. Neurosci. **116**(3), 403 (2002)

Seegmiller, R.A., Epperson, D.L.: Distinguishing thinking-feeling preferences through the content analysis of natural language. J. Pers. Assess. **51**(1), 42–52 (1987)

Silverman, I., Choi, J., Mackewn, A., Fisher, M., Moro, J., Olshansky, E.: Evolved mechanisms underlying wayfinding: Further studies on the hunter-gatherer theory of spatial sex differences. Evol. Hum. Behav. **21**(3), 201–213 (2000)

Tüzün, H., Telli, E., Alır, A.: Usability testing of a 3D touch screen kiosk system for way-finding. Comput. Hum. Behav. **61**, 73–79 (2016)

Van Gerven, D., Schneider, A., Wuitchik, D., Skelton, R.: Direct measurement of spontaneous strategy selection in a virtual morris water maze shows females choose an allocentric strategy at least as often as males do. Behav. Neurosci. **126**(3), 465–478 (2012)

Wang, W. (2014). *Older adults & home medical device interaction: Interface type comparison, display design, and touch gesture analysis.* North Carolina State University

Wright, P., et al.: Using audio to support animated route information in a hospital touch-screen kiosk. Comput. Hum. Behav. **26**(4), 753–759 (2010)

Zheng, M.-C.: Influences of different underground station map designs on map-reading and wayfinding. GeoInformatica **24**(3), 531–555 (2020). https://doi.org/10.1007/s10707-020-003 96-w

Zheng, M., Hsu, Y.: How 2.5D Maps design improve the wayfinding performance and spatial ability of map users. Inform. (Basel) **8**(4), 88 (2021)

Author Index

Printed in the United States
by Baker & Taylor Publisher Services